DIVIDED ARMIES

PRINCETON STUDIES IN INTERNATIONAL
HISTORY AND POLITICS

*G. John Ikenberry, Marc Trachtenberg, William
C. Wohlforth, and Keren Yarhi-Milo, Series Editors*

Divided Armies

INEQUALITY AND BATTLEFIELD PERFORMANCE IN MODERN WAR

JASON LYALL

PRINCETON UNIVERSITY PRESS

PRINCETON & OXFORD

Published by Princeton University Press
41 William Street, Princeton, New Jersey 08540

In the United Kingdom: Princeton University Press
6 Oxford Street, Woodstock, Oxfordshire, OX20 1TR

Library of Congress Cataloging-in-Publication Data

Names: Lyall, Jason, author.
Title: Divided armies : inequality and battlefield performance in modern
    war / Jason Lyall.
Description: Princeton : Princeton University Press, [2020] | Includes bibliographical
    references.
Identifiers: LCCN 2019017537 | ISBN 9780691192437 (hardcover)
Subjects: LCSH: Discrimination in the military–Case studies. | Unit cohesion
    (Military science)–Case studies. | Military readiness–Case studies. |
    Military policy–Social aspects. | Sociology, Military. | Psychology, Military.
Classification: LCC UB416 .L93 2020 | DDC 355.3/3–dc23
    LC record available at https://lccn.loc.gov/2019017537

British Library Cataloging-in-Publication Data is available

Editorial: Bridget Flannery-McCoy
Production Editorial: Sara Lerner
Jacket/Cover Design: Layla MacRory
Production: Erin Suydam
Publicity: Nathalie Levine and Kate Farquehar-Thomson

This book has been composed in Arno Pro

Printed on acid-free paper. ∞

press.princeton.edu

Printed in the United States of America

10 9 8 7 6 5 4 3 2 1

CONTENTS

PART III. EXTENSIONS AND CONCLUSIONS

PART IV. APPENDIXES

TABLES

FIGURES AND MAPS

ACKNOWLEDGMENTS

DURING THE SUMMER OF 2009, I found myself living and working at Camp Julien, an International Security Assistance Force (ISAF) military base nestled on the southern outskirts of a hot, dusty, and crowded Kabul. At the time, I was an assistant professor at Princeton, having made my way to Afghanistan for the first time to try to better understand the dynamics of violence in civil wars, generally, and the Taliban in particular (I'm still trying). The six-week trip, albeit brief, was formative, helping spark a now decade-long research program in Afghanistan. By happy accident, it also led me to question the received wisdom about how armies fight and die on modern battlefields. Indeed, through good fortune Camp Julien was housed within a larger Afghan National Army training facility, one tasked with churning out battalion (kandak) sized units for the escalating war with the Taliban. Here, I thought, was a chance to observe firsthand the birth of the universal soldier as Afghans of all ethnicities and tribal affiliations were stamped into the same mold, their prior affinities now reshaped and replaced by allegiance to the new Afghan state.

Except it never happened. Far from erased, ethnicity appeared only more salient once training began. Military service seemed to create new opportunities for societal hierarchies and prejudices to reassert themselves in myriad ways. Corruption, hazing, even sexual abuse of recruits were all organized across (and sometimes within) ethnic lines; power and powerlessness were dictated in large measure by one's ethnicity. Meanwhile, early battlefield reports revealed that these new units were beset by rampant desertion, widespread refusals to engage Taliban forces, and even side-switching as raw recruits took their rifles and joined (or rejoined) the Taliban. I began to wonder whether these discouraging patterns of battlefield performance could be attributed to preexisting ethnic divisions and resulting status hierarchies— what I term *military inequality*—within the ranks of the Afghan Army. Indeed, perhaps a more general lesson might be derived from this particular instance: Could the perils of military inequality extend beyond the case of the current Afghan civil war to help explain why armies have conquered or crumbled on the battlefields of modern conventional wars?

I returned home certain of the puzzle but unsure of how to proceed. I quickly grew frustrated. Despite a wave of scholarship on inequality across several academic disciplines, the military had largely been ignored as a site of inequality. No measure of military inequality existed, for example. Nor did we have any cross-national data for many of the wartime behaviors I thought important elements of battlefield performance, including desertion, defection, and fratricidal violence. What's more, the study of military effectiveness to date has privileged Western belligerents and wars; theoretical claims are often devised and tested on the same subset of well-known cases like World Wars I and II. Political scientists, historians, and economists have also grown increasingly wary of sweeping theories, preferring now to conduct "microlevel" studies that utilize fine-grained data to explain dynamics in a particular war, battle, or unit, leaving aside questions of whether these findings travel to other cases or actually cumulate in recognizable patterns across belligerents, wars, and time itself.

But I wanted to paint on a broader canvas, even if it meant stepping out of formation with prevailing academic currents (and with, it must be said, much of my own work on civil war). The task, then, seemed simple. Construct a new dataset of belligerents in all conventional wars fought since 1800; build new measures for military inequality and battlefield performance; and then choose more representative cases for close-range investigation of how inequality affected wartime performance, thus offsetting the Western bias in existing scholarship. With Grayson, my newborn son, riding shotgun on my desk in his Baby Bjorn pillow, I set to work building what would become that new dataset, Project Mars, and ultimately, this book. I sketched the anticipated timeline on a loose-leaf piece of paper: two years for data collection, a year for writing up, and then publication. The mixture of naked ambition and blinding naivete is breathtaking, even at this distance. Instead of the projected three years, it took nearly nine. Whether it was worth the effort I leave for you to decide.

What I know for certain is that my intellectual debts began accruing well before I even imagined this book, let alone began writing it. Indeed, the book and its author are both products of three universities. My first debt is to the Government Department at Cornell, where I completed my PhD. I still have no idea what the admissions committee saw in me—I was a raw, first-generation student—but the decision to extend an offer changed my life. I especially thank my dissertation committee of Peter Katzenstein, Valerie Bunce, Matthew Evangelista, and Chris Way for teaching me how to ask big questions. Princeton, where I started my academic career, taught me how to answer those questions. I thank Gary Bass, Tom Christensen, Christina Davis, John Ikenberry, Helen Milner, Andy Moravcsik, and Anne-Marie Slaughter, along with Kosuke Imai, Scott Ashworth, and Kris Ramsay, who collectively kick-started my methods training. Shortly after my arrival at Camp Julien, I officially joined the faculty at Yale, where I started and finished the book. I especially thank Jim Levinsohn and Ian Shapiro for their support and mentorship over the years, and for carving out a space where academic rigor and policy relevance were equally rewarded. I also thank Elisabeth Wood, Oona Hathaway, Jacob Hacker, Susan Stokes, Susan Hyde, Kenneth Scheve, Thad Dunning, Allan Dafoe, Matthew Kocher, Adria Lawrence, Frances Rosenbluth and Jessica Weiss for trenchant criticisms, friendly amendments, and random hallway encounters that suggested new ways of tackling vexing problems.

For helpful conversations, moral support, and the occasional reminder that I belonged, I thank Laia Balcells, Ethan Bueno de Mesquita, Lars-Erik Cederman, Erica Chenoweth, Fotini Christia, Christian Davenport, Christina Davis, Alexander Downes, Matthew Fuhrmann, Michael Horowitz, Kosuke Imai, Ian Johnson, Iain Johnston, Karen Jusko, Joshua Kertzer, Louisa Lombard, Rose McDermott, Catherine Panter-Brick, Stephen Rosen, Elizabeth Saunders, Todd Sechser, Emma Sky, Jessica Trounstine, Nils Weidmann, Jeremy Weinstein, Isaiah (Ike) Wilson III, Andreas Wimmer, Jonathan Wyrtzen, Yang-Yang Zhou, and Yuri Zhukov. Like many, I cannot repay the debt of gratitude I owe to David Laitin, who inexplicably took an interest in my work and has offered encouragement from afar while providing a role model for how to combine rigor with reinvention. I also received valuable feedback from hosts, discussants, and audiences at Columbia University, the Department of Defense, Georgetown University, Princeton University, the University of Chicago, the University of Michigan, the University of Notre Dame, the University of Toronto, and Yale University. Early drafts of several chapters were also inflicted on audiences at annual meetings of the American Political Science Association and the International Studies Association.

I also received an avalanche of advice, and sometimes searing feedback, from a day-and-a-half book workshop at the Jackson Institute for Global Affairs in September 2015. A truly awesome (and intimidating) group of scholars made the trek to New Haven to help improve the book. I am grateful to Stephen Biddle, Jasen Castello, Alexander Downes, Dan Reiter, Erin Simpson, Allan Stam, and Caitlin Talmadge for such a thorough stress-testing of the book's claims and evidence. They may not agree with my argument (still), but I hope they recognize that their contributions made the book stronger in a thousand large and small ways.

Creating Project Mars was an enormous undertaking; the book quite literally would have been impossible to write without the dedicated assistance of a small army of research associates. In total, 134 research associates, drawing on sources in twenty-one languages, worked to collect and clean (Blue Teams) or verify (Red Teams) the thousands of observations that comprise the Project Mars dataset. Some worked on a single cell; others devoted their summers to one of our Changing Patterns of Warfare coding camps; still others stayed with the project for years. I am especially grateful to Nicole E. Pflug, Prakhar Sharma, and Ksenia Anisimova, who served as program managers for the sprawling effort. I also thank Hazal Papuççular, who provided Turkish translations, and Isaias Tesfalidet, who translated Amharic sources, for use in chapters 6 and 7, respectively.

The Project Mars research associates are: Lamis Abdel-Laty, Genevieve Traxler Abele, Nicholas Paolo Accinelli, Isaiah Affron, Akua A. Agyen, Jillian Anderson, Ksenia Anisimova, Walker Atkinson, Helinna Ayalew, Tiraana Bains, Otis Baker, David Bargueno, Paola Barzelatto, Maria Blackwood, Ekaterina Botchkareva, Thomas C. Burke, Louisa Cantwell, Thomas R. Casazza, Billy Cavell, Iwona Chałuś, Henry Chapman, Suparna Chaudhry, Teresa Chen, Nyasha Chiundiza, Jade Chowning, Adam Cimpeanu, Kaitlin Conklin, Luke Connell, Harland Dahl, Ruthie Danny, Ana Teresa del Toro, Noah Daponte-Smith, Hanna Deleanu, Carolyn DeSchiffart, Zachary Devlin-Foltz, Yasmin Barak Eriksson, Ugonna Eze, Stephen Feagin, Della Fok, Gabrielle A. Fong, Fatima Ghani, Armando Ghinaglia, Jennifer Macedo Giang, Shoshanna Goldin, Aparna Gomes, Emily Gray, Megan Harada, Charles Hill, Nikolaj Hoejer, Charlotte Hulme, Virginia Insley, Iman Jaroudi, Shea Jennings, Justin Jin, Nikolaj Joejer, Luka Kalandarishvili, Dipin Kaur, Hannah Kazis-Taylor, Radina Kolev, Matt Kontos, Jesus Ayala Lara, Danielle Larrabee, Charlotte Lawrence, Sona Lim, Georgiy Lomsadze, Marisa Lowe, Vivath Ly, Canning Malkin, Rose Malloy, Allison Mandeville, Joshua Martin, Julian Martin, Chris Meserole, Jake Mezey, Marina Miller, Connor Mills, Jonathan Ng, My Khan Ngo, Peter O'Neill, Bailey Owen, Catherine Padhi, Allegra Pankratz, Hazal Papuççular, Corey Pattison, Ksenija Pavlovic, Lindsay Pearlman, Joseph Peterson, Nicole E. Pflug, Mary Polk, Aula Porca, Chris Price, Leah Quintiliano, Hannah Quirk, Benjamin Rasmussen, Tiffany Rechsteiner, Yerick Reyes, Emily Rice, Adam Rodriques, Gabriel Rojas, Hervé Roquet, Cameron Rotblat, Ruth Schapiro, Madison Schramm, Andrey V. Semenov, Hadia Shah, Sarah al-Shalash, Shaxuan (Lizzie) Shan, Prakhar Sharma, Olivia Shoemaker, Elizabeth Silliman, Julia Sinitsky, Gabriel Morales Sod, Nicola Soekoe, Mariano Stephens, Viktor Miller Stoll, Drew Stommes, Timothy Stone, Isaias Tesfalidet, Griffin Thomas, Eric Tillberg, Joseph Tomchark, Emily Trask-Young, Jessica Trisko Darden, Amaka Uchegbu, Melanie Ullmo, Bo Uuganbayar, Lina Volin, Alissa Wang, Nicolas Wicaksono, Sesen Yehdego, Claire Young, Ruoyin Zheng, and Tatsiana Zhurauliova.

Large data collection efforts like Project Mars are expensive; they hinge on the willingness of organizations and individuals to fund multi-year efforts with false starts, dry spells, and uncertain outcomes. I thank the Air Force Office of Scientific Research (Grants #FA9550-14-1-0072 and #FA9550-09-1-0314), the Institution for Social and Policy Studies (ISPS) at Yale, and the MacMillan Center for International and Area Studies (two Faculty Research Grants and a Director's Award) at Yale for supporting this initiative. I also gratefully acknowledge the Edward J. and Dorothy Clarke Kempf Fund at Yale University for underwriting my book workshop. The findings and conclusions of this book do not represent the official policy or views of the AFOSR, Department of Defense, or the U.S. Government.

Eric Crahan at Princeton University Press maneuvered me into the starting block with an initial meeting at Small World Coffee many moons ago. He encouraged me to chase my narrative wherever it wandered and (hardly) blanched when I eventually submitted a "svelte" 225,000-word version of the manuscript. Bridget Flannery-McCoy assumed Eric's editorial role during revisions and helped drag me across the finish line, gently reminding me that the best books are finished ones. I also owe thanks to two anonymous reviewers, one of whom was apparently so taken with the manuscript that he composed not one but two limericks in its honor. I also thank Alena Chekanov, Sara Lerner, Dimitri Karetnikov, and Meghan Kanabay for skillfully shepherding the book through the production process. Dipin Kaur and Glenda Krupa provided excellent copyediting. I thank Kelly Sandefur at Beehive Mapping for translating my crude sketches into detailed maps.

My final thanks are my most personal. Kevin Cohen, Grace Valenzuela, and Steve Valenzuela are my lifeline back to the old country. The Vasseur clan—Dave, Chaundra, Matthew, Kaelin, and Greyson—provided much-needed sanity checks through a shared backyard. Gord Downie figuratively saved me in a foreign land; Prakhar Sharma literally did so. I'd like to think my Uncle Ken would have enjoyed the book; I only wish I could have written it faster. My mom, Helen, sacrificed everything for her kids; I hope this book makes you proud. To my own children, Grayson and Avery, you are the purpose behind the work. I can't make up for all the time I stole from you to write the book. But I hope you know I was thinking of you the whole time. I dedicate this book to Grace, for everything, forever.

A NOTE TO READERS

SCHOLARS OFTEN LOCK their insights away behind walls of technical jargon and ramparts of methodological sophistication impenetrable to scholars in other disciplines, let alone those unschooled in academia's dark arts. I have endeavored to avoid this path. In the spirit of bridging disciplinary divides, I have relegated much of the book's technical matter to appendixes posted online (www.jasonlyall.com). Central findings from Project Mars, the new dataset of belligerents and conventional wars (1800–2011) that underpins the book, are displayed graphically, while supplemental analyses and robustness checks are available online. The entire Project Mars dataset, along with its codebook, replication files, documentation about its use of Blue/Red teams for data collection and verification, and extensive bibliography of sources consulted for each war and belligerent, can be found on my website.

Since quantitative data can only take us so far, I also draw on nine historical cases from the wider Project Mars universe. The details of how these cases were chosen (using a purpose-built R program) are found on the website, where I also provide a discussion of how Red teams of independent coders were used to interrogate my interpretation of processes and events in these wars. Unless otherwise noted, all French, German, Italian, Persian, Russian, and Spanish translations are my own.

This was an ambitious undertaking, and I welcome feedback and criticism from readers. Revisions, updates, and extensions to Project Mars will be posted to my website.

DIVIDED ARMIES

1

Introduction

What a society gets in its armed services is exactly what it asks for, no more and no less. What it asks for tends to be a reflection of what it is. When a country looks at its fighting forces it is looking in a mirror; the mirror is a true one and the face that it sees will be its own.

SIR JOHN HACKETT, THE PROFESSION OF ARMS, 1983

THE RHYTHM OF HISTORY is set by the clash and din of armies fighting and dying in battle. Yet for all their importance in deciding the fate of nations and empires, the drivers of battlefield performance in modern war are still only poorly understood. This is due partly to the complexity of battle itself, and the near-bewildering variation on display in the ability of armies to generate and deploy coercive violence against their foes. Some armies, for example, have imposed stunning defeat on their adversaries while suffering almost no losses of their own. Outnumbered Anglo-Egyptian forces destroyed an opposing force of nearly 60,000 Mahdist soldiers in a single morning on the fields out-side Omdurman in 1898, a victory so lopsided that some have suggested that its outcome was best characterized as murder, not war. In other cases, armies have staggered back into the fight, showing remarkable resilience after initial setbacks. Bolshevik forces turned the tide against more capable White armies at Petrograd in 1919, carving out a beachhead from which the revolution could be exported and then consolidated throughout Russia. Still other armies struggled simply to field their soldiers, wracked by the twin scourges of deser-tion and defection that thinned their ranks during, and sometimes before, battle commenced. Soldiers of the Spanish Royalist forces, seeking to snuff out the independence-seeking Third Republic of Venezuela (1815–21), often fled military service or switched sides, gutting its combat power and con-tributing to its eventual defeat. Armies have even turned their guns on them-selves to manufacture cohesion through coercion. The Fengtian Clique's Zhili

Army, one of the largest and best-equipped armies of China's Warlord Era, deployed "anti-retreat formations" staffed by teenagers who fired artillery into Fengtian forces if they wavered during the Northern Expedition (1926–28). Repression can sometimes escalate to almost unimaginable levels. Desperation drove the Red Army to backstop its beleaguered forces with blocking detachments that executed an estimated 158,000 of their fellow soldiers from 1942–44, dwarfing total American casualties in the entire Pacific campaign.[1]

This book therefore asks a simple question: What explains battlefield performance in modern war? I argue that the patterns and dynamics of battlefield performance in modern war since 1800 can be explained by the degree of inequality within belligerent armies, or what I term *military inequality*. Specifically, battlefield fortunes are shaped by a belligerent's prewar treatment of its constituent ethnic groups and the ethnic composition of its armed forces, which combine to create predictable patterns in how armies produce violence once they enter combat. The greater the level of military inequality—that is, the more these ethnic groups were subjected to prewar discrimination or repression by the state—the worse a belligerent's expected wartime performance, for two reasons.

First, soldiers drawn from marginalized or repressed "non-core" ethnic groups will be reluctant to fight and die on behalf of the regime and its war. Absent common cause, and possessing strong ethnic ties, these soldiers will use their existing networks to resist or subvert military authorities collectively. Second, military commanders, recognizing the dangers of incorporating these soldiers, will take steps to prevent indiscipline, including the specter of mass desertion or defection. Commanders may rig the ethnic composition of their units to prevent coethnic collusion, and often deliberately simplify their tactics to foreclose opportunities for these soldiers to escape. These measures impose steep penalties, however, increasing casualties by reducing battlefield flexibility and survivability. As inequality rises, wielding violence against one's own soldiers becomes increasingly attractive as armies seek to compel what they cannot command. Groaning under the combined weight of rising casualties, narrowed tactical choices, and embittered soldiers, these divided armies enter battle at a significant disadvantage to more egalitarian foes.

Divided armies, in other words, are flawed by design. Armies, in this view, are political constructions, both reflective of and captive to the identity politics that define a political community. For that reason, divided armies represent conscious decisions to impose limitations on the belligerent's full exercise of military power on the modern battlefield. This characterization

1. Merridale 2006, 157.

stands sharply at odds with prevailing theories of military effectiveness in political science, where armies more closely resemble Emperor Qin's famed terra-cotta warriors: disciplined, obedient, uniform, and silent. Indeed, these theories cast armies as organizations obsessed with efficiency and optimization, of wringing the most from the least, with eyes firmly fixed on the dangers of international hierarchies of military power, not domestic hierarchies of status and belonging. The book's privileging of prewar drivers of military inequality also contrasts with the current preoccupation in the study of political violence (especially civil wars) with fast-moving dynamics to the exclusion of structural factors that shove and shape patterns of wartime violence. My approach shares much with the recent turn toward social history in the study of military affairs, including problematizing the notion of a universal, faceless soldier by considering the "view from below." Yet I part company with its focus on the particular to the exclusion of the general. The argument offered here is designed to explain battlefield performance across all armies, or as many as possible, rather than a single army or individual unit. Military inequality is thus the red thread that runs through the still-unfolding narrative of modern war.

In that spirit, the book seeks to nudge the study of battlefield performance in four new directions. First, it introduces an expanded conceptual framework for understanding battlefield performance, one that integrates previously neglected issues such as desertion, defection, and fratricidal violence. Second, it makes the case for viewing military inequality as an important, if overlooked, independent variable for explaining battlefield performance over the past 200 years. Third, it resets our empirical baseline for battlefield performance by introducing a new dataset, Project Mars, that greatly expands our coverage of conventional wars and belligerents, pushing us away from Western-centric accounts toward a more global view of military affairs. Finally, it aims to shape how we study battlefield performance by adopting a research design that marries diverse streams of qualitative and quantitative evidence with the explicit use of counterfactuals to isolate military inequality's effects across (and within) armies. The book will have achieved its ambition if it persuades others to join in a common effort to build a more global history of battlefield performance, one that recognizes how prewar patterns of inequality can trap divided armies on paths of battlefield ruin.

1.1. Inequality Goes to War

While inequality has waxed and waned throughout the centuries, its current resurgence in the United States and abroad has led academics to sound the alarm about its negative consequences. Economists, who define inequality principally in terms of income and wealth distributions, have linked rising inequality to stunted economic growth, increased crime, worsened health outcomes, and diminished governance.[2] Political scientists have also entered the fray, viewing inequality as a function of access to political power, especially executive decision-making authority, in a given country. Lamenting recent democratic reversals around the world, these scholars have drawn a connection between political inequality and the onset of armed rebellion, full-blown civil war, and even state collapse due to vicious cycles of inter-elite struggles to acquire, or maintain, a stranglehold on power.[3] Historians, too, have issued cautionary tales, warning that economic and political inequalities, once entrenched, can be exceedingly hard to uproot. In one especially troubling reading, inequality can only be beaten back through massively wrenching events such as total wars and pandemics that quite literally level societies for a time before inequality inevitably reestablishes itself.[4]

I share this sense of unease but adopt a different, perhaps more fundamental, view of inequality. I define inequality in terms of membership within a political community rather than the distribution of income or political power. All political communities must answer a basic question: who belongs, and how much? Inequality here refers to the uneven distribution of membership within a given political community across the groups that find themselves nestled within the boundaries of the same territorial unit, whether a state, empire, or other form of political organization. All political leaders construct or inherit collective visions of their political communities that are meant to legitimate their rule. Some political communities are expansive, drawing their boundaries in an inclusive manner that does not single out specific groups for unequal treatment; all groups hold equal status in the community. Some communities are defined more narrowly, relegating certain groups to second-class status that justifies group-based discrimination against them. Other communities have even steeper gradations of belonging, viewing targeted groups as aliens, outsiders trapped within but not members of the broader political community. In these situations, collective violence is deemed permissible to deny or destroy their group claims and sometimes their existence. Inequality here is thus a political construct, one that establishes categories of membership within the community. It is also group-based, not individual-centric, in its focus. Groups are assigned to particular categories of membership from

2. Acemoglu and Robinson 2012; Easterly 2013; Milanovic 2005, 2016; Piketty 2013; Atkinson 2015; Kelly 2000; Deaton 2013.

3. Wimmer 2013; Cederman, Gleditsch and Buhaug 2013; Boix 2015; Ansell and Samuels 2014; Tilly 1999.

4. Scheidel 2017.

which relative societal status is derived. Inequality is therefore relational in nature, establishing a pecking order for groups that defines their rights and obligations to the state, and the state to them. Finally, inequality here is top-down, implemented by political leaders and enforced by the machinery of the state. Inequality, in other words, is official state business. It is intended, not incidental; authorized, not accidental.

Inequality in communal membership takes its shape from the type of group identity (or identities) that leaders make salient for political purposes. Religion, ideology, gender, class, and sexual orientation, among others, can all provide the basis for collectively unequal treatment by the state. Here I concentrate on a particularly powerful form of group identification: ethnicity.[5] Historically, stratification across ethnic lines has been one of the most persistent and durable forms of inequality across all manner of political communities. From the regime's standpoint, ethnicity offers a potent means for identifying its supporters, especially amidst the uncertainty that characterizes initial nation- and state-building campaigns. Presumed shared interests and values among coethnics not only facilitate the redistribution of resources toward one's own group but also make it easier to predict their behavior. From the standpoint of marginalized ethnic groups, ethnicity provides the building block for organizing collective action to challenge the regime's vision that shunts them into second-class status. Ethnicity provides the framework for defining the political community and for potentially challenging its unequal nature if leaders choose to activate latent ethnic cleavages as the basis for their continued rule. Put differently, ethnicity is a group identity that not only defines who you are and your category of membership within the broader community but also what can be done to you by political authorities.[6]

If membership is distributed unequally across ethnic groups, it creates the possibility that militaries will also reflect these underlying status inequalities. To date, scholars have mostly focused on political institutions and national economies as sites of inequality. The military, by contrast, has largely escaped attention, despite the clear connection between citizenship (and membership more broadly) and military service.[7] I therefore seek to close this gap by

---

5. I define *ethnicity* as an identity category in which descent-based attributes are necessary for membership. This definition also encompasses tribal and clan affiliation. In some instances, sectarian identities may operate like ethnicity if viewed as descent-based and if high switching costs are imposed on an individual for changing the identity. See Habyarimana et al. 2009; Chandra 2006; Horowitz 1985.

6. Appiah 2018.

7. Levi 1997.

focusing on *military inequality*, the degree to which membership in the political community is distributed unevenly across the ethnic groups that comprise the military of a national state or other form of political organization.

That militaries themselves are ethnically diverse might seem uncontroversial. Yet our theories of military effectiveness, and international relations more generally, typically treat militaries as functionally equivalent and uniform across states. We affix labels to militaries in a kind of shorthand—the "American" army, "Soviet" soldiers, and the like—that smooth over internal fissures and factions arising from their multiethnic nature. Historically, however, ethnically heterogeneous armies were the norm, not the exception, in world politics. Of the 825 belligerent observations in Project Mars, only a meager ten instances saw the fielding of a monoethnic army. Instead, the typical army fought with an average of nearly five ethnic groups represented in its ranks during wars from 1800 to 2011.[8]

Examples abound. Napoleon's massive 674,000-strong Grand Armée enlisted more non-French soldiers, including Poles, various Germanic populations from the Rhine Confederation, Italians, and Dutch, than it did French soldiers on its fateful 1812 march to Moscow.[9] Qing China's Eight Banner and Green Army formations integrated Han, Mongol, and Manchu populations while also raising auxiliaries from locals, including the Muslim Hui, in nineteenth century wars in Central Asia.[10] France and the United Kingdom routinely assembled armies and fought colonial wars throughout Africa and Asia in which their own populations represented less than a quarter of the forces fielded.[11] Nazi Germany deployed more than two million non-Germans from at least twenty different ethnic groups, including Finns, Poles, and Russians, on the Eastern Front in World War Two.[12] The Red Army, often treated as ethnically Russian in popular accounts, was astonishingly diverse. Its 10,000-strong 45th Rifle Division, for example, had twenty-eight ethnic groups under arms when it decamped at Stalingrad in 1942.[13]

Economists can turn to the venerable Gini coefficient to measure how far a society's distribution of income deviates from perfect equality. We have no such existing measure for the degree of inequality within militaries,

8. This estimate is almost certainly an undercount. Incomplete records, changing identities over time, and the fact that armies often incorporate new groups as they fight, all conspire to reduce the estimated prewar number of ethnic groups within a given army.

9. Zamoyski 2005.

10. Elliott 2001.

11. Vandervort 1998; MacDonald 2014.

12. Stahel 2018; Müller 2012, xxxii.

13. Hellbeck 2015, 464fn187.

however.[14] I therefore introduce a new index, the military inequality coefficient (MIC), that calculates an army's level of inequality across its constituent ethnic groups. It consists of two components. First, I calculate the relative share that each ethnic group represents of the army's prewar personnel. Second, I assign each ethnic group a numeric value based on its position within the political community. Specifically, I denote whether the ethnic group was fully included in the community (a "0"), faced state-sanctioned discrimination (a "0.5"), or suffered collective repression by the state (a "1"). We then interact these two components to generate a value between 0 (perfect equality) and 1 (perfect inequality). This calculation can be summarized in a simple formula:

$$MIC = \sum_{i=1}^{n} pt_i$$

Here, p is the proportion of a belligerent's army that an ethnic group represents, t is the nature of the state's prewar treatment of that ethnic group, and n is the total number of ethnic groups in the army. This logic is best illustrated by example. A belligerent with egalitarian norms of membership for all ethnic groups would score a 0 for its military inequality coefficient, denoting perfect equality. In a more complicated example, imagine a belligerent with an ethnically stratified political community and an army with three ethnic groups divided between a favored group (50 percent of all soldiers), a marginalized group (25 percent), and a repressed group (25 percent). This belligerent would receive a military inequality coefficient of 0.375.[15] Now imagine a belligerent that forcibly drafted 80 percent of its army from repressed ethnic groups, leaving only 20 percent of its soldiers, likely officers, drawn from a privileged ethnic group. This ethnic setup would result in an extremely high coefficient of 0.80. Indeed, it is likely that belligerent armies never reach the theoretical maximum of 1 as this would mean the entire army was staffed solely by repressed ethnic groups. Military inequality may thus be subject to a possibility frontier; the need to maintain control over potentially disloyal soldiers likely imposes an upper bound on inequality, just as income distributions never reach perfect inequality. To anticipate our empirical results, no belligerent records a military inequality coefficient over 0.80.

14. An earlier effort, the military participation ratio (MPR), captured the proportion of the population eligible for military service but did not weight by ethnic groups or prewar state treatment (Andreski 1954, 33–35). More recently, the Ethnic Power Relations (EPR) dataset measured ethnic group access to executive political power since 1945 but excluded the military (Cederman, Wimmer and Min 2010).

15. Formally, $(0.50 * 0) + (0.25 * 0.5) + (0.25 * 1) = 0.375$.

The military inequality coefficient has several desirable properties. It is easily interpreted; higher values indicate greater inequality within the army. Both components are measured before war commences, helping to avoid confounding with wartime processes. Many elements of national power, including the performance of advanced weapons, are shrouded in secrecy and uncertainty. Military inequality, by contrast, is comparatively hard to hide. It also provides a grammar for cross-belligerent comparison and for discussing levels of inequality.[16] Finally, the military inequality coefficient is flexible. It can be applied to estimate the inequality of an entire army, specific divisions and brigades within it, and even small detachments. As a result, the index offers a rebuttal to skeptics who believe structural explanations are unable to render specific predictions about intra-army variation or the behavior of individual units in fast-moving wartime environments.

1.2. Defining Battlefield Performance

We need a clear conceptualization of battlefield performance if we are to make headway in understanding its theoretical drivers and empirical patterns. Unfortunately, no consensus exists over what constitutes military effectiveness, a mark of both its importance and complexity. Indeed, the study of military effectiveness resembles something of a tangled thicket, chockablock with competing definitions and associated indicators that grasp for our attention.[17] The outlines of two broad camps can be identified, however. Some scholars, perhaps the majority, cast military effectiveness in terms of a state's ability to impose relatively greater costs on enemy forces than it suffers. Relative casualties, expressed as a loss-exchange ratio, and organizational tasks associated with survivability and lethality, including questions of tactics, operational art, and force deployment, are emphasized here as measures of military effectiveness.[18] Stephen Biddle's view of military power—"the capacity to destroy the largest possible defensive force over the largest possible territory for the smallest attacker casualties in the least time"[19]—captures this task-centered approach. A second camp focuses on cohesion as the cornerstone

16. To add precision to our discussion, I assign the following military inequality coefficient values to capture gradations (or "bands") of inequality: low (0–0.20), medium (0.21–0.40), high (0.41–0.60), and extreme (≥0.60, which in practice tops out at 0.80).

17. For important examples, see Reiter 2017, 4; Talmadge 2015, 5; Brooks and Stanley 2007, 9; Rosen 1995, 6; Millett and Murray 1988, 2.

18. Grauer 2016; Tuunainen 2016; Talmadge 2015; Boff 2012; Erickson 2007; Strachan 2006; Biddle 2004; Millett and Murray 1988; Beaumont and Snyder 1980.

19. Biddle 2004, 6.

of effectiveness. Cohesive forces are resilient, able to shoulder heavy losses without caving, and exhibit a "will to fight" that stretches the breaking point of armies, prolonging the war.[20] Jasen Castillo, for example, has painted effectiveness in terms of a military's staying power, or the "ability of national leaders to keep the armed forces fighting as the probability of victory begins to fall and the pressures to quit rise."[21] Both camps offer important insights. But by studying military power and cohesion in isolation, we foreclose the possibility that some belligerents may face trade-offs between these two elements when trying to field effective armies.

In the hopes of clearing the conceptual brush, I set aside the term military effectiveness here in favor a new conceptual and empirical framework, what I term "battlefield performance." I define battlefield performance as *the degree to which a state's armed forces can generate and apply coercive violence against enemy forces in direct battle.* This sparse definition has several properties. First, it casts battlefield performance as a trait of a particular military organization or its individual units. Combat provides the setting to observe relative performance, especially since combat represents the collision of opposing forces and their strategies, but performance here is strictly a function of how well the belligerent itself produces and applies coercive violence. Second, this definition concentrates on the tactical and operational levels of the battlefield. Performance cannot be deduced from battle outcomes; defining performance in terms of victory and defeat risks tautology.[22] Instead, this conceptualization draws our eye toward an army's ability to perform certain tasks at the battle level that contribute to victory. There may indeed be a correlation between battlefield performance and battle (or war) outcomes. But the empirical domain here is task completion in battles, which are defined as sustained fights between sizable armed formations of larger armies that aim at destroying enemy forces and securing some objective such as territorial conquest. Battles represent the smallest building block of wartime dynamics, enabling interwar comparisons. Drawing on a battle-level conceptualization avoids excluding belligerents not capable of planning or implementing operations or campaigns; it is an open empirical question whether a belligerent can fight simultaneous battles or orchestrate a series of battles according to a campaign plan, and our theorizing should avoid assuming a level of sophistication that at least some belligerents cannot manage. Some wars, after all, consist of a

20. McNerney et al. 2018; Castillo 2014; Reese 2011; Fennell 2011; Watson 2008; Lynn 1984; Van Creveld 1982; Hauser 1980; Wesbrook 1980; Shils and Janowitz 1948.

21. Castillo 2014, 13.

22. Millett and Murray 1988, 3.

single, decisive battle, while others consist of a series of one-off engagements, situations that would lead to their omission if an operation was the unit of account.[23]

The idea of coercive violence is central to this conceptualization. Fighting has an instrumental logic: it is designed to shape the behavior of a target audience, principally enemy political and military leaders, through the imposition of direct costs and the threat of future ones if their behavior is not altered. The brute force destruction of opposing forces is only a small part of the story; fighting here is seen as aimed at coercing compliance with a belligerent's political demands, even when (especially when) the adversary does not want to comply.[24] Violence is a political tool, not an end state or permanent condition, and reflects an ongoing attempt between enemies to manipulate the costs of continuing with a course of action unwanted by each side. Coercive violence is as much about bending an opponent's will to one's own for political gain as it is the destruction of enemy forces; perhaps more so.[25] I am agnostic about the ultimate ends to which violence is applied. What matters most here is that this conceptualization of battlefield performance is a deeply political one. Both the generation and the application of coercive violence involve political decisions about the nature of the war, how it will be conducted and, crucially for our purposes, who can participate. Political expediency, rather than considerations of efficiency, thus takes pride of place in this view of battlefield performance.[26]

This conceptualization expresses performance in terms of an armed force's proficiency at two central war-fighting tasks: (1) maintain discipline within and control over deployed forces during combat ("cohesion"), and (2) retain the ability to survive and maneuver under enemy fire to inflict maximal casualties on opposing forces for minimal friendly losses ("combat power"). I take each in turn.

Cohesion refers to the shared belief among commanders and soldiers that their primary loyalty lies with the unit, not their specific identity group or individual person, and that all members are willing to sacrifice, even die, for common objectives.[27] Generating a cohesive armed force requires undertaking two tasks. First, soldier compliance with orders must be inculcated until

---

23. For that reason, I do not impose a universal standard for defining a battle. The numbers involved, casualties, territorial gains, and duration, all vary across battles. These engagements are, however, larger than skirmishes that involve only a handful of small units.

24. See especially Schelling 2008, 6–9; Kalyvas 2006, 26–29.

25. Clausewitz 1984, 75.

26. This view contrasts with the prominent efficiency-based conceptualization offered by Millett and Murray 1988, 2.

27. Henderson 1985, 4.

it becomes habitual. At root, this is a question of discipline: "the consistently rationalized, methodically trained and exact execution of the received order in which all personal criticism is unconditionally suspended and the actor is unswervingly and exclusively set for carrying out the command."[28] In an ideal military, discipline is uniform and automatic, the product of prewar socialization that leads soldiers to internalize the need to obey. Duty becomes habit; external enforcement is present but not needed, as motives for compliance in this idealized setting are left unquestioned. In the real world, however, soldier compliance is variable and unevenly distributed both across and within militaries. As a result, we can imagine a spectrum of soldier compliance in wartime that ranges from near total obedience to near total breakdown. Some belligerents field armies that withstand tremendous pressure without disintegrating in a spasm of desertion, side-switching, or panicked retreats. In others, military commanders steadily issue orders and appeal to discipline as their formations slowly crumble under the weight of mounting casualties. Still others collapse after the first blow has landed, and sometimes even before. Some belligerents simply struggle to field their armies at all, dragooning their men to the front lines before they steal away at first opportunity.

Second, armies must possess the ability to monitor and sanction, if necessary, their soldiers for noncompliance. They vary considerably, however, in their ability to enforce order. We can imagine a continuum of institutional mechanisms designed to maintain order that range from routine bureaucratization and military police to more intrusive monitoring regimes to coercive threats levied against soldiers and their families. In some cases, armies have even fielded specialized units known as blocking detachments to manufacture cohesion through the threat (and practice) of fratricidal violence.[29] Our notions of top-down control therefore combine with more bottom-up concerns about soldier discipline to inform two interrelated channels by which coercive power is generated during wartime. This twofold conceptualization alerts us to the possibility that coercive violence can actually be turned against one's own soldiers as a means of enforcing discipline and order on the battlefield.

The application of coercive violence on the battlefield can also be broken into two components. First, we can treat the sophistication of a military's tactics and operational art as running along a continuum from low to high.[30] Tactical proficiency, for example, can be assessed from individual soldiers'

28. Weber 1946, 253.

29. Lyall 2017.

30. Tactics are defined as "the specific techniques used by combat units to fight engagements in order to secure operational objectives" (Millett and Murray 1988, 19). Operations encompass the "analysis, selection, and development of institutional concepts or doctrines for

weapons skills, their ability to use cover and concealment to move under enemy fire, and their ability to integrate with other units to achieve broader objectives. Operational-level judgments revolve around the ability of units to conduct combined arms operations, including the level of coordination across different types of units, to recover from surprise and to exercise initiative when battlefield opportunities present themselves, and to maneuver to undertake risky actions, including exploitation operations that involve decentralized decision-making and a high degree of skill.[31] Assessments of proficiency are therefore context-specific since they involve judging the appropriateness of a chosen tactical or operational solution given the nature of the battlefield problem. Sophistication is a matter of "fit" between problem and solution, a judgment that necessarily involves understanding the menu of options available to commanders at the time and, above all, whether certain paths were foreclosed to them.

Combat power can also be measured as a function of relative casualties among belligerent armies. This is perhaps the most intuitive aspect of the book's notion of battlefield performance. We can imagine a continuum of performance in relative casualties, as measured by the loss-exchange ratio (LER), that ranges from above parity for belligerent A (belligerent A is inflicting more casualties on belligerent B) to below parity (belligerent B is inflicting more casualties on belligerent A).[32] Loss-exchange ratios are clearly influenced by the sophistication of a belligerent's tactics and operational art, though military technology and terrain, to name just two factors, also condition casualties.

1.2.1. Measuring Battlefield Performance

Shifting from conceptualization to measurement, I use four broad quantitative indicators to measure battlefield performance across and within armies. These measures are: the belligerent's loss-exchange ratio, the incidence of mass desertion from the ranks, the outbreak of mass defection to opposing

---

employing major forces to achieve strategic objectives within a theater of war" (Millett and Murray 1988, 12).

31. On the neglect of soldier skill in existing literature, see Biddle 2007.

32. Alternatively, fractional loss-exchange ratios (FLER) can be used to estimate the relative fraction of each side's fielded forces lost to enemy fire. Formally, it is defined as the fraction of belligerent A's forces lost in battle divided by the fraction of belligerent B's forces. From belligerent A's perspective, its relative FLER is defined as:

$$\frac{A_a/A_b}{B_a/B_b}$$

where a represents battle deaths and b represents the number of soldiers fielded by belligerent A and B, respectively.

forces, and whether the belligerent fielded blocking detachments to coerce its own soldiers to fight. Together, these four behavioral measures capture core elements of the production and application of coercive violence in modern war. Each of these behaviors is important in its own right and is analytically distinct; a book could be written about each of them. But there are also important linkages between them; they are not entirely independent of one another. Heavy casualties, for example, may spark mass desertion. The reverse may also be true; casualties may be driven higher because of defensive breakdowns as soldiers desert, thinning the defenders' ranks. Blocking detachments may deter both desertion and defection, but only at the cost of self-inflicted casualties, worsening a belligerent's loss-exchange ratio. Desertion and defection might co-occur as soldiers seek the nearest exit from the army; they may also be substitutes, as soldiers choose their exit based on proximity to the front line. Given that these behaviors might influence one another, it makes sense to consider them collectively rather than alone.

In recognition of their partially intertwined nature, I constructed a *Battlefield Performance Index* (*BPI*), which bundles together these four behavioral measures into a single family index. This index can be applied to summarize the wartime performance of an entire army or a single unit, depending on analytical needs. It also facilitates cross-national comparison by providing a convenient scaffolding for data collection. I scale the index from 0 to 1, where 0 indicates poor performance, 1 denotes excellent performance, and the presence of each of those four battlefield pathologies results in a 0.25 penalty to a belligerent's score. For example, a belligerent whose armed forces experienced mass desertion but maintained an above parity loss-exchange ratio, did not suffer mass defection, and never deployed blocking detachments would earn a 0.75 score. Armies that had both mass desertion and defection would score at 0.50, and so on.[33]

This composite measure offers a comprehensive but not exhaustive look at battlefield performance. It aims to thread the needle between a too-narrow focus on a single wartime indicator and an unwieldy laundry list of disparate measures.[34] The BPI is particularly helpful for congruence testing, where I push the book's proposed argument about inequality and alternative

33. This approach shares similarities with the concept of "repertoires" that civil war scholars use to explain patterns of behavior by armed groups across different types of lethal and nonlethal violence. See Gutiérrez-Sanín and Wood 2017; Hoover Green 2018; Stanton 2016.

34. In one particularly graphic instance, Trevor Dupuy constructed a quantified judgment model that identified variables that explained literally dozens of different combat outcomes, including rates of attrition, casualties, and advance, and the overall winner of the battle (Dupuy 1979).

explanations to account for both these individual aspects of battlefield performance and the overall pattern itself.[35] Using multiple measures creates a formidable set of "hoops" for prospective arguments to jump through, facilitating competitive hypothesis testing.[36] Arguments that only partially explain this congruence, or that fail to account for individual measures of battlefield performance, should be downgraded in favor of those that can predict specific behaviors and the entire bundle of indicators.[37]

Separately and jointly, these measures and index provide the initial scaffolding for our empirical investigation. Not every measure of battlefield performance can (or should) be quantified, however. Accurate measurement under wartime conditions is difficult, especially if the outcomes in question are fast-moving and arising out of dynamic interaction with opposing forces.

I therefore draw on qualitative evidence to render additional judgements about another dimension of battlefield performance: the sophistication and appropriateness of tactical- and operational-level decisions made by military commanders. In particular, I examine the nature of the solutions that commanders deemed available for solving their particular battlefield problems. We want to recover, if possible, the sense of the playbook that commanders employed, including whether certain options had been removed as infeasible given the composition of the deployed forces. Qualitative evidence and methods are also brought to bear on the question of possible trade-offs between combat power and cohesion on the battlefield. For example, did commanders consciously reject tactical and operational solutions that promised better overall performance for fear that these efforts might undercut cohesion? Was innovation avoided for fear of upsetting a fragile balance between the two halves of battlefield performance? And did tactical choices broaden or narrow as the war progressed? These granular assessments of how coercive violence was actually wielded against enemy forces restores a sense of dynamism to the static indicators that comprise the BPI. They also remind us of the possibility that battlefield performance is subject to political pressures that can induce self-imposed constraints on the full exercise of a country's military power. Trade-offs and unforced errors, propelled by political imperatives, can plague battlefield performance, leading to the underprovision of coercive violence on the battlefield. Indeed, as we'll see, many armies slip on tactical straitjackets of their own devising, a fact missed if we solely examine quantitative indicators of battlefield performance.

35. Rosenbaum (2010, 339) recommends congruence testing across multiple indicators, each with their own data-generating processes and problems, to strengthen causal inference.

36. Humphreys and Jacobs 2015.

37. For a discussion of how these indicators were operationalized, see chapter 4.

1.3. The Perils of Military Inequality

The understandable moral concern that inequality provokes nonetheless obscures the fact that its effects on the battlefield are quite ambiguous.[38] Indeed, its general neglect aside, the makings of an important debate about inequality and battle can be gleaned from positions derived from different theoretical camps and traditions.

We cannot exclude the proposition that inequality is actually beneficial for war-fighting, for example. Imagine, for example, an army composed largely of soldiers drawn from repressed ethnic groups. Fielding these forces represents a transference of the war's costs and risks away from favored ruling groups onto the shoulders of the marginalized and victimized. By sheltering politically dominant groups from the consequences of war, leaders may have a freer hand to prosecute long, costly, attritional wars, boosting a state's resilience and staying power. Inequality may also unlock tactical and operational options previously dismissed due to casualty aversion. Willing to discard second-class citizens, military commanders and politicians alike might embrace tactics such as human wave assaults or, more generally, costly frontal attacks, designed to overwhelm enemy positions through the crush of numbers. Prior harm by the state, and the threat of future punishment, might also keep soldiers docile by manufacturing consent through coercion, reducing the likelihood of indiscipline. Unshackling commanders from political constraints due to casualty fears might also produce a more reckless abandon about soldiers' lives, creating a kind of ruthlessness and determination that exceeds an enemy's will to fight, leading to its defeat. Soldiers from privileged groups atop the political community's ethnic hierarchy might also fight harder to defend their status, especially if motivated by nationalism and a fear that if they faltered, domestic unrest from marginalized groups would ensue. Armies might also innovate at faster rates at higher levels of inequality, seeking technological solutions to their internal schisms that increase their lethality and survivability. Inequality might therefore be positively correlated with favorable casualties, tactical innovation, reduced desertion and defection, greater national will to fight, and higher rates of eventual battlefield victory.

It is also equally plausible that inequality is simply irrelevant for explaining battlefield performance. Traditional explanations look to a raft of other, perhaps more prosaic, drivers for battlefield victory. Perhaps the most intuitive explanation for battlefield success is the simplest: victory is won by the belligerent or coalition best able to muster a preponderance of soldiers and

---

38. For a review of the moral objections to inequality, see Scanlon 2018. For a defense of inequality, see Nozick 1974, 160–64.

matériel. "God favors the big battalion," as Napoleon quipped, a view echoed in our theories that cast war as an attritional *Materialschlacht* ("battle of material") that favors belligerents with advantageous force ratios and greater economic wherewithal.[39] Access to superior military technology has long been cited as contributing to success by creating imbalances of killing proficiency and by lowering the costs of seizing territory from less-advanced enemies.[40] Political institutions, too, have been singled out as shaping outcomes. Democracies, for example, have often been extolled as superior war-fighters, whether for their higher levels of social capital (which makes better soldiers) or their representative institutions that threaten electoral defeat for failure to choose winnable wars and battles.[41] In that vein, civil-military relations might also condition the performance of both democratic and autocratic armies. Autonomy from political interference, for example, has frequently been cited as key for creating a proficient, rather than politicized, military.[42] Militaries that have been defanged by a regime's efforts to "coup-proof" itself are likely to fare especially poorly on the battlefield if pitted against less compromised foes.[43] Yet other theories emphasize how ideational factors such as culture, nationalism, and ideology, can influence soldier motivations, military cohesion, and national will to fight. Historians point to distinctive cultural traits among Western nations that translated into centuries of (nearly) unbroken military success.[44] Nationalism may inspire soldiers to new heights, improving their morale and increasing their willingness to sacrifice, perhaps lowering the incidence of mass indiscipline and the need for formal mechanisms of control.[45] Some countries may also possess durable "strategic cultures" that shape beliefs about the utility of military power, including how and when it should be deployed on the battlefield.[46]

There are also good theoretical reasons to believe that this neglect of inequality is justified. A large literature has concentrated on the ability of militaries to socialize new recruits by stripping away preexisting identities and assembling new ones. Boot camp, realistic training, and ideological indoctrination

39. Gilpin 1981; Kennedy 1984, 1989; Desch 2008; Beckley 2010; Rotte and Schmidt 2003; Stam 1996.

40. Van Evera 1999; Glaser and Kaufmann 1998; Brown et al. 2004; Quester 1977.

41. Lake 1992; Bueno de Mesquita et al. 2003; Reiter and Stam 2003, 2002, 1998a.

42. Huntington 1957; Castillo 2014; Talmadge 2015.

43. Pilster and Böhmelt 2012, 2011; Miller 2013; Belkin and Schofer 2003; Quinlivan 1999; Luttwak 1968; Brooks 2006; Feaver 2003; Biddle and Zirkle 1996.

44. Keegan 1993; Hanson 2002; Pollack 2002. But see Lynn 2003 for a culturally based refutation of their arguments.

45. McPherson 1997; Posen 1993. But see Reiter 2007; Collins 2013.

46. Hull 2005; Johnston 1995.

are thought to forge new national or regimental identities that replace narrow ethnic identities and interests.[47] The exigencies of survival on modern battlefields have also been cited as destructive of preexisting status hierarchies and associated identities. Quite literally, prejudices and inequalities are luxuries that cannot be afforded once combat begins. As Tarak Barkawi writes, the battlefield is a place of "extreme constraint [that] thrusts tough choices upon combatants" and ultimately produces conformity so that despite "distinct backgrounds, in different organizations, soldiers acted in remarkably similar ways when caught in similar conditions. Fighting has its own structure."[48] We can take this argument one step further: combat may have generative properties, creating new identities around shared sacrifices so that soldiers come to see each other, and fight for each other, as a "band of brothers." Combat and ensuing small unit dynamics thus create cohesion by knitting soldiers together in strong bonds that trump prewar inequalities.[49] Perhaps for these reasons, nearly all of our leading explanations of military effectiveness tacitly assume that armies are cohesive, a theoretical move that effectively rules out the possibility of inequality-driven internal contradictions.[50]

We therefore have a puzzle on our hands. Military inequality might boost battlefield performance, have no effect at all, or undermine it, as the book claims. What, then, is the actual nature of the relationship between military inequality and battlefield performance? To answer this question, I created Project Mars, a new dataset of 250 conventional wars fought by 229 belligerents between 1800 and 2011.[51] Figure 1.1 plots the relationship between the military inequality of these belligerents (the x-axis) and the predicted probability that a belligerent's army will experience four different types of battlefield outcomes (the y-axis). These four behaviors are: (1) a loss-exchange ratio that drops below parity, indicating a belligerent suffered greater casualties, measured in terms of soldiers killed in action, than it inflicted on enemy forces; (2) mass desertion, in which ≥10 percent of a belligerent's deployed forces abandoned the fight and returned home without authorization; (3) mass defection, in which ≥10 percent of a belligerent's deployed forces switched sides during the war and took up arms against their former comrades; and

47. For a review, see Checkel 2017; Manekin 2017. For a critique, see Krebs 2004.

48. Barkawi 2017, 11.

49. The literature is vast. Key references include Shils and Janowitz 1948; Stouffer et al. 1949; MacCoun, Kier and Belkin 2006; Hamner 2011. For a critical take, see Bartov 2001.

50. Talmadge (2015, 7) makes this assumption explicit, noting that the "requirement to perform basic tactics presupposes the existence of cohesive units to perform them, which in turn assumes that a military has some stock of manpower that can be formed into units."

51. If we divide multifront wars like World War I into separate campaigns, then Project Mars tracks data from 322 separate campaigns.

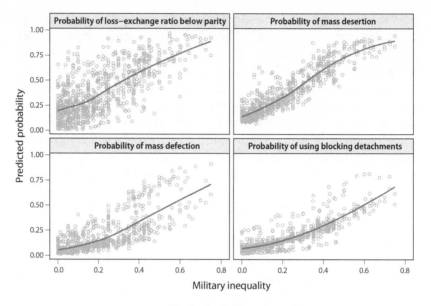

FIGURE 1.1. The Perils of Military Inequality

(4) the deployment of blocking detachments designed to coerce soldiers to fight through threat of fratricidal violence. These measures flow directly from the book's conceptualization of battlefield performance and provide the framework for comparisons across belligerents throughout the book. Each circle represents one of 825 observations of these belligerents collected by Project Mars.

The results are stark. As military inequality increases, so too does the predicted probability that a belligerent's army will experience each of these negative battlefield outcomes.[52] The likelihood that a belligerent's forces will suffer a loss-exchange rate below parity climbs from around 25 percent for belligerents at the low end of the military inequality continuum (near 0) and climbs to a 50 percent chance at 0.40, peaking at over 75 percent predicted probability once a belligerent reaches 0.60. Once a belligerent reaches the outer edges of military inequality (0.80), it is a near certainty that it will experience a below-parity LER. Mass desertion follows a virtually identical pattern, though beginning from a slightly lower predicted probability for low inequality belligerents. The predicted probability of mass defection also rapidly climbs, peaking with about a 70 percent likelihood of occurring once a belligerent reaches a 0.70 value on the military inequality continuum. Unlike

52. For how these estimates were obtained, see chapter 4.

lopsided casualties and mass desertion, however, it never exceeds a 75 percent likelihood of occurring on the battlefield, suggesting that defection is rarer in modern war than its close cousin, mass desertion. The predicted likelihood of blocking detachments being deployed is also low among belligerents with inclusive armies. Once inequality sets in, however, the predicted probability that these detachments will appear also increases, peaking near a 70 percent chance at the highest recorded levels of military inequality. Military inequality clearly confers no battlefield advantages, nor can it be shrugged off as irrelevant. The task now becomes explaining why and how inequality produces such disastrous battlefield outcomes.

1.4. Why Inequality Matters: The Argument in Brief

A political leader's choice about whether (and how much) the prop of ethnic inequality should be relied upon to legitimate his rule has fateful consequences for how armies are constructed. While imposing and enforcing an ethnic status hierarchy might make sense as part of a divide and rule strategy, it complicates the recruitment and staffing of a state's armed forces. Having divided the populace, at least some portion of the armed forces will now consist of individuals with exposure to state-based discrimination or worse. Far from blank slates, these individuals are the carriers of their ethnic identities, and enter military service with collective grievances born of bitter experience with government-sanctioned harm, whether political, economic, or cultural in nature. These ethnic identities are durable and persist despite—and, in some ways, because of—heavy-handed efforts to indoctrinate these new soldiers. Militaries in unequal societies are thus incubators of inequality, reinforcing rather than overturning status hierarchies.

Once these soldiers are incorporated into the ranks, prewar exposure to state-orchestrated ethnic discrimination or violence affects subsequent battlefield performance via three causal mechanisms. First, these policies affect soldier beliefs, sowing doubt about the regime's legitimacy and challenging the notion that favored ("core") and marginalized ("non-core") ethnic groups share a common purpose in the war. Hardened attitudes against political authorities translate into diminished combat motivation and a corresponding interest in redressing grievances by exiting military service. Second, the more severe the prewar abuse, the deeper the erosion of interethnic trust. As a chasm opens between core and non-core groups, the interethnic flow of information dries up, as does willingness to cooperate with non-coethnics. Absent interethnic trust, decision making at higher levels becomes circumscribed as marginalized voices are silenced, contributing to groupthink and the loss of the bonus that results from including diverse perspectives.[53] Third, the greater the inequality, the higher the intraethnic trust, as prewar harm contributes to the building of robust ethnic networks as a survival mechanism. These ties make non-coethnic groups much harder for military authorities to penetrate while also improving coethnics' abilities to mobilize collectively, including to escape from military control. The greater the share of soldiers subjected to unequal state treatment, and the more severe this treatment, the more problems a military will have in producing and applying coercive violence if left unchecked.

Political leaders and military commanders alike are not blind to the dangers of incorporating these soldiers, however. Yet excluding these second-class soldiers is difficult. The mobilization demanded by conventional wars, coupled with the uncertainties of possible substitutes such as mercenaries, conspires to force regimes to prize availability over reliability. Only if these marginalized groups represent a tiny portion of the population do we observe total exclusion.[54] Militaries instead seek to manage these internal contradictions through a combination of four battlefield management strategies. Militaries can manipulate the ethnic composition of their individual units by mixing ethnic groups in the hopes of disrupting intraethnic networks. Battlefield placement also becomes key; units with suspect loyalties can be relegated to rear areas, assigned to quiet sectors, or sandwiched between more dedicated units. Commanders can also be sanctioned for disciplinary breakdowns, encouraging strong-hand policies that reduce opportunities for subversive acts by marginalized groups. Brutality, too, can be unleashed; armies can resort to fratricidal violence to manufacture cohesion through coercion.

Each of these strategies purchases cohesion at the cost of combat power, however. The greater the reliance placed on these strategies, the farther an army deviates from the efficient maximization of its resources and personnel. Armies become increasingly entrapped by their own self-imposed limitations, forced to optimize within the constraints dictated by the need to maintain cohesion. Striving to maintain ethnic balance can mean dispersing loyalists across units that dilutes their presence, weakening the concentration of the group likely to fight hardest for the regime. Hiding units in rear or safe areas can backfire; if enemies discover these forces, then these vulnerabilities can be exploited. Sanctioning commanders not only increases casualties but also instills caution and risk avoidance, creating incentives to cling to past practices

---

53. Page 2017.

54. We must take care to distinguish between marginalized ("non-core") populations and minorities; non-core groups may represent a plurality or even a majority of the population. Marginalized status is a political construct, not a sign of demographic weight.

even if they are suboptimal. In addition to inflating casualties, fratricidal violence also destroys any belief that favored- and second-class groups share a common fate, weakening combat motivation. Interethnic trust also becomes a casualty; an interethnic band of brothers is unlikely to form under these conditions. These trade-offs and costs are intensified by enemy action and by chance but are not created by them. Instead, prewar inequalities set in motion the trade-offs that unfold during wartime.

As a result, we should anticipate that as prewar inequality increases, battlefield performance declines, as illustrated in figure 1.1. Inclusive armies should exhibit the highest degree of tactical and operational sophistication; the most favorable loss-exchange ratio, with the lowest predicted likelihood of having a LER below parity; and the lowest predicted likelihood of observing mass desertion, mass defection, and the use of blocking detachments. As a belligerent's military inequality coefficient rises, these trade-offs should bite deeper, hamstringing tactical and operational choices while increasing the likelihood that these four pathologies will plague their armies. At extreme levels, belligerents should have difficulties simply fielding an army. They should also possess the lowest BPI scores, denoting that these are suffering from multiple inequality-induced problems. Put simply, armies tailor their own straitjackets depending on their ethnic demographics, the nature of prewar treatment of constituent ethnic groups, and their decisions about how to manage potential disloyalty in the ranks. But these dynamics are generalizable, repeating across belligerents in a series of empirical patterns that are visible across the past two centuries.

To be clear, the central driver of battlefield performance is military inequality, not ethnic diversity. In particular, I am not claiming that the underprovision of coercive violence on the battlefield is a function of the number of ethnic groups in the armed forces. Political scientists and economists have long argued that local and national ethnic heterogeneity leads to reduced collective goods provision.[55] Language barriers raise transaction costs and coordination difficulties when crossing ethnic lines, leading to more fragile cooperation and failed collective action. The logic here is seductively simple: the more ethnic groups in uniform, the greater the coordination problems, and the lower the battlefield performance. Yet it falls silent when predicting which ethnic groups are most likely to desert or defect; which groups have sufficient motive to organize collectively to escape military service; and which ethnic groups have dense enough networks to be successful in their

---

55. Alesina, Baqir and Easterly 1999; Miguel and Gugerty 2005; Alesina and LaFerrara 2005. This view has been challenged recently. See, for example, Robinson 2017; Gerring, Hoffman and Zarecki 2018; Wimmer 2018.

attempts to flee. Only by incorporating prewar identity politics, and especially the state's efforts to articulate and enforce the tiers of membership in the political community, can we fill in the how, why, and when of ethnic-based countermobilization. As this book endeavors to show, military inequality, not ethnic arithmetic, is what drives battlefield performance in modern war.

1.5.   Toward a More Global Military History: Introducing Project Mars

This book was born from the belief that tremendous gains could be made to our understanding of the drivers of battlefield performance if we only invested in new data collection. Project Mars was the result of this ambition. Seven years in the making, Project Mars was assembled and cross-validated by 134 coders working with primary and secondary sources in twenty-one languages. We used a model of adversarial coding in which Blue teams gathered initial data and then specialized Red teams subjected these estimates to random audits for quality control and intercoder reliability checks. New measures for military inequality, belligerent traits such as regime type and material preponderance, control variables, and battlefield performance were all collected as part of this coding process. For the first time, we now have cross-national data for wartime behaviors such as fratricidal violence and mass indiscipline that have for too long been neglected or sidelined in our studies of military effectiveness.[56]

Undoubtedly ambitious, Project Mars would still represent something of a missed opportunity if it did not also interrogate existing notions of conventional war. Two concerns were paramount. First, I was convinced that the preeminent dataset used to study military effectiveness, the Correlates of War's Inter-State War dataset, had overlooked or misidentified a substantial number of conventional wars and the belligerents who fought them. With 98 unique belligerents fighting 95 wars (1816–2003) in 337 total observations, COW's Inter-State War dataset contains far fewer wars and belligerents than Project Mars, for example.[57] This difference stems partly from COW's early coding decisions about who counts as a belligerent that unfortunately relegated many non-Western belligerents to non-state status, dropping them from the Inter-State War dataset. This raises a second, broader, concern. Our theories of military effectiveness continue to be devised, tested, and refined on a

---

56. A detailed discussion of the coding procedures and data sources of Project Mars is provided in the online appendix "Sources, Data, Methods."

57. A side-by-side comparison of Project Mars and COW's Inter-State War dataset is also provided in "Sources, Data, Methods."

vanishingly small subset of this (skewed) dataset, with the same wars (especially World Wars I and II) and belligerents (the United States, Germany, Israel) crowding out other, more representative, cases. As Christopher Clark quipped, "The events of 1914 remain…intricate enough to accommodate any number of hypotheses…There is virtually no viewpoint on its origins that cannot be supported from a selection of the available sources."[58] Together, these two trends reinforce the Western and Great Power biases in our studies.[59] By casting its net widely, Project Mars offers something of an antidote, drawing heavily from regions, including Africa, Central Asia, and South America, that have been underrepresented in existing studies and datasets.

Project Mars represents an attempt to reset the empirical baseline of conventional war since 1800 and, in doing so, to craft a more global military history. In the interests of transparency, I briefly detail the understandings of conventional war and belligerents used by Project Mars below.

1.5.1. Scope Conditions

A *conventional war* is defined as armed combat between the military organizations of two or more belligerents engaged in direct battle that causes at least five hundred battlefield fatalities over the duration of hostilities. This is a deliberately sparse definition. It is agnostic about the reasons for the war, belligerents' wartime aims, and its outcomes, including whether the belligerents actually survive the war. Wars may be of variable length and do not require a fixed set of battles to be included. The definition implies that each side has a sufficient level of organization to field armies; that the violence is wielded for broader political purposes; and that armies are organized and applied toward the task of physically destroying, or otherwise incapacitating, an adversary's military power through direct combat. Terrain features are used to mask advances and to augment their defenses, creating spatial differentiation between front lines and rear areas even when combat is mobile in nature. Soldiers in these wars do not hide their identities; they wear distinctive uniforms marking them as combatants, though in some instances, notably during the nineteenth century, this practice was honored only informally. One-sided political violence, including massacres and pogroms, small-scale raids, feuds, and skirmishes, and insurgencies fought against the central government are excluded from this definition.[60]

---

58. Clark 2012, xxi, xxiv.

59. On this Western bias, see Black 2004; Porter 2009; Sharman 2019.

60. The list of included wars is found in the first appendix.

Within this domain, armies exhibit clear evidence of military specialization. In particular, armies embrace a tripartite organization of infantry, cavalry, and artillery branches, and seek to employ these forces as "combined arms" on the battlefield. Combined arms refers to the set of tactics, procedures, and planning that guides the integration of these three branches to maximize each component's lethality and survivability.[61] By integrating these branches, armies can calibrate the effects of their firepower and maneuver to destroy enemy forces while safeguarding their own. The emphasis here is on seizing and controlling ground by defeating enemy forces through either exploitation operations after successful breakthroughs or attrition that renders hostile forces unable to sustain resistance. Flowing from this conceptualization, belligerents had to employ firearm-equipped soldiers to be included in Project Mars. This condition ensures a strict apples-to-apples comparison rather than mixing belligerents that did, and did not, possess firearms. Many of the new belligerents added to Project Mars worked to overcome their technological limits by acquiring firearms, including artillery, through trade (including slaves) with European powers, the creation of indigenous factories, and the hiring of mercenaries. In a few cases, belligerents possessed only partially equipped forces at the war's outset, using initial victories to acquire weapons to outfit their soldiers. In other cases, locally produced weapons were actually of higher quality than European ones, a rude shock to colonial invaders. The Maratha Empire's artillery, which decimated British forces at the 1803 Battle of Assaye, had both longer range and a quicker rate of fire than British cannons, for example.[62]

We cannot treat the modern era (1800–2011) as a single unbroken era of warfare, however. Technological innovations, the rise of nationalism and democratization, and other global trends have altered the costs, if not the nature, of direct battle over time. I therefore divide this time period into the early modern (1800–1917) and modern (1918–2011) eras. The French Revolution, along with Napoleon's initial victories, ushered in the early modern era of mass mobilization and rudimentary combined arms doctrine.[63] Historians date the arrival of the modern system to November 1917, when, at the Battle of Cambrai, British forces first marshaled tanks, aircraft, and artillery to crack German lines.[64] While the principles of conventional warfare and combined arms doctrine do remain similar across these two eras, the advent of the internal combustion engine, the subsequent mechanization

---

61. Citino 2004; House 2001, 4–5; Boff 2012, 5.

62. Cooper 2003, 110–11.

63. Epstein 1994; Esdaile 2008, 10–11.

64. Smithers 1992; Addington 1994, 158–68; Bailey 1996, 140–46; Sheffield 2001, 108–50; Strachan 1988, 223–306; McNeill 1982, 132–53; Biddle 2004, 28–51.

of armies, and the rise of modern communications technology have sharply increased the twin challenges of survival and maneuver on the battlefield. The modern era is marked by greater lethality and fire volume; three-dimensional battles, facilitated by the emergence of aircraft and (later) reconnaissance satellites; often greater mobility and operational speed; more complicated logistics; and greater battlefield decentralization, which complicates the task of maintaining control and discipline on "empty" modern battlefields.[65]

In a sharp break with current practices, this conceptualization of war also includes civil wars if they were fought conventionally. Their curious omission from existing datasets of conventional war is hard to justify on analytical grounds. Moreover, their absence has meant that our theories and empirical findings are silent about some of the most important conflicts of the past two hundred years, including the American Civil War, the Taiping and Nien Rebellions in Qing China, the various campaigns of the Russian Civil War, and the Spanish Civil War. Many of the most destructive civil wars of the post-1945 era—the Biafran War in Nigeria, the Afghan Civil War, and the Second Congo War, for example—were also fought conventionally but are excluded from current "interstate" war datasets.[66]

Perhaps most radically, I define a *belligerent* as a political entity that claims control over, and authority within, a defined territory and populace, and that can field a conventional army. This, too, is a minimal definition, one meant to challenge the idealized Weberian conception of statehood that tacitly underpins existing work on military effectiveness. Control over population need not be absolute. Nor do I require states to possess formal diplomatic recognition from France or Britain, or hold membership in the United Nations, to count as a belligerent.[67] By abandoning this long-standing requirement of diplomatic recognition, we avoid inadvertently introducing selection bias into our data collection. If recognition is only extended to states that win (or survive) their wars, or if there are political machinations behind granting recognition, then we risk excluding relevant belligerents who could (and did) fight conventionally from our universe of cases. In total, 124 new belligerents

65. Project Mars data also reveals that post-1917 wars were more likely to involve democracies; be coalitional in nature; and be a civil war than pre-1918 conflicts. They may also have different escalatory dynamics that condition war-fighting in certain ways (Carson 2018, 11).

66. Nearly one-third of conflicts in Project Mars (n = 83) were civil wars.

67. COW mandates that states must have received diplomatic accreditation at the level of chargé d'affaires or higher from Britain and France in the 1816–1919 era. In the post–World War One era, a state must be a member of the League of Nations or the United Nations or possess accreditation from two Great Powers to be considered a member of the international system. See Singer and Small 1966; Russett, Singer and Small 1968; Singer and Small 1972; Small and Singer 1982.

were added to Project Mars that are not included in COW's Inter-State War dataset.[68] These new belligerents run the gamut from large empires, such as the Durrani Empire, Maratha Empire, the Sokoto Caliphate, and the Mandinka Empire to tiny Central Asian khanates such as Bukhara and Khiva; Bukhara itself was a city-state so small that an intrepid observer estimated its size by walking around its fortified walls.[69] Rebel organizations, including the Taliban, Northern Alliance, the Bolsheviks during the Russian Civil War, and the Taiping Heavenly Kingdom, are also included.[70] This not only provides a more comprehensive account of past wars but are also exactly the type of belligerents that remain especially relevant for contemporary security concerns.

1.6. Research Design

The book also seeks to make a contribution to *how* we study battlefield performance. Adopting a design-based approach, the book integrates quantitative and qualitative evidence in a shared framework.[71] To be certain, there are clear incentives to minimize dry methodological discussions in the hopes of reaching a broader audience. Here, however, I err on the side of transparency, leaving visible much of the book's methodological scaffolding in a bid to convince readers of both the book's core claims and its way of testing them. Put differently, the book's empirical strategy, and in particular the selection and design of its comparative cases, is part of the message. That empirical strategy moves through four stages (table 1.1). First, a theory-building natural experiment is used to road-test and refine initial hypotheses about military inequality's effects as well as to generate the comparative framework used to guide process tracing in subsequent chapters. Second, statistical analyses using cross-national war-level data from Project Mars are employed to test the association between multiple measures of military inequality and battlefield performance in 250 wars since 1800. Third, three pairs of belligerents in controlled comparisons enable close-range process-tracing of the argument and alternative explanations across diverse contexts and historical eras. Finally, I marshal microlevel evidence from four Soviet Rifle Divisions in two paired comparisons during the 1941 Battle of Moscow to test the argument's ability to explain within-army variation in a war unparalleled for its scale and brutality.

68. These belligerents are listed in the second appendix. Formally, a state must suffer ≥1% of casualties or field ≥5% of total deployed forces in a given war to be coded as a belligerent.

69. Schuyler 1877.

70. The emerging literature on rebel governance treats these actors as governing authorities despite their contested sovereignty, uncertain legitimacy, and absence of international recognition. See Mampilly 2011; Staniland 2012; Arjona 2010.

71. Lieberman 2005; Gerring 2012.

TABLE 1.1. Research Design

Purpose	Method	Belligerent	MIC[a]	War	KIA[b]
Theory-building	Natural experiment	Mahdiya	0.01	First Mahdi War, 1881–85	51,405
		Mahdiya	0.67	Second Mahdi War, 1896–99	17,004
Cross-national evidence	Statistical analysis	229 Belligerents		250 Wars, 1800–2011	45.87 million
Theory-testing	Matched comparisons via random selection	Pair A: Sultanate of Morocco	0.01	Spanish-Moroccan War, 1859–60	8,576
		Pair A: Khanate of Kokand	0.70	Russia-Kokandian War, 1864–65	6,262
		Pair B: Ottoman Empire	0.45	Italo-Turkish War, 1911–12	13,111
		Pair B: Austro-Hungarian Empire	0.37	Eastern Front, WWI, 1914–17	2.16 million
		Pair C: Ethiopia	0.24	Ethiopian-Eritrean War, 1998–2000	97,410
		Pair C: Democratic Republic of Congo	0.55	Second Congo War, 1998–2002	16,550
Explain intra-army variation	Microlevel analysis	Soviet Union (16th Army)	0.44	Battle for Moscow, 1941	937,453
		Comparison A: 38th and 108th Rifle Divisions	0.90,0.40	Oct 1941	
		Comparison B: 78th and 316th Rifle Divisions	0.25,0.78	Nov–Dec 1941	

Note: [a] MIC refers to a belligerent's Military Inequality Coefficient. It ranges from 0 (perfect equality) to 1 (perfect inequality).
[b] KIA refer to the estimated mean number of soldiers killed on the battlefield for all belligerents. Wounded, missing, and civilian casualties are all excluded.

This mixed-method research design is built around a Neyman-Rubin potential outcomes framework in which counterfactual observations are used to isolate military inequality's causal effects.[72] The fundamental problem of causal inference here is a simple one: it is logically impossible to observe the same belligerent with high and low levels of military inequality simultaneously. Nor can we randomly assign military inequality to belligerents in a grand experiment to create identical "treatment" and "control" cases with high and low (or no) inequality.[73] We can, however, use a procedure known as matching to identify counterfactual observations. In this application, matching constructs pairs of belligerents that are similar across a wide range of traits thought to dictate battlefield performance but that vary in their levels of prewar military inequality. The closer the matching—that is, the more similar the belligerents—the better our estimate of military inequality's effects, as all other traits are shared across the belligerents and thus cannot explain observed differences in performance. I therefore rely on matching for both quantitative statistical tests and case selection for the paired historical cases. Counterfactuals are directly woven into the fabric of the design, helping to answer the question of how battlefield performance would have improved (or declined) if the belligerent had a lower (or higher) level of prewar military inequality.[74]

The first stage of this multi-method empirical investigation consists of a theory-building study of the rise and subsequent fall of the Mahdiya during the First (1881–85) and Second (1896–99) Mahdi Wars against Anglo-Egyptian forces. While we cannot randomize the assignment of military inequality, we can exploit situations where a sudden exogenous shock rapidly shifts its prewar levels, creating a "natural" experiment of sorts.[75] The Mahdiya offers one such opportunity. Its rise was as remarkable as it was unexpected: within four short years, the Mahdi, an upstart religious leader from a humble background, had forged a nationalist movement that successfully drove out first Egyptian and then British forces from the Sudan, giving rise to the independent Mahdi state in 1885. An inclusive belligerent, the Mahdiya turned in a credible battlefield performance, employing fairly sophisticated tactics that ensured favorable loss-exchange ratios for most of its battles. Desertion was modest; defection, almost entirely absent. At the height of his power,

---

72. On matching, see Neyman 1923; Rubin 2006; Rosenbaum 2002; Ho et al. 2007.

73. For a review of experimental turn in IR, see Hyde 2015.

74. "Counterfactuals, like ghosts, should haunt historians," John Lewis Gaddis has written (2018, 150). Indeed, historians have increasingly recognized the value of counterfactual analysis. See, for example, Gavin 2015; Levy 2015.

75. Mahoney 2010; Dunning 2014, 209–10.

however, the Mahdi was struck down by typhus. His successor, the Khalifa, cast aside ethnic inclusion and moved to entrench his own Ta'aisha tribe as a new ruling class. The boundaries of the political community were violently recast as scores of ethnic groups and tribes within the Mahdiya's diverse population were singled out for repression. Nearly half of the Mahdiya's population was systematically repressed through heavy-handed pacification campaigns, deliberate starvation, and forced population displacement. His military machine reflected these schisms, and his war against Anglo-Egyptian forces in 1896–99 was undone by chronic desertion and defection, disastrous casualties, and an inability to execute even basic tactics and operations. In short, the Mahdi's as-if random death isolates the causal effects of military inequality on subsequent performance since all other explanatory variables were left unchanged. Process tracing across these two variants of the Mahdiya helps refine the book's core claims by uncovering additional auxiliary observations to watch for, especially trade-offs between combat power and cohesion. It also builds out the list of contextual variables that combines with Project Mars data to inform the comparative template used for the remaining historical cases.

Next, the book turns to statistical analysis to conduct a cross-national investigation of military inequality and five measures of battlefield performance. Rather than treating 1800–2011 as a single, undifferentiated era of warfare, these analyses are conducted within the early modern (1800–1917) and modern (1918–) eras of conventional war. Variables drawn from alternative explanations of military effectiveness, including material preponderance and regime type, are also incorporated in these analyses. These cross-national tests are supplemented using a two-control group comparison that pairs high-inequality belligerents with "control" observations drawn first from low inequality belligerents and then medium-inequality belligerents.[76] The central idea here is to observe how the "dosage" of inequality affects battlefield performance across similar belligerents. While military historians are often (rightly) skeptical of quantitative analysis, the method has several advantages. New data on belligerent traits and wartime behavior within an expanded universe of conventional wars helps uncover patterns between military inequality and battlefield performance that are hard, if not impossible, to observe in a single case study. Drawing on hundreds of belligerents and wars establishes the range of variation for both the independent and dependent variable, in turn facilitating the selection of representative case studies for more close-range analysis. The approach is also transparent and replicable. But there are, of course, limitations. Project Mars does not offer time series data; each variable

76. Rosenbaum 2010, 116–18.

is only measured once for each belligerent during a given war. Not every important variable can be measured quantitatively. The quality and quantity of data are also uneven across belligerents and wars. And while regression analysis is ideal for discovering associations between variables, these data are too coarse to capture causal mechanisms at work or the influence of battlefield dynamics. As a result, qualitative case studies are required for process tracing the expected relationship between military inequality, proposed causal mechanisms, and eventual battlefield performance. Case studies are especially important for probing the motives of commanders and soldiers as well as the nature and severity of trade-offs between combat power and cohesion as wartime dynamics unfold over time.

This challenge is tackled in the research design's third stage. I construct three matched pairs in which a treated belligerent is matched with a control belligerent that shares similar traits but has a different level of prewar military inequality. The first comparison pits the Sultanate of Morocco's battlefield performance during the Spanish-Moroccan War (1859–60) against that of the Khanate of Kokand's 1864–65 war with Russia. The second comparison contrasts Ottoman performance during the 1911–12 Italo-Turkish war in Tripolitania with Austria-Hungary's wartime efforts on the Eastern Front during World War I (1914–17). The third comparison draws on Ethiopian battlefield performance during the Ethiopian-Eritrean War (1998–2000) and the Democratic Republic of Congo's campaign during the Second Congo War (1998–2002). For each controlled comparison, I use process tracing to catalogue how military inequality affected battlefield performance during the war, paying particular attention to the causal mechanisms at work and the trade-offs induced by inequality.[77] As an additional test, I spotlight a specific battle for each belligerent, pushing the military inequality argument to account for microlevel dynamics. These narratives are assembled from multiple sources in eight languages, including sanctioned wartime histories, regimental narratives, soldiers' memoirs, journalistic accounts, and internal reports from surveillance and intelligence agencies. Sometimes these materials take unusual form. Captured wartime correspondence, for example, was especially important for understanding Kokand's leader, 'Alimqul, as he implored his reluctant soldiers to stand fast against invading Russian forces in 1864 (they didn't). New battle-level data, including loss-exchange ratios and the timing and severity of mass desertion and defection, rounds out each narrative.

Combining process tracing with a paired comparison approach is somewhat unusual; process tracing is typically deployed within a single case. This makes for a slightly cumbersome chapter organization, for which I can only ask the reader's forbearance. The advantages of a matched pair design are

77. On process tracing, see George and Bennett 2005; Bennett and Checkel 2015.

considerable, however. The controlled comparison eliminates alternative explanations whose values are shared by both cases, helping isolate the proposed causal process while reducing the problem of equifinality, or multiple pathways to the same outcome. We can also observe how the dosage level of inequality affects battlefield outcomes. Each pair of belligerents is separated by a difference in inequality of varying size, allowing us to see the effects of a massive (the Morocco-Kokand comparison), medium-sized (Ethiopia-DRC), and small (Ottoman-Habsburg) difference in military inequality while belligerent traits are identical or similar within pairs. In short, this approach increases our confidence in the value of within-case observations of battlefield performance by disciplining them against a similar case where inequality is at a (far) lower level.[78]

Our findings often hinge on the cases we choose; these are admittedly unexpected cases, let alone pairings. How were they chosen? Drawing on a purpose-built matching software package in *R*, these belligerents were chosen randomly from the Project Mars universe. The matching program combed through the entire dataset to construct pairs of belligerents that shared similar traits across an initial set of thirteen covariates but varied in terms of their level of military inequality. Specifically, belligerents with extreme or high levels of inequality (the "treated" cases) were paired with similar states with low or medium levels (the "controls") to help isolate the military inequality's effects by holding constant leading explanations for battlefield performance. Where multiple counterfactuals were found to be suitable matches for the treated belligerent—which occurred often—the control observation was randomly selected by the matching program, completing the pair.[79] I then conducted a second round of matching on fifteen additional contextual covariates identified as important during the Mahdiya theory-building case. These variables were often difficult to measure quantitatively and thus escaped the first round of matching. Their inclusion helps guard against omitted variables that might drive the analysis and where cross-national data collection might be infeasible or miss important nuances.

Matching and random case selection have a number of advantages over traditional methods. Automating case selection removes discretion from the author's hands, preventing cherry-picking of favorable cases to test the book's argument. The procedure is both transparent and replicable, and can also be

78. In other words, we move past the assumption that the same process is absent (or reduced) in the counterfactual; we actually demonstrate it. On the need to process trace across cases, not simply within them, see Lyall 2015.

79. On using random case selection, see Fearon and Laitin 2008. On matching for case selection, see Nielsen 2014; Weller and Barnes 2014, 88–103. All technical details for this matching are outlined in the online appendix "Sources, Data, Methods."

extended if new data become available. And since treated cases are dropped from the dataset if no appropriate matches are found, it ensures that selected cases are more representative of average belligerents and wars than if outliers with few or no matches were chosen. Ironically, this motley collection of cases, standing as it does outside the mainstream in the study of military effectiveness, provides surer ground for testing the generalizability of the book's claims than focusing solely on the canonical but unrepresentative usual suspects (Germany, the United States, Israel) that dominate existing studies. There are trade-offs with this approach; it can select cases where the historiography is far less developed than other, more well-known, cases. It also hinges on whether important drivers of battlefield performance are omitted from the matching exercise. In our case, the inclusion of additional covariates from the inductive theory building can partially mitigate this problem. Moreover, any omitted variable must be able to explain battlefield performance across and within all of these cases, a difficult challenge.

A final inferential hurdle remains: explaining the behavior of specific units on the battlefield itself. Structural arguments like the one proposed here are often painted as too slow-moving, too coarse, to account for fast-paced battlefield dynamics or the behavior of individual units. After all, isn't military inequality a property of the state, and therefore constant across units? I meet this challenge head-on by examining the performance of four Soviet Rifle Divisions during the brutal Battle of Moscow (October–December 1941). One of the most destructive battles in the most lethal war recorded in Project Mars, at least 937,000 "irrecoverable losses" were suffered by Soviet and German forces in just two months.[80]

I build two paired comparisons from the historical record, seeking to hold factors like terrain, enemy forces, and divisional size and weapons constant, or at least highly similar, across each pair. The first comparison centers around the 38th and 108th Rifle Divisions in October 1941. Both were encircled by fast-moving German forces; only one, the 108th, emerged from the encirclement, while the 38th was destroyed and struck from the Red Army's official roster of divisions. This divergence stemmed from each unit's respective level of military inequality. The 38th was staffed by conscripts from repressed nationalities of the Northern Caucasus, earning an extremely high 0.90 military inequality coefficient. The 108th, by contrast, was recruited from predominantly, though not exclusively, Russian populations in the Western Special Military District, and so had a much lower 0.45 military inequality coefficient. The same pattern repeats with the second comparison between the 78th and 316th Rifle Divisions. The 78th, a so-called 'Siberian' unit from

---

80. Lopukhovsky and Kavalerchik 2017, 37. Soviet forces accounted for 900,000 of these losses.

the Far Eastern Military District, had a low 0.20 military inequality coefficient, reflecting its mostly Russian recruits, and fought well, even managing to spearhead a Soviet counteroffensive in early December. The 316th, however, turned in a poor performance, and was withdrawn from frontline duties in early December. It, too, had an extremely high 0.90 military inequality coefficient; its soldiers were drawn almost exclusively from repressed Kazakh and Kirghiz populations. These microlevel comparisons stitch together divisional narratives for each unit from declassified war logs, military personnel records, General Staff reports, and even newly released Soviet High Command (*Stavka*) maps, the suspected positions of each division marked out in grease pencil.

Taken together, these four stages represent an interlocking set of difficult tests for the military inequality argument and alternative explanations. The motive behind this empirical strategy was a simple one: to devise and then test a generalizable explanation for battlefield performance in conventional wars since 1800. By design, the counterfactual reasoning and comparative setup of the design rejects the contention that all wars are unique and that, by extension, no meaningful patterns can be discerned.[81] Wars and belligerents are not identical, of course, but enough similarity remains, especially when deduced through a clear comparative logic, to detect stable patterns over time. The fact that we continue to observe a negative relationship between inequality and battlefield performance across historical cases that span nearly 150 years, encompass both interstate and civil wars, were waged in vastly different environments, involved belligerents of sharply different strength and regime types, and ranged in lethality from relatively few casualties to the slaughterhouses of World War I and II, should give us confidence that a genuine relationship is at work. In total, this empirical strategy generates estimates of the average population-level causal effects of military inequality; details the related causal mechanisms and microfoundations through process tracing across multiple streams of evidence; renders clear predictions about within-army variation; and engages case-specific explanations and historiography around selected belligerents and wars. The ambition is undeniable, but hopefully so too is the payoff for our understanding of the drivers of battlefield performance.

1.7. Plan of the Book

The book is divided into three parts. Part I, which draws on chapters 2–4, makes the theoretical case for military inequality's effects on battlefield performance since 1800 and provides two initial tests of these claims. Chapter 2 argues for a causal connection between (rising) military inequality and

---

81. For a forceful defense of the view that each war is "utterly unique," see Schake 2018.

(declining) battlefield performance. It does so by first exploring the nature and severity of ethnic inequalities within political communities before detailing how exposure to state policies can affect soldier beliefs and actions. Next, the chapter considers how military commanders, aware of possible issues arising from inequality, adopt a mixture of four strategies to manage soldiers from suspect populations. The chapter then examines how these strategies induce trade-offs between combat power and cohesion that actually undermine battlefield performance. Finally, the chapter considers how enemy actions can intensify these internal contradictions and trade-offs before concluding with a discussion of how several of the arguments' core assumptions can be relaxed. Our qualitative investigation begins in chapter 3 with a theory-building study of the rise and subsequent fall of the Mahdiya during the First (1881–85) and Second (1896–99) Mahdi Wars against Anglo-Egyptian forces. The chapter performs double duty by illustrating the effects of a sudden and unexpected shift from low to extreme military inequality while also building out the matched template used to structure paired comparisons in subsequent chapters. Chapter 4 draws on statistical tests of the linkage between multiple measures of military inequality and five battlefield measures, including loss-exchange ratios, the incidence of mass desertion and defection, the use of blocking detachments, and a composite battlefield performance index. A robust association between military inequality and all of these measures is identified within both the early modern and modern eras of conventional wars. Leading alternative explanations, by contrast, find little empirical support.

Part II, encompassing chapters 5–7, offers close-range investigation of inequality's effects on battlefield performance using three paired historical comparisons spanning 150 years that were randomly drawn from Project Mars. Chapter 5 contrasts the Sultanate of Morocco's strong performance during the 1859–60 Spanish-Moroccan War with the Khanate of Kokand's disastrous outing during its 1864–65 war with Russia. Though similar across twenty-eight covariates, these belligerents were separated by a massive 0.69 difference in military inequality. Kokand's extreme level of inequality, one of the highest recorded in Project Mars, led to mass desertion, lopsided casualties, and the copious use of coercion to force its soldiers to fight. Moroccan forces, despite being outmatched by Spanish weapons, nonetheless managed to turn in a credible performance, exhibiting far greater resilience and tactical skill than Kokand's dispirited soldiers. Chapter 6 compares the Ottoman Empire, a high inequality belligerent, with its medium inequality Austro-Hungarian counterpart, during their respective wars in Tripolitania (1911–12) and on the Eastern Front of World War I (1914–17). Here the gap in military inequality is modest, at 0.08, suggesting that their observed differences should be far less glaring. Indeed, I find that while Ottoman performance was poor, the Austro-Hungarian *k.u.k.* army was only marginally better. Moreover, wartime victimization of its own population pulled Austro-Hungary up the ladder of inequality, resulting in worsened performance that by war's end closely resembled Ottoman shortcomings.

Chapter 7 extends the argument to the modern era by comparing the battlefield performance of Ethiopia and the Democratic Republic of the Congo (DRC) during two of the most destructive conventional wars in the post-1945 era: the Second Congo War (1998–2002) and the Ethiopia-Eritrea War (1998–2000). Despite remarkably similar traits, these belligerents, separated by a substantial 0.32 difference in military inequality, had sharply different wartime outcomes. The DRC's army, riddled with ethnic contradictions, nearly collapsed as a coherent fighting force at the war's outset, leading military commanders to augment regular units with a motley collection of mercenaries, child soldiers, militia, and forces from neighboring Zimbabwe and Angola. For their part, Ethiopian forces waged some of the largest mechanized battles of the post-1945 era and displayed increasing sophistication over time. Mechanized units not only repelled Eritrea's initial invasion but cracked its defensive system in a series of grueling offensives reminiscent of World War I's trench warfare. Though casualties were high, Ethiopian forces displayed a high degree of cohesion and tactical innovation on their way to capturing nearly one-quarter of Eritrea.

Part III consists of two chapters. Taking up the challenge of explaining within-army variation, chapter 8 extends the argument to an outlier case— the Battle of Moscow—to explain the divergent performance of paired Soviet Rifle Divisions during October–December 1941. Reconstructing divisional histories from declassified material, the chapter first chronicles the divergent fates of the 38th and 108th Rifle Divisions after Germany launched Operation Typhoon in October 1941. It then turns to the 78th and 316th Rifle Divisions during the renewed German offensive in early November, its eventual stalling out, and the subsequent Soviet counteroffensive in December. Battlefield outcomes, including the very survival of these divisions, tracks closely with their military inequality coefficients. Indeed, the two units with the highest level of inequality, namely the 38th and 316th Rifle Divisions, were either destroyed completely or driven from frontline duties. Chapter 9 concludes by summarizing the book's main findings before applying the argument to an out-of-sample case, that of Iraqi battlefield performance against the Islamic State in 2014–17. The chapter also teases out the book's implications for international relations theory, proposes a new research program around inequality and war, suggests several policy implications flowing from the argument, and peeks cautiously at the future of war.

PART I

Setting the Stage

THEORY AND INITIAL EVIDENCE

2

Divided Armies

A THEORY OF BATTLEFIELD PERFORMANCE
IN MODERN WAR

Is there anything worse for a state than to be split and disunited?
Or anything better than cohesion and unity?

PLATO, *THE REPUBLIC*, 381 BC

WHILE WE OFTEN PAY lip service to the notion that war is a human endeavor, the soldiers that march and die in our theories of war and battle are typically treated as faceless agents, at once universal and anonymous. We write of battlefield outcomes in terms of the quantity of soldiers in battle or the quality of their weapons; the properties of their political systems, whether democratic or authoritarian; and of the strategies and tactics adopted by commanders and followed, more or less stoically, by their soldiers. Despite periodic warnings from historians,[1] our theories have largely abstracted away the human element of war in search of generalizable insights that, now wrenched free of historical context, can be applied to explain the performance of armies and their interchangeable soldiers across time.

This, I argue, is a mistake. Armies are not uniform, nor are soldiers universal. Indeed, once we peer inside the "black box" of armies, we find that they are shot through with internal contradictions and inequalities, the legacy of prewar nation-building policies enacted by leaders seeking to construct collective identities to legitimate their rule. More specifically, if leaders choose to rule by exploiting ethnic cleavages within their societies, then their armies will also reflect these ethnic inequalities within the ranks, creating inefficiencies and friction that undermines battlefield performance. To tweak Clausewitz,

---

1. Keegan 1976; Lynn 2003; Freedman 2017.

war is viewed here as an extension of domestic identity politics by other means.[2] As a consequence, most armies arrive on the battlefield not as highly optimized and lethal killing machines that our theories expect but instead as hobbled political creatures seeking to fight and survive while trapped within straitjackets of their own devising.[3]

This chapter takes up the challenge of theorizing how prewar military inequality shapes battlefield performance in modern war. Inequality matters in two ways. First, the prewar creation of ethnic hierarchies by leaders, along with their enforcement by the state, creates divided armies as individuals from lower-status groups are folded into the military machine. As a result, these armies are marked by disaffected soldiers among these targeted ethnic groups, shattered interethnic trust across soldiers from groups of different status, and dense intraethnic networks that facilitate collective resistance to military authorities. Second, battlefield management strategies used to triage these problems offer only partial solutions; in some cases, they actually intensify the consequences of inequality. While intended to prevent the breakdown of cohesion, these measures represent self-imposed constraints on tactics and operations that end up hamstringing combat power. In turn, efforts to manage inequality create new vulnerabilities that can be exploited by enemies on the battlefield, increasing the danger of military defeat. Divided armies are, in the end, flawed by design.

The argument is summarized in figure 2.1. To detail each step in the causal argument from prewar inequality to battlefield outcomes, I proceed as follows. First, I examine how national leaders construct political communities for legitimacy purposes. Some collective identities are inclusive, according equal status to all ethnic groups within society. Others, however, use ethnicity as a political cudgel, erecting status hierarchies that stratify membership in the political community along ethnic lines. Second, I discuss how these top-down communal visions enforce the incomplete citizenship of targeted ethnic groups through two kinds of collective punishment, ethnic discrimination and collective violence. Third, I explore how exposure to state-orchestrated collective punishment hardens ethnic identification among coethnics, creating a series of downstream consequences for an army's discipline and cohesion when these groups are incorporated in the army. The intuition here is simple but important: an army's fate is set well in advance of the war, meaning that a too-narrow focus on combat dynamics alone will miss the deeper underlying structural forces at work in constraining battlefield

2. Clausewitz 1984.

3. On the assumption that armies maximize military effectiveness over political considerations, see, for example, Vagts 1959, 13; Millett and Murray 1988; Biddle 2004; Greitens 2016, 31.

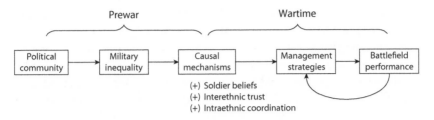

FIGURE 2.1. The Argument

performance. Fourth, I detail the three mechanisms through which hardened ethnic identities set in motion the processes that erode an army's performance once war begins. Fifth, I detail the set of strategies that commanders use to manage the dilemma of difference arising from inequality within their divided armies. I also derive a cluster of testable claims about how military inequality affects the two facets of battlefield performance, namely, combat power and cohesion. Finally, I refine the theory by relaxing core assumptions, including the belief that coethnic solders share uniform preferences and that military inequality is unchanged by wartime dynamics or long-term evolutionary processes.

2.1. Political Communities and Their Hierarchies of Membership

Political leaders face the same basic governance problem: how to construct, and then sustain, a vision of the political community that transfers the primary allegiance of the population from various subnational ("subordinate") group identities to a collective ("superordinate") one and the political organization that claims to represent it.[4] In the modern era, the need for national identification arose from the shift from indirect to direct forms of rule that occurred around the time of the French Revolution.[5] Driven by advances in communication and transportation, this shift to direct rule raised new demands on leaders and subjects alike. Political centralization made it possible for regimes to impose additional burdens on their subjects (and then citizens), including

4. I use the clunky term "political organization" because the post-1800 time period is still home to empires, principalities, duchies, tribal confederations, and other polities, not simply national states. I set aside the (fascinating) question of whether inequality's effects also hold before 1800.

5. Wimmer 2013; Hechter 2000; Mann 1993; Weber 1976; Tilly 1975. On the modernist school of nationalism, see Anderson 1983; Gellner 1983; Hobsbawm 1991.

increased taxation and expectations of military service.[6] For their part, leaders were forced to devise new forms of allegiance that might bind citizens to the state, thereby lowering the costs of rule by dissuading uprisings among an increasingly supportive, nationalistic populace. Military power, too, could be enhanced if leaders could find a way to harness this nationalism behind their war efforts.[7] In exchange, the population would receive a sense of belonging and purpose, a view of a larger collective that defined their place in the world and that established expectations about how leaders would treat them.[8] In the end, these collective identities aimed to supplant existing allegiances with the promise of membership in a broader community that would elevate the station of those who came to identify with (and as) the national identity.

How leaders answer this challenge becomes crucial for the creation of military power. Perhaps the most important question in crafting these collective identities is the simplest: who belongs? Or, more properly, how narrowly should the boundaries of the political community be defined? We can imagine a spectrum that begins with full inclusion for all members of the political organization (see figure 2.2). In this space, all individuals are full (or "core") citizens: their identities are enmeshed with, or absorbed by, the broader political community. These identities often draw on civic conceptions of the community that are stripped of specific group characteristics in favor of a more accessible, perhaps substantively thinner, national identification. Other communal visions, however, are exclusionary, and establish hierarchies of membership that define some groups as incomplete (or "non-core") citizens.[9] Incomplete citizenship can take two forms. Some communal visions, for example, treat targeted groups as second-class citizens, a status enforced by state-imposed restrictions on rights and obligations. Other visions, however, push toward a more extreme outcome, viewing targeted groups as peripheral to, or even outside, the broader community even as they remain within its political boundaries. State rhetoric here is often less than subtle, casting these groups in dehumanizing language like "alien" or worse. Nation-building is thus an exercise in power and the top-down categorization of groups into durable and persistent status hierarchies.[10]

6. Prior colonial legacies can therefore also play an outsized role in shaping ethnic hierarchies for newly independent states.

7. Reiter 2007; Posen 1993; Rosen 1972.

8. Appiah 2018. Instrumental motives, such as access to employment opportunities, may also be at work (Laitin 1998).

9. On "semi-citizens" in democracies, see Cohen 2009.

10. Bendix 1964; Strauss 2015; Wimmer 2018. Status hierarchies shape both equality of opportunity and outcome for ethnic groups (Atkinson 2015).

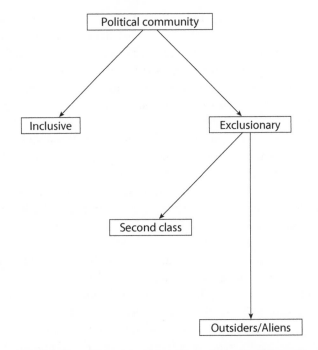

FIGURE 2.2. Political Communities and Their Ethnic Group-Based Status Hierarchies

Leaders can choose from a wide array of possible identity categories or cleavages to construct their status hierarchies, including religion, class, ideology, gender, and region. I focus on ethnicity and its close cousin, race, as the basis for status hierarchies. Ethnicity can be a powerful device for building a political community.[11] As a set of ascriptive traits, ethnicity provides would-be rulers with a template for quickly identifying potential supporters and possible enemies. Exploiting ethnic divisions can also generate powerful us/them dichotomies that rally coethnic supporters to the regime's side.[12] Coethnic networks offer a means for mobilizing supporters against noncoethnic challengers, helping to ensure regime safety. Ethnicity also facilitates the construction of coethnic coalitions that can ensure both the capture of the state and the favorable distribution of resources and services to coethnics.[13] Drawing on ethnic differences also helps leaders render their own societies "legible" for conscription purposes. That is, ethnicity can provide a shorthand for distant rulers to categorize their populations, if only partially, creating

11. Wimmer 2018; Horowitz 1985.

12. Simmel 1898; Coser 1956; Tajfel 2010; Tajfel et al. 1971; Tajfel 1970.

13. Riker 1962.

the possibility of monitoring and policing their citizens.[14] Inequality is thus ethnic group-based and state-imposed, rather than arising out of competition between individuals or households, and centers around the relative status possessed by each group in the regime's vision of the political community.[15]

Ethnic hierarchies, rather than inclusion, might be an attractive option for leaders for several reasons. Downgrading the status of potential ethnic rivals can help maintain control over the distribution of scarce resources, for example.[16] Second-class status might also complicate the ability of rivals to mobilize opposition by restricting access to political and economic levers of influence.[17] Leaders may be driven by cultural motivations such as ethnonationalism that lead to the construction of the state along narrow lines that favor one's own group.[18] Marginalizing non-coethnics can also be a strategy for consolidating power in weak states, where shaky leaders seek to coup-proof their regimes by increasing the costs of rebellion.[19] Leaders might simply be guided by idiosyncratic attitudes that give rise to prejudices dictating the relegation of others to an inferior status in the broader community.

Recognizing the diverse origins of ethnic hierarchies, I take no stake in this debate. What matters here is that some leaders will reach for ethnic cleavages as the architecture for the political community and that substantial variation exists within and across states over time in the nature (and presence) of their ethnic hierarchies. Leaders are not completely free agents in their choice of social identities, of course; they cannot construct hierarchies from whole cloth. Instead, they are constrained somewhat by existing societal cleavages and experiences of the populations they seek to mold. That said, these hierarchies are typically viewed by leaders and population alike as salient and meaningful, bestowing a set of rights and obligations across different groups depending on their position within the community.[20]

Hierarchy is not synonymous with ethnic diversity, however. There is no necessary correlation between diversity, defined as the number of ethnic groups within a population, and a leader's imposition of incomplete citizenship as a tool of rule. Only two groups are needed for a hierarchy to

14. Scott 1998; Blaydes 2018.

15. On the need to treat inequality as group-based ("horizontal"), see Tilly 1999; Stewart 2008; Cederman, Gleditsch and Buhaug 2013.

16. Riker 1962; Bates 1983; Acemoglu and Robinson 2012.

17. Fearon 1999.

18. Cederman, Wimmer and Min 2010; Wimmer 2013.

19. Roessler 2016, 83.

20. This view of identity as fluid and constructed is squarely in the constructivist camp; Anderson 1992, Brass 2003, Chandra 2012. Status hierarchies are backed by political power, however, and so can acquire a sense of permanence until state policies change.

be constructed; conversely, multiple ethnic groups may coexist without a state-imposed ranking. At bottom, my argument is a political one about how (and whether) ethnic heterogeneity is defined, ranked, and enforced by political leaders, not a story about how ethnic diversity drives the underprovision of collective goods and services (in our case, battlefield performance) due to linguistic issues, divergent ethnic preferences, or other transaction costs.[21] It is ultimately a political decision about whether to activate ethnicity as a salient cleavage for the construction of the broader community.[22] These cleavages also revolve around relative group status, not group size. As a result, non-core groups may actually represent a majority of the population, despite their lesser status. Ethnic diversity, in other words, is not destiny, at least on the battlefield.

Nor can these hierarchies be reduced to mere by-products of a state's attributes and factor endowments. Some of the weakest states in the Project Mars dataset—tiny Bukhara, once nestled within contemporary Uzbekistan's borders, had less than a million inhabitants when defeated by Russia in 1873—along with some of the strongest, including the Soviet Union, had high levels of ethnic inequalities. Ethnic inequalities have also been imposed in regime types of various stripes. Democracies, though nominally predisposed toward inclusive notions of citizenship, have nonetheless exhibited durable ethnic and racial hierarchies. The United States meshed formal democratic institutions with persistent discrimination and collective violence against African-Americans for much of its history, for example.[23] Nationalizing democracies like Poland and Czechoslovakia enacted policies bent on "cleansing" ethnic minorities during the 1920s.[24] Two short-lived democracies, the Azerbaijan Democratic Republic and the Democratic Republic of Armenia, devoted much energy to the repression and expulsion of each other's coethnics in the early 1920s despite meeting the requirements for possessing democratic political institutions.[25] Autocracies, too, have exhibited considerable variation in their levels of prewar inequality. In short, we are on safe ground in considering inequality as an independent factor in

21. Alesina and LaFerrara 2005; Miguel and Gugerty 2005; Alesina, Baqir and Easterly 1999.

22. See Posner 2005, 2004. How do we know when ethnicity is salient? Following the Ethnic Power Relations (EPR) dataset, ethnicity is deemed salient when either (1) significant actors claim to act for the group's interests in the national political area, or (2) the group faces systematic discrimination or outright repression by the state in political and economic life. See Wucherpfennig et al. 2011.

23. Foner 1999; Smith 1999.

24. Brubaker 1996.

25. Geukjian 2012; Isgenderli 2011; Hovanissian 1971.

explaining battlefield performance rather than a derivative of other state attributes.[26]

2.2. When Prejudice Becomes Policy: The Role of Prewar Collective Punishment

Ethnic identities provide meaning and assign roles for individuals as they navigate their daily lives. They also define how others, the state included, treat them. Once political leaders answer the question of who belongs in a community, they face a natural follow-on: what to do with the populations that already have strong attachments to subordinate group identities? Here, I view state policies toward ethnic groups as flowing from their relative status and position in the official communal vision propagated by state leaders. Some leaders, for example, anchor their regimes in an inclusive vision in which individuals do not face a choice between national and group identities, either because they are the same or ethnic identities are not politically relevant. Ethnic groups, to the extent they are seen as salient, are not singled out as the basis for official discrimination, let alone violence.

Regarding certain ethnic groups as lower status opens the possibility that the regime will use state resources to institutionalize and maintain these ethnic hierarchies, however. The targeting of lower-status groups can take two broad forms, discrimination and repression. A group's second-class status, for example, can be established and maintained using various discriminatory policies. Access to the state's central decision-making institutions, and the political arena more broadly, may be restricted or blocked entirely. Discrimination can also take on economic shape. Public goods and services might be asymmetrically distributed by the state, for example, while access to market opportunities might be allocated according to ethnic criteria. Discrimination here is viewed as a top-down, state-orchestrated process that can edge up to, but does not include, the use of violence against a particular ethnic group. Rather, the relative distribution of status across ethnic groups is created and reproduced by deliberate state action in service of a broader vision of the political community.

Groups defined as outside the communal vision ("aliens") face the prospect that their low status creates greater latitude for the regime to enforce ethnic hierarchies through collective violence. Relegated to the margins of the community, these groups are often subject to ethnically motivated

---

26. I also use statistical analysis to probe for connections between belligerent attributes and levels of military inequality using Project Mars data. These robustness tests are provided in the online appendix.

TABLE 2.1. Political Communities and Their Prewar Treatment of Non-Core Ethnic Groups

	Inclusive	Exclusionary	
		Discriminatory	Repressive
Citizenship	Citizens	Second class	Outsiders/aliens
Collective Punishment Regime	None	Discrimination	Violence
Military Service	No restrictions ("Meritocratic")	Some restrictions ("Glass ceiling")	Severe restrictions ("Cannon fodder")
National Security	Public good	Club good	Private good

massacres, forced displacement within the state's borders, deliberate famine and starvation, and even genocide. For the regime, violence becomes a management tool, one that maintains the prevailing ethnic hierarchy while also systematically destroying the group's ability to push for greater inclusion. These state-orchestrated campaigns need not destroy the group entirely. Instead, they aim to reduce the likelihood that these low-status groups would find themselves in a position where they could overturn the existing ethnic hierarchy, leading to a status reversal for the dominant core groups.

We can use this inclusion-discrimination-violence typology as shorthand for thinking about how state power maintains status hierarchies within the population (see table 2.1). In this framework, punishment by the state is collective in nature. Given the weakness (or absence) of cross-cutting ethnic ties across core and non-core groups, the regime has limited means for penetrating these groups and selectively targeting specific individuals. Incomplete citizenship reduces the legibility of the non-core population in the eyes of the regime; it can only paint in broad brush strokes because it has truncated ties to non-core populations.[27] Monitoring these populations is by necessity both costly and incomplete. As a result, regimes will employ collective discrimination and repression against these lower-status groups, at once trying to maintain order while also inadvertently hardening ethnic identities as the basis for countermobilization.

Exposure to prewar regime-orchestrated collective punishment has several important effects on targeted groups. It strengthens perceptions that coethnics share a common fate, increasing intragroup solidarity. Collective punishment forces targeted groups to turn inward, finding solace and safety in coethnic ties. Dense networks of ties between coethnics are the result; these same networks will provide the means for escaping surveillance and organizing collective action in wartime. As it stands, the reinforcing of ethnic

27. Habyarimana et al. 2009; Lyall 2010; Roessler 2016; Blaydes 2018.

ties complicates the state's task in monitoring these populations, deepening the problem of identifying problematic individuals for selective punishment and instead forcing the state to rely on indiscriminate actions.[28] Collective punishment also naturally creates grievances against the regime; disaffection, even hatred, becomes commonplace, creating a landscape in which the regime's legitimacy is variable across ethnic groups within the population.[29] Interethnic trust is also a casualty of state-led punishment as state actions generate an us-versus-them dynamic. Differential access to power and wealth, and even freedom from violence, only further drive a wedge between groups as these asymmetries become clear markers of group status. State actions thus construct a framework in which individuals can compare the status of their group against others, highlighting the tangible realities of the official ethnic hierarchy.

Discrimination and violence do not have exactly the same effects on ethnic identification, however. Inflicting harm and property damage on targeted ethnic groups creates stronger group bonds and a sense of collective grievance than does discrimination alone. To be sure, discrimination leads to disaffection and disillusionment with the regime and its communal vision.[30] But collective repression induces a far higher sense of fear among targeted coethnics by demonstrating that group survival, not just status, is at stake. Ethnic identification should be highest among individuals who have directly experienced the state's indiscriminate violence, followed by those that have encountered discrimination. Individuals may have multiple identities, but suffering harm at the hands of the state should lead individuals to emphasize their ethnicity given its external implications. Grievances, a desire for revenge, and a willingness to subvert or escape the state's policies, should all be manifest among individuals who have been violently harmed.[31]

The timing of the collective punishment is also an important part of the story. Scratch the surface of any country's history, even liberal democracies,[32] and one is sure to uncover past exclusionary practices. Rather than emphasize past transgressions, I instead focus on how recent exposure to state-directed

28. Greater solidarity also means that coethnics can police themselves more efficiently, reducing the leakage of information to non-coethnics (see Fearon and Laitin 1996).

29. Enloe 1980.

30. The magnitude of discrimination may also hinge on its form, whether political, economic, or cultural. I treat discrimination as having uniform effects here, leaving aside the question of heterogeneity to future work.

31. At the individual level, we should expect the effects of violence to be largest among those directly victimized, followed by those who have experienced indirect harm (e.g., family or close relatives), and then individuals who are angered by harm done to the entire ethnic group.

32. Marx 2003.

collective punishment shapes group identification. More specifically, I argue that what matters most is whether soldiers and their respective ethnic groups have experienced, or are currently enduring, collective punishment a year before the outbreak of a given war.[33] This narrow temporal window ensures that coethnics have recent exposure to the effects of state policies and that the mechanisms associated with their transfer to battlefield conduct are at work. The argument does not assume that past injustices are carried forward through intergenerational transfers, though these could be present. Soldiers from these targeted groups thus enter battle with the memories of recent injustice, not ancient grievances, on their minds.

2.3.   Building Armies: The Military Inequality Coefficient

We now have the building blocks in place to construct a measure of inequality within the military itself. Individuals, for example, import their identities, relative group status, and treatment by the state into the armed forces as they become soldiers. They are carriers of their identities, so to speak, and come laden with the weight of the state's treatment of their respective groups before they enter the ranks. For their part, political leaders and military commanders must decide on the army's ethnic composition. Together, these two components—the share of soldiers represented by each ethnic group, and their prewar treatment by the state—constitute the Military Inequality Coefficient (MIC).

Formally, the MIC defines the degree to which ethnic groups within the military enjoy full membership in the political community or, conversely, are subjected to state-directed collective discrimination or repression. Generated by a simple equation,[34] the MIC takes values from 0 (perfect equality) to 1 (perfect inequality). As discussed below, the 1 represents the theoretical maximum amount of inequality possible within a given army but one that is rarely approached in the real world. The equation itself is flexible: it can be applied equally to entire armies or individual formations within them. There are multiple paths to particular MIC scores, depending on how a belligerent has structured its army and treated its various ethnic groups. Values beyond

---

33. The statistical tests in chapter 4 and supplemental analyses posted online use 1-year, 5-year, and 10-year windows before war initiation as temporal windows for the measurement of the military inequality coefficient.

34. The formula is $\sum_{i=1}^{n} pt_i$, where p is an ethnic group's share of an army's prewar strength, t represents the regime's prewar treatment of each group, with possible values (0, 0.5, 1) denoting inclusion, collective discrimination, and collective repression, and n indicates the number of ethnic groups within the belligerent's forces.

the midway point of the MIC scale (about a 0.40) can only be attained when a belligerent has engaged in prewar repression of at least one of its army's constituent ethnic groups, however.[35]

The MIC is built around a regime's prewar treatment of ethnic groups within the population. Ethnic hierarchies do not vanish once individuals find themselves within the military, however. Armies themselves are sites for the reproduction of these ethnic inequalities (see table 2.1). Notions of the combat roles that are deemed appropriate for certain ethnic groups (but not others) flow from the cleavages enshrined in the regime's official narrative of the political community. Assumptions about the political reliability and presumed loyalty of these groups also take their direction from the state's treatment of them. Groups that enjoy full inclusion in the political community, for example, are unlikely to face obstacles to their military service once they join the ranks. Civic national identities accommodate, even venerate, ethnic differences, rather than exploiting them for political gain. As a result, inclusive identities are associated with equal opportunities for all groups within the military, an officer corps drawn more or less proportionately from all groups, and service branches accessible to all groups. Contemporary Western democracies such as Canada reflect these practices. Some authoritarian states also rely on patriotism to foster allegiance to their regimes that cross-cut ethnic cleavages.[36]

Groups facing officially sanctioned discrimination will find their paths rocky once their members become soldiers. Suspicions about their motives and loyalty will lead commanders to restrict their roles and responsibilities. These ethnic groups may be underrepresented by design, whether within the officer corps or across the general rank and file, and often experience a "glass ceiling" beyond which they cannot advance. China, for example, passed a Military Service Law in 1984 outlining military service as a duty for all citizens regardless of race and religious creed; Article 55 of its constitution also defines military service as a "sacred duty" and "honored obligation" for all citizens to uphold. Yet Tibetans, Uyghurs, and other ethnic minorities who serve remain few in number. Marginalized groups may also find their roles circumscribed, often shunted into less-prestigious logistical or labor

35. To see why, consider a belligerent that has drawn a maximal 80 percent of its army from an ethnic group that has suffered discrimination but no repression. The coefficient would be calculated $(0.80 * 0.5) + (0.20 * 0)$ for the marginalized non-core and favored core group, respectively, generating a MIC of 0.40.

36. Some groups may not wish to participate in military service. Inclusion is compatible with categorical exclusion if it is consensual, as with ultra-Orthodox Jews in Israel, who do not serve in the Israeli Self-Defense Force by explicit agreement from both parties.

units that remain segregated from the army. The nascent Pakistani military embraced these practices, for example.[37] Bengalis were largely barred from senior positions in the military hierarchy, and were vastly underrepresented in the military as a whole; West Pakistani elites felt Bengalis were "effeminate" and ineffective soldiers because of their presumed closeness to Hindu peoples. By 1959, for example, Bengalis only occupied 2 percent of the military's command positions but represented an estimated 56 percent of the population in the 1951 census.[38] Those few Bengali units that did exist were isolated and received minimal training.[39]

Members of repressed ethnic groups will face even greater restrictions on their military service. They may be relegated to the role of cannon fodder on the battlefield, pushed forward in human wave attacks designed to swamp enemy defenses. Their perceived disloyalty might also lead to their consignment to duties in rear areas, their presence on the front lines proscribed by fears of defection. These groups will be subject to intensive monitoring, and will receive only rudimentary (if any at all) training for fear that military skills and firearms might diffuse to their coethnics in the general populace. Access to weapons may also be restricted; live-fire training exercises are often denied to these groups as well. Armenian soldiers, for example, were withdrawn from frontline combat duties and placed in labor battalions at the rear to facilitate their surveillance by Turkish officers during World War One. Non-Bamana ethnic groups were also driven in near suicidal attacks against Tukulor defenses by trailing Bamana officers during the 1855 war between the Bamana and Tukulor empires.

The unequal treatment of ethnic groups by the regime and within the military raises an important implication for how national security is understood in these countries. Political scientists frequently cite national security as the quintessential "public good," one that is non-excludable (meaning that all share it) and non-rivalrous (use by one individual does not reduce availability to others). Indeed, scholars from Adam Smith onward have cited national security as a pure public good.[40] Implicit in this claim is the assumption that societies, and the militaries that are drawn from them, are cohesive, and that all individuals view their government as the legitimate guarantor of safety and security (a Leviathan) and that the state acts to provide national security to *all* its citizens equally and evenly. This is true for inclusive societies with no or low levels of military inequality. Discrimination, however, changes

---

37. Brass 2003; Talbot 1998; Jalal 1995, 1990.

38. Rahman 1996, 121.

39. Cohen 1998*b*, 42fn11-44, fn13.

40. Samuelson 1954; Smith 2003, part 5, chap. 1.

national security from a public to a club good, where security from external and internal threats is rationed according to the group's relative status.[41] In these instances, the state's commitment to national security still extends to the broader population (i.e., non-rivalrous) but it will do so unevenly, as befitting the relative status of groups within the regime's collective vision. Finally, state-led repression and the divisions it creates changes national security to a private good. Under these conditions, national security is both excludable and its production (or use) can come at the expense of others. Ethnic groups repressed by the state, for example, are not only excluded from the state's protective umbrella but find that the security of the core group is being purchased at the expense of their coethnic soldiers' security and well-being. At high levels of military inequality, national security becomes a private good, one enjoyed by favored core groups while brutally denied to non-core groups.

2.4. Why Not Exclude Non-core Groups from Military Service?

We can anticipate that inviting non-core groups into the military could have potentially disastrous ramifications for battlefield performance. Why, then, do belligerents not simply restrict military service to the core group? Total exclusion, it would seem, is the safe bet, and should be the default position of all non-inclusionary belligerents. Morale among core soldiers might surge, for example, if they are positioned as defenders of the nation against external threats and internal subversion, a boost that might outweigh any reductions in manpower caused by excluding non-core groups.[42] Virulent scapegoating against fifth columnists at home—real or imagined—can exhort soldiers to ever greater sacrifices as the last line of defense.[43] Restrictive manpower policies would also allow militaries to do away with extensive control mechanisms, recouping lost resources that would otherwise be sunk into policing non-core soldiers. Exclusion also eliminates second-order consequences for social order, including the diffusion of combat skills (and possibly weapons) to the non-core population that might fuel anti-regime rebellions. Excising these groups should be especially attractive for regimes with revisionist aspirations toward neighbors that share ties with non-core ethnic groups.[44]

Yet this "radical surgery" option has been relatively infrequent historically. States have typically crafted multiethnic armies, seeking to manage, even

41. Buchanon 1965.

42. Castillo 2014, 11–12.

43. Reiter 2007; Rosen 1972.

44. Mylonas 2012.

exploit, these differences rather than expunge them. Ancient history abounds with examples of multiethnic armies. The Roman Imperial Army *auxilia* included non-citizen soldiers who fought alongside Roman legions.[45] Persia assembled vast multiethnic armies, including that of the much-maligned Darius III, whose forces were crushed by Alexander the Great at the Battle of Gaugamela in 331 BC.[46] And the Mongol Army incorporated defeated populations into its forces using a sophisticated levy system.[47] Heterogeneity, not homogeneity, has been the historical baseline for belligerents for centuries.

There are two main reasons—one pragmatic, one political—why belligerents are unlikely to exclude non-core groups from military service.

Pragmatically, excluding non-core groups completely represents a self-imposed restriction of available manpower, leaving belligerents at a disadvantage relative to rivals. Belligerents may tinker with the ethnic composition of their armies, of course, but likely face mobilization pressures that override exclusionary impulses, especially once the war begins.[48] Unless the non-core group represents only a small fraction of the population, military authorities must opt for managing potential problems rather than shrinking the recruit pool. Leaving behind substantial populations of aggrieved non-core groups while the core-group staffed army sallies forth to wage external war also creates opportunities for domestic unrest. And substitutes for non-core groups carry significant downsides that usually outweigh the troubles associated with incorporating non-core groups. Mercenaries are often unpredictable and unreliable. As Machiavelli famously warned, mercenaries "are useless and dangerous ... for they are disunited, ambitious, and without discipline, unfaithful, valiant before friends, cowardly before enemies.... They are ready enough to be your soldiers whilst you do not make war, but if war comes they take themselves off or run from the foe."[49] Slave soldiers raise similar questions of morale and skill as non-core groups but also generate negative externalities in the form of continual slave-raiding. Both the Asante and Bambara empires relied on forced impressment to staff their armies, for example, a practice that fueled near continual wars with neighboring states as slave-raiding campaigns to acquire soldiers sparked new conflicts.[50]

Pragmatic motivations are not cynical enough by half, however. Using non-core soldiers also has a clear political payoff. From the regime's perspective,

45. Cheesman 1914.
46. Rahe 2015; Briant 2015.
47. Peers 2015; May 2007.
48. Enloe 1980.
49. Machiavelli 1999, chap. 12.
50. McCaskie 1995; Roberts 1987; Bazin 1975.

the lives of non-core soldiers are, by definition, cheaper than those of core soldiers. As a result, non-core soldiers can be employed in less discriminating ways—as "cannon fodder"—without incurring the same political costs as casualties among core soldiers. Shifting the burden to non-core soldiers allows regimes to fight more protracted wars by insulating themselves from domestic opposition among core group supporters. Internal correspondence by Saddam Hussein, for example, illustrates how he maneuvered to protect (core) Sunni soldiers by forcing (non-core) Shia soldiers to advance in bloody frontal assaults against Iranian forces. "The losses should be divided," he ordered, "so that the less courageous [i.e, the Shia] must have a share in them."[51] Foreign battlefields are merely an extension of domestic identity politics; the culling of non-core soldiers by adversaries actually strengthens the regime's nation-building efforts at home.

Given the value of these non-core groups for their militaries, total exclusion should happen only under a fairly narrow set of circumstances. Strong states with capable bureaucracies, small non-core groups, and such overwhelming relative military strength that they can absorb the associated manpower penalties, are the most likely candidates for exclusionary policies. In practice, total exclusion can be extremely difficult to achieve. The canonical example is Nazi Germany's *Wehrmacht*, which barred Jews or those with partial Jewish descent (*Mischlinge*, or "half-caste") from military service under the 1935 Nuremberg Laws. No exceptions were granted; Jews were barred equally from rear area and frontline duties. Still, an estimated 150,000 soldiers of Jewish descent entered German service during World War Two.[52]

Setting these reasons aside, it is also important to examine the direction of the bias that might arise from political leaders and military commanders building their armies in anticipation of fighting certain enemies. Imagine, for example, that rigging the internal composition of armies is commonplace, and that the most disloyal elements are either pulled from the front lines or purged completely. In this case, militaries have "selected" themselves into a lower bracket of military inequality. If true, then the empirical findings that flow from my claims underestimate the true extent of military inequality's debilitating effects by lopping off the top part of the inequality spectrum. Again, while the total exclusion of large non-core groups is rare historically, if this practice were indeed more widespread, then the statistical and qualitative

---

51. "Transcript of Meetings between Saddam Hussein and Iraqi Officials Relating to Tactics," 28–29 December 1980, National Defense University Conflict Records Research Center (CRRC), document no. SH-SHTP-D-000-624.

52. Rigg 2002.

evidence gathered in subsequent chapters are actually conservative estimates that are biased against my own argument.

2.5. Creating Bands of Brothers: Causal Mechanisms

Prewar exposure to state-orchestrated discrimination or repression sets the table for potential problems on future battlefields. What we need, however, is an account of how prior exposure to these state policies affects non-core soldiers once they are sent into battle. I argue that three mechanisms are at work: (1) *soldier beliefs* about whether a "shared fate" exists between their ethnic group and the broader political community; (2) *interethnic trust* between core and non-core groups within the army; and (3) *intraethnic coordination*, the degree to which soldiers possess strong network ties with coethnics inside the military. These mechanisms are conditioned by the magnitude of collective punishment these soldiers faced in the prewar era: the harsher the treatment, the more salient these mechanisms will be, and the greater the army's deviation away from a baseline of optimization for warfare against external foes.[53] Together, these mechanisms drive a process of identification in which coethnics become bands of brothers capable of organizing collective resistance against military authorities. Under conditions of inequality, then, soldier allegiance is to the ethnic group, not a unified "band of brothers" forged through war, as prewar victimization places obstacles on the path to interethnic cooperation. These mechanisms are summarized in table 2.2.

2.5.1. Soldier Beliefs about Shared Fate

Soldier beliefs about a shared fate between his ethnic group and the broader political community provide the initial microfoundations for the effects of inequality. More specifically, do soldiers believe that the consequences of the war's outcome, as well as the costs of fighting, will be shared equally across ethnic groups within the military? Do they share a common fate, or can the war's expected outcome be met with indifference since it will not alter his group's relative status? Inclusive societies and armies are best positioned to draw a connection between the political community and the individual soldier, driving home the importance of fighting well for the common cause.[54] Soldiers need not agree with the stated purpose for the war; instead, soldiers can draw a link between their performance and eventual war outcomes, and

---

53. The effects of prewar victimization should therefore be felt most keenly among those who experienced collective violence, followed by those subjected to discrimination (but not violence) by the state.

54. Moskos 1975, 297.

TABLE 2.2. From Inequality to Battlefield Performance: Causal Mechanisms

Mechanism	Exposure to Prewar Collective Punishment		Wartime Effects
Soldier beliefs about shared fate	Bolsters ethnic solidarity	⇒	Reduces combat motivation Stokes disaffection and grievances Erodes reciprocity and fairness norms
Interethnic trust	Erodes interethnic bonds	⇒	Restricts interethnic information flows Lowers interethnic cooperation Weakens (or eliminates) diversity bonus
Intraethnic coordination	Strengthens intraethnic networks	⇒	Improves in-group policing Improves intraethnic capacity for collective action Increases state's monitoring costs

that these outcomes matter for the political community as a whole. Exposure to collective punishment, however, shreds the idea of a shared fate. Punishment hardens ethnic identities, bolsters group solidarity, and drives a wedge between the regime's efforts to proclaim a common cause and the non-core groups. Cries of "not our war" capture this severing of non-core group interests from that of the broader political community. These doubts about the existence of a shared fate across ethnic groups produces several negative consequences for battlefield conduct.

First, the combat motivation of non-core soldiers plummets once non-core soldiers become convinced that their postwar fate will remain unchanged.[55] Why undertake costly and dangerous action on the battlefield for a regime that has denigrated their group and blocked their individual advancement within the army? Victory itself might be insufficient for the regime to recast its views of the political community and upgrade their relative status. Nor can regimes sitting astride identities credibly guarantee to honor the sacrifices made by non-core soldiers. Their incentives are to valorize the contributions of core soldiers while downplaying those of non-core soldiers, thus minimizing any possible status gains non-core groups might make.

---

55. Following Lynn (1984, 34–35), I argue that prewar "sustaining" motivation carries into wartime to shape soldiers' combat motivation. On theories of morale, see especially Wilcox 2015, 4–14.

Second, and related, unequal treatment within the military reinforces existing grievances against the regime. Discrimination stokes a new round of dissatisfaction: collective violence, even deeper resentment against the regime, and even less willingness to take risks on its behalf.[56] Past and present injustices thus collide to create motivation for non-core soldiers to subvert military authorities and to organize escape from the battlefield. Far from a will to fight, these soldiers, chafing at their unequal status, are primed by state policies to have a will to flee if these opportunities can be manufactured.[57] Finally, collective punishment erodes norms of fairness and reciprocity across core and non-core soldiers. Altruism, the willingness to contribute and sacrifice without expectation of material gain, becomes increasingly conditional in these environments as soldiers become unsure that non-coethnics will reciprocate.[58] Collective punishment thus encourages the crowding out of altruism in favor of in-group parochialism, leading non-core soldiers to believe that self-preservation rather than risk-taking should be the dominant framework for understanding one's role on the battlefield.

2.5.2. Interethnic Trust

Equality sets the preconditions for the development of strong bonds and bridges across soldiers drawn from different ethnic groups. Inequality, however, along with exposure to collective punishment, has the opposite effect: it inhibits the formation of interethnic bonds by eroding interethnic trust. Soldiers from lower-status ethnic groups with firsthand experience of discrimination or repression at the hands of core soldiers will find it difficult to trust non-coethnic soldiers. Stereotypes, prejudices, and grievances combine to form a noxious brew that inhibits the formation of interethnic trust. In turn, low levels of trust deter interethnic cooperation, reducing the ability of units or formations to reach assigned goals cooperatively. Ethnic mistrust lowers task cohesion within a given unit or army.[59] Indeed, evidence from behavioral experiments indicate that exclusionary attitudes toward other groups not only predict prejudicial behavior but that individuals from high-status groups

---

56. On the connection between exposure to violence and risk-taking, see Jakiela and Ozier 2019.

57. For a survey of the vast literature on will to fight, see McNerney et al. 2018.

58. Bowles 2016.

59. I view inequality as reducing social cohesion of a unit, thereby also reducing task cohesion, so the distinction is somewhat artificial between the two. For a review, see MacCoun 1993; MacCoun, Kier and Belkin 2006; Cohen 2016, 26–28.

are willing to forgo gains to maintain their position in the hierarchy.[60] As a consequence, the growth of ethnic mistrust within divided armies can lead to suboptimal behaviors that undermine battlefield performance.

Mistrust, for example, can restrict information flows across core and non-core groups by crowding out opportunities to share news and rumors. Even modest amounts of hesitancy in sharing information has been shown to have major implications for how quickly news travels through networks, especially if individuals are drawn from different ethnic groups.[61] In particular, unwillingness to share across ethnic lines reduces the speed of information sharing, creating battlefield vulnerabilities. A unit's reaction time to surprises, for example, can be lengthened if soldiers are not sharing information or if commanders do not trust their non-core soldiers with critical information. Ironically, initial mistrust may be compounded by commanders who, seeking information about their non-core soldiers, may order enhanced monitoring, heightening mistrust even further. Low interethnic trust, along with pervasive stereotypes unchallenged by new information, also undercuts interethnic cooperation by lowering willingness to work with non-coethnics. Both sides clearly benefit from cooperating to produce military power. Yet mistrust can lead to the underprovision of both combat power and cohesion as parochial biases lead to suboptimal solutions for complex battlefield problems. This mistrust is not necessarily a function of ethnic or linguistic diversity. Instead, its origins lie in the nature of the state's prewar treatment of non-core groups and their relative position in the reigning status hierarchy. Soldiers can be ordered to cooperate, of course, but such cooperation may be partial, slipshod, and accompanied by foot-dragging not found among inclusionary armies.

Generalized mistrust also leaves divided armies unable to access one of the most powerful benefits of inclusion: the diversity bonus. Organizations that possess diversity of identities prove more adept at complex problem-solving because they are able to harness different life experiences and mental models. Identity diversity tracks closely with the creation of new conceptual approaches and tools while also reducing the risk of groupthink. Diverse teams are also better at innovation as well as predicting future patterns and outcomes.[62] Given its highly complex nature, combat is another arena in which diversity could reap dividends. Ethnic mistrust, however, destroys the culture of a shared mission (or fate) that is required to motivate soldiers and

---

60. Enos and Gidron 2018; Hainmueller and Hangartner 2013. Intriguingly, these studies suggest that poor individuals from high-status groups are most likely to succumb to prejudices, suggesting an intraethnic role for class.

61. Larson and Lewis 2017.

62. Page 2017, 5–15, 214.

teams to collaborate in collective problem-solving. Moreover, the top-down nature of military authority, coupled with prevailing status hierarchies, also means that there are few outlets for input into decision-making by members of lower-status ethnic groups. The steeper the inequality, the smaller the incentive to invest in developing new innovative tactics or promoting new solutions since they might upend the existing hierarchy. Mistrust, then, is corrosive of both task cohesion and complex problem-solving, leaving divided armies vulnerable to quick changes on the battlefield.

2.5.3. Intraethnic Coordination

Prior exposure to collective punishment also strengthens intraethnic networks among targeted groups once they enter military service. Violence, in particular, not only increases in-group solidarity through shared experiences but also alters the density of ties between coethnics. That is, violence can rewire coethnic networks by increasing the ratio of links between individuals to the total number that could possibly be present among coethnic individuals.[63] The formation of denser ties acts partly as a defense mechanism, allowing information, including rumors, to flow faster and more freely between coethnics. Denser in-group ties, coupled with mistrust of non-coethnics, accelerate the sharing of information within a group, improving intraethnic coordination.[64] Born from state-directed violence, information asymmetries between targeted coethnics and their non-coethnic minders can organize more responsive and larger collective action than might have otherwise been obtained. Robust networks therefore enable intraethnic coordination around non-cooperative behavior that can subvert battlefield performance.

More specifically, these dense networks produce at least three wartime effects. First, they improve the ability of targeted ethnic groups to police their own members.[65] Dense network ties can thwart the leakage of sensitive information about planned collective acts like desertion to non-coethnics by increasing the likelihood that any would-be leaker would be identified and quickly punished by coethnics. The deterrent effect of network ties in turn boosts the odds of successful coordinated subversive acts against military authorities. Second, these ties enable a larger number of soldiers to participate in collective disobedience. State violence supercharges mass indiscipline; under these conditions, desertion or defection will involve sizable groups of

---

63. Larson and Lewis 2017, 356.

64. On the crippling effect that hesitancy to share across ethnic lines can have on the diffusion of information within networks, see Larson and Lewis 2017, 351.

65. Fearon and Laitin 1996.

soldiers, and sometimes whole units, rather than one or two opportunistic soldiers. These ties act as highways of information about recent battlefield outcomes, prior successes in abandoning the fight, anticipated punishment for trying, and impending attacks or other emerging opportunities that might precipitate preemptive desertion or defection. Taken together, this information increases the odds of successful mass indiscipline among non-core soldiers. Finally, these ties increase the difficulties that military authorities face in tracking soldier attitudes and sanctioning their behavior. As military inequality increases, divided armies will be forced to invest heavily in surveillance and other monitoring mechanisms to counteract the strengthening of coethnic ties that are themselves the legacy of prior state punishment.

2.6. Why Do Inequalities Persist within Armies?

The account offered here assumes that prewar identities and inequalities persist—indeed, are reinforced—within the army. This view stands outside the conventional take on military socialization, however. Militaries are traditionally seen as hothouses of conformity, where a combination of top-down indoctrination and basic training strips away preexisting identities and molds new ones around national values.[66] Prevailing theories emphasize how realistic training exercises can forge new bonds among soldiers from different backgrounds by preaching teamwork, creating allegiance to a primary group (a "band of brothers") that outweighs ethnic or racial identities.[67] In a similar vein, contact theory, first devised by Gordon Allport after observing mixed US Divisions in World World Two,[68] argues that individuals drawn from different groups can break down stereotypes and prejudices through repeated interaction and collective effort at solving a common task. The pressures of combat are also often cited as forcing soldiers to set aside their differences and create strong bonds that compel them to fight hard for one another. These tight-knit groups drive combat behavior more so than ideology or material incentives since they satisfy an individual's needs for recognition, self-esteem, and friendship.[69] Given this combination of prewar indoctrination and training, along with wartime dynamics, it appears unlikely that preexisting attachments could even survive, let alone provide the bases for action, once coethnics find themselves on the battlefield.

66. On the role of ideology, see especially Lynn 1984; Posen 1993; McPherson 1994; Levi 1997; Krebs 2004; Reiter 2007; Castillo 2014; Sanin and Wood 2014.

67. Strachan 2006; Grossman 1996; Goffman 1961; Ardant du Picq 1904.

68. Allport 1954.

69. Marshall 1947; Shils and Janowitz 1948; Stouffer et al. 1949; Henderson 1985; Stewart 1991; Watson 1997; Wood 2003; Weitz 2005; Hamner 2011.

Yet the preconditions for intensive socialization and the recasting of ethnic identities are missing in divided armies. Rather than simply assume top-down ideological indoctrination has uniform effects across all soldiers, we need to consider the possibility that ideology's effects on soldier beliefs and ethnic relations are conditional on a soldier's group allegiance, falling unevenly across soldiers depending on their group status. The same is true, too, when forging a band of brothers; many of the preconditions necessary for transcending interethnic tensions are absent in divided armies.

Contact theory, for example, suggests that intergroup biases and prejudices are overcome only under a narrow set of circumstances. Groups must interact on an equal basis, share goals, be urged to cooperate by an impartial authority, and not be competing with one another.[70] These conditions neatly describe inclusive armies, where the barriers to the formation of primary group bonds and camaraderie are lowest. Divided armies, by contrast, share none of these traits. A legacy of inequality, coupled with the military's own reliance on ethnic hierarchies to establish appropriate roles and duties for its soldiers, all represent serious checks on the emergence of strong intergroup bonds, let alone the recasting of identities of soldiers drawn from groups that have suffered discrimination or repression. Moreover, experimental evidence to date suggests that interventions designed to reduce ethnic or racial prejudice generate substantially weaker effects than other forms of discrimination.[71] Ethnic identities may therefore be particularly stubborn, and any intergroup bonds that do manage to form will be weaker than coethnic ties.

Efforts to socialize non-core soldiers through top-down ideological indoctrination will also meet resistance. Indeed, ideological campaigns can inadvertently reinforce group identities among soldiers who reject the official narrative about the political community and their relative status within it. Heavy-handed indoctrination can actually increase ethnic polarization within the ranks as everyday reminders of their diminished status accumulate. Communication within a polarized environment will fuel additional polarization, leading to a spiral of intergroup competition that leaves each group's boundaries entrenched.[72] Soldiers from groups that have experienced prewar repression will be especially prone to reject or challenge the state's ideology as exclusionary. Socialization efforts can thus backfire, creating an underground river of resentment and apathy that reinforces ethnic identities at the expense of the state's own preferred narrative. Fearing punishment, non-core soldiers

70. Allport 1954; Pettigrew and Tropp 2006, 346.

71. Paluck, Green and Green 2018, 24.

72. Enos and Gidron 2018.

may dissemble and hide their true sentiments.[73] Far from broken, however, these coethnic ties will persist below the surface, frustrating the military's monitoring of its soldiers' attitudes and behavior.[74]

Preexisting inequalities can also compel states to forgo opportunities for bridge-building across ethnic divides. Some armies avoid realistic peacetime training for fear of transferring combat skills to restive populations. Segregating units, or otherwise fielding units where non-core groups are minorities, will render intergroup contact fleeting, with just enough frequency to reinforce stereotypes rather than challenge them. Inequality-induced trade-offs can increase casualties in these units, leading to such high turnover among soldiers that they never have a chance to form strong bonds or overcome prejudices.[75] Finally, belligerents may not even have standing armies that can act as sites of socialization. Indeed, nearly one-third of all 285 belligerents in the Project Mars dataset, including large powers such as the Sokoto Caliphate and Rabah Empire, had no standing armies or were forced, much like Ecuador (1820) and the Republic of Venezuela (1810), to build their armies during the first days of the war.

In short, soldiers are not blank slates to be stamped into conformity by the regime and its military. They carry their ethnic identities and histories with them into the army, where their coethnic ties not only survive but thrive. Militaries are less engines of blind socialization than contested grounds where antipathy, even hatred, of a regime and its communal visions is nourished. Soldiers also have far more agency than top-down accounts of socialization give them credit for.[76] Soldiers can and do resist indoctrination, often emerging from their initial exposure to military institutions with their group identities reinforced, not recast.

2.7.   Managing Divided Armies on the Battlefield

Politicians and commanders are not blind to the drawbacks of incorporating non-core soldiers in the ranks. True, they may lack complete information about the magnitude of these problems, especially without recent wartime experience as a benchmark for future performance. Still, it is plausible that they retain a sufficiently nuanced assessment of their own capabilities and shortcomings to enter war with reasonably accurate expectations about their

73. Kuran 1997.

74. Coethnic soldiers therefore have a "hidden transcript," in James Scott's felicitous phrasing. See Scott 1992.

75. Bartov 2001.

76. On the need for theories of socialization to allow for agency, see Checkel 2017.

TABLE 2.3. Battlefield Management Strategies and Their Trade-Offs

Strategy	Intent	Potential Problems
Manipulate unit composition ("Blending")	Improve monitoring Reduce intraethnic coordination Build interethnic bonds	Hardens prejudices/ stereotypes Disperses core soldiers Imposes tactical constraints
Hide units ("Masking")	Reduce escape opportunities	Creates battlefield vulnerabilities
Sanction commanders	Increase unit discipline	Increases casualties
Fratricidal violence	Increase unit discipline Restore tactical flexibility Manufacture cohesion	Increases casualties Destroys "shared fate" Reinforces intraethnic bonds Reduces interethnic trust

performance. Indeed, we know commanders are concerned about these inequality-induced problems because they invest in battlefield management strategies designed to mitigate or hide the weaknesses of their divided armies. In particular, military commanders have historically adopted four broad strategies for increasing the cohesion of their armies. These include: manipulating the ethnic composition of their units to find an appropriate balance between core and non-core soldiers; hiding (or "masking") the location of non-core soldiers on the battlefield; sanctioning commanders for perceived battlefield failure; and fratricidal violence designed to generate cohesion through fear of punishment. These strategies, along with their strengths and drawbacks, are summarized in table 2.3.

These strategies share the same basic flaw: they all represent second-best solutions to the problem of fielding lethal, coherent armies. Compared to inclusive armies that have little need for such efforts, belligerents with divided armies are forced to adopt these measures to ensure that their armies arrive and fight on the battlefield as cohesive entities. Doing so, however, carries significant downside risk, and even in the best case, these strategies impose constraints on tactical and operational choices that diminish combat power. As Stephen Rosen has noted, some states choose "to be less powerful than they otherwise might be,"[77] a situation that neatly describes belligerents with high levels of inequality. The sometimes ponderous, even tortured, nature

77. Rosen 1996, 1995, 6.

of these battlefield strategies is the direct result of trying to generate combat power within the constraints imposed by military inequality.[78] The higher the inequality, the more severe these battlefield management strategies become, and the farther the belligerent is pushed away from reaching its fullest potential on the battlefield. In short, these strategies may prevent belligerents from crashing into the basement of their (worst) battlefield performance, but at the cost of ensuring that they never reach their ceiling of (best) performance either.[79]

The need to field core soldiers to enforce these management strategies helps explain why military inequality never reaches its formal ceiling of 1. Perfect inequality would represent an army composed entirely of non-core soldiers from repressed ethnic groups, a recipe for surefire battlefield unreliability. In practice, military inequality is subject to a "possibility frontier" that imposes a limit on how high inequality can reach given the need to field some core soldiers to maintain discipline.[80] To anticipate the empirical findings in chapter 4, armies top out at a 0.80 value for military inequality, though individual units can break this ceiling even if the overall army average is lower (see chapter 8). Similarly, short of a robot army devoid of ethnic attachments, it is likely that the floor of perfect equality is also unlikely to be obtained by any belligerent. What matters here, however, is that the state is not officially promoting ethnic discrimination or violence; it does not rule out the possibility of cleavages arising from soldiers informally, which would not be captured by the military inequality coefficient.

Peering inside the military machine to examine these management strategies offers a useful corrective to theories that privilege interaction between armies to the exclusion of interaction between commanders and their soldiers *within* them. Moreover, these strategies help fend off the charge that structural explanations that privilege national level attributes cannot explain battlefield performance within armies because these factors are constant (or nearly so) during war.[81] While it is true that some variables of interest— say, democracy—do not vary across an army's units, that is not the case for military inequality. Variation in the nature of these battlefield strategies

78. On the distinction between combat potential and available combat power, see DuBois, Hughes and Low 1997, 74.

79. There are two implicit counterfactuals here: (1) All else being equal, how much better would a belligerent's battlefield performance be if it had lower military inequality? And (2) How much worse would its performance be if these management strategies were not adopted to prop its army up?

80. On the inequality possibility frontier for income, see Milanovic, Lindert and Williamson 2011.

81. See, for example, Talmadge 2015, 2; Kalyvas 2006. For an exception, see Balcells 2017.

generate clear predictions about unit-level behavior. The ethnic composition of units in particular provides an important bridge between prewar inequalities and the concrete form they take in specific units within the army.[82] Constructing military inequality coefficients for specific units allows us to anticipate the severity of the effects of inequality, the temporal nature of indiscipline (which units will desert or defect first?), and spatial components (where on the front lines are units most likely to break? where are blocking detachments more likely to be deployed?) of battlefield performance right down to the smallest formation. These strategies thus perform double duty: they impart dynamism to the argument in the form of repeated interaction between (wary) commanders and their (reluctant) soldiers while also transmitting the constraining effects of prewar inequality down to the various units and formations that comprise an army.[83]

2.7.1. *Manipulate Unit Composition*

"The darkest fear of every commander," John Keegan once remarked, "is that the latent crowd within his army should be set loose by panic or defeat."[84] Such fears are heightened for commanders of divided armies, who enter battle knowing that elements of their forces are reluctant to fight (at best) and predisposed toward flight (at worst). How to integrate non-core soldiers thus looms as an especially thorny problem. Historically, armies have embraced four different ways of rigging the ethnic composition of their units in a bid to maximize combat power while avoiding breakdowns in cohesion. Some armies settle on one of these approaches; others mix-and-match, experimenting with different solutions across, and sometimes within, wars. Each method represents a new set of opportunities and constraints for how commanders can employ their units on the battlefield; commanders are, in a sense, choosing their own poison, as these strategies are only partial solutions to the problem of cohesion within divided armies.

Broadly speaking, these methods can be arrayed across a spectrum from high to low levels of non-core soldier integration. At one extreme, armies have assembled "blended" units that apportion ethnic representation according to a quota system. Homogenous units are avoided; officers may draw from all ethnic groups. Tsarist Russia fielded blended units on a limited scale after

---

82. McLauchlin 2015, 678.

83. This approach is somewhat in tension with existing microlevel studies of civil war. It recognizes the importance of explaining sub-army variation, but argues that we need theories and research designs that avoid a too-narrow focus on combat dynamics to the exclusion of broader structural factors that shape and constrain these processes.

84. Keegan 1976, 173–74.

universal conscription was introduced in 1874. Units were mandated to be at least 75 percent Slavic, with non-core soldiers drawn from other regions according to their share of the population.[85] Second, belligerents can choose to set core and non-core units against one another in a "cross-guard" strategy that leans into inequality. Under this scenario, subunits (say, regiments) are ethnically homogenous but are folded into the same large organizational umbrella (say, a division). India's fixed-class units, for example, consist of battalions of four ethnically homogenous companies. Each battalion possesses companies from at least two different ethnic groups to counterbalance one another.[86] Third, further decreasing heterogeneity, militaries can construct segregated "national" units composed solely of non-core soldiers but commanded by core group officers. Both Red and White revolutionary armies fielded national units staffed by Latvians, Estonians, Ukrainians, Belorussians, and "Tatar-Muslims," during the Russian Civil War.[87] Finally, militaries can adopt "live and let live" policies, taking no special precautions to offset possible poor battlefield performance. Non-core groups are organized in their own units, nominally subordinate to the overarching military hierarchy but without special sanctioning or monitoring systems. They typically retain their own officers as well. The Qing Empire's Army, for example, was segregated ethnically, with Manchu, Han, and Mongol units, and then further divided into regional commands; no unified army existed. In fact, Qing China fought its 1894–95 war against Japan with only the Beiyang Army (and Navy), as its appeals to other regional forces went unanswered.[88]

Several advantages flow from hugging non-core soldiers to the bosom of their higher-status comrades. The ability of commanders to monitor the attitudes and behavior of non-core soldiers improves as more core soldiers are introduced into the mix, for example. Enhanced surveillance, particularly among the rank and file, can provide tips about possible plots and collective action by non-core soldiers seeking to escape. It may also force non-core

85. Alexiev and Wimbush 1988, 16–18.

86. Even guard duty schedules were apportioned along ethnic lines to ensure soldiers from two different companies held watch at the same time. In the Indian Army, "class" refers to the religious, regional, or caste category used to define recruitment to particular units in the infantry, armored corps, and artillery (Wilkinson 2015, 39, 62).

87. Smele 2015; Mawdsley 2005; Figes 1990.

88. Paine 2005; Elleman 2001. Creating monoethnic units gambles that coethnics will fight harder for each other than non-coethnic commanders, increasing their combat power, and that undisturbed intraethnic networks will not be employed to promote mass indiscipline. Militaries will often resort to national units when they lack the resources for extensive monitoring; better to field these units and hope they fight (and obey commands) than to not have them at all.

soldiers to be more clandestine in their coordination for fear of premature discovery. As a consequence, coordination around collective action will become more difficult, and the number of individuals fewer, as would-be plotters draw their circle of conspirators more closely to avoid detection. Replacing non-core soldiers with core ones will also weaken intraethnic networks simply by removing the number of coethnic nodes and the density of ties among coethnics. This, too, will decrease the likelihood of successful mobilization as well as place limits on the number of participating individuals. Blending these soldiers together also creates the possibility that close quarters and combat conditions will forge new interethnic bonds. A new sense of solidarity might in turn dampen prejudices, convincing non-core soldiers to overlook their past treatment at the state's hands, leading to improvements in their will to fight.

Despite these advantages, some armies have refused to countenance meaningful integration, on the grounds that it dilutes the morale and combat power of the core soldiers involved. Best, it was thought, that units remain segregated, for fear that core soldiers, as the army's backbone, would be dragged down to the level of their lower-status comrades. In 1940, for example, the United States War Department issued explicit instructions that commanders were "not to intermingle colored and white enlisted personnel in the same regimental organizations" since "to make changes would produce situations destructive to morale."[89] Prejudice can run deep, taking some options for battlefield management off the table. There is also no guarantee that increased interaction between groups of different status will break down barriers. Stereotypes and prejudices might simply be reinforced instead. This is especially likely if core officers and soldiers use their own notions of superiority to guide their daily conduct. If new bonds do not form, and if soldiers continue to eye each other warily from their respective ethnic corners, then combat power will suffer even if cohesion is maintained. Without interethnic trust, battlefield cooperation will flag, forcing the adoption of simplified tactics and operations that restrict initiative in the name of solving command and control problems. Cross-guarding during wartime, for example, increases coordination difficulties and places a premium on command and control; if disrupted, these homogenous subunits could flee en masse since their coethnic networks remain undisturbed. This danger is especially acute in national and segregated units, where intraethnic bonds remain strong and monitoring weak. Seemingly mundane issues like the replacement of casualties also become of exceeding importance for mixed units since ethnic balances within

89. President's Committee on Equality of Treatment and Opportunity in the Armed Services (22 May 1950) 1950, 48.

and across formations must be maintained.[90] This fragility can lead to cumbersome manpower policies and snarled delays in sending reinforcements. In turn, uneven exposure to combat by an army's constituent groups creates additional grievances among those forced to plug gaps in the front lines because appropriate replacements could not be found.

2.7.2.   Hide Units

A second method of managing divided armies revolves around the spatial deployment of selected units on the battlefield. Commanders, fearful that adversaries will exploit interethnic differences, can elect to hide ("mask") their vulnerabilities by keeping problematic units out of harm's way. In addition, skillful commanders can even draw on terrain features and interlocking patterns of deploying their units to generate more cohesion.

Perhaps the simplest approach is to shunt non-core soldiers into logistics or labor battalions far from the front lines. This arrangement avoids many, though not all, of the drawbacks of fielding non-core soldiers. Defection, for example, becomes much harder, since would-be turncoats must pass through the full extent of "friendly" forces just to arrive at possible defection routes between the two armies. Many of the tactical restrictions associated with reluctant non-core soldiers are also removed in this model. Pre-1874 Tsarist Russia, for example, fielded national units (*inordnye voiska*) of Kalmyks, Bashkirs, and Tatars that were assigned specific tasks such as protecting rear lines of communication.[91] But this practice does carry risks, including increasing the odds of successful desertion from the rear. Relegating non-core soldiers to support roles obviously diminishes the overall pool of soldiers available for fighting, especially if reliable units staffed by core groups are required to overwatch these logistical units. And if unrest breaks out within these units, belligerents will find themselves with disrupted logistics that circumscribe or rule out certain types of operations. At the extreme, mass desertion, or even widespread passive resistance, from these units can collapse logistics and cripple military operations, imposing delays and driving up casualties among frontline units. Pakistan's war effort in 1971 was hamstrung by the absence of Bengali speakers in the military and the fact that Bengali soldiers took the opportunity to protest their second-class status by deserting,

---

90. The loss of the few soldiers capable of bridging interethnic divides, often due to their language skills, becomes especially damaging for mixed units. This represents a critical vulnerability that enemies can exploit.

91. Alexiev and Wimbush 1988, 16.

crippling logistical systems, especially in the Air Force, where they had been confined to support operations.[92]

Most armies field non-core soldiers with the expectation that they will perform frontline duties. In these instances, the location of their battlefield deployment becomes especially important. Some armies, for example, emplace their problematic units in the first echelons, backstopping them with more reliable units who follow behind. Natural terrain features such as rivers, mountains, and narrow defiladed positions can also be used to hem units in, foreclosing possible desertion and defection routes. Such practices have a long history; Sun Tzu himself noted that "if I am in encircled ground, and the enemy opens a road in order to tempt my troops to take it, I close this means of escape so that my officers and men will have a mind to fight to the death. Throw the troops into a position from which there is no escape and even when faced with death they will not flee."[93] Armies often resort to manufacturing their own obstacles to cut down escape routes. Germany's *Wehrmacht* sowed mines around Romanian and Hungarian positions in the later stages of fighting on the Eastern Front to prevent these formations from fleeing.[94] Commanders may also elect to station units with high levels of military inequality on the flanks to avoid exposing them to the enemy's main effort. This is a risky gambit, however. Enemies, if aware of the ethnic composition of these units, can specifically target them for destruction. Romania's Third and Fourth armies, parked on the flanks of Germany's Sixth Army at Stalingrad, were singled out by Soviet commanders who believed these formations would collapse quickly if struck hard. Their collapse allowed Soviet forces to envelope the Sixth Army from the north and south, encircling and then destroying it.[95] More generally, these actions underscore the absence of a shared fate between core and non-core soldiers, creating additional grievances about the unfair nature of burdens being shouldered by each group.

Compounding these difficulties is the fact that problematic units may find themselves deployed in their own homelands. In these situations, coethnic ties to local populations can facilitate the flow of information, including rumors, as well as fugitives. Non-core units might also be infected by localism and slip away to ensure the safety of their families and property, creating a pull factor that might drive already reluctant soldiers to mobilize and escape. During World War One, for example, the Ottoman Army lost over 500,000 men to desertion, most from non-Turkish units, dwarfing its 175,220

---

92. War Inquiry Commission 2000, 89, 118, 124.

93. Sun-tzu 2009, 133–34.

94. Shils and Janowitz 1948, 291–92.

95. Samsonov 1989.

combat fatalities.[96] Deserters were so ubiquitous, especially among Ottoman Greeks, that they were known informally as "roof battalions" because of their tendency to hide in their (coethnic) houses' roofs to avoid conscription.[97] Armies are thus enmeshed in social terrains, some of which may lower obstacles to desertion among marginalized soldiers. Local inhabitants, if subjected to state discrimination or repression, may also prove unwelcome hosts for the army, a key consideration for many nineteenth-century armies fighting at the end of very long logistical trains. In some cases, the army may actually drag its own social terrain along. A key conduit for would-be deserters in the nineteenth century was the camp followers who trailed the regular army. These extended families followed behind their soldiers to cook food and provide services; in some cases, the number of camp followers dwarfed the main army itself. Black deserters fighting for the Piranti Republic against Brazil during the Farroupilha Revolution (1835–45) were smuggled away through coethnic networks of camp followers, for example.[98] Commanders must therefore not only manage the ethnic composition of their respective units but also their deployment, which can intensify or decrease the trade-offs and inefficiencies associated with military inequality.

2.7.3. Sanction Commanders

As military inequality rises, so too does the temptation to impose a system of strict sanctions to punish commanders for their failures. These measures, designed to heighten commanders' awareness of the dangers of indiscipline, can take several forms. Battlefield autonomy may be reduced; decisions may have to be authorized by more senior officers at distant headquarters or by specially appointed regime proxies such as commissars embedded within specific units. Ahmad Shah Massoud's Northern Alliance built a simple, and widely despised, system of commissars to police unit commanders during the 1992–96 anti-Taliban war, for example.[99] All armies sanction their commanders for poor performance (or should), of course. What separates out these additional measures is their drastic, often extrajudicial, nature. Arrests, forced suicide, and even executions have all been employed as sanctions for commanders who failed to maintain discipline over their soldiers. The Islamic State provides an extreme illustration: it executed dozens of senior and junior commanders after failed desertion attempts, allegedly by feeding them to

96. Erickson 2001, 208–15, 240.
97. Beşikçi 2012, 254.
98. Flores 1995, 63.
99. Giustozzi 2009, 288.

dogs.[100] Fearing sanction, commanders will take extraordinary steps to stiffen the resolve of their men, reduce opportunities for indiscipline, and seek better integration of units during operations to mask or compensate for limitations imposed by the ethnic composition of their units. This top-down tightening of control might be especially effective at preventing laxity or excessive familiarity by officers drawn from non-core groups toward their coethnic soldiers.

Sanctioning commanders for failure carries significant downsides, however. With the threat of punishment hanging over their heads, commanders will embrace simple, conservative tactics that offer better odds of maintaining control of their formations. They may resist the decentralization of authority to their subordinates, restricting their ability to maximize terrain and other advantages. Certain tactics that require high discipline, including night attacks, may be prohibited. More difficult to measure, but no less important, are opportunities lost because the need for authorization led to delayed reaction times. Military authorities might forbid their soldiers from pursuing beaten enemy forces, for example, out of concern that their own soldiers will escape amid the confusion and noise of a sudden advance.[101] Tactical withdrawals might also be ruled out, despite their military necessity, leading to the overrun of defensive positions and needless casualties. On the outskirts of Stalingrad in September 1942, General Vasily Chuikov recounted how "we immediately began to take the harshest possible actions against cowardice [i.e., retreating]. …I shot the commander and commissar of one regiment, and a short while later I shot two brigade commanders and their commissars. We made sure news of this got to the men, especially the officers."[102] Fear of failure can breed conservatism; better to muddle through with inefficient but proven tactics than to risk one's head for innovative approaches that might not work.[103] Enhanced control over their units comes at the cost of groupthink among commanders and a diminished appetite for risk-taking that produces too-predictable tactics and operations.

The unintended consequence of threatening commanders is needless casualties. Seeking to avoid perceived failure at all costs, commanders will exhibit a higher tolerance for casualties, especially if their troops are drawn from marginalized or repressed ethnic groups. Similarly, a reliance on simplified tactics will generate higher losses as these formations suffer from greater exposure to enemy fire. At the extreme, commanders will rely on massed

100. "The Islamic State Executes 9 Commanders," *Difesa and Sicurezza*, 31 August 2018.

101. Wesbrook 1980, 250.

102. Quoted in Hellbeck 2015, 273.

103. Dixon 2016.

frontal assaults that simplify command and control as the solution to cracking enemy defenses. Such crude attacks only create more grievances among non-core soldiers as their cannon fodder status clearly illustrates the absence of a shared fate between unequal ethnic groups. Commanders' incentives to deflect blame for disastrous performances can ignite another round of interethnic recriminations and possible sanctions that undermine the broader war effort. In one graphic example, Enver Pasha blamed his disastrous showing at the Battle of Sarikamish (December 1914–January 1915) on traitorous Armenians in his army (and among locals) during the Ottoman Army's ill-fated Caucasus campaign against Russia. His false testimony added momentum behind plans to unleash genocidal violence against Armenians within the Ottoman Empire.[104]

2.7.4. Fratricidal Violence

Finally, armies can turn their weapons on their own soldiers to maintain cohesion. While scholars tend to be skeptical that such "arid" methods can actually work,[105] belligerents can find themselves entrapped in the seductive logic that cracks within the ranks can be papered over with the liberal use of coercion. The greater the inequalities within an army, the more likely we are to witness commanders investing resources in the erection of a scaffolding of violence and fear aimed squarely at their own soldiers. As Keegan has noted, the fear of punishment can be a powerful motivator: "kill or be killed is the logic of battle, to which the military adds a rider, risk being killed by the enemy or else risk being killed by your own provost-marshall."[106] Indeed, concern over cohesion can reach near-absurd heights, with armies resorting to the deployment of specialized blocking detachments behind regular forces to prevent their desertion, lethally, if necessary.

Napoleon's armies, for example, were accompanied by *colonnes mobiles*, a combination of regular troops, gendarmerie, and other agencies that set about combating the "scourge" (*fléau*) of desertion (*insoumission*) "like a giant posse." On occasion, deserters were executed in front of their units to dissuade future mischief.[107] The Qing Dynasty used dedicated "anti-retreat formations" to backstop their own forces while combating the Taiping Heavenly Kingdom (1851–64), a war that consumed an estimated twenty million lives.[108] The Zhili Clique, which controlled Beijing and the northern

104. Erickson 2013.

105. Henderson 1985; Wesbrook 1980; Castillo 2014; Keegan 1997, 6.

106. Keegan 1997, 6.

107. Blanton 2009, 17–18, 177; Forrest 1989, 169.

108. Platt 2012; Spence 1996.

province of Zhili (now Hebei) of the Republic of China, leaned heavily on the same anti-retreat units during their 1922 and 1924 wars against the northern Fengtian Clique during China's Warlord Era. These battles would be some of the largest, if still nascent, combined arms operations the world had witnessed until the Spanish Civil War, involving armies reaching a quarter of a million soldiers and hundreds of tanks and aircraft.[109]

On paper, blocking detachments offer a lifeline for divided armies. Stationed in rear areas, blocking detachments create an immediate and credible threat of punishment, reducing both incentive and opportunity for soldiers to escape. For armies wracked by desertion or defection, even a partial screen provided by blocking detachments can make the difference between staying upright and complete disintegration. Tactics and operations that were previously ruled out by reason of indiscipline might be restored to an army's menu of options if blocking detachments restore discipline. The threat of sanction should also compel soldiers to fight harder, perhaps gaining a significant edge over adversaries unable or unwilling to resort to such cruelties. Blocking detachments, for example, can drive near-suicidal frontal attacks that swamp an enemy's defenses. A cattle prod of sorts, these formations push reluctant, exhausted soldiers past their natural breaking points, becoming a key asset in attritional contests. These formations also permit armies to shortchange training, sacrificing quality for quantity by using threatened violence rather than socialization as the glue holding units together. Blocking detachments thus provide a framework for action that does not hinge on soldiers' skill, training, or strong bonds, but that generates combat power quickly, if crudely, a kind of exoskeleton for low-skill soldiers that heightens resolve through fear of sanction.

But fratricidal violence is, of course, wildly inefficient, imposing costs in the form of self-inflicted casualties. Iraq, for example, killed hundreds of its own soldiers for desertion in 1984 alone, charging families the cost of the bullet for doing so.[110] The Iranian Army, too, began executing retreating soldiers as early as 1983 to staunch desertion and defection.[111] Beyond increasing casualties, blocking detachments also deepen some of the tensions between combat power and cohesion inherent in divided armies. These formations are hated by soldiers, creating new grievances among them while graphically demonstrating the absence of a shared fate between core and non-core groups. Commanders armed with blocking detachments can be (even more) carefree with their soldiers' lives, feeding a cycle of recriminations

109. Chi 1976; Chan 1982; Waldron 1995.
110. Murray and Woods 2014, 232.
111. Razoux 2015, 268.

and crackdowns that divert increasing resources into disciplining soldiers. These punitive units are typically staffed by highly loyal and skilled soldiers, stripping them from the front lines and leading to diminished performance in combat with enemy forces. The need to maintain close physical proximity to blocking detachments also undercuts the ability of attacking armies to seize opportunities, especially during exploitation operations after breaking through enemy positions.

Fratricidal violence can sometimes slip beyond the boundaries of the battlefield to engulf a state's non-core population. Indeed, embattled regimes saddled with high military inequality frequently open a new front against non-core populations, seeking to hold them hostage to ensure the good performance of their soldiers during wartime. Threats and actual punishment can deter families from encouraging their sons to desert, or from sheltering them when they flee. Moving under the cover of war, some embattled regimes will unleash repressive campaigns against these populations to squash any possible rebellions, real or imagined. These actions, however, only stoke additional grievances among coethnic soldiers, further deflating their morale. Discipline issues will mount as soldiers head for home in the hopes of safeguarding their families or gleaning information about their safety. Efforts to address problems stemming from inequality within the ranks can therefore collapse the distinction between the front lines and the homeland, as the effects of violence are transmitted through networks that bind soldiers, families, and the broader coethnic community.

As resources are shifted from the front to repression on the home front, and as more resources are required to maintain discipline within the ranks, belligerents can find themselves prosecuting two intertwined wars ("double wars") simultaneously, a state of affairs unlikely to contribute to efficient battlefield performance. Take, for example, the case of Ahmadu, ruler of the Tukulor Empire that once stretched across much of today's Mali. Seeking to beat back a French invasion in 1893, Ahmadu found himself in a precarious position. His army's non-Tukulor contingents had begun melting away even before meeting French forces, while unrest among these same peoples threatened to undo the stitches of his patchwork empire. He chose to divert combat power to the task of repressing both his soldiers and their families in a desperate, and ultimately futile, bid to save his rule.[112] Iran, too, found itself not only beating back Iraq's initial foray into Arab-populated Khuzestan that opened the 1980–88 Iran-Iraq War but also repressing the local population simultaneously to prevent their anticipated, but never realized, defection to Iraq.[113]

112. Oloruntimehin 1972, 303–5.
113. Razoux 2015, 121–22, 259.

On occasion, this categorical violence can swell to genocidal levels, as with the Armenian Genocide and Saddam's pursuit of the al-Anfal campaign.[114] Excluding these "double wars" from our analysis of battlefield performance risks overlooking an important feedback mechanism for worsening performance among certain belligerents. It also truncates a range of wartime behaviors, including civilian victimization and forced population displacement, that stem from the decision to nation-build on unequal foundations.

2.7.5. Indiscipline Is Infectious: The Vulnerability of Core Soldiers

These management strategies understandably focus principally on non-core soldiers. But core soldiers are not immune from their effects, either. To be sure, core soldiers, motivated by the twin imperatives of protecting their nation and their place in its hierarchy, are more likely to exhibit greater resilience and lower rates of indiscipline. They are also more likely to be motivated by ideological and nationalist appeals that provide a "cause of doing"[115] than their non-core comrades. Yet the inefficiencies and distortions produced by these management strategies can also render even the most committed soldiers vulnerable to breakdowns in cohesion.

For example, mass indiscipline among non-core soldiers provides core soldiers with information about several aspects of the war effort. Events like mass desertion and defection will cause core soldiers to update their beliefs about the effectiveness of management strategies and, in particular, the likelihood of being caught and punished if one chose to escape. Non-core soldiers are, in effect, canaries in the mineshaft, providing evidence of the dangers and feasibility of flight. Prior collective action by non-core soldiers will also influence soldiers' judgments about the resolve of their own units, raising questions about whether it would hold together under similar conditions that broke non-core units. Fed by rumor mills and nourished by direct experience with these non-core units, core soldiers, though nominally loyal to the regime, will begin to question the ability and willingness of their fellow soldiers to fight and die under worsening conditions.

Most importantly, if these management strategies fail to contain mass indiscipline, then core soldiers will revise their estimates of the probability that the war can be won.[116] The greater the share of soldiers represented by non-core ethnic groups, the more damaging this indiscipline will be perceived by core soldiers, and the worse the anticipated odds of victory. Core soldiers in turn will draw on their own networks to mobilize collectively to

114. Strauss 2015; Black 1993.
115. Wesbrook 1980, 254.
116. Rosen 2005.

abandon the battlefield. Indiscipline is thus a contagion that can jump the firebreaks between core and non-core soldiers in a dynamic, self-reinforcing process.[117] Management strategies might deter or slow these processes. But even if non-core units are completely segregated, their frontline performance cannot be hidden for long from core soldiers. And while frontline experiences are the most comparable, the collapse of non-core units in rear areas can also shape beliefs about the likelihood of victory. Core and non-core soldiers are therefore tied together by an invisible tether of information in which awareness of prior collective action by second-class soldiers diffuses to core soldiers, sapping resolve and making thinkable their own indiscipline. Ironically, belligerents might find themselves forced to apply the same measures against their own favored ethnic groups to prevent this cascade from consuming the entire army.

Taken together, these four management strategies act as a quarantine of sorts to prevent the contagion of indiscipline and defeatist thinking from infecting core soldiers. Since this quarantine cannot be perfect, we should observe a clear sequence of indiscipline that cascades from first movers in homogenous non-core units to blended units that can blunt collective action for a time before succumbing to laggard units staffed solely by core soldiers. The greater the share of an army that is drawn from non-core populations, and the weaker the management strategies, the faster the diffusion of learning across (and within) units and the more likely we are to see processes like desertion and defection infect core soldiers, too. How quickly indiscipline cascades across units is an empirical question: battlefield proximity, the state of communications technology, ruthlessness in suppressing non-core collective action, and the ethnic composition of units will all shape the diffusion of collective indiscipline from non-core to core soldiers.[118]

2.8. Turning the Screws: Combat Dynamics and Feedback Loops

Spotlighting the debilitating effects of prewar military inequality can have the unintended consequence of relegating enemy forces to a minor, offstage role. Yet combat is jointly produced; it is the result of the interaction of two armies seeking to impose their wills on one another through

---

117. Lehmann and Zhukov (2019) argue that mass surrender follows a logic of contagion: soldiers are more likely to surrender if others have done so recently.

118. Diffusion could occur within the same battle, for example, or it could unfold sequentially over a series of them.

violent means.[119] Divided armies therefore enter the arena not only with self-imposed constraints but also facing an adversary bent on exploiting these internal schisms for battlefield advantage. Worse, combat dynamics can amplify inequality's negative effects, cinching an army's straitjacket even tighter, in two ways.

First, political leaders and commanders have long resorted to propaganda and other ploys designed to seize upon grievances in opposing armies. General George Washington, in an 11 May 1776 letter to Congress, mused that "may it not be advisable and good policy, to raise some Companies of our Germans to send among them [British Hessian regiments], when they arrive, for exciting a spirit of disaffection and desertion?"[120] During the Mesopotamian campaign of World War One, British officers specifically targeted non-Turkish units with anti-Ottoman propaganda that called attention to past injustices.[121] Similar Russian efforts to sway Armenian soldiers within the Ottoman Army led Turkish officers to take drastic action. Contemporaries reported that Armenian conscripts were placed in chains and escorted under arms to the front line to prevent their desertion.[122] More recently, American forces dropped millions of leaflets over Iraqi troop concentrations on the eve of the 2003 war, urging Shia soldiers to reject Saddam while providing explicit instructions on how to surrender.[123]

Second, opposing armies can take direct action that targets non-core soldiers in the belief that they will not stand firm. Armies can structure their offensives around delivering a crushing blow along salients held by non-core soldiers, for example. Sometimes subversion over the long haul is preferred. France stoked fires inside the Tukulor army and wider population by supplying non-core groups, notably Bamaman animists who had suffered forcible conversion, with arms during the 1850s–60s. The end result was chronic unrest and mass desertions, making France's eventual conquest of the Tukulor empire much easier.[124] In other cases, adversaries have encouraged defection, folding these fugitive soldiers into their own ranks to bolster their strength at the enemy's expense. During the War of 1812, fought between the United States and the United Kingdom, American commanders encouraged desertion from already undermanned British naval forces by playing upon Irish anti-British grievances—as well as promising "cheap alcohol"—to pry

119. Clausewitz 1984; Kalyvas 2006.

120. "To the President of Congress," in Fitzpatrick 1932, 36.

121. McMeekin 2015, 341–64.

122. Reynolds 2011; Erickson 2001, 98–105.

123. "US Army Chief Says Iraqi Troops Took Bribes to Surrender," *Independent*, 24 May 2003.

124. Oloruntimehin 1968.

them from military service.[125] British officers returned the favor by targeting the fault line in American society between white Americans and African-American slaves. Promoting desertion among black auxiliaries as well as chattel slaves became a cornerstone of British strategy to fan the flames of a wider slave revolt. Defectors who managed to reach British ships were mustered into a Corps of Colonial Marines that scouted and fought in several major battles.

Even seemingly minor tactical decisions about the timing and location of British raids were guided by identity considerations. For example, Admiral of the Fleet Sir George Cochrane ordered Admiral Cockburn in April 1814 to stir up slave revolts:

> Let the Landings you make be more for the protection of the desertion of the Black Population than with a view to any other advantage. … The great point to be attained is the cordial Support of the Black population. With them properly armed & backed with 20,000 British Troops, Mr. Madison will be hurled from his Throne.[126]

The violence of the battlefield establishes a feedback loop between non-core soldiers and the methods of control used by their commanders to enforce discipline. Combat accelerates many of the processes already set in motion by prewar inequalities: the disaffection with the government, the sabotaging of interethnic trust, the renewal of grievances about the war's unfairness, and the strengthening of intraethnic bonds that can facilitate collective escape.[127] For their part, commanders will clamp down even tighter, returning to their toolbox of repressive measures to ensure that non-core soldiers continue to fight. The result is an army at war with itself and with its opponent, seeking to hold itself together long enough to deliver a decisive blow against its foe.

Not every opponent will be able to take full advantage of these internal contradictions. Much depends on the depth of the intraethnic inequalities that plague divided armies. Enemies can overlook these ethnic cleavages or fail to devise compelling enough propaganda to convince soldiers to defect. They may also be wracked by their own inequalities, and thus unable to maneuver with sufficient speed and finesse to exploit these weaknesses. Finally, enemies can make mistakes that foreclose these opportunities.

---

125. Taylor 2014, 198.

126. Quoted in Taylor 2014, 212–13.

127. Evidence from lab, field, and lab-in-the-field experiments converge on the view that exposure to violence can bolster in-group bonds while hardening antipathy toward the out-group (here, the regime and favored core group). See, for example, Lyall, Blair and Imai 2013; Zeitzoff 2014; Canetti and Lindner 2014.

Battlefield savagery, including the killing of prisoners and scorched earth campaigns against civilians, could motivate non-core soldiers to put aside their hatred of their own regime and concentrate on the task of defeating enemy forces. Divided armies may therefore be saved from their own past mistakes by those of a too-eager adversary.

2.9. Battlefield Performance: Hypotheses

Gathering these threads together, the proposed argument generates a set of testable propositions (hypotheses) about the relationship between inequality and battlefield performance in modern war. Drawing on the book's twofold conceptualization of battlefield performance, I derive two sets of empirical expectations about inequality's effects on combat power and cohesion. In addition, I propose a fifth hypothesis that examines how rising inequality causes wartime pathologies to accumulate across these two dimensions, as measured by the combined battlefield performance index (see chapter 1). These hypotheses share the core intuition that as belligerents climb up each rung of inequality, moving from low to extreme values, their battlefield performance should decrease in similar fashion.[128] These hypotheses are couched in terms of outcomes in a specific battle; belligerents with higher military inequality coefficients will have a greater probability of observing these negative outcomes in their performance in any given battle compared to similar belligerents at lower values of military inequality. Yet since battles in wars are not truly independent, and have effects that carry over between them, these hypotheses could also be interpreted as referring to aggregate performance across all the battles of a given war. These hypotheses also take armies as their starting point, but could equally be applied to specific formations and individual units within the broader army.

Beginning with combat power, we should expect that the greater a belligerent's prewar level of military inequality, the lower the tactical and operational sophistication of its army in battle. A combination of low motivation among non-core soldiers, interethnic friction, and the ability of non-core groups to threaten desertion and defection should force commanders to reduce the complexity of their movement to maintain cohesion.

These self-imposed limitations should manifest themselves in several ways.[129] As belligerents shift from lower to higher values of military inequality, we should observe them increasingly struggle to integrate different combat

---

128. Again, "low" is defined throughout the book as a military inequality coefficient between 0 and 0.20; "medium," from 0.21–0.40; "high," 0.41–0.60; and "extreme," 0.61 and above.

129. Not all of these issues need be present at the same time, however.

branches. Decentralization of command authority should also become increasingly rare. Kept on a tight leash, soldiers will struggle to use terrain features for cover and concealment; instead, commanders will favor more straightforward tactics that do not lose sight of their soldiers. Commanders and soldiers alike will be marked by low initiative and risk-taking and an over-reliance on a narrow set of tried-and-true approaches when better solutions are present. Commanders will rule out certain options like night marches or envelopment operations out of fear of encouraging indiscipline. Complicated efforts, including exploitation operations that require independent decision-making and commander autonomy, will be avoided, if not ruled out completely. For armies waging large campaigns, coordination across multiple fronts, as well as across units on the same front, will be inhibited as precautions taken to prevent cohesion problems by each unit complicate planning.

Military inequality also creates observable implications for a belligerent's loss-exchange ratio, the second component of combat power. All else equal, a shift from lower to higher values of military inequality should be associated with reduced capacity to kill enemy soldiers and a decreased ability to safeguard one's own soldiers. More specifically, casualty rates should fall from favorable (above parity) loss-exchange ratios to parity and then to unfavorable (below parity) as military inequality increases.[130]

The argument also suggests two hypotheses about inequality and cohesion. First, as a belligerent's prewar military increases, so too does the likelihood that wartime mass indiscipline will occur within its army. More specifically, we should expect to observe mass desertion and defection as military inequality rises from low to extreme values. The greater the share of soldiers represented by marginalized or repressed soldiers, the greater the numbers of soldiers that should engage in mass desertion and defection. These forms of mass indiscipline should follow the same pattern: units composed of non-core ethnic groups should break first, followed first by mixed units and then units staffed solely by soldiers drawn from core groups. We should also expect variation in the timing of mass desertion and defection to track with whether the non-core group was exposed to collective discrimination or repression. Given the role of violence in hardening ethnic identities and strengthening coethnic networks, groups that have suffered collective repression should be in the vanguard of efforts to desert or defect.

Second, as prewar military inequality rises, belligerents will increasingly turn to formal coercive institutions and practices to maintain soldier discipline on the battlefield. A shift from low to extreme military inequality will result in several steps being taken to deter (or minimize) mass

---

130. Fractional loss-exchange ratios (FLERs) could also be used to measure relative casualties.

TABLE 2.4. Inequality and Battlefield Performance: Indicators and Expectations Summarized

Indicator	Measure	Expected Relationship with MIC
Qualitative		
Tactical-operational sophistication	Perceived solutions available for battlefield problems ("Commander's playbook")	Higher MIC, lower sophistication
Quantitative		
Loss-exchange ratio	Relative battlefield fatalities	Higher MIC, worse LER
Mass desertion	Unsanctioned return home by ≥10 percent of total deployed forces	Higher MIC, greater probability of mass desertion
Mass defection	≥10 percent of total deployed forces switches sides	Higher MIC, greater probability of mass defection
Fratricidal violence	Wartime deployment of blocking detachments	Higher MIC, greater likelihood of fratricidal violence
Battlefield performance index (BPI)	Quantitative measures combined	Higher MIC, lower BPI score

indiscipline among non-core soldiers and to prevent its diffusion to core soldiers. These measures include the deployment of blocking detachments; the use of extrajudicial punishment against soldiers, including executions; the construction of penal battalions drawn from arrested soldiers that are assigned exceptionally dangerous missions as a form of punishment; and, at high or extreme levels of military inequality, the launching of campaigns against non-core groups within the belligerent's own population ("double wars").

Finally, these empirical implications suggest one final hypothesis: as military inequality increases, we will observe the accumulation of these individual pathologies in a belligerent's battlefield performance. The battlefield performance index captures this intuition by measuring a belligerent's performance across four partially correlated pathologies: below-parity loss-exchange ratios; mass desertion; mass defection; and the use of blocking detachments. At low levels of inequality, most of the pathologies, if not all, should be absent. At extreme levels, however, all, or nearly all, of these deficiencies should be observed, reflecting the difficulties that the belligerent is having in maintaining cohesion and the sacrifices to combat power that result. These suboptimal behaviors, in other words, should cluster predictably at high or extreme levels of military inequality. These indicators and expectations are summarized in table 2.4.

Some of these hypotheses are amenable to testing with quantitative data; others will require careful close-range judgment using qualitative evidence. All of these claims are falsifiable, however. For example, if belligerents with low and extreme values of military inequality turn in the same battlefield performance, then the argument is clearly incorrect. Of course, no theory can perfectly capture every nuance of battlefield performance across hundreds of belligerents. Some low inequality belligerents will still exhibit pathologies, while some belligerents with extreme inequality may be able to escape some or most of these battlefield deficiencies. Too many of these cases, however, raises red flags about military inequality's ability to explain battlefield performance.

2.10. Relaxing Assumptions

This discussion so far has relied on three implicit assumptions that deserve closer scrutiny. First, coethnics have been treated as possessing uniform preferences, rendering group boundaries fixed. Second, military inequality is viewed as cemented in the prewar era and thus remains unchanged by endogenous wartime dynamics. Third, the structural nature of military inequality appears to rule out change over time, barring perhaps a crushing defeat that wipes the slate clean for a foreign occupier or successor government. All of these assumptions can be relaxed, however. I discuss the implications of doing so below.

2.10.1. Coethnic Preferences and the Role of Positive Inducements: Fighting for the Future

For simplicity's sake, I have assumed that coethnic soldiers share preferences over outcomes as well as decision-making dominated by coethnic considerations. The argument need not rest on such strong assumptions, however. Indeed, it is flexible enough to allow for mixed motives and opportunism by non-core soldiers that can lead to behavior that sometimes cuts across the grain of their ethnic identities. Inequality predicts overall patterns, but does not necessarily capture each individual's microlevel motives for action. Only if the majority of coethnic soldiers consistently act against their ethnic identities and interests when given a choice would we question the argument's microfoundations.

By relaxing the assumption that a non-core soldier's decision-making is always dominated by coethnicity, we create space for considering the role that material incentives play in driving combat motivation. After all, not every non-core soldier deserts or defects, for several reasons. Military service may represent an avenue for economic advancement, either individually or collectively, for non-core soldiers. They may also be attracted by the prospect of battlefield spoils. Fighting also provides the opportunity to seek revenge against an invading force that inflicted greater harm against a soldier, his family, or his ethnic group than his own government. Revenge-seeking is especially likely if the front lines coincide with the non-core group's "homeland."

Allowing for mixed motives in turn suggests the possibility that ethnic group boundaries are not fixed. Factionalism can indeed appear within ethnic groups during wartime. Some non-core soldiers, along with their respective political elites in the broader population, may view fighting and resulting sacrifices as the road to revising the social contract and improving their group's postwar status. African-Americans, for example, used their military service during the Second World War to advance their claims for redress of grievances and greater equality, particularly in the South, once they returned home.[131] A subset of non-core soldiers may therefore be willing to fight hard to secure a better postwar future. Crafty regimes will fan these hopes, holding out promise that battlefield success will translate into higher status and better treatment in a revised postwar order. Tsarist Russia floated proposals to make Poland and Turkestan independent entities if their populations rallied to the standard during the First World War.[132] Regimes also have incentives to elevate token non-core commanders and soldiers as a means of weakening intraethnic solidarity. In one such example, China's People's Liberation Army has promoted a handful of Tibetans and Uyghurs as deputy commanders, serving under Han officers, in their home military districts.[133]

From a theoretical standpoint, factionalism should appear when the war is going poorly for the regime but victory is not yet out of reach. This Goldilocks situation represents the moment when non-core soldiers have maximal leverage and when the regime is primed for making deals. Conversely, if the war is going well, the regime has little incentive to offer concessions, while a looming defeat might make the regime turn to coercion, not concessions, to maintain the army's cohesion. This loyalist faction should still represent only a subset of the overall non-core soldiers. Many, perhaps most, non-core soldiers are unlikely to overlook past injustices and violence at the government's hands. Nor is interethnic trust between soldiers of favored and second-class groups high, helping quell a cascade of pro-loyal sentiment. Factionalism is also much more likely to appear among volunteers than conscripts due to self-selection into the military. As a result, the presence of some hard-fighting loyalists

131. Parker 2009.

132. Sanborn 2003, 75–77.

133. "Ethnicity factors strongly in PLA promotions," *Asia Times*, 9 September 2017.

should not surprise us. They should, however, remain at best a minority of non-core soldiers unless that group is facing an existential threat from the opposing army.[134] Units with a loyalist contingent should fight better than ones without since these soldiers are motivated to fight harder. The presence of loyalists can also dampen the flow of information within these units since they, too, can access coethnic networks, thus reducing the probability of mass indiscipline.

2.10.2.   Wartime Commitment Problems

The possibility of factionalism within non-core groups raises a second puzzle: why don't leaders simply shift prevailing norms of citizenship in a more inclusive direction to unlock additional military power during the war? The discussion so far has treated military inequality as static in nature, set in concrete before the war and unchanged throughout. Yet we can relax this assumption to explore the possibility of war-induced change to the regime's collective vision and resulting military inequality. It is indeed possible that wartime pressures will force leaders to revisit the ideational bases of their rule. But their ability to enact sweeping reform is likely seriously circumscribed by a credible commitment problem.[135] Rattled leaders, for example, may pledge major reforms in the postwar era, subject to non-core groups fighting hard against the enemy in the present. But these groups will be inherently suspicious (and rightly so) of the regime's willingness to uphold any wartime promises once danger has passed. Non-core groups, for their part, seek to use their leverage during wartime to extract meaningful concessions. Such efforts, however, might empower the non-core groups to overturn the existing ethnic hierarchy that the regime sits atop. Neither side, then, can credibly commit to upholding any wartime deal once the war ends. As a consequence, any concessions made by the regime during wartime will be tactical and limited in nature, representing modest gestures toward greater inclusion but not deeper structural changes.

We should see, then, embattled regimes resorting to grand rhetorical flourishes about greater inclusion, a search for frames that draw non-core groups more closely to the center of the political community, and the extolling of shared hardships imposed by a common (foreign) enemy. Tokenism, too, might be stepped up. Saddam Hussein ordered "distinguished" families— those who lost between three and seven immediate family members—to be recognized with a cash award and medal as a means of acknowledging

---

134. Of course, loyalist motives may not be altruistic. They may seek better assignments, higher salaries, or a prominent position in the new postwar order.

135. Fearon 1995.

the disproportionate share of casualties suffered by the marginalized Shia during the Iran-Iraq War.[136] Substantial overhauls of the existing ethnic hierarchy should be rare, however, and are likely to occur under a very narrow set of circumstances. We should observe extensive reform when the costs of monitoring or repressing non-core groups during wartime is high; when the probability of defeat and violent overthrow by the enemy is high; and when the non-core group is large, compounding the costs of continued repression but also offering promise of additional soldiers, and improved motivation among them, if the group's status is improved.[137] Regimes with discriminatory communal visions are also more apt to shift than those with past histories of collective violence; the credible commitment problem should be less severe in these circumstances. Still, it is likely that there will be more wartime bargaining failures between the regime and its non-core population than successes given the fear of future reneging by both sides.

We cannot assume, however, that war-induced changes will always be more inclusionary. Some leaders, especially those who have maintained their rule through collective violence against non-core groups, may double down, renewing their commitment to high inequality. Wartime might provide the perfect cover for stepping up the collective punishment of targeted groups under the guise of protecting national security. The desire to maintain inequality might also simply trump military necessity, rendering the option of inclusive reform unthinkable. An extreme example of this logic is provided by the Confederate States of America. Rare among belligerents, the Confederacy excluded a large share of its population, African-American slaves, from military service.[138] Despite an unfavorable military balance and mounting casualties, Confederate leaders refused to consider one obvious solution to their worsening battlefield performance: emancipate and enlist African-Americans. Years would pass before the subject was even broached. Finally, in January 1864, Patrick Cleburne, a major general commanding the Army of Tennessee, gathered his senior military advisors and broke the taboo, openly calling for their enlistment. His written assessment of the situation, signed

---

136. Blaydes 2018, 94–99.

137. The logic here is similar to the granting of democratic institutions by autocratic rulers: it dampens unrest while securing their access to decision-making in the future (Acemoglu and Robinson 2006, 23–30).

138. Excluding slaves from military service also generated unintended consequences for Confederate battlefield performance. Fear of slave revolts at home ("the black waits but the opening fire of the enemy's battle line to wake it, like a torpid serpent, into venomous activity" (Alger 1898, 588) led even committed soldiers to desert to ensure that their families and farms were safe (Weitz 2005, 58–59, 71–72; McPherson 2014, 31).

by thirteen of his brigadier generals, pointed squarely to how slavery, and the Confederacy's guiding principles themselves, were proving catastrophic on the battlefield.

> Slavery, from being one of our chief sources of strength at the commencement of the war, has now become, in a military point of view, one of our chief sources of weakness.... The immediate effect of the emancipation and enrollment of negroes on the military strength of the South would be: To enable us to have armies numerically superior to those of the North, and a reserve of any size we might think necessary; to enable us to take the offensive, move forward, and forage on the enemy. It would open to us in prospective another and almost untouched source of supply, and furnish us with the means of preventing temporary disaster, and carrying on a protracted struggle. It would instantly remove all the vulnerability, embarrassment, and inherent weakness which result from slavery.[139]

That it seems far-fetched, even impossible, to conceive of the Confederacy fielding large numbers of African-American soldiers underscores the persistence of ethnic and racial hierarchies even in wartime. Indeed, upon hearing of Cleburne's report, President Davis ordered all copies to be destroyed; as one critic lamented, the proposal "would ruin the efficiency of our Army and involve our cause in ruin and disgrace."[140] But as disaster closed in, Davis relented, broaching the possibility of purchasing 40,000 slaves for noncombat roles, to be emancipated after service, in a message to Congress on 7 December 1864. The modest proposal sparked a firestorm of criticism. "The existence of a negro soldier is totally inconsistent with our political aim and with our social as well as political system," wrote the *Richmond Examiner*, while Brigadier General Howell Cobb argued "if slaves will make good soldiers—our whole theory of slavery is wrong."[141] A watered-down proposal eventually succeeded, but only two companies mustered before the war's end. By contrast, the Union accepted African-American volunteers by July 1862. Some 180,000 eventually took up arms, representing 10 percent of total Union forces while suffering an almost 21 percent casualty rate.[142]

---

139. Reproduced in *Operations in: Southwestern Virginia, Kentucky, Tennessee, Mississippi, Alabama, West Florida, and Northern Georgia, January 1, 1861–June 30, 1865*, 1/v. 52, part 2, serial number 110 in Alger 1898, 590.

140. Quoted in McPherson 2014, 230.

141. Quoted in McPherson 2014, 231, 234.

142. Cornish 1987; McPherson 1997, 125–28.

2.10.3. Persistence, Not Permanence: The Dynamics of Inequality Over Time

The book's argument derives much of its explanatory weight from the fact that prewar structures of inequality are persistent. This assumption does not rule out change over time, however. There are several pathways outside of direct wartime pressures that could produce dynamic, often wrenching, changes in a country's notions of political community and military inequality.

Victory in war, for example, might bring about the conquest of new territories and populations that radically alter a belligerent's internal demography. Victory could also prove disruptive as returning veterans from non-core groups organize for greater political rights and complete citizenship. Similarly, victory might increase the status of the superordinate identity, convincing non-core groups to pursue assimilation as a way of improving their own societal position.[143] Defeat, too, carries consequences. The regime itself might be overthrown, leading to the emergence of a new core group, possibly tied to a foreign intervener, and the imposition of a new communal vision that scrambles the existing ethnic hierarchy. Defeat might also set in motion the search for scapegoats, intensifying collective punishment of targeted groups and increasing inequalities. Even before Germany's defeat in World War I, the ground had been prepared for the legend of the *Dolchstoss* ("stab in the back"), as right-wing politicians and soldiers singled out Jews as responsible for turning the home front against the war. Ominously, a special census was commissioned of Jews in Germany's armed forces to check if they were shirking military service.[144] Finally, defeat might also discredit the dominant communal vision, laying the foundation for the construction of a new national architecture of identities.

Change might also be propelled by gradual waves rather than earth-shaking cataclysms. Rising levels of education, intermarriage, and economic development might all contribute to changing societal norms that recast, or dismantle, ethnic hierarchies. Immigration, too, can reshape categories of membership and belonging in a given political community. Groups may also find their relative positions in the status hierarchy fluctuating over time. The Mahars in India, for example, represented 15 percent of all Indian soldiers in 1875;

143. Sambanis, Skaperdas and Wohlforth 2015.

144. Adam Hochschild, "A Hundred Years After the Armistice," *Atlantic Monthly*, 5 November 2018. The fact that non-core groups have a higher probability of deserting and defecting should not be read as supporting nationalist narratives of traitorous minorities. These accounts typically are silent on how the state's own victimization of these groups set the stage for future battlefield indiscipline.

then were dropped as a "martial" race and by 1892 totally excluded from the Bombay Army; then recruited into a segregated Mahar regiment in World War I, only to be disbanded in 1922, before being reconstituted for service in World War II.[145] Returning veterans from non-core groups may also quietly organize for genuine citizenship, seeking to use their military service as a vehicle for social change. Processes of assimilation may lead to the weakening of ethnic identities or a blurring of the once-harsh boundaries between different ethnic groups with histories of conflict. In short, while ethnic hierarchies and inequalities are backed by political power and thus persistent, they are not permanent, and can exhibit considerable variation over time.

Past inequality, then, is not necessarily a prologue for future inequality. But there is no guarantee that democratization or modernization will propel states along a more inclusive path. While it is possible that mature democracies place limits on the upper bounds of inequality, these gains have been hard fought, often bestowed grudgingly, and are subject to backsliding in the face of populism or xenophobia, even in these favorable conditions. Ethnic inequalities, just like economic ones, are certainly compatible with high levels of economic development; indeed, inequalities of wealth and status may actually be the defining feature of modern capitalist economies.[146] Belligerents will therefore express different levels of military inequality over time, subject to both exogenous shocks and internal dynamics that reshape their societies and their military organizations.

2.11. Conclusion

This chapter has made the case for viewing prewar military inequality as an important driver of battlefield performance in modern wars. The argument has a clear sequential logic, moving from the prewar construction of the political community and the regime's treatment of ethnic groups through to military service. The effects of state discrimination and repression of targeted ethnic groups are felt across three mechanisms that govern soldier conduct within the military: their beliefs about the war; interethnic trust; and intraethnic coordination. Recognizing the negative effects of inequality, military authorities deploy a variety of battlefield management strategies designed to mitigate its downstream consequences. These efforts hold out promise of restoring some, but not all, of the state's lost military power by reinforcing the army's cohesion, albeit at the expense of its combat power.

145. Wilkinson 2015, 72–73.
146. Piketty 2013.

The argument therefore anticipates a general proposition: the higher the pre-war inequality, the more distorted the military machine, and the worse its battlefield performance, whether measured in terms of casualties or different facets of discipline like mass desertion and defection. In this view, militaries are political constructions that reflect domestic concerns and inequalities rather than calculations of maximum efficiency imposed by the demands of survival in a threatening international environment. And while focused on a prewar structural trait of belligerents, the argument is flexible enough to generate predictions about the behavior of units at different levels of analysis, ranging from entire armies to individual units and even small formations. Dynamism can be imparted to the analysis by tracking the changing ethnic composition of specific units over time. Fighting, in other words, reflects prior political decisions about the nature of political communities, their degree of inclusion, and how these norms of citizenship motivate (or fail to) the soldiers that make up an army. While bringing our attention back to the human element of war, the claim here is meant to be generalizable, allowing us to compare within and across armies over time. Whether it succeeds is a matter of empirical investigation, a task I begin in the next chapter.

3

The Rise and Fall of the Mahdi State

A NATURAL EXPERIMENT

Mahdism had died well. If it had earned its death by its inequities, it had condoned its inequities by its death.

G. W. STEEVENS, WITH KITCHENER TO KHARTUM, 1899

PERCHED AT THE HEIGHTS of revolutionary success, Muhammad Ahmad, better known to his followers as the Mahdi ("Expected One"), writhed in agony, his body wracked by typhus. Only forty-two, the Mahdi had first stoked the flames of discontent against an oppressive and corrupt Egyptian colonial overseer and then harnessed these grievances to forge an army. Starting with only 313 soldiers, the Mahdist army swelled to over 60,000 soldiers (*Ansar*) as battlefield successes against Egyptian and Anglo-Egyptian expeditions sent to snuff out the revolution attracted new converts. The hard-earned prize of the First Mahdi War (1881–85) was a newly independent state, the Mahdiya, that stretched across much of contemporary Sudan, and a chastised United Kingdom that had suffered defeat at the hands of "primitive Dervishes." Now, however, the Mahdi's hushed inner circle could only watch helplessly as home remedies—including squirting urine into his eyeballs—were desperately applied, to no avail.[1] On 22 June 1885, the Mahdi died, leaving behind a Mahdiya built on an inclusionary vision that knit Sudan's disparate tribes, clans, and ethnic groups into a shared political community.[2]

---

1. Green 2007, 207.

2. A note on terminology. I use "Mahdiya" and the "Mahdi state" interchangeably. Following recent conventions, I avoid the term "Dervish" and especially the derogatory "fuzzy-wuzzy" and instead use the Mahdi's own preferred *Ansar* ("followers," singular *Ansari*) to refer to Mahdist soldiers. I hew to spellings closest to the original Arabic (the Ja'alin tribe, not Jaalin)

By 1899, the Mahdiya stood in ruins, its leaders hunted down or forced into exile, its armies scattered in the face of slow but steady Anglo-Egyptian offensives during the Second Mahdi War (1896–99). The Mahdiya's eclipse is perhaps more surprising than its emergence: its military was certainly better equipped than during the First Mahdi War, when Mahdist soldiers scavenged for firearms among dead Egyptian soldiers. It was fighting on its home turf against an opponent that it had already defeated. Yet its forces collapsed, with desertion and defection plaguing entire units while its casualties, the oft-cited standard metric of military effectiveness, were among the worst ever recorded in a conventional war. Mahdist forces lost over 11,500 in a few short hours at Omdurman in September 1898 while only killing 49 British, Egyptian, and Sudanese soldiers in return, leading "Omdurman" to become shorthand for the crushing defeat of so-called "primitive" armies by "modern" European ones.

This chapter explores the puzzle of why the nascent Mahdiya achieved battlefield success during the First Mahdi War but failed so miserably during the Second.[3] The answer lies in the content of the Mahdi's and his successor Khalifa's respective visions of the political community. The Mahdi constructed an egalitarian and inclusive notion of the collective Mahdist community that translated into low military inequality. The Khalifa, by contrast, radically reshaped the Mahdiya's social contract, choosing to rule atop an exclusionary ethnocracy that favored his own Baggara tribe and, even more narrowly, his own Ta'isha clan. Military inequality was correspondingly extremely high; many tribes and ethnic groups were subjected to coercion, forced displacement, deliberate starvation, and near-genocidal levels of violence that severed the connection between the regime and its soldiers. While estimates must be treated with caution given gaps in the historical record, the military inequality coefficient swings from 0.01 to 0.65–0.70 after the Mahdi's death, representing a move from low to extreme military inequality.[4]

In social science terms, the Mahdi's unexpected death creates a "natural experiment" in which the Mahdiya's traits remain fixed but the magnitude

---

except when other forms have become more familiar (Omdurman, not Umm Durman, for example).

3. According to the quantitative battlefield performance index, the Mahdiya scored a 1 in the 1881–85 war (denoting the absence of any of the four battlefield problems) but recorded only a 0.25 value in the 1896–99 war (indicating the presence of three of four problems), a dramatic reversal.

4. On the Mahdist army's composition and source limitations, see especially Holt 1970, 248–49.

of its military inequality shifts rapidly from low to extreme.[5] This sudden shock creates a direct comparison between the two Mahdiya states that spotlights the causal relationship between inequality and wartime outcomes by holding other factors constant. Drawing on primary documents, including soldier memoirs, intelligence reports, and accounts by contemporary journalists, I use process tracing to examine how this inequality spike affected the Mahdiya's combat power and cohesion during the First (1881–85) and Second (1896–99) Mahdi Wars against Anglo-Egyptian armies. While the paired comparison between the Mahdi's and Khalifa's versions of the Mahdiya helps screen out most alternative explanations, I also consider remaining counterclaims. In particular, I examine the prevalent view that the Mahdiya was doomed by British military superiority ("whatever happens, we have got the Maxim gun, and they have not"). Together, these cases serve as a theory-building exercise while generating the template used to structure paired comparisons in subsequent chapters.

3.1. Empirical Strategy

This within-Mahdiya comparison was initially identified by the R matching program, which paired the Mahdi- and Khalifa-led versions based on their similarities across thirteen covariates from Project Mars data. Further research in the extensive historiography surrounding these cases uncovered fifteen additional qualitative covariates that other scholars identified as important for explaining battlefield performance in these and other wars. Together, these twenty-eight covariates structure the within-case comparison, helping to "screen out" alternative explanations and pathways that cannot explain the divergence in battlefield performance across the two Mahdiyas. The strength of the design resides in the fact that the central variables for nearly all explanations of battlefield performance are constant, absent entirely, or suggest behavior at odds with actual outcomes, leaving them unable to account for sharply different Mahdist combat power and cohesion. The choice of these two wars was also fortuitous from a theory-building perspective, poised as they are near the chronological midpoint of the Project Mars universe.[6] As a result, they exhibit elements of early modern warfare but also witness some of the first steps toward a distinctively modern form of conventional warfare. The early campaigns of 1884–85 witnessed the use of machine guns,

---

5. On natural experiments, see Dunning 2012; Diamond and Robinson 2010. On the use of leader death (via assassination) as exogenous shock, see Jones and Olken 2009.

6. Both rank in the top 25 percent of wars according to casualties, landing at 28th and 61st out of 250 wars in Project Mars.

breech-loading rifles, the field telegraph, optical range finders, observation balloons, railways, chloroform, and lyddite explosive artillery shells. British forces also deployed a variety of technologies, including more sophisticated machine guns and rifles, armored steamers, tinned provisions, distilled water and ice-making plants, sunglasses, and a worldwide cable system, during the Second Mahdi War.[7]

3.1.1.   Leader Death as a Natural Experiment

The Mahdi's ill-fortune is, somewhat morbidly, our good fortune. His untimely death was not only sudden, random, and unconnected to the Mahdiya's war-making prowess, but also ideally timed. The Mahdi had fostered an inclusive political future for the Mahdiya but state- and nation-building campaigns were still underway as he sought to knit together the new state. Dying at the height of his political power, the Mahdi's death opened the door to a series of rival claimants with competing ideas for how the Mahdiya should legitimate itself.

Indeed, anxious rivals stood vigil, hoping the Mahdi would officially anoint a successor.[8] They also stood in "stunn[ed] shock";[9] the Expected Mahdi was assumed immortal, obviating the need for succession plans. Once the Mahdi succumbed, one of his four Khalifas, Abdallahi b. Muhammad (hereafter simply "Khalifa"), moved swiftly to establish his position. He faced a number of immediate potential challengers in claiming power, not least from the Ashraf who disputed the legitimacy of the eleventh hour transfer of power.[10] He immediately consolidated his position by having potential rivals at Khartoum swear allegiance to him publicly at a hastily called midnight session. He was aided in this endeavor by a quirk of military deployments: his most important challenger, the Ashraf-aligned Red Flag army, was not in Khartoum but was engaged in mop-up operations in remote portions of the Mahdiya. His own Black Flag was stationed in Khartoum, deterring other rivals like the Green Flag from taking action.

The son of a soothsayer from the Ta'isha tribe, a subtribe of the broader Baggara tribe from southern Darfur, the Khalifa moved immediately to recast

---

7. Robson 1993, xvii.

8. The historiography over the Mahdi's succession is divided into two camps. Some scholars argue that the Mahdi whispered a deathbed plea for the Khalifa to assume power (Holt 1970, 134–37). Others suggest that there was a brief debate over succession and that other claimants, especially among the Ashraf tribe, were merely biding their time before making their own push (Nicoll 2004, 230–32; Neillands 1996, 155).

9. Holt 1958b, 283.

10. Holt 1970, 136.

the collective bases of the Mahdiya's legitimacy. Gone was the Mahdi's inclusionary vision, though some of its rhetoric peppered the Khalifa's speeches on occasion. Instead, the Khalifa implemented a sweeping nation-building program that installed his own tribe at the apex of the Mahdiya's social hierarchy. The full weight of the Mahdist army was brought to bear on a wide range of tribes and ethnic groups. Deliberate starvation, state-orchestrated repression, and even near-genocide against selected tribes became the instruments of nation-building. By one estimate, the Mahdiya's population was nearly halved by 1896. The Khalifa had "triumphed by destroying his subjects as he conquered them," creating a "lost paradise of death."[11] As one historian remarked:

> In June 1885, it had been possible to believe that anything could be achieved in the way of nation building; by the autumn, the Mahdi's entire project was on the verge of disintegration. The heart had gone out of the movement and the ascent to supreme power of the Khalifa destroyed collective morale. The clans and tribes that had been brought together in the common struggle split apart again. From a genuine theocracy...the new nation became the fiefdom of one clan and one individual, who cited Mahdist endorsements and precedents to buttress his own rule.[12]

Contemporaries also immediately noticed the recasting of the nature of communal membership along ethnically exclusionary lines. F. R. Wingate, who headed the Egyptian Intelligence Department tasked with monitoring the Mahdiya, noted that "in nominating the Khalifa Abdullah, the Mahdi threw the firebrand of discord amongst the hitherto united ranks of Mahdieh [sic], and thereby greatly weakened his cause."[13] Inequality, rather than inclusion, would now be the Mahdiya's lodestar, setting in motion a chain of countermobilization and repression that would hobble the Mahdiya's once-formidable military machine.

3.1.2.   Historiography

Process tracing within this intra-Mahdiya comparison requires substantial documentation of prewar practices and wartime measures of battlefield performance. Fortunately, the primary and secondary source material surrounding the First and Second Mahdi Wars is extensive; by one count, there have been over three thousand books, memoirs, and articles published on these

11. Green 2007, 210–11.

12. Nicoll 2004, 233–34.

13. Wingate 1892, 186.

two wars.[14] This rich historiography partly reflects the gripping nature of the wars and, for British observers in particular, a stunning story of defeat and redemption. These wars also occurred against a backdrop of surging literacy in the United Kingdom and a corresponding flowering of interest in foreign affairs. Journalists, in turn, now became a fixture on the battlefields, while the advent of telegraphs helped fuel this demand. And the sheer assemblage of outsized personalities in these wars—General Gordon, Lord Kitchener, the Mahdi and Khalifa Abdullali—makes for a crowded historiography. Add the presence of (future) luminaries such as Sir Arthur Conan Doyle—a special correspondent for the *Westminster Gazette* in 1896—and A.E.W Mason (*The Four Feathers*) and even a young Winston Churchill, who fought at Omdurman (1898), and the stage is set for a sprawling historiography that spans generations.

In addition to the voluminous secondary literature, I draw on primary documents from individual combatants and eyewitnesses, especially embedded journalists, from each war. These materials include private diaries and classified intelligence reports as well as more public-facing campaign accounts and memoirs from officers, including several generals, and intelligence analysts.[15] I also incorporate commentary from the rank-and-file soldiers in the form of diaries and short articles published in local newspapers.[16] Over thirty journalists were present for at least some aspect of each war; I include their observations as a useful check on official accounts from military authorities.[17] Even memoirs from Europeans captured by the Khalifa are included,[18] though these sources, with one important exception (Neufeld 1899), drift perilously close to war propaganda designed to justify armed intervention against the Mahdiya.[19]

There are two notable gaps in this historiography, however. First, the perspectives of Egyptian and Sudanese soldiers, as well as Ottoman auxiliaries, serving under British command are almost entirely absent; our impressions are filtered through the viewpoint of their British commanders. Second, and especially important, the Mahdist/Sudanese side of the story is poorly represented. As one historian rued, the Mahdiya's own leaders "remain bit-part

14. Raugh 2008. Classic works include Theobald 1951; Holt 1970; Zulfo 1980. For a historiographical overview, see Raugh 2008; Abu Shouk 1999.

15. Daly 1983; Elton 1961; Wingate 1891; An Officer 1899; Colvile 1889; An Officer Who Was There 1885; Butler 1887; Haggard 1895; Wilson 1886; Verner 1886; Stamford, Alford and Sword 1898; Gleichen 1905.

16. Churchill 1899; Harrington and Sharf 1998; Spiers 2004; Meredith 1998.

17. Emery 1986; Steevens 1899; Bennett 1899a, b; Burleigh 1899, 1898.

18. Wingate 1892; Slatin Pasha 1896; Neufeld 1899; Pugh 2011.

19. Holt 1958a.

players on the stage of their own written history."[20] Particular effort was therefore paid to incorporating the Mahdist viewpoint and sources whenever possible.[21] But much remains to be done. Even biographies of the Mahdi[22] or key players such as his most capable and longest-serving emir, Osman Digna, are few and far between.[23] The sacking of Omdurman in 1898, the destruction of the Mahdiya itself, and the perishable nature of oral traditions have all conspired to tear holes in the fabric of our understanding of the Mahdiya's rise and fall.

Within these constraints, however, there is sufficient evidence to trace the relationship between inequality and battlefield performance and to eliminate alternatives. In the narrative that follows, I note where firm evidence gives way to educated speculation, and triangulate across multiple sources rather than rely on a single account. I also use known historiographical biases to strengthen causal inferences. Belligerents often have incentives to exaggerate their own martial virtues while denigrating those of an opponent. I therefore compare and combine British and Mahdist assessments of each other to cross-validate my own judgments about battlefield performance across the Mahdi's and Khalifa's versions of the Mahdiya.

3.2.   Mirror Images: The Mahdi State(s) Compared

Table 3.1 details the paired comparison. Because it is the template for subsequent chapters, I spend some time detailing why each of these twenty-eight covariates is important theoretically and how they are similar, if not constant, across the two cases.

3.2.1.   Matched Covariates

Matching on these initial covariates helps account for leading explanations that emphasize the role played by material preponderance in shaping battlefield outcomes. In each war, for example, the Mahdiya enjoyed a preponderance of fielded soldiers over its British and Egyptian foes. This material superiority holds true whether power is expressed as a percentage of total soldiers fielded by both sides (*Initial relative power*) or as the average of the estimated maximum number of soldiers the Mahdiya deployed (*Total fielded force*). These average estimates are not only nearly identical but also conceal the fact that the Mahdiya had sufficient organizational capacity to surge

---

20. Nicoll 2004, xxiv.

21. See especially Zulfo 1980; Bedri 1969; Holt 1958a; Nicoll 2004; Paul 1954; Collins 1962.

22. Berman 1932.

23. Jackson 1926.

TABLE 3.1. Matched Pair: The Rise and Fall of the Mahdi State (*Mahdiya*)

Covariates	Mahdi State *First Mahdi War,* *1881–85*	Mahdi State *British-Mahdi War,* *1896–99*
Military Inequality (Coefficient)	Low (0.01)	Extreme (0.67)
From Matching		
Initial relative power	50–55%	65–68%
Total fielded force	50,000	57,500
Regime type	Personalist dictatorship	Personalist dictatorship
Distance from capital	680km	663km
Standing army	Yes	Yes
Composite military	Yes	Yes
Initiator	Yes	No
Joiner	No	No
Democratic opponent	Yes	Yes
Great Power	No	No
Civil war	Yes	No
Non-COW	Yes	Yes
Early modern	Yes	Yes
Contextual Covariates		
Combined arms	Yes	Yes
Doctrine	Offensive	Offensive
Fortifications	Yes (*zariba*)	Yes (*zariba*)
Superior weapons	No	No
Foreign advisors	No	No
Terrain	Desert scrubland	Desert scrubland
War duration	1268 days	1267 days
War birth	Yes	No
Recent war history w/opponent	No	Yes
Facing colonizer	Yes	Yes
Identity dimension	Sufi Islam/Christian	Sufi Islam/Christian
New leader	Yes	No
Population	6-8.5 million	3-5.5 million
Ethnolinguistic fractionalization (ELF)	High	High
Civ-mil relations	Ruler as commander	Ruler as commander
Battlefield Performance		
Tac-op sophistication	Moderate	Poor
Loss-exchange ratio	Moderate (1.29)	Poor (-87.9)
Mass desertion	No	Yes
Mass defection	No	No
Fratricidal violence	No	Yes

soldiers when needed: estimates of up to 60–65,000 soldiers can be found for specific battles in each war, as at Khartoum (1885) and Omdurman (1898). Claims that material superiority drives battlefield performance are thus problematic in this case; the balances are very similar, but the observed outcomes are not. Indeed, if anything, the Mahdiya enjoyed a greater preponderance of fielded forces during the second war but turned in a disastrous showing. Unsurprisingly, the Mahdiya did not meet the Correlates of War (COW) criteria for Great Power status (*Great power*) in either war.[24] Military power is thought subject to a "loss of strength" gradient; the farther a state attempts to project its power, the less its power, as logistical difficulties and terrain conspire to create friction that prevents a state from reaching its full military potential.[25] The distance between a state's capital and the first battle of each war therefore provides an additional measure of a combatant's military power. In this case, the distances involved are remarkably similar. The First Mahdi War's initial engagement was fought 680 kilometers from Khartoum, the Mahdiya's nominal capital, while the Second War opened in 1896 about 663 kilometers from Omdurman. Holding these initial distances nearly constant across the wars helps control for logistical difficulties in resupplying forces as well as opportunities for desertion and defection. The Mahdiya fought alone in both wars. Though a simple point, the absence of allies provides an opportunity for a clean look at its performance without the confounding effects of fighting as a member of an alliance or as a third-party joiner to an ongoing conflict.[26]

These wars were fought only about a dozen years apart, helping to control for weaponry advances while ensuring that they both occurred in the same pre-1917 era of technology, tactics, and balance between offensive and defensive weapons (*Early modern*). While advances were being made—repeating rifles were slowly introduced to British (but not Egyptian) forces, while more sophisticated, if not wholly reliable, Maxim machine guns were also deployed—British tactics remained static. Anglo-Egyptian forces typically fought in "squares," defensive positions designed to maximize force protection and firepower while facing more mobile attackers. Battles in each war were measured in hours, not days, though each war witnessed the occasional siege operation.

24. These measures of fielded forces are preferable to the standard practice of using prewar estimates of total military personnel, as recorded in COW, to measure power balances. There is often little or no correlation between these latent indicators of material power and the number of soldiers actually deployed, especially in colonial wars.

25. Boulding 1962.

26. Weitsman 2014; Downes 2009.

Nor can regime type explain such dramatic differences in battlefield performance. The Mahdiya was born a personalist, theocratic dictatorship, and remained so for its entire existence (*Regime type*). The Mahdi and his successor were advised by a council of high-ranking emirs that had a modest advisory role. Using the coding rules for Polity IV, which ranks political regimes from most democratic (+10) to most autocratic (−10) according to formal constraints on executive power, the Mahdiya was assessed the same value (a −7) on the eve of each war.[27] Since the Mahdiya squared off in each war with the same countries, we can also eliminate the opponents' regime type as a factor explaining Mahdist battlefield performance. The Mahdiya's principal adversary was the United Kingdom which, according to Polity IV data, was a consolidated democracy with a "7" score in the year before each war (*Democratic opponent*). Egypt is considered a formal combatant in the 1881–85 war by dint of its initiation: the Mahdi first declared war against Egypt, forcing a subsequent British intervention in 1882. By contrast, Egyptian forces were not independent in the Second War; instead, they were subordinated to British command and control, with Egyptian units trained and commanded by British officers from the war's beginning. In each case, the Mahdiya was engaged in the daunting task of defeating a democratic Great Power and its local proxy, a fact which makes its victory in the First Mahdi War especially surprising.[28]

Scholars have also cited a military's recruitment system as central to its subsequent performance. Volunteer-based armies, for example, might exhibit more initiative, while conscript-based ones often suffer higher casualties due to the political costs of losing volunteer soldiers.[29] Armies that blend recruitment streams, sometimes drawing from a mix of volunteers, conscripts, mercenaries, and even slaves, could be especially prone to command and control problems, dampening their performance. In our case, however, the Mahdiya's composite recruitment patterns never changed (*Composite military*). Its system meshed volunteers, conscripts from annual tribal levies, defectors, and even a few captured slaves, into a standing army with a modest reserve capacity, though the Mahdi was still constructing his army during initial battles (*Standing army*).

Battlefield differences also cannot be chalked up to changes in Anglo-Egyptian military organization which was largely static across the wars. In

27. Jaggers and Gurr 2004.

28. Neither war is included in COW's Inter-State War dataset; the Mahdiya lacked the requisite diplomatic recognition by London or Paris that COW requires for official statehood (*Non-COW*).

29. Horowitz, Simpson and Stam 2011.

each case, a small contingent of British officers and soldiers, roughly a division's worth drawn from Royal Marines and defense regiments, led and backstopped Egyptian conscripts. During each war, combined Anglo-Egyptian forces also relied on Sudanese auxiliaries and small numbers of (hated) mercenaries known as *Bashi-bazouks* ("damaged heads") that hailed from Albania and Greece.

3.2.2. Contextual Variables

We can draw an even tighter comparison by delving into the historical record for additional factors that are difficult to capture in a quantitative framework. A further fifteen covariates can be identified that might explain the radical shift in the Mahdiya's military fortunes. Once again, these factors are identical, or very nearly so, across both wars, ruling them out as alternative explanations.[30]

Mahdist armies remained wedded to a rudimentary combined arms approach during both wars, for example (*Combined arms*). Cavalry, firearm-equipped shock troops, regular infantry (increasingly outfitted with firearms over time), and artillery provided the building blocks for Mahdist military organization. In each war, Mahdist commanders (emirs) proved capable of conducting envelopment attacks by separate cavalry wings that fixed the enemy in place until shock troops and regular infantry, supported by enthusiastic if sporadic artillery support, converged on enemy positions. Commanders privileged offensive doctrines that favored rapid movement and overwhelming mass at several points of contact to swamp enemy defenses in frontal assaults that promised, though often failed to deliver, quick victories (*Doctrine*). When necessary, however, Mahdist forces were also capable of constructing and besieging fortifications, including building fieldworks such as fairly elaborate trenches and *zaribas*, protective enclosures made from acacia thorn bushes (*Fortifications*).

The Mahdiya also waged each war at the technological disadvantage to Anglo-Egyptian forces (*Superior weapons*). During the First Mahdi War, Mahdist forces managed to claw out a rough parity with enemy soldiers by acquiring weapons abandoned on the battlefield, including modern Remington rifles and artillery pieces, though fewer than half of Mahdist soldiers had a reliable firearm by war's end. If anything, the weapons available to the

---

30. I avoid matching directly on these contextual variables in part because some of them (including *war duration, ethnolinguistic fractionalization,* and even *population size*) may be consequences of military inequality. Matching on them might therefore introduce post-treatment bias into our estimates of the effects of inequality on battlefield performance.

Khalifa's military exceeded that of the Mahdi both in quality and numbers. A greater percentage of the Khalifa's military was firearm-equipped, and his forces had acquired both modern large-caliber artillery and machine guns. As late as the Battle at Omdurman in 1898, Mahdist and Egyptian soldiers fielded the same Remington rifle, though British forces had adopted the far superior Lee-Metford .303 repeating rifle. Indeed, claims that British techno-logical superiority, in the form of Maxim machine guns, Krupp artillery, and armed Nile steamers, was responsible for the lopsided nature of the Mahdiya's defeat are commonplace; I take up this argument below.

Foreign advisors, often drawn from the ranks of European ex-soldiers, pro-vide an additional source of intellectual capital that can boost battlefield per-formance (*Foreign advisors*). Many non-Western combatants in our Project Mars dataset, for example, turned to other states or mercenaries to obtain the skills and technology necessary to master conventional warfare. Some-what surprisingly, despite extensive trade relations with neighboring states, the Mahdiya waged these wars without foreign advisors. It did, however, forcibly impress captured Egyptian gunners into its artillery service.[31] These Egyptian officers had been trained by British forces after the 1882 occupation of Egypt, and so advanced technology and skills diffused to the Mahdiya, albeit in a more circuitous route than directly hiring foreign mercenaries or signing arms contracts with European powers, including Britain's key rival, France.

Difficult terrain can also shape wartime fortunes by slowing movement, crippling logistics, and by providing opportunities for successful desertion (*Terrain*). In our case, however, the terrain was identical across both wars. Nearly every battle took place in the vast areas of thorny scrubland that extends for about 320 kilometers on either side of the snaking Nile River. Battles were fought within a narrow north-south axis ranging from the Nile's second cataract at Wadi Halfa to the sixth cataract, terminating at Khartoum, where the Nile itself divides into the White and Blue Nile rivers. Each war's major battles are illustrated in figure 3.1 and figure 3.3. The Nile tethered com-batants to their logistical systems and to each other; battles not only occurred close to the Nile but often were fought in the same locations, as at Khartoum (1885) and Omdurman (1898). Logistical problems—above all, finding and defending clean water wells—was a defining feature of each war given the difficult terrain and climate. Both wars began during the summer (August and June, respectively) and were fought in extreme heat, with temperatures routinely reaching 40°C.

31. Nicoll 2004, 111; Zulfo 1980, 39.

War duration might also affect wartime fortunes: longer wars favor the better prepared and provisioned combatant, as well as those less sensitive to mounting casualties or economic costs.[32] Similarly, the longer the war drags on, the greater the opportunities for mass indiscipline to appear within the ranks. Yet the First and Second Mahdi Wars, at 1,268 and 1,267 days, respectively, are nearly identical.[33]

Other scholars have suggested that the belligerents' religious or civilizational identities (*Identity dimension*) can influence war's intensity.[34] We might expect that wars pitting combatants across religious or "civilizational" divides tend toward extremes of violence as common norms about restrictions on the use of violence are nonexistent. In our case, the Christian/Islamic division among combatants remained constant across both wars. Given that the Mahdiya was facing the same colonizer (*Facing colonizer*) on its own "home turf," we cannot account for differential battlefield performance by appealing to the nature of the enemy or resolve arising from defending one's homeland.[35] Even the Mahdiya's framing of the wars—that of a jihad against foreign, non-believing enemies—was identical across wars.

Population characteristics, including absolute size (*Population*) and degree of ethnolinguistic fractionalization (*ELF*), might also affect battlefield performance. States with larger populations are thought better able to bear casualties, for example.[36] As societies become increasingly diverse, as measured by the number of ethnic groups within them, they may also experience more frequent civil wars or struggle with interethnic communication, crippling their military power.[37] Given that we are dealing with the same state, population traits are indeed similar, though caution is warranted, as these characteristics are often the outcome of state action, and thus not truly independent variables. At the time of the Khalifa's accession, the Mahdiya had approximately 8.5 million inhabitants.[38] By 1893, however, the population had

---

32. Bennett and Stam 1998.

33. Duration is measured here in days between the first and last battles of the war rather than the public declaration of war and associated cease-fire or peace treaty. The First Mahdi War is coded as occurring from 12 August 1881 to 30 January 1885, denoting the fall of Khartoum. The British are coded as joining the war on 29 February 1884. The Second Mahdi War is coded as occurring between 7 June 1896 and 25 November 1899, with the final Battle at Umm Diwaykarat drawing the war to a close.

34. Gong 1984; Hanson 2002.

35. Mack 1975; Castillo 2014.

36. Rosen 1972.

37. Peled 1998; Cederman, Wimmer and Min 2010.

38. Green 2007, 210.

shrunk by 25–50 percent, victims of regime-orchestrated repression, famine, and displacement, and war with neighboring states.[39] Despite these policies, however, the army's size in each war was comparable, and ethnic diversity remained high throughout.

Finally, relations between civilian leaders and military authorities (*Civ-mil relations*) can shape battlefield performance.[40] Competing priorities, civilian fears of coups, and the curtailing of military autonomy over its training and promotions can all conspire to erode battlefield performance. The Mahdiya, however, fought each war with roughly the same institutional arrangements. Both the Mahdi and the Khalifa were considered the supreme military commander who set strategic priorities and who, when needed, issued operational guidance about when and where to fight battles. Each leader had a stable of emirs, including a senior emir, who handled the daily running of the military and who led forces in battle while the supreme commander observed from a safe distance.

No two cases, even ones featuring the same set of combatants, are identical, of course. These differences, however, generally lead us to expect the Khalifa's military machine to outperform the upstart Mahdi's more rudimentary efforts. The Mahdi, for example, was a new wartime leader (*New leader*), just establishing his credentials and constantly at risk of removal if his military fortunes soured. The Khalifa, by contrast, was a well-established dictator with eleven years under his belt before the opening of the Second Mahdi War in 1896. The Mahdiya itself was literally born of a civil war; by 1896, however, the Mahdiya had formidable, if not completely uncontested, state capacity, including an improved ability to tax its population and devote resources toward its military machine. Nor did the Mahdi benefit from prior experience against British forces. The Khalifa, by contrast, could not only draw on prior experience against Anglo-Egyptian forces but commanded soldiers battle-hardened in wars with neighbors such as Abyssinia, the Congo Free State, and Equatoria in the 1885–96 interregnum. Intriguingly, the Mahdi, but not the Khalifa, initiated his war, which might have tipped the scales slightly in his favor, though the ragtag nature of the Mahdiya's nascent army compared to the Khalifa's seems to stack the deck against observing superior battlefield performance.[41]

---

39. I therefore do not match directly on population size; doing so may inadvertently control for the casual effects of identity type, biasing estimates downward.

40. Huntington 1957; Quinlivan 1999; Talmadge 2013; Castillo 2014.

41. On initiation and favorable war outcomes, see Wang and Ray 1994; Reiter and Stam 1998*b*; Sullivan 2012.

3.3.   Process Tracing: From Inequality to Battlefield Performance

The following sections detail the comparison between the Mahdi-governed Mahdiya and its Khalifa-ruled successor. For each war, I examine the (pre)war nature of the regime's collective vision and explore its recruitment practices and management strategies. I then assess four components of battlefield performance: tactical and operational sophistication; loss-exchange ratios; the incidence of soldier indiscipline, including mass desertion and defection; and the use of violence against the Mahdiya's own soldiers and population. While I broadly follow the chronology of the First and Second Mahdi Wars, the goal here is not to provide a detailed narrative of each skirmish and battle. Instead, I emphasize the arc from prewar inequality to battlefield performance, drawing on evidence from specific battles to demonstrate that the proposed mechanisms are at work. This close-range process tracing has the added virtue of considering paths not taken by the Mahdi and Khalifa as well as identifying additional clues that are consistent with the proposed argument and that cast doubt on remaining alternative explanations.

3.4.   The Rise of the Mahdi State and the First Mahdi War, 1881–85

On the eve of the Mahdi's revolt, the Egyptian Sudan—the name itself is something of an anachronism—stretched from the Red Sea to Darfur's petty sultanates and from the Nile's Second Cataract to the Equatorial Lakes. The area was ripe for revolution.[42] Heavy taxation by a corrupt and heavy-handed Turco-Egyptian regime (the "Turkiyya") had created widespread opposition to Khedival rule. Punitive campaigns aimed at suppressing the Sudan's slave trade created another set of grievances among slaving tribes. A lingering desire for revenge against the "Turk" hovered; payback for the violent conquest of the Sudan was a potentially explosive rallying cry. To make matters worse, the Khedival bureaucracy and judicial system were dominated by the Shaiqaya tribe and Khatmiya sect, stoking a belief among Sudan's mixed population— Muslim and Arab in the north, pagan and black in the south—that they were experiencing alien rule.[43]

Skillfully combining concrete grievances with eschatological precepts, Muhammad Ahmad b. 'Abdallah's declaration that he was the Expected Mahdi

---

42. Holt and Daly 2011; Holt 1970; Theobald 1951.
43. Hechter 2013.

on 29 June 1881 set him on a collision course with Egyptian authorities. Emerging victorious from a short skirmish with government forces at Jazira Aba (12 August 1881), the Mahdi and his small army of followers rattled off a string of quick successes. Victory fed recruitment; by the time of the Battle at Jabal Jarrada (May 1882), the Mahdi commanded fifteen thousand Ansar. Seeking to land a decisive blow, the Mahdi amassed thirty thousand Ansar and struck at the provincial capital of El Obeid on 8 September 1882. The attack was premature, however, and his poorly armed forces were routed. Yet recruitment continued unabated, and in January 1883, El Obeid fell to Mahdist forces after a brief siege (see figure 3.1 for battle locations).

The British occupation of Egypt after the Battle of Tel El Kebir (13 September 1882) ushered in a new phase of the First Mahdi War, one that saw increased British participation. Mahdist forces continued to pile up victories, however, defeating an expeditionary force led by British General William "Pasha" Hicks at the Battle of Shaykan on 5 November 1883. The defeat was decisive: only 500 of 11,000 Egyptian conscripts returned home, and Pasha Hicks himself was decapitated. A second expeditionary force, this time led by British General Valentine Baker, met a similar fate at El Teb (4 February 1884), though the embattled force was rescued at the second Battle of El Teb (28 February 1884) by Sir Gerald Green's 4,500-strong UK contingent.

Debate in Cairo and London now turned to orchestrating a withdrawal from the Sudan. In February 1884, Charles "Chinese" Gordon arrived in Khartoum with instructions to prepare to evacuate remaining besieged Egyptian garrisons at Sennar, Tokat, Sinkat, and Khartoum. Exceeding his mandate, the supremely self-confident Gordon misjudged the Mahdi's strength and ordered a deliberately gradual evacuation of Khartoum. He moved too slowly; on 12 March, Mahdist forces under the command of the Mahdi's father-in-law, Muhammad al-Taiyib al-Basir, cut Khartoum's communications with the north. By the end of March, Khartoum and its 7,000-strong garrison was under siege and subject to daily Mahdist fire. The blockade grew tighter; Mahdist forces, now 60,000 in number, clamped down on the city, starving its inhabitants and leading Gordon to ever-more frantic appeals for relief. At roughly the same time, in February 1884 Major-General Sir Gerald Graham's expedition to Suakin inflicted heavy losses on Osman Digna's Mahdist forces at El Teb and Tamai.

But the real prize was Khartoum. A "Khartoum Relief Expedition" was scraped together under Sir Garnet Wolseley's command and sent to break the Mahdist siege. Wolseley's forces, despite inflicting heavy losses on Mahdist forces at Abu Klea and Abu Kru, were successfully delayed. The relief expedition arrived two days too late; Khartoum had fallen, and Gordon

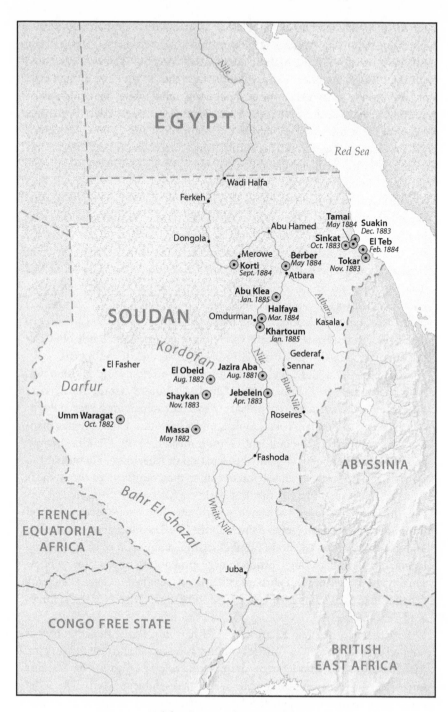

FIGURE 3.1. Mahdiya Sunrise: The First Mahdi War, 1881–85

himself was beheaded, punctuating one of the worst defeats suffered by British forces in its African colonial wars. Though Khartoum's fall typically marks the end of the First Mahdi War, a final expedition under Gerald Graham was launched in March 1885 around Suakin. The Suakin expedition changed nothing, however.[44] Anglo-Egyptian forces completed their withdrawal, abandoning the Sudan to Mahdist forces. The Mahdiya had arrived on the world stage.

Indeed, in the war's aftermath, the Mahdi entered diplomatic correspondence with Egypt, Sultan Hamid II of the Ottoman Empire, and even Queen Victoria, who was enjoined to convert to Islam.[45] India, Tunis, Morocco, Wadai, and the Hijaz all sent delegations to open diplomatic relations. The Mahdiya had a bureaucracy, in part repurposed form the old Turkiyya, a treasury, a small navy, an electric telegraph system, its own currency, and a standing army of at least sixty thousand Ansar. Taxes were collected via annual contributions (*ushr* and *zakat*). A judicial system based on Sharia precepts was imposed throughout the Mahdiya: the use of tobacco, foul language, dancing, playing, and long hair for men were all forbidden. A road-building campaign began in earnest to unite the Mahdiya's diverse and dispersed population. From humble beginnings, the Mahdiya now encompassed up to 8.5 million individuals over 1.6 million square kilometers.

The Mahdiya's victory sent reverberations through the corridors of power. Critics of Prime Minister William Gladstone pounced, using the failure to rescue Gordon as a cudgel, ultimately leading Gladstone to resign. General Wolseley wrote in his private diary that "the conquest of Khartoum had turned the Mahdi into a 'great Military Power'—he will be regarded as irresistible."[46] He warned that subsequent campaigns to defeat the Mahdi would unleash "the most serious war we have undertaken since that idiotic Cabinet of 1854 declared war against Russia"[47] in the Crimea. Contemporaries assumed the upstart state permanent, even extending Geneva Convention protections to it. "It is worth remembering that the Dervishes were not 'savages' ...On the contrary, they satisfied all the requirements for recognition as an 'armed force'—(a) that of being under the direction of a responsible leader, (b) that of wearing a uniform capable of being recognized at a distance, and (c) that of bearing arms openly"[48] wrote one observer. The Mahdiya, it appeared, was here to stay.

44. De Cosson 1886.
45. Holt 1958*b*, 288.
46. Diary entry, 6 February 1885, in Wolseley (1967, 138).
47. Diary entry, 24 February 1885, in Wolseley (1967, 153).
48. Bennett 1899*a*, 26–27.

3.4.1.   The Mahdi's Communal Vision

Muhammad Ahmad b. 'Abdallah's vision of a future state predated both the First Mahdi War and his assumption of the mantle of Mahdi in June 1881 that precipitated it. In broad strokes, he called for an inclusionary Mahdiya that transcended sectarian, tribal, and ethnic ties by appealing to Islam and antiforeign sentiment in equal measure. To use the term "nationalism" would be misleading, at least at this early stage. But he did seek to anchor collective identification around four basic precepts that had widespread appeal, avoiding narrow ethnosectarian language and policies that might antagonize latent identity cleavages in the Sudan.[49]

First, Muhammad Ahmed self-identified as the Mahdi, the prophesied redeemer of Islam whose return was to mark the end of times and the creation of a new order. Consciously mirroring the language and actions of the Prophet Mohammad, he built up support among like-minded tribal leaders who declared their personal loyalty to him by pledging *bay'a*.[50] As the Mahdi, he could access a wellspring of charismatic authority rather than narrowcast his claims to power on the basis of potentially divisive subordinate identities.[51] At its root, the Mahdi's vision was propelled by messianic millennialism; the Mahdi and the movement were both seen as divinely inspired. Pragmatically, a grounding in Islamic ideals created a cross-cutting cleavage that transcended existing identities among the disparate population of the Sudan.

Second, he called for a return to earlier Prophetic models; the Koran and Sunna alone would be the inspiration for a Sharia-ruled order.[52] Prophetic visions and claims to sainthood were also key to mobilizing mass support.[53] Inherent in this conservative vision was a social contract that stood in direct contrast to the corrupt, inauthentic, and even un-Islamic Khedival rule in Egypt. The Mahdi's call for a return to a simpler time, and for pious leaders who ruled justly rather than corruptly, found widespread appeal even among the non-Muslim population that chafed under heavy-handed Khedival control.

Indeed, while appeals to Islam could have been divisive among the Sudan's non-Arab, non-Muslim populations, his collective vision was inclusionary in its call for jihad against the "Turk." In the eyes of many, the Turco-Egyptian

---

49. The best account of the content and symbols of the Mahdi's early state-building is found in Searcy 2011.

50. Searcy 2011, 38.

51. Dekmejian and Wyszomirski 1972.

52. Nicoll 2004; Layish 1997.

53. Searcy 2011, 22–23.

regime was irreligious and illegitimate; the Mahdi's calls represented a chance to throw off the yoke of foreign domination and expel the hated Turks from the Sudan. Jihad, then, represented more than an Islamic revival. It marked the spirit of common cause against an oppressive outsider that had proved deeply invasive of local practices and that had established a narrow ethnosectarian rule over the Sudan that discriminated against Muslims and non-Muslims alike.

Finally, the Mahdi wrapped his collective identity around the principle of strict egalitarianism. He practiced social leveling by calling for the abandonment of tribal identities as well as potentially divisive sectarian ones. He sought to eliminate distinctions between various Sufi orders, instead appealing to a common Sufi identity that suppressed intra-sectarian divisions. He levied socialist policies that proscribed the hoarding of wealth and the payment of exorbitant dowries. These orders even extended to dress: all were to wear the same simple *jubba*, a basic cloth tunic, to hide divisions between wealthy and poor. A stern code of conduct was articulated; harsh discipline was meted out if one Ansari insulted another. "Brothers from another father" encapsulated his understanding of social egalitarianism and his desire to stamp out tribalism.[54]

This inclusive vision was simple enough, and plastic enough, to support multiple interpretations, a great strength when state- and nation-building among a diverse population. The Mahdi and his followers disseminated this vision before and during the war using two channels. The presumptive Mahdi frequently toured key areas in the Sudan such as Kordofan (including El Obeid) to meet with local elders, spread his message through public speeches, and collect pledges of loyalty. He also maintained an extensive system of couriers who disseminated his vision through letters, sermons, and speeches that were read aloud in public spaces throughout Sudan. He continued this practice during wartime, often issuing several letters a day outlining both his broad vision and specific details of daily life when the new Mahdiya was constructed. These missives were not confined to supporters; neutrals and opponents, including enemy officers, were also recipients of his proclamations. Though our records remain incomplete,[55] these letters and other writings were assembled into collected volumes that provided the official narrative of the Mahdi's ideational framework.[56]

Not all tribes and ethnic groups responded immediately to the Mahdi's entreaties; some ethnic and tribal leaders required more persuasion than

54. Kramer 2010.
55. Abu Shouk 1999.
56. Holt 1958a, 1970, 268–69; Searcy 2011, 3.

others, and rallied only after the Mahdi scored initial battlefield victories in 1881. Contingency, too, played its part: the powerful camel-trading Hadendowa tribe joined the movement only after Egyptian authorities reneged on a brokered deal that promised seven dollars for each camel delivered but paid only one.[57] Yet the Mahdi's calls attracted a wide array of supporters even before the first battles, a testament to his inclusionary vision and his avoidance of narrow ethnosectarian favoritism. The vision was thin enough to appeal to multiple groups for diverse reasons but resonant enough to mobilize ever-increasing numbers of followers to take up arms against first the Khedival regime and then its British patron.

3.4.2.   Prewar Practices

Forged in wartime, the nascent Mahdiya had no prewar practices. Instead, its leadership moved quickly to construct a formal military organization that was grafted atop existing practices among its constituent populations. The Mahdiya's Ansar were broadly organized into the three Standards or "Flags" (rayya), each under the command of a designated Khalifa. Standardized uniforms consisting of simple plain cloth tunics were distributed by 1885. The military also exhibited functional specialization, with dedicated shock-action infantry, skirmishers, cavalry (al-khayala), and logistics (al-hagana) units. With the advent of captured firearms and artillery, the Mahdiya constructed a specialized vanguard (Jihadiya) and artillery corps in 1883 to round out its emerging combined arms capabilities.[58]

The Mahdiya embraced an extraordinarily inclusionary form of recruitment, with multiple pathways into military service. Co-opting existing tribal levy systems, the Mahdi raised the bulk of his forces through conscription among tribes in the immediate vicinity of likely battle locations as well as further afield, including in Kordofan, where about half of all Ansar originated. Volunteers, too, were welcomed, as individuals were drawn to the Mahdi's message and his string of early battlefield victories. Defectors from the Khedival Army were especially embraced, as they typically brought not only firearms but much-needed technical expertise. It was standard practice for the Mahdi to fold defeated soldiers into his forces as well. While many of these soldiers undoubtedly preferred service to the alternative, typically imprisonment or execution, we cannot escape the coercive nature of their recruitment. Such coercion was overt with respect to Egyptian artillery gunners; if captured, they were forcibly impressed into the Mahdiya's artillery corps.

57. Paul 1954, 107.
58. Musa 2010, 100.

These separate recruitment channels made for an intriguing, if somewhat bewildering, spectacle for Egyptian and British commanders, as Ansar from all streams converged on the battlefield. The Mahdist order of battle at Abu Klea (17 January 1885), for example, recorded a Berber contingent (horse and cavalry) from three tribes, "turncoat" Egyptians, a levy from nearby Metemmeh drawn from two tribes, and a main force comprised of levies from at least four tribes in Kordofan and Omdurman, along with a Jihadiya vanguard drawn from non-Arab ranks.[59]

Mahdist strategies for managing soldier diversity also took their direction from past patterns of recruitment. Each "Flag" was organized roughly along regional lines, with its subcomponents (rub's, roughly equivalent to "regiments") reflecting specific tribal levies. The Black Flag, for example, was commanded by Khalifa Abdallahi, the Mahdi's eventual successor, and was composed of tribal levies from western Baggara, while the Red Flag gathered its strength from the Ashraf and Nile River tribes. Regiments were typically singular in either ethnicity or tribal affiliation, though in some cases there is evidence of "blended" units that combined two or more neighboring tribes. Some specialization did occur along ethnic and tribal lines; the Baggara, for example, comprised the bulk of the cavalry, a role that reflected material need—they were the predominant horse-faring people in the Sudan—and less an ethnically motivated preference by the Mahdist leadership. Similarly, the Jihadiya was recruited largely from Khedival soldiers captured in battle because of their familiarity with firearms rather than their ethnic composition.[60]

We might imagine that such diversity predisposed the Mahdiya toward both higher soldier indiscipline and greater problems with command and control, especially in the absence of formal mechanisms for prewar socialization. Yet realistic military training was quickly embraced as a means of improving combined action skills and of fostering cohesion. Live-fire drills, including the use of artillery, were conducted to familiarize soldiers and their horses to the noise and confusion of modern battlefields.[61] The Mahdi also enacted a system of spoil-sharing as a means of creating a sense of community within the ranks. One-fifth of all booty went to the Mahdi to fund the war while the remainder was deposited in a communal treasury to finance state-building. This system not only dampened potential inter- and intra-Flag squabbles over spoils but also reinforced the Mahdi's legitimacy as supreme military commander.[62]

59. Snook 2013, 522.
60. Holt 1970, 63.
61. Holt 1970, 72.
62. Nicoll 2004, 97; Kramer 2010, 88–89.

3.4.3. Tactical and Operational Sophistication

The popular image of waves of Mahdist soldiers crashing blindly against stout British formations, only to be mowed down by superior firepower, is difficult to dislodge. Yet it is misleading. Mahdist emirs and their Ansar had a far better tactical and operational acumen than commonly supposed, even in the early days of the Mahdist uprising. The "fanatics-against-Maxims" narrative overlooks the Mahdiya's crafting of its own form of combined arms doctrine as well as the skill of its soldiers in exploiting terrain to offset, if only partially, its technological inferiority.

Early Mahdist offensives integrated the power of massed shock infantry with a vanguard of firearm-equipped soldiers in a bid to overwhelm enemy positions. Cavalry played several roles in these attacks, including initial battlefield reconnaissance, screening the movement of Mahdist infantry toward the enemy, and more long-range interdiction of enemy supply lines, especially their access to water wells.[63] Far from blindly charging enemy positions, Mahdist emirs used envelopment strategies from multiple axes to converge on identified weak points—typically the corners—of Egyptian and Anglo-Egyptian "square" formations. These initial thrusts aimed at tearing a hole in enemy lines, after which swarming soldiers would sow chaos inside the collapsing formation, inflicting casualties and inducing enemy soldiers to retreat or desert. Though early Mahdist attacks were largely one-shot affairs, over time Mahdist emirs sought to maximize shock value by assaulting in successive, closely spaced waves to demoralize tired defenders.

Mahdist tactics also emphasized cover and concealment, seeking to make use of terrain obstacles ("dead ground") to reduce exposure to enemy artillery and rifle fire. In particular, Mahdist emirs made skillful use of covered approaches to reduce Anglo-Egyptian sight lines, often exploiting *khors*, watercourses with sandy bottoms typically dry for most of the year, to move soldiers toward enemy formations unseen. Moreover, Mahdist commanders were tactically creative, able to spring traps through false fronts to set the battlefield on favorable grounds. These traits were on display at the Battle of Abu Klea (17 January 1885). Seeking to block the advance of an Anglo-Egyptian relief column heading to Khartoum, Mahdist forces first made use of skirmishers and harassing fire to slow their enemy's advance. Mahdist emirs then baited the Anglo-Egyptian square into advancing by creating a false front before feigning retreat. As the square lumbered in pursuit of "retreating" Mahdist formations, the main Mahdi group lay concealed behind small hills and within a khor system. Springing their ambush, Mahdist forces

---

63. Holt 1970, 63, 72.

managed to penetrate the square before being driven back, at heavy cost to both sides. Though Mahdi casualties were high, the battle, followed by a second engagement at Abu Kru two days later, delayed the Anglo-Egyptian advance, ensuring Khartoum would fall before the relief expedition could arrive.[64]

Emirs and Ansari alike also demonstrated tactical learning as the war progressed. Though massed assaults remained a staple of Mahdi tactics, emirs experimented with skirmishers and harassing fire to inflict casualties and restrict Anglo-Egyptian movement. Cover and concealment tactics were adapted to exploit weaknesses in the Remington rifle: Mahdi soldiers would bait enemy forces, especially Egyptian soldiers, into voluminous firing, creating dense smoke that masked the movement of Mahdi forces into striking range.[65] Mahdist formations, one contemporary noted, made "maximum use of cover in getting close to the enemy before launching the attack."[66] Retreats, too, were orderly and made good use of terrain: it became standard practice, for example, to leave rearguard units in ambush positions to hamstring pursuing cavalry formations.[67] Innovation even occurred at the operational level. By the fall of Khartoum in 1885, the Mahdiya's military had created a central headquarters system based first in Kordofan, then Khartoum itself, that was able to coordinate offensives across multiple regions and fronts.[68]

Mahdist formations proved flexible enough to fight well defensively, becoming adept not just at creating but also destroying fortified positions. At the first Battle of El Teb (4 February 1884), for example, Mahdist forces constructed shallow earthworks, rifle pits, and fortified buildings protecting the village and its wells. Though they initiated most of their battles, when given time they could construct formidable defenses, as at Metemmeh (21 January 1885), that proved impervious to British artillery bombardments. And the four-month siege of Khartoum demonstrated that they understood the principles of siegecraft and could outlast, if not outfight, their better-armed opponents.

The tactical skills of the Mahdist forces were also frequently remarked upon by senior commanders and soldiers as well as journalists in their correspondence back home.[69] To be sure, we should be cautious in interpreting these claims, given possible incentives to exaggerate Mahdi skills to salve

64. Wilson 1886; Snook 2013.
65. Butler 1887; Brackenbury 1885.
66. Featherstone 2005, 38.
67. Spiers 2004, 104.
68. Featherstone 2005, 29–32.
69. Burleigh 1884.

wounded pride. Yet observers routinely remarked about the "great tactical skill"[70] of Mahdist forces and their mastery of the ambush.[71] In particular, military commanders grew concerned that the Mahdi had identified the core weaknesses of the square formation.[72] Indeed, Major-General Sir Gerald Graham wrote directly to Secretary of State for War Spencer Cavendish in March 1884 about the ability of Mahdi forces, especially those of Osman Digna, to use dead ground and the cover of rifle smoke to achieve surprise. The square formation, it seemed, had become dangerously outmoded in the face of an opponent with such "tactical finesse."[73]

Not that Mahdi forces were tactically flawless, however. Coordination between various combat arms, especially cavalry and infantry, was often poor. Some battles, especially early in the war, were one-shot massed affairs, with little attention paid to masking troop movements or the (attempted) break-through point. The advantages of suppressive fire from captured artillery were not well understood, leaving Mahdist cavalry and infantry to surge into the teeth of waiting defenders. Mahdist commanders still proved too willing to order massed charges across open terrain at distances that gave Anglo-Egyptian forces time to create sustained volleys of fire; Mahdist forces hit an invisible "wall" of volley-fire at distances of 200–400 yards, imposing horrific casualties. To be fair, many African states, not to mention European ones, were struggling with the same question of how their forces would survive on battlefields of increasing lethality. Yet the Ansar compounded this problem by engaging in counterproductive practices. Soldiers unintentionally degraded the range and rate of fire of their rifles, for example, by shortening the barrel, making them easier to carry on long marches. These modifications, along with a tendency to shoot high, meant that Ansar could not take full advantage of their weapons to even the playing field with their foes.[74]

3.4.4. Casualties

A second measure of combat power is the loss-exchange ratio, which simply measures the number of enemy soldiers killed by a combatant for each of its own soldiers killed on the battlefield in return. The United Kingdom maintained excellent records of its own losses as well as those of its Egyptian soldiers. British officers also made creditable efforts to establish the number

70. Harry Pearse, *Daily News* journalist, quoted in Snook (2013, 265).

71. Wilson 1886.

72. Cooper King 1885; Haggard 1895; De Cosson 1886, 183–200.

73. Spiers 2004, 109, 111fn53.

74. An estimated 21,000 Remington breech-loading rifles had been captured from defeated Egyptian forces by mid-1883 (Warner 1973, 226).

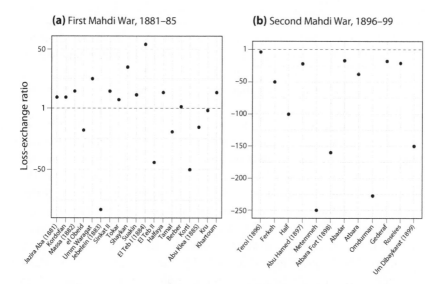

FIGURE 3.2. The Mahdiya's Changing Battlefield Fortunes
Note: Panel (a) illustrates loss-exchange ratios from nineteen major battles from the First Mahdi War, 1881–85. Panel (b) illustrates loss-exchange ratios from twelve major battles during the British-Mahdi War, 1896–99. Positive numbers are enemy soldiers killed for each killed Mahdist soldier; negative numbers indicate the number of Mahdist soldiers killed for each enemy combatant killed. The dashed line at 1 indicates parity. Notably, there are no positive loss-exchange ratios for the Mahdiya in the 1896–99 war.

of Mahdist soldiers killed and wounded in each engagement, sending soldiers out after a battle to count the enemy dead and, on occasion, to dispatch the wounded. That said, Mahdi casualty counts must be treated cautiously: army sizes are notoriously difficult to estimate and subject to inflation by both sides. These issues are compounded by the Mahdi practice of removing their dead and wounded from the battlefield at night, creating a second source of possible bias, albeit one that may partially offset inflationary pressures on estimates of the size of forces engaged.

Panel (a) in figure 3.2 illustrates the loss-exchange ratio for nineteen major battles between Egyptian and later Anglo-Egyptian forces and the Mahdi army. A value of "1" indicates parity; positive values indicate the number of enemy soldiers killed for every Mahdist soldier lost; and negative values indicate the number of Mahdist soldiers lost for every enemy soldier killed.[75] Each loss-exchange estimate is an average derived from multiple

---

75. I chose this format for ease of presentation. Interpreting logged values or ranges from 0 to *y* is not always intuitive when values are less than 1 (a 0.06 LER would mean losing seventeen

sources and excludes wounded, missing, or captured (a rare event) soldiers. The Mahdiya achieved a positive value in twelve of nineteen engagements, indicating that the Mahdi army inflicted greater losses on enemy units than it suffered for the majority of engagements. Overall, Mahdist forces killed 1.29 enemy soldiers for each Ansari they lost. This is a remarkable feat, for four reasons.

First, Mahdi forces were initially heavily outnumbered by Egyptian *fellaheen*; recruitment only gathered momentum after the Mahdi had strung together a series of (unexpected) victories in 1881 and 1882. Second, Mahdist soldiers were forced to beg, steal, or otherwise scourge firearms from the detritus of battles. Mahdist forces were quite literally outgunned for every single battle of the entire war, never having distributed firearms through the entire army before the war's conclusion. Yet, despite this imbalance, an internal British memorandum written in 1883 expressed alarm at the damage inflicted by Mahdist forces: 16,296 British and Egyptian soldiers dead, missing, or captured; 17,669 rifles now in Mahdist hands, along with 16 artillery pieces; and nearly five million rounds of ammunition "lost."[76] Third, the Mahdi actually prohibited firearms (though not their collection) until September 1882, after a failed Mahdist frontal assault against El Obeid, a fortified government town, resulted in the death or wounding of nearly 10,000 Ansar against only 288 Egyptian soldiers killed. Finally, Mahdist forces typically took the battle to Anglo-Egyptian forces, who either fought from defensive formations or from well-defended towns requiring extensive sieges to crack, as at Shaykan (1883) and Khartoum (1885). Attacking into the teeth of defensive positions is by definition costly, demanding a blood price of lopsided casualties.

Achieving a loss-exchange ratio of above-parity when matched against better-trained and better-equipped Anglo-Egyptian forces is a solid achievement. The result should not be oversold: the Mahdi army did struggle once regular British forces entered the fray, resulting in greater losses in some, though not all, post-1882 battles. Still, the defeat of the Hicks and Baker expeditions, as well as the sacking of Khartoum, provide evidence of the Mahdiya's fighting prowess. Parity may be a fairly pedestrian result—it would be scored as "moderate" performance in our indices of combat power—but it stands out in sharp relief compared to the abysmal loss-exchange ratio obtained by the Khalifa's forces against the same enemies in 1896.

---

soldiers for each enemy soldier killed, for example). I therefore use positive (negative) values to indicate greater (worse) relative performance with easily interpretable benchmarks for losses.

76. Nicoll 2004, 142.

3.4.5. Soldier Compliance

Given the Mahdi's need to build both his state and army on the fly, we might imagine that soldier discipline was problematic. Indeed, the absence of social-izing institutions and prewar military training, together with the nascent shape of his identity project and the Mahdiya's diversity, suggests that mass indiscipline should be rife. Yet existing sources indicate the opposite is true: the Ansar were extraordinarily disciplined—"fanatical," according to British officers—both under fire and on the march. No major instances of mass desertion or defection were recorded, for example. Soldiers followed orders; commanders were not faced with collective protests or foot-dragging even as logistical difficulties and tough weather conditions wore soldiers down. Instead, contemporary accounts emphasize how the Ansar were buoyed by the Mahdi's anti-Turkiyya vision and united by a common purpose that tamped down the threat of mass indiscipline. On balance, Mahdist soldiers proved far more disciplined than their Egyptian and Sudanese counterparts in the opposing Egyptian and Anglo-Egyptian armies during the war.

The Mahdiya did not experience mass desertion, for example. Mass deser-tion is defined here (and throughout the book) as the unauthorized with-drawal of soldiers, including entire units, from the battlefield and its rear areas with the intent of abandoning the fight permanently. "Mass" desertion is said to occur when ≥ 10 percent of an army's total deployed forces has decamped for home, a fairly high bar. While we cannot rule out the possibility that a small number of soldiers deserted given source limitations, there is no mention of mass desertion in either British or Mahdist records. The Mahdi did face ini-tial fence-sitting from some reluctant tribes who were waiting to see how the Mahdi fared on the battlefield, but once committed these soldiers and tribes remained within the fold. The combination of an attractive, inclusive, collec-tive vision, along with a benevolent policy of incorporating defeated soldiers into his own ranks rather than executing them, helped swell his ranks.[77] From only a few hundred soldiers, the Mahdi grew an army that gained over sixty thousand adherents in less than four years. Most tellingly, his ranks swelled even after suffering a crushing defeat at El Obeid in September 1882.

Mahdist commanders were able to play upon British hopes of Ansar deser-tion by sending double agents into camps to sow discord among Egyptian and Sudanese soldiers. In late September 1883, General William "Pasha" Hicks, chief of staff of the Egyptian Army, recounted an episode where a Mahdi "deserter" arrived at Hicks's camp and asked to enlist in one of his regiments. After four days, however, the agent stole two months' advance pay, a rifle

77. Clark 1977, 10, 43.

(with 120 rounds), a uniform, and a camel, and returned to the Mahdi with information about Hicks's battle plans and force deployment. "So much for my 'intelligence' officer," Hicks fumed, "not intelligent."[78] The agent also spread rumors about the Mahdi's infallible and immortal nature—assassins' knives could not enter his body, it was said—fueling desertion among Hicks's Muslim conscripts.

Indeed, mass desertion was a problem for the Egyptian and, after 1882, the joint Anglo-Egyptian armies. British commanders routinely complained about it in their dispatches, worried that some of these Egyptian and Sudanese deserters might switch sides, providing an intelligence coup for the Mahdi.[79] For his part, the Mahdi actively encouraged desertion via widely disseminated letters that challenged conscripts to join the fight against the Turkiyya or, at a minimum, to avoid fighting for a corrupt regime in league with Western infidels. General Gordon himself recognized the appeal of the Mahdist vision, writing in his diary, "query, who are the rebels, *we or the Arabs?*"[80] Morale was so poor within the Anglo-Egyptian camp that desertion rarely followed the rhythm of battle, instead occurring before, during, and after engagements with Mahdist forces. Even commanders were dispirited; when ordered to build defensive positions, one commander replied morosely, "we are digging our grave with our own hand."[81]

The Mahdiya's forces also did not exhibit mass defection, despite repeated efforts by British commanders to play up sectarian divisions. Mass defection occurs when ≥10 percent of an army's fielded strength switches allegiance during the war and actively takes up arms against its former state and comrades. Most contemporary accounts stress not only the Ansar's fervor but also their loyalty, even after battlefield setbacks. To be sure, there are scattered references to defecting soldiers in correspondence among senior British commanders. General Gordon's own diary, written daily as he sat besieged by Mahdi forces at Khartoum and later smuggled out by steamship, recounts how "five to seven escaped soldiers" would enter British camps each day during September to December 1884.[82]

78. General Hicks, diary entry, 30 September 1883, in Daly 1983, 99. Emphasis in original.

79. Colvile 1889, 41, 44, 270.

80. General Gordon, diary entry, 4 October 1884, in Elton 1961, 97. Emphasis in original.

81. Holt 1970, 61.

82. References are found in various diary entries by General Gordon in his *Khartoum Journal* in Elton 1961. These include: Diary entry, 15 September 1884 (pp. 44–45); Diary entry, 18 September (p. 51); Diary entry, 20 September (p. 58, 60); Diary entry, 21 September (pp. 61–62); Diary entry, 2 October (p. 92); Diary entry, 7 October (p. 104); Diary entry, 27 October (p. 146); Diary entry, 31 October (p. 155).

Yet caution is warranted here, even for these few references to defection. Existing records are spotty on the numbers and even identities of these would-be defectors. Gordon himself often expressed dismay at his inability to receive actionable, or even accurate, intelligence from these individuals. He openly mused whether these individuals were not actually soldiers but instead grifters driven by the lure of material gains—Gordon paid his informants—rather than displeasure at serving in the Mahdi's army.[83] For "any escaped soldier," he noted, "the belly governs the whole world."[84] Some of these soldiers were also likely returning stragglers from Gordon's own forces rather than soldiers who were genuinely defecting. His Intelligence Department apparently placed little stock in these reports or in the practice of paying for information. General Gordon was probably just grasping at straws; his estimates of deserters and defectors actually *increased* as the Mahdi's forces moved closer to doomed Khartoum.[85]

By contrast, British commanders were well aware of the dangers of defection from their own ranks. Intelligence Chief F. R. Wingate noted the drastic measures necessary to prevent widespread defection and how the ethnic composition of his own forces conditioned the likelihood of defection. Egyptian conscripts, he wrote, "wept in their chains" when forced to deploy to the Sudan. He consoled himself, however, with the knowledge that his Egyptian soldiers were less likely to defect than his Sudanese auxiliaries since "they were strangers to the land—compromise with the Mahdists was beyond their reach."[86] Sudanese soldiers were deemed a chronic flight risk: "As a rule," he lamented, "they only required to be on the stronger side."[87]

British military authorities ultimately underestimated the risk of defection from their ranks. In some instances, entire tribes, such as the Ja'alin, defected to the Mahdi's side, materially shifting the balance of forces against the Anglo-Egyptian expedition. Defection continued before and during battles, as at Bara on 6 January 1883, forcing military authorities to enact drastic measures to maintain discipline (see below). Whole operations were sabotaged by defection. General Gordon's campaign to retake Halfaya, which guarded Omdurman's approaches, foundered with heavy casualties because of treachery among defecting high-ranking officers, Generals Hassan Shallali and Said al-Jimiabi. Anglo-Egyptian forces were finding success driving back Mahdist forces until these officers ordered their own guns to cease fire. They

83. Elton 1961, 74.

84. Diary entry, 12 October 1884, in Elton 1961, 119.

85. Diary entry, 1 November 1884; Diary entry, 6 November 1884 in Elton 1961, 157, 169.

86. Wingate 1892, 74–75.

87. Wingate 1891, 74.

then beheaded the bewildered artillery lieutenant and a bugler who wouldn't sound the retreat and drove their men back from the front line. In the process, they tore a hole in their own defenses, exposing their men to Mahdist attacks and losing valuable artillery pieces, camels, and water in the process. The two were later apprehended trying to make it to Mahdi lines and were executed for treason.[88]

3.4.6. Monitoring and Coercion

The absence of any discussion of the use of blocking detachments, or of wide-spread violence against the Mahdi's own soldiers, is also telling. The Mahdi did construct an elite Jihadiya in 1883 which could have served as a blocking detachment. Instead, it was deployed as a frontline shock formation, leading the charge against the best soldiers among Anglo-Egyptian units rather than policing rear areas.[89] Bolstering the morale of his soldiers was a priority, especially in early battles. But the Mahdi chose to exhort his soldiers by stoking the fires of a millennial Islamism rather than coercion. In one widely distributed message, he admonished his soldiers: "Do not fear the power that stems from their [Egyptian] apparent strength; it is not an inner strength. Do not fear their visible numbers; all power is with Allah. How often, by God's will, has a small force defeated a large army? All is with those who persevere steadfastly."[90]

Evidence of Mahdist coercive practices is also scant among British sources, where incentives nonetheless exist to play up the Mahdi's "uncivilized" nature. General Gordon, for one, did believe that the Mahdi was holding his forces together by threat of punishment. "The Arabs have no conscience," he wrote. "They make my captured soldiers serve the guns and otherwise act against us under pain of death."[91] He also alleged that the Mahdi had spread rumors that Gordon would kill all Mahdi soldiers who defected and that the Mahdi employs "three companies of regulars to bring back deserters."[92]

There is some truth to Gordon's claim that the Mahdiya forced some soldiers to fight. Captured Egyptian artillery officers, though few in number, had critical skills that the Mahdist military lacked, and so were forcibly impressed into service. Gordon himself was hardly an impartial judge, though, and as noted his assessments of the Mahdiya rested almost entirely on purchased

---

88. Nushi 1885, 19–22.

89. Over time, the Khalifa transformed the Jihadiya into a blocking formation (Zulfo 1980, 23n2).

90. Proclamation by the Mahdi (1883), reproduced in Wingate 1891, 92–93.

91. *Khartoum Journal* entry on 26 September 1884 in Elton 1961, 79.

92. *Khartoum Journal* entries on 7 October and 30 October 1884 in Elton 1961, 104, 155.

rumors. In particular, he routinely complained about the weakness of information about Mahdist strength and resolve: "As for knowing the truth in the Sudan it is impossible," he wrote, "for the devils of lying and robbery are riding all over the country."[93] His belief that the Mahdi's military rested on coercion blinded him to the growing sense of purpose and resolve that attracted recruits to the Mahdi's standard. As late as October 1884 he dismissed estimates of Mahdi strength at forty thousand men as "rubbish" and "fudge"—"all Kordofan could not produce this number"—suggesting he had at most three thousand soldiers. At this point, the Mahdi had nearly sixty thousand under arms at and near Khartoum.[94]

The preponderance of evidence from both British military commanders and foreign journalists lies with the claim that Mahdist forces were highly motivated; coercive measures were not necessary. Though often couched in language that grates on modern sensibilities, these accounts brim with admiration for the fighting spirit of "swarming Dervishes" and "awful plucky demons."[95] Major-General H. E. Colvile tipped his cap to the "numbers of the enemy, their bravery, their discipline, and accuracy of fire of those possessing rifles."[96] Perversely, British respect for Mahdist tenacity led to standing orders to kill wounded Ansar: "we shot or bayonetted [sic] all wounded," one Lieutenant Percy Marling admitted, "as it was not safe to leave them as they knifed everyone they could reach."[97]

Colonel J. Colborne, a British officer attached to General Hicks's Soudan Field Force, witnessed the stinging Mahdi defeat at Jebelin (April 1883), where the Ansar traded five hundred soldiers killed for only six enemy soldiers. This brief battle represented the worst defeat suffered by the Mahdiya in the entire war. Yet Colborne's account stressed the highly motivated nature of the Ansar and the absence of any coercive mechanisms for repeatedly driving them forward.

> Onward they came, waving their banners inscribed with the Mahdi's own rendering of the Koran. ...Right up to the cannon's mouth, right up to the rifle muzzle, dauntless they rode, encouraging their followers with the promise of paradise, to break our square. But Nordenfeldts [an organ gun with multiple barrels] and Remingtons are no respecters of creeds or fanatical idiosyncrasies. Sheikh after sheikh went down with

93. *Khartoum Journal* entry on 24 September 1844 in Elton 1961, 75.

94. See entries on 7 and 8 October 1884 in his *Khartoum Journal* in Elton 1961, 106.

95. Spiers 2004, 107; see also Paul 1954, 113; De Cosson 1886; Holt 1970, 60–61.

96. Colvile 1889, 257–60.

97. Quoted in Spiers 2004, 105.

his banner ...and their faithful but misguided followers fell in circles around the chiefs they had blindly followed.[98]

In private correspondence, British officers rated the morale and cohesion of Mahdi units as equal to their own Indian units.[99] By contrast, they issued scathing reports about their mixed Egyptian-Sudanese forces. These units were plagued by poor discipline and even worse morale, forcing officers to rule with near "despotic" levels of coercion. The scene at Cairo's Bulaq dock, where expeditionary forces were first marshaled before transport to the Sudan, underscores the perilous state of the Anglo-Egyptian force at the war's midpoint.

The Egyptian soldiers were placed in vans and cattle-trucks like animals. They quitted the capital without arms, as prisoners, and with all the circumstances of dishonor. ...When subsequently it became necessary to send reinforcements to the Soudan [sic]...Soldiers were again despatched to the front unarmed, beaten, and in chains ...and thereby predisposed to desertion and mutiny.[100]

General Hicks also complained bitterly about his soldiers and their (understandable) penchant for desertion. "All these [soldiers] will be sent up the Soudan in chains—as were the men in the Army I now have! What can one expect from such men? They have not an atom of spirit, pluck, or soldierly feeling. It is 100 to 1 that they bolt."[101] In fact, it would come to light that his own *bashi-bazooks* were selling their weapons to Mahdist forces at $1 per rifle.[102] Egyptian and Sudanese soldiers were often accused of warning Mahdi forces with premature firing to alert them to their presence.[103] British officers sometimes resorted to the use of "crow's feet"—small balls of iron spikes joined together, and tossed in front of formed squares—to deter Mahdist attacks while restricting potential escape routes for fleeing conscripts.[104] And on at least one occasion, at the disastrous battle of El Teb, British officers shot deserting Egyptian commanders and soldiers in an unsuccessful bid to curb their panicked retreat. Egyptian officers even shot their own soldiers to steal their camels in a desperate stampede to escape Mahdist forces.[105]

98. Colborne 1884, 160–62.

99. Colvile 1889, 27.

100. Broadley 1884, 497–98.

101. General Hicks, diary entry, 5 June 1883, Daly 1983, 63.

102. General Hicks, diary entry, 15 September 1883, Daly 1983, 92.

103. Royle 1886, 234.

104. Royle 1886, 237.

105. Royle 1886, 260–66.

3.5.   The Fall of the Mahdiya: The Second Mahdi War, 1896–99

Violence, famine, and forcible displacement became the tools of Khalifa's nation-building campaign in the decade after his unexpected inheriting of the Mahdi's mantle. Entrenching his own Baggara atop the Mahdiya's now steep ethnic hierarchy came at the price of a hobbled military machine that would be ruthlessly undone in the 1896–99 Second Mahdi War, however. Beset by internal rebellion, and wary of his own military and its commanders, the Khalifa had squandered the Mahdi's legacy, saddling himself with a military that proved incapable of defeating Anglo-Egyptian forces or safeguarding the Mahdiya itself.

The Second Mahdi War was sparked by Britain's concern about French and Belgian encroachment into southern Sudan.[106] Led by the cautious Lord Herbert Kitchener, the 25,800-strong Anglo-Egyptian expedition (8,200 of them British soldiers) slowly made its way southward into the Mahdiya. Its advance was facilitated by the impressive construction of the Sudan Military Railroad from Wadi Halfa to Abu Hamed (see figure 3.3). Aided by superior logistics, Kitchener's forces gradually but inexorably penetrated deeper into the Mahdiya, besting the Mahdist army in a series of set-piece battles. The Khalifa's strategy of defense-in-depth collapsed in the face of the restive local populations, his own bitterly divided military, and hammer blows struck at the Battle of Ferket (7 June 1896), Abu Hamed (7 August 1897), Metemmeh (15 October 1897), and Atbara (8 April 1898). Mass desertion from the Mahdist ranks began early and accelerated as heavy casualties were inflicted. Defection, too, emerged, as repressed non-core groups seized the opportunity to switch sides and inflict punishment on the Khalifa's increasingly Baggara-dominated army.

Hemmed in by constraints of his own making, the Khalifa chose to make a last-ditch stand on the outskirts of his capital, Omdurman, on 8 September 1898. The combined Anglo-Egyptian force cut down waves of Mahdist attackers in a brutal spectacle, recording one of the most lopsided victories in the annals of conventional war. Mahdist forces lost an estimated 11,150 killed in action to only 49 British, Egyptian, and Sudanese killed in a few hours on that fateful morning. Subsequent battles at Gederaf (22 December) and Roseires (26 December) against scattered remnants largely ended the Mahdist army as an organized force. The final deathblow, however, was not struck until the Battle of Umm Dibaykarat (November 1899), when a cornered Khalifa, along with his remaining emirs, was gunned down on his prayer mat while

106. Sanderson 1965.

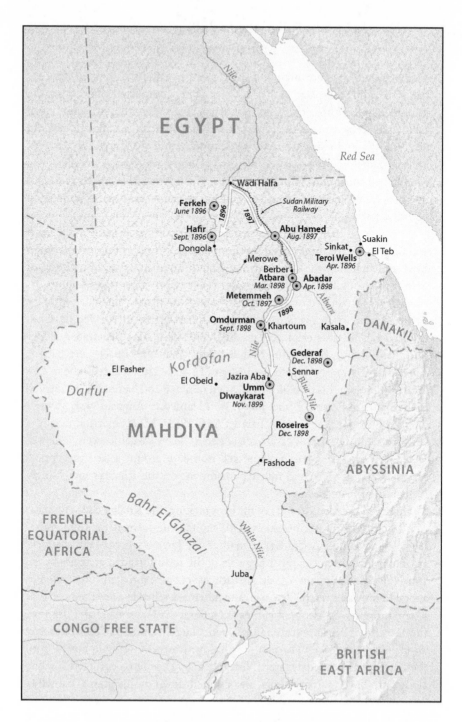

FIGURE 3.3. Mahdiya Sunset: The Second Mahdi War, 1896–99

overseeing the destruction of his remaining forces. The Mahdiya was lost, and the Sudan reverted back to uneasy rule by Anglo-Egyptian condominium.

3.5.1. Redrawing Communal Boundaries Violently

The Khalifa violently recast the Mahdiya's ideational foundations. Favoring the Baggara tribe, and especially his own clan, the Ta'isha, the Khalifa launched a campaign of targeted repression against non-core groups that might challenge this vision. Riverine tribes (*awlad al-balad*), including the Ashraf, the Mahdi's own tribe, and the Ja'alin, were initially singled out since they represented the strongest counterclaim to his authority. Subsequent waves of repression rippled outward to include the Beja tribes, including the Hadendowa, perhaps the best soldiers in his army, and the various black and animist groups of southern Sudan. While paying lip service to the Mahdi's legitimating rhetoric, especially periodic calls for jihad, the Mahdiya's communal boundaries increasingly shrunk, excluding an ever-growing share of the population. By 1891, the Mahdiya had become a garrison state, with non-core groups subject to periodic repression, harsh taxation, and, in some cases, near-genocidal levels of violence. The Mahdiya had become a "tribal dictatorship funded by war."[107]

He first purged Ashraf rivals and their power base among riverine tribes. Muhammad Sharif, a close confidant of the Mahdi with considerable support, was imprisoned. Muhammad Khalid, who commanded the formidable Red Flag Division, was sidelined after making threatening moves toward Omdurman; his forces were absorbed into the Khalifa's own Black Flag and their firearms redistributed away from Ashraf soldiers.[108] Stewing in their political impotence, the Ashraf nurtured their grievance against the Khalifa, continuing to believe his rule was illegitimate since political authority could only be transferred via hereditary succession.[109]

Alone, these efforts to suppress Ashraf rivals might be subsumed under a coup-proofing logic, the usual fare of despots everywhere. Yet the Khalifa went far beyond targeting a handful of rivals. Instead, his nation-building campaign represented a fundamental reordering of the social hierarchy, and physical security, of groups within the Mahdist political community. His heavy-handed imposition of a Ta'isha ethnocracy sparked uprisings in Darfur in 1886–88 that were brutally suppressed. Leaders of these movements were beheaded, their remains mounted on stakes outside Omdurman's walls

107. Green 2007, 227.
108. Searcy 2011, 117.
109. Neufeld 1899, 86.

as a warning.[110] Mass violence was unleashed against selected tribes, including the Juhaina, in early 1887. The Kababish, notable for their economic role as purveyors of camel transports, were also violently singled out when they defected against his rule in 1887, daring to support a brief British incursion in Kordofan.[111] One of the Khalifa's most trusted lieutenants, Osman Digna, was given license to prosecute his own campaigns against potentially suspect populations, including the Amarar, the Ashraf, and his own Hadendowa, with Baggara-infused forces in the Mahdiya's Suakin region.[112] Equatoria in southern Sudan was invaded in summer 1888; the Khalifa not only wanted to drive out the remnants of Khedival rule but also secure another source of slaves for his Jihadiya.[113] The Khalifa also faced popular uprisings from two rival Mahdis, Abu Jummayza and Adam Muhammad, who amassed considerable followings by claiming that they, not the Khalifa (or each other), were the "real" Expected One(s). These movements managed to inflict heavy losses in pitched battles against Mahdist forces in 1888–89 before they, too, were crushed.[114]

Forced population displacement was also a central element of the Khalifa's nation-building campaign. Only days after assuming power, the Khalifa ordered the abandonment of Khartoum in favor of Omdurman. Moving his own tribesmen into favored areas around the new capital, he cracked down on tribes that resisted their forced transfer to the Mahdi's northern reaches, including distant Dongola and Berber. At least one tribe, the Batahin, was massacred for failing to relocate.[115] The Khalifa met initial resistance even from members of his own tribe, who were reluctant to abandon their traditional lands.[116] This strategy was calculated not only to provide economic benefits to favored groups but also to push suspect non-core groups directly into the path of a potential Anglo-Egyptian invasion. These displacements shunted the cost of repelling invaders to non-core groups while preserving Baggara control over Omdurman, the regime's center of gravity, though at the risk of exposing potentially unreliable tribes to outside influence.

Even access to food became a weapon in the Khalifa's hands. A severe famine struck in 1888–89, imposing tremendous hardship throughout much of the Mahdiya. Emaciated refugees jammed Omdurman's crowded streets,

110. Green 2007, 209.

111. Gleichen 1905, 252.

112. Jackson 1926, 114–20.

113. This entire region rose up against the Khalifa during the Second Mahdi War (Collins 1962, 156–72).

114. Clark 1998, 208.

115. Neillands 1996, 155.

116. Zulfo 1980, 29.

desperately seeking relief. Evidence suggests that the Khalifa seized this opportunity to cement his vision by awarding the Baggara preferential access to grain and other foodstuffs, leaving other populations to starve.[117] As late as 1896, E. F. Knight, a special correspondent of the *Times*, remarked upon the mountains of spoiled dates and rotting grain in Mahdist warehouses in Dongola and other non-core regions, deliberately wasted "with the object of keeping the population in an impoverished condition."[118]

By 1889, "an impressive row of once hostile heads grinned on the gallows in Omdurman, or lay discarded in the pit beneath."[119] Theobald's partial tally of heads mounted on public scaffolding outside Omdurman includes leaders of the Kababish, the Rufa'a al-Hoi clan of the Juhaina tribe, several Darfuri chiefs, and all of the Ben Husain tribe's elders.[120] Soldiers drawn from these repressed tribes were among the first to desert or defect during the Second Mahdi War. The early 1890s saw an acceleration of the Khalifa's efforts to stamp out any possible source of opposition, this time among the Shilluk and Nuer populations in southern Sudan. These bloody pacification campaigns would not end until 1894, at the cost of tens of thousands of lives and economic ruin. The constant threat of a recurrence of conflict in these areas, as well as within Darfur, forced the Khalifa to garrison nearly twenty thousand soldiers in isolated posts.[121]

Marginalized political rivals also haunted the Khalifa. Long-simmering anger among the Ashraf boiled over in November 1891, when they, along with other ostracized riverine tribes, revolted. Their coup attempt was quickly snuffed out by the Khalifa's forces before it became threatening, however. The Ashraf's Red Flag was disbanded, leaving their tribe lodged firmly outside the redrawn communal boundaries.[122]

Still, well-informed foreign observers such as F. R. Wingate, the long-serving head of the Egyptian Intelligence Department, believed that the Khalifa had consolidated power by 1892. Wingate, citing eyewitness testimony from a prominent Ja'alin defector, outlined the evolution of the Khalifa's efforts at consolidating his communal vision:

> When the Khalifa first began to rule, he exercised the greatest tyranny over the people, but now that the authority of his own tribes, the Baggara, is undisputed and that internal dissesions [*sic*] have been

117. Theobald 1951, 173.
118. Knight 1897, 306–7.
119. Theobald 1951, 156.
120. Theobald 1951, 146–53.
121. Collins 1962; Mounteney-Jephson 1890.
122. Holt 1970, 141–46, 197–203.

suppressed, he is doing his utmost to establish a more lenient and popular system of government; and his efforts are not altogether unsuccessful. ... The Baggara have become nationalized in their new homes, the other tribes are accepting of the situation, and now there is a more or less general feeling that an advance on part of the [Egyptian] government must be considered as an attempt to interfere with their independence. This feeling is strongest in Omdurman and its vicinity, and weakest among the population immediately in contact with outside influences.[123]

After eight years, the Khalifa had managed to impose his communal vision on the Mahdiya, now a Baggara-dominated ethnocracy predicated on the systematic repression of at least half the population.[124] Talk of political reform was just that, however. The Khalifa did not, and perhaps could not, relax his grip on the reins of political power or the tools of repression. As Wingate himself recognized, "the various conflicting influences at work in Omdurman are apt to give rise to a feeling of insecurity which a period of tranquility would be likely to augment."[125] His memorandum correctly called attention to the fact that the Khalifa had managed to institutionalize a political regime whose allegiance was distributed unevenly across the Mahdiya. It also suggests that it can be difficult to distinguish between tactical acquiescence among targeted groups and genuine acceptance; it is likely that repression had only increased these groups' desire to escape from the Khalifa's grip if an opportunity presented itself. Indeed, Wingate had constructed an elaborate spy network to detect these internal divisions and possibly exploit them if war came.[126]

In truth, the Khalifa had purchased this relative calm at the cost of sowing the seeds of future military disaster. Soldiers from non-core groups, who still represented a large share of the Mahdist army, harbored grievances against the regime, and alienation was widespread among all but the most committed soldiers. Prior repression provided motive for wartime desertion and defection. The contours of the Khalifa's vision also provide clues about which contingents should break, and in what order: we should expect the non-core groups (e.g., the Ashraf, Ja'alin, Beja, Kababish) and coerced Egyptian soldiers (principally serving in the artillery corps) to desert or defect first, followed by southern slave soldiers in the Jihadiya, then the favored Baggara tribes, and finally, the most favored Ta'isha subtribe. The Khalifa entered the Second

123. Intelligence Department report, dated 12 December 1892, quoted in Theobald 1951, 176.
124. Slatin Pasha 1896, 308–12; Searcy 2011, 128.
125. Wingate 1891, 491.
126. Spiers 2007.

Mahdi War faced with the prospect of internal rebellion and unreliable soldiers that handcuffed his military once the threat of Anglo-Egyptian invasion materialized in 1896.

3.5.2. Prewar Practices

The post-1885 army inherited the institutions of its Mahdist predecessor but moved quickly to restructure its composition along lines dictated by the Khalifa's ethnocratic vision. Garrison duties and the suppression of unrest among non-core populations, as well as limited foreign adventures to burnish the Khalifa's jihadist credentials, became the lodestars of the new Mahdist army. The Mahdiya's recruitment patterns shifted to reflect the new collective vision. Non-core groups were still levied, but certain units and functions became off-limits, while the composition of officers and emirs was adjusted to reflect the new Baggara, and especially Ta'isha, dominance. Stark divisions between core and non-core soldiers emerged, permeating larger questions of tactics and operations as well as more mundane affairs. Even pay and rations came to reflect these new realities: non-favored Arab tribes received 3/24ths of an *ardeb* (about 5.6 bushels) of wheat, while the favored Baggara received twice as much.[127]

He moved swiftly to promote Ta'isha and other favored group loyalists into high-ranking positions within the army's Flags, war councils, and Council of Elders. His brother Yaqub was installed as the new executive director of military policy, tasked with running the army's daily affairs. While the Khalifa set the broad strategic parameters, Yaqub issued orders to provincial commands and garrisons; he also was assigned his own Standard (the Black Flag). Though the composition of Flags continued to reflect their local ethnic and tribal identities, their component regiments became "blended" over time as Baggara soldiers were intermixed to ensure unit loyalty.[128] Ta'isha senior officers and their assistants were installed to ensure that command and control remained uninterrupted.[129] Only six years after the Khalifa assumed power, sixteen of seventeen emirs killed during a brief skirmish with Anglo-Egyptian forces at Tokar (1891) were Baggara loyalists sent to command, and monitor, his combined expeditionary force.[130]

127. Warner 1973, 227.

128. For example, the Black Flag recruited principally from western and southern Sudan; the Green Standard, from the White Nile area; and the Red Flag, which was dissolved in 1891, from east-central Jazira.

129. Holt 1970, 247.

130. Paul 1954, 116.

Training, too, was skewed by considerations of group status. The Ta'isha were established as firearm instructors and attached to all Flags; so, too, were Ta'isha "religious instructors." Senior military commanders were appointed as governors of each province; with the lone exception of Osman Digna, all were Ta'isha. Live-fire exercises were forbidden for fear that military training would facilitate insurrection.[131] While ceremonial drills were practiced every Friday at Omdurman, realistic exercises that promoted coordination across (or even within) Flags were rare. Artillery pieces were confined to Omdurman to keep them out of the hands of local commanders. Following the Mahdi's precedent, artillery units remained comprised solely of captured Egyptian soldiers who were fighting under duress.[132] No provision was apparently made for broadening the base of technical skills by either training Mahdist soldiers as artillery crews or acquiring such knowledge from foreign mercenaries.

The need to garrison large numbers of forces to hold down potentially restive populations—and, on occasion, to repress them—also siphoned off a large portion of the Khalifa's available combat power. Even with these garrisons, however, the Mahdiya's vast size meant that large areas, notably Kordofan, were only lightly held. These areas represented a key liability since the opportunity cost for fomenting anti-regime opposition by aggrieved non-core groups was fairly low. "The people of both these provinces [Darfur and Kordofan] were heartily sick of Dervish misrule," noted one Intelligence Department report, "and it was believed that they would welcome with joy a change of masters."[133] Garrisoning a substantial portion of the Mahdist army in remote locations did little to facilitate training; left without adequate supplies, these isolated garrisons spent much of their time raiding local populations for food.

He also created a private guard (the *mulazimin*) that quickly grew in size and importance. Fielded after the 1891 Ashraf revolt, the mulazimin was initially designed to have a vanguard role on the battlefield. Led by Khalifa's son, Shaykh al Din, the unit recruited along a very narrow base: soldiers were drawn from the sons of reliable tribal leaders and from black slaves newly acquired via trade or raids in Fashoda and the western borderlands. Certain tribes, including the Danaqla, along with Egyptians from the former Khedival regime, were excluded. The mulazimin had a dedicated treasury and was granted a disproportionate share of weapons and food supplies. Estimated

---

131. Slatin Pasha 1896; Zulfo 1980, 46fn7. The Khalifa was also concerned about the supply of bullets. The Mahdiya had its own factories but the quality was often poor; shortages were frequent.

132. Zulfo 1980, 39.

133. Gleichen 1905, 256.

to be around nine thousand strong by 1895, these soldiers were tasked with supplementing Baggara cavalry as blocking units, forcing reluctant non-core group soldiers to advance by meting out extrajudicial punishment as a deterrent to indiscipline.[134]

As military inequality increased, and as trust in non-core soldiers and their leaders dropped precipitously, the distortions introduced into the Mahdiya's military by the Khalifa's nation-building campaign intensified. The military, a captive of identity politics, began engaging in self-defeating behavior well before 1896. In perhaps the most glaring case, the Khalifa ordered an invasion of Egypt in 1889 to demonstrate the efficacy of his new ethnocratic vision. Behind the scenes, however, he worked to sabotage that same mission. The invasion force of six thousand soldiers was led by Abd ar Rahman al-Nujumi, one of the Khalifa's best generals who also happened to be an Ashraf, and thus a potential rival claimant to power. Guided by the belief, possibly sincere, that the Egyptians would rise up against their colonial masters, the tiny expeditionary force was deployed without adequate manpower or logistical support. The invaders struggled to execute even basic movements: "it was a medley of tribes and its vast crowd of hangers-on."[135] Desertion began among the repressed non-core soldiers. The Batahin, for example, had witnessed the public hanging or mutilation of sixty-seven of their leaders at Omdurman by the Khalifa in 1888, and now took the opportunity to flee. In the end, the tired and near-famished force was reduced to eating its own pack animals before being nearly totally annihilated by Egyptian forces at the Battle of Tushkah.[136]

Sir Francis Grenfell, the commander-in-chief of the Egyptian Army in 1889, argued that the Khalifa cared little about the war's outcome; instead, it was an opportunity to rid himself of a key rival and his power base. Grenfell played upon this sentiment in a letter written to al-Nujimi on the eve of battle (16 July):

> On my arrival I looked upon your weakness and forsaken condition and I found you were dying of hunger and thirst. I know well your evil state, for the pretender to the *khalifa*, Abdallahi, is disposed to envy you and has found no way to slay you except to send you to us with the Arabs whose ill-will he fears, since he knows for certain that you will quickly be destroyed. So he put his nephew, Yunus, in your place to rid himself of you and your friends.[137]

---

134. Holt 1970, 207.

135. Theobald 1951, 160.

136. For graphic eyewitness account of the failed Egyptian expedition, including the rapid emergence of desertion as supplies and water ran out, see Bedri 1969, 59, 65.

137. Grenfell letter to al-Nujumi, 16 July 1889, reproduced in Holt 1970, 180.

Peter Holt has similarly argued that there is "probably a grain of truth" in claims that the Khalifa was using a foreign battlefield to wage war on domestic opponents: the Khalifa was "able to view the annihilation of an army of *awlad al-balad* [Arab tribes] with more equanimity than if they had been Baggara of the Black Flag."[138] The Khalifa's appointment of Yunus al-Dikaym, a Baggara, as ranking emir for the expedition, and then having him sit safely in Dongola while the invasion force sortied into Egypt, is also telling. Even the most vocal critic of this deliberate sabotage view suggests that the Khalifa's decision to send only five hundred soldiers to reinforce the initial invading force was suspiciously paltry.[139] Viewed from a strictly military perspective, the Egyptian expedition was ruinous: only eight hundred men survived the expedition to return home, while al-Nujumi was killed. In one fell swoop, the Khalifa had destroyed one of his most experienced, if politically suspect, units.

3.5.3. Tactical and Operational Sophistication

Given surging inequality, we should witness a sharp decrease in the tactical and operational sophistication of the Mahdiya's army. This is indeed what happened. The Khalifa-led Mahdiya turned in a far worse performance than its Mahdi-led predecessor despite enjoying several advantages, including a greater number of firearms, considerable combat experience against Anglo-Egyptian and neighboring states, and a decade to prepare for a possible British return.

Tactics, for example, became far simpler, even crude, under the Khalifa's watch. Most battles now consisted of simplistic Mahdi frontal assaults against well-prepared Anglo-Egyptian positions. Mahdist commanders became reluctant to use dead ground and the basic principles of cover and concealment to reduce their exposure to enemy fire. Instead, they played right into the hands of Anglo-Egyptian technological superiority, driving casualties to a level not seen during the first war. Haunted by the twin threat of desertion and defection, military leadership, itself divided by ethnically driven squabbles, embraced simplified tactics and procedures to ease command and control issues across and within the Flags. Tight formations became standard; cramming soldiers together made them easier to monitor and suppressed soldier initiative that, if unleashed, might be turned toward escaping battle rather than winning it.

138. Holt 1970, 182. Holt cites two additional factors—uncertainty about the nature of Egyptian support for liberation, and weak Mahdist logistics—as dooming the expedition.
    139. Theobald 1951, 160.

Coordination across the Flags and the different combat arms proved more problematic than during the first war as well. Some of these issues stemmed from clashing personalities among emirs, a factor not unique to the Mahdiya. Yet cavalry and shock-action units struggled to coordinate their offensives, often working at cross-purposes or failing to support one another once the battle began. Despite firsthand experience with deadly Anglo-Egyptian artillery fire, including its key suppressive role, the Mahdist artillery arm was rarely integrated into battle plans.[140] Poor coordination stemmed from the Khalifa's ban of live-fire exercises and joint training across different combat branches. The Khalifa's fears were understandable: he was wary of providing combat training and firearms to soldiers drawn from suspect non-core groups. But his solution of repurposing Baggara cavalry and the Jihadiya as monitoring and sanctioning units, rather than screening and shock-action vanguard units, meant redistributing most of his combat power to the rear.

Mahdist tactics were noticeably more rigid. Risk-taking, whether in the form of setting ambushes or surprise attacks, was largely discouraged. Mahdist emirs failed to strike when debilitating waves of cholera and dysentery ripped through Anglo-Egyptian forces on several occasions, letting slip a key opportunity to pounce on a weakened foe. The few tactical traps successfully sprung actually stem more from Anglo-Egyptian mistakes— the foolhardy cavalry charge by the 21st Lancers at Omdurman is a classic example—rather than careful Mahdist planning. Tellingly, while Mahdist forces retreated in good order when necessary during the First War, the same forces preferred to remain anchored to poor defensive positions in the Second War. Retreat posed a twofold challenge: abandon positions, and risk not only demoralizing core group soldiers but also creating opportunities for non-core soldiers to slip away in the chaos and confusion of the retreat.

Especially noticeable was the Mahdiya's failure to innovate and learn tactically. Fear of arming the soldiers, or of having too much military firepower concentrated in a single Flag, hobbled the uptake of new weapons systems such as more modern machine guns and kept the military short of fielding entirely firearm-equipped forces despite ravaging the economy to pay for its war machine. Perhaps even more damning was the army's clear inability to update its force employment to compensate for Anglo-Egyptian strengths. For example, the Khalifa's forces had experienced a near carbon copy of Omdurman fighting Abyssinian forces at Debra Sin (near Gondar) as early as 1887. During that battle, Mahdist forces crushed Abyssinian formations

---

140. Mahdist artillery had also fallen into disrepair since the 1881–85 war. Intriguingly, there is no existing record of the Khalifa seeking to acquire foreign weapons despite the clear willingness of European powers, notably France, to sell such weapons.

that rushed in waves across an open plain into Mahdist machine guns and fortified positions. Yet no serious reforms were made to Mahdist tactics; the Khalifa doubled down on massed charges to overwhelm enemy positions, a proposition his military had demonstrated to be costly and ineffective a decade ago.

At the operational level, Mahdist planning centered around a simple defense-in-depth series of holding actions designed to exhaust Anglo-Egyptian forces before a culminating battle at Omdurman. Though sensible, the plan crumbled under the weight of prior decisions: fortifications were located among non-core groups as a result of the Khalifa's forced resettlement, raising questions about the loyalty of the locals and creating logistical difficulties. After Abu Hamed's fall in August 1897, first Berber, then Adamara, and then the entire Berber-Suakin road fell open, as Baggara forces refused to advance into or hold "alien" regions of the Mahdiya. Too far from "home," and now faced with increased defection from his ranks, the Khalifa's repression of non-core riverine tribes now returned to haunt him. The Khalifa continually allowed the slow Anglo-Egyptian combined force to dictate the location and timing of attacks, ceding the initiative to the enemy. As a result, Mahdist forces typically fought on unfavorable ground, allowing the formidable but still vulnerable Anglo-Egyptian army to inflict heavier losses than otherwise might have been the case.

These tactical and operational deficiencies culminated at Omdurman, though the Khalifa's fate was sealed well before the September 1898 battle. He chose to attack an entrenched foe across an open plain in isolated assaults that offered little in the way of cover, a perfect killing ground made even more lethal by his choice of a daytime attack. Had he remained within Omdurman's walls, protected by its fortifications, it may have proven extremely costly to dislodge him; a cautious Kitchener would have been placed in difficulty. This is especially the case if the Khalifa had chosen to occupy Jebel Sorghum, the hill overlooking the plain, rather than leave it undefended. Instead, he chose the worst possible location to mount a last stand, especially since he directed the attack at British forces, not Egyptian and Sudanese ones, and so went after the strongest position.[141]

In addition, he failed to play his best card, a night attack. Kitchener himself thought that the Khalifa's forces would have breached his zariba if he had attacked at night.[142] A nighttime assault would have leveled the playing field by removing the Anglo-Egyptian force's key advantage—the greater range

141. This may represent "mirroring," where the Khalifa is looking at his own army and thinking that if he can destroy the British forces, the remaining soldiers will break.

142. Pugh 2011, 65; Kitchener 1898a, 5726; Steevens 1899, 289.

of their rifles and artillery pieces—reducing it down to about four hundred yards. Concern about the "hideous danger"[143] was rife among the British command: "When the sun rose on 2/9/98," wrote General Sir Archibald Hunter, "I was never so glad in all my days."[144] But a night attack was out of the question; a fear of the loss of command and control, both in terms of coordinating and monitoring forces, outweighed any tactical gains from a surprise attack.[145]

We might conclude that the Khalifa and his army had no chance to defeat Kitchener's combined force at Omdurman. Contemporaries thought otherwise. Had he moved his armies outward to his entrenched forts at Abu Hamed, Berber, and Metemmeh in strength, close enough to reinforce each other, and then conducted an active defense to harass, raid, and interdict enemy, he might have leveled the odds, forcing the Anglo-Egyptian force to disperse to protect vulnerable rail and telegraph lines. This isn't hindsight: his best advisor, Osman Digna, who understood both the capabilities of the Anglo-Egyptian forces and their logistical needs, counseled exactly this strategy.[146] Even the Khalifa's harshest contemporary critics argued that the Mahdiya could have won, or at least performed at a much higher level, than its actual battlefield conduct.[147]

Digna was consistently overruled by the Khalifa, however. The result was predictable: several of the Mahdiya's most capable commanders, including Digna himself, applied initiative to avoiding battles or abandoning them quickly rather than defeating their foes. Digna even advised his own soldiers to desert on the eve of the Battle of Atbara after his advice was dismissed.[148] In the end, the Khalifa squandered many of his advantages; the trade-offs and constraints imposed by his collective vision had trapped his military in a set of predictable and rigid tactics and operations with deadly consequences.

3.5.4. Casualties

Poor tactical and operational practices contributed to a disastrous loss-exchange ratio for Mahdist forces. The price of privileging political expediency over military necessity was staggering battlefield casualties as the hamstrung Mahdist army was dismantled by the powerful Anglo-Egyptian expeditionary force.

143. Theobald 1951, 226.
144. Quoted in Pugh 2011, 65.
145. Neillands 1996, 204.
146. Jackson 1926, 150.
147. Royle 1886, 477; Theobald 1951, 212–22; Clark 1977, 71.
148. Theobald 1951, 151; Royle 1886, 477.

Most accounts of the Khalifa's lackluster battlefield performance fixate on the disastrous battle at Omdurman (2 September 1898). The focus is understandable: the Mahdiya's loss-exchange ratio at that battle was an incredible 227 dead Mahdi soldiers for every British, Egyptian, or Sudanese soldier killed. "The dervish army," noted one eyewitness, "was killed out as hardly an army has been killed out in the history of war."[149]

The rush to discuss Omdurman essentially telescopes history, however. Prior battles and events are either ignored or sandwiched into a narrative where the defeat of the technologically inferior Mahdiya is preordained. Yet these battles offer important clues about the overall performance of the Mahdiya's military. As illustrated in panel (b) in figure 3.2, the Mahdiya never reached parity with Anglo-Egyptian forces in any of the thirteen major battles recorded during the 1896–99 war. On average, the Mahdiya lost an estimated 88 soldiers killed for each soldier it managed to kill among the Anglo-Egyptian forces. Moreover, unlike the Mahdi's Mahdiya, the Khalifa's state never once reached parity with Anglo-Egyptian forces, let alone recorded a favorable balance of casualties. Unsurprisingly, the difference in loss-exchange ratios between Mahdi and Khalifa eras is highly statistically significant.[150]

In fact, the Khalifa's casualties were several orders of magnitude higher than the Mahdi's despite possessing numerical superiority in every engagement. The Mahdiya's worst performance actually came not at Omdurman but at the earlier Battle of Metemmeh (15 October 1897), where British artillery found the Khalifa's forces holed up in fortifications astride the route to Atbara, a strategic defensive position. Rather than attempt to breach Atbara's walls, the British simply bombarded Mahdist forces, inflicting at least 250 KIA (and 750 WIA); Kitchener's force only lost one soldier.[151]

Even one of its best performances, during another engagement at Atbara (8 April 1898), still resulted in a poor loss-exchange ratio, with the Mahdiya losing about 38 soldiers for each enemy killed. The conditions were unusually favorable for Mahdist forces. Anglo-Egyptian forces, some 12,000-men strong, attacked a 15,000-strong Mahdi force that had prior notice of the attack, was ensconced behind multiple trenches, and had artillery support. Nearly all British soldiers, including a young Captain Douglas Haig (later field marshal of the British Expeditionary Force on the Western Front in 1915–18), were experiencing combat for the first time. After an eighty-minute artillery bombardment from twenty-four British guns, they were forced to

149. Steevens 1899, 285.
150. Significant at $p = .006$, $t = 3.29$, 12.85df.
151. Stamford, Alford and Sword 1898, 180.

charge across open terrain in an effort to breach the Mahdist zariba protective enclosure. The Mahdist army exercised fire discipline, waiting until attacking forces were within three hundred yards before opening up fire. Yet while some forces stood firm as combat degenerated into hand-to-hand combat, the Mahdi forces ultimately crumbled, with the Baggara cavalry (commanded by wily Osman Digna) fleeing, precipitating a general rout. At a cost of 79 KIA (and 479 wounded), the Anglo-Egyptian force killed at least two thousand Ansar despite their favorable position. Mahdist military authorities also suffered a grievous blow, losing both a high-ranking emir, Mahmud Ahmed, and the last strong defensive position before Omdurman.[152]

3.5.5. Soldier Compliance

The Mahdiya suffered from near-crippling levels of mass desertion and, to a lesser extent, mass defection during the Second Mahdi War. Though estimates should be treated with caution, some 35–45 percent of the Mahdi's total fielded forces ultimately deserted, including half of the Khalifa's remaining forces at Omdurman in 1898.[153] Though perhaps surprised by the magnitude of desertion, Mahdist commanders were certainly aware of the possibility that soldier indiscipline might become a problem. As early as the disastrous Abyssinian campaign of 1889, the Khalifa ordered his elite Jihadiya to be branded with the letter "J" on their left hand to deter desertion.[154]

It is tempting to ascribe the motives for mass desertion to the staggering, and lopsided, casualties that the Anglo-Egyptian expedition force was imposing on Mahdist forces. But most of the recorded instances of mass desertion occurred *before* battles were fought, not after. Battles at Metemmeh, Atbara, and Omdurman all proceeded against a backdrop of mass desertion that started well before combat began. In the case of Atbara (1898), an estimated three thousand soldiers deserted two days before the battle, representing about 15 percent of the eighteen thousand deployed Ansar. This was a critical loss; without these soldiers, the Ansar were forced to engage a roughly equivalent Anglo-Egyptian force without their reserves.[155] Mass desertion even occurred after the Mahdist army's best performances, as at Teroi Wells (15 April 1896). The trickle of deserters became a flood by the war's third battle at Hafir (19 September 1896). In some cases, Ansar "deserted so quickly they

152. Barthorp 2002, 143–51.

153. Defection, while clearly present, likely did not exceed the 10 percent threshold, and so "mass" defection is coded as absent in Project Mars.

154. Zulfo 1980, 34.

155. Pugh 2011, 60.

left their babies behind,"[156] an allusion to the extensive presence of soldiers' families who followed them from camp to camp.

Mass desertion also followed a predictable sequence. Regiments staffed by repressed non-core ethnic and tribal groups were the first to melt away. The remains of beheaded tribal elders at Omdurman, or the deliberate starvation of their followers, were a bellwether of future wartime discipline that was now being realized, battle by battle. As casualties piled up, intra-Baggara squabbles spilled over, as commanders sought to secure access to dwindling stocks of rifles and artillery to bolster their forces. Cracks within the core group appeared; several Baggara tribes, notionally within the defined core group but still left outside the narrow Ta'isha inner circle, began drifting away or engaging in foot-dragging to avoid fighting. The combination of diminished manpower owing to the exodus of non-core groups and worsening battlefield fortunes simply magnified these intra-Baggara tensions. By Omdurman, the "core" had shrunk to Ta'isha and a select few other tribes; mass desertion, meanwhile, had jumped the firebreak between non-core and core groupings, infecting most units that fought in the Second Mahdi War.[157]

Even when core Baggara regiments resisted desertion, they were beset by chronic malingering. At Omdurman, key reserve formations deliberately arrived late to the battlefield, appearing only after the battle had commenced and too late to affect its outcome. Favored groups, especially the Baggara cavalry, were notorious for breaking from battle, or shirking garrison duties, to pursue spoils among neighboring populations. A sense of entitlement stemming from their privileged position atop the Mahdiya's hierarchy fueled the Baggara's pillaging, leading to missed battlefield opportunities and needlessly diverted resources. Even in life-and-death moments, as at Omdurman, Baggara cavalry still found time to wander after the British camel corps and baggage train in a futile raiding attempt while the Ansar were being mowed down in the thousands.[158]

Non-core soldiers were also much more likely to defect than their core group counterparts. The Khalifa's decision to unleash Baggara regiments against Metemmeh, the Ja'alin tribe's capital, led the entire tribe to defect to Anglo-Egyptian forces (see below). Enough Ansar—estimates range from four thousand to six thousand soldiers—changed sides that Lord Kitchener was able to form his own "Friendlies" formation. These Ja'alin defectors

---

156. Green 2007, 249.

157. In another sign of the breakdown of morale, Mahdist Ansar, including Baggara soldiers, had started to surrender and be taken prisoner by mid-1897, a rare occurrence in the First Mahdi War (Stamford, Alford and Sword 1898, 137–38).

158. Zulfo 1980, 140, 152, 229.

performed reconnaissance and provided valuable intelligence to British officers. They actively fought on the front lines in several battles, including at Shendi, Atbara, and Omdurman. These Friendlies were also implicated in the killing of wounded Baggara soldiers as revenge for their prewar repression and marginalized status. Similarly, the entire Kababish tribe defected. Though often overlooked in the existing historiography, their defection crippled the Mahdiya's logistics: the Kababish represented the majority of cameleers for the Mahdiya's long-distance caravans that fed its deployed soldiers.[159]

The presence of mass desertion and defection raises a puzzle, however. How do we square this view of an undisciplined and slowly unwinding Mahdist army with contemporary accounts of Ansar bravery, even fanaticism, and massed charges? Even at Omdurman, the Khalifa could motivate soldiers to fight and die in large numbers. "One could not but be moved at the heroic bravery displayed by the enemy," wrote one *Reuters* correspondent, as "time after time dispersed and broken masses were re-formed and hurdled against the line until they melted into units, and then ceased to exist."[160]

These views can be reconciled by appealing to selection effects. As non-core soldiers fled, the least committed soldiers were winnowed from the ranks, leaving behind only the most committed, or most luckless, soldiers. The Khalifa managed to continue to field large armies, for example, by relying on threats and coercion to deter further desertion and to root soldiers in place. There was also a pervasive belief that the Baggara, who had come to represent a disproportionate share of the Mahdist army, had burned its bridges with the rest of society. The agent of the Khalifa's violent nation-building campaigns, the Baggara, and especially the Ta'isha, had no exit options. After "half a generation of barbarities," G. W. Steevens wrote, "they know there is no asylum left for them in all Africa: they will die resolutely."[161] Yet commitment was variable even within these die-hard core groups; Baggara soldiers admitted that they feigned injuries to escape the killing fields at Omdurman rather than continue futile assaults.[162] Osman Digna's forces also had an "uncanny flair for judging the right moment at which to quit a stricken field."[163]

Lord Kitchener and his Intelligence Department actively worked to exploit these schisms. Desertion was viewed as a symptom of the weak bonds

---

159. Zulfo 1980, 47fn11.

160. Lionel James, "Dispatches from Omdurman," 2 September 1898, reprinted in Harrington and Sharf 1998, 100–106. Quote on p. 102.

161. Steevens 1899, 247.

162. Bedri 1969, 237.

163. Paul 1954, 107.

between (Baggara) emirs and officers and (non-core) rank and file; solidarity could not form in "mixed detachments" and "composite battalions" since non-core soldiers clearly hated their "alien" officers.[164] F. R. Wingate deliberately played upon these differences by offering a Jihadiya-specific reward of $1, about the equivalent of ten months' pay at prevailing Mahdi rates.[165] Lord Kitchener also fanned the flames of inter-group animosities by playing upon the widespread belief that the Khalifa had constructed a Ta'isha ethnocracy. He routinely sent missives to Mahdist emirs before each battle, pledging his assistance in securing revenge against the Khalifa in exchange for switching sides.

On the eve of the Battle at Ferket (7 June 1896), Kitchener sent a letter to opposing commander 'Uthman Azraq:

> It ought to be clear to you now that this "Call" is not of the Mahdiya at all but is a bloody revolution that has engulfed a tyrant monarch who has now taken command, 'Abd Allahi *the Ta'isha* [emphasis added]. This man has banned every *emir* not of his tribe and has appointed the kinsmen who now oppress you. [We are here] to destroy the foundations of the Ta'isha state and to establish a lawful government based on justice and righteousness.[166]

British intelligence was delighted to receive Mahdist defectors. After the Ja'alin rebellion at Metemmeh, the Intelligence Department noted "a singular lack of cohesion and unanimity had sprung up amongst the Dervish leaders—news of which reached the Sirdar [Kitchener] in due course, to the latter's very considerable satisfaction."[167] A "steady stream" of defectors and otherwise disaffected individuals from repressed groups provided the department with a wealth of information about the tribal composition of the Mahdiya's command structures, helping to fine-tune appeals to possibly wavering emirs.[168] Contemporary accounts suggest that defectors also sketched accurate pictures of Mahdist defenses and force displacements; Anglo-Egyptian forces entered battle with far better intelligence than their Mahdist counterparts.[169] This flow of defectors and information offers a marked contrast from the First

---

164. Stamford, Alford and Sword 1898, 134.

165. Keown-Boyd 1986, 166.

166. Proclamation by the Sirdar, 6 June 1896. Quoted in Zulfo 1980, 58. To twist the knife of ethnosectarian division deeper, he also listed the names of all the non-core emirs the Khalifa had executed or imprisoned.

167. Stamford, Alford and Sword 1898, 174.

168. Neillands 1996, 191.

169. Spiers 2007, 665.

Mahdi War, where General Gordon sat anxiously in Khartoum for a flood of disgruntled Ansar that never materialized.

Despite these efforts, the British failed to capitalize fully on the opportunities presented by intra-Mahdiya schisms. Democracies are often thought better able to induce defection than autocracies because their promises of safe passage and lenient treatment are more credible.[170] Regime type cannot explain why Mahdist soldiers deserted only during the Second Mahdi War, however. Similarly, Anglo-Egyptian forces also committed brutalities against Mahdi soldiers and camp followers during the 1881–85 campaign. General Graham's forces burned villages as collective punishment, killed pregnant women, and ordered wounded soldiers and prisoners to be executed during its 1885 campaign in Suakin.[171]

In this case, Anglo-Egyptian wartime conduct probably gave at least some would-be defectors pause, though primary evidence from Mahdist sources is lacking. Kitchener's steady advance on Omdurman was marked by the first wartime use of "dum-dum" bullets with their tips filed flat to maximize their damage once they hit the enemy.[172] Populated centers were routinely shelled indiscriminately by Anglo-Egyptian artillery, killing scores of women and children, particularly since the Mahdi army marched into battle with thousands of camp followers. Prisoners, including high-ranking emirs, were paraded through conquered towns like Berber.[173] British and Egyptian soldiers alike hunted for souvenirs and trophies among the war dead. No provision was made for the care of wounded on the battlefield. Indeed, wounded Ansar were often killed, including those "waving pond fronds" in a futile attempt to surrender.[174] Even the Mahdi's tomb in Omdurman was shelled to break Mahdi morale.[175] His grave was desecrated by victorious British soldiers and his remains thrown into the Nile save for his skull, which was on its way back to London as a war trophy before the Queen's intervention forced Kitchener to have it reburied unceremoniously in an unmarked grave.[176]

In particular, Kitchener's treatment of wounded Ansar after Omdurman was a major scandal after it was publicly criticized by Bennett and Churchill.[177]

---

170. Wallace 2012; Reiter and Stam 2002.

171. Spiers 2004, 123, 140, 151.

172. Green 2007, 253.

173. Neillands 1996, 196.

174. Green 2007, 254; Spiers 1998, 72–73.

175. Zulfo 1980, 146.

176. Nicoll 2004, 8.

177. Bennett 1899b and Churchill 1899. We'll meet Ernest Bennett again: he was a correspondent for the *Manchester Guardian* while covering the Italo-Turkish War from the Turkish side (see chapter 5).

In fact, a Parliamentary inquiry was launched to determine if the conduct of Kitchener's forces had violated Article VI of the Geneva Convention (1864), which called for the provision of material assistance to wounded or sick soldiers regardless of their nation. Kitchener was found not to have violated this article; he was deemed to have insufficient resources to provide aid and could not be reasonably expected to control all of his camp followers, including the Ja'alin, who stalked wounded Baggara amid the shambles of Omdurman's battlefield.[178]

3.5.6. Coercion

As the threat of soldier indiscipline became reality, Mahdist commanders increasingly embraced a variety of coercive measures to maintain order within their ranks. Baggara cavalry, as members of the loyal core group, were redeployed as blocking detachments to drive reluctant non-core soldiers forward. Imprisonment and even execution became routine. Mahdist forces even opened a "second front" against non-core populations even as they struggled to beat back Anglo-Egyptian advances. Coercion arose as a response to breakdowns of order and discipline, but in turn fed the disintegrative processes tearing at unit cohesion by pitting core and non-core soldiers, and their related populations, against one another.

There are numerous eyewitnesses who testify to the Mahdiya's use of threats and violence against its own soldiers during the Second Mahdi War. As early as the war's second engagement, at Ferket on 7 June 1896, Mahdist emirs had decided on employing the Baggara cavalry as an improvised blocking detachment behind regiments comprised of non-core Ja'alin and Jehadia tribes. One contemporary account of the battle recounts how "at least 75 percent of those at Ferket belonged to the tyrannical Baggara tribe, the others being Ja'alin and Jehadia, who would have willingly deserted to us, but [who] were forced to fight by their masters, the Baggara, in front of whom they were placed during battle."[179] Shifting the Baggara to a rear overwatch position was costly, however, as it degraded the Mahdiya's ability to screen its soldiers movements properly. Reconnaissance capabilities withered, too; a common complaint among Mahdist emirs was their lack of information about Anglo-Egyptian movements, even at Omdurman. The result was an increase in casualties as Mahdist forces were left vulnerable to surprises and to well-prepared Anglo-Egyptian formations untroubled by Baggara cavalry.

---

178. HC Deb, 17 February 1899, vol. 66, cols. 1279–81, House of Commons Debate 1899.
179. Stamford, Alford and Sword 1898, 91.

Observers were quick to point to the differences in soldier motivation across the Mahdi's and Khalifa's armies. W. T. Maud, a leading artist-correspondent for the London-based *Daily Graphic*, wrote in June 1898:

> There is now no Mahdi beside him [the Khalifa] to raise hell in the hearts of his subjects, and send them rushing blindly into battle. Now they must be driven like sheep to the slaughter by his own Baggara bodyguard.[180]

The gradual Anglo-Egyptian advance also disrupted Mahdist logistics, a situation made worse by the Khalifa's refusal to send badly needed supplies, especially food, to the northern settlements guarding the approach to Omdurman. Blessed with mobility, these Baggara cavalry began raiding nearby settlements for food and supplies, treating local non-core populations as conquered enemies rather than fellow citizens. These raiding parties, sometimes lasting for days, weakened the deterrent effect of the blocking detachments and led more and more non-core soldiers to chance desertion or defection. Faced with unreliable blocking detachments, Mahdist emirs lost operational flexibility. At the Battle of Atbara (8 April 1898), for example, Emir Mahmud Ahmed's forces refused to advance outside their fortified camp to engage Anglo-Egyptian forces encamped nearby. Lord Kitchener ordered a brief artillery barrage, followed by a frontal assault that inflicted heavy losses on Mahdist forces. Ahmad recognized the dangers he was facing—an exposed position, unrest within his ranks, and too few Baggara cavalry—but felt retreat was not an option. "To retire would have had such a demoralizing effect upon his forces," one participant wrote, "that he would have lost all control over them."[181]

There is also evidence that Mahdist commanders devised exceptionally cruel measures for ensuring that their non-core soldiers fought. British soldiers at Atbara discovered dead Mahdist soldiers who had been chained to logs in their trenches to prevent them from fleeing or surrendering. "Many unfortunate blacks [non-core soldiers] were found chained by both their hands and legs, in the trenches," an eyewitness recounted, "with a gun in their hands and their faces to the foes—some with forked sticks behind their backs."[182]

Faced with weakening blocking detachments and clear incentives for non-core soldiers to desert, defect, or otherwise malinger, Mahdist commanders

180. William Maud, Letter, "The 1898 Campaign in the Soudan," 7 June 1898, reprinted in Harrington and Sharf 1998, 15–19, quote on p. 17.

181. Stamford, Alford and Sword 1898, 208.

182. Warner 1973, 209.

turned to executions to deter further indiscipline. By April 1898, sentences were inflicted "daily," in part because defectors were supplying Kitchener with valuable information.[183] As a warning to others, executed deserters had their heads mounted on sharpened mimosa tree branches.[184] Coercion was, however, asymmetric in its focus: the risks of execution, or of being chained in firing positions, fell most heavily on soldiers drawn from the Mahdiya's non-core populations. With exposure to risk now unevenly distributed across ethnic groups, any remaining notions of a shared fate were punctured, contributing to a further erosion of morale and a rising desperation to escape the war through collective flight. As military authorities clamped down harder, seeking refuge in desertion or defection became an attractive option; better to take one's chances at flight than to remain and fight (and die) trapped between a repressive Khalifa and a lethal Anglo-Egyptian force.

By contrast, Kitchener's combined Anglo-Egyptian expedition distributed risks across its units evenly, with little regard for ethnicity. "Of course, we shall probably leave a good few behind us [i.e., killed in action], but that can't be helped, and everyone stands the same chance of getting through all right,"[185] wrote one soldier in a letter home. Kitchener's dispatches back to London emphasized the "cordiality and good feeling" between Egyptian and UK soldiers "who have fought shoulder to shoulder."[186] In particular, he singled out the example of Egyptian soldiers carrying wounded British comrades nearly sixty kilometers to the Nile after the battle at Atbara, calling it "a splendid service, which will tend to strengthen the good feeling existing between the two forces, which will be a great advantage in the future conduct of the campaign." We need not accept these statements completely at face value to recognize that the Anglo-Egyptian force was far more cohesive—desertion and defection were nearly entirely absent—than either its predecessor or the Mahdiya itself.

Coercion was not only directed toward the Mahdiya's own soldiers; the Khalifa further twisted his military machine inward as he unleashed a wartime campaign of repression against non-core populations. In perhaps the most glaring example, the Khalifa ordered the evacuation of Metemmeh (June–July 1897), a key fortified settlement that blocked the Anglo-Egyptian advance on Omdurman. Metemmeh was not only a cornerstone of Mahdist defenses, however. It was the Ja'alin tribal capital and, as such, was garrisoned by a Ja'alin detachment. The Ja'alin was politically suspect, however, and so the Khalifa ordered the garrison's replacement with Baggara soldiers and the city's

183. Stamford, Alford and Sword 1898, 208–10.
184. Spiers 1998, 60.
185. Spiers 2004, 150 .
186. *London Gazette*, 24 May 1898, Kitchener 1898*b*, 3233.

evacuation.[187] Abdullah Sa'd, the Ja'alin chief, refused and turned to Kitchener, asking for arms and reinforcements before the Baggara arrived. Though Kitchener did send weapons, they did not arrive in time before the Khalifa's order to cleanse the city. The Ja'alin unit, along with most of the civilian population, was destroyed. At least two thousand Ja'alin soldiers, and untold civilians, were killed.[188]

Metemmeh "sealed in blood" the hatred between the non-core riverine tribes and the Ta'isha monarchy that had been fermenting since the Khalifa's accession.[189] From a military standpoint, the suppression of the Ja'alin was an unmitigated disaster. It not only signaled that non-core soldiers and their families were legitimate targets for state repression but also diverted significant resources away from the task of defeating, or at least slowing, the Anglo-Egyptian force. The Baggara units charged with repressing Metemmeh descended into a frenzy of looting and indiscipline that the Khalifa could not curb. They refused his orders to remove captured booty to Omdurman, breaking with the tradition of communal spoil-sharing. Rather than moving to engage approaching enemy forces, they sat at Metemmeh, abandoning all defensive preparations in favor of sallying forth to raid nearby towns.

The reasons for the Baggara's refusals to advance northward are especially illuminating: they feared being entrapped among a population that was tacitly, and in some cases openly, clamoring for liberation. A legacy of traditional settlement patterns as well as the Khalifa's forced repopulation of problematic non-core groups, the northern reaches of the Mahdiya were seen as "not theirs" by these Baggara regiments. Mahmud, the ranking emir commanding these units, admitted that his army "did not want to go north" because of the "alien" nature of its populations.[190] The Khalifa, too, was wary: he "did not feel confident about the loyalty of the people north of Omdurman." In effect, the Khalifa's narrow ethnocratic vision of the Mahdiya had defined large swatches of its northern reaches as "out of area" for a Baggara-dominated force. The prospect of fighting on alien soil, as well as the difficulty of provisioning forces given the latent hostility of resident non-core groups, led the Khalifa to abandon the region, removing a cornerstone of his defensive scheme.[191]

187. The Khalifa's assessment was mostly accurate. The Ja'alin, as prior victims of the Khalifa's repression, traded with Egyptians despite an official ban and were an important source of information for Wingate's Intelligence Department (Holt 1970, 214).

188. Zulfo 1980, 71.

189. Holt 1970, 232–34.

190. Zulfo 1980, 73.

191. Zulfo 1980, 79.

To make matters worse, the Khalifa's efforts to consolidate the Mahdiya's rule among non-core populations through "fire and sword" in Darfur, Kordofan, and especially southern Sudan led to opportunistic uprisings during the Second Mahdi War. Faced with multiple challenges, the Khalifa resorted to garrisoning nearly twenty thousand soldiers in these areas. In practice, these isolated garrisons were forced into a policy of chronic raiding just to obtain supplies, let alone repress these movements. As the final denouement at Omdurman loomed, the Khalifa, desperate to replenish the dwindling ranks of his soldiers, was nonetheless unable to recall these forces for fear of losing entire regions.[192] While additional men may not have tipped the scales at Omdurman, it is clear that these uprisings depleted Mahdist ranks and sidelined some of the Khalifa's most reliable soldiers.[193]

3.6. Alternative Explanation: The Military Superiority Thesis

While the matched research design eliminates numerous alternative explanations from contention, at least one plausible account remains: the Mahdiya was simply outclassed by the quality of Anglo-Egyptian military technology and tactics.[194] Indeed, Omdurman has become something of a cause célèbre for advocates of the military superiority thesis, which holds that small numbers of European soldiers were able to defeat much larger non-European powers in Africa and elsewhere by virtue of a series of revolutions in technological affairs. Local powers were rendered vulnerable by superior European industrial production that translated into more lethal firearms and artillery as well as more sophisticated types of force employment that local powers had not encountered or could not stand against.[195] As Geoffrey Parker has argued, the "sustained preoccupation of European states fighting each other by land and sea paid handsome dividends"[196] once their lethal tactics and weaponry crashed against unprepared and overmatched local powers.

Though designed to paint the historical landscape with broad brushstrokes, the military superiority thesis is, under close inspection, a series of

192. Collins 1962.

193. Zulfo 1980, 110–14. A minor historiographical debate has raged over the number of Mahdist soldiers present at Omdurman. Kitchener's official dispatch provides an initial estimate of "35,000" but suggests that actual strength was probably closer to "40,000 to 50,000" soldiers. *London Gazette*, 30 September 1898. Kitchener 1898a.

194. Beckley 2010, 54; Boot 2007, 162–65.

195. Thompson 1999; Parker 1996; Headrick 2012; Roland 2016; for a critique, see MacDonald 2014, 23–28.

196. Parker 1996, 154.

interwoven claims, not all of which apply to the Mahdiya. Take, for example, the suggestion that Mahdist forces were unfamiliar with British tactics and technology. The Mahdist military had firsthand experience attacking the British "square" from the First Mahdi War; British tactics overall evolved slowly, if at all, between the two wars. Moreover, the Ansar had recent experience with the devastating, if still unreliable, Maxim machine gun as early as 1889, having encountered it at the Battle of Toski (3 August 1899). Nearly three thousand Ansar—the remnants of a Mahdi invasion force that was slowly dying under the blazing Egyptian sun—were mowed down, along with their general Al-Nujimi, "as if on a parade ground," by the Nile Frontier Force's Maxim guns.[197] And the Mahdist military also had its own Maxim machine guns and Mitrailleuses, suggesting a greater familiarity with these weapons than commonly realized.

The contention that British weapons were qualitatively superior to the Mahdiya's arsenal in the Second Mahdi War finds surer ground. The new Lee-Metford .303 repeating rifle had been distributed to the Anglo-Egyptian force, marking its first combat use. The rifle had an effective range of nearly 730 meters (about 800 yards) and was capable of 20–30 aimed shots per minute. By contrast, the Mahdiya's standard firearm, the Martini-Henry .450 single-shot rifle, was good only out to 370 meters (405 yards). When combined with superior Krupp artillery and murderous covering fire from shallow-draught riverine gunboats, British forces were able to expend over 200,000 small-arms rounds, along with 1,000 artillery shells, in the first hour at Omdurman. Contemporaries held the battle out as graphic evidence of "the terrible effect of modern weapons when used against massed formations."[198] The verdict of modern historians has been equally harsh: a "medieval army had charged frontally into the guns of a modern one and had been annihilated before it could get within range."[199]

At first glance, this qualitative edge might explain the disastrous loss-exchange ratios of the Second Mahdi War and also downstream consequences such as mass desertion and the Mahdiya's need for blocking detachments. But a narrow technocratic focus on the quality of weapons is problematic, for several reasons. First, proponents of the military superiority thesis often miss the fact that Egyptian soldiers, who comprised two-thirds of the entire Anglo-Egyptian expeditionary force, were not equipped with the new .303 rifle. Instead, Egyptian soldiers fielded the same Martini-Henry rifles as their Mahdist counterparts; British officers were afraid that outfitting inaccurate Egyptian soldiers with Lee-Metfords would only vastly increase ammunition

197. Green 2007, 216–17.
198. Neillands 1996, 211.
199. Green 2007, 264.

expenditures.[200] If anything, the qualitative gap was larger during the First Mahdi War, when Mahdist forces were still foraging for weapons, than during the Second War.

Second, restricting our gaze to Omdurman obscures how the same pathologies—disastrous loss-exchange ratios, mass desertion and defection, and tangled command and control—were present during wars with adversaries not equipped with advanced weapons. During the 1887–89 war with Abyssinia, Mahdist forces experienced mass desertion and heavy casualties even when fighting from prepared defensive positions. At the Battle of Gallabat (9–10 March 1889), for example, the Abyssinians attacked Mahdist forces defending a fortified zariba encircling Gallabat. Abyssinian forces had breached the zariba, sparking a cascade of desertions when, in the fog of war, a stray bullet felled Abyssinia's Emperor Yohannes, turning the tide of the battle. The Mahdiya managed to lose fifteen thousand of its most experienced soldiers, and nearly 18 percent of their entire fielded force, when fighting from prepared positions. Abyssinia lost an estimated nine thousand soldiers, about 6 percent of its fielded force, despite having to cross open ground before crashing against the razor-sharp zariba in frontal assaults. Abyssinia managed to exact a terrible price on Mahdiya formations without the benefit of qualitatively superior technology or tactics.

Third, while technological superiority magnifies the costs of battlefield errors, it does not explain why mistakes were made in the first place. One cannot escape the conclusion that Omdurman was the culmination of debilitating processes set in motion years before the September battle. The Khalifa overruled his military advisors and rejected his best option—a night attack—because command and control could not be maintained. Once battle began, he failed to coordinate operations by his Green and Black Flags, throwing away the Mahdiya's manpower advantage by allowing Kitchener to concentrate on each army piecemeal. These errors gave Kitchener breathing room to regroup and pivot his forces when they were scattered around the battlefield. Tactics were simplified to ease command and control burdens, leading to courageous but near-suicidal frontal assaults aimed at the Anglo-Egyptian force's strongest formations. Even the choice of battlefield, a gently rolling plain with little cover, was meant to facilitate the Khalifa's oversight but proved spectacularly ill-advised. "He chose," one historian has argued, "the only spot which spelt certain and total defeat and which denied him any chance of inflicting significant casualties upon the invaders, namely a mass frontal attack in daylight over open ground."[201]

---

200. Keown-Boyd 1986, 228fn8; Royle 1886, 560.
201. Keown-Boyd 1986, 223.

These self-imposed constraints clearly predate the arrival of British forces. They also help address a related issue: why the Khalifa did not take steps in the years after 1885 to offset British advantages in preparation for an eventual Anglo-Egyptian return. As early as 1891, Wingate's spies had confirmed the Khalifa's intention to meet any invading force on the plains of Karari at Omdurman, a plan he never wavered from.[202]

Yet here, too, the Khalifa's freedom of maneuver had largely disappeared. The Anglo-Egyptian attack was facilitated by his practice of placing the most unreliable commanders, along with non-core groups more generally, astride the most likely invasion routes. His scorched earth tactics toward local non-core groups meant that Mahdi forces struggled to secure food, especially corn, from unwilling populations in the war zone. More mobile forms of warfare that could interdict the long and increasingly vulnerable Anglo-Egyptian railway network were ruled out because core units refused to operate "out of area." The Khalifa never managed to cut the telegraph or railway lines during the course of the war, despite the fact that his forces severed these same channels of communication during a minor engagement with British forces at Kosheh in 1885.[203]

Evidence from the battlefield also suggests that mass desertion and defection are not simply the product of casualties but reflect identity-based logics of grievance and collective action. Soldier indiscipline during the Second Mahdi War was tied loosely, if at all, to battlefield casualties, often occurring before combat began, en route to the battlefield, or during raids against locals. Casualties were also comparatively higher against British units during the First Mahdi War than initial encounters with solely Egyptian forces; desertion did not occur in either instance. In fact, it is reasonable to suggest that the Mahdist army's fear of indiscipline, along with its actual outbreak, fueled casualties, not the other way around. The casualties-cause-indiscipline argument also treats all units as uniform in their composition and likelihood of experiencing indiscipline. As a result, this narrative, unlike the identity-based approach offered here, is silent on who deserts or defects and the sequence by which armies disintegrate.

In the end, the Khalifa's repressive ethnocratic vision left his army short of options for addressing the technological imbalance between his forces and the invading Anglo-Egyptian expedition. To be sure, British technological superiority, both in terms of weapons and logistics, increased the magnitude of Mahdiya casualties. But in many ways the military superiority thesis mistakes effects for causes. Advanced weapons did not cause the adoption of simple

202. Pugh 2011, 55.
203. Spiers 2004, 126.

tactics, poor command and control, or soldier indiscipline; they simply allowed Anglo-Egyptian forces to exploit preexisting weaknesses generated by crippling levels of military inequality.

3.7. Conclusion

The Mahdiya's fate provides a stark illustration of the perils of extreme inequality. Designed as a theory-building exercise, the evidence marshaled here provides tantalizing, if necessarily exploratory, clues that the proposed relationship between rising inequality and falling battlefield performance is at work. Driven by his exclusionary vision, the Khalifa's repressive nation-building campaign reduced loyalty to his ethnocratic regime, fed antagonism and mistrust between ethnic groups, and created incentives to escape military service at the first battlefield opportunity. Anticipating trouble, the Khalifa's efforts to manage these divisions—embedding trusted Ta'isha advisors in all units, blending ethnic groups together to prevent collaboration, and killing rival tribal and ethnic leaders—all backfired. Mass desertion and defection, the twin stalking horses of military disintegration, both emerged, forcing commanders to double down on already simplistic tactics to ease command and control burdens. The dynamics of desertion also unfolded as expected, with repressed ethnic groups fleeing first, followed by Baggara now marginalized by the Khalifa's narrow Ta'isha ethnocracy, eventually leaving only a small core of die-hard regime supporters. Blocking detachments like the Jihadiya slowed, but did not stop, the flow of deserters, and at high cost, reinforcing commanders' incentives to abandon previously successful envelopment tactics for simple, brutal, frontal assaults. Unsurprisingly, casualties soared. The Mahdi-era Mahdiya managed to claw itself to a respectable loss-exchange ratio slightly above parity despite its initial paucity of modern firearms and artillery; the Khalifa's army measured its relative losses in dozens of soldiers lost for each foreign soldier killed. Over time, the trade-offs between combat power and cohesion became acute as inequality between soldiers, and between commanders and rank and file, fueled a downward spiral of greater indiscipline and harsher punishment. Perhaps the height of inequality-induced absurdities was the Khalifa's prosecution of a war against targeted ethnic groups within his own population at precisely the same moment he faced an existential threat to his state (and himself) from outside powers. The British, for their part, exploited, but did not create, these battlefield deficiencies. Instead, the Khalifa was merely harvesting the bitter fruits of the seeds of inequality he had sowed upon assuming power more than a decade before the vengeance-seeking British crossed his border.

4

Lessons from Project Mars

QUANTITATIVE TESTS OF MILITARY INEQUALITY
AND BATTLEFIELD PERFORMANCE SINCE 1800

Every military fact is also a social and political one.

ANTONIO GRAMSCI, *THE PRISON NOTEBOOKS*, 1929–35

THE MAHDIYA'S METEORIC rise and shocking collapse lend initial support to the notion that military inequality is bad for business. This chapter takes up the challenge of determining whether this stark pattern generalizes to the wider universe of belligerents and conventional wars fought since 1800. Drawing on Project Mars, this chapter subjects the proposed argument to an increasingly severe battery of statistical analyses to test its robustness across five different measures of battlefield performance. Inspired by the book's conceptualization of battlefield performance as combining elements of combat power and cohesion, these measures include a belligerent's loss-exchange ratio, the incidence of mass desertion and mass defection among its soldiers, and the fielding of blocking detachments designed to coerce reluctant soldiers to fight. A composite index of battlefield performance rounds out these measures. The intuition here is a simple one: our confidence that military inequality is a central driver of battlefield performance is earned by its ability to explain coherence across several different, and imperfectly correlated, behavioral indicators across time and diverse contexts.[1]

The chapter's empirical strategy unfolds over five stages. First, I detail how core variables, including prewar military inequality and battlefield

---

1. Seeking coherence across multiple outcomes and comparison groups can also reduce the sensitivity of findings arising from the non-random nature of military inequality. On this point, see Rosenbaum 2010, 118–20, 339.

performance, were constructed. Alternative explanations, including the relative balance of troops, regime type, and the military's own organizational design, are also detailed, alongside key control variables. Second, I provide simple descriptive statistics about the relationship between military inequality and the various measures of battlefield performance. Third, I subject two different measures of military inequality to a series of statistical tests to examine the strength of this association. I forego long, cumbersome, statistical tables and instead rely on simple figures to convey the substantive importance of military inequality. These tests also break with established practices in quantitative studies of military effectiveness by dividing the 1800–2011 time period into early modern (1800–1917) and modern (1918–) eras. I therefore test for military inequality's effects within these eras rather than pooling observations across them, a move that creates an additional hurdle for the proposed argument but one that better respects the contextual differences in warfare over time. Next, I use matching and a two-control group comparison to investigate how shifts from low to high inequality, and from medium to high inequality, affect battlefield performance within a reduced sample of most similar belligerents. This approach allows us to examine the effects of sudden increases in the "dosage" of inequality while screening out potential differences between belligerents, thereby isolating the effects of military inequality. A final section considers the fate of leading alternative explanations, which receive almost no empirical support within the expanded Project Mars universe.

To preview the chapter's findings, I find considerable support for the claim that prewar military inequality adversely affects battlefield performance across both eras. As inequality increases, the predicted likelihood that a belligerent will suffer lopsided casualties increases substantially. The same is true of both mass desertion and defection, where the effects of inequality are especially damaging in the modern era. Blocking detachments are also far more likely to make their appearance when inequality rises. These four wartime pathologies cluster in predictable fashion. Belligerents saddled with high or extreme levels of military inequality, for example, are far more likely to be wracked by multiple wartime deficiencies simultaneously than are similar belligerents with low levels of inequality. This is not simply a story of ethnic diversity, however. The number of ethnic groups in a given military has at best only a modest effect on battlefield performance. Instead, it is the state's prewar treatment of its constituent ethnic groups that conditions how its soldiers will fight. The roots of military power, these findings suggest, lie not in troop strength or technological advantages but in the political and social realities that mold and shape armies.

4.1. Building Project Mars

The chapter's empirical tests were made possible by the construction of Project Mars, a new dataset of 229 belligerents fighting 250 conventional wars between 1800 and 2011. I have relegated much of the discussion of coding rules, data sources, and auditing procedures to an extensive online appendix ("Sources, Data, Methods"). A few features are worth emphasizing here, however, as they bear on matters of data quality and reliability. A team of 134 coders, combing through materials in 21 languages, worked for nearly seven years to construct and then stress-test a battery of new measures for inequality, battlefield performance, and alternative explanations. Most of these research associates worked as part of Blue team, whose responsibility was to build-out Project Mars by tracking down initial data for its variables. A second, smaller, Red team then subjected Blue team codings to random audits to improve data quality, minimize errors, and raise intercoder agreement on difficult coding decisions. Measures for data quality and our confidence in our judgments were also constructed for core variables, including all measures of military inequality and battlefield performance. We also collected high, low, and mean estimates for core variables to capture uncertainty about these data and to reduce sensitivity to their often-contested, often-incomplete nature.[2] No cross-national effort of this ambition is entirely free of error, of course. These procedures do, however, enable the rigorous study of inequality over a large historical sweep, helping uncover patterns hidden for too long by the absence of relevant data.

4.1.1. Measuring Military Inequality

Coding teams collected two types of data to construct military inequality coefficients for all 825 belligerent observations. First, we took snapshots of each army's ethnic composition by calculating the proportion represented by each group among ground forces on the eve of war. We included all ethnic groups that represented greater than one percent of the army's personnel. For standing armies, we timed our snapshot to one year before the war to minimize the chance that leaders, anticipating conflict, rigged their armies to avoid future problems among restive ethnic groups. For non-standing armies, as well as expeditionary forces constructed to deal with emergent threats, we measured ethnic composition on the eve of the war's first battle, as the

---

2. This follows best practices established by the UCDP/PRIO Armed Conflict Dataset for post-1945 civil wars (UCDP/PRIO 2015).

opposing sides marshaled for armed combat.[3] In all cases, we include only ground forces in our calculations. We also incorporate colonial forces, auxiliaries, and volunteers from other states or groups if they served under the belligerent's command. We cast our net wide, drawing on a variety of sources to construct these demographic data. These include official histories,[4] regimental narratives,[5] formal orders of battle and tables of organization for units at the opening battle,[6] casualty lists,[7] and contemporary reports on the composition of enemy forces by military intelligence,[8] participating soldiers,[9] and enterprising journalists on the battlefield.[10]

Second, we coded the state's prewar treatment of each ethnic group according to the threefold typology outlined in the theory chapter. Inclusion, defined as the absence of state-orchestrated group-based discrimination or violence, was assigned a 0 value. All forms of state-directed discrimination, including political, economic, and within the military itself, were given a 0.5 value. The use of collective coercion and violence by the state against a specific ethnic group was assigned a value of 1. If an ethnic group was subjected to multiple forms of collective punishment, we assigned a 1 value. We generated our narratives of state treatment from political histories of these belligerents. For the post-1945 era, we cross-validated our accounts of ethnic treatment with data contained in the Ethnic Power Relations (EPR) and Minorities at Risk (MAR) datasets. We did not impose a minimum threshold for collective violence. In practice, however, we are capturing bouts of collective violence large enough to be visible in primary documents or secondary sources. These events tend to skew toward large-scale state-directed campaigns rather than one-time events. We anchored our measurement of state treatment in the five years preceding the war; that is, we scanned for evidence of state treatment prior to the war but not in the distant past. This

---

3. For example, we code the ethnic composition of General Gordon's Relief Expedition to Khartoum (1884–85) during the First Mahdi War, not the entire UK Army, using 1884 as a measurement benchmark. As a result, the same belligerent, usually a colonial power, can have sharply different military inequality coefficients depending on the location of hostilities. Staying with the UK example, its forces had radically different ethnic composition during the near simultaneous Boxer Rebellion (1900) in China and War of the Golden Stool (1900) against the Ashanti Empire.

4. See, for example, Airapetov 2014, 2015a, b.

5. See, for example, Bruce 1906.

6. See, for example, Haythornthwaite 2007.

7. See, for example, Lopukhovsky and Kavalerchik 2017.

8. See, for example, Burton 1908.

9. See, for example, McCormick 1859.

10. See, for example, Hardman 1860.

(a) Average military inequality by decade   **(b)** The military inequality possibility frontier

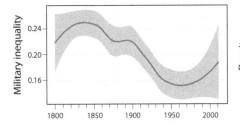
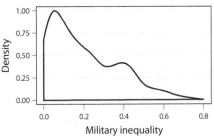

FIGURE 4.1. Summary Statistics: The Military Inequality Coefficient

coding rule ensures that exposure to state discrimination or repression was recent (or still ongoing) for soldiers as they marched into battle. Consistent with the book's argument, we do not assume that intergenerational trauma is at work. Instead, it is the recent lived experience of these soldiers that matters for how they regard the terms of their military service and their willingness to fight and die for the regime.

With these two types of data in hand, the construction of the military inequality coefficient (*Military inequality*) is straightforward. I simply interact each ethnic group's share of the army with its prewar treatment by the regime and sum the totals, creating a point estimate somewhere along a scale that ranges from 0 (perfect equality) to 1 (perfect inequality).[11] We do so for high and low estimates for each ethnic group, thereby constructing high and low estimates of military inequality for each belligerent. All analyses below use the mean values of military inequality.

To provide a sense of military inequality's distribution over time, I plot its mean value by decade for the 1800–2010 era in figure 4.1(a). A quick glance at the curve punctures the notion that military inequality has been crowded out by modernization and democratization globally. True, the mean level of a belligerent's military inequality coefficient has declined somewhat over time, falling from 0.23 in the early modern era to 0.17 in the modern one.[12] But military inequality has been, and remains, a durable feature of the international landscape, fluctuating within a narrow band between 0.24 and 0.16 for

11. The formula is $\sum_{i=1}^{n} pt_i$, where p is the ethnic group's share of an army's prewar strength; t represents the nature of the regime's prewar treatment of a specific group, where possible values are 0, 0.5, 1, representing inclusion, discrimination, and repression, respectively; and n is the number of ethnic groups in the army.

12. This difference is statistically significant at $t = 4.86$, 807.17df, $p = 0.000$.

over two centuries. It also appears to be enjoying something of a renaissance since 1945.

Figure 4.1(b) illustrates the military inequality possibility frontier by plotting the density of military inequality for all 825 belligerent observations. While the mean military inequality coefficient is 0.205, we can see how belligerents tend to cluster predominantly at lower levels of inequality. The number of observations becomes increasingly infrequent as military inequality advances, petering out in the 0.60–0.80 range. This is consistent with the earlier conjecture that armies cannot reach the theoretical maximum of military inequality due to command and control reasons. A basic minimum of soldiers must be drawn from core groups to maintain order, either through passive surveillance or active coercion, and to ensure that the army remains a cohesive fighting force. In practice, the absolute minimum appears to be twenty percent of a deployed force (or 0.80 on the military inequality continuum). Indeed, the highest military inequality coefficient recorded in Project Mars was 0.75, suggesting a natural upper bound for actual inequality.[13]

Empirical reality is messy, of course, and often works to confound our tidy coding protocols. While a fuller discussion of coding rules, along with the codebook itself, has been posted online, two issues deserve flagging here. First, colonial armies, that is, formations staffed principally by soldiers drawn from colonies, pose a particular conceptual challenge, standing at odds with standard renditions of armies as national in character. Put simply, what to do with soldiers of empire? Should Senegalese *tirailleurs* in French service, Eritrean *askari* in Italian employ, and the diverse soldiers of British West Indies and Bengal Army regiments be treated as members of the political community? On the one hand, these soldiers, as second-class colonial subjects, clearly faced ethnic discrimination (or worse), including the inability to command their own units and, of course, access the upper reaches of political power. On the other hand, these soldiers, often volunteers, were usually drawn from groups that enjoyed a greater share of prestige ("martial races") and political power within the colonial possession, suggesting a relatively higher degree of inclusion than other, less favored, groups. To square this circle, I calculated the military inequality scores for these armies twice: once with colonial groups treated as included and assigned a 0 for state treatment, and once as discriminated against, with a 0.5 value assigned.[14] This decision rule has the effect of adding a penalty for colonial status even if these soldiers were (relatively) privileged in their colonial political communities.

13. Individual units within the larger army may, however, exceed this threshold, as chapter 8 demonstrates.

14. If these soldiers were drawn from repressed populations, then a 1 value is assigned instead of the 0.5 value.

Second, some belligerents declared their independence on the eve of war—indeed, it may have been the precipitating event—or during its opening days. As a result, these independence-seeking belligerents lack the political history necessary for evaluating their treatment of ethnic groups within their boundaries. When confronted with a belligerent fighting in the first few years (or days) of its existence, we sought to code its initial treatment of ethnic groups from its first days regardless of whether it survived the war. In doing so, we sought as much temporal separation as possible between the state's treatment of its constituent ethnic groups and the war's opening to prevent inequality being driven by wartime dynamics. We also designated these belligerents with an indicator variable (*war birth*, see below) to demarcate them from the rest of the Project Mars universe for additional robustness checks.

To soften the issues arising from measurement difficulties, I constructed a second measure, *bands of inequality*, that assigns belligerents to one of four "bands" based on their military inequality coefficients. These bands are Low (0–0.20), Medium (0.21–0.40), High (0.41–0.60), and Extreme (≥0.61). This simple classification scheme reduces bias from measurement difficulties while providing a natural grammar for speaking about the magnitude of inequality across belligerents. In the analyses below, I use bands as both a sensitivity check for military inequality and a simple way of interpreting how each increase in the "dosage" of inequality affects battlefield performance.

4.1.2. Battlefield Performance

Following the book's conceptual and theoretical discussions of battlefield performance, I draw on five specific measures to test the relationship between military inequality and wartime outcomes. These include: (1) a belligerent's loss-exchange ratio and, specifically, whether its LER drops below parity; (2) the incidence of mass desertion and (3) mass defection; (4) the use of blocking detachments; and (5) a composite battlefield performance index (BPI) that aggregates these four measures into a single family index. I detail each below.

Loss-exchange ratios are defined as the relative distribution of casualties inflicted versus suffered by a belligerent (or coalition) during a war. More specifically, loss-exchange ratios are calculated as the number of enemy soldiers killed by a belligerent divided by the number of soldiers lost by that belligerent to enemy fire.[15] A LER above one therefore indicates that a belligerent

---

15. For coalitional wars, each coalition's combined loss-exchange ratio is used instead of each belligerent's due to difficulties in assigning responsibility for inflicting casualties during a multiparty campaign or war.

is inflicting greater losses than it is suffering; a one designates parity; and values below one denote that the belligerent's forces are suffering greater casualties than they are inflicting. Care was taken when collecting data to concentrate only on soldier fatalities. Wounded soldiers, prisoners of war, missing individuals, and deaths from disease, a particular problem during the early modern era, were excluded from these counts to the best of our abilities. Civilian deaths, too, were excluded; these ratios are meant as a measure of force-on-force killing, not as an index of the lethality of the war itself. We generated high, low, and mean LER estimates for each belligerent or coalition to reduce sensitivity to competing fatality claims and reporting inaccuracies. To facilitate ease of interpretation, I constructed *LER below parity*, a dichotomous measure that records whether a belligerent's army lost more soldiers to enemy fire than it killed during the war.

Desertion is defined here as the unauthorized wartime withdrawal of soldiers, including entire units, from the battlefield or adjacent rear area with the intention of permanently abandoning the fight. Withdrawal can take two forms. Soldiers may attempt to return to their prewar life by hiding among the civilian population to escape state authorities. Renegade soldiers may also resort to brigandage in rear areas, or even at home, without coordinating with enemy forces. This definition excludes several types of behavior often conflated with desertion. Temporary absences, as when soldiers head home to plant or harvest crops, usually with tacit official approval, but then return when these duties are discharged, are excluded. Such practices were routine among Confederate soldiers during the American Civil War, for example.[16] Trench mutinies, including those that swept through nearly half the French Army after the disastrous Second Battle of Aisne (1917), are also excluded, as soldiers rebelled in place but did not abandon their posts.[17] Refusals to serve, as well as collective protests, are also excluded from this conceptualization. I also distinguish between mass desertion and simply chaotic retreats, where formations collapse under enemy pressure and their soldiers scatter temporarily before reconstituting their units to continue fighting. Libyan forces fighting in the 1978–79 Uganda-Tanzania War were known for their disorganized retreats, for example. Far from home, however, these forces eventually regrouped rather than risk mass desertion among hostile local populations.[18]

---

16. Enough soldiers deserted and remained absent, however, to exceed the 10 percent threshold for mass desertion. See Weitz 2005.

17. Pedroncini 1983; Doughty 2008, 510.

18. Pollack 2002, 373.

Mass desertion is therefore coded as occurring when ≥10 percent of an army's total deployed forces has decamped for home without authorization. This threshold is a pragmatic compromise designed to separate small-scale individual desertions that afflict nearly every army from large-scale desertion that can cripple war efforts.

In similar fashion, I measure *mass defection* as a dichotomous variable indicating whether ≥10 percent of a belligerent's fielded force switched sides during the war with the intention of taking up arms against their former comrades. I exclude side-switching by prominent military commanders if they acted alone. While these defections are important, commanders can shift allegiance for a variety of motives—personal enrichment and safety among them—that do not necessarily apply to the rank and file. In this view, mass defection is a particularly difficult act to complete successfully. Would-be defectors must evade their own fellow soldiers and then cross enemy lines, risking sanction by both sides. For some wars, mass defection may not be a realistic proposition. Suspicious commanders can station potential defectors well away from front lines while inflating the risks of defection, curbing enthusiasm. Enemy forces may not take prisoners or may treat them poorly, foreclosing this option. Desertion and defection are thus often substitutes, rather than complements, for at least some soldiers and wars. Indeed, consigning potential defectors to rear areas may reduce defection opportunities while increasing the odds of successful desertion.

I also constructed a dichotomous measure, *blocking detachments*, that records whether a belligerent deployed specialized armed formations to monitor and sanction its own officers and soldiers during wartime. These formations have five properties. First, these units are formally authorized by senior commanders; they represent official policy even if their origins can be traced to informal practices adopted haphazardly by frontline officers. Second, blocking detachments are typically stationed in the immediate rear of deployed forces to prevent unauthorized withdrawal and to prod reluctant soldiers into attacking. These units do not normally engage enemy forces, instead saving their fire for fellow soldiers. Third, these units have the formal authorization and military capacity to threaten and punish soldiers on their own remit. Potential sanctioning mechanisms include the forced return of soldiers to their units, dragooning into penal battalions, and execution, oftentimes in front of a soldier's comrades. In some cases, blocking detachments have the capacity to punish soldiers' families. Fourth, these units act as barriers between soldiers and rear areas, inhibiting the flow of information about battlefield progress and home-front conditions. Finally, while exceptions do exist, these units are usually staffed by personnel chosen for their perceived loyalty. The Zhili Clique fielded a special unit of exclusively child soldiers (the *Du Jun Dui*) to shoot deserters with cannon fire in its 1925 war against the Fengtian Clique in China, for example.[19]

I did not impose a minimal requirement for personnel size or fatalities inflicted by blocking units. Instead, three criteria were used to decide whether armies deployed blocking units. First, formal orders creating these units were issued by senior political or military officials. Second, these units were actually deployed on the battlefield in at least one major engagement. Third, these units executed soldiers, whether in a formal setting (i.e., a tribunal) or via shooting or bombardment during battle to stem desertion, block retreat, or drive soldiers forward.[20]

Finally, I constructed a summary measure, battlefield performance index (BPI), that pools these four measures into a single index. The BPI ranges from 0 to 1, where 1 denotes maximal battlefield performance, 0 indicates disastrous performance, and the presence of each of these four "pathologies" (LER below parity, mass desertion, mass defection, and blocking detachments) results in a 0.25 penalty subtracted from the belligerent's BPI score. Thus a 0.75 BPI value indicates the presence of one problem; a 0.50, two problems; a 0.25, three problems; and a 0, the presence of all four problems within the belligerent's army during the same war. More than simply a convenient summary index, BPI integrates elements of combat power and cohesion while capturing the intuition that these wartime behaviors may be correlated, at least partially, with one another.

4.1.3. Alternative Explanations

The mandate of Project Mars extended to the construction of new variables to test long-standing theories of military effectiveness. When possible, coding frameworks from existing datasets were applied to new belligerents and wars of Project Mars. In most cases, however, extensive data collection was required to build these new measures from scratch. Though the effort was considerable, so too was the payoff; we are now in a position to test a broad array of alternative explanations with a much deeper evidentiary base. I concentrate on three clusters of alternative explanations here.

As detailed in the introduction, perhaps the most oft-cited explanation for battlefield success is also the most intuitive: belligerents have greater combat power, and fewer cohesion problems, as their relative strength increases.

19. Guo and Qingchang 2003, 316.

20. Variation in the size, organization, and lethality of these units is an important area for future research.

To date, most empirical studies of war draw on the Correlates of War's Composite Index of National Capability (CINC) to measure relative distributions of military power. This index captures six measures of demographic, economic, and military strength, and provides an annual score that represents the belligerent's share of total global capability.[21] I break with tradition here, however, for two reasons. First, the addition of new belligerents to the Project Mars universe, some of them quite powerful, injects substantial measurement error into the calculation of both cumulative global capabilities and an individual belligerent's share. Second, and more fundamental, CINC scores do not provide any information about the military capabilities a belligerent actually deployed in a given war. Knowing a belligerent's relative standing in the global pecking order is unhelpful if they only deployed a fraction of the total strength, recruited armies "off the books," so to speak, by enlisting local or colonial populations, or surged their enlistment and industrial capacities beyond their CINC values during long attritional wars.

I therefore measure *relative forces* using a belligerent's (or coalition's) share of the total number of soldiers deployed during the war's first major ground battle. I focus on the first battle for several reasons. Military planners have traditionally, and often mistakenly, emphasized winning the first battle decisively as an important step to eventual victory.[22] Initially deployed forces are both more relevant than distant factors such as industrial production and have the advantage of not being confounded by endogenous wartime dynamics. That is, we avoid the danger of accidentally controlling for the effects of military inequality by using more aggregate measures, especially the total number of soldiers mobilized during wartime, that are themselves partially shaped by prior levels of military inequality.[23] I also include two additional measures of material power that avoid these inferential problems. *Great power* denotes whether a belligerent was a member of the exclusive club of leading major powers that dominated the international system due to their especially high levels of material capabilities, including militaries with global reach.[24] *Distance to battle* records the distance from the belligerent's capital to the

21. Sarkees and Wayman 2010, 26.

22. Nolan 2017.

23. On post-treatment bias, see Acharya, Blackwell and Sen 2016. In the supplemental analyses, I replace relative forces with the "bad control" of total number of soldiers deployed during the war as a robustness check.

24. United States (1899–); United Kingdom (1800–); France (1800–1940; 1945–); Germany/Prussia (1800–1918; 1925–45; 1990–); Austria-Hungary (1800–1918); Russia (1800–1917; 1922–); China (1950–); and Japan (1895–1945; 1990–) are considered to be Great Powers by the Correlates of War (Sarkees and Wayman 2010, 34–35). Great Powers represent 251 of 825 observations in Project Mars.

war's first engagement in kilometers (logged). This measure performs double duty. It captures a belligerent's ability to project power over distance, a hallmark of Great Powers.[25] Distance also accounts for the presumed decrease in opportunities for successful desertion as soldiers find themselves increasingly encamped among hostile populations and isolated from coethnic networks that can facilitate escape.[26] Alternatively, fighting near home might confer additional benefits, including heightened resolve, if not desperation, that pushes soldiers to fight harder to avoid a defeat that imperils the homeland directly.[27]

A second theoretical tradition centers around how political institutions shape battlefield performance. To measure *regime type*, I draw on the standard Polity2 indicator, where values range from −10 (the most autocratic) to +10 (the most democratic) and are taken in the year preceding the war.[28] Because these data are tied to the COW list of countries, I created new Polity2 scores for each new belligerent in Project Mars. For some, this process was admittedly clumsy. Polity2 scores were not designed with the wide range of political institutions, including tribal confederacies, khanates, and warlords, found among new Project Mars entrants. I also substitute regime type for a simple dichotomous measure of *democracy*, which denotes whether a belligerent's prewar Polity2 was ≥7, the standard threshold for an established democracy. The empirical expectation here is a simple one: the more democratic the belligerent, the better its loss-exchange ratio, the lower its incidence of soldier indiscipline, and the less likely it is to embrace fratricidal violence as official policy. *Democratic opponent* was also introduced to capture the perceived advantages of democracies by indicating whether the belligerent was facing an opponent with a Polity2 score of ≥7. Belligerents faced democratic opponents 121 times in these wars, about 15 percent of all war observations. Following existing theories, adversaries facing democratic opponents should exhibit battlefield problems with greater frequency, and possess lower BPI values, than states fighting non-democracies.

Battlefield performance may also be dictated by whether the belligerent initiated the war, perhaps through surprise attack, or was itself the victim of external aggression.[29] Initiators are likely to have superior loss-exchange ratios and lower incidence of mass indiscipline because they control the timing and pacing of opening offensives. Blocking detachments, too, should be less frequent among initiators than victims. *Initiator* therefore records whether

25. Boulding 1962.
26. McLauchlin 2014.
27. Castillo 2014.
28. Jaggers and Gurr 2004.
29. Slantchev 2004; Wang and Ray 1994.

the belligerent crossed a political boundary with the intent of seeking battle or was the first to openly attack the opposing side and inflict casualties. *Joiner* denotes whether the belligerent entered an on-going war as a third party. Joiners may possess especially high degrees of battlefield performance since they control the timing of their attack and are selectively choosing to engage an already-weakened foe.[30] From this standpoint, democratic initiators should be top performers, a claim I test using an interaction term between regime type and initiator (*regime type*initiator*).[31]

The institutional design of a belligerent's military may also shape battlefield fortunes. I therefore collected data on three dimensions of military organizations. First, *standing* denotes whether the belligerent had a permanent prewar army or whether it was levied for the purpose of attacking or defending. Standing armies are able to generate socialization pressures through persistent training and indoctrination that levied armies cannot match. As a result, standing armies should exhibit superior combat power and cohesion. Second, I built a sevenfold index that tracked how belligerents recruited their armies and specified their primary recruitment channel, from which $\geq$50 percent of its soldiers were recruited, and secondary channels, if present, through which the remaining 10–49 percent of its soldiers were drawn.[32] Two variables were built from this recruitment index. *Full volunteer* records whether the army was staffed solely by volunteers rather than conscripts, mercenaries, or slaves. These armies likely have higher motivation and better skills than their counterparts, resulting in superior combat power and cohesion. Existing theories suggest that conscripts are far more likely to desert and to suffer heavier casualties than professional volunteer armies, for example.[33] *Composite* is a dichotomous measure that records whether a belligerent's army was drawn from two or more different recruitment streams. Blending recruitment paths may render armies more vulnerable to indiscipline since their components may not mesh well together, creating vulnerabilities that opponents could exploit. Historically, colonial and other expeditionary armies were almost invariably composite in nature, drawing on multiple recruitment streams among different populations to recruit soldiers.[34]

30. Downes 2009.

31. Reiter and Stam 2002.

32. Belligerents could identify and mobilize soldiers from within their own societies via four channels: volunteers, conscripts, mercenaries, and slaves (or other coercion-based approaches such as abduction). Three additional channels were added to allow for recruitment outside of a belligerent's own borders or territorial possessions: volunteers, mercenaries, and slaves.

33. McLauchlin 2015; Horowitz, Simpson and Stam 2011.

34. Composite is only weakly correlated with *military inequality* and *bands* at 0.19 and 0.20, respectively.

4.1.4.   Controls

Finally, I add several new control variables that might also influence battle-field performance. *Civil war* denotes whether the war was an armed conflict between two or more sides subject to the same prewar government that resulted in at least five hundred battle-related fatalities. This variable helps account for the possibility that mass desertion and side-switching might be especially prevalent in these kinds of wars given cross-cutting ethnic cleav-ages and the close proximity of soldiers to their families, homes, and support networks. Casualties might also follow a different logic in these wars. *Multiparty* captures whether the war was fought between more than two belliger-ents, which creates different implications for defection and desertion than bilateral conflicts.[35] I also created *war birth*, a binary variable that denotes whether a belligerent was fighting the war within the first two years of its exis-tence. Faced with severe time and resource constraints, these new states might experience battlefield failures at a higher clip than their more established counterparts, especially if they are waging high-stakes wars of independence. These states possess slightly higher levels of military inequality than their peers, though the difference is only statistically significant in the early modern era. There are 79 war birth observations in the Project Mars dataset. A final variable, *non-COW belligerent*, identifies the 124 new belligerents added to Project Mars that are not included in COW's Inter-State War dataset.[36] These belligerents collectively account for 24 percent of all observations in Project Mars (193 of 825).

4.1.5.   Caveats

All large-scale data collection efforts face limitations; Project Mars is no differ-ent. Two caveats deserve special mention here. First, these data provide only a snapshot of each belligerent's aggregate performance in a given war. While valuable for uncovering cross-national patterns, these data do not directly test the argument at the battle level and cannot identify intrawar dynamics.[37] Nor are these data fine-grained enough to test the proposed causal mechanisms, a task better suited for the qualitative paired comparisons detailed in subse-quent chapters. A battle-level dataset remains something of a holy grail for conflict researchers, a truly Herculean endeavor best tackled collectively. As it stands, Project Mars represents the beginning of a conversation rather than the final word on these understudied battlefield outcomes.

---

35. Christia 2012.

36. The correlation between *war birth* and *non-COW belligerent* is modest (0.34).

37. For a similar cross-national approach to studying a sensitive battlefield topic, see Cohen 2016, 67–71.

Second, it is possible that political bias has crept into the data generation process, in several ways. Desertion, defection, and, above all, the use
of violence against one's own soldiers, represent contested, often shameful,
chapters of a nation's history that are usually sidelined in official narratives
of the war. Few political regimes, especially those engaged in nation-building
around wartime sacrifices, are likely to admit that "patriotic" soldiers switched
allegiance or were coerced to fight. Powerful incentives therefore exist to minimize, or deny outright, the occurrence of soldier indiscipline. In extreme
cases, reports of mass desertion and defection, and especially the use of blocking detachments, have been purged almost entirely from official narratives.
To take one example, a growth industry now exists in Russia, fueled by the
declassification of long-buried files, of books on so-called forgotten units
that were overrun or destroyed during the Second World War and subsequently were stricken from official rosters to minimize losses.[38] At the same
time, a victor's bias also exists, in which victorious powers rewrite the war's
narrative to exaggerate the cohesion problems of their enemies while downplaying their own issues. This is especially likely in cases where the adversary
is completely destroyed as an independent state, leaving no one to contest
the skewed narrative.[39] In short, the combination of national sensitivities and
political imperatives collude to sweep these behaviors under the rug. As such,
Project Mars data on the incidence of mass desertion, defection, and blocking detachments likely exhibit a conservative bias that underestimates their
actual frequency on the battlefield. They should, in other words, be viewed as
the floor, not the ceiling, of possible estimates of their battlefield presence.

4.2. Descriptive Statistics

As the opening wedge in our empirical analysis, I summarize Project Mars
data on military inequality and battlefield performance in table 4.1. In total,
there are 825 belligerent observations, each of which summarizes an army's
performance in a given war. Belligerents are sorted according to their respective band of inequality; the mean military inequality coefficient value is also
provided for each band. We can clearly see the military inequality possibility
frontier at work: there are 467 belligerents that entered their wars with low
inequality (56 percent), 216 at medium levels (26 percent), 118 at high levels
(14 percent), and only 24 (or 3 percent) at extreme levels of inequality. These
data underscore the difficulty in fielding armies staffed solely or principally

38. In that vein, a heated, often partisan, debate has recently appeared on the role of blocking detachments and the extent of their violence against Red Army soldiers (Beshanov 2004;
Glantz 2005a; Filippenkov 2016).

39. A state was coded as conquered or destroyed in 113 of 825 observations in Project Mars.

TABLE 4.1. Descriptive Statistics: Battlefield Performance by Bands of Military Inequality, 1800–2011

	Inequality		Battlefield Measures					Observations
Bands	Mean Military Inequality Coefficient	Number of Ethnic Groups in Army	LER Below Parity	Mass Desertion	Mass Defection	Blocking Units	BP Index	N
Low	0.079	4.22	24.6% (115)	21.1% (99)	8.3% (39)	9.4% (44)	0.841	467
Medium	0.286	5.57	45.4% (98)	43.5% (94)	24.5% (53)	24.1% (52)	0.656	216
High	0.461	5.67	66.1% (78)	68.6% (81)	40.7% (48)	33.1% (39)	0.479	118
Extreme	0.651	4.50	75.0% (18)	95.8% (23)	45.8% (11)	45.8% (11)	0.343	24
Mean	0.205	4.79	37.5% (309)	36.0% (297)	18.3% (151)	17.7% (146)	0.726	825

from repressed ethnic groups. The mean number of ethnic groups in each army also varies across different bands of inequality. Belligerents with low inequality and, somewhat curiously, extreme inequality both field armies that contain somewhat fewer ethnic groups than their medium and high inequality counterparts. This may partly reflect the success of inclusive states in fostering attractive national identities that subsume existing ethnic ones or, conversely, the outcome of repressive homogenization in extreme inequality belligerents. Conversely, it may simply be that these states had different preexisting ethnic makeups. I explore whether this difference in the number of ethnic groups, rather than their prewar treatment by the state, is driving variation in battlefield performance in the analyses below.[40]

Subsequent columns outline the percentage of belligerents within each band that suffered below-parity casualties, mass desertion and defection, and deployed blocking detachments during the war. The total number of occurrences for each battlefield pathology is provided in parentheses. Even a cursory glance at these data reveals how rising levels of inequality are associated with declining battlefield performance. Take, for example, the below-parity casualties. Only one-quarter of low inequality belligerents recorded loss-exchange ratios below parity. By contrast, 45 percent of medium inequality belligerents, nearly two-thirds of all high inequality belligerents, and a staggering three-quarters of all extreme inequality belligerents suffered greater casualties than they inflicted on enemy forces. In all, 140 of the 229 belligerents in the Project Mars dataset experienced wartime below-parity casualties at least once. Mass desertion follows an identical pattern. Low inequality belligerents experienced mass desertion in one-fifth of their total observations, compared with 44 percent of all medium inequality observations and two-thirds of high inequality ones. Mass desertion was a virtual certainty among extreme inequality belligerents, with only a single observation (the LTTE during its 1990–2002 war with Sri Lanka) failing to breach the 10 percent threshold denoting mass desertion. A full 127 of 229 belligerents experienced mass desertion at least once, emphasizing its widespread (and understudied) nature. Historically, both Chinese and Russian armies have been prone to bouts of mass desertion, with its occurrence noted in 46 percent (12/26) and 63 percent of their observations, respectively. Brazil, Kokand, and the Mahdiya also recorded mass desertion in nearly all of their wars, suggesting a chronic frailty within their armies.

---

40. The mean difference in the number of ethnic groups between low inequality and the remaining three bands is 1.31. Though substantively small, this difference is statistically significant at $t = 7.49$, $p \leq 0.000$.

Mass defection, too, becomes more common as we move up the rungs of inequality, though it remains less frequent than mass desertion. About 8 percent of low inequality belligerents' wartime observations were marred by mass defection, rising to one-quarter of medium inequality and 41 percent of high inequality belligerent observations. Mass defection occurred in just under half of all extreme inequality belligerents' wartime observations. A total of 89 different belligerents experienced mass defection during at least one of their wars. Some armies faced chronic side-switching: Uruguay, the Yemen Arab Republic, and Hungary all experienced mass defection in two-thirds of their respective wartime observations. China's soldiers defected during 12 of 26 wars, especially during the nineteenth century, while the Russian Army suffered mass defection in 7 of 49 wars. Similar distributions were recorded for the deployment of blocking detachments. Some 10 percent of low inequality belligerent observations saw the emergence of these formations, compared with one-quarter, one-third, and nearly half of all observations by medium, high, and extreme belligerents. Surprisingly, 70 different belligerents resorted to blocking detachments during their wars. The Asante Empire used these formations in three of their four wars; Russia and the Soviet Union did so for nearly 40 percent of their wars; and the Ottoman Empire deployed them in over one-third of its wars.

Finally, belligerents with low inequality score highest on the composite battlefield performance index (BPI). With a 1 representing the best possible performance, low inequality belligerents recorded a mean 0.841 score. Medium inequality belligerents trail far behind, at 0.656, while high inequality belligerents manage only a 0.479 average score, which indicates that two of these four battlefield deficiencies are present. Extreme inequality belligerents bring up the rear, recording a meager 0.343 score, indicating that their armies routinely experience three of these four problems in the same war.

These descriptive statistics provide initial evidence of the dangers of inequality across individual and composite measures of battlefield performance. Each step up the rung of inequality results in diminished performance across measures that are imperfectly correlated with each other, helping build our confidence that we have correctly identified a wide-ranging and robust relationship between inequality and battlefield outcomes.[41] Inclusion does not guarantee battlefield perfection, however. Low inequality belligerents still fall short of the ideal on the battlefield performance index even as they perform comparatively better than belligerents at higher bands of inequality. Intriguingly, these battlefield problems occur with varying probabilities.

---

41. The highest correlation is between desertion and defection (0.34), followed by desertion and blocking detachments (0.23) and defection and blocking detachments (0.17).

Casualties below parity and mass desertion are twice as common among wartime experiences than either mass defection or blocking detachments. Defection arises at only half the rate as desertion, confirming my earlier intuition that would-be defectors face greater logistical and other obstacles than deserters. Blocking detachments also appeared in 18 percent of all observations, a far higher rate of self-coercion than our current theories admit. Finally, these data suggest an upper bound on battlefield dysfunction. Only 14 different belligerents managed to score a 0 on the battlefield performance index; a 0 was recorded on only 20 occasions. Russia holds the unfortunate pride of place for this achievement, reaching this nadir four times in its history.

4.3. Statistical Analysis, Part I: The Military Inequality Coefficient

Descriptive data are useful for drawing initial inferences about military inequality and battlefield performance. We require more sophisticated approaches, however, if we are to test whether this relationship survives in the face of alternative explanations and control variables. I therefore draw on statistical regression (Ordinary Least Squares and logistic regression) to test whether increased military inequality is associated with diminished battlefield performance in the early modern (1800–1917) and modern (1918–2011) eras of conventional war. For each measure of battlefield performance, I first regress military inequality alone, and then introduce a more complicated model that incorporates the full range of alternative explanations and control variables.[42]

Table 4.2 reports the coefficients from these models for all four measures of individual battlefield outcomes as well as the combined battlefield performance index for the early modern era. The results are stark: Military inequality is positively associated with casualties below parity, the outbreak of mass desertion and defection, and the fielding of blocking detachments at the $p \leq 0.001$ level regardless of whether military inequality is alone or tested with the full model. The same holds true for the combined battlefield performance index; military inequality is associated with decreased performance in Models 9a and 10a at the $p \leq 0.001$ level. That these findings change only slightly when the full battery of measures for alternative explanations and controls are added to the mix highlights the robustness of this relationship.

But does it hold in the modern era? Indeed, the same pattern holds when we reestimate the same models for the post-1917 era (table 4.3). Military

---

42. These full models were used to generate figure 1.1 displayed in the introduction.

TABLE 4.2. Battlefield Performance in the Early Modern Era (1800–1917)

	LER Below Parity		Mass Desertion		Mass Defection		Blocking Units		BP Index	
	Alone Model 1a	Full Model 2a	Alone Model 3a	Full Model 4a	Alone Model 5a	Full Model 6a	Alone Model 7a	Full Model 8a	Alone Model 9a	Full Model 10a
Military inequality	4.528***	3.785***	5.145***	5.140***	5.411***	5.860***	4.141***	4.133***	−0.892***	−0.782***
	(0.757)	(0.725)	(0.629)	(0.686)	(0.746)	(0.796)	(0.689)	(0.893)	(0.064)	(0.065)
Regime type		−0.066†		−0.024		−0.017		0.039		0.003
		(0.036)		(0.029)		(0.034)		(0.030)		(0.003)
Initiator		0.180		−0.050		−0.380		−0.501		0.023
		(0.268)		(0.305)		(0.342)		(0.315)		(0.021)
Regime type*initiator		0.002		−0.003		−0.006		−0.042		0.002
		(0.041)		(0.035)		(0.049)		(0.046)		(0.002)
Democratic opponent		1.005**		0.144		−0.536		−0.097		−0.033
		(0.377)		(0.353)		(0.554)		(0.367)		(0.035)
Joiner		−1.083†		−0.042		0.262		0.005		0.015
		(0.623)		(0.466)		(0.591)		(0.711)		(0.043)
Relative forces		1.396**		−0.375		0.039		−0.098		−0.046
		(0.529)		(0.478)		(0.612)		(0.611)		(0.045)
Great power		−0.492†		−0.068		0.537		0.330		0.009
		(0.257)		(0.277)		(0.335)		(0.426)		(0.022)
Distance to battle		−0.183**		−0.041		−0.020		0.010		0.008
		(0.066)		(0.078)		(0.077)		(0.073)		(0.006)

	(1)	(2)	(3)	(4)	(5)	(6)	(7)	(8)	(9)	(10)
Standing army		0.432		−0.492		−0.089		−1.174*		0.040
		(0.383)		(0.430)		(0.575)		(0.487)		(0.037)
Volunteer army		−0.030		0.554		0.904†		−1.416†		−0.020
		(0.426)		(0.440)		(0.532)		(0.762)		(0.035)
Composite army		−0.079		0.114		0.300		0.392		−0.023
		(0.239)		(0.329)		(0.344)		(0.456)		(0.025)
Civil war		−0.325		1.056***		1.248***		0.262		−0.102**
		(0.339)		(0.295)		(0.306)		(0.333)		(0.029)
Multiparty war		−0.713**		0.207		−0.242		−0.014		0.024
		(0.253)		(0.230)		(0.338)		(0.360)		(0.022)
War birth		−0.286		0.059		1.021		0.369		−0.044
		(0.572)		(0.609)		(0.719)		(0.607)		(0.055)
Non-COW belligerent		0.471		−0.629*		−0.470		0.215		0.012
		(0.318)		(0.316)		(0.403)		(0.462)		(0.027)
Constant	−1.519***	−1.404*	−1.648***	−1.092†	−2.971***	−3.501***	−2.664***	−1.812*	0.915***	0.856***
	(0.261)	(0.682)	(0.168)	(0.623)	(0.231)	(0.990)	(0.261)	(0.733)	(0.016)	(0.066)
Wald χ^2	35.76***	127.93***	66.81***	129.88***	52.56***	183.62***				
F Score							36.17***	62.86***	193.90***	36.66***
(Pseudo) r^2	0.107	0.234	0.132	0.176	0.147	0.229	0.091	0.140	0.363	0.423
N	482	482	482	482	482	482	482	482	482	482

Note: Standard errors clustered on 138 belligerents.　*** $p < 0.001$　** $p < 0.01$　* $p < 0.05$　† $p < 0.10$.

TABLE 4.3. Battlefield Performance in the Modern Era (1918–2011)

	LER Below Parity		Mass Desertion		Mass Defection		Blocking Units		BP Index	
	Alone Model 1b	Full Model 2b	Alone Model 3b	Full Model 4b	Alone Model 5b	Full Model 6b	Alone Model 7b	Full Model 8b	Alone Model 9b	Full Model 10b
Military inequality	4.469*** (1.010)	4.158*** (1.1775)	6.616*** (1.079)	6.319*** (1.069)	5.312*** (1.165)	5.132*** (1.152)	5.646*** (1.494)	5.632*** (1.402)	−1.021*** (0.145)	−0.909*** (0.135)
Regime type		−0.029 (0.028)		0.008 (0.026)		−0.073 (0.035)†		−0.070 (0.044)	0.003 (0.002)	(0.002)
Initiator		−0.450 (0.310)		−0.033 (0.258)		0.589† (0.330)		0.435 (0.362)		−0.005 (0.024)
Regime type*initiator		0.003 (0.041)		−0.000 (0.038)		0.0137 (0.039)		0.046 (0.045)		−0.001 (0.003)
Democratic opponent		−1.236*** (0.363)		−0.320 (0.388)		−0.087 (0.505)		−0.469 (0.520)		−0.036 (0.039)
Joiner		−2.350★ (1.110)		−0.662 (0.700)		−0.475 (0.833)		0.127 (0.719)		0.083★ (0.034)
Relative forces		0.387 (0.661)		−0.241 (0.611)		−0.746 (0.810)		0.134 (0.856)		−0.005 (0.071)
Great power		0.284 (0.333)		−0.330 (0.357)		0.173 (0.450)		0.344 (0.518)		−0.012 (0.031)
Distance to battle		−0.132† (0.073)		−0.036 (0.069)		0.145† (0.086)		0.016 (0.092)		0.003 (0.006)

	(1)	(2)	(3)	(4)	(5)	(6)	(7)	(8)	(9)	(10)
Standing army	0.483 (0.514)			−0.341 (0.484)		−0.901† (0.491)		0.559 (0.667)		0.008 (0.052)
Volunteer army	−0.067 (0.389)			−0.480 (0.457)		0.151 (0.456)		−0.450 (0.545)		0.033 (0.038)
Composite army	0.288 (0.284)			0.175 (0.294)		0.843* (0.404)		0.358 (0.450)		−0.042 (0.030)
Civil war	−0.245 (0.332)			0.297 (0.334)		1.432*** (0.396)		0.173 (0.366)		−0.049† (0.028)
Multiparty war	−0.684* (0.279)			−0.090 (0.260)		0.343 (0.306)		−0.066 (0.369)		0.027 (0.027)
War birth	0.022 (0.459)			0.672 (0.421)		0.220 (0.472)		1.334† (0.683)		−0.094 (0.061)
Non-COW belligerent	−0.050 (0.4521)			−0.595 (0.480)		−0.143 (0.406)		−0.289 (0.610)		0.031 (0.046)
Constant	−1.430*** (0.256)	−1.089 (0.855)	−2.058*** (0.270)	−1.223† (0.709)	−2.651*** (0.284)	−4.083*** (0.979)	−2.707*** (0.321)	−4.046*** (1.097)	0.922*** (0.023)	0.917*** (0.084)
Wald χ^2	19.57***					79.91***	14.285**	41.30***		
F Score		90.44***	37.60***	67.14***	20.80***				49.83***	12.93***
(Pseudo) r^2	0.073	0.185	0.147	0.177	0.106	0.217	0.118	0.173	0.315	0.369
N	343	343	343	343	343	343	343	343	343	343

Note: Standard errors clustered on 124 belligerents.   *** $p < 0.001$ ** $p < 0.01$ * $p < 0.05$ † $p < 0.10$.

inequality is once again positively associated with the occurrence of all four battlefield problems and remains statistically significant at the $p = 0.001$ level. This relationship persists even after a battery of measures for alternative explanations and relevant controls are included. Military inequality is also associated with lower scores on the composite battlefield performance index. In fact, the decrease in performance on the BPI is even steeper in the modern era, suggesting that the lethality of modern weapons may be increasing the penalties associated with military inequality. In brief, there is considerable evidence that rising levels of military inequality are associated with a range of negative battlefield outcomes across the early modern and modern eras of conventional war.

While military inequality surmounted the hurdle of statistical significance, it still remains to be seen whether it has substantively important effects on battlefield performance. I therefore turn to figures and percentage changes to illustrate military inequality's effects on each aspect of battlefield performance across each historical era.[43]

Figure 4.2 plots a belligerent's predicted probability of a loss-exchange ratio below parity, the incidence of mass desertion and defection, and the deployment of blocking detachments for armies during the early modern and modern eras. For each battlefield problem, and for each historical era, we can clearly see the positive relationship at work: an increase in military inequality is associated with an increased probability that a belligerent's army will suffer from reduced combat power or cohesion. Loss-exchange ratios, for example, plummet as military inequality increases. At extreme levels of military inequality, it becomes a near certainty that the belligerent's army will suffer lopsided casualties in the early modern era. During the modern era, extreme levels of military inequality are associated with a 75 percent predicted probability that loss-exchange ratios will be unfavorable. The same holds true for mass desertion. Once a belligerent breaches a military inequality coefficient of 0.60, mass desertion appears almost unavoidable in the early modern era and only slightly less likely in the modern one. The odds of mass defection, too, skyrocket in the modern era, with about a 35 percent likelihood at a 0.40 military inequality coefficient but a nearly 60 percent likelihood once the belligerent reaches 0.60. Consistent with the results above, the modern era especially punishes belligerents with high inequality; the likelihood of experiencing mass desertion or defection top out at higher probabilities than during

---

43. I report percentage point estimates in the text without 95 percent confidence intervals for readability; these are plotted on the relevant figures.

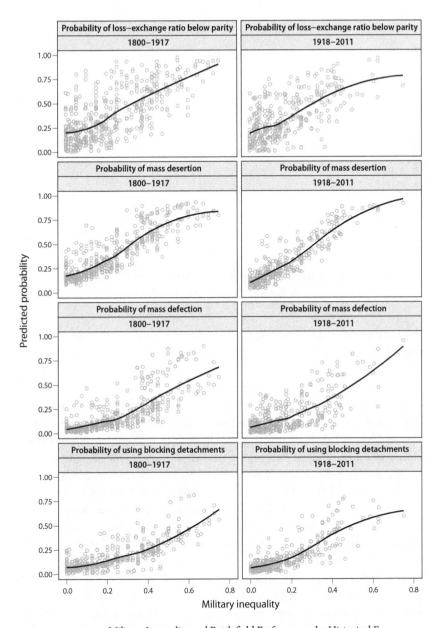

FIGURE 4.2. Military Inequality and Battlefield Performance by Historical Era

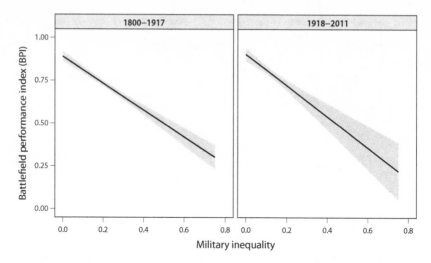

FIGURE 4.3. The Negative Relationship Between Military Inequality and the Battlefield
Performance Index by Historical Era

the early modern era. Relatedly, belligerents turn to blocking detachments at
lower levels of military inequality in the modern era, perhaps a tacit recognition of the greater probability of mass desertion and defection occurring
within their ranks.[44]

Figure 4.3 extends these statistical tests to the composite battlefield performance index. Once again, higher values of military inequality are associated with diminished performance across both eras. Highly inclusive armies
clearly attain the highest BPI values, though it bears emphasizing that these
belligerents do not necessarily obtain a perfect index score. Once belligerents
reach a threshold of 0.20 for military inequality, however, they have already
lost a mean of 0.25 from their BPI score, indicating that their armies experienced at least one of the four battlefield problems tracked by Project Mars.
By 0.40, the average BPI score has dropped to about 0.55, nearly halfway down
the BPI scale. Belligerents with a military inequality score of 0.70 have witnessed their mean performance fall precipitously to about 0.30 on the BPI
scale, a near-disastrous value. The penalties imposed by inequality are again
somewhat higher in the modern era, particularly for those belligerents toward
the more extreme end of the military inequality continuum. Compare, for
example, the mean BPI score for belligerents at a military inequality value
above 0.60 in the early modern and modern eras. These belligerents actually
dip below a predicted mean 0.25 BPI value in the modern era, denoting

44. All predicted probabilities generated using the full regression models outlined in
table 4.2 and table 4.3.

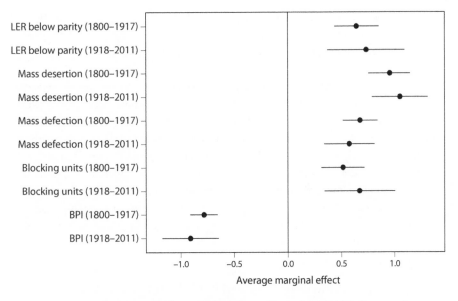

FIGURE 4.4. The Marginal Effects of Military Inequality on Battlefield Performance by Historical Era

a disastrous level of battlefield performance (narrowly) avoided by similar belligerents in the early modern era.

How substantively important is military inequality for explaining these outcomes? Figure 4.4 plots the average marginal effects and associated 95 percent confidence intervals of military inequality on each battlefield outcome for each historical era.[45] Average marginal effects can be interpreted as the predicted likelihood of an outcome given a one-unit change in the variable—here, a shift in military inequality from 0 to 1—while marginalizing over all other covariates. All reported estimates are substantively large, exceeding a 50 percentage point increase in every instance, and are statistically significant. In the early modern era, military inequality is associated with a 64.5 percentage point increase in the likelihood of suffering below-parity casualties; in the modern era, this estimate rises to a 73.6 percentage point increase. Military inequality's predicted effects on mass desertion are even larger, reaching staggering 95.4 and 105.4 percentage point increases in the early modern and modern eras, respectively. Mass defection also records large swings of 67.8 and 57.6 percentage point increases when shifting from perfect equality to perfect inequality in the early modern and modern periods. Blocking detachment deployment also proves sensitive to military inequality,

45. All average marginal effects are determined by a generalized linear model (GLM) using the full complement of measures for alternative explanations and controls.

registering 51.6 and 67.3 percentage point increases in the likelihood of their use during the early modern and modern eras, respectively. The BPI also reflects the negative effects of inequality. Average marginal effects of −0.783 and −0.909 are recorded for the early modern and modern eras, signifying that the shift from perfect equality to perfect inequality results in a near total collapse of battlefield performance for the average belligerent. A −0.783 decrease represents most of the BPI continuum, suggesting that belligerents with extreme inequality will have at least three of these four battlefield problems in the early modern era. The trend is even worse in the modern era; a −0.909 decrease translates into a performance near the bottom of the BPI scale in which almost all problems are present on average. In short, military inequality is not only statistically significant but also substantively important for explaining both individual and aggregate battlefield performance within each of these distinct historical eras.

4.4.   Ethnic Diversity and Battlefield Performance

Can these findings be explained simply by an army's ethnic diversity? Perhaps armies face increased transaction costs and coordination problems as more ethnic groups are represented in the ranks. Language barriers, incompatible ethnic preferences, and disagreement over policies may all increase with the number of ethnic groups under arms, conspiring to drag down an army's battlefield performance.

To test this claim, I reestimated the models above with a new variable, *ethnic groups*, that records the (logged) number of ethnic groups present in the army at the war's outset. Figure 4.5 plots the average marginal effects associated with ethnic groups. For the most part, the substantive effects of the number of ethnic groups are modest and, in several instances, indistinguishable from zero. A one-unit change in ethnic groups—that is, a shift from one to nineteen ethnic groups in the army—results in an 8.8 percentage point increase in the predicted likelihood of suffering a below-parity loss-exchange ratio in the early modern era, for example. The predicted likelihood falls to 6.4 percentage points in the modern era and fails to reach conventional levels of statistical significance. Ethnic groups' largest effects are found on mass desertion, where a one-unit change is associated with an 11.3 and 16.1 percentage point increase in the predicted likelihood that soldiers will abandon the fight and return home. A similarly massive shift in the number of ethnic groups fails to budge the predicted likelihood of mass defection in the early modern era, with only a statistically insignificant 2.6 percentage point increase. Ethnic groups is associated with a 12.7 percentage point increase in the modern era, however. The relationship between the number of ethnic

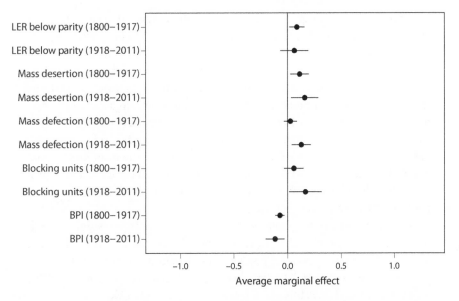

FIGURE 4.5. The Marginal Effects of Ethnic Diversity on Battlefield Performance by Historical Era.

groups and blocking detachments also fails to reach statistical significance in the early modern era; a 16.6 percentage point increase is noted in the modern era. Turning to a belligerent's BPI score, ethnic groups is associated with a slight −0.07 drop in the early modern era and a larger −0.12 decrease in the modern era. In short, the number of ethnic groups does appear to cause some friction, but the effect is dwarfed substantively by military inequality, which retains its expected direction and statistical significance at the $p \leq 0.001$ level or better for all regressions. The state's prewar treatment of ethnic groups, and their demographic weight within the army, are far more important for explaining battlefield outcomes than simply the number of ethnic groups within the ranks.[46]

4.5.   Climbing the Ladder of Inequality: Statistical Analysis Using Bands of Inequality

Due to variation in the quality and quantity of historical evidence across belligerents, there is an unavoidable element of uncertainty around point estimates of military inequality. To mitigate these issues, I employ a second measure, *bands of inequality*, that collapses the military inequality continuum

46. The correlation between military inequality and ethnic groups is quite modest at 0.24.

into four levels ("bands") with clear cutpoints: low (0–0.20), medium (0.21–0.40), high (0.41–0.60), and extreme (≥0.60).[47] This scaled variable helps soften measurement issues while permitting the identification of broad trends across different levels of inequality. It also has the advantage of capturing an intuitive understanding of military inequality as a series of gradations rather than a specific point estimate. In turn, bands sets up a threefold comparison of military inequality's effects when shifting from (1) low to medium bands; (2) medium to high bands; and (3) low to high bands. I use first differences to convey the substantive interpretation of the magnitude of the effects of these cross-band shifts, measured in percentage points, on the predicted likelihood that a given battlefield problem will manifest itself within a belligerent's army in each historical era.[48]

Replacing *military inequality* with *bands* and then reestimating the full models in table 4.2 and table 4.3 returns broader similar results as obtained above. All regressions yield a positive and statistically significant bands at $p \leq 0.001$ or better for each battlefield measure, including the composite BPI, for each era. What does this mean substantively for battlefield outcomes?

Beginning with loss-exchange ratios below parity, a shift from the low to medium band of inequality is associated with a 17.2 percentage point increase in the likelihood that a belligerent will suffer the brunt of casualties in the early modern era. A similar 17.6 percentage point increase is observed when shifting from the medium to high band of inequality. As a result, the shift from low to high levels of inequality is associated with a large 35 percentage point increase in the likelihood that a belligerent's loss-exchange ratio will be unfavorable (see figure 4.6(a)). For the modern era, a shift from the low to medium band of inequality is associated with a slightly smaller 14.1 percentage point increase that is surpassed by a 19.1 percentage point increase when moving from the medium to high band. Shifting from the low to high band is thus associated with a 33.2 percentage point increase in the predicted likelihood of lopsided casualties during the modern era.

---

47. In the following analysis, I combine extreme and high inequality belligerents into the same band due to the small number of belligerents with a military equality value of ≥0.60.

48. First differences were generated by *Clarify* using full models outlined in table 4.2 and table 4.3. All continuous variables except regime type and regime type*initiator were set at their mean to create meaningful values (Hanmer and Kalkan 2013). All dichotomous variables were set at median values; $K = 1000$ simulations were estimated (King, Tomz and Wittenberg 2000; Tomz, Wittenberg and King 2003). The baseline belligerent is a stable autocratic non-Great Power with half of the total fielded forces that possesses a permanent (i.e., standing) and non-volunteer army recruited through composite channels, and that is fighting about 400–450 kilometers from home in a non-civil war.

We find a similar pattern with mass desertion. In the early modern era, a shift from the low to medium band is associated with a 20.6 percentage point increase in the predicted likelihood of mass desertion. This climbs to a 23.2 percentage point increase when shifting from the medium to high band of inequality. Together, a move from the low to high band of inequality is associated with a 43.8 percentage point increase in the likelihood that mass desertion will plague a belligerent's army. The results are even larger for the modern era. Moving from the low to medium band of inequality is associated with a 26.7 percentage point increase; from the medium to high band, a whopping 30.6 percentage point increase. Holding all other variables at their mean, a shift from the low to high band of inequality is thus associated with a 57.3 percentage point increase in the predicted likelihood of mass desertion (see figure 4.6(b)).

The same trends hold true for mass defection, though the magnitude of the changes in predicted probability is smaller than observed for mass desertion. In the early modern era, a shift from the low to medium band of inequality is associated with a 10.8 percentage point increase in the predicted likelihood of mass defection, rising to 22.6 percentage points when moving from the medium to high band. All together, a shift from the low to high band of inequality is expected to increase the predicted likelihood of mass defection by 33.5 percentage points. This relationship attenuates sharply in the modern era, however. Moving from the low to medium band is associated with only a 4.3 percentage point increase, while the medium-to-high shift is predicted to increase the likelihood of mass defection by only 9.5 percentage points. Transitioning from the low to high band is therefore associated with a modest 13.8 percentage point increase (see figure 4.6(c)). These results confirm the earlier intuition that mass defection is harder to coordinate successfully than mass desertion, helping to explain its relatively infrequent nature in Project Mars data. Indeed, would-be defectors must not only escape from their own lines but successfully navigate surrender to enemy forces, a fraught endeavor.

Bands of inequality also shape the predicted likelihood of blocking detachments being fielded, albeit modestly. Beginning with the early modern era, a shift from the low to medium band of inequality is associated with an 8.1 percentage point increase, while a shift from the medium to high band of inequality is associated with another 13.3 percentage point increase. Moving from the low to high band of inequality is thus associated with a combined 21.4 percentage point increase in the predicted likelihood that blocking detachments will be ordered onto the battlefield. The magnitude of these expected probabilities jumps in the modern era. We observe a 10.2 percentage point increase when moving from the low band to medium; an 18.5 percentage point increase

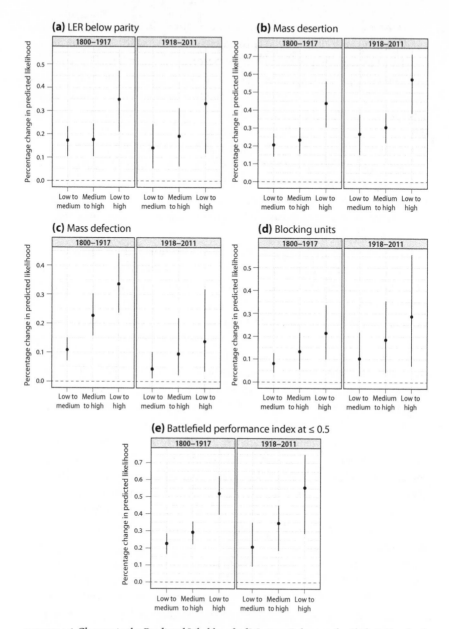

FIGURE 4.6. Changes in the Predicted Likelihood of Wartime Behaviors for Shifts in Bands of Military Inequality

when shifting from medium to high; and a 28.8 percentage point increase when moving from the low to high band of inequality (Figure 4.6(d)).

Finally, we can observe the effects of shifting bands on the aggregate battlefield performance index. Here I set the outcome of interest as the predicted likelihood that a belligerent will manage to score only a 0.50, the BPI's midpoint that denotes two of these four battlefield problems appeared in a belligerent's army. Starting with the early modern era, a shift from the low to medium band is associated with a 22.6 percentage point increase; from the medium to high band, a 29.3 percentage point increase; and a nearly 52 percentage point increase in the likelihood of a middling BPI score when moving from the low to high band. In the modern era, a shift from the low to medium band is associated with a 20.8 percentage point increase; a 34.7 percentage point increase when climbing from the medium to high band; and a massive 55.5 percentage point increase when moving from the low to high band of inequality. These are substantively very large effects. By comparison, sliding from a fully autocratic to fully democratic political regime, a truly enormous shift, is associated with only a paltry 7.7 percentage point increase in a belligerent's BPI score in the early modern era (and *Regime Type* does not reach statistical significance).

These findings collectively provide strong support for the claim that prewar military inequality sabotages a belligerent's subsequent battlefield performance. Both *Military Inequality* and *Bands* uncover the same relationship: rising levels of inequality are associated with the increased likelihood that each of these four problems will appear and that overall performance, as measured by the BPI, will correspondingly fall. These findings also confirm the trend initially noticed in the descriptive statistics: ethnic discrimination, best captured by the medium band of inequality, does exact a toll on battlefield performance. Ethnic marginalization is costly, jeopardizing a state's military fortunes even if collective violence is never wielded against these targeted populations. The expected stepwise pattern is also evident. Each new step up the rungs of the ladder of inequality is associated with a marked, in many cases neatly symmetrical, decrease in battlefield performance. The discontinuous jumps in the predicted probability of mass desertion and blocking detachment deployment in the modern era helps underscore how prewar violence can create incentives for targeted soldiers to escape and for commanders to turn to blocking detachments to force them to remain in place. Again, while low inequality belligerents are not entirely free of battlefield problems, their issues pale in comparison to belligerents that cluster at medium and (especially) high bands of inequality.

4.6. A Closer Look: Two-Control Group Comparison Using Matching

The convergence of findings using *military inequality* and *bands* is encouraging. Yet caution is warranted. It is possible that high inequality belligerents are systematically different than their medium or low inequality counterparts in ways that skew our conclusions about inequality's effects on battlefield performance. Perhaps these belligerents are far weaker or more autocratic than their more inclusive counterparts. If so, then these traits, rather than military inequality, might be driving observed differences on the battlefield. Moreover, if these imbalances are in fact present, then naive statistical analysis alone is likely insufficient to estimate the direction and magnitude of military inequality's effects. I therefore turn to matching to boost our confidence in the association between inequality and battlefield performance that was identified in the preceding analysis. Using a well-known approach called Coarsened Exact Matching, I constructed a balanced sample consisting of "treatment" and "control" belligerents that share similar attributes except for their prewar levels of military inequality. Here, "treatment" cases had high levels of inequality, while "controls" had either low or medium levels.[49] Belligerents with no match from the "control" pool are down-weighted or dropped from the analysis entirely. This procedure leaves behind a balanced sample in which differences in traits between treated and control cases are squeezed out, helping isolate the effects of military inequality.[50]

As an additional hurdle for my proposed argument, I check the robustness of prior findings by comparing high belligerents with two different control groups.[51] I first reestimate the full models in tables 4.2 and 4.3 using *Treatment*, which compares high belligerents to similar low inequality states (Control Group 1).[52] This comparison should illuminate the stark penalties associated with shifting from low to high inequality within the matched sample across all measures of battlefield performance.

I then reestimate the full models in tables 4.2 and 4.3 using medium inequality belligerents as the second control group. This comparison helps isolate the consequences of shifting from medium inequality, which most

---

49. I pool the small number of extreme inequality belligerents with those possessing high levels to create a single treatment group.

50. On matching, see Rubin 2006; Ho et al. 2007; Iacus, King and Porro 2012.

51. On two-control group comparisons, see Rosenbaum 2010, 332-39.

52. Specifically, I use CEM to adjust for imbalances across thirteen covariates from the full models in tables 4.2 and 4.3, with one exception. I swap regime type for the dichotomous democracy measure to facilitate matching; I also created a new interactive term for *Democratic Initiators*. All regressions use the CEM-generated weights.

belligerents achieve through some form of ethnic discrimination, and high inequality, a peak reached only by inflicting collective violence on targeted ethnic groups. We can also use this comparison to detect whether increasing the "dosage" of inequality at higher levels still erodes battlefield performance or, alternatively, if most of the causal action occurs in the comparison between low and high inequality belligerents (as represented as Control Group 1).

What, then, are the battlefield consequences of shifting from low to high inequality (Control Group 1), and from medium to high inequality (Control Group 2)? Figure 4.7 illustrates the average marginal effects that result from each of these comparisons for each battlefield measure across each historical era using only the matched data. Put simply, these results suggest that the average marginal effects of each shift are large and statistically significant across time and (nearly) all measures, indicating once again that military inequality is associated with decreased battlefield performance.

Take relative casualties, for example (figure 4.7(a)). We observe a large 33 percentage point increase in the likelihood that a belligerent will experience below-parity losses when moving from low to high inequality in the early modern era, holding all other variables at their mean. We observe another 15.5 percentage point increase in the same era when shifting from medium to high inequality, indicating that the shift from ethnic discrimination to collective violence imposes additional penalties. In the modern era, the low-to-high comparison is associated with a 27.1 percentage point increase in the likelihood of below-parity casualties, while a medium-to-high shift produces an additional 15.4 percentage point increase (though it dips slightly below conventional levels of statistical significance).

Mass desertion and other cohesion-related battlefield problems exhibit similar patterns. A shift to high from low inequality produces a 36.8 percentage point increase in the likelihood of mass desertion, while a shift from medium to high inequality creates another 20.5 percentage point increase (see figure 4.7(b)) in the pre-1918 era. The effects are even larger in the modern era: a comparison with Control Group 1 increases the likelihood of mass desertion by 46.2 percentage points, while Control Group 2 produces an additional 45.5 percentage point increase. Turning to mass defection, a shift from low inequality to high is associated with a 24.3 percentage point increase in the early modern era. A further 18.2 percentage point increase is associated with a jump from medium to high inequality in the same era. In the modern era, we observe smaller increases of 15.7 and 13.9 percentage points for Control Group 1 and 2 comparisons (figure 4.7(c)). Military inequality affects the likelihood of a belligerent using blocking detachments in similar fashion. Control Group 1 and 2 return near identical 15.5 and 13.3 percentage point increases in the odds of blocking detachments making a battlefield appearance in the

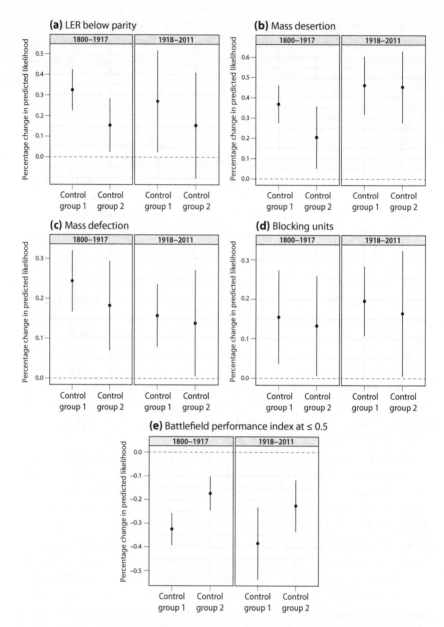

FIGURE 4.7. Average Marginal Effects of High Military Inequality Compared to Low (Control Group 1) and Medium (Control Group 2) Military Inequality Using Matching

early modern era, respectively. In the modern era, a shift from low to high is associated with a 19.6 percentage point increase, and from medium to high a further 16.4 percentage point increase (figure 4.7(d)). These same patterns hold in the aggregate battlefield performance index. In the early modern era, we observe downward shifts of −0.324 and −0.174 for Control Group 1 and 2 comparisons, respectively. In the modern era, the penalties are even more severe, with a −0.384 and a −0.226 decrease in BPI values for Control Group 1 and 2 (figure 4.7(e)), respectively.

In sum, the penalties levied against battlefield performance are highest with Control Group 1, where the disparity in military inequality is largest across belligerents. By contrast, the average marginal effects for Control Group 2 are typically reduced, as befitting the smaller difference in levels of prewar military inequality. Yet penalties still accrue when climbing from medium to high levels of military inequality. While ethnic discrimination imposes battlefield costs, the state's use of collective violence against its own citizens represents an additional distinct tax on its battlefield fortunes. This second set of analyses should be doubly reassuring: we not only recover the same basic relationship within the matched sample as we do the broader Project Mars dataset, but it survives the use of multiple comparison groups, indicating that we have correctly identified a durable empirical pattern.

4.7. Robustness Checks

This chapter has presented a raft of new data and findings. It is only natural to wonder, however, how robust these findings are to alternative model specifications and measurement strategies. While a full accounting can be found in the book's online appendix, I briefly discuss some of the most important robustness checks here. Drawing on the full models in table 4.2 and table 4.3 as benchmarks, a partial list of supplemental analyses includes: (1) reestimating all models with alternative measures for material preponderance, regime type, and military organization; (2) including fixed effects for decades, regions, specific belligerents, and multi-campaign wars;[53] (3) dropping all wars in which belligerents substituted air or naval power for ground forces, minimizing their exposure to casualties and opportunities for mass desertion and defection;[54] (4) reestimating all models with indicator variables for the confidence

53. Belligerents include the Ottoman Empire, United Kingdom, France, USA, Russia, and Germany. Multi-campaign wars include the Napoleonic Wars, World War I, and World War II.

54. Ten wars in total fit these criteria, including the 1999 Kosovo War and the 2001 Afghan War as well as older cases like the Netherlands during the Bombardment of Algiers (1816).

of our judgment in data quality for all battlefield performance measures; (5) sensitivity analysis using different thresholds (5 percent, 20 percent) for defining mass desertion and defection; and (6) replacing the binary variables for below-parity casualties, mass desertion, and mass defection, with mean estimates of their actual values. In all cases, military inequality retained its statistical significance and substantive importance.

Two robustness checks deserve special mention here. First, I conducted a placebo test in which, as a mad scientist of sorts, I randomly assigned new military inequality coefficients to belligerents for all 825 observations. Doing so permits investigation of whether we have correctly identified an association between inequality and battlefield outcomes or, alternatively, we have accidentally captured a spurious relationship due to some hidden process in the data. If an association is truly present, then military inequality should no longer be statistically significant once these new randomly generated values have replaced the original ones. Indeed, this is exactly what happens; military inequality loses statistical significance in nearly every model in table 4.2 and table 4.3, confirming that we have identified a genuine association at work.

Second, perhaps these findings are simply an artifact of the more expansive list of wars and belligerents of Project Mars. Nearly all existing quantitative work draws on the venerable, if smaller, Correlates of War data universe, and so what is needed is a direct examination of military inequality's effects within this more restrictive set of cases. I therefore reestimated the models in tables 4.2 and 4.3 twice, first using only COW-approved belligerents and then drawing only on COW-approved wars. This latter test is especially severe since it discards nearly two-thirds of the (hard-won) Project Mars dataset. In the COW-only belligerent analysis, military inequality remains statistically significant at $p \leq 0.002$ in every single model. Using COW's latest Version 4.0,[55] military inequality remains statistically significant at $p \leq= 0.01$ level in eight of ten models for both historical eras using only COW-approved wars. Only mass defection proves somewhat problematic: military inequality remains statistically significant at the $p \leq 0.05$ level for the early modern era but narrowly misses conventional levels of significance for the modern era. While Project Mars thus provides a more expansive view of conventional wars and their participants, the book's findings can nonetheless be replicated within the dominant COW universe, boosting our confidence in the robustness and generalizability of the relationship between military inequality and battlefield success.

55. Correlates of War 2010.

4.8.   Assessing Alternative Explanations

The quantitative evidence marshaled by Project Mars unfortunately provides little support for leading alternative explanations. Material preponderance and regime type explanations in particular struggle to account for individual measures of battlefield performance and the combined BPI. Moreover, the decision to split the sample into two historical eras exposed inconsistencies in these arguments. It is commonplace, for example, to find that these variables are significant in one time period but not another, or that the direction of the proposed relationship in the early modern era reverses course once we move into the modern era.

Perhaps most surprising is how regime type appears largely irrelevant for explaining battlefield performance. A belligerent's prewar Polity2 scores, the standard measure for regime type, are almost never statistically significant, and the relationship between this variable and certain outcomes often changes direction depending on the historical era. The only time regime type reaches statistical significance is in the early modern era, when a shift from a full authoritarian to full democratic regime is associated with a 23.8 percentage point reduction in the likelihood that a belligerent's army will suffer below-parity casualties. Democracy, a binary variable capturing whether a belligerent had a prewar Polity2 score of ≥ 7, fares somewhat better when replacing regime type in these models. It is associated with a modest 7.8 percentage point reduction in the likelihood of a belligerent fielding blocking detachments and with a 6.8 percentage point increase in the composite BPI in the modern era. But it never reaches statistical significance for any other measure. Facing a democratic opponent is also associated with a 25.2 percentage point jump in the likelihood of suffering below-parity casualties in the early modern era and a similar 22.2 percentage point increase in the modern era. The notion that democracies can induce desertion and defection by credibly promising to treat enemy soldiers well given their commitment to human rights norms is not supported by these data, however.[56] Democratic opponent is not associated with an increased likelihood of mass desertion or defection, and belligerents appear no more likely to resort to blocking detachments to ward off the siren song of democracies. Finally, I find no evidence that democratic initiators are superior at any aspect of war-fighting in either era than their autocratic adversaries.[57]

56. See, for example, Wallace 2012; Reiter and Stam 2002, 79.

57. Democratic initiators are captured by the combined weight of regime type, initiator, and the interactive regime type*initiator term.

Standard indicators of material preponderance and local force ratios also fare poorly. Relative forces is only statistically significant once, where a preponderance of force is actually associated with an increase in the likelihood of suffering below-parity casualties. Shifting from the 25th to 75th percentile of initially deployed forces—imagine a belligerent army moving from being outnumbered 2:1 to outnumbering its opponent 2:1—results in a 16.6 percentage point increase in the odds of experiencing a poor loss-exchange ratio in the early modern era. Taken together, these non-findings confirm skepticism about both the importance of troop strength and of seeking decisive outcomes in the war's first battle through numerical preponderance.[58] Even Great Power status appears to have little connection to battlefield performance; great power is only significant in a single regression, where Great Power status reduces the likelihood of below-parity casualties by 9.3 percentage points in the early modern era. Casualties are, however, somewhat sensitive to how far a belligerent is fighting from its capital city. A 15 percentage point reduction in the likelihood of below-parity casualties is observed when shifting distance from the 10th to 90th percentile (roughly from 50 to 8,200 kilometers from the capital) in the early modern era. The same shift results in a modest 7.8 percentage point decrease in the modern era. If we treat distance from the capital as a proxy for power projection, then casualties do appear at least partly driven by material power. But cohesion problems appear divorced from a belligerent's power capabilities, with none of these measures ever shifting the probability of desertion, defection, or blocking detachments.[59]

New data leads to new insights, however. The traits of military organizations, often neglected in existing theories, emerge as important drivers of battlefield performance. Standing armies, for example, are associated with a 5.3 percentage point decrease in the likelihood of defection in the post-1917 era. These armies are also 15.7 percentage points less likely to deploy blocking detachments in the early modern era. These findings aside, non-standing armies largely hold their own with permanent standing forces, though with so few examples in the modern era we must take care to avoid sweeping generalizations. Composite armies, identified by their multiple recruitment streams, are associated with a small 3.8 percentage point increased likelihood of mass defection in the modern era, but are otherwise not especially vulnerable (or robust) compared to single-stream recruitment. Surprisingly, the

---

58. Nolan 2017.

59. *Non-COW belligerent* also jitters unpredictably across different battlefield measures and eras, rarely reaching conventional levels of statistical significance. These results are therefore not driven by the presumed relative weakness of the new belligerents added to Project Mars.

vaunted advantages of volunteer armies are not apparent in these data. *Volunteer* is only associated with a 6.2 percentage point reduction in the likelihood of using blocking detachments, and only for the early modern era. *War birth*, which denotes that a state was fighting and state-building simultaneously, also has only a weak relationship with these battlefield measures. These states sometimes have a greater likelihood of mass desertion and defection, but the results are sensitive to modeling choices and often inconsistent across eras. The only consistent finding is that war birth is positively associated with a 15.4 percentage point increase in the likelihood of blocking detachment use in the modern era.

One of the most powerful alternative explanations for battlefield performance lies in the political context of the war itself. Civil war is associated with a sharp 21.8 percentage point rise in the predicted likelihood of observing mass desertion in the early modern era. Compared with classical interstate war, civil wars also observe a greater probability of mass defection from belligerent armies. In the early modern era, civil war is associated with a 12.3 percentage point increase in the likelihood of mass defection, falling to an 8.4 percentage point increase in the modern era. As a result, the mean BPI score for belligerents enmeshed in civil wars is lower than belligerents fighting traditional interstate wars in both historical eras. Once again we observe the power of military inequality, which remains consistent in magnitude and statistical significance across both empirical domains.[60] While civil wars increase the risk of cohesion and discipline problems within armies, the proposed military inequality argument offers a unified account that bridges these two domains that have been studied in isolation for too long.

4.9. Conclusion

These statistical tests provide substantial evidence of the association between rising military inequality and declining battlefield performance. Both *Military inequality* and *Bands* remain statistically significant and substantively important across all four measures of battlefield performance as well as the combined BPI. Each new step up the ladder of inequality is associated with an increased likelihood of lopsided casualties, the outbreak of mass desertion and defection, and the fielding of blocking detachments designed to coerce soldiers into fighting. These results also hold across a difficult two-control group comparison test as well as a phalanx of robustness checks and

---

60. In a supplemental analysis, I split Project Mars into two samples (civil war and non-civil war) and reestimated all models. Military inequality remained statistically significant and substantively important in both samples.

alternative specifications. Together, the chapter has assembled a formidable set of challenges for the military inequality argument. Yet it remains the only explanation capable of explaining both individual battlefield outcomes and the overall pattern of performance across two different historical eras. Leading alternative explanations, including those emphasizing material power and regime type, struggle to stitch together compelling narratives for a single measure of performance, let alone the entire pattern. What these tests cannot do, however, is trace the causal processes linking military inequality through the proposed mechanisms to subsequent battlefield conduct. Nor can they capture the trade-offs between combat power and cohesion that commanders face once they field divided armies. As a result, we must turn to our paired historical comparisons for close-range investigation, a task I begin in the next chapter.

PART II

To the Battlefield

HISTORICAL EVIDENCE

5

Inequality and Early Modern War

THE CASES OF MOROCCO AND KOKAND

Men, form squares, and let the music play.

FREDERICK HARDMAN, *THE SPANISH CAMPAIGN*

IN MOROCCO, 1860

HOW DOES INEQUALITY affect battlefield performance? To answer this question, I compare two belligerents, the Sultanate of Morocco and the Khanate of Kokand, that possessed remarkably similar traits but had sharply different levels of military inequality. Drawn at random from the larger Project Mars universe of cases, these states had similar political systems, fielded armies with comparable technologies, and confronted European powers bent on imperialism, among other similarities. Their levels of prewar inequality, however, represent nearly opposite ends of the military inequality coefficient. Morocco's inclusive vision of its political community, coupled with the absence of state-sanctioned collective punishment along ethnic lines, led its army to have a near perfect equality score (0.01). Kokand's leader, 'Alimqul, chose a different path. Emerging victorious from a brutal civil war that violently overturned the existing ethnic and tribal hierarchy, he imposed a narrow ethnocratic vision that was propped up through violence against targeted ethnic groups and tribes. As a result, Kokand's prewar military inequality hovered near 0.70, one of the highest values recorded in Project Mars. The dramatic shift from low to extreme inequality renders the causal effects of inequality on battlefield performance highly visible, facilitating process tracing across (and within) these two belligerent's wartime experiences during the Hispano-Moroccan (1859–60) and Kokand-Russia (1864–65) Wars.[1]

1. A note on terminology. I use "Kokand" rather than "Khoqand" or "Khokand" as this is the most common spelling since 1940 according to Google's Ngram Viewer. The Hispano-Moroccan War has also been variously termed the First Spanish-Moroccan War and the

Given the magnitude of their differences in inequality, we should observe dramatic differences in the battlefield performance of these two belligerents. This is indeed what we find. Morocco turned in a surprisingly credible performance, fielding disciplined forces that inflicted significant losses on the Spanish Army while experiencing little desertion or defection. Kokand, by contrast, recorded one of the worst performances found in Project Mars. Its soldiers deserted and defected in droves, forcing commanders to sacrifice combat power to maintain cohesion by adopting rigid tactics, harsh discipline, and conservative operations that further increased the butcher's bill of casualties.[2] What's especially puzzling about this divergence is the fact that Kokand, not Morocco, held the more favorable position. Facing a small Russian expeditionary force, Kokand enjoyed a 15:1 advantage in soldiers, possessed more artillery of higher quality, and had decades of experience fighting Russian encroachment. By war's end, though, 'Alimqul lay dead and nearly half of Kokand's Western Europe-sized territory was folded into the Russian empire. For its part, Morocco inflicted enough damage on Spain's Africa Army to curb its territorial ambitions, postponing Morocco's slide into colonial possession.

Since little English-language historiography exists for either war, I draw on Spanish, French, and Russian documents to explore how inequality affects battlefield performance.[3] These materials are eclectic and include official commanders' assessments, campaign memoirs, accounts by embedded journalists, unit histories, recorded oral histories, and even captured diplomatic correspondence. I marshal this evidence not with the intent of providing an exhaustive history of each war. Instead, I aim to construct a narrative for each belligerent that demonstrates how inclusion and inequality drive wartime behavior by commanders and soldiers alike. I therefore draw on multiple battles and skirmishes within each war to increase our confidence that the proposed causal pathway between inequality and reduced performance is actually present. Similarly, I highlight how Kokand's extreme inequality soured soldier morale, undercut interethnic trust, and forced its commanders to make wartime trade-offs between combat power and cohesion in an increasingly desperate bid to hold its fractious army together.

Africa War (*La Guerra de África*). The Kokand-Russia War has also been described as the Russian-Kokand War, Russo-Kokand War, and the "Fall of Tashkent."

2. More formally, Morocco scored a 0.75 on the quantitative battlefield performance index. By contrast, Kokand's performance was dismal; its 0.25 value denotes the presence of three of four battlefield pathologies tracked by the index.

3. On the limits of each case's historiography and the opportunities that await additional primary language research, see Barranco 2006; Morrison 2014*a* and Hamedi 2010.

Though random selection of cases has notable advantages, it does run the risk of choosing wars that are unfamiliar to most readers. In recognition of this drawback, the chapter first sets these belligerents and their wars in context. Drawing on the comparative framework established in chapter 3, the chapter then details why Morocco and Kokand can be viewed as similar belligerents across twenty-eight different dimensions. This section also illustrates the nature of each belligerent's prewar political community and associated notions of citizenship and military service. The bulk of the chapter is devoted to constructing narratives for assessing first Morocco's and then Kokand's combat power and cohesion. In each case, the framework provides a sweeping view of battlefield performance before narrowing its scope to focus on illustrative battles—the Battles of Tetuán (4–6 February 1860) and Tashkent (15–17 June 1865)—to highlight military inequality's effects at close range.[4] These cases also generate insights about the limits of inclusion in Morocco and how credible commitment problems prevented 'Alimqul from recasting Kokand's norms of citizenship to unlock increased battlefield performance. The chapter concludes with a discussion of two alternative explanations not eliminated by the matched comparative design.

5.1.   Context

Sandwiched between the Crimean and Austro-Prussian Wars, the Hispano-Moroccan and Russo-Kokandian Wars exhibited many of the traits of the early modern era of combined arms. Both wars witnessed armies struggling to field and coordinate cavalry, infantry, and artillery units together on increasingly lethal battlefields that created new command and control difficulties even as they demanded greater decentralization of initiative. Despite involving non-European states, battles in these wars were marked by direct combat designed to obtain the decisive annihilation of an adversary's deployed forces.[5] Combat, in other words, was not a low-casualty affair waged for symbolic or ritualistic gains, a common feature of so-called primitive war.[6] Battles were often short-lived affairs, measured in days, sometimes a single morning, rather than weeks or months. Fronts, too, were constrained, with distances measured in handfuls, rather than dozens or hundreds, of kilometers. Clashes typically revolved around a key strategic objective, usually a walled city, and

---

4. These battles share similar attributes: (1) Morocco and Kokand were both on the defensive; (2) both had excellent fortifications; (3) they both were fought late in the war; (4) both were among the largest battles of each war; and (5) both had similar duration.

5. Nolan 2017, 12.

6. Turney-High 1942; Black 2004, 67–68.

usually involved 50–60,000 soldiers in a given engagement. Recognition, too, was growing that linear tactics, including the use of "square" formations by Spain and Russia, were becoming outmoded in the face of Moroccan and Kokandian flexibility and firepower. Both Kokand and Morocco fielded excellent field cannons, erected complex defenses that included multiple trenches and walled fortifications, and, in Kokand's case, even had repeating rifles on par with Russian firearms. Logistical concerns also intruded on warmaking; Russia faced enormous distances when resupplying its expeditionary force,[7] while Spain's campaign was weighed down by mountainous terrain and poor roads.[8] In short, these belligerents strove to maximize their battlefield performance—within self-imposed constraints—by harnessing the dictates of early combined arms doctrine to destroy their enemies in direct combat.

5.1.1.   The Hispano-Moroccan War

There was little to suggest that the destruction of a Castilian sigil outside Ceuta, a Spanish enclave on Morocco's Mediterranean coast, by Riffian tribesman would ignite a war. Indeed, the Sultan's official response was one of surprise and disbelief that Spain had "declared war without a cause."[9] The 10 August 1859 attack had, after all, been preceded by decades of pinprick hit-and-run attacks—more nuisance than threat—by Moroccan tribesmen acting independently of the Sultan's authority. Yet this time was different. Prime Minister Leopoldo O'Donnell, seeking to boost his flagging political fortunes by military victory, declared war on 22 October. As one contemporary in Madrid wrote, "Why war? To strengthen us abroad and to unite us at home. If the public mind could be thoroughly engaged with an object of absorbing interest abroad, it would tend greatly to a cessation of the bitter party dissensions at home."[10] O'Donnell, who took personal command of the Army of Africa (*Ejército de África*), ordered the Spanish navy to block Moroccan ports. The Army of Africa assembled in Spain before slowly making its way across the Mediterranean to disembark in multiple waves at Ceuta and nearby (see figure 5.1). The initial force of 8,000 soldiers reached 54,000 by mid-December, along with 3,000 horses, 60 field and mountain cannons

7. Morrison 2014*b*.

8. Mordacq 1900, 8–9.

9. "Circular of Mohamed el Katib to Foreign Representatives at Tangier, and His Correspondence with the Spanish Charge D'Affaires," 25 October 1859, reproduced in *War By Spain on Morocco: Copies of Official Correspondence* 1860, 5.

10. Ross 1860, 25–26. See also Lécuyer and Serrano 1976, 15–17.

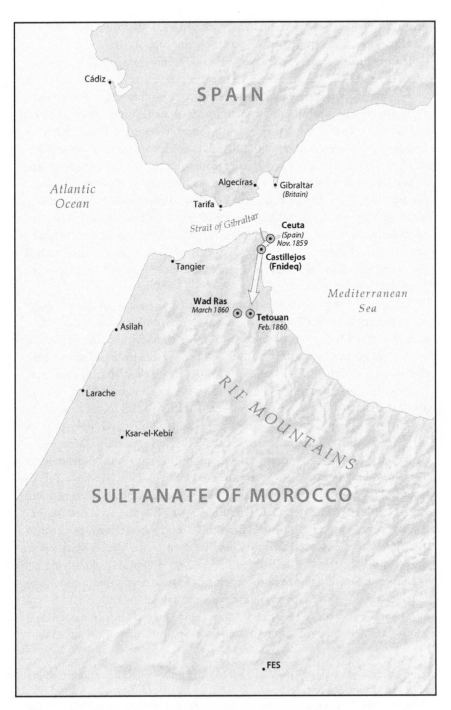

FIGURE 5.1. The Hispano-Moroccan War, 1859–60

of various caliber, and 20 million rifle cartridges.[11] Warships patrolled the coastline, standing ready to provide offshore fire support.

During the war's first phase (November–December), Spanish forces hunkered down at Ceuta, content to fortify their defenses and build roads for an eventual assault on Tetuán, one of Morocco's leading cities. For his part, the Sultan began mustering Moroccan forces, drawing on tribal levies to fill his ranks. Only four days after Spanish forces had disembarked, the war's first armed clash took place at the Serrallo, as Moroccan forces engaged in small probing attacks designed to bait Spanish forces into the open. Four separate Moroccan offensives were launched in November; another eight were conducted in December, all aimed at derailing Spanish road-building efforts while inflicting casualties. These engagements were becoming increasingly costly; on 9 December, Morocco fielded 10,000 soldiers, managing to tally 404 Spanish casualties in a single engagement. By mid-December, Morocco had 50–55,000 men under arms and had managed to slow, but not halt completely, Spanish road construction.[12]

After nearly two months of sitting at Ceuta, the Army of Africa finally made its move toward Tetuán, advancing twenty-one miles in sixteen days to arrive at the valley of Los Castillejos. On 1 January 1860, the Moroccan army crashed into Spanish formations at Los Castillejos in a bid to block the advance to Tetuán. They failed to do so, though Spanish casualties were high, with at least 620 killed and wounded. A second effort to bar the road also fell short at Cabo Negro (14 January). With Spanish forces now at the outskirts of Tetuán, Moroccan forces under Mulay Abbas and Mulay Ahmet launched a major counteroffensive at Guad-el-Gelu (31 January). Momentarily stopped, O'Donnell's forces, despite mounting casualties, moved on to Tetuán, seeking to annihilate Morocco's forces and end the war. On 4 February, the Army of Africa clashed with at least 25,000 Moroccan soldiers in the largest battle to date. After pitched fighting, Spanish forces breached Moroccan trenches, scattering Mulay Abbas's and Mulay Ahmet's armies. Spanish casualties numbered at least 1,108, but the path to Tetuán now lay open. Stripped of its defenses, Tetuán surrendered on 6 February. Surveying his options, the Sultan authorized the opening of peace negotiations, though as much as a stalling action as a genuine expression of interest.

The war's final phase (February–March 1860) kicked off with a surprising Moroccan drubbing of an outnumbered Spanish formation at Melilla

---

11. Mordacq 1900, 51–53. Neither Spain nor Morocco fielded armies larger than 35,000 in a single engagement, however.

12. The best chronologies of the war are found in del Rey 2001, 163–78, and Joly 1910. The war consisted of at least five major battles (Ceuta, Los Castillejos, Guad-el-Gelu, Tetuán, and Guad-el-Ras) and twenty-three smaller armed engagements.

(9 February). Seeking to improve his bargaining position, if not defeat the Spanish outright, the Sultan's commanders launched a series of counterattacks at Samsa (11 March) and Wad Ras (23 March) that inflicted significant casualties. At Guad-el-Ras, for example, Spanish killed and wounded amounted to at least 1,268 soldiers, one of the bloodiest battles in the Spanish Army's post-Napoleonic wars. With both sides battered, an armistice was struck on 25 March. The Treaty of Guad-el-Ras (26 April 1860) officially ended the war, with modest territorial concessions granted to Spain around Ceuta and Melilla. Morocco was also forced to pay a 20 million ducat indemnity (about $4 million in 1861 US dollars); Tetuán was to remain occupied until this charge was fully paid. These terms were far from onerous, thanks in part to the United Kingdom, which exerted diplomatic pressure on Spain and floated a loan to Morocco to speed payment of the indemnity.[13] Spain evacuated Tetuán on 2 May 1862, quietly ceding its most notable battlefield gain. Morocco had blunted Spanish encroachment through force of arms and remained an independent, if somewhat diminished, state until 1912.

5.1.2.   The Kokand-Russia War, 1864–65

Set against the backdrop of Russia's broader campaign to conquer, and eventually absorb, the khanates of Central Asia, the 1864–65 war against Kokand marked Russia's deepest penetration of the steppe region to date.[14] Historians have variously ascribed Russian motives for initiating the war to geopolitical rivalry with the United Kingdom (the "Great Game");[15] a desire for a clearly demarcated and secure frontier;[16] economic imperialism and the drive for open agricultural lands, especially for cotton, a particular fixation of Soviet-era scholarship;[17] and the unplanned but unavoidable drive for glory among various "prancing proconsuls" who took advantage of St. Petersburg's distance to disregard official guidance and carve out their own fortunes.[18] St. Petersburg, hoping to curb Kokand's raiding of trade caravans, initially

13. Long-standing concern that Spanish gains might compromise freedom of navigation of the Straits of Gibraltar sparked British action. See "Mr. Buchanon to Señor Collantes," Diplomatic missive, Madrid, 21 October 1859, in *War By Spain on Morocco: Copies of Official Correspondence* 1860, 39.

14. For overviews of Russian colonial expansion in Central Asia, see Skrine and Ross 1889; Terent'ev 1906; Palat 1988; Sergeev 2012. On the (surprisingly thin) nature of historiography surrounding Russia's conquest of Central Asia, see Morrison 2014a.

15. Sergeev 2012; Ledonne 1997; Yapp 1980; Zagorodnikova 2005.

16. Morrison 2014b.

17. Khalfin 1960, 1974; Beckert 2004; Geyer 1987.

18. MacKenzie 1969, 1974; Marshall 2006; Miliutin 2003, 518–22.

authorized the capture of several forts in Kokand's northern defensive line along the Syr Dar'ia River in 1862 and again in 1863 (see figure 5.2).

Dissatisfied with these results, an expeditionary force under Major-General (then Colonel) M. G. Cherniaev was dispatched to Aulie-Alta (today's Alma Ata in Kazakhstan) from Vernyi in late April 1864. The force was deliberately small, consisting of about 2,500 soldiers, several mounted *sotni* of Cossacks, 12 field cannons, and 4,000 camels. Cost was a major concern; St. Petersburg wanted the campaign conducted on a shoestring budget, forcing Cherniaev to plead constantly for additional funds.[19] A second, even smaller, force commanded by Colonel N. A. Verevkin was subsequently sent eastward from the Syr Dar'ia line. About 4,000 Russian soldiers were now in the field, though not yet under joint command. In a persistent theme of the war, vastly outnumbered Russian forces would repeatedly engage a 50–60,000-strong Kokand army that sometimes fielded 30,000 in a single battle. Six major battles, and at least a dozen smaller engagements, would be fought over the war's first and second phases.[20]

The war's opening phase began on 4 June with Cherniaev's bombardment of Kokand's fortress at Aulie-Alta. The fortress fell quickly, with at least 300 Kokandian soldiers killed; only three Russians were wounded. On 12 June, Turkistan, a major fortified city, fell to Verevkin's forces. The two ambitious commanders promptly constructed a unified system of fortifications (the "New Kokand Line"), though personal enmity continued to rage between them. The fortified city of Chimkent lay astride this new line, however, threatening Russian lines of communication. 'Alimqul chose to make a stand here, and on 13 July, a Kokandian force at least 10,000- strong badly savaged a small reconnaissance party sent by Verevkin to scout routes to Chimkent. Capitalizing on this blunder, Cherniaev cajoled St. Petersburg into appointing him overall commander of the war effort, a position he assumed in August. 'Alimqul continued to defend Chimkent, though an opportunistic invasion by neighboring Bukhara compelled him to lead some of his army away to meet this new threat. On 12 September, Russian forces successfully breached Chimkent's defenses—Cherniaev himself led his soldiers through a narrow sewer pipe to invest its citadel—and occupied the city. Cherniaev now set his gaze on the real prize, Tashkent. His bid to outrace the onset of winter was

---

19. See, for example, "Zapiska gen.-m. Meshcherinova; 29 Sentiabria 1864" and "Voennyi ministr' gen.-gubernatoru Zap. Sibiri; 30 Sentiabria 1864 № 151. (Telegramma)" in Serebrennikov 1914*a*, 116–117.

20. The major battles occurred at Aulie-Alta, Turkistan, Chimkent, Tashkent, Niiazbek, and Tashkent again. This chronology draws on Terent'ev 1906; MacKenzie 1974; Tashkandi 2003; Bobozhonov 2010.

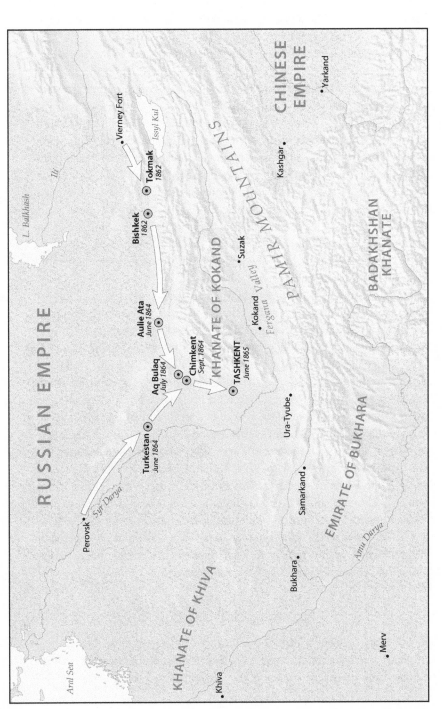

FIGURE 5.2. The Kokand-Russia War, 1864–65

clumsy, however, and he was forced to withdraw after an ill-fated offensive on the city (1 October) met with unexpected resistance.

After a lengthy winter pause at Chimkent, one marked by "terrible boredom from inaction,"[21] Cherniaev ordered his expedition to advance on Tashkent in early May 1865. With only 1,300 soldiers and 12 cannons, he captured Niiazbek, a key fortress that guarded both the southern approach to Tashkent and, crucially, its grain and water supplies. Anticipating a long siege of Tashkent, Cherniaev's forces diverted the Chirchik River, seeking to starve out the Tashkent garrison. Russian reconnaissance operations began probing for the Kokand army, hoping to land a decisive blow. The loss of two additional forts guarding Tashkent convinced 'Alimqul of the need to crush Russian forces. On 9 May, 'Alimqul led at least 6,000 soldiers, plus cavalry and 40 field cannons, in an offensive against the Russian encampment about six kilometers from Tashkent. Yet disaster struck: 'Alimqul was killed by a Russian bullet, but not before he witnessed the bedraggled remnants of his infantry break ranks and flee toward Tashkent.

Kokand's denouement drew near. Russian forces invested Tashkent on three sides; prisoners confirmed that the garrison, and the broader populace, was both starving and pro-Russian. On 9 June, a small Bukharan detachment slipped into Tashkent, taking control of its defenses; that night, Kokand's young khan and his retinue secretly left Tashkent, becoming Bukharan hostages. With only 1,951 soldiers, Cherniaev launched a night attack on Tashkent and its 30,000-strong garrison on 14–15 June. Drawing most of the garrison off with a feint against the Kokand Gate, Cherniaev's vanguard threw scaling ladders against Tashkent's walls near the Kamelan Gate, on the opposite side of the city. Once over the wall, they killed the few sentries still awake and opened the Kamelan Gate. Kokand's army essentially dissolved, defeated both in the field near the Kokand Gate and in bitter fighting within Tashkent's labyrinthian streets. On 17 June, Tashkent surrendered. Nearly half of Kokand's enormous territory had been lost in just over a year. Tashkent was formally annexed by Russia in 1866. A twilight Kokand itself lingered on until 1876 when, after a short war, it too slipped completely under Russian domination, ending its existence as a sovereign state.

5.2.   Empirical Strategy

The Sultanate of Morocco and the Khanate of Kokand admittedly appear, at first glance, to make for strange bedfellows. A closer look, however, reveals startling similarities across many of the factors invoked to explain battlefield

21. Khalfin 1965, 192.

performance. Drawing on the template established in chapter 3, the sections below detail this comparison (summarized in table 5.1). I begin by describing each belligerent's collective identity and military demographics before turning to matched and contextual covariates. While all belligerents (and wars) have unique properties, the closeness of fit across these twenty-eight variables helps isolate the effects of military inequality by screening out alternative accounts.

5.2.1.   Political Community and Military Inequality

On the eve of the Hispano-Moroccan War, Morocco was a theocratic monarchy with a markedly diverse population and a nearly four hundred year history.[22] Tribal groupings, along with multiple Sufi and Sunni orders, offered would-be challengers the normative raw material to foster collective action against a relatively weak state (known as the *Makhzan*). Yet the ruling Alaouite dynasty had successfully articulated an inclusionary "mosaic" vision of the political community that avoided feeding group-based distinctions and tensions. More specifically, the Makhzan crafted its "moral armory"[23] from three shared precepts.

First, the Alaouite family, along with Sidi Mohammad IV, Morocco's Sultan during the war, traced its lineage back to Mohammad, thereby claiming for itself a divine right of rule. This religious sanctioning of the Sultan's authority was buttressed by a second precept: the promulgation of Sharia law as the basis for community membership. Third, the regime justified its rule in terms of its ability to wage jihad against foreign invaders and lawless bandits, including Mediterranean pirates that preyed on coastal shipping. In this communal vision, both the ruler and ruled had a shared duty to protect Morocco and, by extension, Islam itself, creating a strong bond that transcended narrower tribal allegiances. Religion, along with periodic calls for jihad, provided a cross-cutting platform for regime legitimacy that could coexist, rather than supplant, existing identities while avoiding the social conflict that often attends the elevation of one group over another.[24]

The Makhzan also institutionalized this commitment to neutralizing group-based conflict. The Sultan could draw upon a sophisticated system of interlocking patronage appointments that balanced representation and economic benefits across tribes.[25] Tribal leaders typically handed over a portion of the taxes they collected and provided levies in times of war; in exchange,

22. Sahar 2010, 26.

23. Bennison 2002, 161.

24. Bennison 2002, 159–62.

25. Pennell 2000, 37.

TABLE 5.1. Matched Pair: Morocco and Kokand Compared

Covariates	Sultanate of Morocco *Spanish-Moroccan War, 1859–60*	Khanate of Kokand *War with Russia, 1864–65*
Military Inequality (Coefficient)	Low (0.01)	Extreme (0.70)
From Matching		
Initial relative power	66%	66%
Total fielded force	55,000	50,000
Regime type	Absolutist Monarchy (−6)	Absolute Monarchy (−7)
Distance from capital	208km	265km
Standing army	Yes	Yes
Composite military	Yes	Yes
Initiator	No	No
Joiner	No	No
Democratic opponent	No	No
Great Power	No	No
Civil war	No	No
Non-COW	No[a]	Yes
Early modern	Yes	Yes
Contextual Covariates		
Combined arms	Yes	Yes
Doctrine	Offensive	Offensive
Superior weapons	No	No
Fortifications	Yes	Yes
Foreign advisors	Yes	Yes
Terrain	Semiarid coastal plain (rugged topography)	Semiarid grassland plain (rugged topography)
War duration	126 days	378 days
War birth	No	No
Recent war history w/opponent	Yes	Yes
Facing colonizer	Yes	Yes
Identity dimension	Sunni Islam/Christian	Sunni Islam/Christian
New leader	Yes	Yes
Population	8–8.5 million	5–6 million
Ethnolinguistic fractionalization (ELF)	High	High
Civ-mil relations	Ruler as commander	Ruler as commander
Battlefield Performance		
Tac-op sophistication	Moderate	Poor
Loss-exchange ratio	0.43	0.02
Mass desertion	No	Yes
Mass defection	No	No
Fratricidal violence	No	Yes

Note: [a]Morocco enters the Correlates of War State System Membership dataset (v2016) in 1847.

they enjoyed autonomy in their social affairs. Coercion was sometimes still applied toward restive tribes, though such practices had receded into the past; no large-scale state-directed violence occurred in the ten year window preceding 1859.[26] But most violence, when it occurred, was actually inter-group, not state-directed, as the Makhzan preferred jihad and jobs to violent repression.[27]

Morocco's military machine reflected this inclusionary vision. After suffering defeat at French hands in 1844, the Sultan enacted a series of sweeping reforms designed to place the military on a modern footing. Recruitment into the permanent standing army (the *nizam*) was reimagined as a "general and national" process; the "construction of the nizam," noted Bahija Simou, became "a national enterprise whose consolidation was the responsibility of all subjects."[28] These reforms were inspired by contemporary efforts in Tunisia, Egypt, and the Ottoman Empire that viewed the military as a forge for allegiance to the regime's own communal vision. Efforts were also made to emulate Western practices. European drill and uniforms were adopted in 1845, and a deal was struck with the United Kingdom for training and technical assistance, especially with artillery.[29] Pay, too, was apportioned by military branch, not tribal identity.[30] These reforms proved controversial; the Sultan faced criticism that adopting Western ideals, including regular payment of soldiers, was un-Islamic.[31] Yet the Sultan persisted, driven by a belief that "there could be no victory without it [the Western model of warfare] against anyone who has it."[32] And while it would be anachronistic to claim that soldiers were motivated by "nationalism," the regime nonetheless managed to make a case that soldiers should fight to safeguard both their faith and the regime that upheld it. The absence of prewar, targeted, group-based violence by the regime helped make these claims even more credible.

Morocco's army reflected these inclusionary principles. The military itself was composed of three parts: (1) the permanent standing forces (nizam),

26. Morocco did conduct occasional campaigns against coastal Berbers, who were engaged in piracy of European shipping. These populations were de facto and de jure (by 1799 Treaty) outside of Morocco's jurisdiction.

27. Slavery, though waning, was still present in Morocco. An estimated 1–4 percent of the population was a slave or had been manumitted. See El Hamel 2013, 244–45; Godard 1860, 221; and Malte-Brun 1835, 148–49.

28. Simou 1995, 130.

29. Srhir 2004; Rollman 2004; Bennison 2004; Ennaji 1999, 7.

30. Cavalry and artillery were paid ten *mitqals* monthly; infantry, only five *mitqals*. See Simou 1995, 84fn1.

31. Rollman 2004, 213, 216; Simou 1995, 89–90.

32. Cited in Rollman 2004, 216fn31.

which were recruited locally by quota that selected recruits according to their demographic weight in a given area; (2) tribal levies (gu'ish) in several regions that provided the bulk of the cavalry via quota as needed by the Sultan; and (3) the so-called renegades (renégats), a group of French deserters (or their sons) or turncoats who were held captive and had valuable technical expertise, usually with artillery.[33] There was no ethnic favoritism in either promotion or branch; typically, each unit was tribally homogenous and commanded by cotribalists. Demographic estimates must be taken with some skepticism given the lack of complete records. But it is apparent that the military was heavily dominated by Berber tribes (the Riffian and Kabyles in particular), followed by a smaller contingent of Beduin (about 10 percent) and the renegades (about 1 percent). Morocco's military inequality coefficient is therefore either a 0 (denoting total equality) or 0.01, depending on whether the renegades are considered outside the political community entirely or are a repressed subgroup.[34]

For its part, Kokand was the largest and most powerful of nineteenth century Central Asian khanates. Formally established in 1709, Kokand sprawled across a space the size of Western Europe, encompassing much of modern-day Kazakhstan as well as parts of Kyrgyzstan and Uzbekistan. Like Morocco, its population, estimated at about five million by 1864, was extraordinarily diverse, with at least six major ethnic and tribal groupings, and scores of subgroups, present. Contestation across, and sometimes within, these groups pitted sedentary populations (Uzbeks/Sarts, Tajiks, and Karakalpoks) against politically ascendent nomadic ones (Kirghiz/Pamirs, Kipchaks, and Kazakhs).[35] Ethnic and tribal affinity was strong but did not preclude infighting among coethnics nor the emergence of pro-Russian and pro-Bukharan factions that fueled chronic efforts to scramble the ethnic hierarchy by capturing the city of Kokand, the seat of government.[36] Regional tensions also existed between the "older" western lands that had been conquered long ago and newer territorial conquests such as Tashkent and the fertile Ferghana Valley.

Kokand's ruling aristocracy, typically dominated by Uzbeks, invested heavily in legitimating its rule in light of these potential schisms. Three precepts

---

33. Simou 1995, 129–34.

34. Given the absence of a large French population in Morocco at this time, I prefer to exclude the renegades from the calculation of the coefficient. Instead, I denote their coerced service in the recruitment variable. The military inequality coefficient is calculated as Berbers $(0.89 * 0)$ + Beduin $(0.10 * 0)$ + renegades $(0.01 * 0) = 0$.

35. Levi 2007; Manz 1987.

36. Bobozhonov 2010, 244–49.

were central to its ideological vision.[37] First, a succession of ruling khans cast Kokand as the successor to Genghis Khan's empire, harkening back to a glorious past meant to overawe potentially restive populations. Second, Kokand's khans embraced Sunni Islam, often deriving their legitimacy from claims to be Mohammad's direct descendants. Kokand's political and legal system embraced Sharia law, for example, and it was hoped that Islam itself could prove an integrative factor for a spatially dispersed and ethnically fractured society. These first two precepts could potentially have provided the ideational foundation for a broadly inclusionary vision of Kokand. Yet the third precept—that the ruler dictated Kokand's ethnic and tribal hierarchy—sabotaged any integrative effects of appeals to former glories or Islam. Indeed, Kokand had institutionalized a "game of khans,"[38] winner-take-all political system in which a tribe or ethnic group's fate rose and fell with the khan's identity and his ability to hold onto power in the face of certain challenge. Group-based marginalization and repression were thus central to Kokand's communal vision.

'Alimqul's own vision of Kokand's hierarchy centered around a Kipchak-dominated ethnocracy in alliance with the traditional Uzbek aristocracy. He set about constructing this vision in 1862, when his Kipchak forces fought and defeated the ruling pro-Kirghiz khan, Khudaiar Khan, whose tenure was marked by the savage repression of Kipchaks. Some 20–25,000 Kipchaks were massacred in 1853 alone; anti-Kipchak pogroms, sweeping land confiscations, and even open warfare continued in 1854, 1855, and 1858.[39] Once safe behind the throne, 'Alimqul used his position as senior military commander (amir-i lashkar) to overturn Khan's hierarchy. He immediately ordered the execution of nearly 4,000 Kirghiz and assassinated three potential claimants to the throne from his own clan.[40] Echoing the Khalifa's first days as ruler of Mahdiya, he razed Khan's palace at Kokand and ordered the construction of a new one.[41]

Kokand's military was both an instrument and a hostage of these internecine power struggles. By 1830, Kokand's army had transitioned to a regular standing force that received European-style training and equipment, often from foreign advisors who plied their trade in Central Asia.[42] In much the same fashion as Morocco, this permanent force was augmented in times

37. Dubovitskii and Bababekov 2011; Bobozhonov 2010, 679, 681; Beisembiev 2008, 23; Bababekov 2006a, 21–38; Bregel 2009.

38. Bobozhonov 2010, 249.

39. Dubovitskii and Bababekov 2011, 36; Bababekov 2006a, 56–66; Schuyler 1877, 353.

40. Bababekov 2006a.

41. Tashkandi 2003, 6.

42. Galkina 1868, 210–12.

of war with auxiliaries drawn from tribal levies according to a feudal-like system. An estimated 25,000-strong army could be raised and deployed into combat in only twenty days, with additional auxiliaries acting as reserves that could boost Kokand's army to 50–60,000 if needed. Though impressive, these numbers actually represent a decrease in manpower; Khudaiar Khan, for example, was able to mobilize 40,000 soldiers in only twenty days in the mid-1850s.[43] This decrease arose from the deep Kipchak-Kirghiz animosity hardwired into 'Alimqul's military. These nomadic populations provided the bulk of the tribal levies, especially cavalry, and had recently engaged in mass violence against each other at the behest of their respective khans. As a result, these two factions deeply distrusted one another and the Kokand state itself, setting the stage for low combat motivation, mass indiscipline, and even basic coordination problems once war began. Kazakh tribes that had sided with the Kirghiz during 'Alimqul's war for power were also viewed with deep suspicion.

Given state-directed repression of both its Kirghiz and Kipchak mainstays in the immediate prewar era, Kokand's military inequality was naturally quite high. This situation was compounded by a long-standing policy of reserving the top seven ranks (out of fourteen) for Uzbeks only. As a result, all other ethnic and tribal groups face ceiling that restricted their upward mobility, even if they had not been violently targeted by the state.[44] Judged conservatively, Kokand's prewar military inequality was around 0.70, rivaled in its severity only by the Khalifa's Mahdiya (see chapter 3) and likely approaching the suggested threshold for maximum inequality. As with Morocco, this average estimate of military inequality must be treated with caution; no census existed, and the names of the same ethnic group or tribe could vary depending on its geographic location. This estimate views Kokand's military as dominated by nomadic Kipchaks (about 30 percent), Kirghiz (about 30 percent), and Kazakhs (about 5 percent), with sedentary Uzbeks (about 10 percent) comprising senior commanders and Tajiks (20 percent) and Karakalpoks (about 5 percent) providing most of the infantry.[45]

---

43. Bababekov 2006a, 46.

44. Bababekov 2006a, 44–45.

45. Formally, I derive a *high* estimate for Kokand's military inequality coefficient as follows: Kirghiz $(0.25 * 1)$ + Kipchak $(0.25 * 1)$ + Kazakhs $(0.15 * 1)$ + Uzbeks $(0.10 * 0)$ + Tajiks $(0.20 * 0.5)$ + Karakalpoks $(0.05 * 0.5) = 0.775$. I also derive a *low* estimate: Kirghiz $(0.20 * 1)$ + Kipchak $(0.20 * 1)$ + Kazakhs $(0.15 * 0.5)$ + Uzbeks $(0.15 * 0)$ + Tajiks $(0.20 * 0.5)$ + Karakalpoks $(0.10 * 0.5) = 0.625$. This low estimate reflects (1) uncertainty about the exact proportion of each group in military service, and (2) recodes the dominant prewar experience of Kazakhs as marginalization rather than targeted repression. I then take

5.2.2. *Matched Covariates*

Strange bedfellows or not, Morocco and Kokand, as well as the wars they fought, share broad similarities across measures captured by Project Mars. From the standpoint of the material preponderance argument, for example, these belligerents entered their respective wars with almost identical levels of numerical superiority over their enemies. In each case, their forces represented two-thirds of all initially deployed forces. Each could muster armies of comparable size, with estimates of about 55,000 and 50,000 soldiers for Morocco and Kokand, respectively.[46] True, Kokand did enjoy a more favorable balance of forces over time; Russian forces remained small throughout the war, barely exceeding 4,000 total soldiers. Spain, however, sent additional reinforcements across the Mediterranean, reaching about 40,000 total soldiers by the campaign's end. Recalculating these force ratios with total deployed forces swings the balance markedly in Kokand's favor: it possessed nearly 90 percent of all combat forces in the war, while Morocco fielded only 58 percent of the combined armies' strength. Yet this only deepens the puzzle of why we observe divergent battlefield performance if material preponderance determines military effectiveness.[47]

Both states were absolute monarchies with theocratic leanings, helping to eliminate regime type as a possible explanation for divergent battlefield performance.[48] Neither belligerent faced a democratic opponent: both Spain and Russia were well in the authoritarian camp in this era.[49] Both armies fought their opening encounters at remarkably similar distances from their capital cities; the difference is only fifty-seven kilometers between the two cases. This closeness of fit across cases is helpful in reducing the effects that logistical difficulties might have in explaining battlefield performance. Both belligerents possessed a core of professional soldiers in permanent standing formations. In times of war, these regulars, who were often volunteers, were bolstered with auxiliaries drawn from tribal levies that approximated a

the average of these estimates (0.70) as the military inequality coefficient. As with Morocco, I exclude the tiny proportion of soldiers (less than 1 percent) who were slaves (Hopkins 2008).

46. Estimates upwards of 100,000 soldiers were recorded by contemporaries for each belligerent but are not judged as credible by most modern historians.

47. Needless to say, neither state was a Great Power, at least according to the Correlates of War standard. In fact, Kokand is not considered a "state" at all by COW; Morocco squeaks into the international system in 1847.

48. Indeed, their Polity2 scores, where a +10 indicates a full democracy and a −10 indicates a full authoritarian power, are almost identical: Kokand is a −7, while Morocco lags only slightly behind at −6.

49. More formally, Spain had a −5 Polity2 score; Russia, a −10.

feudal-like system. Neither belligerent initiated the war, though increasingly brazen, if inconsequential, attacks by local tribes against soldiers in the Spanish coastal enclave of Ceuta were the immediate *casus belli* for Spanish leaders. And while both states were incompletely consolidated, with periodic domestic upheavals, neither conflict was a civil war. Instead, each state faced foreign invasion by a superior foe only five years apart from one another. Selecting cases nestled closely together in time helps control for macrohistorical trends such as the rise of nationalism or discontinuous jumps in weapons technology that could account for different performance if wars are separated by decades.

5.2.3. Contextual Covariates

The closeness of this round of matching helps ensure that these two belligerents and their wars also share similarities across contextual covariates. Both armies, for example, sought to employ combined arms approaches that integrated firearm-equipped soldiers, large cavalry formations, and specialized artillery units. In particular, each army was able to coordinate cavalry assaults to breach enemy lines while maneuvering multiple infantry formations to exploit these gaps or to outflank enemy units or defenses. Artillery was typically used to disrupt enemy forces while they moved into attack position rather than in direct support of infantry assaults owing to difficulties of real-time coordination, though both armies also made use of counter-battery fire. That these practices resembled contemporary Western-style combined arms approaches was no accident. Kokand and Morocco each had formal agreements with the United Kingdom for training and arms, especially the provision of artillery, signed a decade before these wars. The United Kingdom established a permanent artillery base on Gibraltar to train Moroccan forces, for example. Kokand even received London's permission in 1855 for the use of British Indian soldiers in any future war with Russia.[50] Each military also had several European advisors embedded within their command structures, though not in actual combat units.[51]

Both militaries embraced offensive doctrines, seeking decisive battles against their foes in a series of sharp, short encounters designed to avoid prolonged war. Each army entered their war at a technical disadvantage to their adversaries, though it is easy to exaggerate these differences. There's little question that Spanish and, to a lesser extent, Russian rifled artillery, proved

50. Bababekov 2006b, 15.
51. Dubovitskii and Bababekov 2011, 54–55; Srhir 2004.

superior to cannons fielded by Moroccan and Kokandian forces. Much of Morocco's active artillery rightfully belonged in a museum, which is exactly where Spanish authorities sent captured Moroccan cannons.[52] Kokand, by contrast, did have relatively modern artillery in fairly large numbers. It also managed to acquire sophisticated exploding shells early in the war, much to General Cherniaev's chagrin.[53] The individual firearms of Moroccan and Kokandian infantry were also outclassed by Spanish and Russian weapons, though here differences in quality were marginal. The Spanish Army was equipped primarily with the Modello 1854, a single-shot rifle with an effective range up to 400 meters. Regular Moroccan forces relied upon modern Dreyse needle-guns from Prussia, with an effective range up to 600 meters. Auxiliaries were equipped with *espingardas*, extremely long-barreled, single-shot rifles that needed to be propped up on the ground in order to be fired.[54] Russian infantry used the Six-Line Rifle Pattern 1856 firing Minié ball, a spin-stabilized rifle bullet that inflicted horrific wounds. Despite a theoretical range of 600 meters, most Russian infantry rarely fired at distances beyond 150 meters, as a combination of poor training and ammunition supply difficulties led them to prefer close-range shots. Kokand's Army, for its part, relied on a hodgepodge of smoothbore weapons, including British Land Pattern 1842 muskets (the infamous "Brown Bess"), often acquired via black market from India.[55] These muskets had a range of about 200 meters, though with only limited stopping power.[56] Kokand's military leadership, aware of their weaknesses, had begun a process of modernization but was caught midstream when war broke out in 1864.

We might worry, however, that the discrepancy in war duration— Morocco's war lasted only 126 days, while Kokand's stretched 378 days— might tilt the comparison in Morocco's favor. The longer the war, the greater the possibility that mass indiscipline might occur, and the greater the likelihood of observing the use of blocking detachments. Yet this eight month difference is somewhat misleading. No combat occurred between Kokandian and Russian forces from 3 December, when a Cossack detachment (*sotni*) was ambushed and crushed, to General Cherniaev's 8 May 1865 decision to resume his march on Tashkent. Removing this pause in combat operations leaves us with a war of 223 days, only about three months longer than Morocco's fight. If anything, this lull granted Kokand a temporary reprieve to

52. Hardman 1860, 87.
53. Allworth 1995, 18.
54. del Rey 2001, 239–41, 247–48.
55. Skilakie 2013, 10.
56. Terent'ev 1906, 318.

regroup, providing its army with yet another advantage when considering its battlefield performance relative to Morocco.

New states might also prove especially vulnerable to battlefield defeat given the pressures of simultaneous state-building and war-fighting. Yet neither belligerent was a new state. On the contrary: Kokand was founded in 1709, while the Alaouite Monarchy had ruled Morocco since 1631.[57] As a consequence, they both had recent experience with their eventual adversaries. In a slow but persistent wave of expansion, Russian forces had butted against Kokand's line of fortifications at the Amu Dar'ia as early as 1852. Much of the early 1860s witnessed armed clashes between their armies as Russia continued to encroach on Kokandian lands. Morocco, too, had clashed recently with Spain, albeit indirectly. Raids by irregular tribesmen on Spanish coastal enclaves of Ceuta and Melilla prompted Spain to demand additional territory to protect its autonomous Moroccan cities. When Muhammad IV refused, war was declared. Both states were no strangers to combat with powerful armies. Kokand fought and defeated Chinese armies in the two Khoja Rebellion wars (1826–27, 1830).[58] Morocco clashed with France at Isly in 1844, suffering a stinging defeat that prodded the Makhzan into modernizing its military along Western lines.[59]

In each case, these states were faced with colonizing opponents bent on acquiring some, if not all, of their territory. Political leaders in Kokand and Morocco were therefore in a position where they could motivate soldiers to fight harder to protect their families, if not their state, from a foreign invader.[60] These wars also featured the same identity cleavage, pitting regimes that legitimated themselves through appeals to Islam against Christian (Orthodox) enemies.[61]

Politically, both states were headed by new, potentially vulnerable, leaders. Muhammad IV ascended to the throne after his father's death on 29 August 1859, only two months before war broke out. Kokand's de facto ruler,

57. As a reflection of its status and longevity, Kokand had diplomatic ties with the Ottoman Empire, Russia (by 1830), and Afghanistan. It was also diplomatically recognized by China via its first "unequal treaty" in 1835 which became the model for the subsequent Treaty of Nanjing (1842) with Britain and France (Fletcher 1978; Newby 2005; Karpat 1991).

58. These wars are included in Project Mars. As detailed below, Kokand also initiated a war with China during its 1864–1865 war with Russia.

59. Muhammad IV personally commanded Moroccan forces during this defeat and oversaw subsequent military reforms.

60. For the link between fighting on "home turf" and combat motivation, see Freedman 2005; Castillo 2014, 42.

61. Biddle and Long 2004, 16, find that a belligerent's religious identity, as well as the pairing of religions in a given war, provide a great deal of leverage when explaining loss-exchange ratios.

'Alimqul, had only just consolidated his position after a successful coup in 1852, emerging victorious, if still wary, from the murderous "carousel of khans" that plagued Kokand's politics. Even population sizes and density were roughly similar. Morocco had a population of about 7–8 million, while Kokand's was slightly smaller at 5–6 million subjects. Each belligerent was riven with deep ethnic, tribal, and sectarian divisions that complicated efforts to govern their dispersed populations. Finally, differences in battlefield performance cannot be ascribed to the state of civil-military relations, which were nearly identical in each belligerent.[62] Muhammad IV and 'Alimqul held formal positions as supreme military commanders and had authority to set strategic direction as well as issue battlefield orders. Each ruler also relied on a set of senior commanders who recruited, disciplined, and oversaw their own formations. Both leaders were personally present on the battlefield, a degree of centralization that proved fatal for 'Alimqul, who was felled by a Russian bullet while mounting an unsuccessful defense at Tashkent.

5.2.4. Historiography

Neither of these cases has a particularly robust English-language historiography. Gaps also exist; high levels of illiteracy, along with a reliance on oral traditions, means that the voices of ordinary soldiers are largely absent from the historical record.[63] Yet considerable amounts of primary documents are nonetheless available and can be woven together to construct narratives of each belligerent's battlefield performance. For Morocco, I draw heavily on Spanish- and French-language campaign memoirs and accounts by embedded journalists—the conflict is considered one of the first "media wars"[64]—along with the operational history of the 2nd Division of the Army of Africa's Second Corps and postwar military training manuals.[65] For Kokand, I utilize official Russian correspondence between Petersburg, Cherniaev, and his commanders;[66] 'Alimqul's wartime missives that were intercepted and translated by Russian forces; Kokand's Chronicles, which partially capture

---

62. In terms of the framework proposed by Castillo (2014, 32), these belligerents might best be assigned "medium" levels of regime control and military autonomy, indicating they should have moderate, possibly strong, levels of battlefield performance.

63. Abashin 2014. The destruction of Kokand's archives in 1876 only compounds these difficulties.

64. Martin-Màrquez 2008, 104.

65. Gutiérrez Maturana 1876; Mordacq 1900.

66. In particular, I draw on A. G. Serebrennikov's *Turkestanskii krai: Sbornik materialov dlia istorii ego zavoevaniia*, a 22-volume compilation of official correspondence covering Russia's conquest of Kokand, Bukhara, and Khiva. These materials were housed in the Rossiskaia

Kokand's side of the war, illuminating 'Alimqul's decision-making;[67] participant memoirs; and the operational history of Russia's 4th Turkestan Line
Battalion, the main unit that fought the war.[68]

5.3. Morocco at War

Morocco's defeat in 1860 is often taken as a watershed event that ushered in
modern Moroccan history. In their haste to chart Morocco's postwar developments, however, historians typically overlook the war itself. Yet if we cast aside
the patronizing, if not openly racist, cant of contemporary accounts, we find
that Moroccan infantry, and especially cavalry, performed remarkably well on
the battlefield. Indeed, Morocco's lone blemish on the quantitative BPI was a
loss-exchange ratio below parity. Its forces held together well; mass desertion
and defection were both absent, and cohesion was maintained without the use
of blocking detachments or even substantial monitoring mechanisms. The
sophistication of Moroccan tactics and operations was also quite high. Individual soldier resolve was also strong; pitched battles with Spanish forces were
the norm for all major engagements. The narrative below first outlines the two
dimensions of Moroccan combat power, tactical and operational sophistication as well as its loss-exchange ratio, before turning to elements of battlefield
cohesion.

5.3.1. Combat Power

Moroccan tactics and operational art were of surprisingly high quality
throughout the war. Morocco's army fielded specialized cavalry, infantry,
and artillery units and managed to coordinate their actions, if sometimes
haltingly.[69] Cavalry remained the favored arm; mounted attacks by massed
cavalry from multiple directions were used to probe Spanish squares for
weaknesses in the hopes of achieving breakthroughs to be exploited by
follow-on infantry forces. Skirmishers were also deployed to provide covering fire for cavalry and to increase confusion within Spanish ranks, degrading
their ability to meet cavalry charges. Artillery was used to support Moroccan
infantry assaults from fortified positions, with shells also lobbed into Spanish

---

Natsional'naia Biblioteka (RNB) in St. Petersburg. I thank Ksenia Anisimova for assistance in
acquiring these materials.

  67. The Kokand *Chronicles* are a group of more than forty historical works written during
the nineteenth century that were sponsored by various khans to outline Kokand's history. See
Pantusov 1885; Beisembiev 1987; Tashkandi 2003; Beisembiev 2008; Veselovskii 1894.

  68. Zaitsev 1882.

  69. Mordacq 1900, 18–22.

squares and camps as harassing fire. Moroccan tactics placed a premium on mobility and emphasized the importance of using terrain features and decentralized movements by small groups to reduce vulnerability to enemy fire. Though sometimes maligned as unruly or undisciplined,[70] this system made a great deal of sense when Moroccan forces held the edge in mobility and when Spanish artillery could prove devastating against large concentrations of soldiers caught in open ground.[71]

Favoring an offensive doctrine, initial Moroccan offensives had a probing quality, aiming to lure the Army of Africa from behind its walls at Ceuta and into open combat. "I should rather take their object to be to provoke the Spaniards to move out from their cover," Hardman noted, "to ground where they might afford easy marks for their *espingardas* [long-barreled shotguns]. The Moors have been only too successful in this, and the consequence has been the killing and wounding of hundreds of men without any corresponding advantage."[72] Over time, however, Moroccan commanders updated their tactics, shifting from harassment and probing attacks to direct battle designed to block the Spanish advance from Ceuta to Tetuán. Taken together, these battles witnessed the careful use of terrain to set ambushes and as part of defensive obstacles, the construction of fortification and well-sited trenches, and a remarkable ability to regroup and drive home attacks once initial efforts to crack Spanish squares failed. Indeed, accounts from all major battles, including Los Castillejos, Guad-el-Gelu, Tetuán, and Wad-Ras, emphasize Moroccan ability to regroup under fire and reset for additional attacks.[73] Territorial tug-of-wars were common, with ownership of contested ground exchanging hands multiple times. Moroccan forces did not simply fold after an offensive stalled but instead continued to press home attacks. Retreats, when necessary, were also conducted in relatively good order rather than as headlong rushes to quit the battlefield for good.

Moroccan infantry also exhibited a high degree of technical skill. Observers rated its marksmanship far higher than Spanish counterparts, for example, and much less wasteful of ammunition.[74] Night attacks, too, were common;

70. Al-Nasiri, for example, contrasted the orderliness of Spanish squares with Moroccan decentralization: "The Muslims did not fight in any special order, nor in disciplined form. Rather, they fought while spread out, every which way." Salawi 1917, 64.

71. Joly 1910, 132–33.

72. Hardman 1860, 99.

73. See, for example, "Foreign and Colonial News," *Illustrated London News*, 17 December 1859; "Great Spanish Victory in Morocco," *New York Times*, 20 January 1860; "Foreign and Colonial News," *Illustrated London News*, 25 February 1860; and "The War in Morocco; Capture of Tetuán by the Spaniards," *New York Times*, 25 February 1860.

74. Hardman 1860, 209, 307–8.

Moroccan commanders were evidently unconcerned that their soldiers might slip away under the cover of night.[75] Surprise attacks could also be orchestrated on short notice. On 9 February 1860, the incautious Spanish governor of Melilla, Manuel Buceta del Villar, disobeyed O'Donnell's instructions to avoid combat and sent a 1,200-strong force to pursue Moroccan forces after their defeat at Tetuán. His belief that Moroccan commanders were too demoralized to fight was badly mistaken. His small formation, oblivious to a much larger Moroccan force nearby, was surrounded and crushed. Some 370 Spanish casualties were inflicted; Moroccan losses were negligible. O'Donnell, furious at this insubordination, was forced to order the naval bombardment of several coastal cities to save face.[76]

The sophistication of Morocco's way of warfare, along with the tenacity of its soldiers, was fully on display at the Battle of Guad-el-Gelu (31 January 1860). Seeking to block Spain's advance on Tetuán, Moroccan commanders erected defenses at Guad-el-Gelu, a port city about twenty kilometers to its north. These defenses consisted of fortified camps ringed with trenches and protected by a series of earthen outworks. The terrain itself was potmarked with swamps, creating an additional set of obstacles for the 20,000-strong Army of Africa. Moroccan commanders, notably Mulay Abbas (the Sultan's brother) and Mulay Ahmet, could call on at least 10,000 cavalry along with 16,000 infantry to defend Guad-el-Gelu.[77]

At 10 a.m. on 31 January, Moroccan cavalry, moving in two independent formations, descended on the approaching Spanish army. Their intent was twofold: to disrupt the Spanish squares and to cut them off from the sea by turning their flank and capturing their encampment. In response, the Spanish formed oblique squares ("living machines") and beat back multiple cavalry charges. Unsuccessful at cracking Spanish formations, Moroccan cavalry reset their focus and began probing attacks against trailing Spanish forces. This in turn flushed Spanish cavalry from their rearguard positions and into the fight, where they quickly found themselves bogged down in the marshy soil. Moroccan sharpshooters and artillery inflicted heavy casualties on these stranded units until, in a desperation play, Spanish commanders ordered their artillery forward to clear Moroccan trenches at close range. Under punishing fire, Moroccan soldiers retreated from the trenches. Advancing Spanish soldiers

---

75. Alarcón 1988, 315.

76. "Foreign and Colonial News," *Illustrated London News*, 3 March 1860, 202.

77. Joly 1910, 92–93. O'Donnell believed he faced 25,000 Moroccans. Arrue (1898, 89–90), however, contends that O'Donnell's scouts missed 5,000 new volunteers and 8,000 under Sidi Ahmed's command, bringing the estimated total to 38,000. It is unlikely that these two additional formations took part in the battle.

were met, however, by a counterattack by the elite Black Squadron, which drove them back from the trenches. Four successive Moroccan attempts to overrun the gun positions were driven off, as was a flanking attack sprung from a nearby cemetery. Counter-battery fire by Moroccan artillery was then tried to dislodge Spanish cannons, to no avail. Finally, combined Spanish artillery, infantry attacks, and Congreve batteries—"whose rockets take off like light-ening [sic] bolts, splitting the air with strident noise, penetrating the Islamic masses like snakes of fire"[78]—forced the Moroccan army from the field. Fight-ing continued through the night as Moroccan forces launched several more assaults and kept up considerable harassment fire. Morning dawned on a bat-tlefield littered with 640 Spanish casualties, including Brigadier General Dolz, who was killed while leading his forces, and an estimated 1,000 Moroccan casualties.[79]

This assessment about Moroccan tactical prowess was shared by Spanish military commanders and embedded journalists. Commanders, for example, thought that Morocco's battlefield performance was so good because shad-owy British officers were clandestinely leading its forces in battle. "Scarcely a skirmish occurs," Hardman wrote, "after which a rumor does not prevail that an Englishman assisted in it."[80] Spanish political leaders took up this cause, publicly denouncing Britain for its underhanded assistance to Morocco.[81] In truth, British assistance was minor at best, confined to technical assistance with Moroccan artillery; no British officers are known to have commanded troops in battle. There was also widespread recognition that several of the bat-tles were actually close-run affairs where Spanish fortunes "hung by a thread." At Guad-el-Ras, Hardman noted that "more than one superior officer has since confessed to me that there were moments when he thought the battle lost."[82] Spanish respect for Moroccan combat power even induced doctrinal changes during the war. Alarmed by Moroccan mobility, Spanish comman-ders fielded chains of skirmishers in front of their squares to disrupt cavalry attacks and to prevent flanking maneuvers. After initial encounters, Span-ish rearguard units were also reinforced to prevent Moroccan cavalry from separating the squares from their supplies and camps.[83]

We should not exaggerate Moroccan combat power, however. While indi-vidual soldier quality and initiative was generally high, senior leadership

78. Alarcón 1988, 312.
79. Joly 1910, 92–96; Hardman 1860, 269–70.
80. Hardman 1860, 62.
81. See, for example, "Spain and Morocco," New York Times, 2 January 1860.
82. Hardman 1860, 315.
83. Villalobos 2004, 21.

received poor marks from contemporaries. Commanders often failed to maximize terrain advantages, allowing Spanish forces to move unmolested through rough terrain between engagements. Ambushes and enfilading fire from favorable high terrain, rather than decisive combat in open fields, would certainly have slowed Spanish advances by fouling logistics and inflicting casualties. Hardman captured this sentiment when he argued: "The Moorish generals are surely very stupid people. They allow this army to pass unmolested along paths and through defiles where they might attack it with certainty of causing it much loss, and of suffering little themselves; and three days later they come and attack it in strong positions, when its forces are concentrated, its parapets made, its artillery at hand, and ready to act at five minutes' notice."[84] Al-Nasiri also bemoaned the inability of Moroccan commanders to take advantage of Spanish forces that were wracked by cholera, especially early in the war.[85] A sudden storm also cut Spanish forces off from their naval support and supplies at Asmir, offering an unprecedented chance to encircle and destroy them. Yet no action was taken. "The enemy was stuck between the two rivers and the [Mediterranean] on his left. His supplies were cut off...they were certain to perish if they encountered someone who could seize the opportunity against them. *But where was the strong hand?* [emphasis in original]."[86]

Problems with generalship notwithstanding, Morocco still turned in a somewhat credible performance using our second measure of combat power, loss-exchange ratios. On average, Moroccan forces lost about 2.33 soldiers for each Spanish soldier killed.[87] Casualty estimates are of course more art than science in this instance; cholera deaths may have inflated Spanish totals, while the Moroccan practice of carrying away dead and wounded soldiers renders estimates imprecise. Yet it is clear that Moroccan forces inflicted more casualties on Spanish forces in a single battle at Los Castillejos (about 569 killed and wounded) than Russia suffered in its entire 1864–65 campaign against Kokand. Once again, Moroccan missed opportunities loom large: "Between the lines of Ceuta and the present position of this army, they ought to have killed and wounded as many thousands of Spaniards as they have done hundreds."[88] This loss-exchange ratio is worse than typically recorded for

84. Hardman 1860, 146.

85. Jensen 2007, 28–29.

86. Salawi 1917, 35.

87. Estimates of Spanish KIA range from 1,152–4,000, while 6,000 KIA is the most commonly cited figure for Morocco. Total estimates of Spanish killed and wounded range between 6,498 and 10,000 (see, for example, Mordacq 1900, 9; Villalobos 2004, 22). Morocco suffered 20–25,000 casualties.

88. Hardman 1860, 175.

belligerents with low military inequality, a point I return to below. But there's little doubt that Morocco was punching far above its weight against a technologically more sophisticated foe than its counterfactual, Kokand, managed.

5.3.2.   Cohesion

Despite its ethnically mixed and potentially fractious nature, the Moroccan army exhibited a generally high degree of discipline throughout the war. Diversity was not synonymous with division; the absence of active regime efforts to politicize existing ethnic and tribal differences meant that internal challenges to military cohesion were largely absent. In fact, the Moroccan army was not only well-disciplined but also reasonably resilient, able to stand and trade blows with much better equipped Spanish forces. Indeed, billing the Moroccan army as resilient is perhaps a disservice; many individual commanders, as well as entire units, were positively enthusiastic about the war. A potent combination of religious motives and anti-occupier sentiment fueled combat motivation, leading to pitched fights of an unusually sanguineous nature for the invading power.

Mass desertion, as defined by Project Mars to represent 10 percent or greater of a military's fielded forces, never occurred, for example. Only scattered references to a "handful" of deserters are found in contemporary accounts.[89] Nor did mass defection occur. Not a single mention is made to defectors in any text. Tellingly, General O'Donnell shelved his plans to create a locally staffed auxiliary force given the absence of soldiers willing to switch sides.[90] Somewhat surprisingly, though aware of the ethnic and tribal differences across Moroccan units, Spanish commanders apparently made no effort to exploit these potential cleavages. Perhaps their experience with the few Moroccan soldiers taken prisoner—only five were captured out of at least twenty thousand deployed at the Battle of Castillejos[91]—disabused them of such notions. "Moorish prisoners," it was commonly believed, were driven by "blind fanaticism" to seek revenge on Spanish forces, and thus could not be turned.[92]

The near total absence of major disciplinary issues like mass desertion and defection is remarkable given that Moroccan units were typically homogenous. Rather than blending different ethnic groups and tribal identities, units were organized along preexisting group identities that facilitated their recruitment in times of war. These same group ties could have facilitated collective

89. Alarcón 1988, 441.
90. Hardman 1860, 241.
91. Joly 1910, 161.
92. "Romance XVII—Prisionoros Moros" in Bustillo 1868, 26–27.

action against the war, including flight, had commanders and soldiers wanted to pursue such a course. Cavalry units in particular not only had the ties to do so but the means to escape military authority. Yet such behaviors failed to materialize even when casualties began to mount and the prospects of victory ebbed. Here, the silences in the historical record speak volumes: no mass indiscipline, premature surrender, or even widespread malingering took place. This cohesion is especially impressive given the absence of blocking detachments or even robust monitoring and sanctioning mechanisms. Absent, too, was the use of violence against certain ethnic groups in the wider population once the war turned against Morocco. In this instance, Morocco's low military inequality forces us to widen our understanding of battlefield performance to include processes and patterns that did *not* occur during the war.

Evidence from both Spanish military sources and journalists all indicate that Moroccan forces displayed exceptional resolve. Battles were pitched, often hand-to-hand, affairs, with positions and trenches exchanging control multiple times. At the Battle of Los Castillejos, Spanish eyewitnesses remarked on Moroccan "arrogance" in the face of Spanish artillery and rifle fire.[93] Moroccan resistance was likened to a "horrible tempest"[94] at the Battle of Cabo-Negro; two weeks later, at Guad-el-Gelu, "we could no less than admire the audacity and the tenacity of such a bellicose adversary, as well as its stubbornness and its constancy."[95] At Tetuán, "each Moorish tent," wrote Pedro de Alarcón in his masterful *Diary of a Witness to the War in Africa*, "each flowering tree, each canebrake, each fence, presents a challenge, a personal dispute, a struggle hand to hand."[96] "It was," in other words, "a war to the knife on both sides."[97] As Bahija Simou concluded, the "severity and extent of their cumulative [material] disadvantages did not prevent the Moroccans from showing an impressive ardor in combat."[98]

Battles fought after the stinging Moroccan defeat at Tetuán in February 1860 (see below) are especially informative. We might imagine Moroccan forces to be dispirited, with low combat motivation and even less willingness to offer battle again. Yet all sources converge in a shared view of Moroccan soldiers as highly motivated and eager, perhaps to an irresponsible degree, to return to the battlefield. At the war's final battle, fought at Guad-el-Ras (Wad Ras) in March 1860, an estimated 35–40,000 Moroccan soldiers took

---

93. "Romance XIII—Batalla de Los Castillejos" in Bustillo 1868, 20.

94. "Romance IV—Tras la tempestad la calma—Cabo-Negro" in Bustillo 1868, 24.

95. Alarcón 1988, 294.

96. Alarcón 1988, 341.

97. "The War in Morocco," *New York Times*, 14 February 1860, 1.

98. Simou 1995, 86.

the field, the largest fielded in the entire war.[99] The 2nd Division's operational history notes with weary resignation the need to take up arms again, to "let the blow run again in battle, until the Moor puts off his risky courage, his pride, his proverbial boldness [and] comes submissive to our own field to sign [peace] conditions they rejected with indomitable brio not so long ago."[100] Though a frequent critic of Morocco's leaders and strategy, Hardman wrote glowingly about its battlefield conduct at Guad-el-Ras:

> They have fought well before, but it was hardly to be expected, under all the circumstances, that they should have fought the best at the last. When we remember that they had been invariably defeated during the four months' campaign—often, as I believe, with less damage than their careful, deliberate fire inflicted on the victors, but on some other occasions, certainly, with very heavy loss—that they had not a single triumph to look back upon as a precedent for hope, nor a single gun to oppose to the Spanish artillery, which, with that prodigality of fire that distinguishes it, crushed them with shot, shell, and rockets; remembering all these things, I say, one must regard with admiration the fact that on Friday last they showed a dash and determination even greater than they ever before displayed.[101]

Depictions of the actual fighting at Guad-el-Ras ring with appeals to Moroccan zeal and resiliency. "They fought like wild beasts," one author wrote, "using their rifles as clubs while raining a hail of bullets and projectiles of all types on their enemy."[102] A French account of the battle emphasized how "the Moroccans fought in despair; certain positions were taken and retaken several times; there were bloody battles (des mêlées sanglantes) on a great number of points on the battlefield, and the knife had all the honors of the day."[103] Even the 2nd Division's official history tipped its cap to its Moroccan foes. "Innumerable were the enemies; incredible the boldness with which they returned to the burden after twenty-two previous encounters [battles]; delicious the audacity with which they came again to try their fortune on the same ground on which they were previously trampled."[104]

Ironically, such high combat motivation actually created disciplinary problems for Moroccan military commanders. Soldiers refused to take prisoners,

99. Salawi 1917, 78–80.
100. Gutiérrez Maturana 1876, 257.
101. Hardman 1860, 287.
102. Joly 1910, 126.
103. Mordacq 1900, 89.
104. Gutiérrez Maturana 1876, 261.

for example. As O'Donnell noted, "every individual taken by them is first tortured, then put to death without pity, and his bleeding limbs carried about as trophies among these savage tribes."[105] In an effort to "humanize the war," the Sultan himself offered one hundred ducats for every Spanish prisoner of war brought in alive.[106] The Sultan also faced an unexpected obstacle when seeking peace: his own tribal levies. All post-Tetuán battles were fought principally by new Riffian units that were unbloodied and wanted an opportunity to inflict harm on Spanish forces. In at least one instance, a Riffian contingent disobeyed the Sultan's orders to stand down; it was subsequently crushed at Guad-el-Ras.[107] High resolve among his soldiers meant that the Sultan could underinvest in monitoring and sanctioning mechanisms, though at the possible cost of increased battlefield freelancing by units (over)eager to carry on fighting when strategic imperatives dictated otherwise.

5.3.3.   Battle of Tetuán

The Battle of Tetuán (4–6 February 1860), the war's most significant armed clash, provides an ideal opportunity to examine Moroccan battlefield performance at close range. Moroccan forces fared poorly; in a single morning, the Army of Africa breached Moroccan prepared defenses at Tetuán, an important commercial center, and scattered Moroccan forces in several directions. Worse, after O'Donnell issued a 24-hour ultimatum, a delegation of local leaders ceded Tetuán to Spanish forces, who entered triumphantly, and unopposed, on 6 February. Chastened, the Sultan entered into peace negotiations with O'Donnell, albeit halfheartedly and with an eye toward using the talks to buy time for another offensive. The battle's outcome resonated across European capitals. Madrid heralded the victory as proof of Spain's return to the ranks of Great Powers, while foreign military observers from Prussia, France, and the United Kingdom were present to glean lessons about contemporary warfare.[108] Tetuán thus represents Morocco's worst single-day performance of the entire war.

This may seem a strange position from which to argue for Morocco's relatively robust battlefield performance. Rather than cherry-pick a battle (such as the Battle of Melilla) that casts Moroccan battlefield performance in a highly favorable, and possibly skewed, light, I intentionally stack the deck against my own argument, looking instead for evidence of

105. *Illustrated London News*, 17 December 1859.
106. "Spain," *New York Times*, 20 February 1860.
107. Alarcón 1988, 575.
108. Arrue 1898, 89; Yriarte 1863, 153.

Morocco's comparatively high combat power and cohesion precisely on its darkest day.[109]

After a month of fitful advances, the Army of Africa finally reached the plains before Tetuán on 1 February. Some 25,000-strong, the Army pitched its camp on the plain's eastern edge, wedged tightly between the River Martin (to its south) and the Mediterranean (to the east). Tetuán itself nestled on a series of rolling hills about eight kilometers to the southwest. Befitting its importance, the city was ringed with thick stone walls, parapets, and artillery, an "impregnable" series of defenses that prompted O'Donnell to begin preparations for a lengthy siege.[110] Standing almost equidistant between Tetuán and the Spanish encampment were two fortified Moroccan camps containing 30–35,000 soldiers, including cavalry and at least eight cannons.[111] Each camp was defended by extensive trenches, palisades, and artillery positions. The famed Royal Black Guard of Fez, a highly trained contingent of shock infantry soldiers, had also been dispatched to backstop the twin forces of Mulay Ahmet and Mulay Abbas, a development O'Donnell noted with alarm in his official report.[112] Mulay Abbas's camp, located about a kilometer north of Mulay Ahmet's, encircled the Gheli Tower, which afforded sweeping views of the entire plain.

Frustrated by the halting nature of the Spanish campaign, O'Donnell abandoned his plans to besiege Tetuán and instead sought a decisive encounter that would hasten the war's end. At 8:30 on the morning of 4 February, O'Donnell ordered his forces to break camp and march on Tetuán in two main lines of advance.[113] Crossing the Kantara River via four hastily assembled pontoon bridges, these two formations advanced westward across the plain, seeking to converge on Mulay Ahmet's camp which lay directly astride the route to Tetuán. Each formation had two brigades in echelons of battalions, with an additional two brigades in columns supporting these units. Artillery units were packed into the middle of each formation, with cavalry

109. The explicit counterfactual here is provided by Kokand's disastrous performance at the Battle of Tashkent (see below). Both belligerents faced European powers; fought from prepared defensive positions, including walled cities; had numerical preponderance; and had similar artillery and infantry weapons.

110. On Tetuán's formidable defenses, see Balaguer 1860, 371.

111. Some estimates of Moroccan forces ranges as high as 45–50,000 (Castelar et al. 1859, 264). Most historians and eyewitnesses converge on a lower estimate of 35,000 soldiers, however.

112. Arrue 1898, 90. See his "Parte Oficial de la Accion con Fecha de 8 de Febrero de 1860," reproduced in del Rey 2001, 133–39, quote on 133.

113. Battlefield accounts are drawn from Castelar et al. 1859, 257–63; Gutiérrez Maturana 1876, 191–202; Mordacq 1900, 79–82.

assuming a rearguard role. Spanish forces could call upon forty modern artillery pieces along with Congreve batteries, though these rockets proved of dubious quality and utility.[114] O'Donnell dispatched a third, smaller, formation to the Star Redoubt, a small hill on the northeastern edge of the battlespace, to block any Moroccan cavalry charge against the exposed Spanish right flank.

Moroccan forces responded quickly to Spanish movements. Cavalry were sent to guard the flanks of each camp, waiting like two outstretched arms to envelop the Army of Africa as they crossed the plain. Nearly 3,000 horsemen were arrayed on the left flank of Mulay Ahmet's camp, while some 5,000 sealed the right flank of Mulay Abbas's camp, where they threatened to descend on the army's exposed right flank. Abbas had also hidden infantry, along with sections of the Black Guard, in a thick brushwood forest on his right flank, which afforded his soldiers excellent firing positions. Infantry were also ordered to man the trenches, waiting to fire until Spanish soldiers were entrapped in the marshes that dotted the landscape in front of their defensive positions.

Once Spanish forces closed to within about two kilometers of Mulay Ahmet's camp, Moroccan artillery opened up, raining shells upon the two advancing formations. Casualties remained light, however, due to poor Moroccan aim. Moroccan cavalry stirred, but no charge from the right flank emerged, a missed opportunity to disrupt the Spanish assault that would prove fatal. Still under fire, Spanish artillery were brought forward and, grouped together, began shelling Ahmet's camp from a distance of only six hundred meters. Moroccan and Spanish artillery continued to trade blows until 10 a.m., when O'Donnell ordered his formations to fix bayonets and charge the trenches outside Ahmet's camp, hoping to achieve breakthrough through the shock of a frontal assault.[115] His forces, however, quickly bogged down in the marshy terrain. Seizing their opportunity, Moroccan infantry opened fire against the struggling Spanish, inflicting heavy casualties. The 2nd Division's official campaign report records the scene:

What unforeseen inconvenience stops the thrust of our heroic battalions? What can so bizarrely disrupt such a determined march? The

---

114. "Uncertain and difficult to aim, some failed to launch and some did not explode," noted one review of the battle (Arrue 1898, 98). "Do not expect the hoped-for results in this or other [future] campaigns."

115. O'Donnell's own after-action report views this bayonet charge as decisive in penetrating Moroccan lines and in turning Spanish fortunes around. "Parte Oficial de la Accion con Fecha de 8 de Febrero de 1860," reproduced in del Rey 2001, 133–39, quote on 137. See also Villalobos 2004, 20–21.

death of a hundred of ours! A swamp defends the trenches; a damn swamp where men stagger to the knee, sliding and falling without being able to get up, making unheard-of efforts to get out. [But] they are stuck and losing precious time that the enemy uses to fire deadly discharges.[116]

Spanish forces began to waver under withering Moroccan fire that was "decimating our ranks."[117] Sensing disaster, a desperate General Juan Prim personally exhorted his Catalan volunteers onward, driving his soldiers forward by placing himself at the head of the formation. His soldiers rallied, breaching several lines in Mulay Ahmet's trenches in a scene long since valorized as the height of Spanish martial heroism.[118] Spanish troops poured through the gaps torn in Ahmet's lines, engaging in brutal hand-to-hand combat with surprised Moroccan soldiers. Mulay Ahmet's forces, now reeling, sought to retreat and regroup, only to find their rally points under heavy Spanish bombardment. His forces then attempted to mount a second defense from within the fortified camp itself. These positions, too, were eventually breached, though not without significant Spanish casualties. One Catalan battalion entered the battle with 34 officers and 324 soldiers; attaining breakthrough cost half its unit strength.[119]

Now it was the Moroccans' turn to waver. The sudden breaching of Mulay Ahmet's camp set off a panic within defending forces that quickly spread to Mulay Abbas's still-unchallenged forces. Moroccan soldiers streamed from the camps, seeking refuge either in Tetuán or farther afield, hoping nearby mountains might provide shelter. With no defending army, Tetuán was left to O'Donnell's mercy, a position he leveraged by issuing a 24-hour ultimatum for its leaders to surrender the city or "know the horrors of a city square bombed and taken by assault."[120] Local leaders quickly complied, and O'Donnell's forces marched through the city's gates on 6 February. Morocco's defeat appeared total: some 2,500–3,000 soldiers were killed during the morning assault,[121] while 86 cannons, along with 2,000 shells and a vast stockpile of

116. Gutiérrez Maturana 1876, 198.

117. Alarcón 1988, 335.

118. "Romance XIX Tetuán por España" in Bustillo 1868, 27–28.

119. Alarcón 1988, 340.

120. "Mensaje al Gobernador de Tetuán de 5 de Febrero para Rendir La Plaza," reproduced in del Rey 2001, 133.

121. These figures represent the high end of estimates. Moroccan casualties are notoriously difficult to pin down accurately. One French observer, presumably with less incentive to inflate Moroccan casualties, estimated that only 1,000 Moroccan soldiers were killed or wounded (Mordacq 1900, 83fn1).

gunpowder, were also lost.[122] Seeking a breathing spell to reconstitute his forces, the Sultan authorized the opening of peace negotiations.

Yet despite this battlefield defeat, some elements of customary Moroccan tactical and operational proficiency remained on display. Moroccan trench-works and covering positions were extremely well-chosen; Moroccan soldiers proved adept at channeling Spanish forces into narrow shooting lanes and in specifically targeting officers to sow confusion.[123] As a result, Spanish casualties were considerable. An estimated 1,115 were either killed or wounded during the brief battle; by contrast, Spain suffered about 1,500 casualties in the entire Spanish-American War.

These casualties also reflect the high resolve exhibited by Moroccan soldiers. Tearing holes in the trenches required stubborn hand-to-hand combat and bayonet charges to dislodge Moroccans who "obstinately disputed every foot of ground." Some portions of the trenches changed hands four times before finally yielding to Spanish control.[124] Accounts by Spanish and foreign observers are replete with references to Moroccan courage and tenacity. "They defined themselves with violence and desperation," one account reads, and continued to fight even after a lucky Spanish artillery round detonated a Moroccan ammunition depot, sending up "an immense cloud of smoke and dust."[125] Nearly all Moroccan soldiers died in their positions—O'Donnell refused to consider pursuing the routed Moroccan forces—giving rise to scenes of terrible carnage. "The trenches were littered with corpses," wrote Charles Yriarte, a French eyewitness, "and the cannons marbled with blood: the enemy artillerymen, courageous until suicide, had been killed on their pieces."[126] Small groups of Moroccan soldiers found themselves surrounded by enveloping Spanish formations but consistently refused to surrender.[127] Tellingly, only 25 Moroccan soldiers surrendered.[128] Even these captives gave the appearance of wanting to continue the fight; one Spanish eyewitness wrote of "the blackened and shattered prisoners with the barbarian desire for revenge still glittering in their eyes."[129]

122. Castelar et al. 1859, 273.

123. Hardman 1860, 209.

124. "The War in Morocco; Capture of Tetuán by the Spaniards," *New York Times*, 25 February 1860. See also Griffiths 1897.

125. Yriarte 1863, 148.

126. Yriarte 1863, 150.

127. Desertion and defection were also notable by their absence despite the battle's lopsided nature.

128. Hardman 1860, 213, 218.

129. Balaguer 1860, 372–73.

The 2nd Division's own official account of the battle singled out the bravery of Moroccan artillerymen:

Honor [is due], therefore, because it is a thing of justice, to those savage inhabitants of that mighty empire! Honor those African gunners who, wrapped in a cloud of projectiles, do not cease for one minute in your defense! Honor the commander of the cannon on the right of his line [at Mulay Ahmet's camp] who, heroic like no one else, fired his cannon when the smoke and flames of [Spanish] blasts still enveloped him![130]

These heroics cannot mask the extent of the Moroccan defeat, however. And while contingency certainly played its part—most notably, the lucky Spanish shell detonating a key powder magazine—Morocco's defeat can be ascribed to deeper failures of two of its combat branches. First, Moroccan artillery proved woefully inept, unable to hit slow-moving Spanish formations walking across open ground despite their excellent field positions. Gunners often simply fired in parabolic arcs, causing their shells to bury themselves harmlessly in the soft soil. As contemporaries pointed out, firing with a flatter trajectory would have caused much greater casualties as shells ricocheted within Spanish formations.[131] As Hardman acknowledges, the Spanish caught a break.[132] Second, Moroccan cavalry, typically its most capable branch, turned in an uncharacteristically poor showing at Tetuán. Cavalry formations on Mulay Ahmet's flank hardly moved, providing only nuisance value rather than a concrete threat to advancing Spanish troops. The Black Guard, sent to protect the right flank of Mulay Abbas's camp, was checked by a much-smaller Spanish contingent on the Star Redoubt and declined battle. It is unclear why exactly the cavalry failed to engage; Yriarte contends that Tetuán's strategic importance instilled a conservatism in Moroccan tactics and operations at odds with its strengths conducting mobile offensives.[133]

The Battle of Tetuán also highlights two battlefield behaviors that appear inconsistent with the expectations of the proposed military inequality argument. Though Moroccan soldiers did display considerable resolve, their sudden and widespread collapse, followed by the panicked retreat, is unusual for a belligerent with low military inequality. Spanish commanders themselves were surprised: "Suddenly the enemy everywhere turned his heroic resistance into the most disorderly and humiliating flight that a Christian

130. Gutiérrez Maturana 1876, 196.
131. Yriarte 1863, 148.
132. Hardman 1860, 224.
133. Yriarte 1863, 150.

army could ever witness."[134] Even allowing for artistic license, there is little question that Moroccan forces were rattled by the use of massed artillery and direct frontal assaults on their positions.[135] Mulay Abbas even delayed moving his personal property from Tetuán to avoid inciting further panic among his soldiers.[136] Some retreating soldiers also seized the opportunity to pillage Tetuán, though the details remain contested. Spanish sources predictably cast the pillage of Tetuán as a daylong bacchanalia that destroyed much of the city. Foreign observers, and surviving Moroccan sources, suggest a much more limited affair, with destruction perpetrated by a handful of Riffian auxiliaries, not the main Moroccan force, and confined to the city's small Jewish quarter.[137]

There is also some evidence, though again contested, that Moroccan commanders resorted to extrajudicial punishment to enforce discipline. Sources report, for example, that tribal commanders tried unsuccessfully to compel their soldiers to regroup after the Spanish breakthrough at Mulay Ahmet's camp. As one observer wrote, "in vain the chiefs beat and cursed soldiers within reach, trying to return them to combat.... Those who were in the front ranks saw chiefs in rich costumes strike fugitives with their *gumias* [curved daggers] in a vain effort to bring them back to return to the fire."[138] There are also suggestions, but no hard evidence, that the Sultan ordered his tribal commanders executed after losing Tetuán. According to Spanish sources, "He [the Sultan] ordered the chiefs of all the tribes engaged yesterday [at the Battle of Tetuán] to be decapitated, and many of them, if not all, were accordingly yesterday evening shortened by the head—*pour encourager les autres*, we suppose."[139] If accurate, this is a pattern much more likely to be found in belligerents with higher levels of military inequality than Morocco possessed.

Two points bear emphasizing, however. First, even if true, it is important to note that these executions did not occur along ethnic lines. All commanders deemed responsible were beheaded, at least according to Spanish informants, suggesting the Sultan was not engaged in ethnic scapegoating more familiar to belligerents with higher military inequality. Second, there is reason to doubt that these events even occurred at all. More neutral observers either suggest

134. Gutiérrez Maturana 1876, 200.

135. Salawi 1917, 43, 63–64; Arrue 1898, 109. Not every soldier retreated; harassment fire against Spanish forces continued for hours after the battle (Alarcón 1988, 347).

136. Joly 1910, 102.

137. Al-Nasiri estimates less than thirty individuals were killed during the brief violence.

138. Yriarte 1863, 155.

139. Hardman 1860, 220. See also Alarcón 1988, 440, 449–50.

that such an account was plausible but unlikely or dismiss it as merely a rumor swirling around Tetuán.[140] Intriguingly, al-Nasiri's own account makes no mention of this punishment; instead, his translator inserted a footnote about the supposed beheadings into the original text that was copied nearly verbatim from de Alarcón's classic *Diary of a Witness*.[141]

Setting aside the contested nature of these claims, these mispredictions are helpful in uncovering the limits of the causal links between military inequality and battlefield cohesion. While low inequality belligerents should have correspondingly infrequent outbreaks of soldier panic, this is a probabilistic statement, not an absolute one; even armies without internal ethnic schisms can find themselves vulnerable to battlefield surprise. The proposed theory also takes rational and competent strategy-making as its baseline. Yet in the case of Tetuán, Morocco's relatively high combat power and cohesion were frittered away by senior commanders who made grave errors of judgment, particularly concerning the (non-)employment of Moroccan cavalry. Al-Nasiri pins responsibility for the defeat precisely on emotional, even feckless, decision-making by Mulay Abbas and Mulay Ahmet. "Moroccan soldiers lack a military chief," he wrote, "who can lead them to obtain the victory they desire."[142] Having low military inequality does not guarantee battlefield victory, especially if senior commanders are driven by non-rational motives or, more simply, exercise poor judgment that leads to costly mistakes and errors.

But we should not exaggerate these shortcomings. The defeat at Tetuán proved less than decisive; only three days later, a regrouped Moroccan army inflicted a stinging defeat on Spanish forces at Melilla. And while Tetuán was sold at home as the greatest victory of Spanish arms in the nineteenth century—a fairly low bar—reality soon intruded.[143] Heavy Spanish losses at Tetuán, along with clear evidence that Moroccan forces remained in the field, led to a downward revision of the war's objectives.[144] Dreams of marching on Tangier were postponed indefinitely as the costs and sacrifices necessary became clear. "With sufficient means," the 2nd Division's operational history concluded, "one day [we] could undertake this war, which will last many years, perhaps lasting several generations."[145] Even with its worst

140. See, for example, Schlagintweit 1863, 323–24 and Yriarte 1863, 165–66.

141. Salawi 1917, 44. On the sometimes unreliable nature of al-Nasiri's translator, Clemente Cerdeira, see Calderwood 2012, 399–401.

142. Salawi 1917, 65.

143. Lécuyer and Serrano 1976, 90–91.

144. Mordacq 1900, 83.

145. Gutiérrez Maturana 1876, 53.

performance, the Battle of Tetuán cemented Morocco's reputation for tough-
ness through force of arms, a victory in its own right at a time when many of
its peers were succumbing to imperialist ventures that erased them from the
ledger of sovereign states.

5.4.   Kokand at War

Kokand's battlefield performance was, in a word, poor. Overall, Kokand's
military was wracked by all but one of the four pathologies tracked by the
battlefield performance index. Kokand was on the receiving end of one of the
most lopsided loss-exchange ratios recorded in Project Mars. Desertion was
a constant affliction, one that began with the very first battle with Russian
forces and carried on throughout the war. Defection, too, occurred, particularly among Kirghiz, Kipchak, and Uzbek soldiers whose ethnic communities
had suffered prewar repression. In this case, Kokand narrowly escaped scor-
ing a "1" for the presence of mass defection; Cherniaev's decision to limit the
side-switchers in his employ placed an artificial cap on the number of soldiers
who successfully defected, keeping it below the 10 percent threshold considered "mass" defection. Violence and coercion were also staples of Kokand's
efforts to maintain discipline and cohesion within the ranks. Soldiers and their
commanders from certain ethnic groups and tribes were extrajudicially executed by a dedicated unit, a practice that sometimes extended to elders and
their communities beyond the battlefield. Kokand's tactics and operational art
were also rudimentary at best, with commanders privileging discipline and
control over flexibility and decentralization in the face of widespread soldier
apathy and strong incentives to malinger or worse.

5.4.1.   Combat Power

Kokand's tactical and operational proficiency was remarkably low. 'Alimqul,
who personally oversaw battles in his role as *Amir-i lashkar*, preferred simple
extended line tactics that maximized command and control. He arrayed his
infantry, typically drawn from Uzbek and local populations, in a single thin
line designed to extend beyond enemy flanks, thus protecting against envelopment. Once in position, his forces were tasked with frontal assaults directly
into the teeth of closed Russian formations, relying on the crush of numbers
to overwhelm the square. His cavalry, long the dominant arm in Kokand's
combined arms approach, swept ahead of these infantry charges and attacked
from the flanks in an effort to tear open a hole in Russian defenses. Yet cavalry
and infantry were poorly coordinated. His cavalry formations often surged
far ahead of the infantry, leaving the Russians time to regroup to meet the

exposed soldiers now charging their positions. Kokand's artillery played an important supporting role, often lobbing harassment fire into Russian positions. Technologically superior to Russian cannons, Kokand's artillery was sometimes deployed as a shock weapon, wheeled into combat to charge enemy positions alongside infantry (a maneuver known as a *djilav*).

In a representative address to his soldiers on the eve of the Battle of Chimkent (September 1864), 'Alimqul exhorted his soldiers to smash the Russian square in the name of their Islamic faith:

My cavalry, you are all great warriors (*batyri*)! Your zeal is written on your faces. Do you see, my good fellows, sacred Kuchkar-Ata [on the outskirts of Chimkent]? The infidel's soldiers surround it; let us rail against these lawless forces. After all, we are Muslims, and they are nonbelievers. Do not give up, young ones, while you are still alive, even if it looks like the end of the world has come. Smash the wall [the Russian square] and the defenses of the infidels! Find and pin their commanders; let our horses swim in their red blood, let them trample their corpses as they swim in red blood! Let our heroes break through the center of the infidel soldiers! Beat the drums, blow the horns! Let the battlefield stir with bravery, let red blood pour onto the field, let's sacrifice our souls in the name of our faith. Those killed by the infidels will become martyrs. The infidels' camp will burn. Remember, heroes are ashamed to retreat...if you're a real warrior, then you must not shrink from this. Today will be a great battle! Let us each kill one [infidel], praise God![146]

Vastly outnumbered, Russian forces relied on closed formations to defend themselves from these frontal assaults. Horse-mounted Cossack pickets were stationed on all sides of the square to disrupt Kokandian cavalry charges, while advance guards provided some early warning of an impeding attack, though they often remained close to the main formation to avoid being isolated and enveloped.[147] Russian soldiers had explicit instructions to hold their fire until very close range to maximize stopping power. It was believed, correctly as it turned out, that Kokand's forces would abandon the fight

---

146. Veselovskii 1894, 20–21. Veselovskii (1894) is an important compendium of 'Alimqul's pre-battle speeches reconstructed from postwar oral histories of Kokandian participants and eyewitnesses.

147. Baumann 1993; Marshall 2006, 52–56; Kostenko 1880, endpapers.

early if met with concentrated fire.[148] Artillery and rocket units engaged in harassment fire to disrupt cavalry charges; they also added their firepower to close-range defense of the square.[149] Russian commanders were not averse to temporary withdrawals if they feared being overrun, though such practices were generally discouraged since it was felt that any sign of weakness would embolden Kokand's shaky forces.

Russian tactics were well-chosen. Early battles at Aulie-Alta, Turkistan, and Chimkent revealed that Kirghiz cavalry and Tajik infantry—groups both repressed or marginalized by 'Alimqul's rule—had little desire to press home attacks. Nor did Kipchak cavalry exhibit any willingness to support their bitterly hated Kirghiz foes in any kind of coordinated assault. References to the inability of Kokand's forces to mount prolonged attacks or to regroup if faced with resistance are chockablock in official Russian accounts of these battles.[150] At Turkistan, for example, Kokand's much larger army, which also enjoyed a 10:2 preponderance of artillery, was "met with grapeshot at extremely close distance and they ran with enormous losses, especially in the front ranks [and] thus from that moment their opening assault was already ended."[151] 'Alimqul's forces, even those not yet in combat, broke in "great disorder" and fled for the relative safety of the nearby fortress. Unlike Moroccan forces, Kokand's army was unwilling, or unable, to regroup or innovate around Russian tactics; battles were one-and-done affairs and, as a consequence, were short-lived, typically lasting only a few hours.

'Alimqul himself expressed disappointment at his inability to breach Russian squares despite his highly favorable force ratio. At Chimkent, for example, he noted that "the Russian warriors are few in number. If we launch an attack, the Russians could shoot only once; they don't have time for a second volley and we'll overpower them."[152] Yet upon viewing the initial results of the assault, he remarked that while "there are only a little over two hundred [Russians, an undercount] the surprising thing is that such an army as ours cannot overpower them."[153] In subsequent pre-battle speeches, he harangued his soldiers to "shoot, shoot, and shoot again"[154] in a desperate bid to stop

---

148. Zaitsev 1882, 34; "Komanduiushchii Novo-Dar'inskoi linii komanduiushchemu voiskami. Orenb. kraia: 20 dekabria [1864] № 8424" in Serebrennikov 1914b, 280–81.

149. "Gener. sht. kapit. Meier komanduiushchemu Syr-Dar'inskoi linii 17 iiulia [1864] № 60" in Serebrennikov 1914a, 231–36.

150. See, for example, "Statisticheskii otchet o sostoianii Syr Dar'insk. linii v 1864 godu (Vypiska). 31 dekabria [1864]" in Serebrennikov 1914b, 288.

151. Terent'ev 1906, 280–81, 286, 291.

152. Tashkandi 2003, 65.

153. Tashkandi 2003, 64.

154. Veselovskii 1894, 50.

the one-shot nature of his offensives. Frustrated with the apparent inability of his commanders to revise their tactics, he also routinely sacked commanders while publicly criticizing the negligence of others.

Faced with widespread indiscipline as early as the war's first battle at Aulie-Aata, 'Alimqul was forced to forego more ambitious tactics and operations.[155] Remarkably, 'Alimqul radically truncated his commanders' operational flex-ibility by ruling out offensives in the disastrous aftermath of their defeat near Chimkent in September 1864. Fooled by a faked retreat, Kokand's army was baited into a headlong chase of fading Russian forces when Cherniaev turned the tables, catching Kokand's disorganized formations in mid-pursuit, crushing them. 'Alimqul quickly issued a remarkable edict to his senior commanders: avoid offensives, and instead utilize Kokand's vast manpower advantage by hunkering down in fortresses. "Let him [Mizra Ahmad Quesh-begi, 'Alimqul's commander at Chimkent] henceforth not perpetrate such imprudent and foolish actions," 'Alimqul wrote. "Even if the Russian army approached Tashkent, were defeated, abandoned their artillery, canopies, tents and fled, let him not go out of the fortified walls to seize the spoils. It will be sufficient if he holds onto the Tashkent fortress."[156] These instructions were widely disseminated to his other commanders. He also repeated this injunc-tion even after a Russian reconnaissance effort was beaten back near Tashkent in October 1864.[157]

The lone bright spot was Kokand's artillery. In 1855, Kokand reached an agreement with the United Kingdom to help establish a local arms industry, including the provision of cannon specialists.[158] The agreement also permit-ted Indian soldiers to fight in Kokand's ranks against Russia, though this provision was never implemented.[159] Cherniaev himself was impressed with Kokand's artillery, believing it to be superior in range and quality than his own cannons. In July 1864, Kokand unveiled its high-explosive shells at a skirmish near Aq Bulaq, catching Cherniaev by surprise.[160] "After noon the Khokandians emplaced 3 weapons on the high ground," he recalled, "and

---

155. Radical tactical innovation was also made difficult given the regime's fears of arming unreliable tribes and its use of forced recruitment among locals, who had little time to train properly. See Bobozhonov 2010, 252; Zaitsev 1882, 34.

156. Quoted in Tashkandi 2003, 68.

157. Tashkandi 2003, 69.

158. Dubovitskii and Bababekov 2011, 54–55.

159. 'Alimqul's chief of artillery was, however, a British-trained Punjabi named Djamadar Na'ib (Tashkandi 2003, 64fn236).

160. "Telegramma Voennago ministra komandiru Orenb. korp.; 22 aprelia [1864] № 34" in Serebrennikov 1914a, 107; "Komanduiushchii Syr-Dar. lin. komandiru Orenb. korp.; 9 iiulia [1864] № 140" in Serebrennikov 1914b, 222; Terent'ev 1906, 293.

the first shell which flew through our camp produced a shocking effect on morale—it exploded, and everyone saw that we had business with an enemy the like of which the Syr Dar'ia [i.e., Russian] army had not met before."[161] As with the Spanish in Morocco, Russian commanders falsely believed that British gunners were clandestinely assisting Kokand.[162]

Yet even the occasional success exposed the fragility of Kokand's divided military. At the Battle of Iqan (3–4 December 1864), a small 106-soldier *sotnia* of Cossacks was ambushed and surprised by a nearly 10,000-strong Kokandian formation.[163] The Cossacks were quickly surrounded but unleashed a "disciplined fusillade" that held Kokand's forces at bay. Unable to breach the square, Kokand's commanders ordered the construction of four *qaraburas*, long barriers of thick felt and straw that were each held aloft by 500 men. These shields allowed Kokand's forces to absorb the Cossacks' fire and to penetrate their formation. At least 57 Cossacks were killed; the rest escaped to nearby Turkistan. The dead soldiers were beheaded and their remains scattered across different cities to demonstrate 'Alimqul's martial prowess and to serve as a warning to those considering aligning with Russia.

There's little doubt that the victory at Iqan, however inconsequential militarily, temporarily bolstered 'Alimqul's political fortunes at home.[164] It also emboldened 'Alimqul to dispatch a large contingent of his soldiers to help an upstart leader, Yakub-Beg, in his military campaign against China at Kashgaria.[165] This was ill-advised: he would soon need these soldiers, especially since Kokand's longtime nemesis, Bukhara, was trying to broker a deal with Russia to partition Kokand.[166] But it is the immediate aftermath of the battle itself that is most telling. As 'Alimqul's biographer Mirza 'Alima Tashkandi recounted:

> Immediately after the battle concluded, Kipchak and Kirghiz soldiers turned on each other and began fighting over trophies and the clothing of dead Russian soldiers. As is known, the material incentives for waging Jihad are no less serious than the religious. This need for military spoils arose not from Islamic precepts but rather from the traditions

161. "Komandir Orenb. korp. Voennomy ministru 17 iiulia [1864] № 156 (Telegramma)" in Serebrennikov 1914a, 233.

162. "Nachal'nik Novo-kokanskoi linii komanduiushchemu Sibir. korp. 25 sentiabria [1864] № 1051" in Serebrennikov 1914b, 107.

163. This narrative is constructed from Bobozhonov 2010, 267–69; Beisembaev 2008, 70–71; Pavlov 1910, 118–20; "Nachal'nik Novo-kokanskoi linii Voennomu ministru; 27 dekabria [1864] № 2011" in Serebrennikov 1914b, 279–80.

164. Terent'ev 1906, 288–91.

165. Kim 2004; Bobozhonov 2010, 270.

166. Bobozhonov 2010, 256.

of steppe freemen, where the rule of capture of *uldja* (spoils, trophies) as reward for risk and "military service" dominated. In this case, the modest success at Iqan (which did not have any real military significance) strengthened 'Alimqul's position and for the time being quieted the opposition movement. He triumphantly returned to Kokand.[167]

Poor coordination between combat arms, a reliance on rigid frontal assaults, and fears about battlefield cohesion combined to produce a disastrous loss-exchange ratio. While care must be taken with casualty estimates, Kokand lost an average of 56 soldiers for each Russian soldier it managed to kill.[168] Battles in 1865 were even more lopsided than 1864; at the concluding Battle of Tashkent, Kokand lost an estimated 200 soldiers for each Russian killed.[169] A staggering one-third of all Kokand's forces deployed at Tashkent—including hundreds of cavalry that drowned while fleeing Russian forces—were killed.[170] We cannot, however, ascribe these casualties to Russian technological superiority. While it is true that Russian rifles were superior to Kokand's mixed bag of weapons, Russian doctrine threw away range superiority by having soldiers open fire only at extremely close range. Moreover, Kokand, not Russia, held the technical edge in artillery. And, finally, Kokand's losses were high while on both offense and defense; casualties were steep even when fighting from well-fortified positions. Rather, blame for these losses can be placed on the schisms within Kokand's army that frustrated coordination, demanded simple tactics that drove up casualties, and that induced mass desertion that left fleeing soldiers highly vulnerable to enemy fire.[171]

5.4.2. Cohesion

Given 'Alimqul's narrow ethnocracy and his subsequent reliance on homogenous units to implement painfully simplistic tactics, it is unsurprising that merely fielding coherent forces was a daunting task. Forced to create

167. Quoted in Bobozhonov 2010, 267–68.

168. Estimates of Russian soldiers killed range from 90 to 120, though this likely does not include pro-Russian Kirghiz and Uzbek/Sart soldiers for whom no records exist. Kokand casualties are estimated between 3,657 and 8,567, though 10,000 is not an unreasonable ceiling. Together, LER estimates range from 40.63 to 71.39 Kokand soldiers killed for each Russian killed (mean: 56).

169. Russian forces lost 25 soldiers at Tashkent; Kokand, 4,500–5,500, for a low LER of 180 dead Kokand soldiers for each Russian killed and a high estimate of 220 (mean: 200).

170. Terent'ev 1906, 320.

171. Cherniaev himself credited his battlefield wins to his ability to exploit cleavages within Kokand's ranks. See "Pis'mo Voennogo Gubernatora Turkestanskoi Oblasti General Maiora Cherniaeva Komanduiushchemu voisk Orenburgekovo krai: 7 iiulia [1865]" in Serebrennikov 1914c.

"cohesion out of chaos,"[172] Kokand's commanders faced a raft of disciplinary issues, including mass desertion, sizable defection, and premature surrender, that sapped fighting capacity.

Desertion, for example, was rife, with an estimated 30–40 percent of Kokand's total mobilized army abandoning the fight permanently during the war.[173] Large groups of soldiers, and in many cases, entire formations, exploited battlefield opportunities or nighttime respites to flee.[174] Russian military correspondence to St. Petersburg routinely noted desertion among Kokand's forces, especially its cavalry.[175] Desertion began early; 'Alimqul was already berating "the cowards" in his ranks who "shed their uniforms and tossed their weapons aside" on first contact with Russian forces during the war's opening battle at Aulie-Alta.[176] At Chimkent, widespread desertion was noted even before the battle began. About half of the 30,000 soldiers and con-scripted locals manning Tashkent's defenses ended up fleeing despite facing less than two thousand Russian soldiers.[177]

Mass desertion also unfolded in predictable fashion. Having experienced prewar repression at the hands of 'Alimqul's regime, Kirghiz soldiers, espe-cially cavalry formations, were the first to desert.[178] Kipchak cavalry, partic-ularly those drawn from tribes not favored by 'Alimqul's increasingly narrow vision, deserted next, often expressing twin desires to avoid fighting alongside hated Kirghiz units and to not engage the Russians alone. The downstream consequences of these desertions then rippled out to infantry formations drawn from coethnic Kirghiz and Kipchaks, eventually enveloping more loy-alist Uzbek formations and their commanders.[179] As discipline unraveled, it was often only the ill-trained local forces that remained stranded on the

---

172. MacKenzie 1974, 36.

173. This estimate is derived from multiple sources, including Bababekov 2006*b*, 40–47, Terent'ev 1906, 280–320, and Bobozhonov 2010, 260–69.

174. Bababekov 2006*b*, 19; Tashkandi 2003, 64–65; Terent'ev 1906, 318–20; "Zapiska polkovnika Poltoratskago ob obrazovanii peredovoi Kokanskoi linii; 9 iiulia [1864]" in Sere-brennikov 1914*a*, 218; "Komandir Orenb. korp. Voennomu ministru; 18 iiulia [1864] № 2516" in Serebrennikov 1914*a*, 248–51; and "Nachal'nik Novo-kokanskoi linii Vsennomu ministru; 14 oktiabria [1864] № 1142" in Serebrennikov 1914*b*, 132–36.

175. "Nachal'nik peredovoi Kokan: linii komandiru Sib. korp; 8 avgusta [1864] № 577" in Serebrennikov 1914*b*, 22, 25; "Komandir Orenb. korp. Voennomu ministru; 18 avgusta [1864] № 30" in Serebrennikov 1914*b*, 54, 55; and "Statisticheskii otchet o sostoianii Syr Dar'insk. linii v 1864 godu. 31 dekabria [1864]" in Serebrennikov 1914*b*, 286–87.

176. Quoted in Veselovskii 1894, 26.

177. Terent'ev 1906, 313–20.

178. Zaitsev 1882, 44.

179. Tashkandi 2003, 249.

battlefield, trapped between continuing the fight for their homes or cutting a deal with Russian commanders.[180]

This cascade of desertions is difficult to reconcile with the familiar claim that casualties induce soldiers to quit the fight. Even early in the war, desertion among Kirghiz and non-favored Kipchak cavalry often preceded battle. In some cases, these formations refused to join battle at all. Kirghiz and then some Kipchak cavalry, for example, refused to attack Russian columns marching on the two fortresses at Shur-Tipa that protected Tashkent.[181] As noted above, cavalry charges were often desultory, one-shot affairs, with only minimal casualties taken (especially given overwhelming force ratios) before these units returned to their homes. Unlike their Moroccan counterparts, Kokand's infantry was also willing to countenance premature surrender to avoid casualties. Records are incomplete, but we do know that 370 prisoners were captured during the May 1865 battle at Niiazbek fortress alone, more than Spain managed in the entire Hispano-Moroccan War.[182] Infantry actually laid down in their positions and surrendered at the climatic battle at Tashkent as well.[183]

'Alimqul's pre-battle speeches also reflected a growing concern that appeals to Islam were not enough to bridge the fissures within Kokand's ranks. To be sure, 'Alimqul did not hesitate to draw on Islamic rhetoric and imagery to motivate his soldiers. But his speeches and private discussions with senior commanders betray alarm that his army was only being held together by charismatic leaders who could command loyalty along narrower, subgroup, identities. After one of his emirs was killed on the battlefield, 'Alimqul lamented that "when he fell, they [his soldiers] could not even fight for one day, and they all decided to run. But the deserting Muslim forces ... found only the infidels' bullets."[184] 'Alimqul proved prescient; his own death would set in motion the unwinding of his own army. Gathering after 'Alimqul's death outside Tashkent, his emirs bemoaned that "without him, our spine has been broken. Our leader has become a martyr, and the men will be forced to scatter... our friends have turned into enemies [and] now our people have been torn apart."[185] The need to maintain cohesion by his own example of personal

---

180. 'Alimqul's own speeches often distinguish between local soldiers (*avliya*) and those "foreigners" who came from outside the immediate area (*khuroson*) to form Kokand's army. See Veselovskii 1894, 35fn2.

181. Bobozhonov 2010, 277.

182. Zaitsev 1882, 60; "Vr. komanduiushchii voiskami Orenb. korp. Voennomu ministru; 24 maia [1865] № 226" in Serebrennikov 1914c, 169.

183. Zaitsev 1882, 62.

184. Quoted in Veselovskii 1894, 35.

185. Quoted in Veselovskii 1894, 53.

bravery led him to assume a frontline position where he could exhort his soldiers to fight, even at the cost of increasing both his own risk and that of total disintegration.

Defection, too, occurred, though it was dwarfed by mass desertion. Kirghiz and Kazakh volunteers joined Cherniaev's army in the early days of the war; some estimates suggest as many as one thousand Kirghiz cavalry had defected to Russia even before war broke out.[186] In fact, the war's first armed engagement took place between a Russian-commanded 40-strong Kirghiz unit and Kokand block-posts near the Saurun River.[187] These cavalry screened Russian formations and provided reconnaissance, their local knowledge of terrain and Kokand's internal schisms proving invaluable throughout the war. Kirghiz defectors in particular were repeatedly awarded military decorations for their heroism.[188] Perhaps 3–5 percent of Kokand's total deployed force defected during the war. While insufficient to be considered "mass" defection, the proportion of defectors was large relative to the few soldiers that comprised the Russian expeditionary force.[189]

'Alimqul's own wartime conduct also fueled the dynamics of defection. In the wake of Kokand's early defeat near Chimkent (3 August 1864), he elected to turn his army against the Kazakh beys responsible for the city's defense. 'Alimqul set his sights especially on Baizak, a powerful Kazakh elder from the Dulat subtribe who had sided with the Kirghiz to block 'Alimqul's rise to power in 1863.[190] Russian and Kokandian sources paint the post-defeat scene in remarkably similar detail:

Not seeing any particular zeal among the Kazakhs to support Kokand's power, 'Alimqul seized the Kazakh elders of Chimkent and upbraided them for their indifference to the Muslim cause and their submissive obedience to the Russians. He threatened them with revenge and execution and then, for the sake of setting an example, ordered the oldest elder, the 80-year old Baizak, strapped to a loaded cannon and, in the English manner, shot.... The result, however, was completely unexpected: every Kazakh, with the exception of the arrested beys and sultans, fled to Cherniaev's side, and despite the fact that he refused to

186. Sergeev 2012, 112.

187. "Prikaz po voiskam Orenburgskago kraia 16 iiunia 1865g № 205" in Serebrennikov 1914c, 211.

188. "Prikaz po voiskam Zap. Sibiri; 28 iiunia [1865] № 251" in Serebrennikov 1914c, 235–36.

189. Abashin (2014) argues that Cherniaev deliberately downplayed non-Russian contributions in official reports to maximize his own glory. Kirghiz cavalry may therefore deserve greater credit for Russia's victory than they traditionally receive from contemporaries and historians.

190. Tashkandi 2003, 67fn249.

accept those with poor weapons, even the unarmed pledged to aid him powerfully.[191]

Official Russian correspondence estimated that some ten thousand Kazakhs sought to join Cherniaev's forces after this massacre. He accepted nearly one thousand of these petitioners, bolstering his pro-Russian Kazakh formations. As Cherniaev himself recognized, the Chimkent massacre made it possible "for us to wrap ourselves in the clothes of Kazakh liberators [who were] saving them from fanaticism."[192] This incident underscores an important aspect of defection: unlike desertion, the enemy must accept one's proposal to switch sides, possibly creating an artificial ceiling on the actual number of soldiers who defect. Logistical concerns and a healthy distrust of their loyalty led Cherniaev to cap the number of Kirghiz and Kazakh soldiers he employed. Still, these defectors, along with their broader coethnic networks, provided important information about conditions inside the army, fortresses, and beleaguered cities like Tashkent.[193]

'Alimqul was not unaware of these schisms; he himself had contributed to both their creation and their hardening once war broke out. Coercion and violence therefore became staples of his efforts to enforce discipline among potentially disloyal formations. A dedicated unit of pro-'Alimqul Kipchak cavalry was assigned the task of executing commanders and soldiers for battlefield defeats. Soldiers perceived of committing offenses against 'Alimqul, including minor slights and insults, could wind up the victim of extrajudicial punishment, including beheading.[194] While Kirghiz and Kazakh commanders bore the brunt of this fratricidal violence, 'Alimqul ruthlessly punished any signs of dissent even among friendly Kipchak tribes as the war dragged on. These actions prompted the ruling Kipchak tribal aristocracy to charge that 'Alimqul was an unbalanced man who "constantly went against the advice of his tribe." In the end, however, his blocking detachment had a Goldilocks quality: too eager to pursue "savage reprisals against negligent soldiers"[195] and thus intensify kin-based grievances; too few in number to create an effective deterrent to mass indiscipline.

191. Terent'ev 1906, 285. See also Veselovskii 1894, 16. An unknown but sizable number of Kazakh (and some Kirghiz) elders were killed after they too refused to renew their fealty to 'Alimqul after Baizak's execution.

192. "Pis'mo nachal'nika Zachuiskago otriada: 20 avgusta 1864" in Serebrennikov 1914b, 114–16, quote on p. 115.

193. Zaitsev 1882, 65.

194. Bobozhonov 2010, 272.

195. Tashkandi 2003, 7.

The July massacre marked the beginning of a parallel war against populations suspected of treacherous pro-Russian leanings. Kazakhs now entered into a "new era of strife" with the Kipchak-dominated regime that persisted throughout the war. Paranoia, sometimes justified, led 'Alimqul to punish suspect populations, even those he once favored with forced displacement. In the aftermath of Kokand's lone victory at Iqan, 'Alimqul berated the Sart-dominated city for its support of Russia, noting that even "a few [inhabitants] had found time to help the Russian army" in battle. "You call yourselves Muslims," he chided, "yet you become my enemy."[196] After admonishing tribal elders that their souls were going to hell for their presumed misdeeds, he ordered the city to be emptied. Russian military correspondence reported that 'Alimqul's army "robbed the unarmed inhabitants of their household goods and clothing and, as a result, many perished from exposure to the harsh winter."[197] There is some truth to 'Alimqul's claims; local informants had alerted Russian commanders to the ambush of the Cossacks.[198] But the extension of collective punishment to local populations only further weakened Kokand's unity and military capability by creating incentives to cut side deals with Russia and to avoid fighting if drafted into Kokand's army.[199]

5.4.3.   Battle of Tashkent

The Battle of Tashkent (May–June 1865) sounded the death knell for both 'Alimqul and Kokand itself. Cherniaev's small force—only 1,951 soldiers and twelve cannons—nonetheless bested a 30,000-strong Kokand army that seemed safely ensconced behind Tashkent's formidable defenses, which included not only a deep moat and high stone walls but also at least sixty-three cannons in fortified barbettes and dozens of falconets. Tashkent was a sprawling city of two hundred thousand citizens, stretching eighteen miles at its widest point and dominated by a garrisoned citadel located at its eastern edge. The battle to seize this prized trading entrepôt unfolded over two stages: (1) a series of probing Russian offensives and Kokandian counteroffensives along the approaches to Tashkent (May–early June); and (2) the early morning storming of the city (14–15 June) and its eventual surrender (17 June).

Cherniaev opened his spring campaign in early May with an aggressive thrust toward Shur-Tipa, about eight kilometers northeast of Tashkent. His

196. Quoted in Veselovskii 1894, 41. He specifically singled out "Sarts" as responsible rather than issuing a more general complaint against Ikan's citizens (p. 43).

197. "Voennyi gubernator Turkest. obl. komanduiushchemu voisk. Orenb. kraia. 6 avgusta 1865g. № 2962" in Serebrennikov 1914d, 11.

198. Zaitsev 1882, 51.

199. Bobozhonov 2010, 264.

arrival on 6 May cast a ripple of alarm through 'Alimqul and his advisors. An intelligence report received that day warned 'Alimqul that "General Cherniaev stopped at Shur-Tipa and has begun to isolate Tashkent.... The mood of Tashkent's citizens has changed; they seem to have lost faith [in Kokand's army]."[200] In response, he dispatched a close advisor to Tashkent to "determine the mood of the subjects and report to me in written form for us to act accordingly."[201] He was right to be worried; several envoys had been sent by Tashkent's elders to strike a separate peace deal with the Russians. A second faction had approached Bukhara for assistance. One unlucky envoy was caught by 'Alimqul's spies; as a lesson, his property, including his home, was confiscated and then sold, with the proceeds used to fund jihad against the Russians.[202]

Unwilling to wait as war clouds gathered again, 'Alimqul ordered a large formation of about 6,000 soldiers and forty cannons to Shur-Tipa to block Russia's advance. On 9 May, he issued the fateful, and fatal, decision to attack the Russian encampment. Problems arose immediately. His Kipchak and Kirghiz cavalry, the bulk of his deployed strength, refused to attack. Instead, they lingered on the battlefield's sidelines, resistant to 'Alimqul's entreaties to "do one's duty and to defend the honor of Islam that might easily be lost if we break with our faith and forever blacken its name."[203] A sense of dread now rippled through the awaiting infantry; charging into the now-alert Russian formation without cavalry support held little prospect of success. As B. Bobozhonov wrote, the Kokand army now faced internal destruction, as "clan and local interests took precedence over the necessity of joint action against a common opponent, despite the war's religious trappings."[204]

Seeking to rally his forces, 'Alimqul took up position with his artillery, urging them forward to attack the Russia square. Left with no cavalry cover, however, 'Alimqul's position was exposed, and he was quickly felled by a Russian bullet.[205] Gravely wounded, he implored his reeling forces to stand firm: "Kipchaks, Kirghiz, hold fast together! If the infidels take Tashkent, then your hour of reckoning will come!"[206] He lived just long enough to watch his cavalry squadrons quit the battlefield, retiring to Tashkent where they

200. Quoted in Tashkandi 2003, 75.

201. Quoted in Tashkandi 2003, 75.

202. Bobozhonov 2010, 274fn2. Locals, including Baizak's son, were also providing key information about Tashkent's defenses, especially the vulnerable state of its water supplies, to Russian commanders.

203. Quoted in Veselovskii 1894, 50–51.

204. Bobozhonov 2010, 277.

205. Nalivkine 1889, 249, argues that 'Alimqul's death was caused by the desertion of Kokand's cavalry.

206. Quoted in Veselovskii 1894, 52.

later sacked its treasury before returning to their homes.[207] His infantry fell back, too, though in many cases entire sections of the line simply lay down in their positions and surrendered.[208] Quarrels even broke out among Kokand's soldiers over credit for killing 'Alimqul.[209]

Pressing his advantage, Cherniaev set aside his formal instructions from St. Petersburg to halt combat operations and instead ordered his expeditionary force to besiege Tashkent. As his forces slowly tightened the noose around Tashkent, he authored a remarkable secret report for St. Petersburg that outlined how crippling internal divisions had weakened Kokand's military power. 'Alimqul had tried but failed to unite his people against the Russians, Cherniaev argued, because of deep-seated animosities across and within various clans and tribes. The Great Horde of Kirghiz, located in Kokand's northern areas, was in a state of "almost open confrontation" with the government now, including the more politically connected southern Kirghiz who had aligned with the Kipchaks. The northern Great Horde, he maintained, will be "our advance guard against Kokand." The Uzbek-dominated aristocracy was also tangled in near constant infighting with the southern Kirghiz tribes. The Tajiks, for their part, were now divided into northern and southern clans, though still united in their hatred of the Uzbeks. He even noted the simmering tension between Tashkent and the 'Alimqul regime, a wedge he now sought to exploit.[210]

Cherniaev was also well-informed about developments inside Tashkent. Prisoners of war, as well as delegates from the city itself, spoke of an upswell of pro-Russian sentiment, driven partly by hatred of 'Alimqul and partly because the Russian blockade was slowly starving the population.[211] Cherniaev ordered his camp moved to within five kilometers of Tashkent's southern gates in preparation for an assault. His first attempt, on 6 June, failed, however, as the pro-Russian faction could not wrest control of any of Tashkent's heavily fortified gates. Unnoticed by the Russians, a small contingent arrived from Bukhara during the night of 9 June and took control of Tashkent's defenses. Bukhara's commanders quickly set about reconstituting what remained of Kokand's army at Tashkent in preparation for a Russian frontal assault.

---

207. Bobozhonov 2010, 277.

208. Zaitsev 1882, 62; Skilakie 2013, 21.

209. Tashkandi 2003, 14fn51. The tale is also retold in the contemporary Kirghiz song "Prikhod Russkikh" reproduced in Veselovskii 1894, 68.

210. "Zapiska o mestnykh' usloviiakh' russkoi politiki v Srednei Azii (Sekretno). 1 iiunia 1865g" in Serebrennikov 1914c, 173–83.

211. "Voennyi gubernator Turkest. obl. komanduiushchemu voiskami Orenb. kraia; 11 iiunia [1865] № 2085" in Serebrennikov 1914c, 203.

Cherniaev opted for a surprise attack instead, banking on the fact that Kokand's patchwork army was only holding together through fear and a belief in Tashkent's fortified walls. His forces slipped quietly into action during the night of 14–15 June, arriving at Tashkent's walls at 0200. A small formation under Colonel Kraevskii feigned an attack on Kokand Gate while the main force, under Captain A. K. Abramov, headed toward Kamelan Gate. Two detachments were held in reserve. Scaling ladders were thrown against the wall near Kamelan Gate at 0400. Russian soldiers quickly killed the sentries and threw open the gate to waiting Russian forces. Cherniaev then committed his reserve formations, surging his small army through Kamelan Gate before fanning out into the city. Artillery began providing covering fire as the Russians stormed prepared fighting positions while Tashkent's defenders labored to return fire with falconets.

Recognizing their mistake, the main Kokandian formation abandoned their pursuit of Kraevskii's forces and wheeled back into Tashkent. In a now-familiar pattern, these forces broke almost immediately upon contact with Abramov's detachments. Regular Kokandian infantry scattered "in great disorder and with great losses,"[212] leaving resistance to the locals, who now began erecting barricades—the Russians counted forty or more—in Tashkent's narrow, tangled streets.[213] At about the same time, in perhaps the battle's most iconic scene, Kokand's 5,000 remaining cavalry sought escape from the battlefield after offering only desultory resistance.

[Colonel] Kraevskii received word that enemy [cavalry] fleeing from the city had appeared on his right flank; he immediately galloped off with his Cossacks and four cannons to intercept them. Rounds of grapeshot fired from close range successfully caused these mobs to flee once again. A handful of Cossacks (39 individuals) rushed to pursue them, scattering Kokand's cavalry and putting them to flight. This horde of cavalry, more than 5,000-strong, chased only by a handful of brave Cossacks, tossed their banners to the roadside and rushed in great disorder to cross the Chirchik River, drowning each other in the process.[214]

212. "Voennyi gubernator Turkestan. oblasti komanduiushchemu voiskami Orenb. kraia; 7 iiulia 1865g № 2306" in Serebrennikov 1914*c*, 248.

213. "Zapiska o deistviiakh vzvoda strelkovoi roty 7 Zapando-Sibirskago bataliona pri shturme gor. Tashkenta 15,16, i 17 iiunia 1865g" and "Voennyi gubernator' Turkestan. oblasti komanduiushchemu voisk Orenb. kraia; 7 iiulia 1865g № 2306" in Serebrennikov 1914*c*, 218, 248–51. See also Terent'ev 1906, 318–20; Zaitsev 1882, 75.

214. "Voennyi gubernator Turkest. oblasti komanduiushchemu voiskami Orenb. kraia: 7 iiulia [1865] № 2306" in Serebrennikov 1914*d*, 249. In total, Terentiev (1906, p. 320) concludes that half of Tashkent's 30,000-strong garrison deserted during the storm.

Despite these early (and easy) successes, the Russian assault bogged down near Kamelan Gate as determined locals manned barricades and turned their homes (*sakli*) into sniper positions. Indeed, Cherniaev's main force became separated from Kraevskii's detachment in the noise and confusion of running street battles. Desperate to avoid being overrun, Cherniaev ordered the *sakli* around Kamelan Gate to be burned, creating a semicircle of fire that protected his infantry through the night. In concert, he demanded artillery strikes on enemy positions, including the main garrison lodged in Tashkent's citadel, to disrupt any assaults. Early the next morning, Russian forces charged the enemy barricades, clearing them at bayonet point. By 0730 on the morning of 16 June, the citadel was captured and fighting virtually ceased. The city formally surrendered on 17 June. Resistance was somewhat stiffer than anticipated, though much of the credit for fighting goes not to Kokand's army but to locals who organized their own defenses. Cherniaev was able to capitalize on interethnic factions within Tashkent to dampen this resistance. "Partisans of the Russian orientation played a certain role in the comparatively quick attainment of victory [over Tashkent]," historian N. A. Khalfin wrote, "particularly during the period of assault when Tsarist troops held the city wall, Muhammad Saatbay and his followers called on the Tashkent people to stop their resistance ... and facilitated surrender of the city."[215]

Russian casualties were light: 25 soldiers were killed, and another 85–157 were wounded during the storming of Tashkent. Kokand's army lost 4–5,000 soldiers killed, an estimate that excludes uncounted local defenders. With the fall of Tashkent, the war itself was officially proclaimed over. Tashkent itself fell under Russian suzerainty in 1866; nearly half of Kokand's vast lands were now under Russian control. Badly weakened by the war, with its leadership in disarray and its various tribes jockeying for power, Kokand was in little position to resist further Russian encroachment. In 1868, Kokand was declared a Russian vassal; after a brief war in 1875–76, Kokand was abolished and formally annexed to the Russian Empire.

5.5. Discussion

These cases also help extend our knowledge of the mechanics of how military inequality affects battlefield performance in two ways.

First, despite possessing low prewar military inequality, Morocco still underperformed in its battlefield performance, particularly in its loss-exchange ratio. This disparity suggests there are natural limits to the benefits of top-down inclusionary visions of the political community if they do

215. Khalfin 1960, 201.

not generate bottom-up attachment to the regime and its vision. Community, after all, requires not only the absence of state-sanctioned violence or marginalization but also the manufacturing of positive attachment to the broader community if vertical ties are to be constructed—and if soldiers are to be motivated enough to serve and die for the cause. Without this vertical attachment to an overarching identity, horizontal ties between societal groups or, in Morocco's case, tribes, are likely to be attenuated, and commitment to the political community partial and variable across (and within) groups. While low military inequality is a key building block for battlefield performance, there is likely important variation within the category in the strength of the bond between differential societal groups and the architects of the collective vision.

Al-Nasiri's own assessment of Moroccan performance pinpoints the weakness of the overarching political community, of the idea of Morocco itself, as the wellspring of battlefield problems and eventual defeat. Commitment to the Makhzan was still partial and uneven across the various contingents that made up the Moroccan military, he argued, leaving these forces unable to match the motivation and organization of its Spanish foe. Persistent tribalism and incomplete affinity for the Makhzan introduced substantial heterogeneity of motive and resolve of Moroccan forces that imposed a ceiling on its performance despite the Makhzan's inclusionary vision. He wrote:

> The Moroccan volunteers during this period were of two categories. The first were resolute and zealous ones, who would say: "If the enemy weren't holed up in the mountains and protected by his machine guns, then I would do this and that …"And the others, one of who said: "What's in it for me to walk into their gun fire? Let the people of Tetouan fight for their Tetouan. As for me, until they arrive in my tent in 'Abda or in Dukkala…" Or some such talk, as if he didn't believe that it was incumbent upon him to help the Muslims to victory.[216]

The uneven nature of attachment to the communal vision across different components of the Moroccan military helps explain specific episodes in the war. The sacking of Tetuán's Jewish quarter by certain Riffian tribesmen, for example, points to the weakness of horizontal ties across community members. Similarly, the desire to prolong fighting even despite the Sultan's wishes, which led to the crushing defeat of new Riffian levies at Guad-el-Ras, indicates that certain societal groups had a deeper commitment to the communal vision. And while evidence remains contested, the fact that some coercion was used against wayward soldiers at Tetuán becomes more explicable if

216. Salawi 1917, 37.

attachment to the political community was unevenly distributed. There is an implicit counterfactual here: if the Makhzan had been farther along in its efforts to forge "Moroccans out of Riffians," possibly through greater access to education and widespread literacy, positive effects among its soldiers toward the national vision might have been deeper and more widespread. If we could re-run the Hispano-Moroccan War with this version of Morocco, we should expect an increase in battlefield performance. Put differently, Morocco left some of its potential battlefield performance unrealized even though it was on the correct path of low military inequality.

Second, a closer look at 'Alimqul's decision-making reveals the strength of the credible commitment problem he faced. 'Alimqul recognized early that his specific vision for Kokand was alienating large swathes of the population and, by extension, undercutting his military machine. He appeared willing to make changes, at least on the margins, to the broad contours of his identity project, aiming to nudge it in a more inclusionary direction that might increase his yield of volunteers from non-core groups. In a remarkable series of letters, copies of which were captured by Russian intelligence at Orenburg, 'Alimqul appealed to the leaders of repressed and marginalized tribes to support his nation-building efforts.[217] Mistakes had been made, 'Alimqul acknowledged. In his desire to construct a political community on "correct" Islamic principles, he had been excessively heavy-handed. Now he promised a kindler, gentler rule, pledging official forgiveness and an "amnesty for their past transgressions" to all non-core tribes that increased their supply of soldiers to his army. As Bobozhonov notes, this was a purely pragmatic, if not openly cynical, gesture, one aimed at expanding the army while reducing the strength of potential fifth columnists at home. Perhaps most importantly, these modest changes were not induced by wartime pressures; the letters had been dispatched by early February 1864, well before Russian forces arrived on the steppe.[218]

He found few takers. Tribal levies went partially unfulfilled among these targeted groups, while recruits from these populations often entered service grudgingly. Kokand's army was left smaller than 'Alimqul desired, forcing him to make wartime appeals for "anyone with a weapon" to volunteer, with the promise of battlefield spoils as the main inducement to fight.[219] This open recruitment only created new problems. Many of these volunteers had low

217. The three undated letters were translated and reproduced in "Nachal'nik Ala-taus. okp. komandiru Sib. korp.; 24 fevralia 1864g, № 494" as "Prilozhenie 1" (p. 61), "Prilozhenie 2" (p. 62), and "Prilozhenie 3" (pp. 62–63) in Serebrennikov 1914a.

218. Bobozhonov 2010, 245.

219. Bobozhonov 2010, 269.

levels of commitment and even worse skills. 'Alimqul introduced a crash training program in December 1864 but found himself in a bind: train these soldiers up, and increase the risk of domestic challenge, or provide only rudimentary training, and risk defeat at Russian hands. His inability to escape the confines of his narrow vision of the political community also compelled him to make new demands upon his fast-dwindling Kipchak and Kirghiz supporters. He levied new taxes on these previously exempt groups because the unwillingness of non-core groups to support the war curtailed the flow of badly needed resources and supplies to the military. Wartime setbacks tightened this bind: non-core groups were emboldened to push for additional concessions, or to strike deals with Russia and Bukhara, in a bid to recast the tribal and ethnic hierarchy in Kokand once again.

These constraints produced the spectacle of 'Alimqul, who desperately desired peace, repeatedly sabotaging negotiations out of fear that his pro-war supporters would overthrow him. His early efforts to recast Kokand's political community in a (marginally) more inclusionary direction had failed to bear fruit. His fate was now lashed to the demands of the pro-war party at the core of 'Alimqul's communal vision. On no less than three occasions 'Alimqul reached out to Cherniaev, asking for peace terms: once after the Battle at Aulie-Alta;[220] again after the fall of Chimkent, where he pleaded that he did not want peace terms to be "a test of arms;"[221] and a final effort after his lone victory at Iqan. In each case he ultimately walked away from each proffered peace deal, citing his fear of condemnation by his supporters—whom he derided as "ignorant and militaristic adherents and kinsmen"[222]—if he failed to uphold the Islamic values that he had staked his regime on.

The best account of 'Alimqul's thinking comes from Tashkandi, who brokered the final attempted settlement in December 1864. He recorded 'Alimqul's pleasure with the proposed deal: "This peace proposal is very pleasant and good," 'Alimqul acknowledged, indeed "there is not one better than it…. But there is one circumstance which prevents me from accepting it."[223] He explained:

The people of Turkistan and Ferghana are extremely ignorant, stupid and warlike, with rude temperament, and are unable to tell benefit from harm. If we conclude peace, they will all, due to their ignorance, say:

220. "Za nachal'nika Zachuiskago otriada komandiru Sib. korp.; 23 avgusta [1864] № 835" in Serebrennikov 1914b, 57–58.

221. "Mulla Alimkul' nachal'niku Novo-Kokanskoi linii; ? oktiabria [1864]" in Serebrennikov 1914b, 121.

222. Tashkandi 2003, 12.

223. Tashkandi 2003, 73.

"These two apostates—'Alimqual and Tashkandi—are only concerned
with their own rest and pleasures and have abandoned so many Muslims
in Russian hands to conclude this peace. But had they acted heroically,
then we all could have set out on a holy war and captured all the land
from Orenburg to Shamaia [contemporary Semipalatinsk]." While we
are alive, they will abuse and curse us, and after death our children and
grandchildren.[224]

Torpedoing this initiative, 'Alimqul spent the remaining days of his
rule locked in a quixotic struggle to identify and punish tribal leaders who
were independently seeking their own peace deal with Cherniaev.[225] Take
the case, for example, of 'Abdarrakhman-bik, the head of the Sibzarskii part
(*dakha*) of Tashkent. In late-1864, he held a supposedly secret meeting with
Cherniaev in which he asked for Tashkent to be made a Russian protectorate.
When 'Alimqul found out, he had 'Abdarrakhman-bik arrested and his property confiscated; his house itself was sold off, with the proceeds devoted
to the war effort.[226] Stamping out these various initiatives may have prolonged 'Alimqul's rule in the short term, but at the cost of sacrificing Kokand's
survival as an independent state in a war that 'Alimqul himself wished to
escape.

5.6. Alternative Explanations

The matched comparison used here eliminates many leading alternative
explanations for the sharply divergent nature of these belligerents' battlefield
performance. That Kokand, not Morocco, possessed superior initial starting conditions—a far more favorable force ratio, superior artillery, and an
enemy tethered to long, vulnerable, supply lines—only deepens the puzzle.
No research design is perfect, however, and differences across the cases do
remain. Perhaps the most plausible alternative is one that emphasizes the
much greater degree of political instability in Kokand and, in turn, how fears
of removal led 'Alimqul to coup-proof his military. While Mohammad IV did
face some domestic criticism, 'Alimqul was mired in a long-running political
struggle that claimed dozens of would-be aspirants to power. By one count,
there were twenty-one leadership changes between 1841 and 1864 alone.[227]

224. Cited in Tashkandi 2003, 73–74; Bobozhonov 2010, 273.

225. There were multiple appeals by non-core group leaders to Russia and Bukhara to
eliminate 'Alimqul, secede from Kokand, or establish a protectorate. See Bobozhonov 2010,
263–64.

226. Khalfin 1965, 183; Bobozhonov 2010, 273–74.

227. Beisembiev 2008, 18.

In this view, 'Alimqul was forced to constantly watch over his shoulder, particularly since his predecessor, Khudaiar Khan, was bent on reclaiming his throne.[228] Perhaps, then, 'Alimqul had no choice but to sacrifice military effectiveness on the altar of regime survival by remaking his army as a loyal garrison force unfit for combat against external foes like Russia.

Yet this coup-proofing account does not withstand close scrutiny. For starters, 'Alimqul was not worried about a military coup; he actually worked to strengthen the army on the eve of war with Russia. He also left the preference for Uzbeks in command positions untouched, an odd move if he sought to stack senior ranks with loyal coethnics. His main concern was insurrection and revolt from newly disempowered tribes who could raise their own armies against him. Most importantly, a coup-proofing argument mistakes the symptoms for the cause. Political instability was the natural outgrowth of 'Alimqul's violent efforts to overturn the existing tribal hierarchy and to impose a new one. Rearranging the tribal landscape into new tiers of citizenship within the political community inevitably generated unrest.[229] Had 'Alimqul espoused a more inclusive vision, instability and the chronic jockeying of elites for power would have been far more muted. In turn, Kokand's battlefield performance would have improved. Ultimately, 'Alimqul's concerns about regime survival were driven by his choice of collective identity rather than a separate causal chain leading from coup fears to battlefield performance.

5.7. Conclusion

Though an unusual pairing, Morocco and Kokand nonetheless shared many prewar drivers of battlefield performance, including regime type, material preponderance, and military technologies. Their prewar levels of military inequality differed, however, and locked them onto divergent paths once war began. As expected, Kokand's extremely high military inequality translated into near-disastrous battlefield performance that often resembled late-stage Mahdiya's collapse against British forces. Morocco, by contrast, exceeded expectations, particularly at a time when few states were finding any kind of success against European colonial powers. Kokand's performance provides spades of evidence that prewar military inequality can negatively affect soldier motivation and fan the flames of interethnic distrust while inducing commanders to adopt suboptimal practices to maintain cohesion within, and control over, their soldiers. Tribes subjected to state repression were

228. Indeed, Khan was installed by Bukhara as a puppet on rump Kokand's throne after Russia's 1865 victory.

229. Bobozhonov 2010, 242–45.

the first to desert the battlefield, to defect to the Russians, and to engage in other behavior, including premature surrender, that crippled Kokand's military power. These practices diffused from battle to battle because of close ties within units—nearly all were tribally homogenous—that facilitated both information-sharing and coordination once their commanders decided to abandon the war effort. Wartime repression also spread beyond Kokand's soldiers to various tribes suspected of disloyalty, accelerating the army's collapse as it became mired in a "double war" against its own population.

Extreme inequality also induced several key trade-offs in Kokand's battlefield performance. Compared with Morocco, Kokand's commanders were forced to rely on rudimentary tactics and operations that traded flexibility for increased control. Efforts to motivate soldiers through threats and violence backfired, only enflaming grievances that the bulk of the army already harbored against 'Alimqul. Coercion was at best a partial substitute for training; soldiers could be kept in line with threats, but their skill remained low, reinforcing the need for simple tactics and contributing to increasingly lopsided casualties. These differences cannot be chalked up to varying approaches at managing diversity; both armies largely deployed monoethnic (or tribal) units, and neither military had invested heavily in extensive monitoring. Instead, a high degree of ethnic diversity only became problematic because of prior repression; in its absence, as the case of Morocco illustrates, armies will fight hard even if technologically overmatched.

These wars are also valuable guides because of their representative nature. The study of early modern warfare has been dominated by a handful of cases, notably the Franco-Prussian War and American Civil War, that are clear outliers. By contrast, most wars of this era closely resemble the Hispano-Moroccan and Russo-Kokandian Wars. In fact, there are no statistical differences between these chosen wars and remaining early modern conflicts in terms of lethality, duration, force ratios, the types of regimes involved, and distance to the first battle. These cases, in other words, make for ideal theory-testing grounds. Their value, however, is not confined to their ordinariness. Both wars had far-reaching consequences. Morocco's battlefield performance was good enough to preserve its nominal independence for decades, while Kokand's led to vassalage and its eventual erasure from the ledger of independent states.[230]

---

230. The shadow of Kokand would linger over Russia, however. Tashkent was the epicenter of conscription riots in 1916 as the Tsarist state sought to replace battlefield losses through the impressment of 200,000 men from the Ferghana Valley (Abdullaev, Khotamov and Kenensariev 2011, 76).

6

Forging Armies from Prisons of Peoples

HOW INEQUALITY SHAPED OTTOMAN AND HABSBURG BATTLEFIELD PERFORMANCE

A country of nationalities cannot wage war without danger to itself.

KASIMIR BADENI, MINISTER-PRESIDENT OF AUSTRIA

THE PREVIOUS CHAPTER'S COMPARISON of the Sultanate of Morocco and Khanate of Kokand illustrated how shifting from low to extreme inequality sabotages an army's battlefield performance. What happens, however, if two similar belligerents are separated by only a modest degree of inequality? Would we still observe differences in their performance, or do we only witness such sharp downturns when differences in inequality between them are glaringly large? Some initial evidence, derived from the cross-national tests in chapter 4, indicates that while the belligerent with higher absolute level of inequality should still suffer worse performance than its more inclusive counterpart, the differences between the two should be muted compared to a pair of belligerents at opposite poles of the military inequality continuum. Inequality's relative effects, in other words, should be harder to discern as the belligerent's inequality values converge. Ideally, then, we should examine not only pairs of belligerents with sharply divergent military inequality coefficients but also pairs where differences in inequality are much less stark to see if we still observe variation in the quality of their armies' battlefield performance.[1]

---

1. Readers familiar with a dose-response test will recognize a similar intuition here. Large differences in inequality coefficients should translate into large battlefield differences, holding

Turning again to Project Mars, I take up the challenge of isolating the causal effects of inequality by comparing Ottoman battlefield performance during the Italo-Turkish War (1911–12) with Austro-Hungary's on World War I's Eastern Front (1914–17).[2] The Ottoman Empire entered war with Italy over Tripolitania with a high degree of military inequality (a 0.45 military inequality coefficient). Austria-Hungary's Common Army, by contrast, had a medium level of inequality, at about 0.37, when war broke out against Russia.[3] While both belligerents had significant absolute levels of inequality, the difference between the two was fairly modest, amounting to about a 10 percent "nudge" on the military inequality continuum.

Yet differences in battlefield performance can nonetheless be discerned. As this chapter demonstrates, while both powers struggled to field effective armies, the Ottoman Empire's initial performance was relatively worse than Austria-Hungary's despite similar capabilities. The Ottoman 42nd Independent Division recorded a disastrous loss-exchange ratio while fighting an uninspired Italian Army that was doing all it could to avoid losing soldiers. Austro-Hungary's Common Army, despite facing a relatively stronger opponent in Tsarist Russia, nonetheless obtained a far more favorable loss-exchange ratio.[4] Both struggled with combined arms approaches, but Ottoman tactics and operational art were especially wedded to simplistic frontal assaults, a reflection of the difficulties Ottoman officers had in

----

other factors constant. By extension, small differences in inequalities should lead to correspondingly smaller relative differences in battlefield performance. The attenuation in the effect of inequality when moving from large to small differences is thus evidence of a causal relationship at work.

2. The Italo-Turkish War wears many labels: the Turco-Italian War, the Tripolitan War, the Ottoman-Italian War, the *Guerra di Libia*, and the War of Tripoli (*Trablusgarp Sava i*). For consistency's sake, I use "Italo-Turkish War," though somewhat reluctantly, as it obscures the fact that "Turkish" forces were principally Arab and Berber, not ethnically Turkish, in composition.

3. I use Austria-Hungary, Habsburg Empire, and Dual Monarchy interchangeably, reserving "Austria" for the western half of the dual monarchy (rather than *Reichsrat* or Cisleithania) and "Hungary" as the eastern half (rather than Transleithania). See Judson 2016, ix.

4. Formally, the Common Army was known as Imperial and Royal Army (*kaiserlich und königlich Armee*, or *k.u.k* Army). I use both terms interchangeably. The *Honvéd* (formally, the *koniglich-ungarisch*, or *k.u. Honvéd*) refers to Magyar-dominated forces. The Imperial-Royal *Landwehr* (*kaiserlich-koniglich*, or *k.k. Landwehr*) refers to Austrian (German) formations. The Common Army held about two-thirds of the Empire's infantry, along with its cavalry and artillery. The *Honvéd* and *Landwehr* were intended as second-line national guards but, by 1914, had evolved into first-line forces due to Magyar parliamentary pressures for autonomous units. See Watson 2014b, 114.

maintaining discipline over Arab and Berber levies. Both armies also experienced mass desertion. But Ottoman forces began fraying by the war's first day, while desertion took several months to manifest in the Common Army. Both belligerents also came to rely on coercion to create artificial cohesion, hoping to bind their polyglot forces through the threat, and reality, of punishment. Ottoman forces turned to the lash quickly; by the opening battle at Tripoli, Turkish officers had taken up positions in the rear, driving their soldiers forward with their pistols. Austro-Hungary moved more slowly on this front, though fears over the political reliability of non-core soldiers, along with their initial battlefield performance, gradually led to the adoption of increasingly violent sanctions.

The Common Army also pulls double duty in this chapter by demonstrating what happens when military inequality increases during the conflict. A stunning battlefield defeat at Galicia in August–September 1914 led officials, desperate to find a scapegoat, to unleash violence against targeted ethnic minorities, including Ruthenes and Czechs, within the population. The violent campaign was severe enough to drive the Common Army's prewar military inequality to near-Ottoman levels. As a consequence, the Common Army provides an instructive example of how wartime dynamics can worsen military inequality relative to prewar levels and, in so doing, further degrade an army's battlefield performance. By 1917, any advantage that the Common Army held over its Ottoman counterfactual had eroded away as it too donned a straitjacket of high military inequality that contributed to its battlefield defeat and subsequent disintegration.

This chapter draws on primary documents, including internal memoranda, soldiers' testimonies, and journalistic accounts, to process trace inequality's effects across and within each belligerent's army. In particular, I incorporate new historiography on Austria-Hungary and the Eastern Front to shed light on connections between evolving notions of citizenship, wartime repression, and battlefield conduct. The chapter begins with an overview of each war, then compares the two belligerents using the now-familiar matching template devised in chapter 3. Next, the chapter narrates Ottoman combat power and cohesion during the Italo-Turkish War. The Battle of Tripoli (October 1911) is used as a microcosm to explore trade-offs that beset Ottoman performance during the war. Following the same structure, the chapter then chronicles Austro-Hungarian combat power, cohesion, and trade-offs while fighting Tsarist Russia. The Battle of Galicia (August–September 1914)—the "Stalingrad of World War I"[5]—is then detailed to

5. Tunstall 2010, 212.

examine how military inequality generates unforced errors in tactical choice and sanctioning mechanisms.[6] I also explore how the tyranny of wartime credible commitment problems prevented the Dual Monarchy from implementing a more inclusive vision of its political community. The chapter concludes with a discussion of remaining alternative explanations that survive the comparative research design.

6.1.   Italo-Turkish War

The Italo-Turkish War had a long fuse; Italian military planners had cast covetous eyes on Tripolitania as early as November 1884. War plans were shelved until early 1911, when a confluence of events prodded a reluctant Prime Minister Giovanni Giolitti to approve the annexation of Tripolitania and Cyrenaica. Giolitti faced rising jingoistic sentiment on the home front, with his political opponents organizing demonstrations in favor of imperialist ventures to restore lost Roman glory. The Italian economy had also stalled, further boxing Giolitti in. For its part, the Sublime Porte was serially distracted by uprisings in Yemen and Arabia. At least 110,000 soldiers would be committed to a brutal counterinsurgency campaign in Yemen by early 1911. The Ottoman garrison in Tripolitania was stripped; over half its strength was redeployed to Yemen. As a result, Italian military planners convinced themselves that any war would be short and easy. It was widely believed, for example, that Arab populations would not fight on behalf of their Ottoman overlords. Time, however, was pressing. France and Germany had already reached an accommodation over Tunis, sidelining Italy and leaving only Ottoman Libya as an outlet for expansion. Divining Italian intentions, the Ottoman government sent twenty thousand modern Mauser rifles, two million tons of ammunition, and several light artillery to Tripoli on the steamer *Derna* to reinforce its garrison. The arms shipment arrived 25 September 1911, forcing Italy's hand.

On 27 September, Italy issued an ultimatum to the Sublime Porte, announcing its intention to occupy Tripolitania and Cyrenaica within the next twenty-four hours to safeguard "its dignity and its interests." Though Ottoman diplomats scrambled to meet Italian demands, these efforts were doomed to fail, and war was officially declared 29 September. Meeting minimal Ottoman resistance, the first contingent of the *Regio Esercito* landed

---

6. These battles were chosen for two reasons: historians consider their respective battlefield performance to be *highest* in these battles, thus avoiding "cherry-picking" easy cases of military dysfunction; and (2) they occur early in each war, demonstrating that the observed pathologies were preexisting and not generated endogenously from dynamics in the war's later stages.

ashore at Tripoli on 5 October. The overmatched Ottoman garrison quickly withdrew to Aziza, some forty kilometers south of Tripoli. For the next ten days, Italian expeditionary forces, some 34,408-strong, disembarked at Tripoli and set about digging an extensive trench system ringing its environs. Formal annexation of Tripolitania was declared on 13 October. Amphibious assaults at Derna (17–19 October), Benghazi (19–20 October), and Homs (21 October) consolidated Italian control over the coastlines of Tripolitania and Cyrenaica (see figure 6.1).[7]

The Battle of Tripoli (23–26 October 1911) marked the first sustained clash between the Ottoman Empire's 42nd Independent Division and the *Regio Esercito*. Over the next year, Ottoman forces, an amalgam of Turkish officers and infantry (nizam) and local auxiliaries, would launch at least forty-three major offensives against dug-in Italian forces across these coastal cities, with action concentrated in Tripoli, Ain Zara, and Benghazi. Far more cautious Italian commanders initiated only seventeen offensives over the same period, dedicating their operations to expanding their defensive lines or, more rarely, interdicting Ottoman supply lines to Egypt and only moving when overwhelming numbers could be guaranteed. Italian notions of a quick and cheap victory were quickly disabused; logistical difficulties and Italian missteps conspired to prolong the war. Some 100,000 Italian soldiers were fighting in Ottoman Libya by late-November 1911; a total of 180,000 soldiers served at some point during the war.

Though the war was stalemated by mid-1912, the looming shadow of another conflict persuaded the Porte to sue for peace. Emboldened by apparent Ottoman weakness, Montenegro declared war on 8 October 1912, igniting the First Balkan War.[8] On 18 October, the Porte signed the Treaty of Ouchy in Lausanne, Switzerland, agreeing to surrender Tripolitania and Cyrenaica. Italian leaders were more relieved than triumphant. The war had consumed 47 percent of all state expenditures in fiscal year 1912–13. Nearly 4,000 Italian soldiers had been killed and another 8,000 wounded, depleting the Italian Army on the eve of the First World War.[9] Ottoman regulars, now numbering only 2,600, withdrew, though not before relinquishing all their weapons to their Arab and Berber auxiliaries. These forces, now freed from Turkish control, set off in different directions. Some sought accommodation with Italian rule; others contested it through protracted guerrilla warfare. Italy's grip over Tripolitania and especially Cyrenaica gradually weakened in the face of stiff

7. These operations were accompanied by naval campaigns in the Greek Islands and Dardanelles.

8. Clark 2012, 242.

9. Gooch 2014, 50–51.

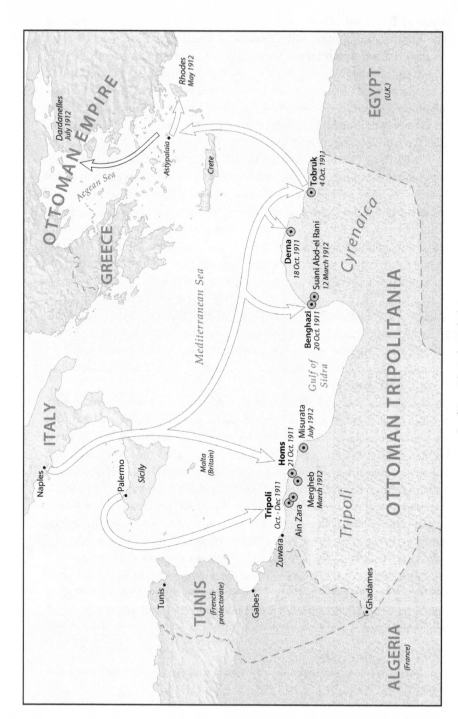

FIGURE 6.1. Sand Box: The Italo-Turkish War, 1911–12

resistance by the Senussi. By July 1915, most of the gains of Italy's 1911–12 "war for a desert" had been lost.

6.2.   Eastern Front, 1914–17

The assassination of Archduke Franz Ferdinand, heir apparent to the Habsburg throne, along with his wife, Sophie Chotek von Chotkowa und Wognin, in Sarajevo on 28 June 1914, set in motion a chain of events that culminated in the First World War. Thrust to center stage, Austro-Hungary, fearful of its growing diplomatic isolation in Europe and alarmed by Serbian assertiveness in Albania and elsewhere, issued a ten-point ultimatum to Belgrade on 23 July. Russia, Serbia's ally, began a partial mobilization in response, encouraging Belgrade to reject the ultimatum. With its demands unmet, Austro-Hungary declared war on Serbia on 28 July.[10] Russia, siding with its Serbian ally, initiated general mobilization, confident that Austro-Hungary's creaking multiethnic structure rendered it weak and vulnerable.[11] On 1 August, Germany, fearing the loss of its Austro-Hungarian ally, declared war on Russia. The widening conflagration would soon engulf the remaining European powers, sparking the largest and deadliest conflict to date, with armies counted in the millions now harnessing the industrial revolution to wage total war.

Unlike the more familiar trench warfare of the Western Front, the Eastern Front's opening campaigns in 1914–15 were marked by enormous encounter battles across vast fronts with only thin defensive works.[12] Austro-Hungary's Military High Command, the *Armeeoberkommando* (AOK), was perhaps the most committed of all European militaries to the ideal of annihilation warfare. As a result, the AOK launched offensive after offensive—in Serbia, Galicia, the Carpathian mountains, and Gorlice-Tarnów—in a bid to destroy the Tsarist Army. Yet advances were modest, while casualties staggering. In early 1916, Austro-Hungary had become a junior partner to Germany, its campaign plans decided in Berlin, its officers overseen by German minders, and its divisions fighting with their own embedded German contingents. Russian last-gasp offensives—the Brusilov and Kerensky Offensives—were both beaten back, though again at terrible cost. Russia, beset with its

10. The origins of World War I, and Austria-Hungary's role in sparking it, have been subject to intense debate. For key recent works on Austria-Hungary's part, see Sked 2001; Williamson and May 2007; Clark 2012; Watson 2014*b*; Benjamin 2014.

11. On Russia's role, see especially McMeekin 2013; Clark 2012.

12. I concentrate here on the Eastern Front and do not discuss the Serbian, Italian, or Romanian fronts. Even though somewhat intertwined, these campaigns are coded separately in the Project Mars dataset.

own internal revolutionary turmoil and its army disintegrating, withdrew from the war for good, signing the humiliating (and short-lived) Treaty of Brest-Litovsk. Nominally victorious, the Austro-Hungarian army was itself in free fall by early 1918, its national minorities no longer willing to fight for the Dual Monarchy. Desperate attempts by Emperor Karl to stem the nationalist tide in mid-1918 fell far short. By the signing of the Armistice in November 1918, the Common Army had largely dissolved, followed swiftly by the demise of Austria-Hungary itself.

6.3. Empirical Strategy

The sections below first outline the nature of their respective prewar collective identities and military inequality before turning to a brief overview of the covariates on which these belligerents are matched.[13] The tighter the matching across belligerents, the more we isolate the causal effects of military inequality. No two belligerents are identical, of course. But our confidence that we have uncovered the correct causal pathway increases with each observation that can only be explained by appealing to divergent levels of military inequality across the belligerents. The matched comparison is outlined in table 6.1.

6.3.1. Political Community and Military Inequality

Though reformist tendencies were present, the Ottoman Empire entered the Italo-Turkish War with high military inequality. In just the five years before the war, Ottoman leaders had authorized categorical violence against different populations throughout the empire. Examples of state-orchestrated collective punishment include the massacre of 20,000–25,000 Armenians at Adana (April 1909); the bloody suppression of insurrection in Kosovo (1910) and Shkoder (1911) *vilayets*; and brutal counterinsurgency campaigns against Arab tribes in 'Asir and Yemen (1906–11) that killed hundreds of thousands.[14]

Politically, its long-standing millet system, which provided autonomy to religious minorities in exchange for second-class citizenship, was under strain

13. As before, this pair was identified using a purpose-built R program to match a belligerent with a similar counterfactual drawn randomly from Project Mars.

14. Lifting our gaze beyond the five-year prewar measurement window, we find additional evidence of exclusionary tendencies at work. The crushing of the IMRO uprising in Macedonia (1903) and resulting refugee flows, the Hamidian massacres that killed 80,000–300,000 Armenians, and the mass killing of an estimated 25,000 Assyrians at Diyarbakir (1895) are all politically relevant events on the eve of the Tripolitan War. See McMeekin 2015, 42–43.

TABLE 6.1. Matched Pair: The Ottoman and Austro-Hungarian Empires Compared

Covariates	Ottoman Empire Italo-Turkish War, 1911–12	Austro-Hungarian Empire Eastern Front, 1914–17
Military Inequality (Coefficient)	High (0.45)	Medium (0.37)
From Matching		
Initial relative power	30.1%	23.6%
Total fielded force	65,000	2.25 million
Regime type	Anocracy (−1)	Anocracy (−4)
Distance from capital	1,085 km	587 km
Standing army	Yes	Yes
Composite military	Yes	Yes
Initiator	No	Yes
Joiner	No	No
Democratic opponent	No	No
Great Power	No	Yes
Civil war	No	No
Non-COW	No	No
Early modern	Yes	Yes
Contextual Covariates		
Combined arms?	Yes	Yes
doctrine	Offensive	Offensive
Superior weapons	No	No
Fortifications	Yes	Yes
Foreign advisors	Yes	Yes
Terrain	Desert/Oasis	Forested Steppe/Hills
War duration	383 days	1,060 days
War birth	No	No
Recent war history w/ opponent	No	No
Facing colonizer	No	No
Identity dimension	Islam/Christian	Christian/Christian
New leader	Yes	Yes
Population	25.4 million	52.1 million
Ethnolinguistic fractionalization (ELF)	High	High
Civ-mil relations	Professional military	Professional military
Battlefield Performance		
Tac-op sophistication	Poor/Moderate	Moderate
Loss-exchange ratio	0.25	1.54
Mass desertion	Yes	Yes
Mass defection	No	No
Fratricidal violence	Yes	No

from the rise of ethnic nationalism on the eve of the Italo-Turkish War. Under the Young Turks, changes were made to the conscription system in October 1908 that formally abolished the millet system's ethnic deferments and existing restrictions on non-Muslims serving in the Ottoman military. The 1909 draft class was the first to reflect this expanded recruitment pool.[15] In practice, however, this nominally more inclusionary basis for military service merely introduced new recruits from non-core ethnic and religious groups that had been subject to prior state repression. Moreover, sharp levels of discrimination still existed within the military. Officers, for example, remained overwhelmingly Turkish, while certain groups, especially Armenians, were singled out for narrowly circumscribed roles, often limited to service in non-frontline labor battalions. Though exact figures for each group's representation are not available, it is possible to estimate the Ottoman Army's prewar ethnic composition. I estimate that the Ottoman Army's military inequality coefficient was 0.40–0.50 in 1910, a high value.[16] Given that the 42nd Independent Division fought in near total isolation for the war, it can be argued that its military inequality is more relevant for battlefield performance than the Ottoman Army's average. Its military inequality coefficient is, however, quite similar, at 0.40–0.45.[17]

For its part, Austria-Hungary entered World War One as a belligerent with medium military inequality. In the preceding years, political leaders,

15. On the Ottoman conscription system, see Zürcher 1998; Beşikçi 2012; Erickson 2001. The 1908–9 reforms, which brought large numbers of Christians and other previously exempt populations into the Ottoman military machine, were met with little enthusiasm by these groups. Greek, Syrian, Armenian, and Bulgarian communities all demanded to serve in ethnically homogenous units with their own officers. These appeals were refused by the Young Turks as antithetical to their (Ottoman) nation-building project. See Zürcher 1998, 447.

16. The low estimate of 0.40 is calculated assuming the following demographic breakdown within the Ottoman Army: Turks (60 percent, inclusive treatment); Arabs (25 percent, collective violence); Christians (7.5 percent, collective violence); and other groups such as Kurds (7.5 percent, collective violence); or $(0.60 * 0) + (0.25 * 1) + (0.075 * 1) + (0.075 * 1) = 0.40$. The high estimate of 0.50 is calculated assuming the following demographic breakdown within the Ottoman Army: Turks (50 percent, inclusion); Arabs (30 percent, collective violence); Christians (10 percent, collective violence); and other groups such as Kurds (10 percent, collective violence); or $(0.50 * 0) + (0.30 * 1) + (0.10 * 1) + (0.10 * 1) = 0.50$.

17. The low estimate of 0.40 is calculated as Turks (20 percent, inclusion) and non-Turkish groups such as Arabs and Berbers (80 percent, collective discrimination), or $(0.20 * 0) + (0.80 * 0.5) = 0.40$. The high estimate of 0.45 is calculated as Turks (10 percent, inclusion) and non-Turkish groups such as Arabs and Berbers (90 percent, collective discrimination), or $(0.10 * 0) + (0.90 * 0.5) = 0.45$.

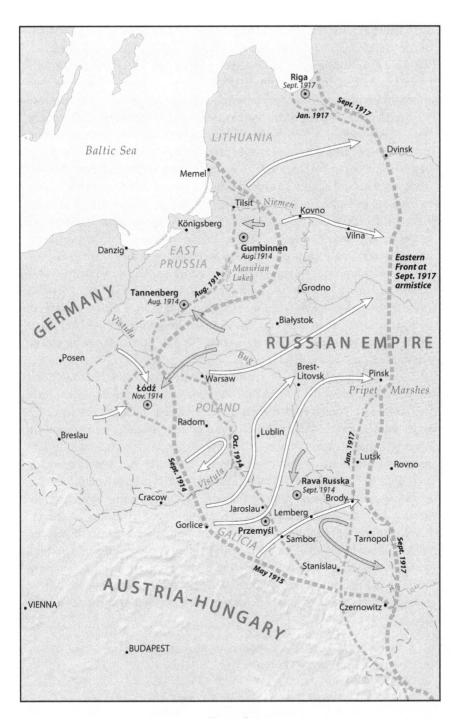

FIGURE 6.2. Eastern Front, 1914–17

especially Emperor Franz Joseph, had worked to cultivate a state-based patriotism (*Staatsidee*) that could unite the Habsburg's multiethnic population.
Decades of historiography have largely dismissed such efforts as fanciful;
viewed from 1918, it seems unlikely that ersatz patriotism could paper over
rising nationalist demands, let alone find genuine support.[18] Yet recent historiography has challenged the conventional view of Austria-Hungary as a
"prison of peoples," a "rotten state,"[19] or, in the words of Germany's Foreign Minister, "that ever increasingly disintegrating composition of nations
beside the Danube."[20] Since 1867, when the Dual Monarchy between German Austrians and Magyars was established, a constitutional order had begun
to develop, one that aimed to defuse nationalist grievances. Patriotic clubs
among veterans were on the rise; civil society among the national minorities
was emerging; and some sense that the Dual Monarchy could also be of benefit for certain non-core groups was slowly coalescing.[21] This is not to dismiss
the severity of challenges issued by nationalist leaders and movements: Poles
wanted reunification with their coethnics in Russian Poland; Czechs wanted
equal status to the Magyars; Ruthenes, Croats, and Slovaks each desired their
own state, as did some Magyars. Instead, we should expect some variation
in the degree of loyalty within various non-German ethnic groups as well as
across them, at least initially.

The Common Army itself carefully reflected broader ethnic divisions
within Austria-Hungary. Divided into sixteen nationalized recruitment areas,
the Common Army wrestled with a set of issues, including demarcating
regimental languages and establishing promotion policies, that reflected its
heterogeneous makeup. Drawing on data from the 1910 recruit intake, the last
prewar year for which data are available, the Common Army had a medium
level of inequality at 0.374. No outright repression of national minorities was
recorded in the five years prior to the war. The officer corps, however, was
heavily skewed toward Germans, who represented 76.1 percent of all officers
but comprised only 24 percent of the overall population (and 25.2 percent
of the entire army). All other ethnic groups were systematically underrepresented in the officer corps: Slovaks, Ruthenes, and Romanians collectively
made up 18.2 percent of the Common Army but only 1.1 percent of the officer
corps. Magyars represented 23.1 percent of the Common Army but only held

18. Namier 1921; Seton-Watson 1926; Kann 1950; Albertini 1952; Kann 1974; Strachan 2001;
McMeekin 2013; for a review, see Deak 2015.

19. Taylor 1948, 232.

20. Quoted in Watson 2014*b*, 14.

21. Deak 2014; Clark 2012; Gumz 2009; Cohen 2007; Healy 2004; Rachamimov 2002;
Cohen 1998*a*.

9.3 percent of officer slots; Czechs were 12.9 percent of the army while only 4.8 percent of officers.[22]

Austria-Hungary's *Staatsidee*, and thus military inequality, underwent a shift during the course of the war, however. As detailed below, prewar suspicion about the loyalty of national minorities led to the construction of an extensive censorship network and mass arrests. Serbian and Ruthenian civilians were subjected to categorical violence by the Common Army during the Serbian and Galician campaigns. In the latter case, more than 25,000 Ruthenians were summarily executed by September 1914. If we code the Serb and Ruthenian soldier contingents as now subject to state-directed categorical violence, the Common Army's military inequality coefficient climbs to 0.434, about the same as the Ottoman Empire's mean value.[23] This intra-case shift in military inequality sets up an empirical expectation that Austro-Hungarian performance should worsen over time.

6.3.2.   Matched Covariates

I build the case for treating these belligerents as comparable by turning first to their military capabilities. Each belligerent was numerically inferior to its opponent at the war's outset, with Ottoman and Habsburg forces possessing less than one-third of forces initially deployed to the combat area (30.1 percent and 23.6 percent, respectively). Both countries found themselves locked into contests in which their principal adversaries had either far larger armies or a greater willingness to deploy them. The total number deployed by each side was sharply imbalanced; the Ottoman war remained localized, with only about 65,000 Turkish and Arab soldiers deployed, while the Habsburg Monarchy threw an estimated 2.25 million soldiers into the fray on the Eastern Front. Even this imbalance across belligerents is useful, however. Since each state experienced bouts of mass soldier indiscipline, it suggests that cohesion is not a function of an army's absolute size but of its composition. More generally, while military power can be difficult to measure precisely, both of these belligerents were derided by contemporaries as "sick" and decrepit empires

---

22. The military inequality coefficient of 0.374 for the prewar Common Army is calculated as: Germans (25.2 percent); Magyars (23.1 percent); Czechs (12.9 percent); Serbo-Croat (9 percent); Poles (7.9 percent); Ruthenes (7.6 percent); Romanians (7 percent); Slovaks (3.6 percent); Slovenes (2.4 percent); and Italians (1.3 percent). Germans are coded as receiving inclusive treatment; all others, collective discrimination. We therefore calculate: $(0.252 * 0) + (0.748 * 0.5) = 0.374$. For estimates, see Rauchensteiner 2014, 57; Watson 2014*b*, 115; Deák 1990.

23. This value is calculated as Germans $(0.252 * 0) +$ all others$(0.627 * .5) +$ Serbs/ Ruthenes$(0.121 * 1) = 0.434$. In this calculation, Serbs are estimated to represent one-half of the 1910 Serbo-Croat share of the Common Army.

that invited partition. Though Austria-Hungary was still nominally a Great Power, it was only barely hanging on to its status, and even its senior political and military commanders were preoccupied with the prospects of a sudden collapse in its power or, equally as important, its prestige. Viewed through the venerable, if imperfect, lens of the Correlates of War's standard Composite Index of National Capability, each belligerent faced an opponent with double its share of global power.[24]

Military power degrades over distance, and so it is important to control for the location of the first battle and the belligerent's capital city. Here, too, the cases are similar. Constantinople was separated from the initial Battle of Tobruk that launched the Italo-Turkish War by 1,085 kilometers. The Battle at Kraśnik, which opened fighting on the Eastern Front, was about 587 kilometers distant from Vienna.[25] Ottoman forces in particular faced formidable logistical challenges. British control of Egypt, along with Italian and Royal Navy control of the Mediterranean, forced the adoption of circuitous smuggling routes to resupply their garrisons with arms and Turkish officers, often via underground routes in Egypt and Tunisia.[26] Logistical difficulties, however, were a hallmark of each belligerent's war effort, continuing to hamper offensives throughout both wars. Each military also had standing and well-established reserve formations. These militaries were composite in nature, drawing their soldiers from multiple recruitment streams, including both mass conscription and volunteers.

Ottoman and Habsburg political systems also paralleled one another in important ways. Both were monarchical in nature, though each had begun experimenting with parliamentary institutions that constrained the ruler's ability to devise and execute policy without interference. Polity IV, the standard dataset for assessing regime type, scores each belligerent as an "anocracy," sharing properties of both democratic and authoritarian political systems. Their Polity2 scores, which range from +10 (consolidated democracy) to −10 (strong authoritarian), are very similar: the Ottoman Empire received a −1 value (in 1910) while Austria-Hungary was judged somewhat more authoritarian at a −4 score (in 1913). According to the expanded regime type framework

24. The Ottoman Empire held 1.73 percent of total global power capabilities in 1910; Italy, 3.06 percent. Austria-Hungary possessed 4.47 percent of world capabilities in 1913; Russia, 11.6 percent. Austria-Hungary did, however, fight the war in coalition with Germany, which helped even the odds even if Russia still enjoyed numerical preponderance on the battlefield.

25. These wars fall squarely in the 50–60th percentiles of distance (in kilometers) between all belligerents' capital cities and their initial battle.

26. Simon 1987.

of Project Mars, both political systems are considered "weak constitutional monarchies."

Austria-Hungary did, however, initiate its war, while the Ottoman Empire was clearly the victim of Italian aggression. While existing studies have found a link between initiation and victory, the statistical analyses in chapter 4 failed to detect any effect of initiator on our four measures of battlefield performance. Moreover, the disastrous state of Austro-Hungarian mobilization—including confused railway schedules, vacillating attack plans, and the spectacularly misguided decision to engage Serbia before (and during) the war with Russia—negates any advantages that might accrue from initiation. Neither side was facing a democratic opponent, helping to control for adversary differences. Neither was a civil war; all belligerents were recognized by COW as having the attributes of statehood; and the fact that these wars were fought nearly at the same time helps control for technological developments in weapons technology. Indeed, industrial warfare and its horsemen—the internal combustion engine, rapid-fire rifles, improved artillery, and wireless communications—were present in battles in the deserts of Tripolitania and the rolling hills of Galicia. The Ottoman Army, for example, struggled to adjust its combined arms approach to Italian military innovations, including the first combat deployment of aircraft for reconnaissance and interdiction missions.[27] The *Regio Esercito* also deployed a wireless telegraphy system to facilitate artillery spotting from tethered balloons and aircraft as well as communications between bases;[28] constructed a logistical fleet of some three hundred lorries; introduced dozens of armored cars at the Battle of Zanzour (8 June 1912); and undertook sophisticated amphibious landings. On the Eastern Front, the scale of battles, often involving armies of hundreds of thousands and fronts measured in tens of kilometers, forced new tactical innovations as well. The rise of defense-in-depth in 1916, best typified by complex interlocking trench systems up to one hundred kilometers deep, led to tighter combined arms coordination and the emergence of new shock troop formations. While technological advances in certain spheres, including combat aviation and especially motorized vehicles, did not reach levels seen on the Western Front, the sharply increased lethality of these armies placed a premium on devising new methods of combined arms that maximized soldier survivability.[29]

27. Italian aircraft flew 712 sorties, dropping "several hundred" bombs. Dirigibles completed another 136 sorties, releasing 360 bombs. See Stephensen 2014, 230.

28. Guglielmo Marconi himself was present in Tripoli to conduct experiments with wireless technology (*radiotelegrafici*).

29. See, for example, Stone 2008; Watson 2014b; Rauchensteiner 2014.

6.3.3. Contextual Covariates

These belligerents also shared broadly similar characteristics across fifteen different contextual covariates. Both had embraced combined arms doctrines, though haltingly, and each was experimenting with technologies, including aircraft, long-range artillery, and motorized vehicles, that would provide the building blocks for modern warfare. Their respective political and military leaders were card-carrying members of the "cult of the offensive," extolling the virtues of first-strike offensives and tactics even as their armies remained ill-equipped to execute them. Both belligerents found themselves entangled with better-armed adversaries. Ottoman forces, for example, lacked aircraft, had inferior artillery, and fewer armored cars than intervening Italian forces. The AOK marched to war with a resource-starved army—the result of Hungarian parliamentary intransigence—that left it with inferior mobilization and military capabilities compared to Russia. In particular, Russian cannons far outranged Austrian ones, leading to horrific casualties in early battles that persisted until the belated intervention of German material support and technical expertise in 1916. Both wars had similar dynamics, opening with battles of movement before degenerating into positional wars centered around extensive trenchworks and fortifications.[30] And, intriguingly, both armies relied on German advisors, both military and economic, to assist with training, war-planning, and the acquisition of modern weapons.[31]

Both belligerents were long-standing empires rather than new states experiencing a "war birth" that might complicate their efforts to field competent forces. By 1910, Austria-Hungary and the Ottoman Empire ranked among the top ten most populous states in the world (at fifth and tenth positions, respectively) and had almost identically sized militaries, with 315,000 and 324,000 soldiers, respectively.[32] Census data from the Ottoman Empire (1905–6) and Austria-Hungary (1911), though imperfect, indicate that both empires clearly had very high levels of ethnolinguistic fractionalization.[33]

---

30. The maneuver phase of the Eastern Front lasted far longer than during the Italo-Turkish War, however.

31. Yorulmaz 2014.

32. Data drawn from COW's "National Material Capabilities" Dataset, Version 5.0 (Singer 1987).

33. From these censuses, I calculate an ELF value of 0.86 for Austria-Hungary and a 0.745 for the Ottoman Empire (Alesina et al. 2003). The 1911 census measured an individual's everyday language (*Umgangssprache*) and so does not provide a perfect ELF score for Austria-Hungary (K.u.k. Hof-Kartographische Anstalt G. Freytag & Berndt 1911). The Ottoman ELF value is also problematic and likely underestimates true fractionalization. The census was unable to

Nor did these belligerents have a recent history of warfare with their eventual opponents. The Kingdom of Italy laid claims to Libya as early as Russia's defeat of the Ottomans in 1878, and in 1902, signed a secret treaty with France that granted Italy freedom of action in Morocco and Tripolitania. No effort was made to fulfill these territorial ambitions until a vocal lobbying campaign in March 1911 by pro-imperial elements awakened the public's appetite for colonial possessions. Even then, however, the Italian government hesitated. Austria, too, had a long history with its eventual foe; Russia and Austria-Hungary were formal allies in the League of Three Emperors until 1887, though tensions, and a simmering rivalry over the Balkans, had flared up in 1908 with Austria-Hungary's formal annexation of Bosnia-Herzegovina over Russia's strong protest. Despite this jockeying for influence, the past one hundred years witnessed far more Austro-Russian cooperation than contestation. Unlike the cases of Kokand and Morocco, Austria-Hungary and the Ottoman Empire were not facing colonizers bent on destroying and absorbing their state. Even Italian aims were limited to the margins of the expansive Ottoman Empire.

Each belligerent was also wrestling with domestic turmoil on the eve of war. The Young Turk Revolution of July 1908 ushered in an era of constitutional reform, including multiple party elections, that unsettled Ottoman policymaking. A brief, abortive countercoup to roll back these constitutional gains was snuffed out in March 1909, leaving Sultan Mehmed V and a variety of ambitious political parties dueling for power immediately before the Italian invasion of Tripolitania. Austria-Hungary, too, was roiled by a leadership crisis in the aftermath of Archduke Franz Ferdinand's assassination that precipitated the Habsburg decision for war against Serbia. Holding key military responsibilities, the Archduke's death created an immediate vacuum in policymaking among senior military commanders that injected unwelcome uncertainty into Austrian war plans.[34] Both Sultan Mehmed V and Emperor Franz Joseph I presided over professional, standing militaries that were subordinate to executive political leaders. Each military, however, was relatively autonomous in its training, though both made careful note of ethnic balances within their forces and tailored recruitment in acknowledgement of these divisions.[35]

---

survey an estimated two to three million inhabitants of Syria. The census also lumped Turks, Arabs, and Kurds into the same "Muslim" identity category (Karpat 1985, 2002, 766).

34. A stricter definition of political upheaval—say, no replacement of the executive leader in the past year—would register "no change" for either belligerent. Sultan Mehmed V assumed power on 27 April 1909 and died on 3 July 1918. Emperor Franz Joseph I assumed power on 2 December 1848 and died on 21 November 1916.

35. Castillo 2014, 31.

Differences do exist across these belligerents, though whether they can account for patterns of battlefield performance is debatable. War duration, for example, varied sharply across the conflicts. The Italo-Turkish War lasted 383 days, while Habsburg entanglement on the Eastern Front stretched for 1,060 days. We might imagine that longer wars create greater opportunities for mass soldier indiscipline to manifest itself, thus stacking the deck against Austro-Hungarian battlefield performance.[36] This bias cuts against the proposed argument, which anticipates that Ottoman, not Austro-Hungarian, forces should first experience mass desertion and defection. Some historians have also argued that battlefield losses crippled Austria-Hungary to a point where it was no longer an independent state, relying heavily on German forces as early as their first combined offensive at Gorlice-Tarnów in May–June 1915. If we take the offensive's 2 May start date as the end of an independent Austria-Hungary war effort, then only 74 days separate the two wars.

Religious identification also differed across belligerents in each of these wars. The Italo-Turkish War pitted belligerents with Islamic and Christian identities, while the Eastern Front was an intra-Christian war of Catholics against Orthodox Christians (and sometimes Orthodox against Orthodox). Fighting across religious divides might decrease opportunities for defection while reducing incentives to desert if the war is interpreted as a civilizational struggle. Finally, battlefield terrain also varied across wars. The desert setting of the Italo-Turkish War likely reduced opportunities to flee given the paucity of oases and populated areas to which soldiers might successfully escape.[37] Casualties might also be higher in desert wars given the relative absence of ground cover that permits units to conceal themselves and take shelter from enemy fire. These factors bear close attention as the process tracing unfolds below.

6.3.4. A Note on Historiography

This chapter takes advantage of new historical research and archival collections timed to the recent centennial of each war. The evidentiary record across these wars is uneven, however. The Italo-Turkish War has long been overshadowed by the subsequent Balkan Wars and First World War.[38] As a result, much of its historiography has centered around questions of Italy's decision

36. Mass soldier indiscipline may actually prolong wars if it remains short of total disintegration by slowing troop movements, delaying offensives, and by preventing the gathering of sufficient strength for a culminating victory.

37. On terrain and desertion opportunities, see McLauchlin 2014.

38. Stephensen 2014.

to invade and its effects on European diplomacy.[39] That said, it is possible to stitch together a credible record of battlefield performance from Italian and Ottoman official histories and documents, though many key Ottoman sources remain sequestered in archives.[40] Moreover, a lively, if highly partisan, set of correspondents and military observers were embedded with Italian and Turkish-Arab forces, providing contemporary eyewitness accounts about the nature of fighting and the motives of the soldiers involved.[41] These sources are biased, but predictably so. Evidence that runs counter to these known biases—say, a pro-Arab journalist notes widespread desertion among Arab soldiers—thus increases our confidence that mass desertion occurred compared to a similar report by pro-Italian observers.

The Eastern Front, once described by Winston Churchill as the "forgotten war,"[42] has seen a surge of new research that challenges prevailing conceptions about broader wartime dynamics as well as Austro-Hungarian strategy and tactics.[43] These studies cast new light on the social dynamics within the Austro-Hungarian empire before and during the war, capturing the regime's increasingly frantic efforts to modernize within the confines of tradition.[44] Concerns about regime legitimacy, both from above and below, figure prominently in these accounts. New research on the Habsburg Empire's "double war" against Serbia and Russia as well as its own populations adds another dimension to its military strategy that previous accounts overlooked. Above all, the view of Austria-Hungary that emerges is one where its defeat was not inevitable but instead a product of its own efforts to hold its forces together—and feed its starving population—under mounting wartime pressures that ultimately destroyed the state itself.[45] As a result, I draw on this research to provide a more nuanced account of Austro-Hungarian military inequality and battlefield performance than the "autocratic state in irreversible decline" caricature found in older historiography.[46]

39. Askew 1942; Childs 1990.

40. Tittoni 1914; Ministero della Guerra 1922, 1928; Romano 1977.

41. For pro-Italian positions, see, for example, Irace 1912; McClure 1913. For pro-Turkish positions, see Wright 1913; McCullagh 1913.

42. Churchill 2015.

43. Leonhard 2018; Herwig 2014; Afflerbach 2014; Jeřábek 2002; Stone 2008; Buttar 2014; Wawro 2014; Watson 2014b; Showalter 2004; Lein 2014b; Schindler 2015.

44. The seminal study here is Healy 2004.

45. Stone 2015; Lieven 2015; Airapetov 2014; Watson 2014b; Wawro 2014; Buttar 2014; McMeekin 2013; Deak 2015, 264.

46. For German language historiography, see especially Cole 2014; Judson 2016; Deak 2014, 2015; Rauchensteiner 2014. Quote in Cole 2014, p. 7.

6.4.   A Box of Sand: The Italo-Turkish War, 1911–12

While summary judgments do obscure subtle nuances, Ottoman battlefield performance can best be characterized, somewhat charitably, as middling. Drawing on the now-familiar battlefield performance index, the Ottoman Army scored a middling 0.50 value for its efforts in Tripolitania. Ottoman forces suffered loss-exchange ratios below parity, for example, and experienced mass desertion from the ranks. This assessment understates the problems that arose within the Ottoman military campaign, however. Side-switching was also a problem, though it did not reach the 10 percent threshold that demarcates "mass" defection. Turkish officers also resorted to threats and occasional violence against their Arab soldiers but did not deploy formal blocking detachments, a decision imposed by the small size of the Turkish officer corps rather than moral qualms. Soldier indiscipline also complicated tactical choice, leading to the adoption of simplistic frontal assaults that drove up the costs of each attempt to breach fortified Italian positions. I provide a narrative of Ottoman battlefield performance below, focusing first on combat power before turning to issues of cohesion, drawing on battle-level observations to identify patterns of outcomes and possible trade-offs at work.

6.4.1.   Combat Power

The sole Ottoman unit in Tripolitania on the eve of the Italian invasion was the 42nd Independent Division, widely panned as "one of the worst units in the whole empire."[47] The understrength division, its manpower siphoned off to quell revolts in Arabia and Yemen, consisted of about 5,000 soldiers that provided the nucleus of resistance once Tripoli was seized by Italian forces on 2 October 1911. Regrouping after this initial defeat, the division reconstituted itself by raising tribal levies among local, marginalized populations, including Arabs, Berbers, Senussi, and Beduin tribes. These non-core groups were organized in formations of approximately 150 soldiers and placed under Turkish command, with tribal chiefs acting as palliative figureheads in second-in-command roles. Turkish volunteer officers, collectively known as the *Fedai Zabitan* ("self-sacrificing officers"), were also smuggled into the country along contraband routes.[48] Turkish commanders, recognizing the problems inherent in fighting with a mixed force, manipulated the ethnic composition of

47. Vandervort 2012, 73.

48. Enver Bey, the future Minister of War and leading member of the "Three Pashas" triumvirate that ruled the Ottoman Empire from 1913–18, and Mustafa Kemal Atatürk, the first Prime Minister of Turkey, were among these officers.

units to ensure that they were (nearly) ethnically homogenous. Senior leadership in all units was held by Turkish officers, who were also seeded throughout the units to stiffen their resolve. Non-Turkish soldiers were earmarked for light infantry and cavalry roles; Turkish soldiers acted as heavy infantry while also commanding artillery units. By late October, the Italian Expeditionary Force found itself engaged with Ottoman units capable of launching combined arms assaults against their lines. This was a most unwelcome surprise; Italian military planners had not anticipated meeting substantial resistance, holding Ottoman and (especially) Arab military prowess in low regard.[49]

This organizational structure reflected prewar military inequality and the resulting mistrust across ethnic groups that frustrated deeper coordination. Despite the practice of backstopping each formation with Turkish officers and infantry, coordination problems within and across different formations remained a constant feature, leading to "disjointed fighting."[50] Turkish officers were themselves divided over how best to incorporate non-core levies; internecine political struggles among these officers hampered coordination even further.[51] Matters were made worse by the absence of a common language between Turkish officers and their non-core soldiers.[52] Turkish commanders routinely decried the apparent absence of discipline among non-core units. "They are people," one officer argued, "who have never heard of organization or tactics. They have not the faintest idea of discipline. They are just savages."[53] As a result, "these volunteers, impatient of inaction, and unused to discipline, are very hard to control."[54] This "instinctive mistrust that separates the Turk from the Arab,"[55] in the words of one officer, cropped up even at the level of individual soldiers' kit and supplies. Modern weapons were provided to these levies, for example, but officers restricted access to ammunition to ensure their continued loyalty.[56]

Turkish commanders were also keenly aware that their non-core volunteers were driven by different combat motivations. Arabs, Berbers, Senussi, and the like were not fighting to safeguard the Ottoman Empire. Nor had they overlooked its past repression against their ethnic groups and families, stories of which had become part of tribal oral histories. Instead, these soldiers had mixed motives for answering Turkish appeals for tribal levies. Many tribal

49. Vandervort 2012, 50; Stephensen 2014, 46–49.
50. McClure 1913, 164.
51. Childs 1990, 132.
52. Simon 1987, 192, 330.
53. Quoted in Abbott 1912a, 201.
54. Abbott 1912a, 105.
55. Quoted in Abbott 1912a, 202.
56. Simon 1987, 196.

leaders interpreted the Italian invasion in religious terms, citing the need to wage jihad against an infidel as motive enough to join Turkish forces.[57] "What does life matter?" went a common refrain at early war meetings among tribal chiefs and volunteers. "Paradise is found with death in the Italian trenches."[58] Yet a shared religion was insufficient to forge tight bonds between Turks and these tribal levies. Instead, tribal chiefs viewed their Turkish commanders with suspicion, judging them insufficiently devout in religious matters given their often only glancing familiarity with Islam.[59]

Non-core motivations were thus rooted in an alternative group-based patriotism that clashed directly with appeals to Ottoman identity or sovereignty. Georges Rémond, a French journalist traveling with Ottoman forces, captured this sentiment when he asked a young Turkish lieutenant what motivated his non-Turkish soldiers. They fought, he argued, for three reasons:

(1) A certain territorial patriotism, less alien than is believed to the Arab soul, (2) hatreds excited by the harsh repression exercised by the Italians on the morrow of the uprising in the oasis [October 1911], and (3) finally the assertion, repeated a thousand times, that [Italians] are the poorest people in the world, and that they come, hungry at home and driven by misery, to despoil the Arabs of their fields, their barley, and their sheep.[60]

Tribal recruitment was also driven by more prosaic considerations. Turkish commanders, Italian military observers, and journalists embedded with both armies all emphasize that the prospects of winning battlefield spoils weighed heavy in soldiers' calculations for joining and fighting. "Everyone was glib talking of the retaking of Tripoli with rifles and swords," wrote H. C. Seppings Wright, a journalist reporting from Ottoman field positions, "of what loot they would get, and how the warriors had all come to get an Italian rifle to carry back to their homes."[61] There is a pervasive sense among journalists that tribal chiefs viewed the Turks, and the war itself, as an unexpected but welcome opportunity to make money. "War is a good deal (*une bonne affaire*) for them," Rémond remarked, as "they receive money from various Islamic societies in Europe and Asia, occasionally plunder the Italians or the Arabs who have submitted to them ... and thus pass the time in Allah's grace."[62]

57. Jihad was formally declared on 23 January 1912. See Stephensen 2014, 96.
58. Rémond 1913, 49.
59. Simon 1987, 193.
60. Rémond 1913, 64.
61. Wright 1913, 52.
62. Rémond 1913, 58.

Ethnic mistrust, along with the fact that about 90 percent of the Ottoman army in Tripolitania was non-Turk, subsequently undercut tactical and operational flexibility. Turkish commanders privileged simple massed frontal assaults against Italian trenches and fortifications that aimed at overwhelming Italian defenses to achieve breakthrough. Cavalry would provide initial screens, masking the approach of the main body of troops by feigning attacks and drawing Italian fire. Artillery was often used, though sparingly, as Ottoman cannons were dated, short of range, and suffered from irregular supply of shells.[63] Battles were typically short-lived affairs, lasting about 8–12 hours, though on occasion stretched over a few days.

These frontal assaults lessened the burden of coordination and reduced the complexity of Turkish overwatch of Arab and Berber units; commanders often stationed Turkish forces in the rear of these units to ensure that they maintained discipline in the face of enemy fire. Momentum was difficult to sustain, however. Even successful breakthroughs saw offensives stall as Arab soldiers broke ranks in pursuit of spoils. Simple tactics thus made sense from a command and control perspective, ensuring that non-Turkish soldiers arrived at the point of attack on time while limiting pre-battle opportunities for desertion or indiscipline during exploitation operations in case Italian lines were successfully breached. Given less than complete Turkish oversight, tactics and operations emphasized single-shot offensives in which units were committed simultaneously, or nearly so. Multiple waves of attackers, along with more complex envelopment operations, were largely avoided, again because of Turkish mistrust of non-core soldiers and their desire to limit opportunities for non-core soldiers to exercise initiative.

Recognizing these coordination issues, senior Ottoman commanders constructed a series of training camps for their levied soldiers. These commanders walked a fine line: they wanted to bolster Arab and Berber modern combat skills and discipline while weaning tribal levies away from their more familiar raiding style of hit-and-run warfare. They did not, however, want to increase combat skills enough that they might then challenge Ottoman rule once Italy was ejected from Tripolitania. Commanders therefore mandated three-week training for all non-Turkish soldiers that provided a cursory introduction to the tenets of modern warfare.[64] Eyewitness accounts suggest that the lessons were at least partly absorbed. Wright remarked how tribal levies "now fight with more caution; they even take cover sometimes, and

63. Artillery shells were prioritized for shipment along smuggling routes since it was the principal means for harassing fire against Italian-held cities like Tripoli and Derna.

64. Barbar 1980, 216–17.

shoot from behind it."[65] G. F. Abbott, also embedded with Turkish forces, wrote that after their training programs, "I saw them learn to take cover, to fire in an extended line and not massed, to attack noiselessly."[66] Not all credit should flow to these training programs; tribal levies were quick to devise their own countermeasures against Italian aerial reconnaissance and bombing, for example.[67]

The strengths, and self-imposed limitations, of this divided force were on display at the Battle of Gargaresch (8 January 1912), one of the Ottoman Army's best performances in the war. Gargaresch, a small village anchoring a oasis some seven kilometers west of Tripoli, was a key bulwark in the Italian defensive ring encircling Tripoli and sat astride Ottoman smuggling routes to Tunis. A combined Ottoman force of 2,000–3,000 launched an early morning assault against a 3,000-strong Italian column ensconced behind defenses consisting of three trench lines with 300-meters separation, barbed wire, and pits sown with spikes.[68] Italian cruisers prowled offshore; the entire defensive works lay within range of their guns. Seeking to turn the Italian flank, the Ottoman assault began with probing cavalry attacks on the right wing of Italian defenses. These attacks were quickly beaten back. Infantry, largely unsupported by artillery, then crossed no-man's-land between Ottoman and Italian positions, maintaining good order ("a superb contempt of danger"[69]) while under heavy artillery and naval fire. Italian forces slowly gave way, surrendering each tier of their trenchworks.[70]

Stunned by this apparent setback, Italian forces withdrew that night, ceding Gargaresch to jubilant Ottoman troops. The victory was a costly one; Ottoman casualties ran in the hundreds, a product of Turkish fears of insubordination among non-coethnic soldiers that led to charging well-fortified Italian positions in tight groupings to ease command and control difficulties. Hasty training also betrayed itself. Arab shooting was derided as ineffectual by

65. Wright 1913, 112.

66. Abbott 1912a, 106.

67. Wright 1913, 112–14.

68. Italian forces consisted of the 57th Infantry Regiment, reinforced with a battalion of grenadiers, a battery of mountain artillery, a half-battery of field artillery, and the 2nd and 4th squadrons of the 19th Cavalry (Guide) Regiment. See Stephensen 2014, 130.

69. Pol Tristan, "Le combat de Gargaresch," *L'Ouest-Éclair*, 24 Fevrier 1912.

70. The exact number of trenches cleared remains a matter of historical debate. Pro-Italian sources argue that Italians only surrendered the first line of defenses, retreating in good order to protect their forward-deployed artillery (McClure 1913, 121). Pro-Turkish sources contend all three trench lines were cleared and that a full rout was only narrowly prevented by the timely arrival of Italian reinforcements. See Pol Tristan, "Le combat de Gargaresch," *L'Ouest-Éclair*, 24 Fevrier 1912.

observers; "Arab fire, as usual, [was] much too high."[71] Nor were Turkish officers able to consolidate tactical gains at Gargaresch into durable strategic ones.
Arab and Berber forces, their job done, refused to remain in place and withdrew, ceding their hard-won gains. On 20 January, an even larger Italian force
reoccupied the oasis unopposed and set about improving its defensive works
to deter any future Ottoman attacks. None would be forthcoming, however. The window of opportunity for breaching Italian lines around western
Tripoli, already closing, was now firmly shuttered.

These same weaknesses were exposed when Ottoman forces conducted
defensive operations. At the Battle of Ain Zara (4–5 December 1911), 18,000
soldiers of the *Corpo d'Armata Speciale*—nearly half its total strength—
sortied from Tripoli in three columns. Their objective was to fix and destroy
a 4,000-strong Ottoman concentration hunkered down in and around Ain
Zara and its nearby oasis. Each column consisted of reinforced brigade-sized
units, their joint movements supported by cavalry, mobile mountain guns and
fixed long-range Krupp artillery, naval shellfire directed by a tethered observation balloon, and even crude aerial bombardment of the Turkish camp
by Blériot XI and Nieuport IV G aircraft. Ottoman forces, commanded by
Colonel Neshat Bey, had established a simple but extensive trench system
consisting of both main and reserve lines, along with zigzag saps connecting
trenches to shelters, to blunt the expected Italian advance. They were seriously outnumbered; estimates suggest 3,000–4,000 Ottoman soldiers were
spread across a nearly five kilometer front. But the Italians were forced to
advance across difficult terrain—thunderous rains the night before rendered
many *wadis* impassable—that canalized their approach to Ain Zara, simplifying the defenders' task.

Outgunned and outmanned, Ottoman forces quickly surrendered their
first line of defenses but continued to resist doggedly, albeit unevenly, despite
mounting casualties. Surveying their forces, Turkish officers resisted calls for
retreat because they feared their Arab and Berber soldiers would become
demoralized and desert, unraveling their force entirely.[72] Yet remaining fixed
in place while bracketed by Italian artillery was a losing proposition. Around
1500, after hours of bombardment, the order was given to conduct a fighting withdrawal. Chaos ensued. Units fractured; some Arab soldiers refused
to acknowledge the order, unwilling to relinquish their positions to infidel
Italians ("we could not make out why"[73]). Others were only too happy to
escape the killing ground of Ain Zara, making for the rear in a "comically

71. Abbott 1912a, 22.
72. Abbott 1912a, 52.
73. Abbott 1912a, 56.

lazy" retreat that echoed the worst fears of their Turkish officers. Arab and Berber soldiers, intermingling with thousands of camp followers, slowly filtered to the rear "like an East End mob going home after a day on Hampstead Heath. There was no hurry...the soldiers just strolled away."[74] Officers tried to quicken their pace, but to little avail. "Belated Arabs straggled beside the ranks of marching Turks," one eyewitness chronicled, "a fainting rabble followed in the army's wake, and the desert way for close on twenty miles was strewn with discarded horse-gear, cooking pots, a chair or two, and miscellaneous litter from the Arab tents."[75] By 0435 on 5 December, the last few stragglers had left Ain Zara.

Defeat at Ain Zara had far-reaching consequences. Ottoman forces lost their bridgehead for threatening Tripoli; their main base of operations was now reconstituted at Azizia, some forty kilometers distant. Despite fighting from prepared positions against plodding Italian brigades confined to predictable routes, Ottoman casualties were decidedly lopsided, with hundreds of soldiers killed in exchange for 17 killed and 94 wounded Italians. The entire detachment of Ottoman field cannons was also lost in the confusion of the withdrawal and recovered by Italian soldiers. Command and control problems, at once reflecting and exacerbating ethnic divisions across ranks and within units, conspired to increase the costs of mounting a defense while undercutting the odds of successfully executing complex operations like fighting withdrawals—or even orderly ones.

These two battles provide initial clues that Ottoman forces bore the brunt of casualties regardless of whether they were attacking or defending. Pooling known casualties from all battles, the Independent Division lost an average of about four soldiers for each enemy soldier they managed to kill. Estimates of Ottoman soldiers killed in action range from 8,189 to 12,600, though figures as high as 14,800 have been cited.[76] Using this (very) high estimate, Ottoman loss-exchange ratios climb to 4.24 soldiers lost for each enemy soldier killed. The discrepancy in estimates reflects the difficulties in tracking casualties among Arab and Berber soldiers given their practice of removing their dead from the battlefield after each engagement. By contrast, Italian forces lost between 1,432 and 4,000 soldiers to Ottoman action.[77] These imbalances reflect in part the cautious nature of Italian tactics. Risks were to be avoided; individual initiative was often discouraged. Instead, Italian commanders

74. Abbott 1912a, 57.

75. Ostler 1912, 82.

76. Gooch 2014, 48.

77. By historical standards, the Ottoman 0.246 loss-exchange ratio ranks in the 15th percentile of all belligerents in wars from 1800 to 2011.

sought refuge behind their fortifications and artillery superiority, content to let Ottoman forces dash themselves against their trenchworks.[78] Yet most of the blame for the lopsided nature of Ottoman casualties must be placed on the rigid, simplistic tactics that were dictated by command and control problems arising from mistrust between Turkish officers and their non-core soldiers. Concerned with the prospects of mass indiscipline, Turkish officers worked to maintain the reliability of their forces at the cost of becoming predictable, driving up casualties.

6.4.2. Cohesion

Given divergent motives and morale across Turkish and non-Turkish soldiers, it is perhaps unsurprising that ethnic divisions eroded cohesion within Ottoman forces. Discipline within tribal levies remained a problem throughout the war. Desertion, for example, began early. An entire garrison of Arab levies deserted Tripoli—"the Turks suddenly found themselves alone"[79]—in the face of a small Italian landing party on the opening day of the war. Armed bands drawn from these deserters even ambushed Turkish forces in an attempted robbery as they withdrew from Tripoli's outskirts.[80] A conservative estimate is that between 10 and 20 percent of total deployed Ottoman strength deserted during the war.[81] Desertion was almost solely confined to Arab and Berber levies; there are no recorded instances in the existing historical record suggesting either Turkish officers or nizam deserted.[82] Tribal desertion was also group-based; typically, large segments of the levy, if not the entire unit, collectively disappeared, often on the eve of battle.[83] Even minor desertion could cripple successful Ottoman offensives. At the second battle of Ain Zara (5 January 1912), Ottoman forces breached Italian trenches but could not exploit their breakthrough because of a shortage of soldiers. Italian units were able to regroup, calling down artillery to chase off the outnumbered Ottoman forces. Noting the pre-battle desertion of some Arab auxiliaries, Wright wrote that "I heard afterwards that a couple of thousand of these hardy

78. By March 1912, the *Regio Esercito* was shipping water, along with stone for its defenses, from Italy rather than venture beyond its defensive perimeters around Tripolitania's and Cyrenaica's coastal cities (Gooch 2014, 14).

79. Abbott 1912a, 114.

80. Abbott 1912a, 114–15.

81. This qualifies as "mass" desertion as defined in chapter 3.

82. Vandervort 2012, 136.

83. Simon 1987, 188. Some desertion also occurred around holidays (Wright 1913, 63) and seasonal harvesting (Childs 1990, 133), though the majority was driven by wartime processes.

warriors would have well turned the scale, and would have completely cut off the retreat of the Italians back to Tripoli."[84]

Side-switching did occur as well, though on a relatively small scale that did not reach the 10 percent threshold used by Project Mars to denote "mass" defection. Shortly after the war began, but before Ottoman efforts to recruit locally had kicked off, some urban Arab tribes known as the *Efendiya* openly cast their lot with the Italians. Members of these tribes served as Italian spies, often right inside Ottoman camps; the Italian Expeditionary Force was often well-apprised of Ottoman movements and, equally as important, morale. On rare occasions, *Efendiya* acted as guides for Italian military columns, though the limited number of Italian offensives meant their effects on battlefield outcomes were marginal.[85]

Other forms of military indiscipline also appeared within tribal levies. Fire discipline, for example, remained uneven at best.[86] Arab levies in particular were famous for wasting ammunition, their apparent chronic inability to aim their weapons, and their blunt refusal to follow Turkish orders in battle. Tribal levies also refused to take prisoners among Italian soldiers. Indeed, captured Italian soldiers were not only executed but their bodies were often mutilated. Rumors circulated among foreign correspondents that non-Turkish levies were paid by their chiefs for executing prisoners.[87] These practices infuriated Italian commanders, though their soldiers also refused to take prisoners, setting up a vicious dynamic of inhumane treatment and execution of prisoners on both sides. Turkish commanders, for their part, had hoped to fight the war along "civilized" lines but found themselves unable to rein in their nominal subordinates on this issue.

In his unpublished memoirs, Hajj Mohammed Khalifa Fekini, the principal overseer of Arab tribal levies as well as chieftain of the Rojeban tribe, identified Arab-Berber antagonisms as another key source of indiscipline. He continually clashed with Suleiman al-Baruni, the Berber leader, who had designs on creating, and controlling, an autonomous Berber enclave within the Ottoman *vilayet*. Fekini documents how al-Baruni quietly worked to place his men in charge of paying tribal levies, which he then systematically looted, leaving Arab levies without pay.[88] In reply, Arab morale plummeted

<hr>

84. Wright 1913, 66.

85. Barbar 1980, 198–99. Mohammed Fekini makes mention of small numbers of Arabs fighting alongside an Italian detachment at the Battle of Wadi Melah, for example. See excerpts reproduced in del Bocca 2011, 174–75.

86. Rémond 1913, 54.

87. Irace 1912, 169.

88. del Bocca 2011, 32. Fekini believed that senior Turkish commanders were also complicit in this corruption.

while incentives to use combat for seeking spoils intensified. "His mendacity," Fekini wrote of al-Baruni, "provided the enemy a great service at a low-cost, because he had dealt a murderous blow to the enthusiastic esprit of the fighters, who were now disheartened."[89] Arab soldiers protested their unequal treatment and "began to avoid combat." These pay issues, and the wider Arab-Berber schism they represented, had an outsized effect on joint Ottoman battlefield performance since Arabs represented the bulk of the levies. Fekini also maintained that Italian forces and their spies were aware of these tensions and deliberately targeted Arabs in their operations to exacerbate this bad blood.[90] Furious, Fekini wrote long letters to Neshat Bey, the Caliph, the Turkish Prime Minister, and various tribal leaders denouncing al-Baruni and calling (unsuccessfully) for his dismissal.[91]

To tamp down these disciplinary issues, Turkish officers adjusted their force employment to ensure that they were in position to monitor non-Turkish battlefield conduct. When attacking, for example, Turkish officers were deployed behind tribal levies to drive them forward and to reduce opportunities for unsanctioned withdrawals or departures from the operational plan. "It is pretty certain that they [Turkish officers] will still confine themselves to forcing the poor Arabs to the front," wrote one pro-Italian correspondent Tullio Irace, "while they wait at a convenient and safe distance in the background, ready to take to their heels the moment that victory decides against them."[92] This practice was augmented by leavening tribal units with regular Turkish infantry, though most levies fought as homogenous units. Dedicated blocking detachments were not created, a function of insufficient numbers of Turks rather than absent willpower.

Indeed, Turkish officers were unafraid to bludgeon reluctant tribal levies into fighting. "We have been told by friendly men among them that these people [Arabs] were forced by the Turks to march in front to the attack of our trenches," Irace continued, "the Turks themselves keeping in the rear, holding the Arab women as hostages, and threatening to massacre the lot of them should they fail to break through the Italian line. Such is the Turk's usual method."[93] "Cuffing and kicking,"[94] for example, remained a basic staple of Turkish disciplinary practices on the battlefield, while desertion was

89. Mohammed Fekini, Diary Entry, reproduced in del Bocca 2011, 32.

90. He blames the Ottoman defeat at Zanzour (8 May 1912) to specific Italian targeting of "demoralized" Arab levies that induced their lines to break, for example.

91. del Bocca 2011, 35.

92. Irace 1912, 290–91. See also McClure 1913, 181.

93. Irace 1912, 158.

94. McClure 1913, 267, 271–72.

punishable by death.[95] As a result, "a good many of the Arabs had little stomach for the fight, in spite of the exhortations of a number of marabouts, and the more direct methods of persuasion adopted by Turks who were scattered among them as officers."[96] Savage reprisals against soldiers and even whole communities caught fighting for the Italians, or even providing them with material support, were also ordered as a means of deterring mass indiscipline within the ranks.[97]

Italian commanders, aware of the divided nature of Ottoman forces, tried to drive a wedge between Turkish and non-Turkish soldiers. Leaflets were dropped from Italian aircraft over Ottoman positions that highlighted the gulf between Turkish and non-Turkish motives and sacrifices in the war.[98] One leaflet distributed near Aziza in early January 1912 made the Italian case in blunt language:

> We are addressing this to you so that you may no longer take part in the war with the Turks, and let yourselves be killed to no purpose, and perish as the dust scattered by the wind. Do you not know that a weak State cannot resist a powerful nation? Do you not know that "iron is subdued only by iron?" War is like this. You are simple inhabitants, and know not the art of war. There is no doubt that, with God's help, we shall drive the Turks out of this country. In that event, what will become of you, if you persist in fighting with the Turks? ... Therefore, leave us to settle the question with the Turks, and then we shall say, "Let bygones be bygones." Whoever gives up fighting from this moment need never fear of being punished.... If you are grateful to us, we also shall be grateful to you. The Italian Government is your father, and you are its children. Therefore, beware of those who wish your ruin. Have you not seen that in fighting you are placed in the first line, while the Turks march behind you, so that they may flee from the battlefield and expose you to the fire of our guns and rifles?[99]

Recognizing these interethnic fissures is only a halfway house to exploiting them, however. Belligerents must also adopt their tactics and operations to

95. Abbott 1912a, 24.

96. McClure 1913, 115.

97. Bennett 1912, 188, 255.

98. Beehler 1913, 54.

99. "O Dwellers and Wanderers," Italian leaflet dropped near Aziza, 5 January 1912. Reproduced in Abbott 1912a, 193–94. Abbott notes that the Turks seized all the documents "so that their contents might not poison the minds of those to whom they were addressed ... carefully calculated to widen such dissension as there is between Arab and Turk." For their part, the Arab soldiers seemed to think these pamphlets were bank notes (Abbott 1912a, 194–95).

capitalize on the weaknesses buried within an opponent's military. In this case, Italian commanders not only failed to seize advantages created by these discipline problems but inadvertently damped them through mistaken tactical choices. Italian soldiers, for example, quickly discovered that tribal soldiers were unwilling to shoot if human shields drawn from the same populations were used, fueling hostage-taking as quasi-official policy. Prisoners of war were often executed or forcibly deported. Collective punishment was applied to villages caught within Italian lines; the homes of suspected snipers were routinely demolished. Medical parties and burial crews were shelled by Italian artillery after battles.[100]

Defectors were also dismissed rather than welcomed. After the battle of Ain Zara in December 1911, some Arab tribes sought to defect, sending envoys to Italians to pledge their allegiance. Yet Italian military commanders "refused to treat with these rebellious, ferocious, defeated Arabs. They were sent back to their villages, with orders to await the fate that we should think fit to impose on them."[101] Lieutenant-General Gherardo Pántano, in a frank assessment of Italian tactics, lamented that "our officers demonstrate feelings of great resentment, hostility, and hatred against the Arabs and do not know how to distinguish between friends and foes, or, rather, between those who we should fight and those we should protect.... Arabs found seriously injured are covered in gasoline and burned, or thrown in wells... others are shot with no other reason than that of a cruel whim."[102]

To make matters worse, these counterproductive tactical choices were being made in the shadow of Italy's earliest, and worst, misstep: its massacre of thousands of civilians during and immediately after the Battle of Tripoli in October 1911. Some portion, likely small, of Tripoli's population took up arms after Ottoman forces breached Italian lines on 23 October and began sniping from the rear. Once the initial wave of Ottoman attackers was beaten back, Italian soldiers turned on the local population. Ostensibly seeking to root out remaining Ottoman soldiers, at least four thousand civilians were executed in a "veritable carnival of carnage."[103] Word of the atrocity quickly spread through tribal networks—"the country rings of tales"—and to the wider world. "These tales," wrote journalist Francis McCullagh, "have now penetrated into the ends of the Desert and the Sudan (whence reinforcements are consequently beginning to arrive in larger and larger numbers) and they

---

100. McCullagh 1913, 243–44.

101. Irace 1912, 242.

102. Quoted in Stephensen 2014, 148.

103. Thomas Grant, "Italian Soldiers With Batches of Arab Prisoners, Whom They Are Treating With Indescribable Brutality," *Daily Mirror*, 2 November 1911, quote on p. 3.

have aroused in their believers an undying hatred of the Italians."[104] The massacre became a potent rally cry given close tribal ties: "There is hardly one of them [Arab levies] who has not had some friend or relation butchered in the oasis."[105] Putting aside their dislike of Turkish officers, and of the wider Ottoman project, these once-ambivalent tribes now sought vengeance against Italy, heeding Ottoman calls for volunteers. Absent Italian barbarism, it is likely that Arab and Berber desertion and defection would have been even higher, and the 42nd Independent Division even more constrained on the battlefield, than its actual performance in the Tripolitan war.

6.4.3. Case Study: Battle of Tripoli, 23–26 October 1911

The two Ottoman offensives that collectively comprise the Battle of Tripoli offer a microcosm of the compromises and trade-offs that haunted Ottoman battlefield performance throughout the war.[106] Desperate to drive the Italian Expeditionary Army from its Tripolitan beachhead, the 42nd Independent Division, now augmented with its first crop of tribal volunteers, initiated an early morning assault on 23 October. With hindsight, the four-day battle that ensued represents the high-water mark of Ottoman battlefield performance.

Italian forces, now 20,000-strong, had encircled the oasis of Tripoli with an elaborate system of layered trenches, firing pits, and terrain obstacles that stretched for nearly twenty kilometers from Tripoli's western edges to its southern approaches before turning abruptly north in a straight line to the Mediterranean. With their backs to the sea, the Italians had precious little defensive depth; only four kilometers separated the southernmost point of their defenses and the Mediterranean. Farms, gardens, patchy forests of palm trees, and several hamlets were trapped within these defensive lines, adding a second set of jumbled obstacles to would-be attackers. The First Aeroplane Flotilla, outfitted with nine or ten single- and dual-seated aircraft, was also stationed in Tripoli. Its arrival marked the first time an aviation unit had been deployed to an active combat theater. Armored cruisers steamed offshore, ready to provide covering fire in advent of an Ottoman attack. None was expected, however. Indeed, Italian artillery, its decisive advantage over Ottoman forces, was still crated, awaiting offloading from transport ships in the harbor.

104. McCullagh 1913, 295.
105. McCullagh 1913, 296.
106. Some historical accounts divide the Battle of Tripoli (or "October Surprise") into two separate battles, one at Shara Shatt (or Henni-Sciara Sciat, 23 October) and a second at Sidi Mesri (or Henni-Bu Meliana, 26 October).

Ottoman forces, estimated at nearly 8,000-strong, began advancing into attack positions in the predawn gloom, undetected by at least two circling Italian reconnaissance aircraft.[107] At 0700, feints and probing attacks were launched along the western limits of Italian defenses. Succeeding in drawing off Italian forces, the main Ottoman force, consisting of the 6,000-strong 8th Infantry Regiment (commanded by Neshat Bey himself) and some Arab cavalry, crashed against the Italians' weakly held eastern flank. The front now stretched six kilometers, ranging from Fort Sidi Messri to the Mediterranean. Italian defenders, the 11th *Bersaglieri* Regiment (1,800 men), were caught by surprise and quickly crumbled under Ottoman advances, gashing a large hole in their defenses.[108] In a preplanned operation, a small contingent of infiltrating nizam linked up with local residents, sniping Italian soldiers from the rear. Confusion reigned as Ottoman forces, now pouring through multiple breakthroughs in Italian defenses, fanned out, picking off panicking Italian soldiers. Turkish officers divided their forces, sending their nizam to capture the 11th's fortified headquarters at al-Hani. Arab and Berber forces surged into the oasis, interdicting Italian reserves moving up to plug defensive gaps. Two companies of the 2nd Battalion (the 4th and 5th) were badly mauled, their wounded summarily executed by Arab forces.

After nearly eight hours, the Ottoman offensive finally petered out. The HQ at al-Hani proved too fortified to crack without additional artillery support, while the Italians succeeded in sending reinforcements to stabilize their defensive lines. Bey ordered a withdrawal, leaving behind 503 dead Italian soldiers (including 21 officers), the largest single-day loss for the entire war. The Ottoman cost was high: an estimated 1,500–2,000 soldiers were killed. But the price was judged worthwhile by Ottoman political and military leaders, confident that the Italians had suffered a profound psychological shock that had dashed their hopes for an easy conquest of Tripolitania. Ottoman diplomats were keenly aware of the importance of this opening battle as a moral victory that produced a "great depression" among Italian policymakers. "It's now that the war begins," noted one observer.[109] They now turned to ensuring that contraband smuggling routes remained open while monitoring Western media for estimates of Italian casualties.[110]

107. Ottoman forces were roughly divided evenly between nizams and Arab and Berber tribal levies. Four field and two mountain artillery batteries provided fire support.

108. The 11th Regiment consisted of 1st and 3rd Battalions (between Sidi Messri and al-Hani) and the 2nd Battalion (at al-Hani to the sea).

109. Fuad Simavi Bey à Assim Bey, le 26 octobre 1911, Dépêche No. 34 897/693 in Kuneralp 2011, 280–81.

110. See, for example, Nihad Bey à Assim Bey, le 27 octobre 1911, Dépêche No.482/221 in Kuneralp 2011, 286; Tevfik Pacha à Assim Bey, le 28 octobre 1911, Télégramme chiffre No.733 in

The Italian reply to the "October surprise" was swift. House-to-house searches began for civilians who had taken up arms as well as Arab soldiers trapped behind Italian lines. Beginning on 24 October, several massacres unfolded, with nearly 4,000 locals killed and another 3,750 deported. These actions continued even as an official Ottoman envoy arrived outside the Italian defensive perimeter on 25 October, seeking their surrender and withdrawal. This offer was rebuffed, and the now-chastised Italian Expeditionary Force set about fortifying its positions, including deploying over forty artillery cannons and doubling aerial patrols.

Ottoman forces were not idle, however. Regrouping, the 8th Infantry Regiment, now with approximately 6,000 soldiers, initiated a second offensive in the early morning hours of 26 October. Reversing direction, Bey ordered a series of feints at eastern Italian positions (at Shara Shatt and al-Hani) at 0500. He then directed the bulk of his forces to strike at the southern edge of Italian lines, near Kemal Bey's House, a prominent landmark 1.5 kilometers west of Fort Sidi Messri. Once again, Ottoman forces successfully breached Italian lines. In a near-repeat performance, Turkish nizams began attacking the rear of the 4th and 6th companies of the 84th Regiment while Arab levies moved deeper into the oasis. Heavy machine gun and artillery fire blunted the assault, however, and Bey reluctantly ordered a withdrawal. Another 26 Italian soldiers were killed (and 107 wounded); at least 250 Ottoman soldiers died as well. Sporadic fighting continued over the next few days as stranded Arab levies commandeered houses to continue fighting from within Italian lines. These soldiers were eventually quieted, though not before Maxim machine guns and two batteries of field guns were committed to dislodging them. Alongside these mop-up operations, Italian soldiers embarked on a second round of reprisals among the local population, killing scores.

Contemporary observers, Italian and non-Italian alike, judged the outcome of the Battle of Tripoli as a second Adwa, the epic defeat of Italian forces by Ethiopia in 1896 ("a disaster to which Adwa would be as but a street accident").[111] Poetic license aside, the battle did have far-reaching consequences. On 28 October, General Caneva requested an additional 30,000 soldiers even as he shortened his defensive perimeter, abandoning eastern key forts at Sidi Messri, Shara Shatt, and al-Hani. In doing so, he unwittingly revealed evidence that Italian soldiers had hanged and mutilated Arab soldiers—who were not considered lawful belligerents by Italian military

---

Kuneralp 2011, 286; and Assim Bey aux Missions Ottomanes, le 31 octobre 1911, Circulaire en télégramme en clair No. 9946/323 in Kuneralp 2011, 297.

111. McCullagh 1913, 250.

command—when Ottoman forces reoccupied these locations.[112] These atrocities created a new set of grievances among Arab and Berber soldiers that made desertion, let alone defection, less likely. As Caneva himself recognized, the conduct of his forces had created a "ditch of blood that we have unfortunately found ourselves obliged to dig between ourselves and our future subjects."[113]

Though outnumbered and outgunned, Ottoman forces did reasonably well to identify and exploit weaknesses in Italian defenses. The Italian General Staff's own internal account called this battle a "severe trial" for Italian solders, as they "repulsed an adversary strong in numbers, masterly in deceit, tenacious in close quarters, and who took advantage of all the cover afforded by the terrain."[114] Caution became the watchword for Italian movements after October 1911. Wary of risk, the Italian Expeditionary Force rarely conducted offensives, remaining mostly content just to sit within range of their artillery and cruisers and brush back Ottoman assaults.[115]

Care must be taken not to exaggerate Ottoman martial prowess, however. Fear among Turkish officers that Arab and Berber levies were unreliable led to the adoption of simpler tactics and operations to facilitate greater commander control. Though feints were used, much of the action centered on straightforward frontal assaults that crashed against entrenched Italian positions until a weakness was found. Coordination between infantry, cavalry, and artillery remained rudimentary, with artillery tasked with independent fire unconnected to the movement of Ottoman forces during the assault. Simple tactics did facilitate command and control, as did the practice of stiffening Arab units with handfuls of Turkish officers. Predictable tactics in turn exacted a steeper price in terms of casualties. Ottoman casualties remained far higher than Italian ones in each action of the Battle of Tripoli, a legacy of interethnic mistrust and the resulting reliance on simple frontal assaults.

Turkish officers were right to be concerned about indiscipline within non-Turkish ranks. Despite breaching Italian lines, momentum was lost on both 23 and 26 October because Arab soldiers, no longer under tight Turkish supervision as they headed deeper into Tripoli's oasis, turned to widespread looting. Eyewitnesses reported that Arabs "scattered through the oasis on the hunt for loot" from retreating Italians, "hunt[ing] singly or in small groups. Some of them proceeded to strip the corpses of the Italian dead, to seize the rifles and

---

112. del Bocca 1986, 18; del Bocca 1911, 45–52.

113. Quoted in del Bocca 2011, 27.

114. Tittoni 1914, 26, 29.

115. Herrmann 1989.

ammunition of the fallen, to plunder the regimental stores."[116] This "craze for loot" turned Arab victory into defeat: "many Arabs were shot down ...while industriously stripping corpses instead of trying to meet the counter-attack of the Italians." Italian commanders half-jokingly counseled their soldiers to scatter tins of hardtack biscuits around the trenches to distract and slow advancing Arab units on the prowl for spoils.[117] "I should not be at all surprised if, before the war ends, the Arabs are all dressed in Italian uniforms," concluded one correspondent.[118]

Tribal leaders themselves recognized that this indiscipline had proven costly. Fekini ruefully admitted that "unfortunately, our fighters are not as well organized as their adversaries and had no notion of military discipline. I was obliged to intervene in order to put some order into the ranks and to impose discipline."[119] Even in the context of limited success, the methods of maintaining sufficient order and discipline to mount attacks created new grievances among non-core soldiers that festered throughout the war. The official Italian military history of the battle recounts how Turkish practices of monitoring their Arab levies was already sparking interethnic friction:

Arab inaction [after 26 October] could be attributed to disagreements that arose between tribes and between Arabs and Turks about assigning responsibility for the battle outcome [as well as] complaints about why the Turks always maintained a prudent distance from the front line, leaving the weight of all the fighting to the Arabs. It was rumored that at Ain Zara, after the battle of the 26th, many [Arab] leaders had told the Turkish commander that they would not give any more help if he did not distribute food and payroll more equitably, and if Turkish soldiers did not also fight on the front lines.[120]

Even at the height of its battlefield success, the Ottoman Army was hamstrung by simplified tactics, high casualties, poor discipline, and reliance on coercion to maintain soldier discipline; all familiar pathologies of high military inequality. Italian mistakes at Tripoli aided Ottoman advances and helped paper over the internal divisions that threatened the Ottoman Army. These interethnic tensions never remained far below the surface, however, and conspired to hobble Ottoman battlefield performance until the war's conclusion in October 1912.

116. McCullagh 1913, 133–34.
117. McCullagh 1913, 219.
118. McCullagh 1913, 217.
119. Mohamed Fekini, Diary Entry, quoted in del Bocca 2011, 23.
120. Ministero della Guerra 1922, 147.

6.5. Austria-Hungary: Unforced Errors and the Limits of Mechanical Cohesion on the Eastern Front

The performance of the Austro-Hungarian Common Army on the Eastern Front was, in a word, disastrous. According to the conservative battlefield performance index, Austro-Hungarian forces clawed their way to a 0.50 value—the same as Ottoman forces. Its overall performance was penalized by both the outbreak of mass desertion and reliance on fratricidal violence, including blocking detachments, to force soldiers to fight. As with the Ottoman assessment, however, the BPI understates the problems that beset the Common Army. National minorities, especially Czechs, Ruthenes, and Poles, switched sides during the war, though defection fell far short of 10 percent of total deployed forces. Its loss-exchange ratio, too, was artificially propped up by a combination of German officers and, later, whole divisions, that bolstered Austro-Hungarian tactical and technical capacities. As a static, one-time measure, the BPI also misses the cascading nature of Austro-Hungarian military disintegration as its political and military leaders transitioned from prewar discrimination to the wartime implementation of targeted repression against suspect national minorities. Below I sketch the nature of Austro-Hungarian combat power and cohesion across several Eastern Front campaigns. I then explore the Battle of Galicia (23 August–11 September 1914), which offers a clean look at Common Army performance given the absence of German forces.

6.5.1. Combat Power

Concerns about the political reliability of national minorities were intimately bound with Austro-Hungary's decision for war in 1914 as well as its battlefield tactics. In the wake of the 28 June assassination of Archduke Franz Ferdinand in Sarajevo, Austro-Hungarian elites, including Emperor Franz Joseph himself, argued that only war with Serbia (War Plan-S) and its nominal protector, Russia (War Plan-R), could dispel the specter of nationalism now openly stalking the Austro-Hungarian empire. "Thus I must intervene," Emperor Joseph declared, "to win through force of arms the guarantees that are essential to secure for my state's internal tranquility and a lasting external peace."[121] His Chief of the Army, General Franz Conrad von Hötzendorf, along with the rest of the *Armeeoberkommando* (AOK), thought external war necessary to prevent, in Conrad's words, "internal fighting which would inevitably result in the disintegration of the polyglot Monarchy."[122] War at

---

121. Quoted in Watson 2014b, 70.
122. Quoted in Watson 2014b, 22.

least held the promise of reinvigorating the bonds between a still-popular monarch and the empire's peoples, even if interethnic ties were increasingly strained.

Yet war held risks; as early as 1906, Conrad had warned of "corrosive nationalist elements, especially in Bohemia, Bosnia-Herzegovina, Galicia, and the South Tyrol,"[123] that threatened the cohesion of both Austro-Hungary and its military. So concerned was the AOK about fighting a war with divided forces that it retained a plan to invade Hungary to reunify the Dual Monarchy (and its Common Army) as late as 1914.[124] Viewing non-German soldiers of his Common Army as especially prone to disloyalty, Conrad embraced campaign plans that called for wildly ambitious offensives designed to knock Serbia and Russia from the war in a matter of weeks.[125] Quick battles of annihilation, rather than plodding attritional contests, were the means by which Conrad and the AOK could wage war without jeopardizing Austro-Hungary's domestic stability. Though (rightly) derided as woefully out of touch with modern tactics, weaponry, and logistics, even Conrad recognized the long odds involved. "I believe more and more," he lamented, "that our purpose will merely be to go under honorably, like a sinking ship."[126]

Even the mobilization process—the Habsburg Army grew from 450,000 to 1,687,000 in less than a month[127]—was fraught with ethnic tension. Unsure of popular allegiances, Habsburg authorities resorted to a double-barreled mobilization, issuing patriotic appeals but also dressing the call to arms in the language of ethnicity.[128] Or, in this case, in fifteen different languages, as authorities turned a blind eye as Czech, Ruthene, Polish, and even Magyar units assembled and then marched with flags from their national communities rather than official Habsburg symbols. Draft-dodging was an early concern and followed predictable contours, with Austrians the least likely to skip service (only 3 percent of recruits) and Slavs and Ruthenes from the Balkans and Galicia the highest (at about 33 percent).[129] Some grumbling within the ranks was already evident. A Czech unit, for example, marched to the beat of "Red-colored handkerchief, wave through the sky, we fight the Russians, though

---

123. Quoted in Rachamimov 2005, 160. See also Judson 2016, 390.

124. Nolan 2017, 333.

125. Conrad's views may have been shaped early on by his family history. His father, a cavalry officer, watched his regiment, recruited principally from Hungarians, revolt against Vienna in 1848 (Buttar 2014, 71–72).

126. Quoted in Buttar 2014, 83.

127. Watson 2014b, 73.

128. Watson 2014b, 95.

129. Watson 2014b, 117.

we don't know why."[130] The AOK itself believed that at least one-quarter of its 1914 army went to war politically unwilling to "do their duty to the Emperor."[131] Assessments of soldier attitudes are also colored by the fact that the AOK unleashed a wave of mass arrests targeting Slavic and non-Magyar populations, seeking to root out potential subversives.[132] Most worrisome for the AOK, however, was the fact that many non-core soldiers reported for duty because they felt that wartime service would lead to political reform. "The war," as Pieter Judson argues, "offered them opportunities to reshape the empire according to their particular vision."[133] The process of double mobilization thus managed to reinforce ethnic group solidarity and raise official suspicions about disloyal soldiers simultaneously. As a result, many soldiers were sent off to war with combat motivations that sharply diverged from the stated goal of preserving the Dual Monarchy.[134]

This subversive undercurrent of ethnic mistrust and suspect loyalties heavily constrained Habsburg tactical choices and operational art in the war's opening campaigns in Galicia, the Carpathian mountains, and Gorlice-Tarnów.[135] Driven by a fervent belief in the cult of the offensive, Habsburg and Russian military authorities, joined in mid-1915 by their German counterparts, unleashed sweeping wars of maneuver across the plains and highlands of modern-day Ukraine in wheeling battles designed to enfold and then annihilate opposing forces in enormous "cauldron battles." Historians converge on an unflattering view of Habsburg tactics in these campaigns.[136] Typical Habsburg offensives revolved around frontal assaults by closed formations directly into the teeth of prepared Russian defenses with only rudimentary fire support. Combined arms approaches, including coordinating artillery barrages with infantry assaults, were ruled too complex for Slavic soldiers to master. "Ethnically German generals did not think illiterate Slavic peasants could make complex maneuvers or fight independently outside the view of

---

130. Quoted in Agnew 2004, 164.

131. Cornwall 2000, 31.

132. Judson 2016, 391–94.

133. Judson 2016, 385. As late as January 1917, the Czech National Socialist Party argued that "this inner loyalty of ours, the realization that we have capably performed our duties to the empire and the dynasty, must strengthen our firm, unshakeable faith in future justice, even if it is inconvenient to a few German nationalists." Quoted in Judson 2016, 406.

134. Ironically, had Austria-Hungary won the war, it would have annexed millions of non-Germanic subjects, deepening its interethnic tensions.

135. The Battle of Galicia was fought 23 August–11 September 1914; the Carpathian mountains campaign was in reality three separate offensives initiated on 23 January 1915, 27 February 1915, and 22 March 1915; and the Battle at Gorlice-Tarnów lasted 2 May–22 June 1915.

136. DiNardo 2010; Tunstall 2010; Stone 1975; Watson 2014b; Rauchensteiner 2014.

officers," one historian noted, "so they massed the infantry instead of advancing in less vulnerable open order."[137] Advancing in tightly packed formations facilitated monitoring, helping German officers to close possible desertion avenues. Close monitoring ensured that soldiers actually fired their weapons; units with large proportions of non-core soldiers often proved reluctant to fire or to advance without officers prodding them forward.[138] Initiative was strictly rationed; units made little use of battlefield terrain for concealment since it could provide cover for desertion or defection. The AOK also resisted night attacks and marches for the same reasons, sacrificing flexibility and initiative to ensure continued control.

Ethnic mistrust also crippled Habsburg training. Wary of the reliability of their own soldiers, and especially concerned that the Hungarian *Honvéd* might form the nucleus of an independent army, the AOK drastically curtailed prewar training. "An army that distrusted half of its soldiers," Norman Stone observed, "naturally had little interest in training them in initiative or independence."[139] Retrograde actions—the ability to retreat in good order while under heavy enemy fire—were left unpracticed, abandoned out of fear that these maneuvers could provide cover for desertion or shirking.[140] Digging proper defensive entrenchments also went by the wayside; trenches were irrelevant given the AOK's desire to fight a quick, short war. "Don't bother teaching them to fight," one Habsburg general remarked, for "they learn that in battle; teach them to *obey*."[141] This weakened training regime came at the cost of soldier skill; many Habsburg soldiers could barely fire their weapons, let alone master complex tactics, before they debouched at the front lines.[142] Buckling under the weight of staggering casualties, the AOK further slashed training; by 1915, many replacement (*Marsch* battalions) recorded only five weeks of training before entering combat.[143]

Even routine matters such as rotating units or sending reinforcements to the front were greatly complicated by ethnic considerations. Units were far from interchangeable; careful attention was paid to the ethnic composition of both line and replacement units. Nor could units be slotted into their respective areas of responsibility without consideration of the ethnic makeup of neighboring units. Pack too many suspect units together, for example, and

137. Nolan 2017, 334–35.
138. Wawro 2014, 361.
139. Stone 1975, 308.
140. Schindler 2015, 249.
141. Quoted in Wawro 2014, 354.
142. Watson 2014*b*, 255.
143. Watson 2014*b*, 119.

the AOK risked cascades of poor performance across these units that could unravel an offensive or collapse key defensive positions. As a result, the front became a patchwork quilt comprised of ethnically diverse units with varying degrees of loyalty, willingness to fight, and combat capability. At Gorlice-Tarnów, for example, the AOK, amid a backdrop of Czech-dominant units surrendering en masse (see below), grew concerned about the loyalty of a replacement battalion of Infantry Regiment No. 35, a unit that was 60 percent Czech. In June 1915, the battalion had complained that its new commanding officer, a Hungarian, could not speak Czech, a level of dissent deemed sufficiently worrisome that the entire regiment was ordered to the rear. It was replaced by Infantry Regiment No. 69, a Hungarian-dominant unit, one less-than-pleased to discover its new frontline role. IR No. 69 was forced to curtail its training—it had less than eight weeks—to plug the gap in the front.[144] Multiplied across many infantry regiments, the practice of ethnic micromanagement contributed to impoverished training and tactics while creating new grievances among units most likely to be loyal.

The campaigns of 1914–15 also decimated the small Habsburg officer corps. One of every eight prewar officers had been killed, while large numbers had been captured or were missing.[145] In total, nearly half of the Habsburg Army's officers had been lost, forcing the AOK to rely heavily on up-jumped reservists, the so-called War Officers (*Kriegoffiziere*). These officers had far less training than their prewar counterparts, and their youthfulness created friction among the Habsburg's seasoned *grognards*. Unlike the carefully curated prewar officer corps, these war officers typically possessed only a single language and thus found themselves isolated from, and unable to communicate with, their soldiers. Tactical flexibility and skill suffered; miscommunication raised significant barriers to the adoption of more sophisticated tactics and to regrouping if a formation was surprised by a Russian attack.[146] War officers, while still predominantly of German ethnicity (56.8 percent), had far more Hungarians (24.5 percent) and Czechs (10.6 percent) than the prewar officer corps.[147]

144. Rauchensteiner 2014, 946.

145. Bundesministerium für Heereswesen und Kriegsarchiv 1930, 56; Jeřábek 2002, 158–59; Watson 2014*b*, 281.

146. Tunstall 2016, 117; Stone 1975, 127.

147. Though suspicion over the loyalty of Czech officers was high, military necessity, along with the Czech population's relatively large, educated middle class, forced the AOK's hand (Watson 2014*b*, 285–96). Czechs, along with every other national group except Germans, remained underrepresented in the war officers relative to their proportion of soldiers. On the language composition of the army in 1915, see Plaschka, Haselsteiner and Suppan 1974, 35.

Despite suffering staggering losses—an estimated 2.7 million soldiers were killed, wounded, or incapacitated by frostbite and disease—the Habsburg Army entered 1916 with a sense of cautious optimism. A sustained recruitment drive had nearly tripled the army's size, now at 4.88 million, though questions of quality and loyalty remained.[148] The influx of German officers, as well as much tighter coordination with German armies, gave the AOK some confidence that its soldiers would fight harder, even as its subordinate status to the German General Staff rankled. The Eastern Front, too, had seemingly stabilized. Weary Russian and Habsburg forces now turned to constructing extensive defensive trenches, a move welcomed by the AOK since its soldiers would now be easier to monitor. The "Habsburg Army didn't get any better," noted Geoffrey Wawro, "it just got easier to police"[149] in 1916. Training, too, was curtailed in favor of make-work projects, including featherbedding the officers' defensive locations. Fear of ethnic disloyalty remained constant. Prewar ethnic stereotypes were amplified by wartime examples of Slavic soldiers, especially Ruthene- and Czech-majority units, engaging in mass surrender and desertion during these opening campaigns. As the commander of IX Corps noted in October 1915, "German and Hungarian units were also breached and lost prisoners, but the number of missing compared with the number of deaths and wounded is as far as I know never in a similar proportion to that of the infantry regiments with Czech personnel."[150] Wartime repression of Serbs and Ruthenes in 1914 also signaled to all national minorities that the regime was intent on doubling down on collective punishment rather than recasting its ideational bases in a more inclusionary direction.

Russia's Brusilov Offensive (4 June–20 September 1916) shattered this illusion, however. Importing French-style "Joffre tactics," General Aleksi Brusilov sought to penetrate Austro-Hungarian defenses using a combination of short artillery bombardments to drive k.u.k. soldiers to their shelters while specialized shock troops punctured enemy lines, racing to beat the emerging defenders. Brusilov made efficient use of aerial reconnaissance to map defensive works; Russian soldiers then practiced against mocked-up defensive emplacements. His opening gambit on 4 June, which pitted 632,000 Russian soldiers against 500,000 Austro-Hungarian and German soldiers, met with initial success, catching the AOK by surprise and gashing large holes in at least four sectors.[151]

---

148. Estimates are found in Watson 2014*b*, 282, 280.

149. Wawro 2014, 376. See also Rothenberg 1976, 195–96.

150. Quoted in Rauchensteiner 2014, 945.

151. On the Brusilov Offensive, see Wawro 2014; Stone 1975; Dowling 2012, 2008; Bundesministerium für Heereswesen und Kriegsarchiv 1933, 660–65.

These gains were made possible by two vulnerabilities created by increased military inequality within the k.u.k. Army. First, two-thirds of all available Austro-Hungarian forces, including reserves, were concentrated in the first set of "lines" of the defensive trench system. The AOK's use of a "thick frontline" system meant that most sectors only had a kilometer of depth, making the odds of being overrun dangerously high if Russians penetrated the initial defensive layer.[152] Such a disposition was warranted, however, by concern over mass indiscipline; packing soldiers into narrow sectors helped new officers monitor their charges.[153] Second, Brusilov, aware of these internal schisms, "hammered into his subordinates' heads" the need to target "Slavic" units because they would have "less inclination to resist."[154] In each sector, Czech- and Ruthenian-dominated units were identified as breakthrough points. His foresight paid off: the 2nd Infantry Division (mostly Czech) and the Moravian 8th Infantry Regiment surrendered en masse, while the entire 4th Army collapsed on 6 June, rending a twenty-kilometer-wide gash some seventy-five kilometers deep beyond Austro-Hungarian lines. The 7th Army soon followed, losing 76,200 of its 194,200 soldiers after only four days.[155] A cascade of increasingly panicked and disorganized retreats ensued as remnants of units fled to the rear, surrendered en masse, or simply melted away.

By the end of July, the k.u.k. Army had lost 475,138 soldiers, including 265,931 captured or otherwise missing. Yet the Brusilov Offensive was petering out. Russian forces had far exceeded their supply lines, limiting exploitation operations, while heavy losses (about 495,000 casualties, including 60,000 killed), bureaucratic infighting, and the lack of reinforcements barred further advances. The damage was done, however. By September 1916, the reeling Habsburg Army shackled itself to the German Army, forfeiting its independence. "It is probably not an exaggeration," Stone remarked, "that the Austrian army survived, now, by grace of the Prussian sergeant-major."[156]

German officers, now entrenched in all senior commander positions, quickly concluded that k.u.k Army's failings stemmed from unreliable Slavic units. Some Czech-dominated units—the 79th Honvéd Infantry Brigade and

---

152. Stone 1975, 249.

153. These vulnerabilities were magnified by the AOK's decision to strip many of its best regiments from the Eastern Front to launch a massive "Punishment Expedition" against Italy at Trentino.

154. Rauchensteiner 2014, 526. On this point, see especially Airapetov 2015a, 123–33, and Dowling 2008, 44, 63, 70, 72.

155. Stone 1975, 254.

156. Stone 1975, 254.

the 42nd Honvéd Infantry Division in particular—had indeed offered little resistance before fleeing. Two additional Czech-dominated units, Infantry Regiments No. 18 and No. 98, actually switched sides during battle. Ruthenians, too, did not escape German ire; "the woeful Ruthenians," one report lamented, "deserted once more in droves."[157] As part of their post-Brusilov lessons learned, German commanders demanded that all Czech units be disbanded. When the AOK, citing manpower shortages, balked, these commanders repositioned their divisional cavalry behind suspected unreliable troop formations to enforce order.[158]

German commanders also rammed through a sweeping overhaul of k.u.k Army tactics and operations. Specialized storm battalions (*Sturmtruppen*) were created, for example, to infiltrate Russian lines quickly, without plodding frontal assaults that required days of preparatory artillery bombardments. Regiments were downsized somewhat to increase tactical flexibility and decentralize decision-making. Production of artillery cannons and machine guns of higher quality was accelerated, and closer attention was paid to their tighter integration with infantry assaults.[159] Conrad himself was sacked in February 1917 and replaced as Chief of General Staff by Arthur Arz von Straussenburg. Yet military inequality remained high; these reforms foundered on the fact that an increasing share of officers and soldiers no longer identified with the Habsburg cause. In the wake of the February Revolution in Russia, new questions about Habsburg war aims, and especially the wisdom of continuing the war now that the Russian Army was slowly dissolving, arose. German commanders increasingly viewed Hungarian formations as politically suspect, no longer willing to be "punched down" into other troop bodies but instead becoming increasingly nationalistic.[160] In May 1917, German General Hans von Seeckt, Chief of Staff of Army Group "Erzherzog Joseph," warned that Hungarians had turned their eyes toward independence. "The self-confidence and the deep aversion of the Hungarians," he concluded, "soon increasing to hatred, soon increasing to contempt, against the current [German] Army Command had grown strongly,"[161] and their reliability could no longer be guaranteed.

Russia's Kerensky Offensive (1–23 July 1917) provides a final opportunity to assess Habsburg tactical and operational sophistication. Meant as a last-ditch effort in Galicia to prop up the fledgling Provisional Government

157. Quoted in Rauchensteiner 2014, 528.
158. Rauchensteiner 2014, 947. On the quarrelsome nature of military relations between Germany and Austria-Hungary, see Craig 1965; Shanafelt 1985.
159. Nolan 2017, 394.
160. Rauchensteiner 2014, 754.
161. Ibid.

in Petrograd, the Kerensky Offensive combined shock troops and the heaviest preparatory barrage witnessed on the Eastern Front.[162] Initial results were encouraging; most, though not all, of the badly demoralized Russian soldiers followed their officers, and combined Austro-Hungarian and German lines were penetrated in several sectors. German forces shortened their lines in good order; Austro-Hungarian forces, predominantly in a Czech-held sector, broke in disarray. Some units, notably the Czech-dominated Infantry Regiments No. 35 and No. 75, defected to the Russians at the Battle of Zborov (1–2 July). To seal breaches in their defensive lines, German commanders ordered the removal of ethnically suspect units (including the 19th Infantry Division and the Hungarian 15th Honvéd Infantry Division) and their replacement with ethnically German formations. Senior commanders actually drafted plans to remove all Romanian, Ruthenian, Serbian, and Czech soldiers from the Eastern Front entirely to eliminate these liabilities.[163]

By 16 July, however, the Russian offensive was staggering beneath the weight of poor morale, high desertion, and fouled logistics. On 19 July, combined Austro-Hungarian and German forces counterattacked, punching through disorganized Russian formations to reach the Zbruch River. Over the next three days, the Russian Army, or what remained of it, retreated nearly 240 kilometers. Much of the credit for this pushback is due to the German Army; Austro-Hungarian forces contributed relatively little to the actual fight, more content to ride German coattails than to seek independent action even against a badly weakened foe. Indeed, the AOK spent much of 1917–18 simply bunkering down, hoping to maintain its control over an exhausted and disillusioned rank and file weakened by near starvation level rations. Even victory over Russia, as codified in the Treaty of Brest-Litovsk (3 March 1918), did little to stem the k.u.k. Army's collapse. Between March and November 1918, the army simply melted away, as desertions, mutinies, and even defection gutted its ranks. The death of the army was quickly followed by that of the state itself, as Austria-Hungary slipped beneath the waves of ethnic nationalism unleashed by the war.

Given the poor state of Austro-Hungarian tactics for much of the war, it is perhaps surprising to discover that the k.u.k Army's loss-exchange ratio is, at first glance, quite good. Treating the Eastern Front as a single campaign, Austro-Hungarian forces killed 1.54 Russian soldiers for each of their own.[164] This above-parity loss-exchange ratio is far better than a typical high, or even

---

162. Airapetov 2015*b*, 263–71.

163. Rauchensteiner 2014, 756–58.

164. This estimate is the mean derived from estimates of Austro-Hungarian (550,000–601,000) and Russian (775,400–1,005,000) killed in action from the Galicia campaign to the signing of the treaty at Brest-Litovsk.

medium, inequality belligerent, and far outpaces that of the Ottoman Empire. Yet this summary statistic is misleading, for two reasons.

First, the k.u.k Army fought with substantial German material and technical assistance from mid-1915 onward. If we concentrate solely on the initial campaigns in Galicia and the Carpathian Mountains, when Austria-Hungary largely faced Russia alone, then its loss-exchange ratio falls to near-parity (1.08).[165] This result is consistent with the performance of most medium inequality belligerents, and is fairly damning considering the poor state of the Russian Army in these campaigns. By early 1915, only 1.2 million of 5 million Russian soldiers actually had a rifle, for example.[166] Yet the average tour of duty for an Austro-Hungarian soldier at the Carpathian front was a mere five to six weeks before being killed, wounded, or captured, a reflection of near fanatical adherence to offensives even when outnumbered and unprepared to carry them out.[167] What's worse is that the AOK turned in this performance while able to intercept Russian radio communications in near-real time. Russia continually sent its radio messages *en clair*, allowing the AOK to pilfer unencrypted Russian messages at the same time as their intended recipients by as early as August 1914, including at Galicia. The AOK had the world's most sophisticated signals intelligence (SIGINT) effort, with eleven mobile wireless telegraphy units dedicated to intercepting Russian correspondence and with sending false messages designed to confuse Russian forces. This intelligence provided early warning of enemy movements and operational designs, especially once AOK code-breakers cracked Russian ciphers, gaining access to high-level Russian communiques.[168] Yet these advantages did not translate into overwhelming tactical and operational advantages or lopsided loss-exchange ratios, a testament to how deep-seated the dysfunction was within the k.u.k. Army.

Second, prisoners of war are excluded from these totals. Austria-Hungary lost an estimated 2.77 million soldiers to Russian prisons over the course of the war, the largest POW losses of any belligerent in World War One.[169] "It was evident," Manfried Rauchensteiner has noted, "that the men fighting in the Imperial and Royal Army were far more willing to raise their hands in surrender or desert than the soldiers from any other power fighting in the

---

165. Mean casualties (killed and wounded) are 1.1 million for Austria-Hungary and 1.19 million for Russia from the opening of the Galicia campaign to the final battle of the *Karpathenkrieg* at Mezölaborcz in April 1915. See Stone 1975, 91, and Tunstall 2010, 212.

166. Nolan 2017, 369.

167. Tunstall 2010, 12.

168. Schindler 2015, 227–28, 262–63.

169. Rachamimov 2005, 158.

war."[170] Adding POW estimates to each belligerent's losses drives the Austro-Hungarian loss-exchange ratio down to levels consistent with the expected performance of high inequality belligerents throughout history.

6.5.2. Cohesion

Indiscipline spread throughout the ranks in two-step fashion. Ethnic groups that faced prewar restrictions on military service and had only second-class status within the Dual Monarchy—notably, Czechs, Ruthenians, Serbs, Romanians, and Poles—were the first to engage in collective indiscipline. Wartime repression of internal Serbian and Ruthenian populations worsened indiscipline among these groups as the Dual Monarchy shifted from medium to high military inequality. As the war dragged on, a second wave of mass indiscipline, this time from the two core groups, Magyars and Germans, roiled Habsburg ranks. Nearly every form of collective indiscipline imaginable, from desertion and defection to mutinies, self-mutilation, and preemptive surrender, was observed on the Eastern Front. Desertion, for example, was rampant; nearly 5 percent of the entire fielded Habsburg force deserted in the final weeks of the war alone.[171] High profile cases of defection also occurred, though too few soldiers switched sides to meet the strict 10 percent threshold for mass defection. To prevent the further erosion of discipline, the AOK decided to field specialized formations, typically stationed behind politically suspect units, to force them to fight. Coercion, it turned out, was a poor substitute for cohesion. Prewar ethnic networks, reinforced by wartime violence, proved durable even on the battlefield, facilitating the unraveling of the Common Army.

A caveat is in order, however. Nearly all historians do agree that ethnically motivated mass indiscipline was an enormous problem for the Habsburg Army. We also should be careful of potential biases. AOK commanders had incentives to exaggerate, if not invent wholesale, "stabbed in the back" myths to excuse their own poor performance. A core primary text, the official five-volume history of the war, *Österreich-Ungartens letzter Krieg 1914–1918*, is littered with references to "traitorous Slavs" but is also written by partisan former wartime commanders.[172] Nor did every unit with non-core soldiers fight poorly, as nationalist historians bent on identifying early resistance to the Dual Monarchy have claimed. In the war's early days, some fought doggedly, with some infantry regiments virtually annihilated in place. The claim here is

---

170. Rauchensteiner 2014, 321.

171. Rauchensteiner 2014, 954.

172. Österreichischen Bundesministerium für Heereswesen und Kriegsarchiv 1930.

a simpler one: non-core units had a higher probability of deserting or defecting, and of doing so earlier in the war, than units staffed principally by core groups. Casualties, hunger, poor leadership—these factors, too, shaped mass indiscipline. Yet even these factors were often viewed through an ethnic lens by non-core soldiers. Staggering casualties at Galicia and the Carpathian campaign among Czechs, Ruthenians, and Serbs were cited as proof that (core) officers did not care about their (non-core) men, reducing their willingness to fight for a regime that saw their lives as cheap.

Mass desertion among Ruthenian, Serb, and especially Czech-dominated infantry regiments began as early as the August 1914 campaign in Galicia. Taking advantage of the confusion and noise of the battlefield, these soldiers coordinated their actions and typically deserted or surrendered in small groups of 10–20 individuals.[173] During the 1915 battles in the Carpathian mountains and at Gorlice-Tarnów, desertion from these units reached staggering levels. Twelve companies' worth of Czech soldiers had disappeared entirely from the 2nd Army by 14 March 1915; by 21 March, only two of sixteen companies of the 8th Infantry Regiment could be mustered.[174] Some Czech-dominated units, notably the 26th and 28th Regiments, simply melted away. Czechs, along with Ruthenians and Serbs, were singled out as desertion threats in the 2nd, 3rd, and 4th Armies on the Carpathian front by mid-spring 1915. Plans were mooted to have these soldiers relegated to road construction, and instructions were issued to ensure that these regiments were flanked by more reliable elements. The 21st Infantry Regiment mutinied at Gorlice-Tarnów *after* Russian forces had been pushed back; the neighboring 36th Infantry Regiment did so as well. A roll call of the 36th Infantry Regiment found only 893 soldiers remaining out of a paper-strength 2,571 despite the absence of severe fighting. In September 1915, the heavily Czech 19th Division fell apart so spectacularly that two entire Russian Army Corps were outfitted with weapons abandoned by deserting soldiers.[175] For the AOK, "the Czechs time and again fared badly when compared to the troops of different national origins."[176]

Facing the same enemy on the same front, and armed with the same tactics and weapons, k.u.k. Army units displayed considerable variation in their

---

173. France's foreign intelligence service, the Deuxième Bureau, had already concluded that Czechs were "less heroic" and had a greater tendency to surrender prematurely than other soldiers by November 1914. See Rauchensteiner 2014, 346. In fact, French, British, Russian, and German intelligence agencies had converged in their presumably independent views of Czech, Polish, and Ruthenian soldiers as especially prone to desertion by late 1914.

174. Rauchensteiner 2014, 345–46.

175. Schindler 2015, 279.

176. Rauchensteiner 2014, 240.

desertion rates depending on the ethnic composition of a given unit.[177] Soldiers, of course, desert for many reasons, and desertion itself is a complicated process. Yet many of the behaviors observed among Slavic units, but not within core-staffed units, are consistent with the military inequality argument. These soldiers complained vocally about their officers, especially war officers, who they believed cared little for their safety because they were not coethnics. Mistrust and miscommunication found fertile soil in units where officers did not speak the regimental language(s). The use of ethnic slurs, or even slights such as an officer mispronouncing a soldier's name, were enough to generate grievances. Most importantly, these soldiers believed they were second-class citizens with the army and broader political community. A Czech soldier, Frank Prošek, neatly encapsulated this sentiment when he was apprehended leaving his unit:

> I'm an enthusiastic soldier ... but I am forced to labor under a serious and unjust disadvantage. As a Czech, I am subject to discrimination and ill treatment. Promotions only go to Austrians. What chance did I have in this army; my race damns me in the eyes of my superiors.[178]

Mass desertion might have been manageable had it been confined to a small portion of the k.u.k. Army. By 1915, however, Germans and Magyars made up less than half (49.1 percent) of the army's rank and file. As a result, commanders grew worried that non-core soldiers could be catalysts for a contagion of disloyalty that might sweep through reliable units. Brigadier General Artur von Mecenseffy, commander of the 10th Infantry Division, echoed this fear in April 1915:

> As well as the requisite level of training, the [non-core] troops lack ... the necessary discipline and inner moral stability; this applies in particular to troops of Czech nationality, who—as I have already reported—in

177. Several scholars have dismissed claims that non-core soldiers were especially prone to desertion (Rachamimov 2002, 43–45; McNamara 2016, 53). They cite Russian POW records that, while incomplete, indicate that Czechs, Ruthenians, Poles, and other non-core communities were only slightly overrepresented within the prison population, and thus were no more likely to break than Germans or Magyars. Setting aside the unhelpful conflation of desertion and surrender, these arguments overlook selection bias in the data, which arises from two sources: (1) desertion to the rear reduced the opportunities and numbers of non-core soldiers "eligible" to surrender; and (2) commanders shifted "minority-majority" units away from key sectors, and sometimes the front lines themselves, to reduce surrender opportunities. Given these biases, it is remarkable that non-core soldiers were still present in proportionate numbers within Russian camps.

178. Quoted in McNamara 2016, 52.

many cases [are] politically contaminated [and] only unwillingly follow the call into the field.[179]

AOK commanders were right to worry that the plague of desertion might jump the firebreaks they had built to safeguard still-reliable units. The costs and trade-offs imposed by the demands of continually patching the now-threadbare quilt of the Common Army eventually undermined Hungarian Honvéd units as well. Because of their presumed loyalty, they were continually used to backstop, or replace entirely, unreliable units in the most dangerous sectors.[180] Unsurprisingly, Hungarian soldiers bore a disproportionate share of casualties relative to their share of mobilized soldiers, souring morale while providing grist for nationalists now calling for outright independence. Hungarian soldiers also came to resent the (German) commanders imposed by the German Army. By summer 1918, at least 200,000 deserters from the Hungarian-dominated Honvéd roamed Galicia alone. AOK hopes that ethnic intermixing would tamp down desertion were also dashed. By 1918, first Hungarian and then finally German soldiers engaged in, rather than suppressed, collective indiscipline, emulating their non-core counterparts. Take, for example, the case of the 111th Infantry Regiment, on its way to the front in the war's final days:

> The 111th Infantry Regiment (Czechs, Germans) arrived at the Graz camp yesterday with a strength of three battalions and was supposed to continue to Larici later in the day. When the regiment was about to depart, the second battalion refused to follow orders.... The unit consists of 80% Czechs and 20% Austrian Germans. The latter have declared their solidarity with the former.[181]

The problem of defectors (*Überläufers*) also bedeviled Habsburg commanders. Nearly 125,000 soldiers, mostly Czechs and Poles but also including Serbs, Romanians, and Ruthenians, took up arms against former Habsburg comrades during the war. Defection undercut Habsburg battlefield performance in several ways. Defectors provided Russians with information and early warning about Austro-Hungarian movements, troop strength, and plans, including about the Gorlice-Tarnów offensive, for example.[182] Even the threat of defection was enough to induce complications into troop deployments and rotations; neither officers nor units could be swapped interchangeably given the prospect that a particular unit might switch sides in

---

179. Quoted in Rauchensteiner 2014, 349.
180. Rauchensteiner 2014, 954.
181. AOK Memorandum, quoted in Kerchnawe 1921, 105.
182. Afflerbach 2014, 252.

mid-battle. Managing this threat meant diverting badly needed manpower from direct combat to monitoring roles at a time when the Common Army was outnumbered in nearly every battle.

Defection occurred via two pathways. In some cases, large groups of men, and on occasion entire units, switched sides during combat. Two battalions of the Czech-dominated 15th Infantry Regiment crossed Russian lines in November 1914, for example. Martial law was imposed on the remainder of the regiment; it was subsequently withdrawn from battle. In another well-known, if still contested, incident, the 28th Infantry Regiment (95 percent Czech) defected in April 1915 during a Russian offensive. Soldiers apparently sang the well-known song "Hey, Slavs!" to avoid being shot by Russian sentries. AOK action was swift; the 28th was officially disbanded, though the decision was later overturned on account that it might generate additional grievances among Czech soldiers. The subsequent parliamentary inquiry lay the blame for the unit's conduct squarely on its ethnic composition.[183]

In addition, up to one hundred thousand POWs were organized by Russia, in contravention of existing international law, into a Czech Legion fighting for an independent Czechoslovakia.[184] The Legion was deployed during the 1917 Kerensky Offensive and was responsible for sparking additional defections from Czech-staffed units when they met on the battlefield at Zborov. Similarly, the AOK's decision to create a Polish Auxiliary Corps in September 1916 from volunteers backfired when it, too, defected. Its leader, Josef Pilsudski, had managed to extract a promise from the Central Powers that Poles would be granted an independent postwar state. The Central Powers, however, reneged on this concession at the Treaty of Brest-Litovsk. In response, the Auxiliary Corps crossed Russian lines and linked up with the Russian-created First Army Corps. This joint formation, about 8,000-strong, fought against the Common Army at the Battle of Rarańcza (15–16 Feburary 1918) in Bukovina. They also clashed with German forces at the Battle of Kaniów (10–11 May), where they were defeated in detail and subsequently disbanded.[185]

Austro-Hungarian commanders and, later on, their German minders, moved swiftly to manage the negative consequences arising from the wavering loyalty of various non-German groups. "Unfortunately," Emperor Joseph I lamented in August 1914, "our armed forces are not all stamped from the

---

183. Revisionist historians have recently argued that side-switching by the 28th IR was due more to poor officers, who first panicked and then surrendered when surprised by a Russian offensive, than to soldier ethnicity. See Lein 2014*b*, *a*.

184. Smith 2014, 205.

185. Herwig 2014, 358.

same press."[186] Steps would need to be taken to anticipate, deter, and, if necessary, punish mass indiscipline to ensure that the AOK continued to field organized armies. Next to the Soviet Union (see chapter 8), Austria-Hungary constructed the most elaborate system of monitoring and control of all the belligerents examined in this book's qualitative cases. These multi-pronged efforts were guided by, and reinforced, ethnic stereotypes; in many ways, this ham-fisted campaign opened a second front against its own soldiers that precipitated the collective action it was meant to suppress.

By early 1915, for example, the AOK had erected a far-reaching surveillance apparatus to assess soldier morale and determine which units were most likely to crumble in battle. Standardized questionnaires were sent to senior officers asking whether "national-chauvinistic or other destructive tendencies [were] apparent in our officers" and whether "the seeds of ethnic and antimilitary agitation"[187] had been planted before the war. Monthly reports on the morale and physical status of soldiers were compiled to anticipate which units would prove unreliable. As part of this predictive exercise, an extensive surveillance and censorship apparatus was built to monitor the enormous POW population in Russian camps. At its height, the system employed over one thousand censors and read millions of letters from captive soldiers to their families and loved ones back in Austria-Hungary; some 8,000 letters were handled in September 1914, growing to 455,000 by November 1916 in thirty-five different languages. Censors were given a strict methodology—calculate the number of prisoners captured without wounds, as identified by the soldiers' own letters—to use as evidence of the loyalty of different ethnic groups. Predictably, Czechs, Italians, Serbs, and Ruthenes were singled out as especially likely to have been captured without wounds.[188] These "insights" were fed back into campaign planning and used to guide decision-making about troop movements and emplacements.

The AOK also decreed that some, though not all, monoethnic units be disbanded and their non-core soldiers scattered among other, more reliable, units. The introduction of German Army officers to k.u.k. Army units, too, was rationalized as necessary for maintaining stricter control over problematic divisions and regiments. This latter measure proved wildly unpopular, however.[189] Even Conrad admitted "I cannot begin to tell you how disgusted I am with the infiltration of German troops, but the head must rule quietly over

186. Quoted in Wawro 2014, 163.
187. Wawro 2014, 368.
188. Rachamimov 2005, 158–67.
189. Watson 2014*b*, 507–9.

the heart."[190] These measures proved only partially successful in disrupting preexisting ethnic networks. Desertion attempts receded in 1916–17 among non-German and non-Magyar soldiers, though this time period also coincides with the "sitting" phase of the war that witnessed few Austro-Hungarian offenses. It is clear, though, that these practices led to increased antagonism between war officers and their soldiers, particularly if German officers were present. Nor did attempts to shatter ethnic bonds lead to the formation of new social networks or "band of brothers."[191] Instead, targeted ethnic minorities appear to have experienced greater harassment that worsened morale. The commander of the 93rd Infantry Division, Brigadier Adolf von Boog, suggested in a classified memorandum that distributing Czechs throughout his Hungarian-dominant Honvéd unit was counterproductive:

> No-one can doubt that the Czech [soldier] must hear some hurtful remarks. That fills one with bitterness. One can tell from the peoples' faces and must put oneself in their shoes: such a man has no-one he can talk to, he feels lonely, outcast, and the severity of war service must hit him doubly hard.[192]

Waging war as a "prison of peoples" meant that the AOK eventually turned to coercion and violence to manufacture cohesion. POW testimonies often allude to officers "driving the troops into battle with their pistols," as one captured Hungarian soldier complained. "They [the officers] spend their whole time menacing their own men."[193] Threats and punishments were not universally administrated; instead, they fell disproportionately on national minorities. "The Czech must, like, I believe, all Slav people, constantly feel the lash. He is either a domestique or an anarchist," concluded von Boog.[194] As early as the Galicia campaign, entire units were escorted to the front-lines by military police in white armbands to ensure that soldiers did not desert en route.[195] Though records remain incomplete, military courts sentenced soldiers to death to combat widespread shirking (*druckebergerei*) in the ranks.[196] In some cases, entire divisions were singled out for punishment;

190. Quoted in Tunstall 2010, 203.
191. Watson 2014a, 186.
192. Quoted in Rauchensteiner 2014, 946. Intriguingly, he proposed pooling his Czech soldiers into a Czech-only regiment to improve morale. He did, however, also counsel severe repression if the regiment showed any signs of indiscipline.
193. Wawro 2014, 149.
194. Quoted in Rauchensteiner 2014, 946.
195. Schindler 2015, 229.
196. Wawro 2014, 227.

the 27th and 28th Infantry Divisions were apparently decimated by their own blocking detachment due to poor battlefield performance.[197] In the late stages of the war, the AOK turned auxiliary militia loose on mutinying units, taking care to pit different ethnic groups against one another.[198]

Coercion might have forestalled some desertion and defection, at least on the margins. But the AOK itself recognized the declining effectiveness of such efforts over time. A January 1918 memorandum concluded that "it is not possible to scream and apply the revolver more than the AOK is already doing."[199] Violence also generated grievances among soldiers, motivating collective action. "We all had had enough of that suffering, hunger, berating, and hitting our commanders subjected us to, and a thought about an end to all of this torture was secretly growing inside us,"[200] said Czech soldier Josef Křepala, who surrendered to Russian forces. Maintaining a strict enforcement regime was also costly. Seven divisions were diverted from the front to internal security duties in a bid to hunt down and return the estimated 550,000–600,000 deserters in Galicia and Austria proper in early 1918.[201] The collective and indiscriminate nature of AOK-initiated violence against non-core soldiers created additional incentives to escape punishment by fleeing, even if these soldiers individually held pro-Habsburg sympathies. "The harshness of these countermeasures," Stone concluded, "did much to create the situation which they were trying to prevent."[202] In the end, Austro-Hungarian battlefield performance was undone by the combination of variable loyalty among non-core ethnic groups and the costs and inefficiencies of efforts to manage these divisions under the strain of modern war.

6.6. Case Study: War Case "R" and the Battle of Galicia, 23 August–11 September 1914

The Battle of Galicia, though often overlooked in traditional accounts that privilege the Western Front, was one of the most consequential clashes of World War I. Waged across the forests, hills, and swamps of contemporary Poland and Ukraine, the battle itself consisted of four interconnected encounters at Krásnik (23–25 August), Komarów (26 August–2 September), Gnila Lipa (29–30 August), and Rawa-Ruska (3–11 September). Austro-Hungarian

---

197. Wawro 2014, 354.
198. Rauchensteiner 2014, 892.
199. Quoted in Rauchensteiner 2014, 887.
200. Quoted in McNamara 2016, 53.
201. Watson 2014*b*, 538.
202. Stone 1966, 103.

forces scored modest successes in the first two engagements. The final two engagements, however, were disastrous, with Austria-Hungary losing control over Galicia's capital at Lemberg (Lviv) on 2 September before ceding nearly all of Galicia by mid-September. Aside from its historical significance, the battle offers a window into how prewar ethnic discrimination, coupled with wartime fears over the political reliability of targeted groups, undercut battlefield performance. Fear of national minorities led to simplified tactics that increased casualties, reinforcing non-core soldiers' desire to escape the battlefield, creating a demand for enhanced surveillance and sanctioning mechanisms. Each turn of the screw meant sacrificing additional combat power in a losing bid to manufacture enough cohesion to knock Russia from the war.

Following War Case "R," Conrad aimed to strike a decisive blow against gathering Russian forces before they had time to mobilize completely. This ambitious strategy was misguided in several respects, however. Conrad dithered in deploying his own forces, and had too few railway carriages, further slowing deployment. Worse, he ordered his forces to detrain far from the emerging front; in some cases, divisions were forced to march nearly 100 kilometers over three days simply to reach their staging points. Perhaps worst of all, he ordered the diversion of substantial forces to the ongoing Serbian campaign (War Case "S"), where Austro-Hungarian forces would suffer a humiliating defeat.[203] This decision left his forces at a sharp material disadvantage against much larger Russian forces. His erstwhile ally, Germany, declined to advance against Russia, content to hunker down in East Prussia while fighting on the Western Front. Conrad was thus left without the expected German northern offensive that was designed to split Russian forces. Instead, the k.u.k Army faced the full brunt of a rapidly mobilizing and numerically superior Tsarist Army.

By mid-August, Conrad had assembled the 1st, 3rd, and 4th Armies, nearly 950,000 soldiers and 2,000 guns in total, along a 280-kilometer front to the north and east of Lemberg.[204] They were met by Russia's 3rd, 4th, 5th, and 8th Armies, some 1.2 million soldiers and at least 3,000 guns, under the command of General Nicolai Ivanov. Enacting Plan 19-A, Ivanov arrayed his forces in a vast semicircle arcing nearly 800 kilometers, with a northern concentration

203. Gumz 2009.

204. These Armies were joined on the battle's eve by two additional formations, the 2nd Army and Army Group Kövess, each understrength from heavy action in Serbia. This order of battle is drawn from "Gliederung der für den nördlichen Kriegsschauplatz bestimmten Streitkräfte," in Österreichischen Bundesministerium für Heereswesen und Kriegsarchiv 1930, 69-80.

(the 4th and 5th Armies) and an eastern one (3rd and 8th Armies). At the opening collision on 23 August, the k.u.k. Army could draw on 37 infantry divisions and 10 cavalry divisions; the Tsarist Army, a pool of 53.5 infantry and 18 cavalry divisions.

Looming over the entire Galician campaign was a fundamental tension: Conrad was concerned about the political reliability of large portions of his army, yet fervently believed that Russian preponderance in men and machines could be offset by his soldiers' "high morale." He was right to be worried. Conrad had already received reports of nationalist grumbling during mobilization and the march to the front lines. Alarmingly, on 17 August, the 5th Honvéd Cavalry Division panicked during an aborted skirmish with Russian forces and unraveled completely. After multiple fitful skirmishes with Russian cavalry screens, the Austro-Hungarian 1st Army met the Russian 4th Army at Krásnik on 23 August. The brief three-day battle, in which Austro-Hungarian forces enjoyed local numerical superiority, was a fluid affair, with neither side left with time to dig extensive trenchworks. Conrad launched a second offensive on 26 August at Komarów, hoping to destroy the Russian 5th Army with his slightly larger 4th Army. In each case, the Common Army managed to inflict somewhat greater casualties on Russian forces, though it was now seriously overstretched and forced to strip soldiers from Lemberg's defenses to replace casualties.

These modest gains masked a deeper problem with Habsburg force employment. As noted above, the fear of ethnic disloyalty led AOK commanders, including Conrad himself, to embrace massed frontal assaults with little or no prior coordination with artillery units. Russian defenses at Krásnik and Komarów often consisted only of a main trench and perhaps a secondary line, with artillery batteries in support. They nonetheless made extensive use of terrain features to minimize their exposure to Habsburg fire and to maximize their chances of enfilading approaching Austro-Hungarian units. For their part, Common Army units advanced to *Stumdistanz* in battalion columns— deemed easier for officers to control and monitor—and then fixed bayonets, charging the remaining distance. Some units lost nearly half their strength in these advances. Little wonder, then, that German military observers derived such "ruinous tactics" that treated soldiers as "cannon fodder."[205] A Russian colonel captured at Komarów echoed this sentiment, claiming that his soldiers "would never attack like *that*."[206]

Devoted believers in the cult of the offensive, Habsburg officers initially chose to lead their assaults, hoping to serve as examples to less-committed

205. Quoted in Wawro 2014, 192.
206. Quoted in Wawro 2014, 199.

non-core soldiers. Predictably enough, these officers were killed at a murderous rate. These casualties created their own second-order effects. Replacement war officers that began reaching frontline units after these initial two battles often lacked the skills to lead, or understand, their men. The 37th Honvéd, for example, reported severe communication issues among war officers and rank and file.[207] Soldiers accused these officers of having a cavalier "Heute rot, Morgen tot" ("here today, gone tomorrow") attitude toward casualties.[208] Discipline problems, particularly in units with high concentrations of Czech, Ruthenian, and Romanian soldiers, now began to appear despite battlefield success. The 13th Landwehr, staffed by Czech and Ruthenian soldiers but commanded by ethnic Germans, disintegrated at Komarów, its soldiers seeking escape through desertion. The AOK ordered their war officers to "reinforce discipline before it's too late," going so far as to impose the death penalty for even acknowledging Russia's numerical edge in soldiers.[209] Internal AOK estimates suggest that the Common Army lost 10 percent of its strength each day at Komarów to "straggling" soldiers fed up with nonsensical orders and forced marches and who harbored subversive doubts about the war's purpose.[210]

Despite these initial victories on the northern salient, the Common Army had too few divisions to cover the expanding front. Habsburg armies now began to separate, becoming lost in space as a gap opened between the northern thrust and the secondary concentration around Lemberg. Russian forces were now sliding around the weakened Habsburg right flank at Lemberg, seeking to turn the corner and emerge behind the armies on the northern front. Saddled with poor reconnaissance, Conrad was largely unaware of the true strength of the opposing Tsarist armies—"we'd walk right into Russian positions that we hadn't even seen"[211]—but, true to form, launched another offensive. His overmatched forces struck Russian lines at Gnila Lapa (the First Battle of Lemberg), about 40 kilometers from Lemberg. His fifteen weak divisions, about 145,000 men with 828 artillery pieces, now had to grapple with sixteen strong Russian divisions, about 300,000 soldiers with 1,304 artillery pieces.

Strategic miscalculations and identity-induced tactical compromises might be shrugged off as nuisances, if costly, when Habsburg forces held the numerical advantage. Now, however, they were tangling with much larger

207. Wawro 2014, 190.
208. Wawro 2014, 197.
209. Wawro 2014, 212.
210. Internal AOK Memorandum in Wawro 2014, 207.
211. Quoted in Wawro 2014, 221.

Russian armies. And they were doing so with massed formations seeking breakthrough using direct frontal assaults, tactics the soldiers derided as "straight up the gut"[212] (*gradaus*). Local offensives repeatedly ground to a halt under withering Russian artillery and machine gun fire. The new war officers may have lacked experience, but even they knew that their units could no longer advance; indeed, they were in danger of breaking. Soldiers had "now recognized the stupidity of their commanders,"[213] and open dissent soon followed. In reply, officers were instructed to tighten discipline. Abandoning their frontline role, war officers shifted to the rear of their formations, where they "spade and rifle in hand, employ[ed] lethal force against any of the men who hung back and refused to attack."[214] Entire units, typically those with high concentrations of Czechs, Ruthenians, and Romanians, were escorted to the front by armed military police.[215] Yet by 30 August the 3rd Army was on the verge of collapse; the 2nd Army soon followed. Mere rumors of advancing Russian Cossacks were enough to set whole battalions to flight.[216] Some cavalry even turned their weapons against their own Czech- and Romanian-staffed baggage trains to stop their panicked retreats.

His armies exhausted, his logistics train horribly snarled, and with only fragmentary evidence on his own troop locations, Conrad did what came naturally: he ordered another offensive. Austro-Hungarian forces struck at Rawa-Ruska (the Second Battle of Lemberg) on 3 September, only to be defeated in detail by Russian counterattacks. The seams in his forces were now exposed. War officers struggled to retain control over their formations. A scattershot system of replacing soldiers and units in the front lines had jumbled together soldiers of different nationalities, creating "bad feelings"[217] and miscommunication that slowed reaction times while contributing to tactical rigidity.[218] Preemptive surrender now entered the toolkit of non-core soldier resistance to military authorities. Two Czech battalions of the retreating 3rd Army—some 2,000 men in total—surrendered to a Russian patrol of just six men.[219] A special force of 1,600 military policemen was created to sweep up 3rd Army soldiers making use of the battlefield confusion to desert.[220] Shirking, too, became endemic. "Why is it that after every clash with

---

212. Wawro 2014, 227.
213. Ibid.
214. Ibid.
215. Schindler 2015, 229.
216. Wawro 2014, 218.
217. Schindler 2015, 257.
218. Buttar 2014, 255–61.
219. Wawro 2014, 242.
220. Schindler 2015, 226.

the enemy," the AOK heatedly asked, "*thousands* of stragglers circulate in the rear of our army, far from the fighting? You must discover the cause of this phenomenon and correct it."[221] Officers were again reminded of their duty to shoot malingering or deserting soldiers.[222] Rearguard actions against pursuing Russian forces were scrapped in favor of ordering soldiers to comb the ground for rifles tossed away by preceding Austro-Hungarian soldiers during the retreat from Rawa-Ruska.[223]

By 11 September, it was clear even to Conrad that the Common Army could no longer hold Galicia. Ordering a general retreat behind the San River, however, only accelerated the forces of disintegration. Many units with high concentrations of non-core soldiers, including the 23rd Honvéd Division, the 3rd, 8th, and 30th Infantry Divisions, and the 97th Trieste Division, abandoned the fight.[224] Czech-dominated units were especially singled out in the official war history as prone to disloyalty. Conrad himself maintained that these units' propensity to engage in "spontaneous retreats"[225] undercut the Habsburg offensive. For its part, the official AOK account chronicles numerous examples of minority-dominated units that simply refused orders to advance or that collapsed outright. "A remarkable number simply fled,"[226] it concluded. Ruthenian soldiers, too, were labeled as Russophile by their German officers; portions of the 11th Infantry Division, with a large allotment of Ruthenians, just melted away or surrendered after only brief exposure to Russian shelling.[227] Wartime violence hardened other ethnic stereotypes as well. Romanian soldiers, long suspected of disloyalty, came to be identified with self-mutilation as a means of escaping the front.

When order was restored, Austro-Hungarian front lines had been driven back nearly 160 kilometers into the Carpathian Mountains. Russian forces now set about besieging the strategic fortress at Przemysl. Galicia itself had been lost. Germany, now concerned that the k.u.k. Army could not withstand another blow, shifted the center of gravity of its war effort from the Western Front to save Austria-Hungary. Petrograd, too, believed that the war would be over by Christmas.[228]

Habsburg losses were grievous: an estimated 320,000–340,000 soldiers had been killed or wounded, while another 100,000–130,000 found themselves

221. Internal AOK Memorandum in Wawro 2014, 248.

222. Watson 2014*b*, 157.

223. Wawro 2014, 236, 249.

224. Rauchensteiner 2014, 219, 337.

225. Internal AOK Memorandum in Wawro 2014, 244.

226. Bundesministerium für Heereswesen und Kriegsarchiv 1930, 337–38.

227. Bundesministerium für Heereswesen und Kriegsarchiv 1930, 326.

228. McMeekin 2013, 85.

in Russian prison camps. Together, these losses amounted to one-third of Austria-Hungary's prewar standing army.[229] The small prewar officer corps was especially hard-hit. The result would be increased interethnic miscommunication and antagonism, diminished control, and worsening battlefield performance. As one surviving officer lamented: "Our normal tactical units have been so ripped apart in the fighting thus far that command is extremely difficult. I have far more strangers under my command than familiar old comrades."[230] Prewar Russian campaign planners had recognized the vulnerability created by the need for a multilingual officer corps and set about targeting it. "From the opening of the campaign, the Common Army will [need] to work on its mechanical cohesion," the General Staff concluded, "but how this will be produced in case of failure is difficult to foresee."[231] To help destroy this mechanical cohesion, Russian soldiers were ordered to target Habsburg officers. "Take off those yellow officer leggings you wear," a captured Russian colonel advised his Habsburg counterpart, because "we see them from far away and we fire at them."[232]

The consequences of defeat in Galicia did not stay confined to the battlefield, however. Combat had breathed new life into prewar ethnic stereotypes, and now military commanders opened a second front against suspect civilian populations behind the front lines. The Ruthenian population in Galicia, long accused of being Russophile, now made a convenient scapegoat for the battle's disastrous outcome. Retreating soldiers, especially from Hungarian Honvéd Divisions, cut a swathe through Galicia, conducting savage reprisals against whole villages suspected of harboring spies or merely pro-Russian sympathies. Hostages were taken to ensure good behavior; priests and peasants alike were hanged along roadsides, grisly signposts marking the Common Army's retreat.[233] Some thirty thousand citizens were killed by their own army in Galicia in the days after Conrad's September order to withdraw. Even the AOK was shocked at the brutality of this "double war." Conrad himself ruefully acknowledged, but did little to stop, the carnage: "We fight on our own territory as in hostile land," he wrote. "Everywhere Ruthenes are being executed under martial law."[234]

---

229. Russian casualties were estimated at 225,000–250,000 killed and wounded; another 40,000 soldiers were captured as POWs. Drawing on the mean of casualty estimates, the Common Army had an unfavorable 0.72 loss-exchange ratio at the Battle of Galicia.

230. Quoted in Wawro 2014, 251.

231. Glavnoe upravlenie General'nogo shtaba 1912, 126.

232. Quoted in Wawro 2014, 199.

233. Watson 2014*b*, 150, 152.

234. Quoted in Watson 2014*b*, 154.

Fusing the homeland to the front lines, the defeat in Galicia laid bare the second-class status of national minorities within the broader Austro-Hungarian *Staatsidee*. Defeat unleashed a wave of refugees, partly manufactured by Russian design, that further destabilized the Dual Monarchy. Drawing on prewar ethnographic surveys linking ethnicity to loyalty,[235] Habsburg authorities began systematically housing and rationing food to refugees according to their presumed political loyalty. Nearly a million refugees—"unwelcome co-eaters"[236]—fled Galicia, only to be quarantined in camps along national lines. Food and reintegration back into the homeland was stratified along ethnic and national lines; Ruthenians, Jews, and Czechs were especially singled out for poor treatment. Rations and payments to a soldier's family were stopped if he was suspected of desertion or premature surrender, a burden that fell most heavily on national minorities.[237] Galicia, then, was a watershed moment, rendering apart the vision that held Austria-Hungary together and precipitating a slide into a more exclusionary communal vision. Future battles would be fought amid a rising tide of non-core soldiers' grievances, now fueled by poor treatment of their coethnics on the home front, and increased violence by war officers desperate to hold the line against mass indiscipline.

6.7.   Discussion

"The most dangerous moment for a bad government," de Tocqueville once wrote, "is when it begins to reform."[238] Austria-Hungary offers a case in point: imperial authorities recognized that reforms were necessary to bolster the flagging allegiance of non-core groups but faced a severe credible commitment problem. Having swiftly overturned the hard-won gains and rights of national minorities in the war's first months, imperial authorities, most notably in the Austrian half of the state, were compelled by wartime setbacks to offer at least piecemeal concessions to emerging Serbian, Croat, Ruthene, Polish, and Czech nationalist movements. Such efforts were hamstrung, however, by the entirely understandable belief among nationalist leaders that imperial authorities might simply claw back any wartime concessions once danger had passed.[239] Repression in Serbia and Galicia in 1914, along with persistent inequalities in food distribution among a population now slowly

---

235. Watson 2014*b*, 171.
236. Quoted in Watson 2014*b*, 198.
237. Rachamimov 2005.
238. Tocqueville 1856, 214.
239. Cole 2014, 318.

starving under Allied blockade, made nationalist leaders wary of any deals. Anton Korošec, a Slovene and president of the Yugoslav Club in the Austrian parliament, put it succinctly: "What has happened already is enough to make us distrust you."[240] Instead, nationalist leaders sought to exploit this possibly fleeting moment of regime vulnerability to drive home their own, increasingly ambitious, plans for autonomy, if not independence.

Bargaining began in earnest after the death of Emperor Francis Joseph on 21 November 1916. His successor, Charles I, was bent on modernization that allowed for some nationalist gains but that preserved the overarching Habsburg imperial framework. He broached the idea of Trialism (a tripartite Austria-Hungary-Poland) at his first cabinet meeting (12 January 1917), reopened the shuttered Austrian Reichsrat (Imperial Assembly), and forced the resignation of Hungary's Prime Minister István Tisza, a key obstacle to reform. But nationalist leaders only increased their demands. A public "May Declaration" calling for unification of all South Slavs in an independent Yugoslavia was followed quickly by appeals for an independent Czechoslovakia. Polish demands for territorial reorganization, at Ruthenian expense, were met by dueling Ruthenian calls for Polish territory. Imperial authorities sank deeper into a morass of competing, often zero-sum, territorial demands that threatened to swamp their more modest reform efforts. Indecision grew; Charles and his advisors were aware of the dangers now gathering but were chained to the existing Habsburg imperial vision. Tisza, for example, resembled a man "who suddenly notices an abyss at his feet, is caught by vertigo, but cannot make a step either forward or backward."[241]

Negotiations ground on fitfully against a backdrop of widespread starvation, rolling labor strikes, and continued battlefield setbacks. Yet the gap between imperial necessities and nationalist aspirations only grew wider. An April 1918 Congress for Suppressed Nationalities, held in Rome, proclaimed the right of Yugoslav, Romanian, Polish, and Czechoslovak communities to their own independent states at the war's conclusion. Their hopes were bolstered by British, French, and American statements during summer 1918 recognizing the inevitability of independent successor states Yugoslavia, Poland, and Czechoslovakia. Charles countered with a last-ditch proposal to federalize Austria on 2 October 1918 that was easily brushed aside by nationalist leaders. Its armies in tatters, and its ability to protect, let alone feed, its citizens, no longer assured, the imperial Habsburg vision had visibly and irrevocably failed to bind together its citizens. One by one, nationalist committees spent October 1918 scrambling to supplant imperial authorities and to secure the

240. Quoted in Haslinger 2014, 85.
241. Quoted in Galántai 1989, 310.

foundations for independence. By Armistice, the Imperial Army, and the state itself, had dissolved, with former Habsburg troops now pledging allegiance to the armies of their respective national homelands.[242]

These reform efforts also directly affected Habsburg battlefield performance. The willingness of non-core soldiers to sacrifice for the regime fell with each new concession extracted from Emperor Charles by nationalist leaders. Imperial authorities granted amnesty to political prisoners, including deserters, in July 1917, in the hopes that Czech, Ruthenian, and other populations would be assuaged by this political gesture. The amnesty was seen as a last-ditch effort to curb the interethnic tensions that were not only crippling the war effort but also threatening the stability of the empire itself. Foreign Minister Ottokar Czernin, himself an ardent critic of the amnesty, nonetheless recognized its necessity: "The Monarchy must be in order domestically before peace is made," he wrote, "otherwise the peace negotiations would also address our internal affairs and we would have a regulation [treaty] dictated to us."[243]

But the relaxation of penalties predictably caused desertion rates among national minorities to skyrocket; an 80 percent increase was reported in some regiments.[244] The AOK managed to reverse this policy in early 1918 while also introducing labor battalions as a further deterrent to desertion among the national minorities. Yet mutinies were now so widespread among some Slavic units that the AOK ordered these formations to be transported to the front in sealed railway cars.[245] In some cases, entire regiments of Slovene, Serb, Croat, Czech, and even Hungarian soldiers deserted en masse, creating a "deserter plague" that wrested large swathes of agriculturally rich lands in Galicia, Slavonia, and Croatia away from Vienna's control.[246] Prisoners of war, released under the terms of the Treaty of Brest-Litovsk that formally, if temporarily, concluded war on the Eastern Front, mutinied upon discovering that they were being sent to the Italian front.[247] As a reflection of these realities, the AOK created new P.U. ("Politically Unreliable") units that were confined to internal security tasks to prevent defection and desertion.[248] Lurching between concessions and coercion, the AOK lost control of its forces,

242. See Healy 2004; Cole 2014; Judson 2016; Deak 2014, 2015.

243. Quoted in Rauchensteiner 2014, 751.

244. Cornwall 2000, 33–34.

245. Deák 1990, 202. These mutinies were crushed using auxiliary forces staffed by non-coethnics, further enflaming interethnic tensions. An estimated 133,040 incidents of "withdrawal and non-compliance" were recorded in May 1918 alone. Rauchensteiner 2014, 892–93.

246. Lein 2014b; Watson 2014b, 505.

247. Rachamimov 2005, 172.

248. Rauchensteiner 2014, 948.

unable to beat back the tide of nationalism that was swamping the imperial project. When the November Armistice was signed, only one-sixth of the AOK's nominal strength was still engaged in combat; the rest of its forces had deserted, mutinied, or been assigned to internal duties to prevent further dissolution.[249]

6.8. Alternative Explanations

The chapter's matched pair design helps rule out many competing explanations for Ottoman and Habsburg battlefield performance. One remains, however. Perhaps these empires simply found themselves overmatched, both materially and technologically, by stronger adversaries. Ottoman and Habsburg forces did fight at a numerical disadvantage for most of their battles, for example. And Italy and Russia did field advanced weapons, especially artillery and aircraft, in greater numbers and sophistication than those found in Ottoman and Habsburg arsenals.

This view finds some support among both historians and contemporaries. "Simply put," one historian has argued, "the Austro-Hungarian army was blasted off the battlefield by Russian artillery."[250] More colorfully, G. F. Bennett, a correspondent covering the Italo-Turkish War, asked: "Are these bare-footed scalliwags able to oppose an army provided with the latest pattern of the magazine rifle, with artillery, with aeroplanes and everything necessary for war?"[251]

Though its simplicity is appealing, this material preponderance counterargument paints with too broad a brush. It stumbles, for example, when trying to explain why Austro-Hungarian and Ottoman loss-exchange ratios diverged so sharply, both from one another and in contrast to their foes. A narrow focus on relative troop strength or weapons quality also misses the ethnically concentrated nature of desertion and defection (and, in the Austro-Hungarian case, premature mass surrender). In this case, as with other chapters, crude measures of military power do not map cleanly onto battlefield outcomes in straightforward ways.

More broadly, the claim that Italy and Russia had technologically superior weapons is only partially true. That Russian and Italian forces fielded superior

---

249. Déak (1990, p. 202) estimates that only five hundred thousand of three million enlisted soldiers were still at the front lines in early November 1918.

250. Schindler 2015, 258.

251. Abbott 1912b, 258. Abbott actually concluded, yes, "these volunteers are more than a match for any number of disciplined, liberally fed, and scientifically trained conscripts that is likely to be brought against them."

artillery is unquestioned.[252] Aircraft, however, were marginal to battlefield fortunes in each war. Austro-Hungarian forces actually enjoyed better communications and signals intelligence than the Russian Army, especially early in the war. Standard-issue infantry rifles were comparable across belligerents. Ottoman infantry were equipped with the five-round Model 1893 German Mauser rifle that outranged and had greater stopping power than Italy's new six-round magazine rifle, the Modello 91. "The Modello," del Boca noted, "was not bad for the time but no better than [that] in use by the Turks."[253] Tribal levies were less well-equipped, often relying on the older British Martini-Henry, a single-shot breechloader, though many acquired Modello 91s ditched by fleeing Italian soldiers.[254] For their part, the Common Army relied on the Mannlicher M1895 bolt-action rifle that also had a higher rate of fire and effective range (600m to 500m) than the standard Mosin-Nagant M1891 rifle in use by most Russian infantry. Given these differences, it is difficult to assign material preponderance or military superiority arguments much more than a marginal role in explaining battlefield performance.

Prewar patterns of military inequality within these belligerent armies also help explain why these material imbalances existed in the first place. For example, internecine negotiations between German and Magyar politicians starved the Common Army of both men and material. Periodic reform efforts foundered in the "never-never world" of Habsburg politics, marked by "Hungarian obstruction, threats of abdication, followed more prosaically by juggling of half-percentages and promises of petty payments to nationalist blackmailers, until a few coppers rattled through the machine to reward the soldiers for trying."[255] The Common Army went to war with fewer infantry battalions than in 1866 despite a population increase of some twenty million;[256] tiny Serbia had more artillery pieces.[257] Indeed, Hungarian politicians continually sought to purchase artillery pieces for the Honvéd rather than the Common Army. Austrian politicians, fearing the creation of two separate armies, and reluctant to cede control over these weapons, continually resisted their acquisition. In return, Hungarian politicians blocked budgets and starved the Common Army. In the end, the k.u.k was hostage to the

252. Contemporaries did question, however, the usefulness of Italian artillery, arguing that Italian gunners were poorly trained and tended to waste shells at a fearsome rate (Wright 1913, 62).

253. del Bocca 1986, 102.

254. Tribal levies also purchased Italian weapons in markets near Italian positions (Bennett 1912, 163). See also Vandervort 2012, 59fn144.

255. Stone 1975, 71.

256. Stone 1975, 71.

257. Schindler 2015, 123.

divided nature of the imperial Habsburg project and the continued need to thread the needle between antagonistic ethnic groups more inclined to retreat into their respective communities than to make common cause.

6.9. Conclusion

This chapter has marshaled evidence to trace the causal pathway between prewar military inequality and battlefield performance in the fading light of the early modern era of conventional warfare. Prewar marginalization and, in the Ottoman Empire, violence, lowered combat motivation among targeted ethnic groups and contributed to their desire and means for escaping wartime service. Indiscipline, especially mass desertion, was typically concentrated in these groups, though it did not always remain confined to them. In the case of Austria-Hungary, a clear sequence of breakdown, beginning with non-core groups such as Czechs, Ruthenes, and Serbs and then shifting to Magyars and eventually Germans, can be observed. Uneven motivation and loyalty across these groups forced Turkish and Habsburg military commanders to make tactical concessions, sacrificing combat power for cohesion. Simplistic frontal assaults and rigid formations with scant regard for terrain were the hallmark of both Ottoman and Habsburg tactics and operations. Innovation on these fronts was stunted by the need to maintain cohesion at all costs. Each belligerent experimented with different strategies of management, seeking to vary the ethnic composition of units to ensure, or at least improve, their cohesion. That each belligerent also embraced coercion against its own soldiers indicates the limits of unit-level tinkering to fix structural problems. Manufacturing a credible coercive threat proved elusive, too. The imposition of mechanical cohesion through violence generated new grievances, particularly against officers, reinforced ethnic stereotypes about loyalty, and diverted resources from the battlefield itself.

These cases also provide evidence of the predicted attenuation of the effects of military inequality when shifting from medium to high military inequality. Neither belligerent was an exemplar of battlefield performance; far from it. But while Ottoman forces remained wedded to their rigid tactical principles, Austro-Hungarian forces did demonstrate some tactical innovation in 1916–17, albeit more haltingly than European counterparts and only at the behest of its German ally. The Common Army's loss-exchange ratio was also far more favorable than the Ottoman Army's, at least when taken as an aggregate measure. Extreme Ottoman losses were a reflection of the almost nonexistent prewar training that tribal levies were given; Austria-Hungary, for all its problems, at least provided some basic level of training to non-core populations. Still, these differences are less sharp than if the Ottoman Empire was judged against a comparable belligerent with low military inequality. As anticipated, Austro-Hungarian battlefield performance also degraded once political and military leaders authorized the collective punishment of national minorities. As the war unfolded, the AOK took the war to its own people, whether in Serbia, Galicia, or the home front itself, further poisoning the well of support among targeted nationalities. By the war's end, the increased military inequality in the Common Army yielded nearly identical results as the Ottoman Empire.

Though middling, the battlefield performance of these two belligerents might have been even worse. Terrain, the opponent's strategy, and other contextual factors imposed a floor on how badly they could perform, preventing their embedded pathologies from reaching full expression. Take the issue of defection. Italian forces chose to turn away potential side-switchers, removing mass defection from our scorecard of battlefield performance. Italian repression of the civilian population, as well as poor treatment of captured soldiers, cratered Arab and Berber willingness to desert or defect, easing Ottoman recruitment woes. Rather than sitting behind Tripoli's walls, Italian commanders might have adopted more aggressive operations, imposing greater casualties on Ottoman forces. Similarly, Austria-Hungary's performance was propped up by German tactical assistance, the infusion of German commanders into Habsburg units, and their joint operations, where their divisions fought alongside one another. The Tsarist Army, too, was saddled with a high level of military inequality, undercutting its performance. This floor effect jibes with the quantitative findings in chapter 4; few states score poorly on every measure of the BPI. Much has to go right (or wrong) for states to plumb the depths of battlefield performance as captured by our index.[258]

A final look at the wartime dynamics in these cases suggests extensions to the military inequality thesis. While the proposed argument anticipates vertical conflict between (core) officers and (non-core) soldiers along ethnic lines, horizontal conflict was also present across non-core groups as well. Tensions between Berbers and Arabs, for example, complicated Ottoman command and control, ruled out tactics and offensives requiring high degrees of coordination, and shifted regular Turkish infantry into policing roles behind these formations. Friction between different national minorities also increased problems of trust and cohesion within mixed Austro-Hungarian units. In some cases, such as Hungarian Honvéd units operating in Galicia,

---

258. This discussion suggests an implicit counterfactual: how much worse would Ottoman and Austro-Hungarian battlefield performance have been if opponent strategy, capabilities, and terrain permitted the full exploitation of their inherent vulnerabilities?

ethnic antagonism spilled over into open violence, fueling additional spirals of mistrust across groups while further complicating force employment and frontline replacement policies. In the late stages of the war, the AOK manipulated these tensions, hoping to ward off disintegration by pitting alienated groups against one another, though always at the expense of combat power. Mass indiscipline also jumped the fence in the Common Army, as war-weary Germans and Hungarians sought refuge in mass desertion. The fact that non-core soldiers represented a majority of Common Army soldiers, along with deliberate interethnic mixing by the AOK, spread the contagion of mass desertion. Nor could political leaders appease nationalist grievances; credible commitment issues loomed large as war fortunes faded and ethnic mistrust intensified. Finally, the Common Army's collapse at a relatively high level of military inequality (0.434) may demarcate the lower bound of a danger zone of disintegration for belligerent armies; the Mahdiya (0.67) and Kokand (0.70) fell apart at much higher levels.

7

African World Wars

ETHIOPIA AND THE DEMOCRATIC REPUBLIC
OF CONGO ON THE MODERN BATTLEFIELD

Group feeling produces the ability to defend oneself, to offer opposition, to
protect oneself, and to press one's claims. Whoever loses it is too weak to do
any of these things.

IBN KHALDUN, *THE MUQADDIMAH*, 1377

THE HISTORICAL EVIDENCE marshaled so far has been drawn exclusively
from the "early" (pre-1917) era of modern war. What remains to be demonstrated, however, is whether military inequality can help explain battlefield
performance in more contemporary wars. Equally shaped by advances in military technology and combined arms doctrine, the modern battlefield is far
more lethal than its pre-1917 forerunner. Armies and their soldiers must be
capable of independent maneuver while under fire; practice decentralized
decision-making among dispersed formations; combine and coordinate different weapons systems; and maximize their ability to exploit terrain advantages to stay alive long enough to destroy their enemies.[1] Given this hostile
environment, it is possible that ethnic prejudices and prior treatment by the
state may fall by the wayside, abandoned as peacetime luxuries that cannot
be afforded by favored nor second-class groups if they are to survive on modern battlefields. Alternatively, the penalties associated with clinging to prewar
patterns of discrimination or repression may be even higher now, as self-
inflicted coordination miscues and tactical constraints are ruthlessly exposed
by adversaries.

---

1. Smithers 1992; Addington 1994, 157–58; Bailey 1996, 140–46; Sheffield 2001, 108–50;
Strachan 1988, 223–306; McNeill 1982, 132–53; Biddle 2004, 28–51.

I therefore return to Project Mars and match two similar belligerents fighting wars in the post-1945 era: Ethiopia during the Ethiopia-Eritrea War (1998–2000) and the Democratic Republic of the Congo (DRC) during the Second Congo War (1998–2002). The Ethiopia-Eritrea War, which began as a minor skirmish over the dusty border town of Badme, quickly escalated into one of the deadliest wars of the twentieth century. Foreign observers watched with horror as the war's early battles descended into a First World War–style hellscape of massed frontal assaults against trenches, albeit fought now with modern tanks, artillery, and aircraft.[2] The Second Congo War, also known as Africa's First World War, began with a similarly minor confrontation at Goma. Within weeks, however, the war became a maelstrom that pulled in six neighboring states while birthing an estimated twenty militia and rebel organizations.[3] Though not obvious at first glance, these belligerents share similar traits. Both had recently exited from civil wars and had only begun the process of nation-building when they were sucked back into war. Both started their wars on the defensive, responding to armed incursions by neighboring states that they nonetheless dwarfed in terms of population and economic size. Both were rebuilding their armies on the eve of war, and relied on the same military equipment, including modern tanks and armored vehicles, from the same suppliers, especially Russia. Both wars are also unjustifiably neglected in the traditional canon in the study of military effectiveness. Yet the Ethiopia-Eritrea War witnessed the largest tank battles in Africa since the Second World War, while the Second Congo War earned the dubious distinction of the deadliest civil war of the post-1945 era.

Despite these similarities, Ethiopia and the DRC sharply diverged in their performance on the battlefield. Ethiopia not only managed to recover from the unexpected invasion but also steadily improved over time. By the war's third year, the Ethiopian Army successfully executed a multi-front combined arms operation that recorded some of the fastest advance rates for mechanized forces since 1917. Prewar discrimination against non-Tigrayan nationalities did increase casualties in early battles as officers proved willing to accept losses among these marginalized groups. But the army proved cohesive, with no

2. On the Ethiopia-Eritrea (or Badme) War, see Negash and Tronvoll 2000; Plaut and Silkes 1999; Lato 2003; Woldemariam 2015; Abebe 2014; Kissi 2006; Tareke 2009; Jacquin-Berdal and Plaut 2004; Fessehatzion 2003; Murphy, Kidane and Snider 2013; Tronvall 2009; Campbell 2014.

3. On the Second Congo War, (or "Africa's World War"), see Stearns, Verwijen and Baaz 2013; Roessler 2011; Reyntjens 2009; Cohen 2016; Autesserre 2010; Baaz and Stern 2008; Baaz and Verwijen 2013; Cooper 2013; Gordon 2015; Stearns 2011; Sanchez de la Sierra 2015; Roessler and Verhoeven 2016; United Nations 2010; Clark 2002; Prunier 2009.

mass desertion or defection. The same cannot be said for the DRC's army, the Forces Armées Congolaises (FAC), which turned in a disastrous performance comparable to that of Kokand or the Khalifa's Mahdiya. Plagued by rampant desertion and defection, and forced to resort to extrajudicial punishment to maintain discipline, the FAC relied heavily on external patrons like Zimbabwe and Angola just to field a coherent fighting force. The FAC also turned to various militia, notably the Army for the Liberation of Rwanda (ALiR), as both complements to and substitutes for its own ramshackle forces.

Their battlefield fates were decided by their levels of prewar military inequality. Ethiopia's military inequality coefficient (0.24) was at the lower end of the medium scale; the DRC, by contrast, was a high military inequality belligerent (at 0.54). This comparison allows us to assess the effects of a medium-sized shift in military inequality (0.31) on battlefield performance. For comparative purposes, this 0.31 difference is larger than that between Habsburg and Ottoman empires (chapter 6) but not so steep as that between Morocco and Kokand (chapter 5). The comparison also illuminates the difference between inequality constructed through prewar ethnic discrimination (Ethiopia) versus collective violence (DRC).

I stitch together narratives of each belligerent's battlefield performance from multiple sources, including journalists, human rights organizations, self-published memoirs (for Ethiopia), and arbitration claims by the fact-finding Eritrea-Ethiopia Claims Commission. Despite the importance of these wars, historiography surrounding their conduct is surprisingly thin. Even standard military histories ("tick-tocks") are scarce. Much of the existing work on the Ethiopia-Eritrean War focuses on its origins and centers around the assignment of blame for its initiation. The Second Congo War has attracted the attention of political scientists studying rebel organizations, but the FAC has been largely neglected, an understandable if regrettable gap given its near collapse. Archives for all belligerents involved remain sealed. As such, this chapter represents an initial foray, not a definitive assessment, of the role of inequality in shaping battlefield performance in these wars.

I open with a discussion of why we can treat Ethiopia and the DRC as comparable belligerents. I then provide a brief overview of each war as well as each belligerent's prewar notions of political community and citizenship norms. The bulk of the chapter is devoted to tracing inequality's effects on each belligerent's combat power and cohesion. Rather than exhaustive histories, I draw on different facets of each belligerent's wartime experience to highlight how inequality shaped battlefield conduct and possible trade-offs between combat power and cohesion. Each narrative also highlights a specific operation—Ethiopia's Operation Sunset (February–March 1999) and the

DRC's Third Offensive (October–December 2000)—to highlight inequality's distorting effects at close range. These operations permit a cross-case comparison at the operational level because they share similar properties. Both belligerents initiated the offensive; faced dug-in defenses, including trenches; utilized a combined arms approach, including fielding mechanized infantry; and possessed favorable force-to-force and force-to-space ratios at the point of attack. The chapter concludes with a discussion of new wrinkles that these cases add to the military inequality argument.

7.1.   The Ethiopia-Eritrea War of 1998–2000

The war began on 6 May 1998, when at least two brigades of Eritrean infantry, supported by tanks, armored personnel carriers, and helicopters, crossed the border and, after a brief firefight, seized Badme, a small town nestled near the contested border (see figure 7.1). The ensuing war unfolded across three fronts—Western, Central, and Eastern—and in three phases.[4] The first phase (May–June 1998) was marked by continued Eritrean advances, desperate attempts by the surprised and unprepared Ethiopian forces to stop their advances, and an increasingly bold series of airstrikes against each other's capitals and airports. A June 1998 cease-fire temporarily halted fighting. Rather than seek peace, however, the belligerents used this respite to dig in, creating extensive trenches and defensive positions along all three fronts that recalled the First World War's Western Front. Ethiopia also accelerated its mobilization, bringing nearly 300,000 men under arms. Each side signed extensive arms contracts with Russia to supply modern tanks, APCs, and aircraft, including top-tier MiG-29 (Eritrea) and Su-27 (Ethiopia) fighter-bombers. The war's second phase opened on 6 February 1999 and lasted until 19 June 1999, when another (again temporary) cease-fire took hold. This phase was marked by multifront Ethiopian offensives designed to dislodge Eritrean forces and regain lost territory, occasionally through costly frontal assaults against entrenched Eritrean defenders. Limited gains were made; the Western Front near Badme, for example, was pushed back nearly twenty kilometers after a successful Ethiopian drive. Eritrean counterattacks were largely driven back. This second phase concluded with Ethiopia back in control of most of

---

4. The Western Front encompassed southwestern Eritrea/northwestern Ethiopia along the Mereb and Setit rivers and covered the Gash Barka region of Eritrea and the Tigray Regional State of Ethiopia, including Badme. The Central Front (Alitiena-Mereb) covered parts of the Southern Region of Eritrea and northern parts of the Tigray Regional State on Ethiopia's side of the border. The Eastern (Burie/Assab) Front covered the Afar region of northeastern Ethiopia and southeastern Eritrea, including its Southern Red Sea Region.

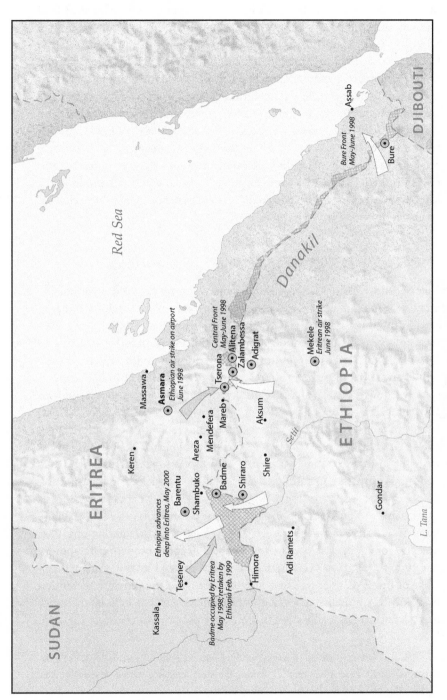

SUDAN

ERITREA

Kassala

Teseney

Keren

Areza

Shambuko

Barentu

*Ethiopia advances
deep into Eritrea, May 2000*

*Badme occupied by Eritrea
May 1998; retaken by
Ethiopia Feb. 1999*

Himora

Adi Ramets

Badme

Shiraro

Mendefera

Shire

Aksum

Gondar

L. Tana

Setit

Mareb

Tserona

Alitena

*Central Front
May–June 1998*

Zalambessa

Adigrat

Massawa

Asmara

*Ethiopian air strike on airport
June 1998*

ETHIOPIA

Mekele

*Eritrean air strike
June 1998*

Red Sea

Danakil

*Bure Front
May–June 1998*

Assab

Bure

DJIBOUTI

FIGURE 7.1. The Ethiopia-Eritrea War, 1998–2000

the territory it lost in 1998, especially on the Western Front. The war's final phase occurred between 12 May and 18 June 2000. A multifront Ethiopian offensive smashed through Eritrean defenses, forcing them to retreat in the face of a combined arms assault that included pincer attacks with mechanized forces. Ethiopian operations stretched up to 50–60 kilometers on each front and relied on heavy artillery bombardments to support massed infantry and tank operations. By 18 June, Ethiopia had conquered one-quarter of Eritrea, displacing nearly 650,000 refugees, and had shattered much of Eritrea's infrastructure. The war was concluded by the Algiers Agreement, which largely returned the belligerents to the prewar status quo, with only minor territorial adjustments. Casualties were staggering for such minimal gains: Ethiopia lost between 34,000 and 70,000 soldiers killed in action, while Eritrea lost an estimated 19,000 to 51,500 soldiers.[5]

7.2.   The Second Congo War, 1998–2002

The Second Congo War was extraordinarily complex, with a formidable array of states pitted against each other in two main coalitions centered around the warring DRC and Rwanda (see figure 7.2). Complicating matters, however, was the creation of militia and proxy forces by each side to fight alongside, and as substitutes for, conventional armies. At least twenty militia and rebel organizations arose during the conflict, turning an interstate war fought inside the DRC into a civil war in which local dynamics and complex informal alliances often drove patterns of violence.[6] Fighting itself took several forms; conventional combined arms operations often coexisted with guerrilla attacks and one-sided violence against civilians as weapons in each coalition's arsenal. The war was fought across the DRC's enormous expanse, frustrating a clean narrative, especially as militia and soldiers swapped sides, creating a "war within the war" dynamic. Here I focus specifically on the FAC's actions and impose a three-phase structure on the war's evolution. The war began in August 1998 with the mutiny of a FAC unit in Goma and lasted until the Luanda Accords brought a temporary cease-fire in July 1999. This initial phase was marked by the near total collapse of the FAC as a coherent fighting force and the timely intervention by the DRC's principal allies, Zimbabwe and Angola, to help blunt Rwandan advances. These allies began a training program to resurrect the FAC

---

5. Casualty estimates remain highly politically charged for both belligerents. UCDP's Battle-Related Deaths Dataset (Version 18.1), among the most reputable sources of casualty data, suggests that 97,410 soldiers were killed during the war.

6. König et al. 2007.

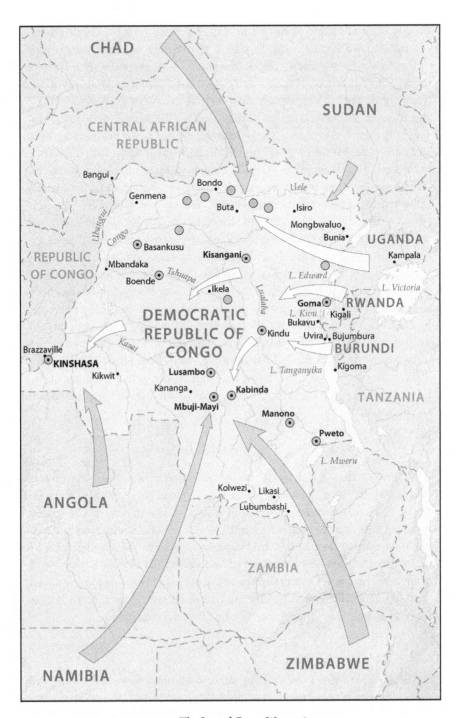

FIGURE 7.2. The Second Congo War, 1998–2002

even as their small forces fought rearguard actions across multiple fronts, seeking to hold Rwanda and its militia at bay long enough to train new cadres. With the breakdown of the Luanda Accords, the war's second phase began, with fighting once again occurring across multiple, now mostly static, fronts. Little territory changed hands; instead, proxy battles between DRC- and Rwanda-aligned militia now intensified, with civilians increasingly targeted for their perceived political allegiance as well as for battlefield pillage and rape. The war's final phase opened in September 2000 with a series of DRC offensives designed to showcase its new military might and to reclaim lost territories from an increasingly disenchanted Rwanda and its quarrelsome militia. These efforts were largely failures, however. The FAC collapsed repeatedly on the battlefield. Desertion and defection remained rife, and the FAC struggled to mount coherent offensive operations. The disastrous outcome of its Katanga Offensive nearly led to the loss of the DRC's second-largest city and contributed directly to the assassination of President Laurent-Désiré Kabila on 16 January 2001. The war dragged on in desultory fashion until several peace agreements removed neighboring belligerents one by one from the country. Total losses were staggering, whether measured by lives lost or infrastructure destroyed. The war's effects continue to echo today; the central government remains weak, while large portions of the population are still preyed upon by various militia, the ghostly vestiges of the FAC's war-fighting strategy. Little was accomplished by the war, but much was destroyed.[7]

7.3. Empirical Strategy

As with other chapters. these two belligerents, drawn from the wider Project Mars universe, were randomly paired using a dedicated matching software program. The paired comparison itself is summarized in table 7.1. I begin by outlining the nature of each belligerent's prewar political community and military inequality. I then justify the comparison between these belligerents by examining the framework of matched and contextual covariates devised in chapter 3. This paired comparison is both a means of isolating the presumed causal pathway between inequality and battlefield performance and a vehicle for testing, and eliminating, possible alternative explanations.

---

7. Drawing on multiple sources, I estimate about 16,550 battlefield casualties were inflicted during the war on all sides. This is close to the UCDP's Battle-Related Datasets (Version 18.1) own estimate (12,452). An estimated 350,000 civilians were also killed between 1998 and 2001 (Roberts 2001).

TABLE 7.1. Matched Pair: Ethiopia and the DRC Compared

Covariates	Ethiopia *Ethiopia-Eritrea War,* *1998–2000*	DRC *Second Congo War,* *1998–2000*
Military Inequality (Coefficient)	Medium (0.24)	High (0.55)
From Matching		
Initial relative power	49.9%	64.9%
Total fielded force	310,000	55,000
Regime type	Anocracy (1)	Anocracy (0)
Distance from capital	639 km	1,572 km
Standing military	Yes	Yes
Composite military	Yes	Yes
Initiator	No	No
Joiner	No	No
Democratic opponent	No	No
Great Power	No	No
Civil war	No	Yes
Modern	Yes	Yes
Contextual Covariates		
Combined arms	Yes	Yes
Doctrine	Offensive	Offensive
Superior weapons	No	No
Fortifications	No	No
Foreign advisors	Yes	Yes
Terrain	Rugged/arid/desert	Mixed plateau/highland/ rugged/jungle
War duration	751 days	1,599
War birth	No	No
Non-COW	No	No
Prior war history w/opponent	Yes	Yes
Facing colonizer	No	No
Identity dimension	Christian/Christian	Christian-Muslim/ Christian-Muslim
New leader	Yes	Yes
Population	60 million	48 million
Ethnolinguistic fractionalization (ELF)	Moderate	High
Civ-mil relations	Praetorian	Praetorian
Battlefield Performance		
Tac-op sophistication	Moderate	Low
Loss-exchange ratio	0.65	0.46
Mass desertion	No	Yes
Mass defection	No	Yes
Fratricidal violence	No	No

Note: Estimates for the DRC's total fielded force exclude militia, foreign armies, and mercenaries. DRC scores a "low" on its reliance on coercion measure because it never fielded formal blocking detachments. It did, however, forcibly recruit children into its regular forces and affiliated militia.

7.3.1. *Political Community and Military Inequality*

In June 1991, the combined forces of two rebel coalitions, the Tigray People's Liberation Front (TPLF) and Eritrean People's Liberation Front (EPLF), finally overthrew Ethiopia's socialist-military dictatorship, ending a brutal sixteen-year civil war.[8] The TPLF moved quickly to form a coalition with other Ethiopian movements, creating the Ethiopian People's Revolutionary Democratic Front (EPRDF). The EPLF, for its part, assumed power of a newly independent Eritrea. Nation-building began in earnest in both countries. The EPRDF, nominally a multiethnic coalition spanning all of Ethiopia's nationalities, was in practice still dominated by TPLF leaders. As such, they set about constructing a political community of unusual hues, dabbling in nationalist appeals to shared "Ethiopianness" and Marxist-Leninist commitments to social leveling while also enshrining a formal commitment to ethnic federalism in the new constitution.[9] All self-defined ethnic groups were granted the right to secede from the ethnofederal state.[10] Yet the political system, and especially executive power, remained firmly in Tigrayan hands. Though not entirely an ethnocracy—the Amhara, for example, were treated as near-equals—the Tigray held most political positions despite representing only 6 percent of the population. Non-Tigray were viewed as second-class citizens, subject to regime-sanctioned exclusion from most channels of political and economic power.[11] In addition, the Oromo were singled out as a secessionist threat, and its political wing, the Oromo Liberation Front (OLF), was subjected to a state-orchestrated campaign of mass arrest and killing during 1992–94.[12]

The Ethiopian National Defense Force (ENDF), and particularly its army, was at center stage of this nation-building. Mostly disbanded after 1991, the military was slowly reformed around Tigrayan dominance. On the eve of the 1998 war, an estimated 80 percent of all senior officer positions were earmarked solely for Tigrays or Amhara. By contrast, the Oromo, Afar, Somali, and other southern ethnic groupings experienced discrimination, shut almost completely out from most officer ranks along with important occupations like tank crews.[13] There was a push, however, to implement reforms designed

8. On the close ties between the TPLF and EPLF, see Negash and Tronvoll 2000; Henze 2001; Tareke 2009.

9. Levine 2010.

10. Abebe 2014; Kissi 2006; Tareke 2009.

11. Shinn and Ofcansky 2013, xxviii; Zwede 1998, 284.

12. Woldemariam 2018, 193–99.

13. "Post 1991 Military Leadership: The Total Domination of the Ethiopian Army by Ethnic Tigrean Officers," Ginbot 7: Movement for Justice, Freedom and Democracy, 30 May 2009.

to achieve "national balance" within the army even before war broke out. This trend accelerated after the disastrous campaign at Badme in 1998, when it became clear that the army needed to expand rapidly. Recruitment was thrown open to all ethnic groups, Tigrayan dominance was down-weighted, and even political prisoners with valuable technical skills from the former Derg regime were reenlisted.[14] With no general conscription system, the army relied mostly on ethnic recruitment, hoping to activate former TPLF militia connections to drum up fighters.[15] This loosening of the ethnic shackles on military service in late 1999 coincided with the regime's efforts to harness Ethiopian nationalism to bolster public support for the war. Promises were issued that the social contract would be revised after the war, with a more inclusive political system and a redress of outstanding ethnic grievances proffered in exchange for military service.

Estimates of the army's prewar ethnic composition are somewhat imprecise. But we can nonetheless discern the broad contours of Ethiopia's military inequality coefficient from published sources. Drawing on multiple estimates, I calculate that Ethiopia had a military inequality score of 0.24, at the lower end of a medium level of inequality on the eve of Eritrea's invasion.[16]

Much like Ethiopia, the Democratic Republic of the Congo found itself deeply enmeshed in the throes of nation-building on the eve of its 1998–2002 war with Rwanda, Uganda, and their various militias.[17] Emerging victorious from the aftermath of the First Congo War, President Laurent-Désiré Kabila set about constructing a new vision for the multiethnic DRC. Adopting the rhetoric of Congolese nationalism, Kabila moved aggressively to establish a highly personalistic and kleptocratic administration— "organized like a loose band of freebooters or a hunting pack"[18]—that

14. Tegegn 2014, 32–46. This rapid expansion led Eritrean officials to conclude that the Ethiopian army was staffed by raw recruits and thus vulnerable to a surprise attack. See Asrat 2014, 269, and Connell 2005.

15. Hammond 2004, 233fn11; Dias 2011, 35–36; "New Recruits Join Ethiopian Army," *Voice of America*, 29 June 1998.

16. More specifically, I generate a low estimate of Ethiopia's military inequality with the following breakdown: Tigray $(0.30 * 0)$ + Amhara $(0.30 * 0)$ + southern nations $(0.20 * 0.5)$ + Oromo $(0.15 * 0.5)$ + Afar $(0.025 * 0.5)$ + Somalis $(0.025 * 0.5) = 0.20$. I also generate a high estimate, which acknowledges that state-orchestrated violence occurred against the Oromo in 1992–94 and may still have been occurring at low levels by 1997 (Woldemariam 2018, 196.). Tigray $(0.30 * 0)$ + Amhara $(0.30 * 0)$ + southern nations $(0.20 * 0.5)$ + Oromo $(0.15 * 1)$ + Afar $(0.025 * 0.5)$ + Somalis $(0.025 * 0.5) = 0.275$. The mean estimate is therefore 0.2375.

17. On the role of intervening powers, see especially Turner 2013, 46–73.

18. Prunier 2009, 210.

institutionalized a narrow ethnocratic agenda. He initially aimed to elevate the Katanga and Kasai, including his own Luba tribe, above all other groups. Other ethnic and tribal groups, including the Tutsi Banyamulenge and Banyarwanda, began facing systematic barriers to political power and military service as "doubtful citizens."[19] Still others, notably tribal groupings from eastern Congo, were exposed to deliberate campaigns of collective violence, either by the state or through its militia proxies. As the war progressed, Kabila's desperation grew, and he turned to anti-Tutsi, anti-Rwanda xenophobia to gin up patriotic fervor.[20] The Banyamulenge and Banyarwanda, suspected of divided loyalties, were largely driven from political life, while the Katanga and Kasai-Luba gripped the reins of power even tighter. Inequality in the DRC, like that in Ethiopia, shifted during the war. But the two belligerents were moving in opposite directions, and so ended up even farther apart than their prewar inequality scores would indicate.

The Armed Forces of the Republic of the Congo reflected this ethnic hierarchy. It was also powerfully shaped by regionalism that, in the absence of strong institutions and material resources, led to the construction of parallel armies, each with their own brand of ethnic communalism. As Jason Stearns noted, the FAC was a "hulking, decrepit edifice" and a "shambles"[21] that managed to both privilege and discriminate against nearly every ethnic group depending on where its garrison was located. Unusually, foreign advisors, principally from Rwanda, were embedded within the DRC's command structure, including chief of staff, until the eve of the war. Conflict arose each time Kabila sought to consolidate his control over these various factions. In early 1998, hundreds of Banyamulenge troops deserted following a dispute over plans to distribute them throughout different units.[22] In fact, the key event sparking the Second Congo War was a ham-fisted attempt to integrate the soldiers of a mostly Banyamulenge unit at Bukavu throughout the entire military to create a more favorable ethnic balance. Much as the Khalifa in the Mahidya (see chapter 3), Kabila sought to anchor his loyalists throughout units staffed by non-favored ethnic groups to solidify command and control. His efforts backfired, and the FAC entered the Second Congo War in a state of near "total confusion" as ethnic factionalism tore it apart in the war's first days.[23]

19. Alida 2017; Huening 2013; Jackson 2007; Vlassenroot 2002.

20. Shirkey 2012, 107; Carayannis 2003, 242.

21. Stearns 2011, 272.

22. Reyntjens 2009, 151.

23. Carayannis 2003, 12.

Given Kabila's discrimination and, in some cases, actual repression of multiple ethnic groups, it is unsurprising that the FAC began the war with (very) high military inequality. I derive estimates of the DRC's military inequality coefficient from the Forces Armées Zaïroises' (FAZ) demographics in 1997 as well as the composition of specific FAC brigades. The DRC entered hostilities with a military inequality coefficient of 0.55, near the threshold between high and extreme levels of inequality.[24] Due to changing recruitment patterns, specifically the near elimination of Tutsi Banyamulenge from the army and the surge of victimized *kadogo* soldiers, the DRC's military inequality coefficient likely hit near 0.65 by late 1999, one of the highest recorded in our case studies.[25] These calculations are necessarily imprecise; no complete accounting of the exact ethnic breakdown of the FAC at its inception exists. Nonetheless, the magnitude of the estimated coefficient clearly tracks with qualitative accounts of inter- and intraethnic tensions with the FAC during the Second Congo War.

7.3.2. Matched Covariates

A glance at table 7.1 reveals that these belligerents are remarkably similar across many traits commonly cited to explain battlefield performance. Unlike the Habsburg and Ottoman empires, Ethiopia and the DRC were at least evenly matched with their adversaries in terms of soldiers deployed (50 percent and 65 percent share of the soldiers initially deployed, respectively) during the war's first battle. The total number of soldiers each deployed during the war was admittedly different: Ethiopia mustered an estimated 310,000 soldiers, while the DRC managed only about 55,000. Yet the DRC's estimate is somewhat misleading, in two ways. It does not acknowledge that the DRC was fighting a coalitional war in which at least four other countries (Zimbabwe, Namibia, Angola, and Chad) committed 19,000 additional

24. The prewar estimate is calculated: 20 percent Congolese Tutsi (Banyamulenge, Banyarwanda); 40 percent Katangan (non-Baluba, Baluba); 10 percent Kasai (Luanda, Luba); 20 percent drawn from multiple groups in North and South Kivu (collectively, the kadogo); and 10 percent Mango/Kongo. Formally, we obtain: Congolese Tutsi ($0.20 * 0.5$) + Katangan ($0.30 * 0.5$) + Kasai ($0.2 * 0$) + kadogo ($0.20 * 1$) + Mango/Kongo ($0.10 * 0.5$) = 0.55, where the Tutsi, some Katangan groups, and the Mango/Kongo had all experienced state discrimination (0.5) and the kadogo were exposed to state violence.

25. The late-1999 estimate is calculated: Congolese Tutsi ($0.0 * 0.5$) + Katangan ($0.20 * 0.5$) + Kasai ($0.1 * 0$) + kadogo ($0.50 * 1$) + Mango/Kongo ($0.10 * 0.5$) = 0.65. This coding reflects the exclusion of Congolese Tutsi, consistent with the regime's anti-Rwanda, anti-Tutsi wartime rhetoric, and increased recruitment among supposedly loyal kadogo to replenish the ranks after mass desertion and defection thinned them.

soldiers. These totals also exclude the DRC-created and DRC-affiliated militia that fought alongside regular forces and that bolstered their ranks by at least 50,000, and possibly 100,000, additional soldiers. These include the Mayi-Mayi (20,000–30,000), the Interhamwe (20,000–30,000), and the ALiR (10,000–15,000), among others. This imbalance is also helpful for causal inference; we might anticipate that as army size increases, principal-agent problems also increase, raising the odds of observing mass soldier indiscipline. Yet it was the FAC, and not Ethiopian forces, that experienced mass desertion and defection.[26]

More generally, neither belligerent was a Great Power, as designated by the Correlates of War, though each did possess sizable military assets, including large fleets of Soviet (and later Russian) T-62 and T-54/55 tanks, BRDM-1/2 armored patrol cars, and heavy artillery. They also possessed small quantities of modern fighters and helicopters, though maintenance issues bedeviled both militaries.[27] Each army relied on a similarly unorthodox blend of recruitment streams, drawing on conscripts, volunteers, a handful of foreign mercenaries, and, in DRC's case, the impressment of unwilling children to fill out the ranks. Both militaries were technically standing armies, though each had experienced upheaval in the preceding interwar years and had fallen into disrepair in terms of both men and material.

The wars also began in similar fashion. Neither the DRC nor Ethiopia initiated these wars, nor did they join an ongoing conflict. They were also pitted against similar adversaries, at least as expressed by their political systems. Polity IV, the standard dataset for coding regime type, assigned Eritrea a −6 value, denoting a stable dictatorship. Rwanda and Uganda, the DRC's principal foes, are nearly identical at −6 and −4, respectively.[28] According to our Project Mars expanded regime type codings, Eritrea is a considered a "boss" regime, while Rwanda (a "machine") and Uganda (a "boss") mirror each other closely.[29] Ethiopia and the DRC themselves shared similar political systems. Both were personalist dictatorships with Polity IV scores that denote their status as "anocracies" lodged halfway between democracies and autocracies. Indeed, their Polity2 scores, which range from +10 (consolidated democracy) to −10 (strong authoritarian), are almost identical:

---

26. Their respective force ratios are also tilted in the DRC's favor. Ethiopia was outnumbered 1.2:1 to Eritrean forces, while the DRC enjoyed a more favorable 1.4:1 manpower advantage, when measured by total soldiers deployed during the war. Local force-to-force ratios (FFRs) varied considerably across battles, however.

27. "Ethiopia's Army Gets Some Muscle," *Agence France Presse*, 5 February 1999.

28. Jaggers and Gurr 2004.

29. Weeks 2014.

Ethiopia received a 1 value while DRC was a 0 (both in 1997).[30] Finally, both wars occurred nearly simultaneously, helping to control for trends in weapons technology and other time-dependent factors that might explain battlefield performance.

No two wars or belligerents are identical, of course. It is unclear, however, whether remaining imbalances are sufficient to explain the observed divergence in battlefield performance. For example, the Ethiopia-Eritrea War was an interstate war, while the Second Congo War was an internationalized civil war that mixed methods of fighting. Civil wars do tend to be associated with increased risk of mass desertion and especially defection (see chapter 4), suggesting that the playing field might be tilted toward observing mass indiscipline within the DRC's ranks. This is indeed what we find. In this case, however, it is arguable that one of the main drivers for the civil war was the ramshackle nature of the military itself. Disastrous efforts to force integration, coupled with an equally inflammatory decision to use militias given military weakness, fueled the dynamics that led to ethnic countermobilization and a descent into civil war. Distance between the belligerent's capital and the first armed clash also differed across belligerents. Ethiopia's opening battle at Badme was 639 kilometers from Addis Ababa; Kinshasa, by contrast, was separated by 1,572 kilometers from the initial engagement near Goma, though the conflict quickly spread throughout the country.[31] Given the DRC's size, it is clear that the FAC faced more difficult logistical issues than Ethiopia's military, possibly contributing to diminished battlefield performance.

7.3.3. Contextual Covariates

The closeness of fit across many of these initial covariates helps ensure broad similarities across other, more contextual, covariates. For example, both belligerents exhibited a commitment to combined arms, though they each struggled to implement it (especially the FAC). Both were wedded to an offensive mentality that privileged rapid attacks. Neither belligerent possessed a qualitative edge in military technology. In Ethiopia's case, Russia was selling nearly identical weapons to both sides (i.e., the Su-27 for Ethiopia and MiG-29 to Eritrea, in nearly the same quantities). The FAC, too, faced adversaries with comparable tanks and armored vehicles. Each side was capable of building elaborate layered defenses when called upon, though in neither case

30. Project Mars expanded coding classifies Ethiopia as a "machine" and the DRC as a "strongman" state. Both clearly existed in the twilight world between democracy and autocracy.

31. Ethiopia's distance is at the 50th percentile of all wars; the DRC's at the 65th percentile, so the difference may be more apparent than substantively meaningful.

were fronts organized around the defense of fortifications as in Morocco or Kokand. Foreign advisors from former Soviet bloc countries were present in each case; the FAC was especially dependent on foreigners, including North Korea, for campaign planning, training, and weapons expertise. Both belligerents had prior (and recent) history with their adversaries. Identity cleavages between belligerents, sometimes cited as responsible for determining the fighting quality of soldiers (a monadic argument) or prowess against certain foes (a relational argument), are nearly identical in these cases. Notably, both Ethiopia and the DRC are Christian dominant countries; each has a significant share of Muslims as well. Neither belligerent faced a colonizing power. Population size, a common measure of raw military potential, was similar across belligerents. Ethnically diverse, each belligerent had a high degree of ethnolinguistic fractionalization. With a maximal value of 1, denoting complete certainty that two individuals drawn randomly from the population would be of different ethnic groups, Ethiopia scored a 0.694 and the DRC a remarkable 0.902.[32] Drawing on the Ethnic Power Relations 3.01 dataset, both regimes excluded ethnic groups from executive political power. Each also had separatist movements. These two indicators are among the most salient for predicting civil war onset, suggesting weak state capacity and likely negative effects on battlefield performance.[33] Finally, these belligerents shared a praetorian model of civil-military relations in which the military cast a long shadow over policymaking even if not formally part of the government.[34] New leaders were also scrambling to cement their legitimacy; their experience and precarious existence might also contribute to poor battlefield performance. Indeed, both belligerents had leaders that had assumed power less than three years prior to war's outbreak. In the DRC, Kabila took power on 29 May 1997, only a year before the war. In Ethiopia, Negasso Gidada assumed power 22 August 1995 after Ethiopia's first elections, which were boycotted by most opposition parties.

Again, there are some differences across the wars. At 1,559 days, the Second Congo War lasted much longer than the Ethiopia-Eritrea War (751 days).[35] Longer wars may increase the odds of observing mass soldier indiscipline; by their nature, they may favor attritional slogs that increase casualties. We need to be careful, however, in ascribing too much to this difference. It is plausible that the Second Congo War was much longer precisely because of desertion

32. Data drawn from the Ethnic Power Relations 3.01 dataset (Wimmer, Cederman and Min 2009).

33. Cederman, Gleditsch and Buhaug 2013, 75–76.

34. Perlmutter 1969.

35. These totals represent the 80th and 92nd percentile of all wars.

and defection; that is, duration was a function of mass indiscipline, not its cause.

7.4. Ethiopia at War

Confounding the low expectations of foreign observers, Ethiopia's battle-field performance was surprisingly good, much to the chagrin of their too-confident Eritrean foes.[36] Recovering from the shock of the initial invasion, the Ethiopian Army became increasingly proficient at combined arms. The war's third and final act in May 2000 witnessed Ethiopia's orchestration of a combined arms offensive across multiple fronts with four tank divisions, 22 infantry divisions, extensive artillery, and close air support from modern fighter-bombers. Such efforts were not perfect by any stretch, however. Ethiopia's forces struggled to exploit the holes they tore, at great expense in casualties, in Eritrean defenses. Logistical support was cumbersome at best. Some assaults were also made possible only by deliberately simplifying combined arms operations. Tanks, for example, were often held in reserve, while infantry, sometimes reliant on pack animals like donkeys for resupply, were sent forward to storm Eritrean positions in scenes reminiscent of the First World War's Western Front. Overall, the Ethiopian Army only exhibited one of the four pathologies tracked by the battlefield performance index. Its only blemish was a below-parity loss-exchange ratio, a function of over-reliance on massed frontal assaults in early battles. Cohesion, however, was high; no mass desertion or defection occurred in the war. In fact, only a handful of soldiers are known to have deserted during the war. Nor were blocking detachments used to maintain control. Together, this pattern is consistent with our expectations about battlefield performance for a "low medium" inequality belligerent. I explore the Ethiopian Army's combat power and cohesion in greater detail below before turning a more focused treatment of its Operation Sunset (February–March 1999) that it unleashed near the war's midpoint.

7.4.1. Combat Power

Surprised by the Eritrean invasion, the unprepared Ethiopian Army scrambled to improve its tactical and operational acumen in the midst of combat operations. It largely succeeded in doing so, though progress was often purchased at heavy cost. Transitioning from initial defensive operations in 1998, the army's first efforts at conducting offensive operations in February–March 1999 (detailed below) were something of a mixed bag. Combined arms assaults,

36. On Eritrean overconfidence, see especially Woldemariam and Young 2018, 695–96, and Wrong 2006, 369.

enabled by large-scale purchases of over one hundred main battle tanks, self-propelled artillery, and new fighter-bombers from China, Russia, and Eastern Europe, initially succeeded in cracking stubborn Eritrean defenses.[37] Critics derided Ethiopian tactics as primitive, however. The use of successive waves of infantry against mined Eritrean trenches and defensive positions led to perhaps inevitable comparisons with the First World War. Indeed, the parallels proved irresistible for foreign journalists; the "First World War with modern weapons" remains the caricature of the war even today.

> The Ethiopian commanders' strategy was simple. Deploying tens of thousands of barely trained recruits along a 3-mile front, they drove them forward, wave upon wave, with the sole mission of blowing themselves up on minefields until they had cleared a path to the Eritrean front line for better trained infantry, mechanized forces and armor. In the third or fourth wave, about 5,000 peasants came with them, their mules and donkeys bearing food and ammunition for an Ethiopian breakthrough. It didn't work. The doomed men hardly raised their weapons, but linked hands in a despairing communal solace in the face of certain death.[38]

We must be cautious here, however. The absence of reporters embedded with Ethiopian forces, coupled with the presence of Eritrean minders, means that we only receive a partial, curated view of the war. Questions swirl around the true extent of casualties in these early battles, about whether minesweepers (the *aglay*) in the waves were really unarmed and untrained, and even whether these suicidal human wave assaults actually occurred.[39] What remains undisputed is that the Ethiopian Army managed field tanks, infantry, and preparatory artillery bombardments in coordinated attacks that breached Eritrean defenses in a matter of days, and did so only a year after the war's unexpected opening.

Moreover, the analogy to World War One overlooks considerable evolution and improvement in Ethiopian tactics and operations. On 12 May 2000, the army unleashed its final "Third Offensive" against Eritrean forces; by 18 June, one-third of Eritrea was in Ethiopian hands. After a two-day artillery bombardment of Eritrean positions on the Western Front, Ethiopian forces crossed the Mereb River at multiple points. Armored spearheads struck dead center at the Western Front, seeking to capture Shambuko and Shelalo as

---

37. Stockholm International Peace Research Institute (SIPRI) 2000.

38. "Human waves fall as war aims unfold," *Guardian*, 17 May 1999.

39. "Eritrean disaster looms as a million flee from rapidly advancing Ethiopian forces," *Independent*, 20 May 2000.

stepping stones toward seizing Barentu, the capital of Eritrea's Gash Barka region. This opening gambit was a feint; it was meant to compel Eritrea to shift its reserves away from the Central Front, where the real blow was to fall around Zalembassa. But Eritrean forces quickly collapsed on the Western Front, as defensive positions around Tokombia, Bishuka, Mailem, and then Molk toppled like dominoes. A furtive Eritrean counteroffensive was quickly turned aside. Ethiopian forces seized Barentu on 18 May, having traversed the 50 kilometers from Shambuko in only two days. Seeking to exploit the Eritrean collapse, the army sent its crack 15th Division for a westward sprint to Tesseney, overrunning rear bases before meeting resistance at Haykota on 27 May. Tesseney fell to the 15th on 28 May; the mechanized division had advanced 120 kilometers into Eritrea in only eight days, averaging 15 kilometers a day. Only a last-ditch effort by Eritrean reserves halted its progress on 4 June. Yet the 15th merely turned southward, linking up with three additional divisions to capture first Um Hagar (Omhajer) before shifting northward again to recapture Tesseney on 14 June. This improvised regrouping and (re-)assault of Tesseney covered 250 kilometers in just ten days, a very rapid rate of advance for mechanized units.

Even these notable offensives were eclipsed by the army's swift drive into eastern Eritrea. The (first) fall of Tesseney on 28 May kicked off the second phase of the operation, with a massive artillery bombardment unleashed at Zalembassa. Capitalizing on near total air dominance, the Ethiopian Air Force (ETAF) jerry-rigged Antonov An-12 transports to drop barrel bombs over Eritrean fortifications. Surging mechanized infantry divisions to the Central Front, the Ethiopian Army quickly overwhelmed Eritrean defenses. Eastern Eritrea lay open. On 2 June, a large Ethiopian armored contingent sprinted from Bure deep into Eritrea, halting only 37 kilometers from the Eritrean port city of Asseb on 14 June. In about two weeks, this formation had covered almost 1,000 kilometers, or nearly 83 kilometers a day, far exceeding the historical average of around 10 kilometers per day for lightly engaged mechanized forces.[40] Perhaps unsurprisingly, Eritrea agreed to Ethiopia's peace proposal on 18 June, signing a Cessation of Hostilities agreement in Algiers.[41] Or, as Haile Woldense, then Eritrea's Foreign Minister, remarked, "it is only telling the truth if I say that Ethiopia made us wet ourselves during this invasion."[42]

These improvements notwithstanding, Ethiopia still recorded a less-than-favorable loss-exchange ratio for the war. Lopsided casualties stemmed partly from Ethiopia's need to breach Eritrea's defense-in-depth across desolate,

40. Helmbold 1990, 4–48.
41. On Eritrea's view of the "crushing" nature of this defeat, see especially Bahta 2014, 239.
42. Weldetinsae 2001; Woldemariam 2015, 180.

arid landscapes that provided little cover. Outside Eritrea's initial invasion, Ethiopia was nearly constantly on the offensive, a demanding set of challenges at a time when it was still receiving and integrating new equipment from foreign suppliers.[43] Most importantly, prewar ethnic discrimination also shaped the nature of fighting and the resulting casualties. Prejudice on the part of Tigrayan officers toward targeted minorities, particularly the Oromo, likely influenced their decision-making, especially their tolerance of casualties. Commanders were willing to launch direct frontal assaults even when, as in March 1999, Ethiopian forces did not possess anywhere near enough soldiers to penetrate Eritrean defenses. Moreover, Ethiopian forces in 1998 and 1999 were beset by coordination problems across different types of units. Modern combined arms is of course complex, and coordination problems are a constant concern. What makes these coordination issues especially salient, however, is the fact that they occurred across Tigrayan-dominated tank divisions and their predominantly non-Tigrayan staffed infantry units. Waves of infantry were sent forward to act as screens for tanks, protecting them from anti-tank fire. But the tank crews sat too far back, content to let the infantry bear the brunt of the assault. As a result, gaps emerged between the two, leaving each formation unsupported and vulnerable to murderous Eritrean defensive fire.[44] In a counterfactual world, the absence of ethnic prejudices within the officer corps might have produced tighter coordination and integration, reducing fatalities.[45]

7.4.2. Cohesion

Ethnically diverse, and comprised of recruits with strong ethnic ties to populations in Eritrea, the Ethiopian Army nonetheless remained a cohesive and unified fighting force throughout the war. Neither mass desertion nor mass defection occurred during the war.[46] There are only scattered reports

43. Russian advisors provided technical assistance, particularly on anti-aircraft systems, and even flew Ethiopian aircraft, though their actual role in combat operations remained modest. See "World Class War: UN envoy Mohammed Sahnoun mediates while the world ignores its biggest war," *Africa Confidential* 40(9): 6–7.

44. Fontanellaz and Cooper 2018, 54–59.

45. In this regard, the sophistication on display in May–June 2000, when the army was most inclusive, is instructive.

46. As a reminder, Project Mars defines mass desertion as the unauthorized withdrawal of 10 percent or greater of an army's fielded force, where soldiers quit their service with the intent of returning home and abandoning the fight. Mass defection is said to occur when 10 percent or greater of an army's fielded force decides to switch sides, taking up arms against their former comrades.

of handfuls of soldiers deserting or prematurely surrendering.[47] I found no credible evidence of side-switching during the war.[48] Had it occurred, Eritrean politicians and military commanders would have feted these defectors given their obvious propaganda value. Some Eritrean commanders had apparently concluded that the multiethnic nature of the Ethiopian Army left it vulnerable to a sudden blow, as at Badme, that would tear apart its fragile interethnic tapestry. Summarizing Eritrea's thinking, one analyst noted that "Eritrea reached the wrong conclusion regarding the fundamental objective circumstances of Ethiopia. If their baseless position were correct, Ethiopia would have completely lost its unity; the people would have accepted their "Ethiopianness" against their wish; and, therefore, Ethiopians would have disintegrated and dispersed." If this view were correct, he concluded, "those nations and nationalities of Ethiopia like the Amhara, Oromo, Somali, Southern Peoples, Wollayta, Sidama, Afar-Gumuuz, Berta, Anguak ... would have abandoned the Tigrayans and the Tigrayans would have had to stand by themselves."[49] But they did not.

That said, we should not exaggerate the degree of interethnic solidarity and harmony within the ranks. Prewar ethnic discrimination against many of these non-Tigrayan groups, coupled with their marginalized status within the army itself, certainly produced grievances among these soldiers. Glimpses of this disquiet can be captured in interviews with Ethiopian prisoners of war. One journalist who managed to interview four POWs in February 1999 noted that "they are from far-flung corners of Ethiopia, and say that the war is 'not ours.' Kadir Abdulkadir, 16, from Jigiga, the Somali region of Ethiopia, says he was forcibly recruited from school. Abbas Mohamed, an Oromo, says he surrendered—'the Ethiopian government is only fighting for itself.' "[50] These clues are suggestive, if only that, of the view that prewar ethnic discrimination can bleed over into wartime conduct.

More broadly, it is plausible that ethnic resentment against the regime and its war simmered just below the surface of the army's apparent cohesiveness. Yet it did not produce collective indiscipline. Indeed, its absence is telling. Prewar marginalization likely soured these soldiers on the regime but did not lead many of them to openly challenge military authorities. Such a stance is consistent with the expectations of the military inequality thesis; discrimination was resented but, compared to exposure to violence, provided less motive and

47. "Eritrea Claims 22 Ethiopian Soldiers Defected," *Africa News*, 13 February 1999.

48. Moreover, Eritrea only captured about 1,100 Ethiopian soldiers for the entire war, ruling out POWs as a possible source of defectors (Murphy, Kidane and Snider 2013, 269).

49. Enquay 2005, 196.

50. "Eritrea set for war of attrition," *Independent*, 10 February 1999.

means for soldiers to organize collective escape. A more cynical take, however, might suggest that such discipline was simply coerced, that these soldiers were merely cowed into submission by loyalist units and commanders. I have found no evidence that the army ever fielded blocking detachments, however. Moreover, I uncovered only two mentions of extrajudicial punishment meted out to force soldiers from targeted ethnicities to fight; both refer to the same disastrous Ethiopian offensive in March 1999 (see also below). "All the captured soldiers," one Eritrean source recounted, "said that when the invasion began, their officers stood behind them and ordered them into battle calling up company after company. Soldiers attempting to retreat were shot by officers in the back line. The soldiers said they were shocked by the amount of corpses of fellow soldiers they trampled over and said they felt lucky to have succeeded in coming out alive."[51] Similarly, a Western journalist reported that "it was Oromo peasants [the army] selected as human minesweepers, and Tigrayan officers who shot them from the rear."[52]

Blocking detachments are generally the hallmark of belligerents with high-to-extreme military inequality; their appearance here would represent a misprediction for the argument. Assuming these accounts are true, however, it is entirely within the expectations of a belligerent with a 0.24 military inequality coefficient to experience some extrajudicial violence aimed at targeted ethnic groups like the Oromo. The violence here appears to have been a one-time event, possibly orchestrated by local commanders rather than army-wide policy, and did not involve formal specialized units. Cohesion in a belligerent verging on medium levels of inequality is thus a messy affair, with anti-regime grievances jostling with a desire to revise the social contract through public sacrifice on the battlefield. Violence, along with tactical adjustment to minimize desertion opportunities, also helped maintain cohesion, though at the cost of greater casualties.

7.4.3.   Case Study: Operation Sunset, February–March 1999

"Even if the sun doesn't set," Eritrea's President Isaias Afwerki boasted in a July 1998 television broadcast, "we will never withdraw from Badme."[53] Ethiopia's answer would come eight months later, in the form of Operation Sunset (February–March 1999). Designed to wrest Badme away from Eritrean control, Operation Sunset amassed the greatest concentration of soldiers,

---

51. ERINA Update, 10 March 1999.

52. "Human waves fall as war aims unfold," *Guardian*, 17 May 1999. He also noted, however, that the army "showed hardly less contempt for its own people. Local Tigrayan villagers were pressed into that suicidal baggage train, and mainly Tigrayan soldiers died in the tanks that were entrusted to no other nationality."

53. "Eritrea Says Will Never Withdraw from Borderland," *Reuters*, 9 July 1998.

armored vehicles, and artillery in Africa since the Battle of Tunisia during the Second World War.[54] The operation serves as a microcosm of the highs and lows of Ethiopian battlefield performance at the war's midpoint, marking the Ethiopian Army's first offensive against Eritrean forces.

On 6 February, Ethiopian forces began a series of small-scale probing operations on the desolate Western Front near Badme, provoking several skirmishes. Simultaneously, Ethiopian forces feinted a larger assault at Tsorena (Tserona) on the Central Front. To confuse Eritrean defenders, Ethiopian commanders shifted their military reserves, first sending them to the Western Front, then rapidly redeploying to the Central Front, only to recommit them to the Western Front in a bid to overwhelm Eritrean forces. Eritrean commanders mistakenly committed their own reserves to the Central Front, drawing at least 50,000 soldiers from the Western and Eastern fronts. As a result, Eritrean forces were vulnerable to a sudden concentration of Ethiopian forces, which fell like a hammer on depleted Eritrean lines on 23 February. Led by Brigadier Samora Yunis, a combined force of tanks and mechanized infantry ("a seemingly endless river of thousands of troops"[55]), supported by heavy artillery and helicopter gunships, crashed against Eritrean trenches along a sixty-kilometer section of the Western Front.

Badme was their central objective. The fight would not be easy; Eritrean forces had spent the past eight months digging an extensive trench system across the entire Western Front. Tens of thousands of Egyptian-made anti-personnel and anti-tank mines were strewn in front of the trenches, while T-54/55 tanks were employed as defensive pillboxes. Eritrean artillery had also dialed in their killing zones across wide swathes of the front, including at Badme. Overconfident Eritrean commanders had led them to shortchange their own defenses, however. In many locations, their trench system consisted of only a single line, with no defense-in-depth prepared.[56] Still, the local force-to-force ratio (FFR) of 1.67:1 for Ethiopia fell far short of the customary 3:1 thought necessary for successful offensives against entrenched defenders.[57] It is estimated that Ethiopia deployed 125,000 soldiers on the Western Front for Operation Sunset; Eritrea had about 75,000. Given Eritrea's linear defenses, the local force-to-space ratio (FSR) was about 2,083 soldiers per kilometer, a density far above those recorded in World War II.[58]

---

54. Negash and Tronvoll 2000, 2; "World Class War: UN envoy Mohammed Sahnoun mediates while the world ignores its biggest war," *Africa Confidential* 40:9 (1999): 6–7.

55. Palut 2005, 97.

56. Last 2004; Palut 2005, 98.

57. Mearsheimer 1989.

58. See Biddle 2004, 118.

Yet after only three days of fighting, Ethiopian forces had broken through at Badme, tearing a deep gash nearly twenty kilometers wide in Eritrean defenses. Fearing encirclement, Eritrean commanders ordered a general retreat. Thousands of stranded soldiers were captured by fast-moving Ethiopian formations. At the end of their (short) logistical tethers, however, these divisions halted and turned their attention to consolidating their new positions.[59] These quick victories were purchased at a high price, however. Conservative estimates place Eritrean and Ethiopian casualties at 5,000 and 10,000, respectively.[60] The true extent of Ethiopian casualties may be far higher, though Eritrean claims of inflicting 50,000 fatalities are fanciful. Mines proved especially deadly; an estimated 150,000 had been sown across the Western Front as a first line of defense. Some 20–30 tanks were also destroyed as they charged across open terrain in support of infantry assaults.

Above all, Ethiopian tactics and operational art contributed to these high casualties. Seeking to solve the puzzle of breaching entrenched defenses, commanders struck upon the same idea as their European predecessors: massed frontal assaults into the teeth of Eritrean fortifications and trenches. Ethiopia's reputation, only partly deserved, for relying on "human wave" attacks to overwhelm Eritrean defenses was created during this initial three-day offensive. It is true that Ethiopian commanders ordered successive waves of soldiers to storm Eritrean defenses at Badme. The notion that infantry were unsupported is belied by the sustained use of artillery for preparatory and covering fire during the assault as well as the burned out hulks of armored vehicles that dotted the battlefield once combat petered out. Nor can credible evidence be mustered to confirm the allegation made by Eritrean observers (and some, but not all) Western journalists that ill-equipped troops were sent ahead of better-trained ones to clear mines and absorb enemy fire.

Instead, even Eritrean commanders and soldiers begrudgingly admitted that Ethiopian forces fought with unexpected determination and skill. One Eritrean prisoner of war lamented that "we were told that Ethiopian armed forces are fragmented along nationality lines and [thus] weak and divided,"[61] a claim debunked at Badme. Another admitted "that our leaders never tell the truth, and I think I understand this fact better now. We were told the Ethiopian army is weak, that they don't know how to fight; that [our] army has the best fighters in the world; that the Ethiopians don't know how to use big weapons;

59. The Ethiopian Army had also made substantial logistical improvements under Brigadier General Hailu Tilahun, who released former regime officials with military experience from prison. See Smith 1999, 7.

60. Sundberg and Melander 2013.

61. Quoted in Amlak 2001, 220.

that the soldiers from different nationalities are divided along their national lines and there is no unity among them—and they hate [their government]. Thus we were told that the battle wouldn't last long."[62]

Perhaps most tellingly, Eritrea's Ministry of Defense publicly conceded the fall of Badme on 26 February. A day later, Eritrea accepted the Organization for African Unity's proposal for a negotiated settlement to the war.[63] The Defense Minister was sacked, while at least four divisional commanders were also dismissed for their failure on the Western Front.[64] For its part, the Ethiopian public welcomed the victory at Badme; the streets of Addis Ababa were packed with an impromptu celebration that hailed the outcome as a second Battle of Adwa, in which Ethiopians decisively defeated an invading Italian Army in 1896.[65]

Difficulty often lies, however, in converting military gains into political ones. Mistakenly sensing an opportunity for greater territorial gains, Ethiopian commanders seized upon the idea of a lightening offensive on the Central Front (Operation Westwind). On 13 March, Ethiopian artillery and air support struck Eritrean defenses near Zalembassa on the Tsorena flank of the Central Front. Hoping to catch Eritrean forces unaware, this preparatory bombardment was deliberately cut short to allow four Ethiopian divisions (about 44,000 soldiers) to surge in successive waves against thirty kilometers of fortified Eritrean positions on 14 March.[66] The odds were highly unfavorable; Ethiopia possessed a bare 1.1:1 manpower advantage, and had local force-to-space ratio (1,467 soldiers per kilometer) far less than it enjoyed at Badme. Moreover, Eritrea had redoubled its defensive efforts after Badme; most positions now had three layers of prepared defenses. In a brutal slugfest, these Ethiopian divisions, under the command of Brigadier General Abdullah Gemada, managed to penetrate the first line of trenchworks but stalled soon thereafter.[67] Despite committing its new Su-27 fighter-bombers to the effort, the Ethiopian offensive was called off on the morning of 17 March, having failed to regain any territory. Worse, casualties were enormous.[68] While estimates again must be treated with caution, credible reports of up to

62. Quoted in Amlak 2001, 220.

63. "Eritrea accepts OAU peace agreement after border incursion," *Associated Press*, 27 February 1999.

64. Smith 1999, 7.

65. "Ethiopians Celebrate Victory over Eritreans," *Associated Press*, 2 March 1999.

66. "Ethiopia continuing attacks: Eritrea," *Agence France Presse*, 8 March 1999.

67. "Ethiopia Confirms Cross-Border Shelling On Tsorona Front," *Africa News*, 14 March 1999.

68. "Bodies of Ethiopian soldiers litter battleground in border dispute," *Associated Press*, 19 March 1999; "Eritrea claims victory on Tsorona battlefront," *Associated Press*, 16 March 1999.

15,000 Ethiopian soldiers have been cited, against only 2,000 Eritrean losses.[69] Anti-tank defenses claimed up to 57 tanks and armored vehicles.[70]

Western journalists, accompanied by Eritrean minders, were escorted to the battlefield to witness the aftermath.[71] As one recounted:

> A few Ethiopian corpses lay behind the earthworks, but that was nothing compared to the sight that awaited me as I walked through a gap in the front line. On my immediate right, in a space of 10 yards, fifteen Ethiopian soldiers lay dead on and around the earthworks, some were lying in the trench dug into the ground in front of the mounds of earth. Looking along the trench in both directions, the bodies continued. Some were half buried, some had heads missing, some were bloated, killed in the first wave of attacks two days before, some had only died that morning.... I saw at least three hundred Ethiopian dead in two hundred meters.... The horrific thought, which would not leave me, was that these three hundred Ethiopian dead were the ones that had actually made it across the 3 km to this small part of the line while under constant artillery, tank, mortar, machine gun and even rifle fire. The area of fiercest fighting 15 sq. kms, yet I only saw 200 meters. The Ethiopian Army was using First World War tactics with First World War results.[72]

There are few more challenging endeavors in modern war than to assault a defense-in-depth, especially when the attacker does not possess overwhelming superiority at the decision point. In that sense, the failed Ethiopian offensive in March is understandable, even predictable. Yet it is also hard to escape the conclusion that these successive waves were propelled by more than simple military necessity or difficulty in mastering the modern system. These frontal assaults are exactly what we would expect from an officer corps with prejudicial beliefs about targeted ethnic groups within the army. The cavalier attitude toward casualties; the acceptance of risk and the near-certainty of heavy casualties when launching an offensive with insufficient forces (as in March); and the subtle canalizing of the attack to reduce possible desertion avenues are all consistent with the military inequality thesis. Sometimes absences speak loudest; there were few armored personnel carriers among the ruins, suggesting an unwillingness to commit the resources necessary to protect infantry during their assaults.

69. Sundberg and Melander 2013.

70. Palut 2005, 99; "Ethiopia accuses Eritrea of propaganda campaign," *Reuters*, 17 March 1999.

71. Last 2004.

72. Quoted in Last 2004, 68–69.

In a 200-yard stretch, reporters from Britain, Switzerland, China and other countries counted the bodies of 300 Ethiopian soldiers, some halfway into the Eritrean trenches they died assaulting. The infantry apparently approached Eritrea's heavily fortified positions on foot, either behind or beside Soviet-made tanks. Twenty such tanks lay wrecked in an area that a BBC reporter described as the size of a soccer field. Two ruined bulldozers were also visible—but only one armored personnel carrier, the heavily armored vehicle that modern armies rely on to protect their infantry from withering fire.[73]

To be sure, Tigrayan-dominated armor units fought and suffered losses during Operation Sunset; marginalized ethnic groups like the Oromo were not entirely consigned to their fate alone. That mass indiscipline did not occur under these brutal conditions was due to the nature of their prewar treatment at the hands of the state. Facing discrimination but not overt state-sanctioned violence, ethnic ties were weaker, and grievances less salient, than if these groups had been exposed to collective violence. In that sense, the Eritrean POWs had it right: Ethiopian forces were, for the most part, united in their cause. Indeed, evidence suggests that voluntary recruitment among these groups spiked after the March debacle. Resentment over their second-class status was tempered with the realization that fighting well could lead to a revision of the social contract, as promised by the regime. Nonetheless, systematic discrimination was enough to distort Ethiopia's tactics and operations during Operation Sunset, producing a near-reckless disregard for casualties that made gains far more costly while narrowing the gap between victory and defeat in battle. Even at a (low) medium level of military inequality, the distorting effects of ethnic prejudice and inequality were apparent on the battlefield.

7.5. Shoestring Army: Assessing the DRC's Battlefield Performance

The FAC was wracked by three of the four problems captured by the battlefield performance index. More specifically, the FAC suffered greater casualties than it imposed on enemy forces. It also suffered both mass desertion and defection, as defined by Project Mars. Blocking detachments were never deployed, perhaps a function of the DRC's institutional and fiscal weakness, though extrajudicial punishments were levied against some of the most marginalized groups, including kadogo child soldiers from North and South

73. "Old Tactics, New Arms, Lethal Result," *Washington Post*, 21 March 1999.

Kivu. I explore the FAC's combat power and cohesion below before turning to the pivotal Katanga Offensive (October–December 2000), which neatly illustrates the dangers of high military inequality. Overall, the FAC's battlefield performance was among the worst recorded in our case studies, ranking near Kokand and late-stage Mahdiya in terms of unforced errors and self-imposed constraints.

7.5.1. Combat Power

The FAC's combat power is challenging to assess, for two reasons. First, the FAC rarely fought alone. Instead, limited training and rampant desertion, coupled with generally poor unit discipline, forced Kabila to enlist Zimbabwean and Angolan combat units to backstop his own efforts. Zimbabwean airstrikes were especially important for stiffening FAC resolve and beating back combined Rwandan and Burundian offensives.[74] "Kabila is like a man who starts six fires when he's only got one fire extinguisher," Jason Stearns noted. "The firefighters are the Zimbabwean Army."[75] Second, Kabila recruited and funded various militia, including the ALiR, FDD, and Mayi-Mayi, to act as both complements and substitutes for FAC forces.[76] These militia were variously tasked with controlling rear areas, guarding (and stealing from) mineral wealth, fighting behind the front lines in Rwandan-held territories, and participating in joint operations on the front lines, where the FAC was mostly confined. Hutu mercenary formations, often composed of ex-Interhamwe fighters, were also recruited to augment FAC combat power.[77] The fielding of these additional units frustrates a clean look at FAC performance, though their very presence is a clue that the FAC was struggling simply to maintain itself in the field, let alone excel at complicated tactics and operations.

Event data from ACLED, for example, reveals that the FAC fought 345 separate engagements with enemy forces from August 1998 to November

74. Rupiya 2002.

75. International Crisis Group 2000, 64.

76. The Army for the Liberation of Rwanda (Armée pour la Libération du Rwanda, ALiR) was a Hutu rebel organization that was aligned with Kabila and conducted guerrilla attacks against Rwandan forces in eastern Congo. The Forces for the Defense of Democracy (Forces pour la Défense de la Démocratie, FDD) was another pro-Kabila Hutu rebel organization most active in and around the mineral deposits of South Kivu and Katanga. The Mayi-Mayi were community-based militia that defended their local territories against Rwanda in eastern DRC.

77. The Interhamwe was a Hutu paramilitary organization that conducted ethnic cleansing against Tutsi during the Rwandan Genocide with the backing of Rwanda's Hutu-led government.

2002. Underscoring its battlefield difficulties, the FAC is only recorded as defeating its foe and regaining territory in 45 of these encounters (13 percent). The remaining incidents are either outright defeats that resulted in territory changing hands (64, or 19 percent) or stalemates (236, or 68 percent).[78]

The major battles of the war's opening phase (August–November 1998) also highlight the FAC's low combat proficiency. These battles took place in disjointed fashion by isolated FAC units and their foreign backers along front lines that were steadily creeping westward across the DRC. Take Rwanda's Operation Musako, launched in the Kivus in eastern DRC on 16 August 1998, for example. Seizing on Banyamulenge defection from local units, including the FAC's supposedly elite 12th Brigade, left remaining FAC soldiers unable to resist the advances of Rwanda's 75th Battalion. Its five brigades quickly overran FAC forces at Goma and Uvira; captured kadogo soldiers executed their own commanders and then joined Rwandan forces. Kabila's demonizing of the Tutsi Banyamulenge as pro-Rwanda led to their defection to advancing Rwandan units, taking with them some of the most experienced and skilled FAC soldiers. Indeed, the capture of the Goma and Uvira garrisons had been preceded by the spectacle of Katanga and kadogo soldiers sacking local Banyamulenge villages and executing members of their own units. Similar events transpired at Kalemie; its capture left North and South Kivu under Rwandan control with only light casualties.

The loss of eastern DRC compelled Zimbabwe to step up its intervention. Even with Zimbabwean reinforcements, however, the FAC struggled to mount sustained resistance to Rwandan advances. At the Battle of Kindu (5 October 1998), an ill-fated FAC offensive stalled out when entire FAC units melted away, though not before engaging in the systematic slaughter of civilian Tutsis. Despite outnumbering Rwandan forces, the FAC ended up ceding Kindu and its key airport to Rwandan troops. In a repeat performance, FAC forces lost control of Kalemie (November 1998) as its soldiers panicked under modest Rwandan rocket fire and abandoned their positions. Fear of indiscipline made FAC tactics brutally simple: FAC units were to follow a Zimbabwean advance guard into battle, and instructed not to exercise independent decision-making. Many of these units were still composed of ethnic groups that had been marginalized or ostracized by Kabila. His plan to seed the FAC with loyal Katangans—themselves divided into factions with variable allegiance to Kabila—had yet to be fully implemented. In fact, these initial efforts created a mismatch between Katangan officers and rank and file drawn from populations that had been targeted by Kabila or that had been lost to Rwanda in the war's opening phase.

78. Raleigh and Karlsen 2010.

By 1999, the FAC had settled upon a somewhat improved array of tactics and operational art. FAC forces would now be deployed behind newly recruited Hutu mercenaries and in front of Zimbabwean and Angolan armored formations. This sandwich pattern was designed to boost combat power by foreclosing opportunities to defect forwards or desert backwards. A new recruitment drive brought additional Katangans and kadogo into the fold while reducing Banyamulenge presence. Training was bolstered; these new soldiers were deemed somewhat more reliable than the previous ethnic distribution. Kabila also tried to whip up Congolese nationalism by decrying Rwandan invaders and their Tutsi fifth column. Yet despite these changes, and the continued heavy use of airpower, the FAC still lost ground, suffering defeats at Manono and Lusambo (June 1999). The outcome at Lusambo was especially crushing; a large FAC force had been caught with only minimal Zimbabwean (and Namibian) support, and disintegrated under Rwandan fire. Shocked, Kabila sought a reprieve at the negotiating table, signing the Lusaka Cease-fire Agreement, pausing hostilities until a more propitious time.

Relative casualties, the second component of combat power, are also difficult to estimate with precision. Yet it is clear that the FAC never approached parity with Rwandan or Burundian losses. Even with heavy air support, foreign assistance, and the participation of various militia, the FAC still lost about 2.2 soldiers for every enemy soldier they killed. The need to simplify tactics to deter desertion and defection, along with the inherent difficulties of coalitional war, all conspired to drive up casualties. It is also worth noting that while Rwandan forces were quite proficient, they suffered from their own coordination problems, unfavorable force ratios, the absence of airpower, and increasingly long and complicated logistics, not to mention the need to fight off militia attacks. As a result, the legacy of prewar discrimination and collective violence was a hobbled military that struggled to stay in the field against weaker opponents. By the end of 1999, the DRC had lost nearly half its territory to Rwanda and its allies.

7.5.2. Cohesion

It is fitting that the Second Congo War began not with a skirmish but a mutiny over army reform.[79] The warning signs were there; even in the prewar era, the FAC's ethnic composition was deemed "explosive," as nearly all of its constituent ethnic groups resented the hierarchies of inequality that persisted within and outside the "new" army. The fuse was lit on 23 February 1998,

---

79. The DRC is one of eight African cases where (partial) army dissolution led to subsequent war in the 1990s alone. See Young 2002, 25.

when soldiers of the 10th Brigade mutinied in response to efforts by Kabila's handpicked officers to scatter the unit's Banyamulenge majority across different brigades throughout the DRC.[80] Matters were complicated by the continued presence of Rwandan soldiers in the DRC—nearly universally reviled by the populace and soldiers alike—and the embedding of Rwandan officers in the FAC's senior leadership. Suspecting that Kabila would move against Rwandan officers, the chief of staff of the 10th Brigade, a Rwandan named James Kaberbe, began stacking its ethnic deck. He decreased pro-Kabila kadogo child soldiers (nearly all drawn from North and South Kivu) and bolstered the ranks of those opposed to Kabila, including non-Baluba Katangans, Banyarwanda Tutsi from North Kivu, and Banyamulenge. The 10th Brigade grew to nearly sixteen thousand soldiers, all of uncertain loyalty to Kinshasa. On 27 July, Kabila demanded the withdrawal of all Rwandan forces from the DRC, including the army. On 2 August, the 10th Brigade mutinied (again), throwing their allegiance behind Rwanda while requesting its aid in overthrowing Kabila.[81] They didn't have long to wait; on 3 August, Rwanda invaded in a daring aerial assault at Kitona that was led by Kaberbe himself. The war was on.[82]

Ethnic hierarchies within the FAC also created problems with coordination and unit discipline. For example, a recurrent theme in postwar interviews with ex-FAC soldiers is how hatred of their mostly Katangese officers corroded morale and bred indiscipline. "We are hungry. We don't get anything. They cheat us," recounted one soldier. "According to the rules we are supposed to get rations, food, medical care, but now there is nothing. So tell me, how can we be disciplined? They all cheat us. Our superiors cheat us. We die and our children die."[83] Another argued that "there are no bad soldiers. It is our leaders/superiors [mikonzi] that are bad. They don't care about us. We don't get anything, no food, no training.... They are bad. And if there is one rotten orange in a bag, it will make all oranges in the sack rot."[84]

Mass indiscipline was thus deeply woven into the FAC's fabric. By one estimate, the FAC lost up to 60 percent of its soldiers to desertion or defection during the war.[85] Mutinies were also a constant danger; twenty-six were

80. On the ties between the military and business in the Kivus, see Verweijen 2013.

81. On the defection of the 10th Brigade, see especially Carayannis 2003, 242; Prunier 2009, 175–84; Cooper 2013, 7; Roessler 2016, 337–56. The elite 22nd Brigade, stationed in South Kivu, also defected on 2 August.

82. Subsequent efforts to mix units ethnically among the FDD in 2000 were also met with mass desertion. See Kisangani 2003, 63.

83. Quoted in Baaz and Stern 2008, 76.

84. Quoted in Ibid., 77.

85. Stearns 2011, 272.

recorded by ACLED in 1998 alone.[86] Curiously, blocking detachments do not appear to have been deployed, a somewhat unusual decision for a belligerent with such high military inequality. It is possible that the Zimbabwean, Angolan, and Namibian forces that deployed to the rear of FAC units (by late 1999) might have acted as substitutes for blocking detachments. These units acted as security blankets to reassure FAC contingents while also prodding them forward. Zimbabwean airstrikes might have performed the same role, manufacturing greater cohesion by encouraging FAC units to stand and fight. Fratricidal violence was not totally absent, however. An unlucky FAC commander was arrested after he ordered his troops to withdraw in the face of Rwandan attacks at Lubao in January 1999. He was subsequently arrested, along with dozens of his soldiers; twenty-seven were executed. The Military Order Court (Cour d'Ordre Militaire) also sentenced soldiers to death for perceived cowardice and desertion, sometimes after simply following orders to retreat.[87] In fact, the turn to child soldiers was driven partly out of belief that they would be easier to manage than adults, cutting down the risk of desertion and defection.[88]

Finally, indiscipline manifested itself in the form of predation on the civilian population. FAC soldiers and deserters alike engaged in widespread looting and pillage among local populations to sustain themselves. Roadblocks and taxes also became important tools for starved units to feed themselves. Violence, too, was unleashed on locals, generating a double war in which FAC units were simultaneously fighting foreign armies and ransacking local populations. Event data from ACLED captured forty-nine incidents of the FAC engaging in one-sided violence against civilians during 1998–2001; the true count is likely far higher, given the ubiquity of roadblocks and checkpoints in villages near the frontlines.[89] These campaigns undercut military preparedness and increased grievances against the regime among soldiers whose coethnics fell victim to these FAC excesses.[90] By comparison, soldiers in the accompanying Zimbabwean Army did engage in petty corruption, often selling their rations on the black market in nearby villages.[91] But these units never approached the level of violence and corruption that were a hallmark of most FAC units.

86. Raleigh and Karlsen 2010.

87. Amnesty International 2000, 8.

88. "The Calm in the Eye of Congo," *Christian Science Monitor*, 7 May 2001; Stearns 2011, 272.

89. Raleigh and Karlsen 2010.

90. Laudati 2013.

91. Maringira 2017.

These cohesion problems predated the war itself and did not stem from heavy casualties, which were fairly light in an absolute sense. Like the late-stage Mahdiya's army, the FAC found itself waging war with a dwindling group of regime loyalists. By mid-1999, if not well before, most of the ethnic groups that comprised the FAC had been sidelined (non-Baluba Katangans), discredited and then repressed (the Tutsi Banyamulenge), or recruited precisely because of their marginal social status (the kadogo). Systematic abuse of local populations by the FAC and its militia created a feedback loop in which grievances were reinforced against the Kabila regime, further sapping willingness to fight. Kabila did adopt the rhetoric of Congolese nationalism, but it was a thin gruel for members of victimized groups. Ethnic identities not only persisted in the new FAC; they appear to have been hardened by participation in its ranks. Kabila even sabotaged the inter-Congolese dialogue mandated by the Lusaka Cease-fire Agreement.[92] In doing so, he shuttered the last remaining avenue for credible movement toward a more inclusive foundation for the DRC's political community and its army. The result would be weak ties between the regime and soldiers, disillusionment with the war, and a renewed sense of grievance that produced indiscipline on a massive scale.

7.5.3. Case Study: The Katanga Offensive, October–December 2000

The Katanga offensive witnessed the largest, and last, major battles of the Second Congo War. By October 2000, the ragtag FAC was stationed in clumps across a 2,250-kilometer front line that stretched from Mbankada on the DRC's western border to Kananga before terminating at Pweto, perched on the shore of Lake Mweru in southwestern DRC (see figure 7.2). Embattled, and desperately seeking a quick win, Kabila was intrigued by the sudden unilateral withdrawal of Rwandan forces in Katanga province in September 2000. He demanded a lightning offensive against the suddenly exposed remaining Rwandan and Burundian forces that hunkered down in fetid trenches that crisscrossed the lightly populated region between Lake Mweru and Lake Tanganyika. "This time," Kabila promised, "we will break their back."[93] His generals were less confident; his son, General Joseph Kabila, was even less so, and accepted his promotion to command the FAC offensive with alarm. Kabila's most important ally, Zimbabwe, was tired of war, having cratered its economy supporting Kabila's campaigns.[94] Kabila nonetheless

---

92. "Congo Looks for Leadership; Isolated Kabila Can't Win War, but Can't Face Peace," *Washington Post*, 30 October 2000.

93. Quoted in Stearns 2011.

94. Rupiya 2002.

shook $20 million loose to support the operation and began marshaling forces near Pweto. The next two months would ruthlessly expose the problems imposed by high military inequality. The FAC had more soldiers and better equipment than its foes, and enjoyed both air superiority and the advantage of choosing the time and place of its opening blow. Yet its initial gains were quickly reversed, gradually giving way to the spectacle of FAC brigades being chased 170 kilometers by light Rwandan infantry, with soldiers abandoning their equipment and deserting in droves.[95] The collapse of the FAC stands in sharp contrast to Ethiopia's impressive Third Offensive launched earlier that same year.

By early October, the FAC had positioned eight brigades of mechanized infantry, about 10,000 soldiers in total, for their assault near Pepa. Most of these soldiers were kadogo, drawn principally from North and South Kivu.[96] They were sandwiched between Hutu brigades, staffed mostly from ex-Interhamwe mercenaries, who formed the spearhead of attacking forces, and Zimbabwean armored units, who brought up the rear, providing fire support from Type-59 and Type-62 tanks, howitzers, and Cascavel armored cars. Zimbabwean aircraft, including Hawks and Chinese Chengdu J-7s, provided close support along with Mi-35 Hind helicopters and a handful of FAC Su-25 ground attack aircraft. Opposing these forces was a combined Rwanda-Burundi force of about 3,000 infantry, with no air support and only crew-served weapons. The decisive blow was to land at Mutoto Moya, a small town near Pepa, about 170 kilometers north of Pweto, where the two sides occupied opposing trench lines that stretched thirteen kilometers. Rwandan and Burundian forces were clearly spread thin, with only 231 soldiers per kilometer in a single trench line with no reserves, and they were outnumbered over 4:1 by approaching FAC units.[97]

On 15 October, these FAC brigades, tucked in behind a Hutu vanguard, advanced across the two kilometers of no-man's-land that separated the opposing forces at Mutoto Moya. Crushed by overwhelming numbers, Rwandan and Burundian forces retreated, falling back in good order to Pepa, about 45 kilometers distant. The fortified town, squatting amidst an enormous cattle ranch perched near the southern tip of Lake Tanganyika, was invested by trailing FAC forces on 16 October. Once again led by Hutu formations, the eight brigades charged across the rangeland, followed closely

95. "Desperate Battle Defines Congo's Warlike Peace," *Washington Post*, 2 January 2001.

96. These FAC units were mostly monoethnic. See Carayannis 2003, 234–35.

97. Unusually, militia and irregular forces played only a minor role during the offensive, typically providing follow-on or holding forces. Rwanda, for example, had forced its RCD allies to withdraw, citing their poor conduct. We therefore are able to assess FAC's performance in a more straightforward fashion. See Scherrer 2002.

by Zimbabwean mechanized forces. Overrunning foxholes and defensive fortifications, attacking FAC forces pushed Rwandan and Burundian forces from the town. "They were coming in big numbers, really very big numbers,"[98] said Lt. Col. John Tibesigwa, Rwanda's commander at Pepa. Pressing home their advantage, FAC detachments seized the hill that loomed over Pepa as Rwandan forces withdrew, regrouping at Moba and Moliro. The offensive stalled, however, as episodic skirmishes and airstrikes failed to dislodge Rwandan detachments still encamped near Pepa. Worse, kadogo soldiers, beginning to tire of seemingly unending sacrifices for little gain, started to slowly melt away.

The FAC would advance no farther. Some 6,000 Rwandan and Burundian reinforcements began arriving on 1 November. Their commanders were explicitly warned of the price—"Don't even try to come back to Rwanda"[99]— of failing to capture Pepa. On 5 November, Rwanda kicked off a four-day battle to wrest Pepa away. In some of the most intense fighting of the war, Rwandan infantry were tasked with charging up the FAC-controlled hill, into the teeth of mortar and artillery fire without the benefit of counter-battery fire or covering airstrikes. Waves of infantry were simply mowed down; "it was like those movies I saw of the Americans at Iwo Jima,"[100] recounted one participant. Two days and hundreds of casualties later, Rwandan commanders changed their approach. They ordered a light mobile battalion, stripped of everything but their weapons, to outflank FAC positions and attack from the rear. A frontal assault would keep the defenders occupied while the battalion slipped behind. Covering ground in a night march, the battalion emerged unnoticed, breaking through the FAC's weak rearguard and pinning their main formation between the two advancing Rwandan-Burundian forces. Outmaneuvered, FAC forces tried to surrender but were killed by revenge-seeking Rwandan forces. Most FAC soldiers managed to slip away, streaming back to Pweto, where the FAC's HQ (and General Joseph Kabila) was located. On 5 November, Pepa was once again in enemy hands.[101]

Bedraggled FAC formations, along with their Hutu and Zimbabwean minders, now began a slow, halting retreat from Pepa to Pweto, a nearly 170-kilometer journey along a single road through cattle country. Their armored vehicles tethered them to the road, a liability not shared by the

98. Quoted in "Desperate Battle Defines Congo's Warlike Peace," *Washington Post*, 2 January 2001.

99. Stearns 2011.

100. Quoted in Stearns 2011.

101. "Rwandan army, DRCongo rebels recapture eastern town," *BBC Monitoring*, 10 November 2000.

Rwandan and Burundian mobile light infantry units now in pursuit. For three weeks, a running battle of sorts unfolded, with FAC forces pursued by day and then ambushed from the roadside's flanks at night. FAC cantonments were set up on high ground above the road at night, with soldiers bedded down in fox-holes and bunkers for protection. Opposing forces easily maneuvered around sentries, outflanking FAC camps from the surrounding woods to catch iso-lated units in deadly cross fire. As one FAC soldier recounted, "The Rwandans are very strong; they do flanking actions. They get around behind people. That's how they fight. They used the right tactics. They came when we were resting, and we'd be distracted."[102] Every village stop along the way was an occasion for a firefight; half these villages had prepared defenses, but all were abandoned in panic. "We would pursue them very closely," said a Rwandan commander. "That's the secret. We don't give them any time."[103]

Developments occurring off-stage in Kinshasa also contributed to the unraveling of the FAC offensive. On 21 October, Kabila ordered the arrest of Anselme Masasu Nindaga, a spiritual advisor to the kadogo and one of the founding members of the guerrilla forces that helped Kabila overthrow Mobutu in 1997. Half Tutsi, and suspected of plotting a coup against Kabila, Nindaga became a rallying cry for the kadogo. They rioted in Kinshasa, forcing Kabila to order a wave of mass arrests that sparked firefights with local authorities. An estimated thirty-six kadogo were killed, while hundreds more were arrested or sought refuge in Brazzaville. Of those arrested, ninety-three from the Kivus and Maniema province were tortured and executed as co-conspirators.[104] And, in a ploy reminiscent of the Khalifa at Metem-meh (1897) or 'Alimqul at Chimkent (1864), Kabil had Nindaga transported to Pweto. There, he was executed on 24 November, just as the first groups of kadogo soldiers arrived in the city. The gambit (predictably) backfired; kadogo morale, already strained, now broke, and dozens of soldiers deserted as news spread of Nindaga's murder.[105]

On 1 December, Rwandan and Burundian forces had reached Pweto's outskirts. After brief skirmishes, panic began to ripple through jittery FAC forces.[106] Desertion now spread through the kadogo brigades.[107] On

102. Quoted in "Desperate Battle Defines Congo's Warlike Peace," *Washington Post*, 2 January 2001.

103. Ibid.

104. On the kadogo and child soldiers in DRC, see Cheuzeville 2003.

105. There is some speculation that Kabila, worried about his control over the kadogo, had initiated the Katanga operation as a means of culling his potential opponents, much like the Khalifa during the 1887 Egyptian expedition (see Chapter 3).

106. UCDP data records only 230 casualties for the battle at Pweto, suggesting most soldiers were more intent on fleeing than fighting.

107. Reyntjens 2009, 162.

3 December, Rwandan forces entered Pweto for the first time, encountering a spectacle of 50,000 civilians fleeing along clogged roads, abandoned and burning armored vehicles, and remnants of FAC and Zimbabwean units doing their best to blend in with refugees heading for the nearby Zambian border. FAC commanders had made an especially egregious mistake; they had shipped all their armored vehicles into Pweto on a single, rickety ferry. Desperate to evacuate, panicked soldiers tried to load a 40-ton T-62 tank on it but misjudged their approach, capsizing the ferry. Now stranded, FAC soldiers set alight their neat rows of tanks and armored scout cars, burning thirty-three in all before Rwandan forces could capture them. Other vehicles were disabled and then shoved ignominiously off the roads to clear escape routes. Some soldiers drowned in their haste to ford the nearby river. The HQ staff burned their Mi-17 helicopter—its fuel had been siphoned off and sold on the black market—and fled, abandoning their soldiers.[108] Compounding the confusion, a contingent of kadogo chose this moment to switch sides.[109] Only a last-ditch intervention by Zimbabwean forces using CASA STOL transports managed to recover their soldiers, though they were forced to abandon their equipment and ammunition.[110] "We are victims," one FAC commander lamented, "of our own ineptitude."[111]

In total, at least 5,000 FAC soldiers, mostly kadogo, along with 2,000 Hutu mercenaries and about 300 Zimbabweans sought sanctuary in neighboring Zambia.[112] Their brief internment pulled back the curtain on rarely seen internal FAC practices and, in particular, how inequality conditioned treatment of rank and file by their mostly Katangese commanders. Logistics and resupply, for example, were poor, as the kadogo were deemed far more expendable than soldiers from favored ethnic groups. One kadogo who deserted at Pweto recalled his predicament: "We were waiting for food and supplies, for we were running short of ammunition and had no food at all. They only sent us two trucks full of beer and oranges."[113] Corrupt officers also siphoned off soldiers' salaries; many kadogo reported that they had not been paid since Kabila took power.[114] Unsurprisingly, the interned soldiers expressed little support for either Kabila or his war: "Our feeling is to have been deceived by this

108. Prunier 2009, 252–53; Cooper 2013, 55–56.

109. "Rebels capture key city in Congo," *The Guardian*, 11 December 2000.

110. "Zimbabwe reports 'serious fighting' in southeastern DR Congo," *BBC Monitoring*, 6 December 2000.

111. Quoted in Stearns 2011.

112. International Crisis Group 2000. "Zambia Gets New Influx From Congo," *Reuters*, 20 December 2000.

113. Tshiband 2009, 24.

114. IRIN Update #1076 for the Great Lakes, 19 December 2000.

man who showed almost no interest in our own lives."[115] Even officers from favored groups expressed war weariness. As one FAC commander reported in January 2001, "We're tired of Kabila's war and we don't even know why we're fighting."[116]

Perhaps the most shocking microlevel expression of inequality's effects on the battlefield is how it skewed medical treatment for wounded soldiers. Ndongala Kasiswa, a former FAC captain who renounced his military service while awaiting repatriation in Zambia, reported that Kabila had issued standing orders to officers to kill their own wounded soldiers:

> If a man is wounded, that man is as good as dead. We have received orders from our command to kill every wounded man, and we have been told that it is too expensive to fly them to hospitals in Kalemie or Lubumbashi. We have an order to end their lives. I killed them and I know that many have been killed.[117]

One undoubtedly relieved kadogo soldier proclaimed that "we are bitter but happy to have ended our military roles."[118] Kabila, however, was not quite finished with his kadogo soldiers. He ordered deserters, as well as his own son, to be arrested, even as he commanded a fresh infusion of FAC and Zimbabwean forces to shore up defenses between Kasenga and Pweto.[119] Pressure from the United States and United Nations on Rwanda to stay its hand likely saved the FAC from even greater battlefield losses, including potentially all of Katanga province and Liumbashi itself.[120] International pressure could not save Kabila himself, however. In a fitting coda to the Katanga offensive, Kabila presided over the execution of forty-seven kadogo soldiers on 15 January. It would be one of his final official acts as president. The next day, he was assassinated by a teenage kadogo soldier angered by the crushing defeat at Pweto and Kabila's cavalier treatment of his kadogo units. Kabila's war was over; the consequences of his disastrous decisions, however, continue to be felt.[121]

115. Quoted in IRIN Update #1076 for the Great Lakes, 19 December 2000.

116. Ngolet 2011, 114.

117. "Congo troops say ordered to kill wounded comrades," *Reuters*, 18 December 2000.

118. Ibid.

119. Stearns 2011, 307; Scherrer 2002, 289; Reyntjens 2009, 200.

120. "UN Council Urges Rwanda, Uganda to Withdraw Troops," *Chicago Tribune*, 29 December 2000.

121. "Revealed: how Africa's dictator died at the hands of his boy soldiers," *Guardian*, 10 February 2001; "Make or break for Congo's new Kabila," *Mail & Guardian*, 19 January 2001. For an overview of theories about Kabila's death, see Roessler and Verhoeven 2016, 403–5.

7.6.   Discussion

These cases provide new insights into how military inequality can affect two wartime processes. Evidence from the other chapters supports the claim, for example, that as military inequality increases, so too do the odds of witnessing a belligerent's use of violence against targeted ethnic groups within its own state during wartime. These so-called double wars were observed in Austria-Hungary (0.374), Khalifa's Mahdiya (0.67), and Kokand (0.70). The DRC's wartime experience is also consistent with this trend, as both the FAC and FAC-aligned militia engaged in systematic and widespread victimization of the civilian population, typically across ethnic lines, for much of the war. As we approach the midpoint of the military inequality coefficient, it appears that the likelihood of state-orchestrated categorical violence during wartime also increases. This is a conjecture that requires additional testing, of course. Yet it is instructive that Ethiopia, too, chose to expel a small number of Eritreans at the start of the war. It also denaturalized some individuals, though it did not do so collectively.[122] As a result, it is possible that the Ethiopian case demarcates the line where wartime collective targeting begins to be considered as state policy. Lower levels of inequality may be associated with more administrative and targeted efforts; at higher levels of inequality, states turn to violence, drawing once again on prewar patterns of mass-based violence and repression.

Much of the book's theoretical discussion and empirical evidence has focused on how armies use "in-house" solutions to manage the downstream consequences of inequality. The FAC suggests that another pathway is possible, namely, reliance on foreign backers and extra-institutional militia as an exoskeleton—or a set of crutches—to maintain combat power and cohesion.[123] Without recourse to these strategies, the FAC likely would have disintegrated entirely, possibly in the war's opening days. These substitution strategies are decidedly inefficient. Reliance on Zimbabwean and Angolan units introduced an assortment of coordination problems, interoperability issues, mixed motives, and even language difficulties. Control over the various militia was beset by principal-agent problems, rogue commanders (and soldiers), inter-militia rivalries, and forced recruitment drives. In short, these strategies created as many problems as they appeared to solve, or at least postpone, for FAC commanders. That commanders felt that militia were a viable,

---

122. Murphy, Kidane and Snider 2013, 304–61.

123. On the dynamics of non-state armed group formation and violence during the war, see Fjelde, Hultman and Nilsson 2019; Lake 2017; Richards 2014; Autesserre 2010.

indeed necessary, option is an indication of just how badly military inequality can distort and undermine a belligerent's army.

7.7. Conclusion

This chapter has extended the military inequality argument to the modern era by drawing on two similar belligerents, Ethiopia and the DRC, that were mired in the throes of state- and nation-building. Existing theories struggle to explain the divergence in their battlefield performance. After all, the belligerents both enjoyed material preponderance over their much smaller neighbors, had similar political systems, fought with identical weapons systems purchased from the same suppliers, and had foreign advisors embedded within their command structures. They both launched near simultaneous offensives in which they enjoyed favorable local force-to-force and force-to-space balances. It's true that the Ethiopian Army was likely more "coup-proofed" than the FAC; efforts to impose central control over FAC units through forced integration ultimately produced mutiny. But the observed difference in battlefield performance between these two belligerents is the opposite anticipated by a coup-proofing argument; it is the successfully coup-proofed military that should struggle on the conventional battlefield (by design).[124] A focus on military inequality, by contrast, alerts us to the possibility of sharp battlefield variation between Ethiopia (0.24) and the DRC (0.55). Prewar ethnic discrimination did influence Ethiopian tactics and operations, helping to promote a callousness to marginalized ethnic groups that ballooned casualties needlessly. But Ethiopia did manage to escape the binding constraints imposed by higher levels of military inequality. The FAC's rapid breakdown, its cycles of consolidation and collapse, and its chronic problem of mass indiscipline all arose from Kabila's prewar decisions to build his army, and his state, atop a narrow ethnocratic vision that grew increasingly xenophobic and bigoted as the war dragged on.

---

124. Talmadge 2015; Pilster and Böhmelt 2012, 2011; Miller 2013; Belkin and Schofer 2003; Quinlivan 1999; Luttwak 1968; Brooks 2006; Feaver 2003; Biddle and Zirkle 1996.

PART III

Extensions and Conclusions

8

The Battle of Moscow

MICROLEVEL EVIDENCE

Victory is forged before battle.

GENERAL IVAN VASIL'EVICH PANFILOV, 1941

AS DAWN BROKE on the morning of 17 November 1941, Abdrasit Ziiaev, a twenty-seven-year old Red Army infantryman, found himself bundled tightly against the cold in a narrow slit trench outside the tiny village of Sloboda, some fifty kilometers due west of Moscow.[1] His unit, the 78th Rifle Division, hummed with activity around him. Tasked with defending the key Volokolamsk-Moscow highway, the 78th Rifle Division, along with its sister divisions in the 16th Army, had borne the brunt of the renewed offensive that Germany had unleashed on 15 November. Since its opening gambit on 22 June 1941, the German Wehrmacht had driven the Red Army back hundreds of kilometers, right to the outskirts of Moscow itself. In less than six months, the Red Army had suffered 2.12 million casualties; German losses totaled 135,221.[2] Operation Typhoon, launched on 2 October, had pushed the Red Army to the brink of collapse. Now the Wehrmacht sought to deliver the final blow that, in Chief of Staff General Franz Halder's words, would "break the back"[3] of the Red Army, leaving Moscow exposed and the Soviet regime imperiled. The outcome of the Second World War "now hung in the balance."[4]

Desperate to slow the German advance, if only temporarily, the 78th Rifle Division's commanders ordered a late-morning counteroffensive on the

1. "Zhurnal boevykh deistvii voisk Zapadnogo fronta za noiabr' 1941 g.," TsAMO Fond: 208, Opis': 2511, Delo: 219, List: 1, s.106

2. Lopukhovsky and Kavalerchik 2017, 71.

3. Quoted in Hartmann 2013, 51.

4. Roberts 2011, 175.

seventeenth, spring-boarding from Sloboda to strike German forces clustered near Mikhailovskoe.[5] Ziiaev never reached Mikhailovskoe, however. Amidst the confusion of the counterattack, which raged for three days until the 78th was driven back, he disappeared (*propal bez vesti*).[6] His disappearance could, of course, be chalked up to the unpredictability of an ever-shifting battlefield and the destructive nature of high-intensity warfare. Yet a closer look at the circumstances of his disappearance suggest a different story. Ziiaev was an Uzbek, born in the Ferghana Valley, a hotbed of resistance to Soviet power as well as the site of exceptionally brutal forced collectivization. On the day he went missing, at least seventy other soldiers also failed to join the counterattack, one of the largest single-day episodes of disappearances recorded by the 78th.[7] Nearly all were fellow Uzbeks who were recruited from the same few urban centers in the Uzbek Soviet Republic. They were also marshaled into military service from the same training centers. Rather than a lone unfortunate case of a soldier's disappearance, Ziiaev example alerts us to the possibility that strong coethnic networks, forged by shared prewar experiences with Soviet repression, might be robust enough to survive even the harsh conditions of the Battle of Moscow.

This chapter takes up the challenge of demonstrating how military inequality explains the battlefield performance of individual Soviet rifle divisions and their soldiers during one of the most important, and lethal, battles of the twentieth century. The scale of the Battle of Moscow (October–December 1941) defies easy description. It involved some of the largest concentrations of soldiers and armored vehicles in history, with 1.1 million casualties recorded during these fateful two months.[8] Remarkably, this butcher's bill of casualties approximates the 1.5 million battle fatalities recorded in *all* wars from 1989–2015.[9] The battle's high political and military stakes pose a difficult test for the book's military inequality argument. Existing theories suggest that high-intensity wars are characterized by extreme constraints on soldier decision-making and choices. Preexisting ethnic identities are thus liabilities

5. "Zhurnal boevykh deistvii voisk Zapadnogo fronta za noiabr' 1941 g.," TsAMO Fond: 208, Opis': 2511, Delo: 219, List: 1, s.113,119.

6. His service file (ID: #51994460) can be found at TsAMO Fond: 58, Opis': 818883; Delo: 1113.

7. As detailed below, these data are drawn from declassified personnel records from the 78th Rifle Division archived by the OBD Memorial project (https://obd-memorial.ru/html/).

8. Lopukhovsky and Kavalerchik 2017, 37.

9. Melander, Pettersson and Themnér 2016. Credible estimates suggest 16.7 million soldiers were killed on the Eastern Front, 1941–45 (Hartmann 2013, 157; Erlikhman 2004, 20–21; Krivosheev 2009, 85). By contrast, an estimated 16.2 million battle fatalities were inflicted during all civil wars fought from 1945 to 1999 combined (Fearon and Laitin 2003, 75).

in these environments if they undercut the efficient production of violence, and so should be abandoned as soon as the costs of attachment outweigh their benefits. Moreover, the Eastern Front in general, and the Battle of Moscow in particular, has been a touchstone case for theories of military effectiveness that privilege alternative factors such as Soviet manpower advantages, ideology, technological advances such as the modern T-34 tank, and the role of Lend-Lease in bolstering Soviet battlefield fortunes.[10]

By contrast, I treat the Soviet Union as a multiethnic empire simultaneously engaged in nation-building and nation-destroying. Soviet institutions not only encouraged the creation of national minorities and their attendant identities but also worked to entrench a specific ethnic hierarchy, one with Russians entrenched firmly at the top.[11] Designed to transcend "narrow" preexisting nationalisms, and faced with a diverse population, Soviet leaders sought to redefine the political community around Communist principles that would bind allegiance to the new regime. Such efforts were inherently violent. Between 1925 and 1939, Lenin and then Stalin brought the full weight of the Soviet state to bear on targeted ethnic groups. These campaigns included: a counterinsurgency campaign against Chechens and Ingush in the Northern Caucasus;[12] the systematic targeting and destruction of the *kulak* class, an ideological category dominated by Ukrainians and Belorussians; a near-genocidal campaign of famine that killed millions of Ukrainians[13] and Kazakhs;[14] the forced movement of minority populations, including Germans, Koreans, Poles, and Jews away from borderlands;[15] and a long-running campaign against Turkish *Basmachi* in Soviet Turkestan.[16]

The Red Army mirrored the divided and unequal nature of the Soviet political community. An estimated eight of the thirty-four million soldiers mobilized for war from 1941 to 1945 were non-Slavic.[17] The proportion of non-Russians among soldiers who saw combat was even higher, with ethnic

10. The literature on the Eastern Front is vast. Key English-language works include: Glantz and House 2014; Citino 2012; Stahel 2012; Hardesty and Grinberg 2012; Reese 2011; Citino 2007; Merridale 2006; Glantz 2005*b, a*; Glantz and House 1999; Erickson 1999*b, a*; Glantz and House 2015.

11. Harris 2013; Brandenburger 2011, 2002; Martin 2001; Slezkine 1994.

12. Gapurov, Izraiilov and Tovsultanov 2007.

13. Snyder 2010; Danilov, Manning and Viola 2006; Conquest 1986.

14. Cameron 2018; Carmack 2015.

15. Naimark 2010.

16. Gusterin 2014; Broxup 1983; Olcott 1981.

17. Glantz 2005*b*, 548–51, 604.

Russians representing between 51 and 60 percent of fielded forces.[18] Soviet rifle divisions, the basic building block of the Red Army, also exhibited substantial variation in their degree of ethnic heterogeneity, creating comparisons that can be used to estimate the effects of inequality on divisional battlefield performance.[19]

I therefore draw on the battlefield experiences of four similar rifle divisions of the 16th Army, the largest of seven armies that the Soviet General Staff had amassed to bar German advances toward Moscow on the Western Front's right wing. I focus mainly on Germany's initiation of Operation Typhoon and its eventual stalling out (2 October–5 December 1941). The first comparison pairs the 38th and 108th Rifle Divisions, two units fighting nearly side by side to blunt the opening thrusts of Operation Typhoon. The 38th was quickly overrun and so thoroughly destroyed that its very existence was scrubbed from official Soviet accounts. The 108th, however, fought its way out of encirclement, maneuvering some 320 kilometers over two weeks to resurface in the Soviet rear, though having lost nearly two-thirds of its solders as battlefield casualties. Next, I compare the 78th and 316th Rifle Divisions over a three-week period (15 November to 5 December). The 78th emerged from these battles as a highly decorated Guards Division, its soldiers mostly fighting tenaciously against larger German formations, though with occasional bouts of large-scale desertion. Its counterpart fared less well. Though the 316th would also be awarded Guards designation, its soldiers were more prone to desertion and its commanders far more reliant on coercion, including blocking detachments (*zagraditelnye otriady*), to force its soldiers to fight. While the 78th spearheaded the Soviet counteroffensive (6–25 December), the 316th, beset by discipline problems and depleted by heavy casualties, was pulled from the front lines and relegated to reserve status. Together, these divisions run the gamut of performance from decorated to destroyed, a pattern driven by their respective levels of military inequality.

To compare these units, I weave together daily narratives for each division from multiple declassified Soviet sources. These include General Staff and Western Front headquarters' operational summaries for the 16th Army;[20]

18. From these estimates, we can derive high (0.49), low (0.40), and mean (0.445) estimates for the Soviet Union's military inequality coefficient, with all non-Russian ethnic groups treated as experiencing state-directed repression in the five years before the war.

19. The Red Army mobilized and deployed 222 rifle divisions between July and December 1941. See Askey 2016, 264.

20. For General Staff (*GenShtab*) records, see especially Zhilin 2001*a, b*. For Western Front (*ZapF*) records, see the Central Archive of the USSR Ministry of Defense (hereafter, TsAMO) archival repository maintained by "Pamiat' Naroda" (https://pamyat-naroda.ru/). I cite these documents using TsAMO's Fond/Opis' Pamiat'/Delo/List classification system.

daily "war logs" for each division;[21] and thousands of individual records for each division's soldiers, which provide basic personal information as well as their fate, whether killed, wounded, missing, or punished by military authorities.[22] I supplement these materials with once-secret material from state security agencies and participant memoirs.[23] Especially helpful were declassified maps drawn by General Staff and Western Front headquarters staff that tracked the emplacement and movement of these divisions over time.[24] Despite my best efforts, there are still holes in these narratives. Some files remain sealed or are inaccessible to foreigners. The chaos of 1941 battlefields rendered reliable record-keeping of casualties and even unit locations a secondary concern for divisional staff.[25] Soviet propaganda, both during the war and after, has also distorted the historical record, especially concerning the 316th Rifle Division.[26] These caveats aside, sufficient evidence exists to trace how inequality-induced pathologies explain both each division's performance and the patterns of resilience and retreat across these units.

8.1. Setting the Stage: The 16th Army, October 1941

On the eve of Operation Typhoon, the Red Army assembled 1.25 million soldiers, 849 tanks, 7,600 artillery pieces, and 936 aircraft across a front that stretched from Leningrad to the Crimea, nearly 730 kilometers in total. Arrayed against them was the Wehrmacht's powerful Army Group Center, with 1.929 million soldiers (1.8 million of whom actually participated in the operation), along with at least 1,700 tanks and 1,387 aircraft.[27] As these balance of forces suggest, the Red Army, far from a colossus of unlimited manpower and equipment, was continually outnumbered during this winter

21. See, for example, "Zhurnal boevykh deistvii. Daty sozdaniia dokumenta: s 1.10.1941 po 31.10.1941 g.," TsAMO, Fond: 208, Opis': 2511, Delo: 216.

22. These files are maintained by the ODB Memorial project (https://obd-memorial.ru/html/), which has archived over eighteen million Red Army service personnel cards.

23. On state security agencies, see especially Patrushev 2000a, b. For important memoirs, see Zhukov 2013; Konev 2014; Rokossovsky 1970; Momysh-uly 1998; and Usenov, Snegin, and Bulatov 1985.

24. See, for example, "Karta polozheniia voisk fronta na 5 oktiabria," TsAMO, Fond: 208, Opis': 2511, Delo: 511.

25. The best account of missing data and political bias in Soviet casualty estimates is Lopukhovsky and Kavalerchik 2017.

26. Grigor'ev and Akhmetova 2014; Iazov 2011.

27. Sokolov 2015, 112; Soviet General Staff 2015. These figures may underestimate German tank superiority. New research suggests that the Wehrmacht fielded as many as 2,139 to 2,470 armored vehicles, nearly all tanks, during Operation Typhoon (Liedtke 2016, 143).

offensive. Soviet forces were bunkered down in a defensive system with variable depth; most locations had two levels of defenses, though often hastily constructed. The 16th Army occupied a central position on the Western Front that stretched from Viaz'ma to Briansk. Charged with defending the Voloko-lamsk highway, the 45,000-strong 16th Army consisted of four rifle divisions on 2 October—the 38th, 108th, 112th, and 214th—along with three artillery regiments, a tank brigade, and substantial anti-tank formations. It was joined later by reinforcements, namely the 316th and 78th Rifle Divisions, on 14 October and 1 November, respectively. As a whole, the 16th Army would be dislodged from its initial defenses near Iartsevo, suffer near disaster at Viaz'ma, and then be driven steadily backwards until it consolidated its position in a line stretching from Krasnaia Poliana to Kriukovo before terminating at Istra. From here, it mounted a counterattack on 6 December, pushing overex-tended German forces back until the Soviet offensive petered out around 25 December.[28]

The 16th Army was commanded by General Konstantin Rokossovskii, generally considered one of the best Soviet commanders. He offers a fasci-nating example of Soviet nationalities policy at work. Half-Polish, his career in the Red Army was derailed by accusations during Stalin's 1937 purges that he was a spy. He refused to sign a (false) confession and was tortured for his truculence. His wife and young daughter were subsequently sent into internal exile. Rokossovskii himself languished in prison until he was released, appar-ently without explanation, on 22 March 1940 by Stalin's direct order.[29] He quickly found himself on active duty as a major general in command of the 9th Mechanized Corps when war broke out in 1939. Stalin personally appointed him to command the 16th Army in September 1941. He had only just assumed his duties when Operation Typhoon commenced. Despite a sometimes prickly relationship with General Georgii Zhukov, then the Stavka's represen-tative for the Western and reserve fronts, Rokossovskii earned praise for his ability to rally retreating units and to mount stubborn defenses. He also had a reputation among his soldiers as a "gentleman" commander; he was far more reluctant to punish or execute subordinates than most other Soviet generals. He retained command of the 16th Army throughout the Battle of Moscow, helping hold senior leadership qualities constant throughout these divisional comparisons.[30]

28. Technically speaking, this is the second formation of the 16th Army; its first formation was wiped out at the Battle of Smolensk and officially disbanded on 8 August 1941.

29. Rokossovskii devoted little attention to his prewar career in his memoir (Rokossovsky 1970).

30. Sokolov 2015, 10–11. On tensions between Rokossovskii and Zhukov, see Rokossovsky 1970, 78–80, and Zhukov 2013, 38–39.

8.1.1. Introducing the Paired Comparisons

The logic of comparison here mirrors the matched approach used in previous chapters. These four rifle divisions are set into pairs in which divisions with extreme levels of military inequality are paired with similar units that have (much) lower inequality. In addition, these units were all elements of the same 16th Army. This within-army setup has several notable advantages. It holds constant a series of important potential drivers of battlefield performance, including regime type and ideology, civil-military relations, the quality of senior leadership, the nature of the campaign plan, and the prevailing set of tactics, training, and procedures. Since the persuasiveness of our inferences hinges on how similar these paired divisions are, I detail the comparative framework here. The approach is summarized in table 8.1.

These four rifle divisions had sharply different levels of military inequality owing to the nature of their recruitment areas. Beginning with the first comparison, the 38th Rifle Division was recruited almost exclusively from the North Caucasus Military District. An estimated 90 percent of its soldiers were drawn from the Checheno-Ingush Autonomous Soviet Socialist Republic (ASSR) and Dagestan ASSRs. All of these ethnic groups had experienced collective repression at Moscow's hands in the five years preceding the war, creating an extremely high military inequality coefficient of 0.90.[31] The 108th Rifle Division, by contrast, was drawn from the Smolensk Military District in western Russia, not far from its eventual position on the front lines of the Western Front. While complete records are unavailable, a slim majority (about 55 percent) of its soldiers were ethnically Russian, followed by Ukrainians and some Belorussians. These national minorities had all experienced collective repression in the immediate prewar period. This ethnic composition yields a military inequality coefficient of about 0.45, creating a sizable 0.45 difference in military inequality coefficients between the two divisions.

For the second comparison, the 78th Rifle Division was a vaunted "Siberian" unit drawn from the Far Eastern Military District, and was the most ethnically homogenous of the four units, with about 75 percent of its soldiers ethnically Russian. This combination of prewar treatment and ethnic demography generates a military inequality coefficient of 0.25. The 316th was assigned to the Transcaucasian Military District (headquartered in Alma Ata, Kazakhstan) and was drawn mostly from reservists in the Kazakh and Kirghiz SSRs, with a few Ukrainians also present. A minority of soldiers, between 10

---

31. This is the highest military inequality coefficient recorded in the entire book. It also surpasses the hypothesized inequality possibility frontier of 0.80, offering an important reminder that individual units may exceed the average values of their armies.

TABLE 8.1. Paired Comparisons: Four Rifle Divisions (RD) of the 16th Army, October–December 1941

	Comparison A (2–15 Oct.1941)		Comparison B (15 Nov.–25 Dec.1941)	
	38th RD (North Caucasus MD)	108th RD (Western Special MD)	78th RD (Far Eastern MD)	316th RD (Transcaucasian MD)
Military inequality coefficient	0.90	0.45	0.25	0.78
Unit Traits				
Soldiers (approx.)	9,836	10,095	11,500	11,000
Guns and mortars	68	43	190	257
Front (linear km)	4	6	15	14
Force-to-space ratio (linear km)	2,459	1,683	767	786
Force-to-force ratio (USR:GER)	1:2	1:2.1	1:2.2	1:2.1
Battlefield Performance				
Irrecoverable losses	90–95%	65–70%	50–60%	75–80%
Cohesion	Low	Medium	High	Low/Medium
Blocking detachments	No	No	No	Yes
Towns recaptured	0	0	14	2
Rate of advance (km/day)	0	0	2.89	0.88
Outcome				
Overall performance	Totally destroyed, Colonel Kirillov executed	Fights out of encirclement	Awarded 9th Guards designation	Awarded 8th Guards designation
Status in Dec.1941	Disbanded and struck from roster	Active combat (reformed in Nov.1941)	Spearheads Dec.1941 counteroffensive	Assigned to Stavka Reserve, Dec.1941

and 33 percent, were ethnically Russian.[32] Kirghiz and especially Kazakh soldiers had experienced the full brunt of Soviet repression, with agricultural collectivization producing mass starvation and famine, widespread population displacement, and forced relocation.[33] I calculate a mean military inequality coefficient of 0.78 for the 316th, resulting in a large 0.53 difference in inequality across the 78th and 316th. Together, these four divisions cover nearly the full range of the military inequality continuum (from 0.25 to 0.90). As we will see, they also span the range of battlefield performance from mostly proficient to total collapse.[34]

These divisions are remarkably similar within their pairs across key dimensions touted by scholars as drivers of individual unit performance. As table 8.1 details, these units shared a similar number of soldiers, field artillery, and mortars, and defended similar lengths of front (measured in linear kilometers).[35] In comparison A, each division was bunched up in a forward defense, with a defense-in-depth overruled by Stavka, leaving only a thin secondary line behind the main effort. In comparison B, the two divisions had a more established defense-in-depth, with a second line of defensive works up to five kilometers behind the main effort. As a result, within-pair differences across force-to-space (FSR) and force-to-force (FFR) ratios are modest and unlikely to explain battlefield performance.[36] The comparison is strengthened further by the fact that these extreme inequality divisions fought in close proximity with their paired counterfactual. At most, the 78th and 316th were thirty kilometers apart on the Western Front; the 38th and 108th, considerably closer. Being battlefield neighbors helps control for a host of microlevel factors that might drive outcomes, including terrain, weather, the timing of German assaults, and, to a certain extent, German capabilities and skill, since

32. The high estimate is derived from Glantz 2005b, 594. The low estimate stems from "Prikaz Narodnogo Komissara Oboroni Soiuza SSSR," (18 noiabria 1941 g. № 339, reproduced in Grigor'ev and Akhmetova 2014, 143.

33. Cameron 2018.

34. Note that both the 78th and 316th received Guards designations during November 1941. The 316th became the 8th Guards Rifle Division on 18 November; the 78th became the 9th Guards Rifle Division on 26 November. I retain their original designations to avoid confusion.

35. Soviet divisions had a paper strength of up to 14,000 soldiers but few in practice reached this size in 1941. By 2 October, both the 38th and 108th had already experienced serious combat losses. Soviet rifle divisions each had three regiments of infantry; each regiment had three battalions; and each battalion had three companies.

36. FSRs measure the number of soldiers in a given unit over the length of the front (in kilometers) the unit must defend. FFRs measure the ratio of Soviet to German soldiers at the main point of attack. These estimates are taken from the first day of each German offensive (2 October and 15 November) but were fluid during the battle.

these units were attacked by formations often from the same army or Panzer Group. Where imbalances do exist—the 316th had a greater complement of anti-tank weapons than the 78th, along with an additional two weeks of combat experience—they are typically biased against the favored military inequality argument.[37]

Three additional contextual factors bear emphasizing. First, all four divisions largely fought these battles cut off from regular contact with Stavka, the 16th Army's own headquarters, and each other.[38] German aircraft specifically targeted command and control bunkers as well as communication lines during both offensives, leaving these divisions with only intermittent (at best) radio and telephone connections. The collapse of communication networks unmasked divisional capabilities by forcing their commanders to rely on their unit's own organic skills and traits rather than seek direction and material assistance from HQ. In particular, the 38th and 108th were largely without regular contact with Stavka or the 16th Army HQ for most of the 2–15 October period. Lev Lopukhovsky captures the confusion that entailed: "The troops were receiving conflicting orders from the commanders, the HQ they left behind, as well as from Stavka. At the same time, as commanders were searching for their HQ, the HQ were seeking their commanders, and the Stavka was trying to locate its commanders and their HQ."[39] Moreover, the 16th Army's headquarters was also ordered to pull back, severing communications with division and brigade commanders (the movement of the HQ is illustrated in figure 8.1). As Rokossovskii recounted in his memoir, he barely escaped encirclement while in a village looking for his divisions.[40] General Staff and Western Front operational logs frequently recount how couriers and light aircraft were often dispatched to find particular units and deliver orders.[41]

Second, with one exception, these divisions were operating within the same coercive framework established by Stalin and Western Front commanders. On 16 August, Stalin issued order № 270, which extended authority

---

37. Both the 38th and 108th were "second formations" as their predecessors were wiped out in June–July cauldron battles. As a result, they were entering combat with similar levels of combat experience and divisional "age."

38. Lopukhovsky 2013, 175.

39. Sokolov 2015, 115.

40. Rokossovsky 1970, 82–84.

41. See, for example, "Izvlechenie iz operativnoi svodki № 211 General'nogo shtaba Krasnoi Armii (5.10.41g)" in Zhilin 2001a, 235–36; "'Zhurnal boevykh deistvii voisk fronta za oktiabr' 1941g," TsAMO Fond: 208, Opis': 2511, Delo: 216, List: 1, s.41, 44, 49. Rokossovskii actually demanded that his orders to evacuate the 16th Army's HQ (received by telegram) be delivered in writing by aircraft. See Rokossovsky 1970, 49.

to commanders to shoot deserters and arrest their family members. It also prohibited encircled soldiers from surrendering and authorized the battle-field cashiering of hesitant, incompetent, or just plain unlucky officers. On 5 September, Stalin consented to the deployment of blocking detachments on the Southwestern Front, though not the Western Front, a decision that became policy one week later with Stavka directive 001919.[42] The divisions were therefore operating without the presence of blocking detachments, allowing us to observe their relative performance absent the forcing function they provided. The one exception is the 316th Division. Declassified documents (see below) reveal that its commander had struck upon their informal use on at least one occasion to help beat back the renewed German assault in mid-November. Given the division's 0.90 military inequality coefficient, it is unsurprising that this unit turned to such measures while its lower inequality counterpart did not. Rokossovskii also turned to violence on occasion to maintain discipline in the 16th Army. He issued an order, distributed to all senior 16th Army commanders, that two deserters who cast their weapons away on 25 October were to be shot in front of their regiment. He also noted that their families were to be stripped of any benefits.[43] Finally, secret police units also trolled rear areas, seeking stragglers and deserters. These units had already detained an estimated 657,364 soldiers, arrested 25,876 soldiers, and executed 10,201 by 10 October 1941.[44]

Finally, we might worry that specific divisions, especially the 38th and 316th, were purposely selected by the Germans as the focal points of their attacks. Perhaps German planners recognized that these divisions were vulnerable and built their campaign plans around striking these weak points in Soviet defenses. Or, alternatively, perhaps Stavka deliberately placed their weaker divisions as obstacles in the path of the most likely German attack, seeking to wage an attritional contest on the backs of national minorities. Neither fear is warranted, however. German intelligence did not have a clear enough picture of Soviet units and locations to identify specific divisions for attack. Captured Wehrmacht planning documents for Operation Typhoon reveal, for example, that German staffers could only identify the 16th Army's location crudely, and those of specific units not at all accurately.[45] German intelligence also completely missed the arrival of reinforcements, including the 316th and 78th Divisions, on the battlefield.[46] For its part,

---

42. Daines 2008, 423.

43. "Prikaz voiskam 16A," TsAMO, Fond: 3467, Opis': 0000001, Delo: 0001, List: 194, s1.

44. Toptygin 2002, 121.

45. "Skhema 4. Polozhenie voisk storon (po nemetskim dannym) k iskhodu 2.10.41g." Reproduced in Lopukhosky 2013, Plate 4.

46. Hartmann 2013, 53.

Stavka failed to guess correctly the central thrust of Operation Typhoon and appeared to use reinforcements to plug gaps in defenses based on available units rather than their demographic characteristics. The 78th and 316th, for example, were committed to the same battlefield location at nearly the same time.

8.2.   Comparison A: The 38th and 108th Divisions (2 October to 15 October)

Morning broke over the 38th and 108th Rifle Divisions on 2 October as they sat nearly side by side, awaiting the impending German offensive in hastily prepared positions. Soviet intelligence had caught wind of German preparations, though the exact location and scale of the opening assault still surprised Soviet commanders. Only ten days later, the Red Army had suffered a catastrophic military defeat, perhaps the worst suffered during the entire war. In fact, the defeat was so total that much of the history of Operation Typhoon, particularly its dual "cauldron battles" of encirclement at Viaz'ma and Briansk, was largely excised from official narratives of the war until recently.[47] The entire 16th Army, along with the 19th, 20th, 24th, and 32nd Armies, were all encircled by surging Army Group Centre forces under the command of General Fedor von Bock. Though hampered by mud, logistical difficulties, and local Soviet counterattacks, the Wehrmacht moved aggressively to destroy these trapped armies. Yet the sheer size of Soviet forces meant that gaps inevitably appeared in German containment, allowing groups, and in some cases entire battalions, to escape the closing pincers. Still, observers, including Stalin himself, feared the Red Army's collapse. Out of desperation, Zhukov authorized the shooting of "cowards and panic-mongers" on 13 October to stem the tide.[48] Plans were also made to abandon Moscow.[49] By 20 October, the Red Army had lost at least 673,000 soldiers and nearly 1,300 tanks in the twin Viaz'ma and Briansk pockets alone.[50] By the time the German offensive ground to a halt on 30 October, seven of fifteen army field commands, along with sixty-four of ninety-five rifle divisions, had been encircled and destroyed. Only the remnants of the remaining thirty-two divisions, some

47. On the revival of interests in these "forgotten" battles, see Glantz 1999; Beshanov 2004; Lopukhovsky 2013; Daines 2008; Glantz and House 2015.

48. "Prikaz voiskam zapadnogo fronta," TsAMO Fond: 208, Opis': 2511, Delo: 24, List: 2–3.

49. Patrushev 2000b, 207–8.

50. Hartmann 2013, 51.

reduced to 10 percent of their original strength, escaped.[51] Against this bleak backdrop, the sections below detail the divergent paths of the 38th and 108th Rifle Divisions (see figure 8.1).

8.2.1. The 38th Rifle Division

The absence of detailed information about the 38th Rifle Division is our first clue that its battlefield performance was disastrous in October 1941. Masking deeper truths, the battle's first day did end well for the 38th, however. An early morning assault by the Wehrmacht's 255th Infantry Division was disrupted by divisional artillery and mortar fire at Kholm, about four kilometers from the division's main defenses at Iartsevo.[52] Yet this was only a feint. On 3 October, the first wave of the German assault crashed against the division's positions at Iartsevo, Novosel'e, and Zadnia. Communication lines and radio transmissions were immediately disrupted; ties between Stavka and 16th Army HQ, as well as between Rokossovskii and his regimental commanders, were severed.[53] The 38th began retreating almost immediately. By 5 October, the 38th's three regiments, now acting more or less independently, had retreated to the eastern bank of the Vop' river, hoping to establish some semblance of a new defensive line.[54] Forced to dispatch orders by aircraft, Rokossovskii was tasked with evacuating the 16th Army's HQ to Viaz'ma, where it was to regroup with several divisions, including the 38th.[55] This order only added to the command and control confusion, however, and on 7 October, the new line at the Vop' collapsed under heavy German pressure.[56] Remnants of the 38th Division, now operating in company-sized groups of soldiers or smaller, began streaming toward Viaz'ma. Steady communications between the 16th Army HQ and Stavka were only established on 11 October, much too late to organize any potential breakout or regrouping. The 16th Army HQ, along with Stavka itself, kept sending orders via radio transmissions and couriers to the 38th, like a phantom limb they were desperate to reconnect with, but received no answer. The Western Front headquarter's daily war logs dated

---

51. Lopukhovsky 2013, 393.

52. "Zhurnal boevykh deistvii voisk fronta za oktiabr' 1941g.," TsAMO Fond: 208, Opis': 2511, Delo: 216, List: 1, s.17; Lopukhovsky 2013, 118. See also Shaposhnikov 2006.

53. See, for example, "Izvlechenie iz operativnoi svodki № 218 General'nogo shtaba Krasnoi Armii (8.10.41g)." in Zhilin 2001а, 264–65.

54. "Zhurnal boevykh deistvii voisk fronta za oktiabr' 1941g.," s. 34–35.

55. Lopukhovsky 2013, 222.

56. "Zhurnal boevykh deistvii voisk fronta za oktiabr' 1941g.," Fond: 208, Opis': 2511, Delo: 216, List: 1, s.41,44.

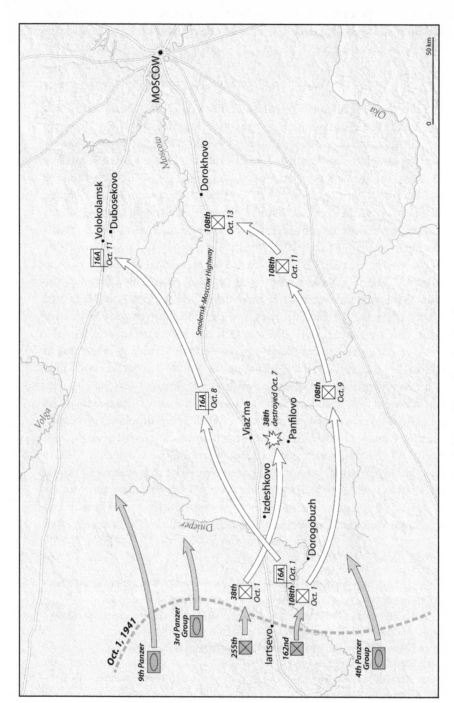

FIGURE 8.1. Divided Fates: The 38th and 108th Rifle Divisions, 2–15 Oct. 1941

from 9 October ominously warned that "information about the 38th's position was not received due to lack of communication."[57]

Indeed, by 11 October, it was too late. The division had ceased to exist, completely encircled and destroyed in the Viaz'ma pocket. In a particularly haunting piece of historical evidence, intelligence analysts on the General Staff had continued to plot the 38th's suspected location on a daily series of 1:500,000 scale maps. On 11 October, some anonymous staffer had marked the last suspected location of the division near the small village of Batishchevo, south of Viaz'ma. The division is depicted as surrounded on three sides by German forces and alone, separated from the retreating 20th Army to the south by a wall of German steel. Faint pencil etchings denote the date (11 October) and time (19:00).[58] After this date, the division no longer appears in either the 16th Army's war logs or Western Front HQ operational summaries. There is but a single, perhaps wishful, thought that the 38th might have joined the 20th Army after all; a map dated 19 October places the 38th under the 20th Army's command structure. But, in a concession to reality, no individual division marker was placed on the map.[59] The 38th Rifle Division was gone.

This battlefield verdict was later conceded by Soviet authorities themselves. On 27 December, the People's Commissar for Defense officially disbanded the division after its "total destruction by Fascist forces." The division itself was erased from official histories as well as the Soviet order of battle.[60] Responsibility for the division's poor performance fell heaviest on its commander, Colonel Maxim Gavrilovich Kirillov. One of the few soldiers of the 38th to escape encirclement, he was arrested by Soviet authorities and subsequently put on trial for his alleged failings. In his defense, he argued that his soldiers had deserted or surrendered en masse, and that he was unable to maintain discipline once his units scattered. His efforts to form a partisan band ("Death to Fascism") also floundered, his soldiers unwilling to fight while behind enemy lines. Accused of "mediocrity and indecision" in the face of the German assault, Kirillov was executed by firing squad on 2 September 1942.[61]

57. "Zhurnal boevykh deistvii voisk fronta za oktiabr' 1941g.," Fond: 208, Opis': 2511, Delo: 216, List: 1, s.49. There are no reports of its location after 13 October. "Izvlechenie iz operativnoi svodki № 224 General'nogo shtaba Krasnoi Armii (11.10.41g.)," reproduced in Zhilin 2001a, 293.

58. "Karta polozheniia voisk 16 i 20 A na 11 oktiabria' (1941 g.)," TsAMO Fond: 208, Opis': 2511, Delo: 670.

59. "Karta polozheniia voisk fronta na 11–19 oktiabria' (1941 g.)," TsAMO Fond: 208, Opis': 2511, Delo: 517.

60. The designation "38th Rifle Division" was later granted to a new unit from the Central Asian Military District on 1 January 1942.

61. Zviagintsev 2017a, b, 177–79.

The seeds of this disaster were sown even before the opening German assault, however. On 27 September, Rokossovskii presented the 16th Army's plan of defense to the Western Front commander, General I. S. Konev, that called for its three divisions to mount an active mobile defense given German numerical superiority. Rokossovskii called for building a defense-in-depth around three echelons; the 16th Army's rifle divisions could inflict maximal damage on attacking German forces, then withdraw to the next echelon before being overrun, slowing German Progress. Konev immediately overruled these plans. His reasons for doing so are instructive. He "couldn't allow even thoughts of conducting a possible fighting withdrawal *with the troops entrusted to him* [my emphasis]."[62] He singled out the 38th as a flight risk if it were ceded authority to conduct a mobile defense on its own initiative. Instead, he ordered the 38th to concentrate all its soldiers in a single echelon and "conduct a tenacious defense of the present line on the Vop' river. ... Fight stubbornly. Eliminate any thought of a mobile defense."[63] Rokossovskii was forced to abandon his proposed plan, rendering the 38th Rifle Division more vulnerable to encirclement and overrun. Ironically, the fear of indiscipline bred a reliance on inflexible tactics that actually magnified the shock of the German offensive, thus contributing to the very outcome that Konev wished to avoid.

8.2.2.   The 108th Rifle Division

The 108th Rifle Division was also staggered by the initial German onslaught, which pinned its regiments down at the villages of Starozavop'e, Skrushevskie, and Buianovo. Unlike the 38th, however, the 108th not only maintained its cohesion but mounted a stubborn defense for the next four days until 7 October, when it retreated in good order to new defensive positions south of Viaz'ma.[64] Having regrouped, the 108th launched a fierce counterattack later that day from three villages against German formations at Panfilovo, some 17 kilometer south of Viaz'ma.[65] Official German operational summaries made special note of this counterattack, describing the 108th as offering

62. Quoted in Sokolov 2015, 96. Rokossovskii's account is found at Rokossovsky 1970, 46–47.

63. TsAMO Fond: 208, Opis': 2511, Delo: 191, List: 54.

64. "Zhurnal boevykh deistvii voisk fronta za oktiabr' 1941g.," Fond: 208, Opis': 2511, Delo: 216, List: 1, s.34–35.

65. "Zhurnal boevykh deistvii voisk fronta za oktiabr' 1941g.," Fond: 208, Opis': 2511, Delo: 216, List: 1, s.41, 44. "Izvlechenie iz operativnoi svodki № 216 General'nogo shtaba Krasnoi Armii (7.10.41 g.)," in Zhilin 2001a, 252–53.

"stubborn resistance" that was disrupting the German timetable.[66] Unable to defeat German forces, the 108th once again retreated, pursuing a scorched earth strategy that left a wake of devastation in its trail.[67] On 10–11 October, the division halted, turned about-face, and launched a series of coordinated counterattacks against German positions at Panfilovo, Vypolzovo, Nesterovo, and Volodarets.[68] Communication between the division and Western Front headquarters still remained spotty; the division was largely on its own. In one of the few messages received by the Western Front HQ, General N. I. Orlov, commander of the 108th, reported heavy casualties on 11 October and requested resupply to make up for severe shortages of ammunition and fuel. This was the last message received; after 11 October, the 16th Army lost all contact with the division. Intelligence units sent to reestablish communications never returned.[69]

This was not the end of the story, however. On 13 October, lead elements of the division, having slipped past blocking German units, emerged near Dorokhovo, some 320 kilometers from its original defensive position near Iartsevo. For the next six days, stragglers streamed into Dorokhovo, often in small groups, sometimes alone. By 17 October, the battered division had already reestablished its headquarters a kilometer north of Kriukovo, strung communication lines with the 16th Army HQ, organized provisional defenses, and engaged small German formations in sporadic firefights.[70] Two days later, the last of the division's encircled soldiers rejoined the unit. In total, some 1,200 soldiers survived, about 12 percent of its pre–Operation Typhoon strength.[71] As one survivor recounted, "It took me two weeks to work my way out. I covered nearly 200 miles behind the German lines, and on 19 October I got out to Dorokhovo. As I learned later, few of our boys managed to get out."[72] Despite these heavy losses, the division still retained a high degree of cohesion and discipline. A declassified hand-drawn sketch dated 1 November reveals that the division had managed to reconstruct a relatively sophisticated

66. Stahel 2015, 85–86.

67. Lopukhovsky 2013, 205.

68. "Zhurnal boevykh deistvii voisk fronta za oktiabr' 1941g.," Fond: 208, Opis': 2511, Delo: 216, List: 1, s.50,53.

69. "Zhurnal boevykh deistvii voisk fronta za oktiabr' 1941g.," Fond: 208, Opis': 2511, Delo: 216, List: 1, s.53. "Izvlechenie iz operativnoi svodki № 224 General'nogo shtaba Krasnoi Armii," in Zhilin 2001a, 293.

70. "Operativnaia svodka shtaba 108 SD," TsAMO Fond: 460, Opis': 5047, Delo: 120, List: 267, s.1.

71. "108 strelkovaia diviziia," Boevye deistviia Krasnoi Armii v VOV, http://bdsa.ru /strelkovye-divizii/5062-108-strelkovaya-diviziya.

72. Quoted in Braithwaite 2006, 195.

defense, with its three understrength regiments situated behind natural cover to provide interlocking fields of defensive fire.[73] Compared to the fate of the 38th, this martial order appears remarkable.

Given the price paid for slowing the German advance, it is perhaps understandable that the 108th's own official history largely sidesteps this period. Only two pages are devoted to the events of 2 October to 21 November. It recounts, for example, how the division met the initial German attack of 2 October with sustained artillery fire and close-quarters fighting. The 1st Battalion of the 407th Regiment was especially singled out for its fighting, which left "over a thousand corpses of these dogs lying on the right bank [of the river Vop']." The history is openly dismissive of German efforts from 2–5 October, claiming that they "achieved nothing but huge losses" for the Wehrmacht. It pins the blame for defeat on other units; "ruptures by the Germans of our neighbors' [defensive] lines resulted in our encirclement." The division, however, "continued to fight as it withdrew and in November took a short spell to gather itself for the coming fight with its sworn enemy furiously striving for Moscow." Though clearly written (and censored) by committee, the narrative credits the relative success of the 108th to the presence of Stalinist commissars and their "Bolshevist agitation" within the division. They provided instruction about German ways of war that stiffened morale by teaching soldiers that the Germans were not invincible but instead could be beaten. These lectures also taught soldiers how to maintain discipline while encircled. Commissars also conducted after-action reviews following each battle to identify and disseminate best practices throughout the division's regiments.[74]

Perhaps most remarkably, the battered division was only pulled from the line briefly, just long enough to onboard new soldiers, before being sent back into the fight. Operational summaries reveal that the 108th saw combat as early as 21 November.[75] The 108th was transferred to the 5th Army and took up defensive positions in the Pavlovsk-Slobodsk area between the cities of Zvenigorod and Istra. It soon found itself in the thick of fighting; for fifteen days, the division fought fierce battles as it slowly retreated, one kilometer a day, toward Moscow.[76] By the time the German offensive stalled

---

73. "Skhema raspolozheniia chastei 108 SD," TsAMO Fond: 208, Opis' 2511, Delo: 34, List: 52.

74. "Rukopisi po istorii 108 SD," TsAMO Fond: 1298, Opis': 0000001, Delo: 0002, List:1, s11–13.

75. "Zhurnal boevykh deistvii voisk Zapadnogo fronta za noiabr' 1941g.," Fond: 208, Opis': 2511, Delo: 219, List: 1, s.147, 154, 161.

76. "Zhurnal boevykh deistvii voisk Zapadnogo fronta za noiabr' 1941g.," Fond: 208, Opis': 2511, Delo: 219, List: 1, s.255.

on 5 December, the 108th had regiments where less than 150 soldiers were still alive. A shell of its former self, the division was nonetheless tasked with supporting the Soviet counteroffensive led by the 78th Rifle Division on 6 December.

8.3. Comparison B: The 78th and 316th Rifle Divisions (15 November to 6 December)

On the eve of renewed operations, a newly reconstituted 16th Army was the largest of seven Soviet armies stationed on the Western Front. Holding down nearly seventy kilometers of front, the 16th Army possessed 287 field guns, 180 anti-tank weapons (far more than any other army), and 150 tanks, along with 50,000 infantry organized into four rifle divisions.[77] On 15 November, the 78th Rifle Division was responsible for fifteen kilometers of the front near Voloko-lamsk, while the 316th Rifle Division defended almost fourteen kilometers to the east of Ruza (see figure 8.2). These divisions were separated by about thirty kilometers, with only the 18th Rifle Division and the 2nd Guards Cav-alry Division between them. The 316th was stationed at the top of the 16th Army's curved front; the 78th anchored the bottom. Despite reinforcements, including a large shipment of anti-tank weapons to the 316th, the stench of des-peration hung over the Western Front. On 1 November, Zhukov once again threatened to punish wayward soldiers, calling for commanders to "ruthlessly crack down on cowards and deserters, thus ensuring discipline and organi-zation." Cohesion was key: "In this decisive battle for the motherland and for glorious Moscow, all forces of the Western Front must unite to deliver crushing blows to the fascist hordes ... blood for blood! Death for death!"[78]

On 16 November, the second phase of Operation Typhoon was launched, with German forces striking in strength along the Volokolamsk axis. In a coincidence of timing, Zhukov had ordered the 16th Army to attack German positions that same morning, with the 316th spearheading offensive oper-ations. While the 78th made modest inroads near Vishenki, the 316th was thrown back, creating a pinwheel effect of sorts in which German forces crashed through the seam between the 316th and General Lev Dovator's cavalry group.[79] Four Panzer divisions, totaling some 350–400 tanks, now

77. Soviet General Staff 2015, 37.

78. "Prikaz voiskam Zapadnogo fronta № 051," reproduced in Vzvarova and Emel'ianova 1989, 18–19.

79. The 78th faced IX Corps's 78th and 87th Infantry Divisions (each had about 9,000 sol-diers), along with the 10th Panzer Division (75–100 tanks). The 316th principally fought the 35th Infantry Division (about 17,000 soldiers) and the 5th Panzer Division (75–100 tanks).

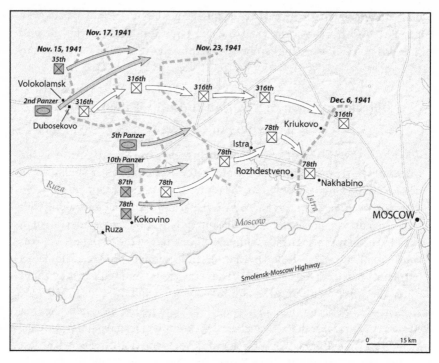

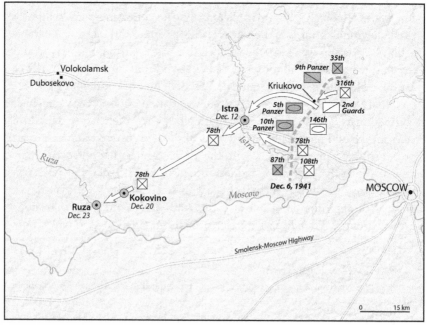

FIGURE 8.2. The 78th and 316th Rifle Divisions in Action, 15 Nov.–25 Dec. 1941

drove the 16th Army, including both the 78th and 316th Rifle Divisions, backwards.[80] Over the next three weeks, the 16th Army conducted a fighting retreat eastwards of about 60 kilometers until a new defensive line stretching from Kriukovo to Rozhdestveno was established. The 78th and 316th, having suffered tremendous casualties, would end up on 5 December only fifteen kilometers from one another on the newly consolidated Kriukovo-Rozhdestveno line.

8.3.1. The 78th Rifle Division

Commanded by Lieutenant-General Afanasii Beloborodov, the 78th Rifle Division arrived on the Western Front on 1 November, having proceeded directly to the front lines after disembarking from long baggage trains in Moscow. The division was quickly bloodied, acquitting itself well in the series of initial skirmishes. Taking up positions on the front line near Mara, Gorodishche, Barynino, Kholshcheviki, and Kostrovo, the division spent its first five days preparing an offensive. On 6 November, the order was received to attack, and the 78th pushed forward, capturing control of the highway leading south of Lyskovo and seizing most of the strategic town of Mikhailovskoe. A spirited counterattack by German infantry detachments, supported by thirty tanks, was then driven back on 8 November. The 78th was back in action on 11 November, consolidating its control over the important Mikhailovskoe-Lyskovo highway.[81]

The morning of 16 November once again found the 78th in a series of well-designed, if shallow, defenses, tasked with maintaining Soviet control over hotly contested Mikhailovskoe. Zhukov, seeking to break up the concentration of German forces along the Volokolamsk axis, ordered an ill-timed offensive by the 16th Army that saw the 78th again engage German forces on the outskirts of Mikhailovskoe. Divisional operational summaries and personnel files bear witness to intense fighting by both sides. By 1700, at least 102 of the division's infantry had been killed, along with a further 21 listed as missing.[82] A General Staff after-action review chastised Zhukov for ordering the offensive, which had been designed by his staffers in a single night. The attack took place too late in the morning (1000) to achieve surprise; some 16th Army units did not arrive at their appointed locations until 1230. Divisions

80. Soviet General Staff 2015, 59.

81. "Zhurnal boevykh deistvii voisk Zapadnogo fronta za noiabr' 1941 g." TsAMO, Fond: 208, Opis': 2511, Delo: 219, List:1, s.5,26,31,35,42,49,55,68,75,83,98.

82. "Zhurnal boevykh deistvii voisk Zapadnogo fronta za noiabr' 1941 g." TsAMO, Fond: 208, Opis': 2511, Delo: 219, List:1, s.106

were left with no time to prepare; cavalry units reported less than 50 percent of their horses had been shoed. In a familiar refrain, the 16th Army HQ had poor communications with its divisions, some of which lacked any telephone connections at all.[83]

The 78th, as a leading wedge of this offensive, found itself in a less than ideal set of circumstances. Yet alone among the 16th Army's divisions, the 78th won some modest battlefield gains, pushing German forces backwards near Mara, Sloboda, and Gorodishche. Inching forward, the division found itself locked in a desperate battle around Mikhailovskoe, Vaiukhino, and Barynino.[84] Personnel logs from the day's fighting recorded another 118 soldiers killed and 70 missing. The 6th Panzer Division's own operational summary singled out the encounter with the "78th Siberian Division" as the most difficult battle of its entire eastern campaign so far: "Men were said to fight to the last and that in the recent battle for Gorodishche no less than 812 enemy soldiers were counted in and around the village."[85] While the fog of war may have shrouded the true number of casualties, there is little question that the 78th was engaged in a stubborn, if slowly collapsing, defensive stand. The 78th even managed to reverse some Wehrmacht gains and take prisoners, though German documents allege that the division massacred wounded German soldiers who had surrendered.[86]

The Wehrmacht was now advancing across a 30–40 kilometer front, driving most of the 16th Army's divisions slowly backwards. German Panzers played a key role, with tank density averaging 10–12 tanks per kilometer and rising to a crushing 30 per kilometer near the main Volokolamsk axis.[87] The 78th held out until 20 November, when Rokossovskii ordered it to withdraw, fearing its destruction. Fighting from 18–20 November in and around Gorodishche, Onufrievo, and Rakovo had killed another 203 soldiers, while another 178 were missing. Running battles continued on 21 November, as the division struggled to break contact in multiple villages, including Kholuianikha, Shibanovo, Krasino, Petrovo, Bolsheviki, and Dubrovskii. The powerful German motorized assault continued advancing on Istra, one of the largest towns and a key logistical center, while the 78th sought to slow

83. Soviet General Staff 2015, 57. "Izvlechenie iz operativnoi svodki № 263 General'nogo shtaba Krasnoi Armii (16.11.41 g)," in Zhilin 2001a, 630.

84. "Zhurnal boevykh deistvii voisk Zapadnogo fronta za noiabr' 1941 g." TsAMO, Fond: 208, Opis': 2511, Delo: 219, List:1, s.113,119,130.

85. Quoted in Stahel 2015, 151.

86. Ibid.

87. Soviet General Staff 2015, 59. "Izvlechenie iz operativnoi svodki № 264 General'nogo shtaba Krasnoi Armii (17.11.41 g)," in Zhilin 2001a, 643–44.

its advance. The 126th Rifle Division, which held the central sector of the Western Front, collapsed, however, falling back raggedly toward Klin. The 78th and 316th were now imperiled, as German forces threatened to curl in behind them through the gap now created by the missing 126th.[88]

Alarmed by this turn of events, the Western Front's headquarters issued a remarkable set of orders to the 16th Army. The first telegram was directed at Rokossovskii: "We categorically confirm to you the order to consolidate on the present line and to not take a single step back without our authorization— if need be, up to and including the sacrifice of the unit and formation."[89] A second dispatch was sent directly to divisional commanders, warning that "there is nowhere left to fall back, and no one will allow you to do so. By using any and the most extreme methods, you must immediately bring about a turning point, to cease withdrawing and not only not surrender for any reason Istra, Klin, and Solnechnogorsk, but drive the Fascists from these occupied areas."[90] In case the commanders missed the urgency of the situation, Zhukov sent a third missive reminding them of his standing orders that authorized the immediate execution of commanders for unauthorized withdrawal of their units.[91]

While the motivational nature of these orders can be debated, the 78th continued to offer dogged resistance as it slowly retreated toward Istra. On 22 November, the division continued to hold positions in three villages while waging an intensive battle in another four (Dedeshino, Kholshcheviki, Frolovskoe, and Telepnevo) that resulted in 114 soldiers killed and 16 missing. By 25 November, the division had established new defensive positions near the Istra reservoir. While the 16th Army's remaining divisions crossed the Istra river, the 78th remained on its western bank, defending the town and its vital highway to Moscow. Slowly driven back toward Istra, the 78th waged urban combat against superior German forces, trying to hold a defensive line up to 15 kilometers in length. With too few soldiers, the 78th was forced to withdraw at dawn on 27 November, its formations chased in dogged pursuit by Luftwaffe Ju-87 Stuka dive-bombers seeking to break the division. For the next three days, the 78th lost another 114 soldiers (with 22 missing) due to fierce fighting across eight different villages. Spread dangerously thin, the 78th was perhaps saved by the fact that the 16th Army's front had collapsed from its

88. "Zhurnal boevykh deistvii voisk Zapadnogo fronta za noiabr' 1941 g." TsAMO, Fond: 208, Opis': 2511, Delo: 219, List:1, s.137,145.

89. Quoted in Soviet General Staff 2015, 66.

90. Quoted in Soviet General Staff 2015, 68.

91. "Prikaz," TsAMO, Fond: 208, Opis': 2511; Delo: 24; List: 78–80.

original 67–70 kilometers to only 35–40 kilometers, preventing the Germans from breaking through its operational depth.[92]

Battered German forces continued their advance, though problems of logistical resupply and heavy casualties were stealing much of their momentum. Ragged fighting over 1–3 December cost the 78th another 107 killed and 45 missing soldiers. On 3 December, the Wehrmacht captured Zhenevo and Rozhdestveno, inching closer to the final defensive lines guarding Moscow. Miraculously, the 78th counterattacked, seeking to recapture Rozhdestveno, losing another 78 soldiers killed on 4 December. Though managing to recapture two small villages, the 78th could not hold them, retreating another 15 kilometers to final defensive positions between Rozhdestveno and Nakhabino.[93] Here, however, the defenses held, with the 78th now responsible for a five-kilometer swatch of the 16th Army's greatly diminished front. Army Group Centre's offensive had stalled; its exhausted and depleted forces, wracked by frostbite amid bitter –30°C temperatures, could go no farther. German officers now watched ominously as "masses of Russians suddenly appeared. The sheer number of them left us speechless. There were endless marching columns... and tanks, artillery units, and countless motor vehicles."[94] The Soviet 1st and 20th Reserve Armies had arrived. Operation Typhoon was now cancelled.

Outnumbered and outgunned, the 78th nonetheless turned in a credible performance during the 16 November–5 December phase of Operation Typhoon. Despite heavy losses, it retained the ability to stage phased withdrawals from multiple villages in reasonably good order. In total, it retreated about 55 kilometers over 18 days, slowly giving ground while also mounting sustained, if ultimately unsuccessful, counterattacks. In particular, its ability to coordinate multi-village offensives, and even seize and hold key territory temporarily, was unusual among its sister rifle divisions of the 16th Army. And while there is little doubt it suffered a lopsided loss-exchange ratio, it nonetheless continued to offer stubborn resistance that degraded Wehrmacht combat strength, casualties that would ultimately force Bock to order his soldiers to prepare for the inevitable Soviet counteroffensive. They would not have to wait long; Zhukov ordered a massive counterattack across the Western Front the next day.

92. "Zhurnal boevykh deistvii voisk Zapadnogo fronta za noiabr' 1941 g." TsAMO, Fond: 208, Opis': 2511, Delo: 219, List:1, s152,160,167,177,186,191,200,207,216.

93. "Zhurnal boevykh deistvii voisk Zapadnogo fronta za noiabr' 1941 g." TsAMO, Fond: 208, Opis': 2511, Delo: 219, List:1, s.222,229,236,244,255.

94. Quoted in Stahel 2015, 308.

INTRA-78TH RIFLE DIVISION VARIATION

We can use the 78th's personnel records to conduct an additional test of the military inequality argument's ability to explain patterns of battlefield performance *within* the division itself. The ratio of killed to missing soldiers offers a simple measure of how hard the division was fighting and its relative degree of cohesion.[95] Pooling these data, at least 926 soldiers were killed between 15 November and 5 December; a further 390 went missing. This generates a killed-to-missing ratio of 3.2:1, indicating that the division retained a significant degree of cohesion despite losing nearly one-tenth of its initial strength in only three weeks. Reports on the "political conditions" within the division that were filed to the Western Front's headquarters generally confirm a high level of cohesion. "The morale of soldiers and commanders is strong," one report dated 5 November reads, "as soldiers, commanders and political commissars alike all yelled 'for the motherland! for Stalin!' when charging to attack the enemy."[96]

A closer look at these data reveal an interesting wrinkle, however. We can use these same records to identify whether certain ethnic groups were more (or less) likely to appear among the dead or missing. Recall that the division was about 75 percent ethnically Russian. If soldiers were killed or disappeared at random, we should expect these ethnic groups to be represented at or about their proportion of the division's overall strength. I therefore plot the ethnic composition of killed and missing soldiers by ethnic group (Russian and non-Russian) for the five largest episodes of soldier disappearances in this three-week period in figure 8.3. Collectively, these five dates represent 73 percent of all known soldiers who disappeared, along with 36 percent of all divisional casualties. The dashed line represents the proportional share that non-Russians should represent of casualties and disappearances.

Several patterns emerge. First, non-Russian soldiers, nearly all of whom were Uzbeks, are slightly underrepresented among killed soldiers and sharply overrepresented among missing soldiers. On the battle's opening day, 16 November, 47 soldiers were reported killed, with another 21 deemed missing. Non-Russians represented 25 percent of the casualties but one-third of

95. Soviet personnel records use "missing" to denote a range of politically sensitive behaviors, including surrender, desertion, defection, and genuine disappearances. The measure is thus a noisy one and is best treated as a rough proxy for indiscipline than any single category of behavior. Definitions of "missing" are consistent across units, however, enabling comparison across divisions.

96. "Zhurnal boevykh deistvii 9 Gv. SD. za period 1 noiabria 1941 g. - 1 sentiabria 1942 g.," TsAMO, Fond:1066, Opis':1, Delo: 6, List:1 (quote on s.5).

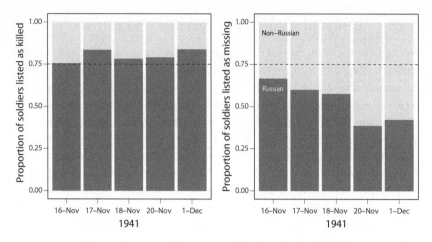

FIGURE 8.3. Proportion of Russian and non-Russian Soldiers Reported Missing and Killed in
Daily 78th Rifle Division Personnel Records by Selected Date in 1941

the disappeared. The next day, as a fierce battle raged near Mikhailovskoe,
118 soldiers were reported killed and 70 missing. Non-Russians represented
only 18 percent of the casualties but 40 percent of the missing. The pattern
repeats on 18 November, when 98 soldiers were killed and 59 went missing.
Only 22 percent of the casualties were non-Russian; 42 percent of the missing, however, were non-Russian. On 20 November, after the 78th had received
its orders to withdraw from the outskirts of Gorodishche and Rakovo, personnel logs recorded 24 soldiers killed but 101 missing. Twenty percent of
the casualties were non-Russian; a whopping 61 percent of the disappeared
were non-Russian. The last major surge of disappearances was recorded on
1 December: of the 34 soldiers reported missing, 20 were non-Russian, while
only 18 percent of the 45 killed soldiers were non-Russian. Notably, these
bursts of disappearances are only weakly correlated with overall casualties;
the 20 November incident, for example, saw disappearances outrun soldier
deaths by a five to one ratio.

Instead, there appears to be a strong group dynamic at work. Of the 142
non-Russians who disappeared, 115 were Uzbek by ethnicity. Focusing solely
on the mass disappearance on 20 November, 57 of the 62 missing soldiers
were Uzbek. We can also reconstruct the outlines of their coethnic networks
from their personnel records. Nearly all of the recruits were within eight years
of each other, and had been recruited in two birth year "waves" (1907–10
and 1911–15). On average, these soldiers were twenty-eight years old, much
older than the typical recruit. Nearly half of these soldiers came from just two
birthplaces: the Samarkand oblast and the Ferghana Valley. They were also

recruited into the Red Army at the same recruitment stations. It is reasonable to propose that these soldiers knew one another prior to their army service, and that these shared connections survived throughout their (brief) military service. These soldiers were also old enough to experience directly the waves of repression and collectivization that Stalin unleashed during the late 1920s and early 1930s in Samarkand and the Ferghana Valley. In fact, many of these soldiers were of the exact age to experience the imposition of Russian language instruction in school as well as the mass closure of mosques. Large-scale agricultural collectivization resulted in widespread famine through the Uzbek Soviet Socialist Republic in the 1930s. And in the late 1930s, Stalin ordered the purging and subsequent execution of the republic's entire leadership; they were replaced by Russians.[97] Strong coethnic ties, as well as exposure to Stalinist violence, could provide both motive and means to escape military service under the cover of battle. By contrast, when daily disappearances are few in number, Uzbeks are almost entirely absent; Russian soldiers were far more likely to disappear in singles and pairs than their Uzbek counterparts, who appear to have sought safety in numbers.[98]

8.3.2. The 316th Rifle Division

A bloodied veteran of the mid-October struggle over Volokolamsk, the 316th was the strongest and perhaps most experienced of the 16th Army's remaining rifle divisions. With the largest allotment of anti-tank weapons, including new PTRD anti-tank rifles, the 316th was tasked with leading the counteroffensive against German forces on 16 November. As we know, the two belligerent armies kick-started their offensives nearly simultaneously. Like the 78th, the 316th found some initial success, stepping off its defensive lines at Popovkino, Avdot'ino, Chentsy, and Dubosekovo to capture the German-held villages of Borniki, Sof'evka, and Bludi. Heavy fighting also raged at Khrulevo and Davydkovo.[99] The 316th was quickly pushed backwards, however, with scenes of extremely heavy fighting around Dubosekovo as the 1075th Rifle Regiment fought a desperate holding action against the 2nd Panzer Division and the 46th Panzer Corps. Facing dozens of German tanks with no armor support, the 4th Company of the 1075th Regiment waged a feverish four-hour

---

97. Aminova 1977; Golovanov 1992.

98. The fact that we observe larger numbers of Russians disappearing when Uzbeks do as well provides circumstantial evidence that Russians may be gauging their odds of victory and defeat by the actions of marginalized soldiers. This pattern is consistent with a "contagion" of indiscipline moving from marginalized to favored status soldiers.

99. "Zhurnal boevykh deistvii voisk Zapadnogo fronta za noiabr' 1941 g." TsAMO, Fond: 208, Opis': 2511, Delo: 219, List:1, s.82,97,105.

pitched battle using only anti-tank rifles, grenades, and Molotov cocktails to slow the German advance. In a statement destined to become a staple of Soviet wartime propaganda, political officer Vasilii Klochkov famously rallied his men with the cry "Russia is a vast land, yet there is nowhere to retreat—Moscow is behind us!" He then strapped explosives on and detonated himself against a German tank.[100] Newspaper reports by *Krasnaia Zvezda* journalists credited up to eighteen tank kills to this plucky band of 28 heroes ("the 28 Panfilov") who sacrificed their lives to delay the German advance (but see below). According to divisional personnel logs, at least 116 soldiers were killed (surely an undercount) and another 31 went missing on 16 November alone.[101]

Much was made in Soviet propaganda of the multiethnic nature of the 28 Panfilov heroes and the division as a whole. An excerpt from the General Staff's official history of the Battle of Moscow provides a flavor of this sentiment:

> In the frozen trench near the Dubosekovo station the Guards troops swore to each other to fight the enemy to their last drop of blood. Among them were Russians, Ukrainians, collective farm workers from Talgar in Kazakhstan, and Kazakhs from Alma-Ata. Their warrior's comradeship, made fast by blood, became the embodiment of the combat friendship of the peoples of our countries, who rose up against their mortal enemy.[102]

Despite these apparent heroics, the 316th was forced to retreat in the face of superior German forces. Communications had once again broken down, and the division scrambled to reset its defensive posture. Over the next eighteen days, the division would end up retreating 65 kilometers (about 3.6 kilometers a day) until the Soviet defensive line finally solidified along the Kriukovo-Rozhdestveno axis. Before reaching that destination, however, the division would suffer the loss of General Panfilov, killed by shrapnel from a mortar round as he exited his field headquarters on 18 November.[103] A German attack that same day pushed the division back to Efremovo, Golubtsovo, and Shishkino, though a rare night counterattack did succeed in driving the Germans from Shishkino. Losses were again heavy, with 99 soldiers reported killed and another 24 missing during this counterattack. On 20 November, the 316th (now officially the 8th Guards Rifle Division, having received notice

100. Bek 1943, 1965; Iazov 2011; Grigor'ev and Akhmetova 2014, 119–25.

101. "Zhurnal boevykh deistvii voisk Zapadnogo fronta za noiabr' 1941 g." TsAMO, Fond: 208, Opis': 2511, Delo: 219, List:1, s.105,112.

102. Soviet General Staff 2015, 55.

103. "Pamiati general-maiora I.V. Panfilova," *Krasnaia Zvezda*, 21.11.1941 g.

of its new status on 18 November) retreated to new defensive positions at Zalevo, Aksenovo, and Maloe Nikolskoe.[104] Another 26 soldiers were killed, and 53 went missing, during this fighting retreat. Eleven sappers of the 1077th Regiment engaged in a five-hour delaying action against overwhelming odds, including German tanks, to help the division escape. They were wiped out to a man.[105]

Brutal fighting continued during 22–25 November, with the 316th forced yet again out of a series of defensive positions at Ustinovo, Rybushki, Rozhdestveno, Yakunino, Sizhevo, and Martiushino. With the 316th beginning to break down into small groups of soldiers fighting localized battles, the Wehrmacht, enjoying clear material superiority, captured the important city of Klin on 24 November. Zhukov ordered an immediate riposte at Solnechnogorsk but the battered 316th was too weak to counterattack, which left the division in an even more precarious state.[106] After a series of hammer blows against its defensive positions in late November, the 316th finally reached Kriukovo, which became its main effort. Beginning on 3 December, the 316th waged a costly campaign to wrest Kriukovo from German control, experiencing a substantial number of casualties while failing to dislodge German forces entirely from Kriukovo and its outskirts. On 5 December, the German offensive stalled out, leaving a battered 316th Division desperately in need of resupply and retrofit.[107]

Compared with the 78th, the 316th exhibited a lower degree of combat power and cohesion, our two hallmarks of battlefield performance. On the defensive side of the ledger, the 316th was prone to disorganized retreats, losing soldiers along the way as it raced to stay ahead of pursuing German armored columns. Problems appeared when launching offensives, too. The 316th engaged in fewer overall counterattacks than the 78th, and when it did manage to launch them, they typically had much less staying power than the 78th. The 316th also had a far worse killed-to-missing ratio. Personnel records indicate that at least 578 soldiers were killed in action from 16 November to 5 December. An additional 436 soldiers disappeared. This results in a 1.2:1 ratio, suggesting that cohesion was far more of an issue for the 316th than the

104. "Zhurnal boevykh deistvii voisk Zapadnogo fronta za noiabr' 1941 g." TsAMO, Fond: 208, Opis': 2511, Delo: 219, List:1, s.118,129,136. Shaposhnikov 2006, 80–82.

105. "Iz politdoneseniia komissara 1077-go strelkovogo polka 316-i strelkovoi divizii komissary 8-i gvardeiskoi strelkovoi divizii" reproduced in Vzvarova and Emel'ianova 1989, 29.

106. "Zhurnal boevykh deistvii voisk Zapadnogo fronta za noiabr' 1941 g." TsAMO, Fond: 208, Opis': 2511, Delo: 219, List:1, s.152,159,166,176.

107. "Zhurnal boevykh deistvii voisk Zapadnogo fronta za noiabr' 1941 g." TsAMO, Fond: 208, Opis': 2511, Delo: 219, List:1, s.228,235,243,254.

78th Division. In a particularly alarming sign for divisional commanders, a large group of 140 soldiers disappeared on a day (5 December) when the division had only experienced some skirmishes (with 18 killed in action). Despite possessing key advantages over the 78th—including its much larger arsenal of anti-tank weapons and more favorable force-to-space ratio—the 316th proved less resilient than its counterpart.

MISPREDICTION? THE CURIOUS CASE
OF THE 316TH DIVISION

In one sense, the military inequality argument correctly anticipated that the 78th Rifle Division would outperform its more divided counterpart. Yet the 316th Rifle Division, for all its shortcomings, still seems to have punched above its weight. While the 316th never matched the 78th's cohesion or ability to organize timely counterattacks, its soldiers did appear to exhibit surprisingly high combat motivation and resilience, most notably at Dubosekovo. Indeed, the legend of the 28 Panfilov heroes was hallowed ground for Soviet wartime propaganda, a patriotic call to arms that still resonates today in Russia and Kazakhstan. In 2016, for example, the newest metro station on the Moscow Central Circle, Panfilovskaia, was opened. Kazakh President Nursultan Nazarbayev similarly unveiled a monument to General Panfilov in Astana's Zheruyik Park in May 2015. While no theory can explain every case, mispredictions can be important for theoretical development by identifying the scope conditions and blind spots of a given explanation.[108] Given its sky-high military inequality score (0.78), why did the 316th still continue to perform reasonably well on the battlefield? Why, in other words, did it not simply collapse, like its close cousin, the 38th Rifle Division?

The events of 16–17 November at Dubosekovo cast a long shadow over assessments of the 316th's battlefield performance, so it makes sense to begin our investigation with the 28 Panfilov heroes. Most historians now agree that these heroic deeds never happened.[109] Instead, they were complete fabrications by two journalists whose newspaper articles purportedly describing these events just happened to catch Stalin's eye, fueling another round of

---

108. Kalyvas 2006, 302.

109. The best overview of this controversy is Statiev 2012. The most recent (official) attempt to rehabilitate the reputation of the 28 Panfilov is *Vklad uchenykh-istorikov v sokhranenie istoricheskoi pamiati o voine* 2015. The director of Russia's State Archive was fired for confirming that the incident had been fabricated. See "Razoblachenie falsifkatora izgotovlennoi im fal'shivki neizbezhno," *Kommersant"*, 20 April 2015, 4.

mythmaking.[110] Errors abound in the initial newspaper accounts; the wrong regiment was cited, for example, while 6 of the alleged 28 Panfilov, whose names appear to have been chosen randomly from casualty lists, turned out to be alive, including one who had embarrassingly defected to the Germans.[111] No record of a sustained battle at Dubosekovo can be found in German operational logs. On the Soviet side, many of the relevant documents remain classified or were destroyed in a mysterious fire.[112] Key participants in these November battles have recanted their testimony. This includes I. V. Kaprov, the former commander of the 1075th Rifle Regiment, who claimed in a secret 1948 report that "there was no battle with German tanks at the Dubosekovo junction on the 16 November—it is a complete fiction. On this day, 2nd company fought German tanks of the 4th [Panzer] Group. Over 100 were killed from the company, not the 28 that they wrote about in the paper."[113]

A closer look at the documentary record also reveals that the 316th had morale problems in the run-up to Operation Typhoon's November restart.[114] Fearing its collapse, the 316th's commanders had established a robust monitoring system to keep tabs on soldier attitudes. A secret 27 October report by the 16th Army's political commissar to the military commissar of the 316th warned that "I have data that individual servicemen of the Division entrusted to you express negative moods, show cowardice and there are cases of drunkenness." He went on: "For example, a soldier of the 1st platoon of the 1075th Rifle Regiment said of his fellow soldiers: 'They want to die with hunger. The Red Army treats us like dogs. We were sent for slaughter.'" Another soldier from the 1077th argued that "fifty percent of the farmers are opposed to the Soviet regime. Our generals shout that we will beat the enemy on foreign territory, and is done. ... The opposite is true. The Russian people were sold by the

110. V. Koroteev, "Gvardeitsy Panfilova v boiakh za Moskvu," *Krasnaia zvezda*, 27 November 1941, 3, and Aleksandr Krivitskii, "Zaveshchanie 28 pavshikh geroev," *Krasnaia zvezda*, 28 November 1941, 3.

111. My first clue that something was amiss turned out to be the official commendation for the fallen 28 heroes. In a division dominated by Kazakhs and Kirghiz, 17 of the 28 awardees were Russian; only 4 Kazakhs and a lone Kirghiz were included in the list of 28. See Zhilin 2001a, 150–59.

112. Belov 2014, 27.

113. Belov 2014, 29. "Spravka-doklad glavnogo voennogo prokurora N. Afanas'eva 'O 28 panfilovtsakh,'" GA RF Fond: R-8131. Available at http://statearchive.ru/607.

114. Official investigations for why the 316th lost Volokolamsk in late-October 1941 partly emphasized its command and control problems arising from the "uncertain" nature of its soldiers. See, for example, "Donesenie nachal'nika operativnogo otdela shtaba zapadnogo fronta o boevykh deistviiakh 16-i armii sd 15 no 28 oktiabria 1941 goda," reproduced in Knyshevskii 1992, 175–80. See also Safranov 1958.

generals." A third said that "we must stop fighting." The commissar ordered that "all appropriate measures" should be taken to "eradicate the above facts and restore order."[115]

Well before soldiers went missing during the mid-November battles, the 316th's regimental and company commanders had already instituted a policy of executing deserters. Baurdzhan Momysh-uly, the famed Kazakh who commanded a battalion of the division's Talgarsky Regiment (the 1073rd), ordered a fellow Kazakh executed by a firing squad after he deserted, mutilated himself, and then returned to the unit. Momysh-uly wrote that he was forced to kill his 'son' [Barambaev, the deserter] for the sake of hundreds of 'sons' [his battalion]."[116] Viewing "fear as a parasite, an infection that must be destroyed by discipline," Momysh-uly later also prevented 87 stragglers from joining his battalion out of concern that they would further strain the internal cohesion of his own unit. In one remarkable sequence in late October, General Panfilov cashiered several commanders for failing to control their "panic-stricken mobs" (21 October), issued orders that "cowards are to be shot on the spot" (23 October), and then executed at least two deserters (24 October) in order to prevent mass panic.[117] The 316th also executed at least one soldier in a public show trial on 16 November, the same day as the alleged battle at Dubosekovo, to prevent mass panic within the 1077th Regiment.[118]

Most importantly, the 316th was an early adopter of blocking detachments to maintain cohesion. A 300-man unit—even larger than what Stalin would order in mid-1942—was already in place by 24 September.[119] As the 316th suffered casualties, the need for such a large unit was reduced, and so the blocking detachment shrunk to 150 soldiers by 18 November.[120] While we might question whether a blocking detachment of that size could generate a credible threat of sanction, it should be noted that the depleted 1075th Rifle Regiment was about the same size. Panfilov appears to have adopted this company-sized blocking detachment out of fear that panic might rip through his ranks, leading to the division's disintegration. Tucked into the 316th's record of daily orders is a terse note dated 18 November calling for the deployment of this unit to the 316th's rear to prevent collapse. The 1077th Regiment, it was noted, was

115. "Rasporiazhenie chlena voennogo soveta 16-i armii," reproduced in Knyshevskii 1992, 184.

116. Bek, "Panfilovtsy," 207–8.

117. Grigor'ev and Akhmetova 2014, 64–77. See also Bek, "Volokolamskoe shosse," 178–81, for execution of soldier Pashko, a beloved soldier who was thought to be spreading panic.

118. The executed soldier was Egor Konstantinovich (ID.75592714), TsAMO Fond 33, Opis' 594258 Dela 36.

119. Statiev 2012, 779.

120. Daines 2008, 174.

at half its pre-battle strength; the 1073rd, down to only 200 men, with another 2,334 believed to be scattered in retreat along the roads; and the 1075th had only 250 men. The 690th, a volunteer regiment attached to the 316th, had shattered; only 40 percent of its soldiers had emerged from encirclement and were now thought to be hiding in the forest.[121]

This reliance on coercion helps explain why the 316th was able to retain some semblance of cohesion despite its extreme level of inequality. Even under these conditions, however, we cannot deny that the 316th's leadership, especially Panfilov and Momysh-uly, worked to construct a sense of shared identity as a bulwark against disorder. Both leaders appealed to Kazakh national pride and worked to refine the "motherland" as their families and the Kazakh SSR rather than Moscow or the Soviet Union. Momysh-uly in particular aimed to build a counter-narrative to official propaganda even as he worked within the strictures of the Russian-dominated Red Army. When asked to define the motherland, he replied, "The Motherland is you [ty]! Kill those who are trying to kill you! Who needs to do this? You do! Your wife, father and mother, your children need you to do this! The Motherland is you yourself, your family, your wife and children."[122] Panfilov, too, presents an unusual profile. By all accounts, he was beloved by his soldiers, in part because of his own personal history: he had served in a variety of official capacities in Central Asia since 1924, including as the military commissar for the Kyrgyz SSR, and so knew the region and its cultures. In short, while the 316th lacked the cohesion and combat power of the 78th, it still retained some measure of battlefield proficiency through its heavy reliance on coercion and a dollop of positive inducement as outsiders with the opportunity to raise their social standing by fighting well.

8.3.3.   The Red Army Counterattacks, 6–25 December 1941

The post–Operation Typhoon period offers a final illustration of the divergent battlefield performance of the 78th and 316th Divisions. Seeking to deliver a crushing blow to exhausted German forces, Zhukov ordered a massive counteroffensive on 6 December across the entire length of the Western Front. Parked on the front's right wing near Istra, the newly reinforced 16th Army was the most powerful of the ten Soviet armies now under Zhukov's central command. With 55,000 soldiers in its four rifle divisions, the 16th Army boasted more field (320) and anti-tank (190) guns, along

121. "Boevoe donesenie komandira 316-i strelkovoi divizii komanduiushchemu 16-i armiei zapadnovo fronta (18 noiabria 1941 g.)" reproduced in Vzvarova and Emel'ianova 1989, 28.

122. Bek, "Panfilovtsy," 212.

with tanks (125), than any other army.[123] The 316th was stationed to the east of Kriukovo; the 78th was holding the southern sector of the 16th Army's front, near Brekhovo. The two divisions were separated only by about eight kilometers. They faced depleted but skilled German forces capable of erecting robust hasty defenses, including converting settlements into strongpoints that required close-quarters combat to dislodge dug-in units. Conditions were also poor; each division peered out into a snowscape marked by poor visibility, short days, deep snow, and temperatures that routinely dropped below −20°C.

How did these divisions perform? The 78th collided with German units near Rozhdestveno, where it quickly bogged down trying to breach defensive positions using frontal assaults.[124] In at least one instance, regimental commanders ordered their soldiers to conduct bayonet charges against German lines.[125] Though initially unsuccessful, by 11 December the 78th had overcome German defenses and was about to reach Istra. Retreating German forces detonated the reservoir near Istra, masking their retreat with a flood, slowing the 78th's advance for about four days. It continued to grind on, however, slowly recapturing fourteen villages on its way to Kokovino and then Ruza by 23 December.[126] By 25 December, the Wehrmacht had retreated nearly fifty-five kilometers, giving the 78th a rate of advance of about three kilometers per day. The division also managed to capture some of the largest totals of German motor vehicles, guns, and tanks of any division during the fight near the Istra reservoir area (16–20 December).[127] According to its personnel records, the division lost 246 soldiers killed and another 104 missing during this three-week operation, a ratio somewhat worse than it recorded during defensive operations in November. Indeed, Zhukov complained about the 78th's simple tactics: "These frontal assaults," he noted, "lead to excessive losses and a slowing of the pace of the offensive."[128] In short, the division performed well, especially being understrength, but still wrestled with conducting more complicated offensive operations and with protecting its own soldiers while maneuvering.

123. Soviet General Staff 2015, 168.

124. "Zhurnal boevykh deistvii voisk Zapadnogo fronta za noiabr' 1941 g." TsAMO, Fond: 208, Opis': 2511, Delo: 219, List:1, s.244,255.

125. Soviet General Staff 2015, 178.

126. "Nastuplenie 16 A na Istrinskom napravlenii v dekabre 1941 goda," Fond: 208, Opis': 2511, Delo: 1043, List: 77.

127. Soviet General Staff 2015, 195.

128. Zhukov, 2013. "Prikaz voiskam zapadnogo fronta," TsAMO Fond: 208, Opis': 2524, Delo: 10, List: 235–236.

The performance of the 316th paled by comparison. Like the 78th, it too participated in the initial Soviet offensive, meeting heavy resistance near Kriukovo.[129] After advancing about three kilometers over three days, the 316th managed to drive German forces from the center of Kriukovo. That victory would mark the high water of its efforts, however. On 9 December, the Western Front HQ ordered the division to withdraw from combat and take up a position in the second echelon of Soviet defenses near Kriukovo.[130] Despite its vaunted Guards designation, the division appears to have been suffering from high rates of indiscipline. Personnel records indicate that the number of soldiers gone missing had spiked; 115 individuals disappeared just between 7 and 12 December. Soldiers continued to disappear even after the division was pulled from the front line; 46 went missing on 10 December alone, for example. With only a fraction of the 78th's combat time, the 316th managed to lose far more soldiers to disappearances. With a total of 154 missing soldiers against only 57 killed soldiers, the 316th's ratio of killed to missing was 1:2.7, almost the complete inverse of the 78th's ratio for this period. Recognizing that it was unfit for combat, the Western Front HQ pulled the division from the front entirely on 16 December. It was reassigned to Stavka's reserve and sent for refitting, where it took on 4,000 new soldiers.[131] As before, these soldiers were drawn almost entirely from Central Asia, particularly the Kazakh SSR. The division did not return to combat duty until 18 January 1942, when it was assigned to the north Western Front.

8.4. Combat Dynamics and the Lessons of 1941

These paired cases not only underscore the dangers of inequality for battlefield performance but also its path-dependent nature; inequality, in some senses, is destiny. Yet an emphasis on structural inequality does not mean excluding a role for combat dynamics. Rather, these divisions were fighting and dying within the confines of their own tailored straitjackets that restricted, but did not dictate completely, their tactical and operational choices. Moreover, the Battle of Moscow convinced Stalin and the Stavka of the need to make important macrolevel changes to better manage the battlefield pathologies arising from prewar inequalities. In effect, endogenous

129. Soviet General Staff 2015, 178. "Izvlechenie iz operativnoi svodki № 284 General'nogo shtaba Krasnoi Armii (7.12.41 g)," in Zhilin 2001b, 33. The last mention of the 316th in the daily General Staff readouts is "Izvlechenie iz operativnoi svodki № 290 General'nogo shtaba Krasnoi Armii (13.12.41 g)," in Zhilin 2001b, 83.

130. Grigor'ev and Akhmetova 2014, 202–4.

131. Iazov 2011, 138.

wartime dynamics arising from the experience of combat created a feedback loop of policy changes driven by recognition among senior leaders that ethnic inequalities had to be tempered, or innovated around, if Soviet battlefield performance was to improve enough to defeat the Wehrmacht.

For example, Stalin, seeking to improve the combat motivation of his soldiers, deliberately softened the edges of his Communist-inspired vision of the political community. As early as November 1941, he began a gradual but steady evolution in his public rhetoric, drawing far more on the imagery of Russian nationalism to help tamp down anti-regime sentiment among soldiers and citizens alike.[132] Pushed to the wall, Stalin recognized that he needed to barter for support of his own populations given German conquest of western Russia.[133] Though unwilling (or unable) to overturn the Soviet Union's ethnic hierarchy, he also modified his appeals toward national minorities, particularly Central Asian populations. His vision of "national Bolshevism," for example, relied on appeals to an ethnically ambiguous motherland (*Rodina*) that could be interpreted variously by these populations as referring to their own ethnic homelands. He also cleverly encouraged hopes that the status of these groups would be elevated in the postwar order. Military service thus represented both a pathway to a better future and an opportunity for victimized populations, especially Ukrainians and Belorussians, to exact revenge on German invaders. This flowering of national Bolshevism was brief, really lasting only from late 1941 to late 1944, driven by military exigencies and discarded once danger had passed. Such efforts represented tactical modifications, not wholesale changes, but did manage to increase recruitment among Central Asians. On the margins, then, national Bolshevism represented a gesture toward greater inclusion that may have encouraged at least some soldiers to fight harder to secure equality in a new postwar order.[134]

Fearful of genuine reform, and unsure whether such promises would be seen as credible by their intended audiences, Stalin supplemented the carrot of positive inducements with the stick of institutionalized coercion. Inspired by the improvisation of field commanders, Stalin officially entrenched blocking detachments as the centerpiece of efforts to maintain cohesion within the Red Army. On 28 July 1942, he released Order № 227, which called for the immediate creation of 200-man blocking detachments to be staffed by Red Army soldiers and positioned in the rear of all units. Written by Stalin himself,[135] Order № 227 decreed that these units were to establish positions

---

132. On Stalin's sensitivity to public criticism, see Kotkin 2017, 902.
133. Dallin 1956; Reese 2011, 11.
134. Slezkine 1994; Brandenburger 2011, 2002, 2001; Martin 2001.
135. Khlevniuk 2015, 223.

2–3 kilometers behind the front lines to fulfill three tasks: return straggling or lost soldiers to their units; prevent desertion and defection through fear of sanction; and to imprison or kill commanders or soldiers that deserted, defected, exercised poor judgment, or otherwise represented a threat to cohesion.[136] The final piece of a broader interlocking system of secret police (NKVD), surveillance and censorship, and penal battalions for officers (*shtrafbaty*) and companies for soldiers (*shtrafroty*) was now set in place.[137]

These units functioned as a catch-and-release program that steered the majority of wayward soldiers—stragglers, those absent without authorization, malingers—back to their units. While filtration points channeled suspected deserters and defectors into prison camps or public executions, the majority of soldiers went right back to their units, boosting Soviet manpower enormously. Between 1 August and 15 October 1942, an estimated 140,755 soldiers were detained by 193 blocking detachments (38,600 soldiers) across all fronts. In 1943, the NKVD detained 158,585 soldiers for "straggling behind," another 42,807 men for unauthorized departure, and 23,418 for suspected desertion just in the immediate rear area (extending 25 kilometers behind the front line). Another 18,000 soldiers were sent to penal units or the Gulag.[138] In total, some 1.25 million soldiers were caught away from their units without authorization and returned to the front lines during 1942–43. For a small investment in soldiers, these detachments could have large effects. An estimated 51,728 soldiers, or 37 percent of total Red Army soldiers deployed on the Stalingrad and Don fronts, were detained for suspected desertion or unauthorized leave from their units in 1942 by 41 detachments that had only 8,200 soldiers.[139]

Blocking detachments may have prevented a mass exodus of Red Army soldiers, but they did so at a terrible cost. While estimates vary, scholars now believe that 158,000 Red Army personnel died at the hands of these units by

136. The best Russian-language discussions of blocking detachments are: Orlov (2012); Telitsyn (2010); Daines (2008); Pyltsyn (2007); Zolotarev 1996, 330.

137. See Lyall 2017 for the historiographical debates surrounding the effects and effectiveness of these units. Order No. 227 was preceded by a flurry of increasingly draconian orders tasking NKVD units with curbing mass desertion from the ranks. See, for example, "Dokladnaia zapiska No. 1/955" (22 October 1941), "Direktiva NKVD SSSR No. 283 o meropriiatiiakh po bor'be s dezertirstvom" (6 December 1941), and "Pis'mo NKVD SSSR v NKO SSSR" (26 December 1941), reproduced in Patrushev 2000 (vol. 2), pp. 235–36, 391–92, 473–75.

138. Reese 2011, 174–75.

139. "Spravka OO NKVD STF v UOO NKVD SSSR o deiatel'nosti zagraditel'nykh otriadov Stalingradskogo i Donskogo frontov [Ne ranee 15 oktiabria] 1942 g.," Pogonii (2000, 230–31); 36,109 soldiers were detained on the Don Front, and another 15,649 were detained at Stalingrad.

1944.[140] Soldiers quickly came to resent their presence, speaking openly of a "Second Front" being organized against them.[141] Soldiers clearly understood the stakes: "The organization of blocking detachments, that's the Second Front. On the front line we'll be shot by the Germans, and from the rear by the blocking detachments."[142] In turn, hatred of these units gave rise to fears of armed mutiny; scores of officers were fragged by their men.[143] These units also conspired to narrow battlefield flexibility by design: to remain a credible deterrent, these units needed to be tethered to regular line units. As a result, Soviet commanders embraced simplified, rigid, tactics that assumed military cohesion would suffer if a gap emerged from regular units and their minders. The need to preserve this linkage created incentives to rely on costly frontal assaults where blocking detachments could maintain near-constant surveillance. Similarly, exploitation efforts were curbed for fear that attacking units might become separated from their blocking detachments. The fact that blocking detachments also targeted officers created incentives to rely on tried-and-true, if costly, tactics and operations and to eschew more innovative but riskier approaches that might save lives. Fearing sanction if seen as insufficiently aggressive, commanders launched many mistimed offensives that stalled out in part because they felt pressured to take action even if their men and materiel were depleted. Through both direct and indirect channels, these units raised Red Army casualties.

This reliance on blocking detachments also helps explain why we observe less tactical and operational innovation among Red Army divisional commanders than expected. The combination of high (or extreme) inequality and coerced fighting made the adoption of new tactics sluggish at best even when faced with crushing battlefield pressures. Red Army commanders, for example, continued to favor frontal assaults throughout the war, driving up the costs of each offensive. As David Glantz has argued, the Red Army "continued to make dreadful errors right until the end, and those errors contributed as much as anything to the horrendous losses that it suffered." Despite some

140. Daines 2008; Telitsyn 2010; Orlov 2012.

141. See, for example, "Dokladnaia zapiska OO NKVD STF v UOO NKVD SSSR 'O reagirovaniiakh lichnogo sostava chastei i soedinenii na prikaz Stavki No.227, 14/15 avgusta 1942 g.," in Pogonii 2000, 191.

142. "Spetssoobshchenie OO NKVD STF v UOO NKVD SSSR 'Ob otritsatel'nykh vyskazyvaniiakh otdel'nykh voennosluzhashchikh Stalingradskogo fronta v sviazi s izdaniem prikaza Stavki No.227' 19 avgusta 1942 g.," Pogonii 2000, 187.

143. See, for example, "Spetssoobshchenie OO NVKD STF v UOO NKVD SSSR 'Ob otritsatel'nykh vyskazyvaniiakh otdel'nykh voennosluzhashchikh Stalingradskogo fronta v sviazi s izdaniem prikaza Stavki No.227, 19 avgusta 1942 g.," in Pogonii 2000, 190–92. On fragging, see Merridale 2006, 192.

improvements over time, Soviet tactics and operational art remained fairly simple, if not crude. This was true of both Stalingrad and Kursk, where even the most innovative commanders—often in armor units—continued to rely on frontal assaults and basic maneuvers rather than more complicated operational art such as mobile defense or double envelopment. In other words, the stereotype of the Red Army as a "monolithic and rigid force that employed artless steamroller tactics to achieve victory regardless of cost" was largely correct. The Red Army sought to absorb German offensives and then shift to the attack once their momentum had been halted, moving "in painstakingly rigid fashion while on the offense, often artlessly and regardless of cost."[144] The notion of armies and their commanders continually updating their approaches in light of new information won through combat may therefore be somewhat misplaced; innovation may be crowded out as the level of inequality within specific units increases.

While Stalin and his generals worked to reduce inequality-induced vulnerabilities, we must also recognize that German failures, both of omission and commission, placed a cap on the limits of damage inflicted. To be sure, the Wehrmacht punished the Red Army savagely for its self-imposed constraints. But rather than capitalize fully on these limitations, German strategy seemed calculated to drive soldiers from marginalized ethnic groups, and even Russian victims of Stalinist repression, back into Stalin's hands. Criminal conditions in German prisoner of war camps, where over half of the 5.7 million captured soldiers died from starvation, disease, and abuse, discouraged side-switching by would-be defectors.[145] Similarly, the execution of 5,000–10,000 commissars also sowed doubts about the likelihood of successful surrender.[146] Brutal counterinsurgency policies towards civilians likewise generated new grievances among Ukrainian and Belorussian populations that were most likely to support liberation from Stalin.[147] Nazi racial policies toward Slavic peoples, which dictated forced population resettlement, coerced labor, and the confiscation of property and goods, likely reduced substantially the number of Russians and other groups willing to collaborate with the Nazi occupiers.[148] A blinding commitment to the Final Solution in Eastern Europe may also have had second-order consequences for German war-fighting. Fouled logistics, especially railways, and the diversion of critically needed soldiers to

144. Glantz 2005*b*, 618.

145. Schneer 2005.

146. Hartmann 2013, 91.

147. Rutherford and Wettstein 2018, 118–47; Kay, Rutherford and Stahel 2012; Sinitsyn 2010, 167–209.

148. Rutherford 2014; Snyder 2010; Mazower 2009.

prosecute the Holocaust may have undercut the Wehrmacht's performance in at least four major campaigns against Soviet forces.[149] The full costs imposed by military inequality may not be realized if enemies are unable (or unwilling) to take advantage of these own goals, either because they are unaware of them or because their own ideological blinders prohibit timely action.

8.5.   Conclusion

Structural explanations often stumble when asked to explain why battlefield performance varies within armies. Yet a shift to the microlevel helps confirm that the logic of military inequality is operating both across and within armies. In fact, the differential rates of soldier disappearances from the 78th Rifle Division suggest that the argument is also able to handle intra-division variation in cohesion and combat power. Whether these findings generalize to the other 218 rifle divisions mobilized and deployed during 1941 remains an open question, of course.[150] This pattern of decreased cohesion as inequality rises is nonetheless consistent with broader empirical findings about the overrepresentation of non-Russians among prisoners of war and deserters during the war.[151] A microlevel turn also confers certain advantages. Its close-range nature opens up new measures of battlefield performance, including rates of advances, towns (re)captured, and the ability to escape encirclement, that are difficult or misleading to estimate for entire armies. An emphasis on microlevel dynamics also restores agency to individual soldiers, spotlighting their decisions to fight or flee, and their capacity for collective action. In doing so, it breaks down the assumption that armies are unitary and homogenous actors; local processes of producing and wielding violence are particular to the ethnic composition of the units doing the fighting.

Highlighting endogenous wartime dynamics should not blind us to the importance of prewar politics, however. The short-lived nature of some of these divisions (especially the 38th), along with replacement policies geared toward maintaining prewar ethnic balances, help ward off concerns that inequality was endogenous to combat. Yes, combat is messy, and potentially transformative. But these prewar ethnic divisions remained durable; ethnic identities were not so fluid that they were continually reshaped during the war.

---

149. Pasher 2014.

150. The military inequality argument does well to anticipate aggregate Soviet performance. With a military inequality score of 0.445, the Soviet Union was predicted to have a battlefield performance index (BPI) value of 0.57, indicating that it had about two of the four pathologies tracked by the index. In fact, it had three: a LER below parity; mass desertion; and the deployment of blocking detachments.

151. Schneer 2005; Edele 2017; Reese 2011.

Identities were also sticky at the macrolevel. Stalin was largely entrapped by a credible commitment problem, having lashed his regime (and himself) to the mast of a Soviet vision that foreclosed a more egalitarian political community. Stalin's inability to shift the bases of the Soviet community in a genuinely inclusive direction dictated increasingly draconian policies that further drove up the costs of the war, pushing the Soviet Union to the brink of defeat. Military inequality thus offers a bridge between macrolevel politics of community and the microlevel dynamics of war-fighting right down to individual units on the battlefield itself.

9

Conclusion

On the actual day of battle naked truths may be picked up for the asking; by the following morning, they have already begun to get into their uniforms.

IAN HAMILTON, *A STAFF OFFICER'S SCRAP-BOOK DURING THE RUSSO-JAPANESE WAR*, 1905

SUCCESSFUL ARMIES ARE INCLUSIVE; unsuccessful ones largely die by their own hands, wracked by the poison of inequality that kills them, sometimes slowly, sometimes quickly, from the inside out. Combat is, of course, the collision of armies seeking to impose their wills on each other through coercive violence and brute force. Yet the battlefield fate of many armies was set long before the first battle. As this book has demonstrated, the prewar nature of a belligerent's political community and, above all, whether its leaders exploited ethnic differences as a tool of rule, helped dictate its subsequent battlefield performance. Once certain ethnic groups become identified as incomplete citizens and subjected to either discrimination or, worse, outright repression, the state's military machine becomes increasingly distorted. Prewar military inequality sours morale among soldiers drawn from these targeted populations, lowering their combat motivation while increasing their desire to subvert or escape military service. It also breeds interethnic mistrust, tossing away the advantages of diversity, while strengthening intraethnic bonds and communication avenues that can facilitate escape. In turn, belligerents are forced to adopt suboptimal strategies to manage these soldiers, whether through manipulating the ethnic composition of units, altering their battlefield employment, or fielding murderous blocking detachments. Trade-offs between combat power and cohesion, the two bulwarks of battlefield performance, become increasingly acute as levels of military inequality rise. The result is often mass desertion and defection, unfavorable loss-exchange ratios, and fratricidal violence, leading to battlefield defeat and, in some cases, the complete disintegration of the army itself. Low inequality is not necessarily a guarantee of success—no one factor can credibly promise that—but the historical odds favor societies and armies that embrace inclusive citizenship as the basis of military service. The greater the deviation from this ideal, the more likely armies will succumb to unforced errors and self-induced vulnerabilities that opponents ruthlessly exploit. In the end, armies are experiments in social engineering on a grand scale, and they sometimes fail.

9.1.   Key Findings

To test and support these claims, I devised a mixed-method research design built explicitly around counterfactual reasoning and paired comparisons to isolate inequality's effects on battlefield performance. I also invested heavily in new data collection. The result, Project Mars, expanded our universe of conventional wars and their belligerents. It also made possible an examination of wartime behaviors, including mass desertion, defection, and fratricidal violence, that had existed for too long on the margins of our theories. Project Mars provides a more balanced, less Western, view of warfare, reducing our dependence on the same few cases that currently dominate our theories and empirical findings about the drivers of battlefield performance since 1800.

Our empirical investigation opened with a fortuitous event: the sudden and unexpected death of the Mahdi in 1885, a shock that catapulted the Mahdiya's military inequality from low to extreme levels. This marked shift across nearly the entire spectrum of military inequality (a full 0.66 increase) led to a dramatic collapse in the Mahdiya's military fortunes. The Khalifa's decision to rule atop a narrow tribal and ethnosectarian base transformed a once-successful army into a shell of its former self in less than a dozen years. Faced with British forces in 1898–99, the Khalifa's military experienced mass desertion and defection, used copious violence to maintain discipline in the ranks, and, at eighty-eight soldiers lost for each British or Egyptian soldier killed, recorded one of the worst casualty imbalances in the Project Mars dataset. The chapter not only served as a theory-building exercise but also generated the template used in subsequent chapters to test the explanatory weight of the military inequality argument against alternative explanations.

Next, I employed statistical tests at the war level to explore the relationship between military inequality and multiple measures of battlefield performance. Both measures of inequality, *military inequality* and *bands* of inequality, return similar findings across both eras of modern war. In the early modern era, a full shift in military inequality results in a 64.5 percentage point increase in the predicted likelihood that a belligerent will suffer below-parity casualties; a 95.4 and 67.8 percentage point increase in the likelihood of mass desertion and defection, respectively; and a 51.6 percentage point increase in the likelihood of fielding blocking detachments. In the modern era, the same patterns hold, with a 73.6 percentage point increase in the likelihood of lop-sided casualties; a staggering 105.4 percentage point increase in the likelihood of mass desertion; and similar 57.6 and 67.3 percentage point increases in the likelihood of a belligerent deploying blocking detachments. The combined battlefield performance index (BPI) also drops precipitously, with reductions of −0.783 and −0.909 recorded in the early modern and modern eras when sliding across the entire military inequality continuum.

Moving from low to high bands of inequality also results in diminished bat-tlefield performance across every measure. In the pre-1918 era, a shift from low to high inequality results in a 35 percentage point increase in the pre-dicted likelihood of a below-parity LER; a 43.8 and 33.5 percentage point increase in the likelihood of mass desertion and defection, respectively; and a 21.4 percentage point increase in the likelihood that blocking detachments will be deployed. In the post-1918 era, the same shift across bands of inequal-ity results in 33.2, 57.3, 13.8, and 28.8 percentage point increases in the predicted likelihood of below-parity casualties, mass desertion, mass defection, and the use of blocking detachments, respectively. The predicted likelihood that a bel-ligerent will score a middling 0.50 or lower on the BPI also increases 52 and nearly 56 percentage points when shifting from low to high inequality in the early modern and modern historical eras, respectively.

The design's third stage involved process tracing inequality's effects through paired comparisons drawn and matched at random from Project Mars. Collectively, these six cases span 140 years, were fought around the world from North and Central Africa to Central Asia and Eastern Europe, and run the gamut from small conflicts to the First World War's Eastern Front. These cases also help nail down inequality's effects since they encompass pairs of belligerents where the differences in inequality are large (0.69 for Morocco and Kokand), medium (0.31 for Ethiopia and the DRC), and modest (0.08 for the Ottoman and Habsburg Empires). Drawing on primary documents and secondary sources in multiple languages, these cases enable close-range examination of the mechanisms through which military inequality affected battlefield performance. Marginalized and repressed soldiers, for example, deserted and defected at a higher rate than their core counterparts, and typ-ically did so earlier in the war. Armies with medium to extreme inequality sought to avoid breakdown by simplifying their tactics, increasingly relying on crude massed frontal assaults at higher levels of inequality. They were also more likely to face trade-offs between cohesion and combat power, including more tangled command and control, a deliberate avoidance of decentraliza-tion that in turn increased casualties, and the use of blocking detachments that increased resentment among targeted groups. Having backed themselves into a corner, these belligerents often sacrificed combat power in the hope they might manufacture enough cohesion to remain in the fight. Every belligerent in these cases with a military inequality coefficient of at least 0.43, about the midway point of the continuum, also turned their arms against their own population in "double wars," using the cover of conflict to prosecute prewar nation-building ambitions.

Evidence for the argument is also found in battlefield dynamics within each case. These battles ranged from dozens of soldiers near Iqan in 1864 to the million-strong armies that clashed during the 1916 Brusilov Offensive. Fronts ranged from a few kilometers (Tetuán, Tashkent) to dozens (Badme, Tripoli) to hundreds (Katanga, Galicia) in breadth. Sometimes the chosen armies were on the offensive; other times, they fought from defensive positions. Technology, too, varied across these battles, spanning single-shot rifles and primitive rocket batteries to modern tanks, aircraft, and artillery. In some cases, history rhymed eerily; Kokand's and DRC's armies, saddled with high military inequality, threw themselves into ill-fated offensives that saw their retreating forces drowned in nearby rivers in a desperate bid to escape. The stakes, too, differed. Little was won or lost by Ethiopia during its Operation Sunset at Badme, for example. Yet the fates of Kokand and Austria-Hungary, and to a lesser extent Morocco, were shaped by the fortunes of their armies. At Katanga, Galicia, and Chimkent, high military inequality belligerents diverted substantial resources into repressing local populations despite the poor performance of their own armies. As a whole, these battles represent an important inferential test of the argument's ability to capture both macrohistorical patterns across belligerents and to make clear predictions about conduct in specific battles.

Together, these cases highlight the expected negative relationship between military inequality and battlefield performance. Figure 9.1 plots this relationship using the BPI, where a 1 denotes a "clean sheet"—the belligerent did not experience mass desertion, defection, deploy blocking detachments, or have a loss-exchange ratio below parity—and a 0 denotes that all four problems were present.[1] Moving left to right, we find that battlefield performance falls as military inequality rises, culminating in the sad-sack performance of Kokand and the Mahdiya at the far end of the distribution. If anything, their battlefield performance was artificially propped up by the fact that defection from their armies was insufficient in size—largely due to the reluctance of their enemies to accept would-be defectors—to be coded as "mass"

---

1. A 0.75 is thus associated with the presence of one problem; a 0.50 with two problems; and a 0.25 with three problems present.

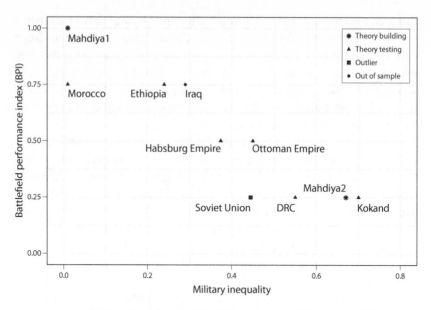

FIGURE 9.1. Military Inequality and Battlefield Performance: The Historical Cases

by Project Mars. A less restrictive threshold for mass defection would push these belligerents to the cellar of the BPI.[2] This is the exact same relationship we uncovered in figure 4.3 using the entire Project Mars dataset.

The research design's final stage is perhaps its most ambitious. Nested inside the most lethal war in Project Mars, the chapter details the fate of four Soviet rifle divisions in two paired comparisons during the Battle for Moscow in October–December 1941. The battle, like the Eastern Front itself, is a clear outlier, whether measured in casualties (at least 1.2 million), tanks deployed (over 5,000), the length of the front (nearly 700 kilometers), or sheer brutality, making it a difficult test for the proposed argument. Yet it is hard to explain the divergent fate of these divisions without reference to the prewar treatment of their constituent nationalities. The neighboring 38th and 108th Rifle Divisions were both caught in the jaws of Operation Typhoon; both had to fight their way out of envelopment with roughly comparable men and materiel. The 108th, with its forces drawn from the largely Russian Western Special Military District, waged a running ten-day battle to escape encirclement, though at terrible cost. The 38th, its forces recruited from the North Caucasus Military District, quickly shattered, its soldiers deserting, surrendering, or going

2. The same is true of the Soviet Union, where only 5–6 percent of the Red Army's deployed strength defected (Edele 2017, 21).

missing. The entire division was struck from the official Soviet battle roster, erasing it from the historical record. Similarly, the famed 78th "Siberian" Division conducted a masterful fighting retreat once Operation Typhoon restarted in mid-November. It retained enough combat power to first stabilize Soviet defenses before spearheading a counteroffensive that recaptured lost territory and drove the Nazi defensive line backwards. The 316th, despite the best efforts of Soviet propagandists, actually fought poorly, its regiments experiencing unsustainable losses in the first days of the renewed Nazi campaign. Drawn from the Transcaucasus, the division was judged too unreliable, and too depleted, to participate in the counterattack. It lasted only a few days in its defensive positions before it was transferred to Stavka's reserve formations, an ignoble end for a supposedly vaunted Guards Division. These within-army comparisons offer an important rebuttal to skeptics who charge that structural explanations are unable to keep pace with fast-moving battlefield dynamics.

9.2. Beyond Project Mars: Explaining Iraqi Battlefield Performance, 2014–17

As a final test, I extend the book's argument to a more recent case, that of the Iraqi Army's 2014–17 war against the Islamic State (ISIS).[3] Though a full investigation must await another day, the war provides an opportunity to step outside the original historical evidence used to devise, refine, and test the book's theoretical propositions. Passing this test should increase our confidence that the negative relationship between rising inequality and falling battlefield performance generalizes to an important out-of-sample case and is not merely an artifact born of overfitting Project Mars data (1800–2011).

On 1 January 2014, ISIS, with nearly one-third of Syria under its control, launched a mechanized assault into northern Iraq, seizing Fallujah and striking Ramadi in quick succession. The Iraqi Army offered only desultory resistance, its soldiers often deserting and abandoning equipment, including thousands of tanks, armored vehicles, and trucks, merely at the appearance of ISIS forces.[4] A series of halfhearted and poorly led government counterattacks (March–May) managed to slow, but not stop, ISIS's advance. In June, Mosul,

---

3. This account draws on Weiss and Hassan 2015; Stern and Berger 2015; Lister 2015; Fishman 2016; Mccants 2016; Hashim 2018.

4. "Exhausted and Bereft, Iraqi Soldiers Quit Fight," *New York Times*, 11 June 2014, A1 and "Islamic State now controls resources and territory unmatched in history of extremist organizations," *Washington Post*, 4 August 2014.

a city of nearly 1.8 million inhabitants, was captured by ISIS in a lightning campaign. Iraqi Army units offered only token resistance; in some cases, entire formations collapsed, deserted, or switched sides. Anbar Province itself fell under ISIS sway until June 2015, when the front stabilized. ISIS forces were then slowly dislodged and driven back, ceding Fallujah, Ramadi, and finally Mosul. At the time of writing (winter 2018), ISIS no longer exists as a quasi-state fielding a conventional army, though fears remain that it will reemerge from the underground as an insurgent organization.

The seeds of Iraq's shaky performance were sown by its Prime Minister Nouri al-Maliki's decision to pursue an ethnosectarian political program that marginalized Sunni and Kurdish citizens. Rather than cast an inclusionary net, al-Maliki pursued a Shia-dominated vision of the political community that relegated non-Shia to second-class status. In response, as early as mid-2008, Sunni soldiers that had joined the Sons of Iraq movement were already targeted for state-sanctioned violence in Baghdad and Diyala province. Mass arrests of Sunni Baathists followed; the Sons of Iraq movement was tossed aside rather than properly integrated into the Iraq Army. Mass protests by Sunni tribes against the "Shiafication" of the government and the broader community began in December 2012.[5] In response, al-Maliki ordered the purging of Sunni commanders from the local police and the army's senior ranks, including many of the most experienced officers. These actions incited further countermobilization. In April 2013, the army opened fire on Sunni demonstrators, sparking open war as Sunni tribes sought revenge for their dead co-kin. The army then launched a bumbling offensive, leading tribes to mobilize ever-larger counter-demonstrations. On the eve of the war, the al-Maliki regime had alienated most Sunni and Kurdish citizens, facilitating the rise of ISIS by leading Sunni to cast their support for the terrorist organization as a bulwark against an oppressive regime.

Poisonous identity politics, especially supercharged ethnosectarian polarization, inevitably warped the nascent postwar Iraqi Army. Technically, Article 9 of Iraq's 2005 constitution prohibited group-based discrimination within the military: "The Iraqi armed forces will be composed of the components of the Iraqi people with due consideration given to their balance and representation without discrimination or exclusion." Yet this quota system (*muhasasa*) only applied to the officer corps. Moreover, by 2006 it was already being violated as Sunni and Kurdish commanders were purged and replaced by Shia loyalists. Shia militia, some tied directly to Iran, were increasingly integrated into the Iraq Army. In 2011, al-Maliki staked a claim to greater control over the military by creating a new Office of the Commander in Chief in

5. Sky 2015, 345–63.

2011 that afforded him direct control over recruitment and promotion.[6] Death squads, rumored to be sanctioned by al-Maliki, began hunting down and executing former Saddam-era officers and soldiers. Conditions became so bad within the military that "we have even seen Sunni officers pretending to be Shiites."[7] Such measures are a standard part of the autocrat's coup-proofing toolkit, though in this case it is neither clear that al-Maliki was worried about a specific coup threat nor whether he accepted an increased risk of civil war as the cost of stacking the military with his loyalists.[8] The result, however, was skewed recruitment and heightened military inequality, which I judge to have reached about 0.29 when war broke out in January 2014.[9]

Given the patterns uncovered in prior chapters, we can anticipate that a medium level of inequality will translate into one, possibly two, pathologies within the Iraqi Army as tracked by the battlefield performance index. Our safest bet is assuming that mass desertion, the most common of the battle-field problems tracked by Project Mars, will occur within the Iraqi Army. Mass defection, too, might be an issue, though blocking detachments are unlikely; they typically appear at levels of military inequality greater than 0.40, as in Kokand, the Soviet Union, and late-stage Mahdiya. These cohesion problems should in turn generate battlefield trade-offs in the form of simplified tactics and operations. If past practices are accurate bellwethers of future conflict, then Iraqi casualties should hover near parity.

All told, there is a remarkable degree of congruence between these theoretical expectations and the Iraq Army's empirical realities. As illustrated in figure 9.1, a conservative, perhaps charitable, coding indicates that at least one battlefield pathology was present, earning the Iraqi Army a 0.75 score (out of a maximum score of 1) on the battlefield performance index. Mass desertion plagued the army from its very first battle with ISIS. At both Fallujah and Ramadi, understrength Iraqi formations abandoned their positions and equipment, shedding their uniforms in a desire to hide among the population. The 7th Iraqi Division, a Sunni-majority formation, was only at 60 percent strength during its first clash, already gutted by corruption, "ghost" soldiers,

6. Florence Gaub, "An Unhappy Marriage: Civil-Military Relations in Post-Saddam Iraq," Carnegie Middle East Center, 13 January 2016.

7. Quoted in ibid.

8. Roessler 2016, 303–6, views al-Maliki as caught in a coup–civil war trap, though it is important to recognize that Iraq was already mired in a civil war during Maliki's rule and that ISIS invaded from Syria.

9. This mean estimate is derived from low and high estimates of military inequality. At the "low" end, I derive: Shia $(0.75 * 0)$ + Sunni $(0.20 * 1)$ + Kurds $(0.025 * 0.5)$ + Yazidi $(0.0125 * 0.5)$ + Turkmen $(0.0125 * 0.5) = 0.225$. At the "high" end, I derive: Shia $(0.60 * 0)$ + Sunni $(0.30 * 1)$ + Kurds $(0.05 * 0.5)$ + Yazidi $(0.025 * 0.5)$ + Turkmen $(0.025 * 0.5) = 0.35$.

and disillusionment with Baghdad. After its first fight, the 7th was down to 30 percent strength as deserters fled. Locals, too, resented Baghdad's perceived pro-Shia agenda. "When [ISIS] presented itself, people said, 'Well, it may be possible to save us from the government, from the army which is not a professional national army, but one that killed and arrested Sunni.' "[10] Indeed, the "people started to look at the army as an enemy rather than as a national army."[11] Enough soldiers deserted in the first six months alone to exceed the 10 percent threshold of Project Mars for coding "mass" desertion.

Compounding these difficulties, Sunni soldiers also defected during these initial battles. In fact, many Sunni tribes had already shifted their allegiance away from the government into a more neutral, or even pro-ISIS, stance during the 2011–13 interregnum. ISIS also used social media during 2013 to announce that no quarter would be given to soldiers who resisted. Those willing to "repent," however, could register with ISIS and have their safety guaranteed. To encourage defections, ISIS conducted an assassination campaign ("Soldiers Harvest") against security forces to create incentives to join ISIS and escape a similar fate.[12] Since side-switching was confined to Sunni forces, and because much of it occurred prior to the 2014 war, the number of wartime defections probably does not reach the 10 percent threshold used to denote "mass" in Project Mars. I therefore conservatively do not lower Iraq's BPI score to 0.50 (indicating two problems were present).

The army's fissures were ruthlessly exposed during the sacking of Mosul by ISIS forces in June 2014. It took only a week for a 1,500-strong ISIS detachment to wrestle Mosul away from army and police detachments that, on paper, had a combined strength of almost 60,000. The army's 2nd Division, about 80 percent Kurd and 20 percent Sunni, dissolved almost immediately. Kurdish soldiers withdrew to Kurdistan; Sunni soldiers and especially local policemen, fearing for the safety of their families, fled deeper into Anbar province or sought refuge in Baghdad.[13] "[Local officers and soldiers] are the first to be under ISIS's fire," one soldier lamented. "ISIS can easily reach them and the army does very little to protect them."[14] Some Sunni defected, joining tribal

---

10. Quoted in Malkasian 2017, 179.

11. Quoted in Malkasian 2017, 179.

12. Knights 2014, 4; Fishman 2016, 198.

13. Contemporary accounts suggest that Kurdish withdrawal prompted a "panic" among Sunni soldiers. "Iraq May Turn to Iran for Help, Maliki Aide Says," New York Times, 13 June 2014.

14. Abbas and Trombly July 1, 2014; "Exhausted and Bereft, Iraqi Soldiers Quit Fight," New York Times, 11 June 2014, A1; "Islamic State now controls resources and territory unmatched in history of extremist organizations," Washington Post, 4 August 2014.

uprisings aimed at pushing remaining army detachments from the city.[15] The Naqshabandi Army, staffed principally by Saddam-era military veterans, also took in defectors.[16] Desertion and defection were also fueled by a pervasive belief among Sunnis that the government, not ISIS, was the real enemy. As one local explained: "You see, when Sunnis fight ISIS, people blame them for fighting Sunnis who are protecting you, while no one is fighting Shi'a militias that are killing our brothers."[17] An American observer with Iraqi forces remarked that "there is no sense of nation. The republic goes no farther than Baghdad."[18] In short, "no one wants to die for something he doesn't believe in."[19] Amid the chaos of collapsing units and attacks by explosive-laden ISIS trucks, those few soldiers who remained in their positions suffered heavy casualties.[20] Maliki's refusal to authorize Kurdish peshmerga to reinforce eastern Mosul compounded the disaster.[21] The result was the "most significant operational success for any jihadi group since 2011."[22]

Equally as striking as these early defeats was the process of institutional reform that the Iraqi Army implemented to offset these deficiencies. Sunni-dominated units were sidelined as unreliable in favor of Popular Mobilization Units (*al-Hashd al-Shaabi*) drawn almost exclusively from Shia populations.[23] Remaining Kurdish soldiers were transferred to peshmerga units outside the formal chain of command. In effect, the Iraqi Army became far more homogenous across ethnic and sectarian cleavages, lowering its military inequality sharply. Elite special forces units, including the famed Golden Division, were created to spearhead urban offensives while regular forces manned cordons around targeted cities and villages. Notably, these small detachments were built along inclusionary lines, integrating Sunni, Shia, and Kurdish soldiers. American airpower was then enlisted to support these revamped formations. Between August 2014 and November 2017, at least 14,097 airstrikes were conducted against ISIS targets in Iraq while another

15. ISIS even named the operation after a turncoat Sunni military officer (Fishman 2016, 202).

16. "The Iraqi Army Was Crumbling Long Before Its Collapse, U.S. Officials Say," *Washington Post*, 12 June 2014, A12.

17. Quoted in Malkasian 2017, 188.

18. Quoted in Malkasian 2017, 187.

19. Abbas and Trombly July 1, 2014.

20. Estimates range as high as 2,500 Iraqis killed (and 4,000 POWs) to only 105 ISIS soldiers killed.

21. McGurk 2014, 2.

22. Fishman 2016, 199.

23. Renad Mansour, "Your Country Needs You: Iraq's Faltering Military Recruitment Campaign," *Diwan: Middle East Insights From Carnegie*, 22 July 2015.

14,332 took place in Syria.[24] Airpower not only created the space for these institutional reforms to be enacted but also bolstered the morale of battered Iraqi units. Airpower thus substituted for ground forces, helping restore Iraqi combat power by propping up sagging casualty ratios without forcing new, and often poorly trained, PMUs to bear the brunt of anti-ISIS offensives.[25]

The Iraqi Army was also aided by ISIS's brutal conduct toward conquered populations. ISIS commanders began executing Sunni tribal leaders once their usefulness had ended, dampening enthusiasm for defection. ISIS also engaged in a "double war" against civilians under their control, singling out ethnic and religious minorities such as the Yazidi for execution and forced displacement. Shiite populations in these areas were also victimized, fueling revenge-seeking recruitment into the army or PMUs. An influx of foreign fighters to ISIS also inadvertently created a hierarchy of privilege within ISIS's forces—including better pay and weapons—that had ethnic underpinnings. In many ways, ISIS came to resemble the late-stage Mahdiya; its political and military leaders, much like the Khalifa, were presiding over an increasingly narrow ethnosectarian vision even as its army, and the populations under its control, grew increasingly diverse. The Iraqi Army, for its part, was shifting in a more inclusionary direction, albeit by excluding marginalized Sunnis. ISIS, by contrast, was saddled with rising military inequality, creating friction within its forces that eventually culminated in mass desertion, some defection to other armed groups, and fratricidal violence.

The straitjacket of even modest levels of military inequality is not so easily shed, however. Mistrust within the Iraqi Army between remaining Sunni soldiers (and officers) and their Shiite counterparts reduced cross-unit coordination. PMUs had high morale but low training, forcing them to rely on simple, if brutal, smash-mouth tactics to breach fortified ISIS positions. Airpower could compensate somewhat for these deficiencies, but casualties remained heavy. These losses in turn forced commanders to over-rely on elite commando formations that were rapidly depleted by sustained operations.[26] The liberation of western Mosul, for example, made extensive use of unrelenting airstrikes to clear a densely populated urban area given understrength commando units. Airstrikes not only created a sizable refugee population but also inflicted

24. Airwars.org data, accessed 24 November 2017, https://airwars.org/.

25. Given Iraq's prior reliance on blocking detachments to maintain discipline, it is also possible that airpower acted as a substitute for such drastic measures at a time when the army faced disintegration.

26. By January 2017, the Golden Division was estimated to have suffered 50 percent attrition. "Mosul Op: 6,500 Iraq soldiers killed in 3 months," *MEMO: Middle East Monitor*, 21 January 2017.

significant civilian casualties while destroying a large portion of the city.[27] Shiite militia also victimized Sunni populations in newly liberated areas, punishing Sunni civilians suspected of being informants or harboring pro-ISIS sympathies.[28] Army recruitment has predictably cratered among Sunni and Kurds; appeals to patriotism have largely fallen on deaf ears, and recruitment benchmarks are continually missed.[29] As the war winds down, the Iraqi Army, and Iraq as a whole, face another critical challenge: the construction of an inclusive political community that reduces ethnosectarian inequality within the army and the society from which it is drawn.

9.3. Theoretical Implications

Theories of military effectiveness tend to stand aside from more general theories of international relations. This need not be the case, however. A focus on military equality sheds light on several important questions in the study of world politics.

War, for example, plays a central role in most theories of state formation. Indeed, warfare has often been cited as both increasing state capacity through centralization ("war makes the state, and the state makes war") and promoting the homogenization of identities as wartime experiences foster national solidarity.[30] Nationalism is thus a consequence of fighting and a prelude to new, more deadly, rounds, as leaders draw on increasingly nationalistic sentiments and larger pools of enthusiastic soldiers.[31] Yet these accounts miss how these processes can be distorted, if not disrupted, by military inequality, in two ways. First, existing theories build their insights (understandably) atop the experiences of states that survived their wars. To do so, however, ignores the many belligerents that did not survive to enter standard war datasets. As captured by Project Mars, 104 belligerents experienced violent state death since 1800, demonstrating that war can also destroy states, not simply consolidate them. That these belligerents typically possessed high-to-extreme levels of

27. Azmat Khan and Anand Gopal, "The Uncounted," *New York Times Magazine*, 16 November 2017.

28. "Iraq: New Abuse, Execution Reports of Men Fleeing Mosul," *Human Rights Watch*, 30 June 2017.

29. "Iraq's elite special forces struggle to regroup after bloody fight for Mosul," *Washington Post*, 21 June 2017; Mansour, "Your Country Needs You: Iraq's Faltering Military Recruitment Campaign," *Diwan: Middle East Insights From Carnegie*, 22 July 2015.

30. Sambanis, Skaperdas and Wohlforth 2015; Brubaker 1996; Mann 1993; Tilly 1992; Coser 1956; Simmel 1898. For a review, see Hall and Malešević 2013; Malešević 2010. For a critique of this view, see Giddens 1985; Hutchinson 2005.

31. Posen 1993; Van Evera 1999; Keegan 1993, 46. But see Collins 2013.

military inequality is perhaps unsurprising. Second, violence on the home front failed to foster solidarity, at least in the short to medium term. Instead, campaigns of collective punishment reinforced ethnic divisions that spilled over on the battlefield. Many leaders, including some of the most despotic, continually worried about national solidarity despite frequent wars. Rather than assume violence and war have uniform effects, we need to theorize the scope conditions under which these factors can consolidate or divide national identities and capabilities. Violence, war, and victory likely all have differential effects depending on the underlying distribution of inequality within societies and armies.

A theoretical framework built around military equality also challenges the widespread view that armies are "optimized" to respond to the pressures of an anarchic international system. Theorists of various stripes, including realists, rationalists, and formal modelers, treat the construction and mobilization of armies as driven by the nature of external threats, the balance of offensive and defensive technologies, and the inherent uncertainty of other states' motives and capabilities.[32] Armies are thus investments; they are assumed to be coherent, standing entities, where soldiers are functionally interchangeable within and across states and increased capabilities simply a matter of investing additional resources. The book's findings suggest otherwise, however. Armies reflect societal divisions, less so international factors; politics trump anarchy. Inequality conditions the ability to exploit and defend against military technologies; far from exogenous, the ability to field certain technologies hinges on domestic constraints, including their anticipated effects on ethnic divisions. Neither technological uptake nor mobilizational capacity is uniform across belligerents, and calculations of cost are heavily conditioned by current inequalities. States are unlikely to update to changes in their security environment effortlessly; for many armies, reform is a wrenching process, one that may lead to systematic under-responses to external pressures. In short, as military inequality rises, states become increasingly myopic, less sensitive to international pressures than their own domestic needs. The presumed baseline of rationally updating states may only hold for a subset of states, those with low enough levels of inequality to make adjustments without running afoul of their own self-imposed political constraints.

The book's theoretical argument also intersects with the burgeoning study of secrecy in international relations.[33] Leaders reasonably have incentives to misrepresent their state's true military capabilities. Moreover, it can be difficult to assess relative military strength absent actual fighting that reveals

---

32. For a review and extension of these literatures, see Fearon 2018.
33. See Carson 2018, 7–8, fn13 for an extensive review.

capabilities. Together, these two factors generate uncertainty over capabilities that has been variously cited as creating security dilemmas between states, sparking unintended wars, inhibiting prewar bargains, and creating credible commitment problems that torpedo efforts to end wars.[34] What if, however, relative capabilities can be divined accurately, if not perfectly, from prewar military inequality? To be sure, policymakers may miss these clues. But it is possible that uncertainty over capabilities has been exaggerated in our studies of war and conflict. Not all states can harness offensive technologies successfully; not all states can manage to build threatening breakout capabilities. Escalation dynamics, too, are likely variable depending on a leader's confidence in his or her army's anticipated performance. Moreover, it is difficult to hide prewar military inequality, once analysts know to look for it. As a result, security dilemmas may be neither as pervasive nor as binding as suggested by these theories. Prewar bargains, too, may be easier to strike than imagined. Alone, uncertainty over capabilities may be insufficient to drive war initiation without importing assumptions about a state's motives.

Finally, many of the findings uncovered here pose a stark challenge to existing theories of military effectiveness. Consider the long-held notion that democracies are superior war-fighters, for example.[35] The combination of new democracies and wartime measures suggests that there is only a weak, at best, relationship between democracy and battlefield performance. These (non-)findings will hopefully spur renewed efforts to assess regime type effects using new data flexible enough to capture the range of non-Western political systems in the expanded Project Mars dataset. Similarly, simple indicators of numerical preponderance, while more appropriate than the commonly used (and crude) prewar indices of national capabilities, fared poorly. Numbers of soldiers are unlikely to shape battlefield outcomes like desertion and defection even in attritional wars.[36] Nor do material preponderance arguments explain why the effects of manpower advantages are so variable across historical eras. Civil-military relations and coup fears also appeared to play only a modest role in some of the historical cases. Instead, poor civil-military relations were a downstream consequence of failed imagined communities and high levels of military inequality rather than an independent variable. Rather than settle these debates, the evidence gathered here suggests new

34. Fearon 1995; Jervis 1978.

35. Lake 1992; Bueno de Mesquita et al. 2003; Reiter and Stam 2003, 2002, 1998a; Biddle 2007; Biddle and Long 2004; Scheve and Stasavage 2012; Stasavage 2011.

36. Gilpin 1981; Kennedy 1984, 1989; Desch 2008; Beckley 2010; Rotte and Schmidt 2003; Stam 1996.

avenues of inquiry for these long-standing explanations, including the need for additional theorizing and data collection.

9.4. Avenues for Future Research

The book's quiet ambition has been to break new ground about the drivers and dynamics of battlefield performance in modern war. In doing so, it has uncovered a host of new theoretical and empirical puzzles that, taken together, could launch an interdisciplinary research program that reinvigorates the study of neglected aspects of conventional warfare. I offer ideas about avenues of future research across three levels of analysis: leaders and their decisions about inequality; specific units and their internal structures; and individual soldiers and their networks.

9.4.1. Leaders and Inequality

Seeking to explore the effects of inequality, I largely sidestepped the question of why leaders embrace exclusionary nation-building strategies in the first place. Many leaders, after all, choose to forgo the considerable battlefield advantages of inclusionary nation-building, relegating non-coethnics to marginal positions within the political community. Ethnic diversity alone does not condemn belligerents to poor battlefield performance; instead, it is a calculated decision (and a choice) by leaders to exploit interethnic differences for political gain. Opening the black box of elite decisions therefore remains a key task for future research. Doing so would also shed light on the possibility of differential pathways to inclusion and inequality. For example, there may be important differences in battlefield performance arising from decisions about how to construct an inclusionary political community. Soldier beliefs about common cause with the regime in particular are likely affected by whether inclusion was attained through forced (but non-violent) assimilation, through a "mosaic" model where differences are celebrated, or through prior violence that erected a communal vision atop the wreckage of rival ethnic groups. Many of today's inclusionary communities were founded atop histories of exclusionary nationalism that only gradually softened over time.[37] How these historical memories of past treatment might be passed down through generations as rallying cries for countermobilization remains an important issue for future research. So, too, is the question of when regimes backslide on their commitment to full citizenship and military equality. Inclusion might not be a final way station on a journey but merely a temporary resting place for some states.

37. Marx 2003.

Nor does ethnicity exhaust the possible cleavages that opportunistic lead-ers could exploit. The concept of military inequality introduced here could be wrenched free of its ethnic moorings and expanded to other identities.[38] Historically, governments have manipulated the magnitude and salience of ideological, class, and gender differences within their populations. These identities might in turn affect battlefield performance in much the same man-ner as ethnicity and race. It remains an open empirical question, however, whether these cleavages are durable enough to survive military socialization processes and salient enough to foster group-based grievances and foment countermobilization.[39] That soldiers possess multiple identities sets up an intriguing possibility: these cleavages may be mutually reinforcing in some instances and cross-cutting in others. Soldiers exposed to state-sanctioned violence across two or more cleavages—perhaps ethnic and sectarian identi-ties closely overlap in a given community—may be especially prone to engage in mass desertion and defection, and do so earlier in the war. The possibil-ity of cross-cutting cleavages may also create opportunities for the regime to increase cohesion by pitting marginalized groups against one another. Postwar reforms might be promised to the group that fights the hardest, cre-ating incentives to perform well despite the obvious credible commitment problem.

There is also a curious duality to the notion of inequality articulated here. On the one hand, inequalities appear durable and persistent, which provides leverage for causal inferences about how these divisions affect wartime con-duct. This is true even in wartime; faced with setbacks, some leaders simply double down on their communal visions, reinforcing ethnic hierarchies with violence against both their own soldiers and populace. On the other hand, these hierarchies of inequality sometimes appear more malleable, as wartime pressures induce leaders—notably, 'Alimqul and Stalin—to make gestures, if perhaps marginal, to future reform. Why tactical concessions are offered and, more broadly, when inequality itself is overthrown, in times of war and peace remains to be examined. Victory and defeat can equally be powerful inducements to change, though the direction of that change is ambivalent, as these outcomes spark new debates about who counts, and who does not, as a citizen. Citizenship norms are not simply endogenous to war outcomes, though. Gradual change can also be propelled by evolving societal norms and

---

38. Wimmer (2014, 185) makes a similar appeal for sociologists to consider non-ethnic cleavages when studying the causes and conduct of war.

39. Since these non-ethnic identities typically lack ascriptive traits, it is harder for states to target group members. Individuals may also be able to "pass" as members of the core group more easily than if ethnic cleavages are politically salient.

attitudes toward both newcomers and traditionally marginalized or repressed ethnic groups. Immigration flows, too, can act as exogenous shocks to a political community that fuel contestation about citizenship norms and the nature of military service. What seems clear, however, is there is no natural progression toward greater equality as a function of macrohistorical changes such as victory in war or economic development. There is, in other words, no Kuznets curve in which military inequality first rises and then declines automatically as economic modernization advances. Instead, the persistence of inequality appears tied to the warp and woof of political struggles at home and their extension to battlefields abroad.[40] These propositions make clear the importance of gathering additional time series data for each belligerent to enable the study of drivers of change and persistence in hierarchies of military inequality.

9.4.2. Unit Structure and Battlefield Management

From the outset, the book's argument has emphasized how the ethnic composition of units, along with the nature of their officer corps, is an important bridge between prewar military inequality and subsequent battlefield performance. Yet more can be done. Indeed, an entire research program could be built around unit-level characteristics and their role in shaping wartime conduct and effectiveness.[41] The book's cases, for example, only hint at the relative effectiveness of varying strategies for managing ethnic differences. Are there best organizational practices for reducing the fallout from high military inequality? Can units become sites of socialization in which allegiance around regimental or other practices fosters a collective identity among members of unequal groups? Even more mundane practices—imagine the complexities of wartime replacement of casualties in ethnically balanced units—become important when viewed through the lens of military inequality. As demonstrated with the Soviet rifle divisions in chapter 8, a mesolevel research program multiplies the opportunities for observing trade-offs within and across different units. It also expands the number of observations within a conflict, creating a more rigorous set of empirical tests. It may well be impossible to collect data on the specific units for each of the belligerents in Project Mars. But a shift toward units and their respective battles as the focus of our investigations could reap similar rewards as the earlier move made by civil war scholars to place rebel organizations and their production of violence (captured by georeferenced reports of attacks) at the center of their analyses. At the very least,

40. Kuznets 1955.
41. McLauchlin 2015; Cohen 2016.

linking prewar factors like inequality to concrete organizational design at the unit level helps reintroduce missing structural factors into our understanding of wartime dynamics. In turn, unit composition offers predictions about how specific units will perform, helping answer the charge that slow, big, structural factors like inequality cannot explain fast-moving wartime events and processes.

Moreover, while the index of battlefield performance introduced here was designed to be comprehensive, it was not exhaustive of unit-level wartime conduct. The historical cases suggest, for example, that premature surrender is another means by which disgruntled soldiers can punish military authorities. Soldiers' willingness to obey orders concerning the capture and safeguarding of enemy prisoners, an issue during both the Hispano-Moroccan War and the Italo-Turkish War, provides an additional measure of soldier discipline. Other forms of collective action, including protests, strikes, and conscription riots, might also be considered. We know little about these practices, in part because of data scarcity. Data collection could also be expanded to provide more fine-grained indicators of unit disintegration. Weekly time series data at the unit level on the incidence of desertion and defection would be especially useful for disentangling the complex relationship between casualties and mass indiscipline. Evidence from our cases suggests that, contrary to folk wisdom, desertion often preceded battle rather than followed it. In fact, panicked retreats and abortive desertion efforts increased, rather than reflected, casualties, as in Kokand, the Democratic Republic of Congo, and the 38th Rifle Division.

The explicit incorporation of unit characteristics like ethnic composition would also facilitate the extension of the military inequality argument to a new domain: irregular wars. Project Mars sought to bridge the gap between international and civil wars but excluded insurgencies from its remit. Yet it is plausible that both counterinsurgents and insurgent organizations are negatively affected by increased military inequality. Internal cohesion has long been thought a key determinant of insurgent behavior and resiliency, for example.[42] Though loss-exchange ratios are less relevant for these types of war, the twin dangers of desertion and defection are clearly a challenge for both states and rebels. Insurgent organizations, including the Islamic State, have also resorted to the use of blocking detachments to maintain cohesion, again suggesting parallels with the belligerents studied here. From the counterinsurgent perspective, military inequality might condition the likelihood of desertion and defection within its ranks, especially if these soldiers are drawn from the same population as the insurgents. The willingness of soldiers to

42. Wood 2008; Christia 2012; Staniland 2014; Cohen 2016.

fight coethnics, or to share information and cut side deals with them, might hinge on prior state treatment and their role within the armed forces. Bolstering inclusion by integrating defectors or civilians that share ethnicity with insurgents can also improve information gathering and the application of selective violence that can unravel rebellions.[43] Military inequality might then serve as a unifying theory linking conventional and insurgency wars that are currently treated as separate domains.

9.4.3. Soldiers and Their Networks

If military units represent the missing middle in most theories of military effectiveness, then the soldiers themselves are nearly invisible. I have sought to restore some measure of their agency; soldiers are not merely automatons conditioned by brute force socialization and numbed by combat.[44] Instead, the historical evidence marshaled here suggests that prewar grievances outlast state-imposed political education. Soldiers typically emerged from boot camp and training with their coethnic networks intact, if not reinforced, by state efforts to recast their identities. We only catch glimpses of soldier beliefs and interethnic trust in the book's cases, however, a function in part of the paucity of existing sources written by soldiers themselves, especially in the nineteenth century. As a result, many questions remain. Under what conditions can prewar military socialization or wartime experiences tamp down, rather than enflame, existing ethnic grievances? How can inclusive militaries best harness the benefits of diversity? Can realistic training exercises create enough bonding experiences for interethnic networks to be forged? If exposure to combat and wartime trauma increases intraethnic trust, as new research now suggests,[45] does that necessarily come at the expense of relations with non-coethnics? In the final analysis, can soldiers victimized by their own state ever truly trust their non-coethnic commanders and make common cause with the state, or will bribes and the threat of the lash always be necessary to motivate these soldiers?

A "bottom-up" focus on the everyday experiences and identities of soldiers opens up several new research possibilities. Network-based approaches, for example, hold particular promise for teasing out the structure of intra- and interethnic ties within military units.[46] Mapping the density of ties, membership within cross-cutting cleavages, and the number of critical individuals

43. Lyall 2010; Roessler 2016, 56–57.

44. On the omission of actor agency in our dominant models of socialization, see Checkel 2017.

45. For a review, see Bauer et al. 2016.

46. On information-sharing within ethnic networks, see Larson and Lewis 2017.

("nodes") within each unit would shed light on the process by which grievances are translated into collective action against military authorities. Different types of ethnic networks may exist within individual units that condition how information flows, the speed at which new information is shared, and how exposure to wartime violence affects within-group coordination. If desertion and defection truly unfold in contagion-like fashion, we should observe information (and rumors) ricocheting inside intraethnic networks far more quickly than across ethnic groups. In addition, scholars could examine how coethnicity can provide a bridge for coordination across military units, helping to explain why we sometimes observe near-simultaneous desertion and defection from units separated on the battlefield.[47]

Encouragingly, these questions are amenable to diverse research methods. Experiments could be devised, for example, to examine how information spreads via word of mouth within military units of varying ethnic composition.[48] Behavioral experiments could also be devised to explore how well soldiers in units with variable levels of military inequality (or ethnic heterogeneity) perform collective tasks.[49] War diaries and letters home, for example, could provide everyday histories of how non-core soldiers viewed the state, their fellow coethnics, soldiers from the core group, and the war itself.[50] Tracing the life histories of individual soldiers from prewar service to wartime would be invaluable for establishing that grievances predated the war and that combat intensified these anti-state feelings. There are, of course, limits to these sources; censorship of wartime correspondence almost certainly rises as military inequality increases, and only certain belligerent armies will have enough literate soldiers to be viable candidates for this approach. Still, archival materials, including surveys, could also be leveraged to assess soldier beliefs and combat motivation. We might even imagine using predictive modeling to forecast a soldier's likelihood of deserting or defecting based on his individual attributes, including the salience and intensity of his identification with coethnics and the broader political community.

47. Network ties might be fairly weak and yet robust enough to facilitate the flow of rumors and true information about the intentions and behavior of other units. Scott (2018) provides a model for tracing communication networks among deserters and (runaway) slaves and their role in rebellion.

48. Even more ambitious would be randomizing the composition of the units as well as the nature of the information to be shared.

49. See Habyarimana et al. 2009. One simple treatment could be the random assignment of a verbal or visual prompt reminding subject soldiers of the existing status hierarchy.

50. On everyday history as a methodology, see Fitzpatrick 2000; Healy 2004, 300. On its use in wartime, see Merridale 2005; Fennell 2011; Boff 2012.

A focus on combat motivation from below also promises to shed light on why some soldiers from second-class communities still fought for the regimes they hated. Coercion is surely an important part of the explanation. Eighteen percent of all belligerents built and deployed blocking detachments during their wars, suggesting that their military commanders viewed coercion as a viable policy instrument. Now armed with Project Mars data, future research could seek to account for the institutional variation observed across blocking detachments. The number of units deployed, the size and composition of these units, and differences in the timing of their introduction to the battlefield both within and across wars all remain to be explored. Similarly, the extent to which these detachments engaged in civilian victimization behind the front lines or in newly occupied territories remains unknown across cases. The appearance of these units on the battlefield also likely jump-starts a process of tit-for-tat retaliation that leads to wartime barbarization. Driven forward by their own countrymen, soldiers are likely to seek vengeance against their enemy for their plight, corroding norms about the taking and treatment of prisoners of war.[51]

Some marginalized soldiers fought, however, from a conviction that their wartime service would lead to a better postwar fate for their coethnics and families. Not all Czechs deserted or defected from the Habsburg Army in World War I; some soldiers from repressed tribes under the Mahdiya continued to fight even though defeat was imminent. Some individuals from victimized non-Russian minorities still volunteered for the Red Army despite Stalin's ruthless persecution of these populations before (and during) World War II. As Roger Reese notes, "for the outcast, the great reward of service was acceptance into the national community and acknowledgement of citizenship."[52] Material incentives, even if distributed unequally, appeared to help bridge the shortfall in soldier morale. Kokand's cavalry, the Khalifa's own Baggara formations, Ottoman Arab levies, and DRC-aligned militia all engaged in looting, often from their own populations, even breaking off combat to chase lucrative spoils. Enemy actions also pushed reluctant soldiers into fighting; a desire to avenge killed comrades or victimized coethnics could be a powerful driver, as the Italian Army discovered at Tripoli. Future research examining when alternative motivations trump military inequality among these groups of soldiers would help specify the scope conditions for when (and if) military inequality's effects on soldier beliefs can be trumped by material or other inducements.

51. Lyall 2017.
52. Reese 2011, 125.

9.5. Policy Implications

This book was conceived in the spirit of basic research and grounded in the effort to reset our baseline expectations about battlefield performance and its drivers over the past two hundred years. But the book's findings also speak to contemporary policy debates about the creation of military power and its potential application in future wars.

Intelligence agencies and their uniformed counterparts wrestle, for example, with making accurate prewar net assessments of an adversary's military power. Though absent from these analyses today, military inequality possesses several traits that makes it ideal for anticipating a potential foe's likely battlefield performance. Prewar military inequality is highly visible and difficult to mask, making it relatively easy to track through open sources, including in near-real time through social media. Even classifying a state's prevailing notions of citizenship and military service along the simple inclusive-marginalization-repression spectrum provides useful forecasts about likely combat power and cohesion. With sufficient data, traditional tables of equipment and organization at the unit level could be supplemented with military inequality coefficient scores. This fine-grained approach could prove invaluable for identifying units prone to break under pressure or those that will stand and fight, helping shape campaign plans before the war begins. Unit ethnic composition and the regime's plans for managing interethnic divisions should therefore be folded into net assessments as they provide clues about potential wartime vulnerabilities of both adversaries and allies. Doing so may also avoid unwelcome battlefield surprises. Asked to comment on ISIS's unexpected success, Chuck Hagel, the US secretary of defense (2013–15), noted that "it wasn't that we were blind in that area. We had drones, intelligence, monitoring of these groups. But when two Divisions of the Iraqi regular forces drop their weapons and run [at Mosul] ... I'm not sure how you predict that."[53] This is, of course, exactly the outcome that the book's argument would expect.

Once identified, inequality-induced vulnerabilities could be exploited for significant battlefield gains. Propaganda could be tailored toward specific units to capitalize on anti-regime grievances or interethnic mistrust to encourage indiscipline and frustrate command and control (C2). Astute commanders could also carve out escape corridors and credibly commit to proper treatment of prisoners to encourage desertion and defection among soldiers from targeted ethnic groups. Failure to consider how interethnic animosities might shape performance can also unknowingly foreclose battlefield opportunities. For example, the encirclement of ISIS units by Shia-staffed

---

53. PBS *Frontline* Season 35: Episode 2 ("Confronting ISIS"), 11 October 2016.

PMU formations at Mosul in 2016–17 forced otherwise reluctant ISIS (Sunni) soldiers to fight tenaciously, greatly increasing casualties among storming Iraqi counterterrorism units. Campaign plans could also target an opponent's battlefield management strategies. As one example, blocking detachments introduce a specific form of C2 vulnerability. With their distinctive profiles easing identification problems, blocking detachments could be degraded or destroyed, possibly through airstrikes and electronic warfare, blowing holes in an adversary's monitoring and sanctioning capabilities. This in turn would create new opportunities for desertion and defection, possibly leading to the unravelling of entire formations. Hunting an opponent's blocking units would compromise their capacity to coerce fellow soldiers, including their ability to respond quickly to sudden collapses, by forcing them to disperse to avoid destruction.[54] Such targeting should extend beyond the "proper" battlefield itself to include blocking detachments victimizing populations in rear areas. Without a credible threat to repress coethnics for poor behavior, non-core soldiers may be more inclined to risk desertion or defection given that punishment would no longer fall on their families and communities.

To turn the tables, belligerents saddled with high or extreme military inequality could improve their fighting chances with several reforms. Tactical political concessions to some members of marginalized or repressed groups might create a loyalist faction that drives a wedge into an ethnic group, reducing its capacity for collective action. Investing in technological solutions that maximize firepower while minimizing manpower—especially airpower and mechanized forces to replace wavering soldiers—might soften trade-offs between cohesion and combat power. Blocking detachments, perhaps aided by modern surveillance technologies, should be fielded, and countermeasures adopted to increase their survivability. Urges to open a second front against civilian populations should be ignored. These campaigns only divert resources away from the fight while angering their coethnics within the army, fueling their desire to shirk or escape service, creating a vicious cycle of escalating costs. Increasing pay, and ensuring its timely delivery, might also compensate for low combat motivation among some non-core soldiers. Suggestive evidence also indicates that these belligerents should avoid constructing homogenous units from non-core populations, especially if oversight mechanisms are weak. Though perhaps slightly more combat proficient, these units carry heightened risk of cohesion problems, including wholesale desertion and defection. The Common Army's transition to mixed

54. A key component of the US air campaign against Iraq in 2003 was to fix and, if possible, destroy, the Special Republican Guard, Special Police, and regular Republican Guard units that Saddam Hussein had deployed behind Iraqi units to shoot would-be deserters.

units during World War I was belated and halfhearted but does appear to have delayed mass indiscipline.[55]

Even belligerents with low military inequality may find themselves ensnared by identity-induced inefficiencies and trade-offs if they partner with local proxy forces. Since 2001, the marriage of Western airpower and special forces with local militia has been a hallmark of warfare in Afghanistan, Libya, Mali, and against ISIS in Syria and Iraq. Local forces beset by high military inequality are likely to experience indiscipline, "ghost" soldiers, and heavy casualties, especially if pitted against more inclusionary enemies. Such forces may require a greater-than-anticipated use of foreign (Western) soldiers to provide training and to stiffen resolve. Cohesion will be especially worrisome if violence cannot be wielded against militia members for ethical reasons and if they are fighting in their home areas, where network ties can facilitate escape. Worse, Western forces are likely to have only weak oversight, lowering the costs of desertion and defection while increasing the likelihood of human rights abuses against civilians in combat zones. These actions can spark reprisals that reignite war, fuel subsequent dynamics of the conflict, and make a lasting political settlement much harder to achieve and maintain.

Similar issues arise when attempting to rebuild armies in the aftermath of civil war or foreign intervention.[56] Much of the existing literature has emphasized technocratic solutions such as ethnically balanced recruitment and well-designed demobilization campaigns. Yet these reforms will fail if political leaders do not offer an inclusionary vision of the political community, one that embraces universal norms of citizenship and military service. Without such an ideational foundation, the military will simply reflect a tiered system of incomplete citizenship that will curb its battlefield performance. As Iraq demonstrated, no external power can impose an inclusive vision, at least not successfully; the solution lies within the population itself.[57] Afghanistan, too, has demonstrated the perils of building a military where the imagined community is contested. Questionable regime legitimacy, perceived second-class status among non-Pashtuns, and skewed ethnic and tribal recruitment patterns have converged to produce an Afghan Army wracked by high desertion, side-switching, unsanctioned battlefield truces, and low combat power. Technocratic solutions cannot, in the final analysis, answer fundamentally

55. The Forces Armées Congolaises' (FAC) disintegration in response to forced ethnic integration is a cautionary tale here, however.

56. By one count, 40 percent of all civil wars fought between 1945 and 2006 ended with settlements mandating the integration of insurgents into the national army (Hartzell 2014).

57. Lake 2016.

political questions about identity, citizenship, and their intersection with military service.

Finally, a word about inclusion. As this book has demonstrated, armies have a long history of justifying barriers to full inclusion of targeted groups on grounds of unit cohesion and concern about disorder.[58] Ironically, the problem isn't diversity but instead the state's own ham-fisted politicization of identity-based differences. The evidence here is overwhelming; states and armies alike should abandon these practices and embrace radical inclusion.[59] Put differently, bigotry and racism are threats to national security. Ethical and military considerations thus lead to the same conclusion: stoking the fires of group-based hatred and antagonism as official policy only diminishes battlefield performance. In the United States, we still hear echoes of official concern about the inclusion of homosexual, female, and transgendered individuals in combat roles. Yet marginalizing or outright excluding these groups throws away military power. Removing structural barriers to their full inclusion in society and the military will muster new skills, produce new diversity bonuses, decrease intergroup biases and prejudices, and build more cohesive teams with superior problem-solving capabilities. Rather than misplaced fears about unit cohesion, political and military leaders should be devoting their efforts to harnessing the advantages unleashed by tearing down remaining obstacles to full, meaningful inclusion for these groups.

9.6. The Future of War

Offering predictions about the future of war is something of a poisoned chalice. Yet there is value in lifting our gaze from historical patterns, if only to identify emerging trends that might diminish the importance of military inequality for explaining performance on future battlefields.

Perhaps the most obvious challenge to the book's thesis is the simplest: conventional wars are a dying breed, with few major interstate wars expected in the future. A vocal and growing number of "declinist" scholars have concluded that conventional wars are now something of a historical curio, having largely been "snuffed out"[60] of existence since 1945.[61] This claim is hotly contested, however.[62] It may be simply too early to draw conclusions about

58. Kier 1999; Schaefer et al. 2016.

59. Dempsey and Brafman 2018.

60. Pinker 2011, 303.

61. Scheidel 2017; Morris 2014; Human Security Report Project 2010; Pinker 2011; Goldstein 2011; Levy and Thompson 2011; Sheehan 2008; Gat 2006; Kaldor 1999; Keegan 1993; Mueller 1989.

62. Braumoeller 2019; Mann 2018; Gleditsch and Pickering 2014.

whether this decline is real or merely an artifact of incomplete data, poor measures of decline, or simply the elapse of too little time since 1945 to draw a definitive conclusion. In the meantime, conventional wars short of total war, including Russia's invasion of Crimea, the anti-ISIS fight in Syria and Iraq, and the grinding war in Yemen, continue to be waged. All major powers, including the United States, China, India, and Russia, continue to prepare to wage conventional war through arms procurement rivaling Cold War heights. The diffusion of tactical skills to rebel organizations—partly a legacy of America's forever wars in Iraq, Afghanistan, and elsewhere—also raises the possibility of new (or continued) civil wars fought along conventional lines. Finally, mass mobilization wars like World Wars I and II have always been rare. Most of the wars recorded in Project Mars were not total in nature for at least one of the belligerents (and often both). Shifting our mental image of war away from these devastating but rare conflicts and toward the more frequent, if less deadly, conventional wars, helps ensure that we are positioned to explain these smaller conflicts as they arise in the future, as they undoubtedly will.

A related charge is that a revolution in military affairs is currently underway that will do away with concerns about military inequality. Technological advances now unfolding may soon render industrial-era mass armies obsolete. Indeed, the rise of precision standoff weapons, persistent surveillance systems, artificial intelligence, swarms of armed drones, and dispersed but networked units may well be changing the very nature of war. Future wars may be short-lived affairs, this view suggests, as speed and precision place a premium on striking a decisive blow at the war's outset, eliminating the need for plodding attritional slugfests.[63] Future robot armies and scalable artificial intelligence to control them offer a radical solution to the problem of military inequality: replace human soldiers entirely. Such an army would not only sever the link between citizenship and military service but would eliminate all ethnic inequalities and associated trade-offs between combat power and cohesion.[64] From the futurist's viewpoint, divided armies are anachronistic, increasingly unlikely to accomplish their objectives, or even survive, on battlefields of the not-so-distant future.[65]

Standing atop the mountain of evidence gathered here, however, a different view emerges. We risk distraction or worse by focusing solely on technological changes, no matter how revolutionary, missing instead deeper continuities that have persistently shaped war across the past two centuries.[66]

63. Nolan 2017, 579–81.
64. Ferejohn and Rosenbluth 2017, 9–24.
65. Freedman 2017, 239–53; Scheidel 2017, 436–37.
66. On this point, see especially Freedman 2017.

The realization of robot wars marked solely by machine-machine interaction remains distant. Moreover, the rise of biased algorithms suggest that this robotic solution may be infeasible. Algorithms devised from machine learning on past human behavior have shown a remarkable ability to absorb human biases.[67] Though speculative, it is possible that robots could develop identities, possibly based on their morphology or function, that approximate ethnicity in humans. Self-realizing robots might then undertake purposive action to advance or defend their positions in a status hierarchy that could lead to disobedience, desertion, and the use of coercion by a central AI to force robotic soldiers to fight. Imagine, for example, disputes over the assignment of credit for solving common tasks, or drones designed for high-risk suicide operations that become self-aware enough to reject their designated role. We are far from transcending military inequality through better robotics; we may, in fact, only end up inadvertently re-creating these same problems in future robot armies.

Futures are also unevenly distributed; not all countries will be able to field robot armies even if technically feasible. For the immediate future, new technologies will likely alter the severity of the trade-offs between combat power and cohesion but will not enable belligerents to escape them completely. Human-machine interactions, rather than machine-machine interactions, will likely predominate in the near future, especially within armies. New biometric technologies, for example, could be employed by commanders to monitor the exact location of their soldiers, closing down avenues for desertion and defection. Drones, too, could be used in overwatch roles to surveil one's own soldiers. The ability to track soldiers in real-time might lift constraints on using non-core soldiers in complex decentralized operations. Biometric data could be paired with automated blocking detachments to enhance the credible threat of punishment if soldiers misbehave or shirk. Ruthless belligerents could therefore stack their armies with marginalized groups and mitigate at least some of the risk of mass indiscipline through persistent surveillance and sanctioning mechanisms. Such measures may, of course, fail under battlefield conditions. Belligerents with high military inequality may resist implementing these complex systems, especially if these tools could "leak" to targeted populations and facilitate anti-regime collective action. Reliance on these emerging control technologies will also create new vulnerabilities. Automated blocking detachments or surveillance could be disrupted, co-opted, or destroyed via lethal or non-lethal (i.e., hacking) means. In short, new technology might place more obstacles on the path

67. O'Neil 2016; Crawford et al. 2016; "Biased Algorithms Are Everywhere, and No One Seems to Care," MIT *Technology Review*, 12 July 2017.

between grievances and mass indiscipline, but it is unlikely to be foolproof, and creates the risk of critical failure if compromised by enemy action.

One final issue remains. The military inequality argument detailed here assumes that ethnicity will remain a salient political cleavage in the future. It is possible, however, that leaders will abandon efforts to construct their communal visions around politicized ethnicity. Legitimacy may be obtained through other means, whether appeals to an inclusive cosmopolitanism or through rising economic development that lessens the competition for public goods and services.[68] There is some evidence that ethnicity is losing its salience. Ethnic civil wars, for example, have declined since 1990.[69] And it is likely that belligerents with high-to-extreme levels of military inequality will continue to fall at the hands of more inclusionary states, forcing surviving belligerents to ratchet their levels of military inequality downward to escape destruction.

Yet ethnicity's demise is likely a long ways off. Historically, ethnic differences have proven to be a powerful and popular means for leaders to mobilize support. Political headwinds are now buffeting even Western democracies as tribalism, populism, and (white) nationalism all have reared their heads. These forces threaten to swing the pendulum back toward greater levels of military inequality as certain identity groups are relegated to second-class citizenship. Progress toward inclusion is thus not guaranteed; so long as ethnic differences or other identity cleavages remain politically salient, the possibility of military inequality and reduced battlefield performance will remain.

This discussion of the future brings us full circle. Armies are, in the end, political constructs that reflect prewar choices by leaders about how to define the boundaries of their imagined communities. The book does not, of course, suggest that battlefield performance is governed by an iron law able to explain every belligerent's wartime fortunes. Chance, an enemy's skill, the fog of war—some of it self-inflicted—all take their toll. But the evidence marshaled here illuminates the power of radical inclusion for shaping how armies have fought and died over the past two centuries. Political communities marked by openness and tolerance, that extend the benefits and protections of military service to all without consideration for ethnic identity, typically field powerful militaries that escape the straitjacket that confines belligerents with divided armies. Meaningful inclusion creates lethal armies; military inequality divides them, destroying them from within. Safeguarding inclusion against those who would exploit group differences for political gain will remain paramount for ensuring that these societies and their armies emerge victorious on the future battlefields of still-unimagined wars.

68. Wimmer 2018.
69. Cederman, Gleditsch and Wucherpfennig 2017.

PART IV

Appendixes

Project Mars

LIST OF CONVENTIONAL WARS, 1800–2011

TABLE A1. Conventional Wars, 1800–2011

War	Belligerents	Included in COW Ver. 4.0?[a]	Civil War?
Napoleonic: Second Coalition, 1800	Austrian Empire v. France	No	No
Napoleonic: Second Coalition (Naval), 1801	UK v. France, Denmark	No	No
Tripolitan War, 1801–1805	Barbary States v. USA	No	No
War of the Oranges, 1801	France, Spain v. Portugal	No	No
Russo-Persian War, 1803–1813	Russia v. Persia	No	No
Second Maratha War, 1803–1805	UK v. Maratha Confederacy	No	No
First Serbian Uprising, 1804–1813	Serbia v. Ottoman Empire	No	Yes
Napoleonic: Third Coalition (Bavaria), 1805	France v. Austrian Empire, Russia	No	No
Napoleonic: Third Coalition (Italy), 1805	Austria v. France	No	No
Asante-Asin-Fante-UK War, 1806–1807	Ashanti Empire v. Asin Confederacy, Fante Confederacy, UK	No	No
Napoleonic: Prussian Campaign, 1806	Prussia v. France	No	No
Napoleonic: Russian Campaign, 1806–1807	Russia v. France	No	No
Russo-Turkish War, 1806–1811	Ottoman Empire v. Russia	No	No
Anglo-Turkish War, 1807–1809	UK v. Ottoman Empire	No	No
Napoleonic: Finnish War, 1808–1809	Russia v. Sweden	No	No
Napoleonic: Peninsular War, 1808–1814	France v. Spain, UK, Portugal	No	No

TABLE A1. (*continued*)

War	Belligerents	Included in COW Ver. 4.0?	Civil War?
Napoleonic: Fifth Coalition, 1809	Austria v. France	No	No
Napoleonic: Walcheren Campaign, 1809	UK v. France	No	No
Argentine War of Independence, 1810–1818	Junta of Buenos Aires v. Spain	No	Yes
Venezuelan War of Independence I, 1810–1812	First Republic v. Spain	No	Yes
Wahhabi War, 1811–1818	Egypt v. First Saudi State	No	No
Napoleonic: Russia, 1812	France v. Russia	No	No
Venezuelan War of Independence II, 1812–1814	Republic of Venezuela v. Spain	No	Yes
War of 1812, 1812–1815	USA v. UK	No	No
Chilean War of Independence, 1813–1820	Chile v. Spain	No	Yes
Durrani Empire-Sikh War, 1813	Durrani Empire v. Sikh Kingdom	No	No
Napoleonic: Sixth Coalition, 1813–1814	Russia, Austria, Prussia, Sweden v. France	No	No
Gurkha War, 1814–1816	UK v. Nepal	No	No
Napoleonic: Seventh Coalition, 1815	France v. Prussia, Russia, UK	No	No
Neapolitan War, 1815	Kingdom of Naples v. Austria	No	No
Venezuelan War of Independence III, 1815–1821	Spain v. Republic of Venezuela	No	Yes
Bombardment of Algiers, 1816	UK, Netherlands v. Algeria	No	No
Third Maratha War, 1817–1818	Maratha Confederacy v. UK	No	No
Durrani Empire-Sikh War II (Multan), 1818	Sikh Kingdom v. Durrani Empire	No	No
Fifth Cape Frontier War, 1818–1819	Xhosa v. UK	No	No
Durrani Empire-Sikh War III (Kashmir), 1819	Sikh Kingdom v. Durrani Empire	No	No
Ecuadorian War of Independence, 1820–1823	Ecuador v. Spain	No	Yes
Peruvian War of Independence, 1820–1824	Spain v. Peru	No	Yes
Greek War of Independence, 1821–1829	Greece v. Ottoman Empire	No	Yes
Turko-Persian War, 1821–1822	Ottoman Empire v. Persia	No	No
Brazilian War of Independence, 1822–1823	Portugal v. Brazil	No	Yes
Durrani Empire-Sikh War IV, 1822–1823	Durrani Empire v. Sikh Kingdom	No	No

TABLE A1. (*continued*)

War	Belligerents	Included in COW Ver. 4.0?	Civil War?
Ashanti-British War, 1823–1826	UK v. Ashanti Empire	No	No
Franco-Spanish War, 1823	France v. Spain	Yes	No
First Anglo-Burmese War, 1824–1826	Burma v. UK	No	No
Argentine-Brazilian War, 1825–1828	Argentina v. Brazil	No	No
Siege of Bharatpur, 1825–1826	UK v. Bharatphur Princely State	No	No
Khoja Rebellion I, 1826–1827	Kokand (Khanate) v. China	No	Yes
Second Russo-Persian War, 1826–1828	Persia v. Russia	No	No
Vientiane-Siam War, 1827	Lao Kingdom v. Siam	No	No
Argentine Unitarian-Federalist War, 1828–1831	Liga del Interior v. Liga del Litoral	No	Yes
Gran Colombia-Peru War, 1828–1829	Gran Colombia v. Peru	No	No
Russo-Turkish, 1828–1829	Russia v. Ottoman Empire	Yes	No
French-Algerian, 1830	France v. Algeria	No	No
Khoja Rebellion II, 1830	Kokand (Khanate) v. China	No	Yes
November Uprising, 1831	Russia v. Congress Poland	No	Yes
First Turko-Egyptian, 1832	Egypt v. Ottoman Empire	No	Yes
Siamese-Vietnamese War, 1833–1834	Siam v. Kingdom of Cambodia, Vietnam	No	No
Farroupilha Revolution, 1835–1845	Piranti Republic, Juliana Republic v. Brazil	No	Yes
Texas Revolution, 1835–1836	Texas v. Mexico	No	Yes
Afghan-Persian (Siege of Herat), 1836–1838	Persia v. Herat	No	No
Afghan-Sikh War (Jamrud Campaign), 1837	Kingdom of Kabul v. Sikh Kingdom	No	No
War of the Confederation, 1837–1839	Peru-Bolivia Confederation v. Argentina, Chile	No	No
Uruguayan Civil War, 1838–1847	Argentina v. Uruguay, France, UK	No	Yes
First Anglo-Afghan War, 1839–1842	UK v. Kingdom of Kabul	No	Yes
First Opium War, 1839–1842	UK v. China	No	No
Second Turko-Egyptian, 1839–1840	Egypt v. Ottoman Empire	No	Yes
Bolivia-Peru War, 1841–1842	Peru v. Bolivia	No	No
Siamese-Vietnamese War II, 1841–1845	Siam v. Vietnam	No	No
Sino-Sikh War, 1841–1842	Jammu (Dogra Dynasty) v. China, Tibet	No	No

TABLE A1. (*continued*)

War	Belligerents	Included in COW Ver. 4.0?	Civil War?
Anglo-Baluch, 1843	Sindh v. UK	No	No
Gwalior War, 1843	UK v. Gwalior	No	No
First Dominican War, 1844	Dominican Republic v. Haiti	No	No
Franco-Moroccan War, 1844	France v. Morocco	No	No
First Anglo-Sikh War, 1845–1846	Sikh Kingdom v. UK	No	No
Second Dominican War, 1845	Haiti v. Dominican Republic	No	No
Mexican-American War, 1846–1847	USA v. Mexico	Yes	No
Seventh Cape Frontier War, 1846–1847	Xhosa v. UK	No	No
Austro-Sardinian War, 1848	Austria v. France, Italy, Sardinia	No	No
First Schleswig-Holstein War, 1848–1850	Prussia v. Denmark	Yes	No
Hungarian War of Independence, 1848–1849	Hungary v. Austria, Russia	No	Yes
Second Anglo-Sikh War, 1848–1849	Sikh Kingdom v. UK	No	No
Austro-Venetian War, 1849	Austria v. Republic of Venice	No	Yes
Third Dominican War, 1849	Haiti v. Dominican Republic	No	No
War of the Roman Republic, 1849	Roman Republic v. Austria, France	Yes	Yes
Eighth Cape Frontier War, 1850–1852	UK v. Xhosa	No	No
First Egba-Dahomey War, 1851	Kingdom of Dahomey v. Egba Kingdom	No	No
La Plata (Ejército Grande), 1851–1852	Brazil, Entre Rios and Corrientes, Uruguay v. Argentina	Yes	No
Taiping Rebellion, 1851–1864	Taiping Heavenly Kingdom v. China	No	Yes
Montenegrin-Ottoman War, 1852–1853	Ottoman Empire v. Montenegro	No	No
Tukolor-Tamba War I, 1852–1853	Tukolor Kingdom v. Tamba Empire	No	Yes
Crimean War, 1853–1856	Russia v. Ottoman Empire, France, UK, Italy	Yes	No
Nien (Nian) Rebellion, 1853–1868	Nien Movement v. China	No	No
Fourth Dominican War, 1855–1856	Haiti v. Dominican Republic	No	No
Tibet-Nepalese War, 1855–1856	Nepal v. Tibet	No	No
Tukolor-Bambara War II, 1855	Bambara Empire v. Tukolor Kingdom	No	No

TABLE A1. (*continued*)

War	Belligerents	Included in COW Ver. 4.0?	Civil War?
Anglo-Persian, 1856–1857	UK v. Persia	Yes	No
Central American National War, 1856–1857	Costa Rica, Guatemala, Honduras, El Salvador v. Nicaragua	No	No
Second Opium War, 1856–1860	UK, France v. China	No	No
Franco-Tukulor War, 1857–1859	Tukolor Kingdom v. France	No	No
Indian Rebellion, 1857–1858	Sepoy Movement v. UK	No	Yes
Hispano-Moroccan War, 1859–1860	Spain v. Morocco	Yes	No
Papal States, 1860	Italy v. Papal States	Yes	No
Tukulor-Bambara War III, 1860–1861	Tukolor Kingdom v. Bambara Empire	No	No
Two Sicilies Insurrection, 1860	Italy v. Sicily	Yes	No
American Civil War, 1861–1865	Confederate States of America v. USA	No	Yes
Franco-Mexican, 1862–1867	France v. Mexico	Yes	No
Montenegrin-Ottoman War, 1862	Ottoman Empire v. Montenegro	No	Yes
Central American War, 1863	Guatemala v. Honduras, Nicaragua, El Salvador	No	No
Ecuadorian-Colombian, 1863	Colombia v. Ecuador	Yes	No
Paraguayan War (Lopez), 1864–1870	Paraguay v. Brazil, Argentina, Uruguay	Yes	No
Russia-Kokand War, 1864–1865	Russia v. Kokand	No	No
Second Egba-Dahomey War, 1864	Kingdom of Dahomey v. Egba Kingdom	No	No
Second Schleswig-Holstein, 1864	Prussia, Austria v. Denmark	Yes	No
Sino-Kuchean Muslim War, 1864–1865	Kuchea v. China	No	No
Russia-Bukhara Khanate War, 1865–1868	Russia v. Bukhara	No	No
Sino-Kokand War, 1865	Kokand v. China	No	No
Austro-Prussian War, 1866	Prussia, Italy v. Austria, Saxony, Wurttemberg, Hanover, Baden, Bavaria	Yes	No
Boshin War, 1868–1869	Japan v. Satsuma Prefecture	No	Yes
British Abyssinian Expedition, 1868	Abyssinia v. UK	No	No
Sino-Jahriyya Order War I: Gansu, 1869–1871	China v. Jahriyya Order of Gansu	No	No
Franco-Prussian War, 1870	France v. Baden, Bavaria, Prussia, Wurttemberg	Yes	No

TABLE A1. (*continued*)

War	Belligerents	Included in COW Ver. 4.0?	Civil War?
Kashgaria-Urumchi Dungan War, 1870–1872	Urumchi Dungans v. Kashgaria	No	No
Ottoman Conquest of Arabia, 1870–1871	Ottoman Empire v. 'Asir, Yemen	No	No
Second Ethiopian War, 1871	Abyssinia v. Tigray	No	Yes
Sino-Jahriyya Order War II: Hezhou, 1872	China v. Jahriyya Order of Hezhou	No	No
Aceh War, 1873–1874	Netherlands v. Aceh	No	Yes
Anglo-Ashanti War, 1873–1874	Ashanti Empire v. Fante Confederacy, UK	No	No
Russo-Khivan, 1873	Russia v. Khiva	No	No
Sino-Jahriyya Order War III: Suzhou, 1873	China v. Jahriyya Order of Suzhou	No	No
Egypt-Abyssinian, 1875–1876	Egypt v. Abyssinia	No	No
Russia-Kokand Khanate War, 1875–1876	Kokand v. Russia	No	No
First Central American, 1876	Guatemala v. Honduras, El Salvador	Yes	No
Montenegrin-Turkish War, 1876–1878	Montenegro v. Ottoman Empire	No	Yes
Sino-Kashgarian War, 1876–1877	China v. Kashgaria	No	No
Ninth Cape Frontier War, 1877–1878	Xhosa v. UK	No	No
Satsuma Rebellion, 1877	Japan v. Satsuma Prefecture	No	Yes
Russo-Turkomen War, 1878–1881	Russia v. Teke Turkomen	No	No
Second Anglo-Afghan War, 1878–1880	UK v. Afghanistan	No	No
British-Zulu, 1879	UK v. Zulu Kingdom	No	No
War of the Pacific, 1879–1883	Chile v. Bolivia, Peru	Yes	No
First Mahdi War, 1881–1885	Mahdist State v. Egypt, UK	No	No
Anglo-Egyptian, 1882	UK v. Egypt	Yes	No
Sino-French (Tonkin) War, 1883–1885	France v. China	Yes	No
Ethiopian-Mahdi War, 1885–1889	Abyssinia v. Mahdist State	No	No
Second Central American, 1885	Guatemala v. El Salvador	No	No
Serbo-Bulgarian War, 1885–1886	Serbia/Yugoslavia v. Bulgaria	No	No
War of Dogali, 1887	Italy v. Abyssinia	No	No
Mahdi-Egyptian War, 1889	Mahdist State v. Sudan	No	No
Franco-Dahomean War: First Campaign, 1890	France v. Kingdom of Dahomey	No	No

TABLE A1. (*continued*)

War	Belligerents	Included in COW Ver. 4.0?	Civil War?
Chilean Civil War, 1891	Congressist Junta v. Chile	No	Yes
Fifth Franco-Mandingo Campaign, 1891–1892	France v. Mandinka Empire	No	No
Congo Arab War, 1892–1894	Congo Arab Confederacy v. Belgium	No	No
Franco-Dahomean War: Second Campaign, 1892	France v. Kingdom of Dahomey	No	No
Bornu Empire-Rabah Empire War, 1893	Rabah Empire v. Bornu Empire	No	No
First Matabele War, 1893–1894	Kingdom of Ndebele v. UK	No	No
France v. Tukulor Empire, 1893	Tukolor Kingdom v. France	No	No
Mahdist-Italian War, 1893–1894	Mahdist State v. Italy	No	No
Melilla War, 1893–1894	Rif Confederacy v. Spain	No	No
First Sino-Japanese War, 1894–1895	Japan v. China	Yes	No
First Italo-Abyssinian War, 1895–1896	Italy v. Abyssinia	No	No
Japanese Invasion of Taiwan, 1895	Japan v. Taiwan	No	No
Portugal v. Gaza Nguni, 1895	Portugal v. Gaza Empire	No	No
Second Franco-Hova War, 1895	Merina Kingdom v. France	No	No
British-Mahdi War, 1896–1899	UK v. Mahdist State	No	No
British-Sokoto Caliphate War, 1897	UK v. Sokoto Caliphate	No	No
Greco-Turkish War, 1897	Greece v. Ottoman Empire	Yes	No
Eighth Franco-Mandingo Campaign, 1898	France v. Mandinka Empire	No	No
Spanish-American, 1898	USA v. Spain	Yes	No
Franco-Rabah Empire War, 1899–1901	France v. Rabah Empire	No	No
Second Anglo-Boer War, 1899–1900	Boer Republic v. UK	No	No
Thousand Days' War, 1899–1902	Liberal Party of Colombia v. Colombia	No	Yes
Venezuelan Civil War, 1899	State of Táchira v. Venezuela	No	Yes
Boxer Rebellion, 1900–1901	Austria-Hungary, France, Germany, Italy, Japan, Russia, UK, USA v. China	Yes	No
Russo-Chinese (Manchuria), 1900	Russia v. China	Yes	No
War of the Golden Stool, 1900	Ashanti Empire v. UK	No	No
British Expedition to Tibet, 1904	UK v. Tibet	No	No
Russo-Japanese, 1904–1905	Japan v. Russia	Yes	No

TABLE A1. (*continued*)

War	Belligerents	Included in COW Ver. 4.0?	Civil War?
Third Central American, 1906	El Salvador v. Guatemala	Yes	No
Fourth Central American, 1907	Nicaragua v. El Salvador, Honduras	Yes	No
Wadai War, 1908–1911	Ouaddai Empire v. France	No	No
Second Spanish-Moroccan War, 1909	Spain v. Morocco	Yes	No
Tripolitanian War, 1911–1912	Italy v. Ottoman Empire	Yes	No
Xinhai Revolution, 1911	Chinese Revolutionary Alliance v. China	No	Yes
First Balkan War, 1912	Bulgaria, Greece, Serbia/Yugoslavia v. Ottoman Empire	Yes	No
First Sino-Tibet War, 1912–1913	Tibet v. China	No	No
Second Balkan War, 1913	Bulgaria v. Greece, Romania, Ottoman Empire, Serbia/Yugoslavia	Yes	No
Second Revolution, 1913	Kuomintang v. China	No	Yes
WWI: Caucasian, 1914–1917	Ottoman Empire v. Russia	No	No
WWI: Eastern, 1914–1917	Austria-Hungary, Germany, v. Russia, Romania	Yes	No
WWI: Western, 1915–1918	Germany v. Belgium, UK, France, Australia, Canada, USA	Yes	No
WWI: Italian, 1915–1918	Italy v. Austria-Hungary, Germany	No	No
WWI: Salonika Front, 1916–1918	Bulgaria, Germany v. France, UK, Greece, Serbia/Yugoslavia	No	No
WWI: Serbian, 1914–1915	Austria-Hungary, Germany, Bulgaria v. Serbia/Yugoslavia, UK, France	No	No
WWI: Sinai-Palestine, 1915–1918	Ottoman Empire v. Australia, UK	No	No
National Protection War, 1915–1916	National Protection Army v. China	No	Yes
WWI: Mesopotamia, 1914–1918	UK v. Ottoman Empire	No	No
WWI: Mesopotamia (Russian Front), 1916	Russia v. Ottoman Empire	No	No
Estonian War of Independence, 1918–1920	Soviet Russia v. Estonia	Yes	Yes
Finnish Civil War, 1918	Red Finland v. Germany, Finland	No	Yes

TABLE A1. (*continued*)

War	Belligerents	Included in COW Ver. 4.0?	Civil War?
Latvian War of Independence, 1918–1920	Soviet Russia v. Estonia, Latvia, Germany	Yes	Yes
Lithuanian War of Independence, 1918–1919	Soviet Russia v. Lithuania	No	Yes
Polish-Ukrainian War, 1918–1919	West Ukrainian People's Republic v. Poland	No	No
Russian Civil War: Cossack, 1918–1920	White Don Army v. Soviet Russia	No	Yes
Russian Civil War: Southern Front, 1918–1920	White Volunteer Army/AF of South Russia v. Soviet Russia	No	Yes
Russian Civil War: Siberia, 1918–1920	White Siberian Army v. Soviet Union	No	Yes
Russian Civil War: North Russia, 1918–1919	UK, USA v. Soviet Russia	No	Yes
Second Sino-Tibet War, 1918	China v. Tibet	No	No
Czech-Polish War, 1919	Czechoslovakia v. Poland	No	No
Franco-Turkish War, 1919–1921	France v. Ottoman Empire	Yes	No
Hejaz War, 1919–1925	House of Saud v. Hashemite Kingdom	No	No
Hungarian Adversaries War, 1919	Hungary v. Czechoslovakia, Romania	Yes	No
Soviet-Polish War, 1919–1920	Poland v. Soviet Russia	Yes	No
Third Anglo-Afghan War, 1919	Afghanistan v. UK	No	No
Waziristan Campaign, 1919–1920	Waziristan v. UK	No	No
Azeri-Armenian War, 1920	Democratic Republic of Armenia v. Azeri Democratic Republic	No	No
Polish-Lithuanian War, 1920	Poland v. Lithuania	Yes	No
Russian Civil War: Outer Mongolia, 1920–1921	Bogd Khanate v. China	No	Yes
Turkish-Armenian War, 1920	Democratic Republic of Armenia v. Ottoman Empire	No	No
Warlord Era: Anhui-Zhili War, 1920	Anhui v. Fengtian Clique, Zhili Clique	No	Yes
Rif War, 1921–1926	Spain, France v. Republic of the Rif	No	Yes
Russian Civil War: Outer Mongolia, 1921	Bogd Khanate v. Soviet Union	No	Yes
Soviet-Georgia War, 1921	Soviet Russia, Turkey v. Georgia	No	No
Warlord Era: First Zhili-Fengtian War, 1922	Fengtian Clique v. Zhili Clique	No	Yes

TABLE A1. (*continued*)

War	Belligerents	Included in COW Ver. 4.0?	Civil War?
Warlord Era: Second Zhili-Fengtian War, 1924	Fengtian Clique v. Zhili Clique	No	Yes
Warlord Era: Anti-Fengtian War, 1925	Guominjun v. Fengtian Clique, Zhili Clique	No	Yes
Warlord Era: Northern Expedition, 1926–1928	Kuomintang, Guominjun v. Fengtian Clique, Five Province Army, Zhili Clique	No	Yes
Sino-Soviet Conflict (CER-Manchuria), 1929	Soviet Union v. China	Yes	No
Warlord Era: War of the Central Plains, 1930	China v. Guangxi Clique, Guominjun, Shanxi Clique	No	Yes
Second Sino-Japanese War, 1931–1932	Japan v. China	Yes	No
Battle of Shanghai, 1932	Japan v. China	No	No
Chaco War, 1932–1935	Paraguay v. Bolivia	Yes	No
Kashgar War of Sinkiang, 1933–1934	Tungan 36th Division v. China, Soviet Union	No	No
Kashgar-FET War, 1933–1934	Tungan 36th Division v. First East Turkestan Republic	No	No
Saudi-Yemeni War, 1934	Mutawakkilite Kingdom of Yemen v. Saudi Arabia	Yes	No
Second Italo-Abyssinian, 1935–1936	Italy v. Abyssinia	Yes	No
Spanish Civil War, 1936–1939	Nationalists, Germany, Italy v. Spain, Soviet Union	No	Yes
Third Sino-Japanese, 1937–1945	Japan v. China	Yes	No
Battle of Lake Khasan (Changkufeng), 1938	Japan v. Soviet Union	Yes	No
Battle of Khalkhin Gol (Nomanhan), 1939	Japan v. Soviet Union	Yes	No
WWII: Poland, 1939	Germany, Soviet Union v. Poland	Yes	No
WWII: Winter War, 1939–1940	Soviet Union v. Finland	Yes	No
WWII: Belgium, 1940	Germany v. Belgium	Yes	No
WWII: East African Campaign, 1940–1941	Italy v. UK	No	No
WWII: France, 1940	Germany, Italy v. France, UK	Yes	No
WWII: Greco-Italian War, 1940–1941	Italy, Germany v. Greece	No	No
WWII: Netherlands, 1940	Germany v. Netherlands	No	No
WWII: North Africa, 1940–1943	Italy, Germany v. UK, USA	No	No
WWII: Norway, 1940	Germany v. Norway	No	No
WWII: Vichy France-Thai, 1940–1941	Thailand v. France	Yes	No

TABLE A1. (*continued*)

War	Belligerents	Included in COW Ver. 4.0?	Civil War?
Peruvian-Ecuadorian War, 1941	Ecuador v. Peru	No	No
WWII: Anglo-Iraqi War, 1941	Iraq v. UK	No	No
WWII: Continuation War, 1941–1944	Germany, Finland v. Soviet Union	No	No
WWII: German-Yugoslav, 1941	Germany v. Yugoslavia	No	No
WWII: Great Patriotic War, 1941–1945	Germany, Hungary, Romania, Italy, Bulgaria v. Soviet Union, Romania	Yes	No
WWII: Pacific, 1941–1945	Japan v. Australia, New Zealand, USA	Yes	No
WWII: Hong Kong, 1941	Japan v. Canada, UK	No	No
WWII: Malaya-Singapore, 1941–1942	Japan v. Australia, UK	No	No
WWII: Burma, 1941–1945	Japan v. China, UK	No	No
WWII: Syria-Lebanon Campaign, 1941	Australia, UK v. France	No	No
WWII: Sicilian/Italian Campaign, 1943–1945	Canada, UK, USA, Italy v. Germany, Italy	No	No
East Turkestan: Gulja Incident, 1944–1945	Second East Turkestan Republic v. China, Soviet Union	No	No
WWII: Lapland War, 1944–1945	Finland v. Germany	No	No
WWII: Operation Overlord, 1944–1945	Germany v. Canada, France, UK, USA	No	No
WWII: Soviet-Japanese War, 1945	Soviet Union v. Japan	No	No
Chinese Civil War, 1946–1949	China v. Communist Party of China	No	Yes
India-Pakistan War, 1947–1949	Pakistan v. India	Yes	No
1948 Palestine War, 1948–1949	Egypt, Iraq, Jordan, Syria v. Israel	Yes	No
Operation Polo, 1948	India v. Hyderabad	No	No
Korean War, 1950–1953	People's Republic of Korea, China v. UK, USA, Republic of Korea	Yes	No
First Taiwan Strait Crisis, 1954–1955	China v. Taiwan	Yes	No
Suez Crisis, 1956	France, Israel, UK v. Egypt	Yes	No
Second Taiwan Strait Crisis, 1958	China v. Taiwan	Yes	No
North Yemen Civil War, 1962–1969	Egypt, Yemen Arab Republic v. Mutawakkilite of Yemen	No	Yes

TABLE A1. (*continued*)

War	Belligerents	Included in COW Ver. 4.0?	Civil War?
Sino-Indian War, 1962	China v. India	Yes	No
Laotian Civil War, 1964–1973	Democratic Republic of Vietnam v. USA, Laos, Republic of Vietnam	No	Yes
India-Pakistan War, 1965	Pakistan v. India	Yes	No
Vietnam War, 1965–1973	USA, Republic of Vietnam, Cambodia v. Democratic Republic of Vietnam	Yes	No
Nigerian-Biafran War, 1967–1970	Nigeria v. Republic of Biafra	No	Yes
Six Day War, 1967	Israel v. Egypt, Jordan, Syria	Yes	No
Football War, 1969	El Salvador v. Honduras	Yes	No
War of Attrition, 1969–1970	Egypt v. Israel	Yes	No
Black September War, 1970	Syria v. Jordan	No	Yes
Bangladesh War, 1971	Pakistan v. India	Yes	Yes
Yom Kippur War, 1973	Egypt, Iraq, Jordan, Syria v. Israel	Yes	No
Turko-Cypriot War, 1974	Turkey v. Cyprus	Yes	Yes
Angolan Civil War, 1975–2002	South Africa, UNITA, FNLA v. Cuba, MPLA	Yes	Yes
Lebanese Civil War, 1975–1976	Lebanese National Movement v. Lebanese Front, Syria	No	Yes
North Vietnam-South Vietnam, 1975	Democratic Republic of Vietnam v. Republic of Vietnam	No	No
Vietnamese-Cambodian War, 1975–1979	Cambodia v. Democratic Republic of Vietnam	Yes	No
Ogaden War, 1977–1978	Somalia v. Cuba, Ethiopia	Yes	Yes
Uganda-Tanzania War, 1978–1979	Uganda v. Libya, Tanzania	Yes	No
First Sino-Vietnamese War, 1979	China v. Democratic Republic of Vietnam	Yes	No
Yemen Border War II, 1979	Yemen People's Republic v. Yemen Arab Republic	No	No
Iran-Iraq War, 1980–1988	Iraq v. Iran	Yes	No
Falklands War, 1982	Argentina v. UK	Yes	No
Lebanon War, 1982	Israel v. Syria	Yes	No
MNF in Lebanon, 1982–1984	France, Lebanon, USA v. Amal, Progressive Socialist Party, Syria	No	Yes
Tigrean and Eritrean War, 1982–1991	Eritrea, Tigray v. Ethiopia	No	Yes
Second Sino-Vietnamese, 1987	China v. Democratic Republic of Vietnam	Yes	No

TABLE A1. (*continued*)

War	Belligerents	Included in COW Ver. 4.0?	Civil War?
Toyota War (Aozou Strip), 1987	Chad v. Libya	Yes	No
Iraq-Kuwait, 1990	Iraq v. Kuwait	No	No
Sri Lanka-Tamil War I, 1990–2002	LTTE v. Sri Lanka	No	Yes
Croatian War of Independence, 1991–1995	Serbia/Yugoslavia v. Croatia	No	Yes
Georgian-Ossetian War, 1991–1992	Georgia v. Russia, South Ossetia	No	Yes
Persian Gulf War, 1991	Kuwait, UK, USA, Saudi Arabia, Egypt, v. Iraq	Yes	No
Bosnian War, 1992–1995	Serbia/Yugoslavia v. Bosnia-Herzegovina, Croatia	Yes	Yes
Transnistria War, 1992	Moldova v. Russia, Transnistria	No	Yes
Nagorno-Karabakh War, 1992–1994	Armenia v. Azerbaijan	Yes	No
Afghan War I, 1994–1996	Taliban v. Islamic State of Afghanistan	No	Yes
Rwanda War, 1994	Rwandan Patriotic Front v. Rwanda	No	Yes
Yemen Civil War, 1994	Yemen Arab Republic v. Democratic Republic of Yemen	No	Yes
Afghan War II, 1996–2001	Islamic State of Afghanistan v. Taliban	No	Yes
Ethiopian-Eritrean War (Badme), 1998–2000	Eritrea v. Ethiopia	Yes	No
Second Congo War, 1998–2002	Rwanda, Uganda v. Angola, DRC, Zimbabwe	Yes	Yes
Kargil Conflict, 1999	Pakistan v. India	Yes	No
Kosovo War, 1999	Serbia/Yugoslavia v. USA	Yes	Yes
US-Afghan, 2001–2002	USA v. Taliban	Yes	No
US-Iraq, 2003	USA v. Iraq	Yes	No
Israel-Hezbollah War, 2006	Hezbollah v. Israel	No	No
Georgia-Russia War, 2008	Georgia v. Russia	No	Yes
Sri Lanka-Tamil War II, 2008–2009	Sri Lanka v. LTTE	No	Yes
Libyan Civil War, 2011	National Transitional Council, UK, USA, France v. Libya	No	Yes

[a]Refers to the Correlates of War Inter-State War dataset (version 4.0).

APPENDIX II

Project Mars

NEW BELLIGERENTS,
1800–2011

TABLE A2. Project Mars: Non-Correlates of War (Non-COW) Belligerents

Belligerent	Contemporary Location
Aceh Sultanate	Indonesia
Amal (Movement of the Disinherited)	Lebanon
Anhui	China
Ashanti Empire	Benin, Ghana, Côte d'Ivoire
Asin Confederacy	Ghana
'Asir	Yemen
Azeri Democratic Republic	Azerbaijan
Bambara Empire of Karta	Mali
Bambara Empire of Segu	Mali
Bharatpur Princely State	India
Barbary States	Morocco, Algeria, Tunisia, Libya
Boer Republics	South Africa
Bogd Khanate	Mongolia
Bornu Empire	Chad, Niger, Nigeria, Cameroon
Bukhara	Uzbekistan
Chinese Revolutionary Alliance	China
Communist Party of China	China
Confederate States of America	United States
Congo Arab Confederacy (Tib Empire)	Democratic Republic of the Congo
Congress Poland	Poland
Congressist Junta	Chile
Democratic Republic of Armenia	Armenia
Democratic Republic of Yemen	Yemen
Durrani Empire	Afghanistan, Iran, Pakistan, NW India, Tajikistan, Turkmenistan, Uzbekistan
Egba Kingdom	Nigeria
Entre Ríos	Argentina
Fante Confederacy	Ghana
Fengtian Clique	NE China (Manchuria)

TABLE A2. (*continued*)

Belligerent	Contemporary Location
First East Turkestan Republic	China (Xinjiang)
First Republic of Venezuela	Venezuela
First Saudi State	Saudi Arabia
Five Provinces Alliance	China
National Liberation Front of Angola (NLFA)	Angola
Gaza Empire	N Mozambique, SE Zimbabwe, South Africa
Gran Colombia	Colombia, Venezuela, Ecuador, Panama, N Peru, W Guyana, NW Brazil
Guangxi Clique	China
Gwalior	India
Hashemite Kingdom	Saudi Arabia
Herat	Afghanistan
Hezbollah	Lebanon
House of Saud	Saudi Arabia
Hyderabad	India
Islamic State of Afghanistan	Afghanistan
Jahriyya Order of Gansu	China
Jahriyya Order of Hezhou	China
Jahriyya Order of Suzhou	China
Jammu (Dogra Dynasty)	India
Juliana Republic	Brazil
Junta of Buenos Aires	Argentina
Kashgaria	China (Xinjiang)
Khiva	W Uzbekistan, SW Kazakhstan, Turkmenistan
Kokand	Parts of Kazakhstan, Uzbekistan, Krgyzstan
Kingdom of Cambodia (Khmer Empire)	Laos, Thailand, S Vietnam, Cambodia
Kingdom of Dahomey	Benin
Kingdom of Kabul	Afghanistan
Kingdom of Naples	Italy
Kingdom of Ndebele	Zimbabwe, South Africa
Kucha Kingdom	China (Xinjiang)
Kuominchun/Guominjun	China
Kuomintang	China
Lao Kingdom of Vientiane	Laos, Thailand
Lebanese Front (Phalangist)	Lebanon
Lebanese National Movement	Lebanon
Liberal Party of Colombia	Colombia
Liga del Interior/Unitarians	Argentina
Liga del Litoral (Federal Pact)	Argentina
LTTE	Sri Lanka
Mahdist State (Mahdiya)	Sudan, Ethiopia

TABLE A2. (*continued*)

Belligerent	Contemporary Location
Mandinka Empire	SW Guinea
Maratha Confederacy	India, Pakistan, Bangladesh, Nepal, Afghanistan
Merina Kingdom	Madagascar
Montenegro	Montenegro
Mutawakkilite Kingdom of Yemen	Yemen
National Protection Army	China
National Transition Council	Libya
National Union for the Total Independence of Angola (UNITA)	Angola
Nationalists (Bando Nacional)	Spain
Nien Movement	China
Ouaddai Empire	Central African Republic, Chad
Peru-Bolivia Confederation	Bolivia, Peru
People's Movement for the Liberation of Angola (MPLA)	Angola
Piratini Republic	Brazil
Progressive Socialist Party	Lebanon
Rabah Empire	Chad
Red Finland	Finland
Republic of Biafra	Nigeria
Republic of Formosa	Taiwan
Republic of the Rif	Morocco
Republic of Venezuela	Venezuela
Republic of Venice	Italy
Rif Confederacy	Morocco
Roman Republic	Italy
Rwandan Patriotic Front	Uganda
Satsuma Prefecture	Japan
Second East Turkestan Republic	China (Xinjiang)
Sepoy Rebel Movement	India
Shanxi Clique	China
Siam	Cambodia, Laos, Malaysia
Sikh Kingdom	China, India, Pakistan
Sindh	Pakistan
Sokoto Caliphate	Burkina Faso, Cameroon, N. Nigeria, Niger
South Ossetia	South Ossetia
State of Táchira	Venezuela
Taiping Heavenly Kingdom	China
Taliban	Afghanistan
Tamba Empire	Senegal
Teke Turcomen	Turkmenistan
Texas	United States
Tibet	China

TABLE A2. (*continued*)

Belligerent	Contemporary Location
Tigray	Ethiopia
Transnistria	Transnistria
Tukolor Kingdom	Mali, Senegal
Tungan 36th Division	China (Xinjiang)
Urumchi Dungans	China (Xinjiang)
Vietnam (Indochina)	Vietnam
Waziristan	Pakistan
West Ukrainian People's Republic	Poland, Ukraine
White Don Army	Russia
White Siberian Army	Russia
White Volunteer Army	Russia
Xhosa	South Africa
Yemeni State (until 1872)	Yemen
Zhili Clique (Zhili Province)	China
Zulu Kingdom	South Africa

BIBLIOGRAPHY

Abashin, Sergei. 2014. "The 'fierce fight' at Oshoba: a microhistory of the conquest of the Khoqand Khanate." *Central Asian Survey* 33:215–31.

Abbas, Yasir and Dan Trombly. July 1, 2014. "Inside the Collapse of the Iraqi Army's 2nd Division." *War on the Rocks*.

Abbott, G. F. 1912a. *The Holy War in Tripoli*. London: Edward Arnold.

Abbott, G. F. 1912b. "The Tripolitan War from the Turkish Side." *Quarterly Review* 217:249–66.

Abdullaev, Ravshan, Namoz Khotamov and Tashmanbet Kenensariev. 2011. Colonial Rule and Indigenous Responses, 1860–1917. In *Ferghana Valley: The Heart of Central Asia*, ed. Frederick Starr. Armonk, NY: M. E. Sharpe, pp. 69–93.

Abebe, Semahagn Gashu. 2014. *The Last Post-Cold War Socialist Federation: Ethnicity, Ideology, and Democracy in Ethiopia*. Burlington, VT: Ashgate.

Abu Shouk, Ahmed Imbrahim. 1999. "A Bibliography of the Mahdist State in the Sudan (1881–1898)." *Sudanic Africa: A Journal of Historical Sources* 10:133–68.

Acemoglu, Darren and James Robinson. 2006. *Economic Origins of Dictatorship and Democracy*. Cambridge: Cambridge University Press.

Acemoglu, Darren and James Robinson. 2012. *Why Nations Fail: The Origins of Power, Prosperity, and Poverty*. New York: Crown Business.

Acharya, Avidit, Matthew Blackwell and Maya Sen. 2016. "Explaining Causal Findings Without Bias: Detecting and Assessing Direct Effects." *American Political Science Review* 110: 512–29.

Addington, Larry. 1994. *The Patterns of War since the Eighteenth Century*. Vol. 2. Bloomington: Indiana University Press.

Afflerbach, Holger. 2014. The Eastern Front. In *The Cambridge History of the First World War: Global War*, ed. Jay Winter. Vol. 1. Cambridge: Cambridge University Press, pp. 234–65.

Agnew, Hugh. 2004. *The Czechs and the Lands of the Bohemian Crown*. Palo Alto, CA: Stanford University Press.

Airapetov, O. R. 2014. *Uchastie Rossiiskoi imperii v Pervoi mirovoi voine (1914–1917)*. Vol. Tom 1: 1914 god. Nachalo Moskva: ID Universitet knizhnyi dom.

Airapetov, O. R. 2015a. *Uchastie Rossiiskoi imperii v Pervoi mirovoi voine (1914–1917)*. Vol. Tom 3: 1916 god. Sverkhnapriazhenie Moskva: Kuchkovo Pole.

Airapetov, O. R. 2015b. *Uchastie Rossiiskoi imperii v Pervoi mirovoi voine (1914–1917)*. Vol. Tom 4: 1917 god. Raspad Moskva: Kuchkovo Pole.

Alarcón, Pedro Antonio de. 1988. *Diary of a Witness to the War in Africa*. Memphis: White Rose Press. Translated by Bern Keating.

Albertini, Luigi. 1952. *The Origins of the War of 1914*. Three Volumes. Oxford: Oxford University Press.

Alesina, Alberto, Arnaud Devleeschauwer, William Easterly, Sergio Kurlat and Romain Wacziag. 2003. "Fractionalization." *National Bureau of Economic Research* Working Paper No. 9411.

Alesina, Alberto and Elina LaFerrara. 2005. "Ethnic Diversity and Economic Performance." *Journal of Economic Literature* 63:762–800.

Alesina, Alberto, Reza Baqir and William Easterly. 1999. "Public Goods and Ethnic Divisions." *Quarterly Journal of Economics* 114:1243–84.

Alexiev, Alexander and S. Enders Wimbush, eds. 1988. *Ethnic Minorities in the Red Army: Asset or Liability?* Boulder, CO: Westview Press.

Alger, Russell, ed. 1898. *The War of the Rebellion: A Compilation of the Official Records of the Union and Confederate Armies*. Vol. LII. Operations in: Southwestern Virginia, Kentucky, Tennessee, Mississippi, Alabama, West Florida, and Northern Georgia, January 1, 1861– June 30, 1865. Washington, D.C.: Government Printing Office.

Alida, Furaha. 2017. "'Where do we belong?' Identity and autochthony discourse among Rwandophones Congolese." *African Identities* 15:41–61.

Allport, Gordon. 1954. *The Nature of Prejudice*. Addison-Wesley: Reading, MA.

Allworth, Edward. 1995. Encounter. In *Central Asia: One Hundred Thirty Years of Russian Dominance, A Historical Overview*, ed. Edward Allworth. Third ed. Durham, NC: Duke University Press, pp. 1–59.

Aminova, R. Kh. 1977. *Osushchestvlenie Kollektivizatsii v Uzbekistane (1929–1932 gg.)*. Tashkent': Iz. Fan Uzbekskoi SSR.

Amlak, Gethahun. 2001. The Battle for Badme. In *Dispatches from the Electronic Front: Internet Responses to the Ethio-Eritrean Conflict*, ed. Walte Information Center. Addis Ababa: Walta Information Center, pp. 220–23.

Amnesty International (31 May 2000). *Democratic Republic of Congo: Killing human decency*. AI Index: AFR 62/07/00. https://www.amnesty.org/en/documents/afr62/007/2000/en/.

An Officer. 1899. *The Sudan Campaign, 1896–1899*. London: Chapman and Hall.

An Officer Who Was There. 1885. *Suakin, 1885: Being a Sketch of the Campaign of this Year*. London: Kegan Paul, Trench and Co.

Anderson, Benedict. 1983. *Imagined Communities: Reflections on the Origins and Spread of Nationalism*. Revised ed. New York: Verso Books.

Andreski, Stanislav. 1954. *Military Organization and Society*. Berkeley: University of California Press.

Ansell, Benjamin and David Samuels. 2014. *Inequality and Democratization: An Elite-Competition Approach*. Cambridge: Cambridge University Press.

Appiah, Kwame Anthony. 2018. *The Lies That Bind: Rethinking Identity*. New York: W. W. Norton & Company.

Ardant du Picq, Charles. 1904. *Études sur le combat: combat antique et combat moderne*. Paris: R. Chapelot.

Arjona, Ana. 2010. *Social Order in Civil War*. Unpublished Ph.D. Dissertation, Yale University.

Arrue, Francisco. 1898. *La Guerra de África de 1859 a 1860: Lecciones Que Explico En El Curso de Estudios Superiores del Ateneo de Madrid*. San Lorenzo: Imprenta del Cuerpo de Artilleria.

Askew, William. 1942. *Europe and Italy's Acquisition of Libya, 1911–1912*. Durham, NC: Duke University Press.

Askey, Nigel. 2016. *Operation Barbarossa: The Complete Organizational and Statistical Analysis, and Military Simulation*. Vol. IIIA. The Soviet Armed Forces, Mobilization, and War Economy from June to December 1941. Morrisville, NC: Lulu Publishing.

Asrat, G. 2014. *Sovereignty and Democracy in Ethiopia*. In Amharic. Washington, D.C.: Signature Book Publishing.

Atkinson, Anthony. 2015. *Inequality*. Cambridge, MA: Harvard University Press.

Autesserre, Severine. 2010. *The Trouble with the Congo: Local Violence and the Failure of International Peacebuilding*. New York: Cambridge University Press.

Baaz, Maria and Judith Verwijen. 2013. "The Volatility of a Half-Cooked Bouillabaisse: Rebel-Military Integration and Conflict Dynamics in the Eastern DRC." *African Affairs* 112: 563–82.

Baaz, Maria and Maria Stern. 2008. "Making Sense of Violence: Voices of Soldiers in the DRC." *Journal of Modern African Studies* 46:57–86.

Bababekov, Khaidarbek. 2006a. *Istoriia Kokanda*. Tashkent: Institut istorii narodov srednei azii imeni Makhpirat.

Bababekov, Khaidarbek. 2006b. *Istoriia zavoevaniia Srednei Azii tsarskoi Rossiei v sekretnykh dokumentakh*. Tashkent: Institut istorii narodov srednei azii imeni Makhpirat.

Bahta, F. T. 2014. *The Hidden Party*. In Amharic. Addis Ababa: Negarit Media.

Bailey, Jonathan. 1996. *The First World War and the Birth of the Modern Style of Warfare*. Camberley, England: British Army Strategic and Combat Studies Institute.

Balaguer, Victor. 1860. *Jornadas de Gloria: Los Españoles en África*. Madrid: Liberia Española.

Balcells, Laia. 2017. *Rivalry and Revenge: The Politics of Violence during Civil War*. Cambridge: Cambridge University Press.

Barbar, Aghil Mohamed. 1980. The Tarabulus (Libyan) Resistance to the Italian Invasion: 1911–1920. PhD thesis. University of Wisconsin-Madison.

Barkawi, Tarak. 2017. *Soldiers of Empire: Indian and British Armies in World War II*. Cambridge: Cambridge University Press.

Barranco, Juan José Lopéz. 2006. *El Rif en armas: La narrativa española sobre la guerra de Marruecos (1859–2005)*. Madrid: Mare Nostrum.

Barthorp, Michael. 2002. *Blood-red Desert Sand: The British Invasions of Egypt and the Sudan, 1882–98*. London: Cassell.

Bartov, Omer. 2001. *The Eastern Front, 1941–45, German Troops and the Barbarisation of Warfare*. Second ed. New York: Palgrave Macmillan.

Bates, Robert. 1983. Modernization, Ethnic Competition, and the Rationality of Politics in Contemporary Africa. In *State Versus Ethnic Claims: African Policy Dilemmas*, ed. Donald Rothchild and Victor Olorunsola. Boulder, CO: Westview Press, pp. 152–71.

Bauer, Michal, Christopher Blattman, Julie Chytilova, Joseph Henrich, Edward Miguel and Tamar Mitts. 2016. "Can War Foster Cooperation?" *Journal of Economic Perspectives* 30:249–74.

Baumann, Robert F. 1993. The Conquest of Central Asia. In *Russian-Soviet Unconventional Wars in the Caucasus, Central Asia, and Afghanistan*. Fort Leavenworth: Combat Studies Institute, pp. 49–89.

Bazin, Jean. 1975. Guerre et servitude à Ségou. In *L'esclavage en Afrique précoloniale*, ed. Claude Meilasoux. Paris: Librairie François Maspero.

Beaumont, Roger and William Snyder. 1980. Combat Effectiveness: Paradigms and Paradoxes. In *Combat Effectiveness: Cohesion, Stress, and the Voluntary Military*, ed. Sam Sarkesian. Vol. 9. Newbury Park, CA: Sage, pp. 20–56.

Beckert, Sven. 2004. "Emancipation and Empire: Reconstructing the Worldwide Web of Cotton Production in the Age of the American Civil War." *American Historical Review* 109:1405–438.

Beckley, Michael. 2010. "Economic Development and Military Effectiveness." *Journal of Strategic Studies* 33:43–79.

Bedri, Babikir. 1969. *The Memoirs of Babikr Bedri*. Volume one. Oxford: Oxford University Press. Translated from the Arabic by Yousef Bedri and George Scott.

Beehler, William. 1913. *The History of the Italian-Turkish War, September 29, 1911–October 18, 1912*. Annapolis, MD: William H. Beehler.

Beisembiev, Timur. 1987. *Ta'rikh-i Shakhrukhi kak istoricheskii sbornik*. Alma-Ata: Nauka.

Beisembiev, Timur. 2008. *Annotated Indices to the Kokand Chronicles*. ILCAA: Research Institute for Languages and Cultures of Asia and Africa.

Bek, Aleksander. 1943. "Panfilovtsy na pervom rubezhe." *Znamia* 5–6:199–234.

Bek, Aleksander. 1965. *Volokolamskoe shosse*. Moskva: Izdatel'stvo "Khudozhestvennaia literatura."

Belkin, Aaron and Evan Schofer. 2003. "Toward a Structural Understanding of Coup Risk." *Journal of Conflict Resolution* 47:594–620.

Belov, S. I. 2014. "Problemnye aspekty izucheniia temy boia 28 panfilovtsev." *Bylye Gody* 31: 26–31.

Bendix, Reinhard. 1964. *Nation-building and citizenship: Studies of our changing social order*. New York: Wiley.

Benjamin, Marvin. 2014. "A Life and Death Question": Austro-Hungarian War Aims in the First World War. In *The Purpose of War—War Aims and Strategy during the Great War, 1914–1918*, ed. Holger Afflerbach. Munich: Oldenberg.

Bennett, Andrew and Jeffrey Checkel, eds. 2015. *Process Tracing in the Social Sciences: From Metaphor to Analytic Tool*. Cambridge: Cambridge University Press.

Bennett, D. Scott and Allan Stam. 1998. "The Declining Advantages of Democracy: A Combined Model of War Outcomes and Duration." *Journal of Conflict Resolution* 42: 344–66.

Bennett, Ernest. 1899a. "After Omdurman." *Contemporary Review* 75:18–35.

Bennett, Ernest. 1899b. *The Downfall of the Dervishes: Or, The Avenging of Gordon; Being a Personal Narrative of the Final Soudan Campaign of 1898*. London: Methuen and Co.

Bennett, Ernest. 1912. *With the Turks in Tripoli: Being Some Experiences in the Italian War of 1911*. London: Methuen and Co.

Bennison, Amira. 2002. *Jihad and Its Interpretations in Pre-Colonial Morocco*. New York: RoutledgeCurzon.

Bennison, Amira. 2004. "The 'New Order' and Islamic Order: The Introduction of the Nizami Army in the Western Maghrib and Its Legitimation, 1830–73." *International Journal of Middle East Studies* 36:399–420.

Berman, Richard. 1932. *The Mahdi of Allah: The Story of the Dervish Mohammed Ahmed*. New York: Macmillan Company.

Beshanov, Vladimir. 2004. *Tankovyi Pogrom 1941 goda: Kuda Ischezli 28 Tysiach Sovetskikh Tankov?* Moskva: Izdatel'stvo AST.

Beşikçi, Mehmet. 2012. *The Ottoman Mobilization of Manpower in the First World War: Between Volunteerism and Resistance*. Boston: Leiden.

Biddle, Stephen. 2004. *Military Power: Explaining Victory and Defeat in Modern Battle*. Princeton, NJ: Princeton University Press.

Biddle, Stephen. 2007. Explaining Military Outcomes. In *Creating Military Power: The Sources of Military Effectiveness*, ed. Risa Brooks and Elizabeth Stanley. Palo Alto, CA: Stanford University Press, pp. 207–27.

Biddle, Stephen and Robert Zirkle. 1996. "Technology, Civil-Military Relations, and Warfare in the Developing World." *Journal of Strategic Studies* 19:171–212.

Biddle, Stephen and Stephen Long. 2004. "Democracy and Military Effectiveness: A Deeper Look." *Journal of Conflict Resolution* 48:525–46.

Black, George. 1993. *Genocide in Iraq: The Anfal Campaign Against the Kurds*. Washington, D.C.: Middle East Watch (A Division of Human Rights Watch).

Black, Jeremy. 2004. *Rethinking Military History*. New York: Routledge.

Blanton, Harold. 2009. Conscription in France during the era of Napoleon. In *Conscription in the Napoleonic Era: A revolution in military affairs?*, ed. Donald Stoker, Frederick Schneid and Harold Blanton. New York: Routledge, pp. 6–23.

Blaydes, Lisa. 2018. *State of Repression: Iraq Under Saddam Hussein*. Princeton, NJ: Princeton University Press.

Bobozhonov, B. 2010. *Kokandskoe khanstvo: vlast', politika, religiia*. Tashkent: Institut Vostokovedeniia akademii nauk Respubliki Uzbekistan.

Boff, Jonathan. 2012. *Winning and Losing on the Western Front*. Cambridge: Cambridge University Press.

Boix, Carles. 2015. *Political Order and Inequality: Their Foundations and Consequences for Human Welfare*. Cambridge: Cambridge University Press.

Boot, Max. 2007. *War Made New: Weapons, Warriors, and the Making of the Modern World*. New York: Gotham.

Boulding, Kenneth. 1962. *Conflict and Defense: A General Theory*. New York: Harper.

Bowles, Samuel. 2016. *The Moral Economy: Why Good Incentives Are No Substitute for Good Citizens*. New Haven, CT: Yale University Press.

Brackenbury, Henry. 1885. *The River Column: A Narrative of the Advance of the River Column of the Nile Expeditionary Force, and Its Return Down the Rapids*. Edinburgh: William Blackwood and Sons.

Braithwaite, Roderic. 2006. *Moscow 1941: A City and Its People at War*. New York: Knopf.

Brandenburger, David. 2002. *National Bolshevism: Stalinist Mass Culture and the Formation of Modern Russian National Identity, 1931–1956*. Cambridge, MA: Harvard University Press.

Brandenburger, David. 2011. *Propaganda State in Crisis: Soviet Ideology, Indoctrination, and Terror Under Stalin, 1927–1941*. Palo Alto, CA: Stanford University Press.

Brass, Paul. 2003. *The Production of Hindu-Muslim Violence in Contemporary India*. Seattle: University of Washington Press.

Braumoeller, Bear. 2019. *Only the Dead: The Persistence of War in the Modern Age.* Oxford: Oxford University Press.

Bregel, Yuri. 2009. The new Uzbek states: Bukhara, Khiva, and Khoqand: c. 1750–1886. In *The Cambridge History of Inner Asia: The Chinggisid Age*, ed. Nicola Di Cosmo, Allen Frank and Peter Golden. Cambridge: Cambridge University Press, pp. 392–411.

Briant, Pierre. 2015. *Darius in the Shadow of Alexander.* Cambridge, MA: Harvard University Press.

Broadley, Alexander. 1884. *How We Defended Arabi and his Friends: A Story of Egypt and the Egyptians.* London: Chapman and Hall.

Brooks, Risa. 2006. "An Autocracy at War: Explaining Egypt's Military (In)Effectiveness." *Security Studies* 15:396–430.

Brooks, Risa and Elisabeth Stanley, eds. 2007. *Creating Military Power: The Sources of Military Effectiveness.* Palo Alto, CA: Stanford University Press.

Brown, Michael, Owen Coté, Sean Lynn-Jones and Steven Miller, eds. 2004. *Offense, Defense, and War.* Cambridge, MA: MIT Press.

Broxup, Marie. 1983. "The Basmachi." *Central Asian Survey* 2:57–81.

Brubaker, Rogers. 1996. *Nationalism reframed: Nationhood and the national question in the New Europe.* Cambridge: Cambridge University Press.

Bruce, George. 1906. *The twentieth regiment of Massachusetts Volunteer Infantry, 1861–1865.* Boston: Houghton Mifflin Company.

Buchanon, James. 1965. "An Economic Theory of Clubs." *Economica* 32:1–14.

Bueno de Mesquita, Bruce, Alastair Smith, Randolph Siverson and James Morrow. 2003. *The Logic of Political Survival.* Cambridge, MA: MIT Press.

Bundesministerium für Heereswesen und Kriegsarchiv. 1930. *Österreich-Ungarns letzter Krieg.* Vol. Vom Kriegsausbruch bis zum Ausgang der Schlacht bei Limanowa-Lapanów; 1. Das Kriegsjahr 1914 Wien: Verlag der Militärwissenschaftlichen Mitteilungen, 1930–1938.

Bundesministerium für Heereswesen und Kriegsarchiv. 1933. *Österreich-Ungarns letzter Krieg.* Vol. Die Ereignisse von Jänner bis Ende Juli 4: Das Kriegsjahr 1916 Wien: Verlag der Militärwissenschaftlichen Mitteilungen, 1930–1938.

Burleigh, Bennet. 1884. *Desert Warfare: Being the Chronicle of the Eastern Soudan Campaign.* London: Chapman and Hall.

Burleigh, Bennet. 1898. *Sirdar and Khalifa; Or: The Re-Conquest of the Soudan, 1898.* London: Chapman and Hall.

Burleigh, Bennet. 1899. *Khartoum Campaign, 1898: or, The Reconquest of the Sudan.* London: Chapman and Hall.

Burton, R. G. 1908. *Wellington's Campaigns in India: Division of the Chief of Staff, Intelligence Branch.* Calcutta: Superintendent Government Printing, India.

Bustillo, Eduardo. 1868. *Historia de la gloriosa guerra de África en 1859: escrita y dividida en romances.* Cuarta edicion ed. Madrid: Despacho de Marés y Compañia, Juanelo 19.

Butler, W. F. 1887. *The Campaign of the Cataracts: Being a Personal Narrative of the Great Nile Expedition of 1884–1885.* London: Sampson Low, Marston and Company.

Buttar, Prit. 2014. *Collision of Empires: The War on the Eastern Front in 1914.* London: Osprey Publishing.

Calderwood, Eric. 2012. "The Beginning (or End) of Moroccan History: Historiography, Translation, and Modernity in Ahmad B. Khalid's Al-Nasiri and Clemente Cerdeira." *International Journal of Middle East Studies* 44:399–420.

Cameron, Sarah. 2018. *The Hungry Steppe: Famine, Violence, and the Making of Soviet Kazakhstan*. Ithaca, NY: Cornell University Press.

Campbell, John. 2014. *Nationalism, Law, and Statelessness: Grand Illusions in the Horn of Africa*. New York: Routledge.

Canetti, Daphna and Miriam Lindner. 2014. Exposure to Political Violence and Political Behavior. In *Psychology of Change: Life Contexts, Experiences, and Identities*, ed. Katherine Reynolds and Nyla Branscombe. New York: Psychology Press, pp. 77–94.

Carayannis, Tatiana. 2003. "The Complex Wars of the Congo: Towards a New Analytic Approach." *Journal of Asian and African Studies* 38:232–55.

Carmack, Roberto. 2015. "A Fortress of the Soviet Home Front": Mobilization and Ethnicity in Kazakhstan during World War II. PhD thesis. University of Wisconsin-Madison.

Carson, Austin. 2018. *Secret Wars: Covert Conflict in International Politics*. Princeton, NJ: Princeton University Press.

Castelar, D. Emilio, D. F. Canalejas, D. G. Villaamil and D. Morayia. 1859. *Crónica de la Guerra de África*. Madrid: Imprenta de v. Matute y B. Compagni.

Castillo, Jasen. 2014. *Endurance and War: The National Sources of Military Cohesion*. Palo Alto, CA: Stanford University Press.

Cederman, Lars-Erik, Andreas Wimmer and Brian Min. 2010. "Why do Ethnic Groups Rebel? New Data and Analysis." *World Politics* 62:87–119.

Cederman, Lars-Erik, Kristian Gleditsch and Halvard Buhaug. 2013. *Inequality, Grievances, and Civil War*. Cambridge: Cambridge University Press.

Cederman, Lars-Erik, Kristian Gleditsch and Julian Wucherpfennig. 2017. "Predicting the Decline of Ethnic Civil War: Was Gurr Right and for the Right Reasons?" *Journal of Peace Research* 54:262–74.

Chan, Anthony. 1982. *Arming the Chinese: The Western Armaments Trade in Warlord China, 1920–1928*. Vancouver: University of British Columbia Press.

Chandra, Kanchan. 2006. "What Is Ethnic Identity and Does It Matter?" *Annual Review of Political Science* 9:397–424.

Chandra, Kanchan. 2012. *Constructivist Theories of Ethnic Politics*. Oxford: Oxford University Press.

Checkel, Jeffrey. 2017. "Socialization and Violence: Introduction and Framework." *Journal of Peace Research* 54:592–605.

Cheesman, George. 1914. *The Auxilia of the Roman Imperial Army*. Oxford: Clarendon Press.

Cheuzeville, Hervé. 2003. *Kadogo: Enfants des guerres d'Afrique Centrale*. Paris: L'Harmattan.

Chi, Hsi-Sheng. 1976. *Warlord Politics in China*. Palo Alto, CA: Stanford University Press.

Childs, Timothy. 1990. *Italo-Turkish Diplomacy and the War over Libya, 1911–1912*. New York: Brill Academic Publications.

Christia, Fotini. 2012. *Alliance Formation in Civil War*. Cambridge: Cambridge University Press.

Churchill, Winston. 1899. *The River War: An Account of the Reconquest of the Soudan*. New York: C. Scribner's Sons.

Churchill, Winston. 2015. *The World Crisis*. Vol. V: The Unknown War. London: Bloomsbury Revelations.

Citino, Robert. 2004. *Blitzkrieg to Desert Storm: The Evolution of Operational Warfare*. Lawrence: University of Kansas Press.

Citino, Robert. 2007. *Death of the Wehrmacht: The German Campaigns of 1942*. Lawrence: University Press of Kansas.

Citino, Robert. 2012. *The Wehrmacht Retreats: Fighting a Lost War, 1943*. Lawrence: University of Kansas Press.

Clark, Christopher. 2012. *The Sleepwalkers: How Europe Went to War in 1914*. New York: Harper Perennial.

Clark, John. 2002. *The African Stakes in the Congo War*. New York: Palgrave Macmillan.

Clark, Peter. 1977. *Three Sudanese Battles*. Khartoum: Institute of African and Asian Studies, University of Khartoum.

Clark, Peter. 1998. The Battle of Omdurman in the Context of Sudanese History. In *Sudan: The Reconquest Reappraised*, ed. Edward Spiers. London: Frank Cass, pp. 202–22.

Clausewitz, Carl von. 1984. *On War*. Princeton, NJ: Princeton University Press.

Cohen, Dara Kay. 2016. *Rape During Civil War*. Ithaca, NY: Cornell University Press.

Cohen, Elizabeth. 2009. *Semi-Citizenship in Democratic Politics*. Cambridge: Cambridge University Press.

Cohen, Gary. 1998a. "Neither Absolutism nor Anarchy: New Narratives on Society and Government in Late Imperial Austria." *Austrian History Yearbook* 29:37–61.

Cohen, Gary. 2007. "Nationalist Politics and the Dynamics of State and Civil Society in the Habsburg Monarchy, 1867–1914." *Central European History* 40:241–78.

Cohen, Stephen. 1998b. *Pakistan Army*. Berkeley: University of California Press.

Colborne, Colonel John. 1884. *With Hicks Pasha in the Soudan: Being an account of the Senaar campaign in 1883*. London: Smith, Elder.

Cole, Laurence. 2014. *Military Culture and Popular Patriotism in Late Imperial Austria*. Oxford: Oxford University Press.

Collins, Randall. 2013. Does nationalist sentiment increase fighting efficacy? A skeptical view from the sociology of violence. In *Nationalism and War*, ed. John Hall and Siniša Malešević. Cambridge: Cambridge University Press, pp. 31–43.

Collins, Robert. 1962. *The Southern Sudan, 1883–1898: A Struggle for Control*. New Haven, CT: Yale University Press.

Colvile, H. E. 1889. *History of the Sudan Campaign: Compiled in the Intelligence Division of the War Office*. Nashville: Battery Press.

Connell, Dan. 2005. *Conversations with Eritrean Political Prisoners*. Lawrenceville, NJ: Red Sea Press.

Conquest, Robert. 1986. *The Harvest of Sorrow: Soviet Collectization and the Terror-Famine*. Oxford: Oxford University Press.

Cooper King, C. 1885. "Soudan Warfare." *Journal of the Royal United Services Institution* 131: 887–908.

Cooper, Randolph. 2003. *The Anglo-Maratha Campaigns and the Contest for India*. Cambridge: Cambridge University Press.

Cooper, Tom. 2013. *Great Lakes Conflagration: The Second Congo War, 1998–2003*. Solihull, West Midlands: Helion and Company.

Cornish, Dudley. 1987. *The Sable Arm: Black Troops in the Union Army, 1861–1865*. Lawrence: University Press of Kansas.

Cornwall, Mark. 2000. *The Undermining of Austria-Hungary: The Battle for Hearts and Minds*. London: Macmillan Press.

Correlates of War. 2010. *Inter-State War Data: Version 4.0*. URL: http://www.correlatesofwar.org/

Coser, Lewis. 1956. *The Functions of Social Conflict*. New York: Free Press.

Craig, Gordon. 1965. "The Military Cohesion of the Austro-German Alliance, 1914–1918." *Journal of Modern History* 37:7–30.

Crawford, Kate, Meredith Whittaker, Madeleine Clare Elish, Solon Barocas, Aaron Plasek and Kadija Ferryman. 2016. *The AI Now Report: The Social and Economic Implications of Artificial Intelligence*. Technical report tabled with the White House Office of Science and Technology Policy for their Future of Artificial Intelligence Series.

Daines, Vladimir. 2008. *Shtrafbaty i zagradotriady Krasnoi Armii*. Moskva: Iauza.

Dallin, Alexander. 1956. "The Soviet Reaction to Vlasov." *World Politics* 8:307–22.

Daly, M. W., ed. 1983. *The Road to Shaykan: Letters of General William Hicks Pasha written during the Sennar and Kordofan Campaigns, 1883*. Occasional Paper Series No.20. Durham, England: University of Durham.

Danilov, V. P., R. T. Manning and L. Viola, eds. 2006. *Tragediia sovetskoi derevni: Kolletivizatsiia i raskulachivanie, 1927–1939*. Vol. 5. Moskva: ROSSPEN.

De Cosson, E. A. 1886. *Fighting the Fuzzy-Wuzzy: Days and Nights of Service with Sir Gerald Graham's Field Force at Suakin*. London: J. Murray.

Deák, István. 1990. *Beyond Nationalism: A Social and Political History of the Habsburg Officer Corps, 1848–1918*. New York: Oxford University Press.

Deak, John. 2014. "The Great War and the Forgotten Realm: The Habsburg Monarchy and the First World War." *Journal of Modern History* 86:336–80.

Deak, John. 2015. *Forging a Multinational State: State Making in Imperial Austria from the Enlightenment to the First World War*. Palo Alto, CA: Stanford University Press.

Deaton, Angus. 2013. *The Great Escape: Health, Wealth, and the Origins of Inequality*. Princeton, NJ: Princeton University Press.

Dekmejian, Richard and Margaret Wyszomirski. 1972. "Charismatic Leadership in Islam: The Mahdi of the Sudan." *Comparative Studies in Society and History* 14:193–214.

del Bocca, Angelo. 1911. *A un passo dalla forca: Atrocità e infamie dell'occupazione italiana della Libia nelle memorie del patriota Mohamed Fekini*. Milano: Baldini Castoldi Dalai.

del Bocca, Angelo. 1986. *Gli Italiani in Libia: Tripoli bel suol d'amore: 1860–1922*. Vol. I. Milano: Mondadori.

del Bocca, Angelo. 2011. *Mohamed Fekini and the Fight to Free Libya*. New York: Palgrave Macmillan.

del Rey, Miguel. 2001. *La Guerra de África, 1859–1860*. Madrid: Grupo Medusa Ediciones.

Dempsey, Martin and Ori Brafman. 2018. *Radical Inclusion: What the Post-9/11 World Should Have Taught Us About Leadership*. New York: Missionday.

Desch, Michael. 2008. *Power and Military Effectiveness: The Fallacy of Democratic Triumphalism*. Baltimore: Johns Hopkins University Press.

Diamond, Jared and James Robinson. 2010. Afterword: Using Comparative Methods in Studies of Human History. In *Natural Experiments of History*. Cambridge, MA: Harvard University Press, pp. 257–76.

Dias, Alexandra. 2011. "The Conduct of an Inter-state War and Multiple Dimensions of Territory: 1998–2000 Eritrea-Ethiopia War." *Cadernos de Estudos Africanos* 22:21–41.

DiNardo, Richard L. 2010. *Breakthrough: The Gorlice-Tarnow Campaign, 1915*. Santa Barbara, CA: Praeger.

Dixon, Norman. 2016. *On the Psychology of Military Incompetence*. New York: Basic Books.

Doughty, Robert. 2008. *Pyrrhic Victory: French Strategy and Operations in the Great War*. Cambridge, MA: Harvard University Press.

Dowling, Timothy C. 2008. *Brusilov Offensive*. Bloomington: Indiana University Press.

Dowling, Timothy C. 2012. The Brusilov Offensive. In *Essays on World War I*, ed. Graydon A. Tunstall. New York: Columbia University Press, pp. 89–110.

Downes, Alexander. 2009. "How Smart and Tough Are Democracies? Reassessing Theories of Democratic Victory in War." *International Security* 33:9–51.

DuBois, Edmund, Wayne Hughes, Jr. and Lawrence Low. 1997. *A Concise Theory of Combat*. Monterey, CA: Institute for Joint Warfare Analysis.

Dubovitskii, Victor and Khaydarbek Bababekov. 2011. The Rise and Fall of the Kokand Khanate. In *Ferghana Valley: The Heart of Central Asia*, ed. Frederick Starr. Armonk, NY: M. E. Sharpe, pp. 29–68.

Dunning, Thad. 2012. *Natural Experiments in the Social Sciences: A Design-Based Approach*. Cambridge: Cambridge University Press.

Dunning, Thad. 2014. Improving process tracing: the case of multi-method research. In *Process Tracing: From Metaphor to Analytic Tool*, ed. Andrew Bennett and Jeffrey Checkel. Cambridge: Cambridge University Press, pp. 211–36.

Dupuy, Trevor. 1979. *Numbers, Predictions, and War: Using History to Evaluate Combat Factors and Predict the Outcomes of Battles*. New York: Bobbs-Merrill Company.

Easterly, William. 2013. *The Tyranny of Experts: Economists, Dictators, and the Forgotten Rights of the Poor*. New York: Basic Books.

Edele, Mark. 2017. *Stalin's Defectors: How Red Army Soldiers became Hitler's Collaborators, 1941–1945*. Oxford: Oxford University Press.

El Hamel, Chouki. 2013. *Black Morocco: A History of Slavery, Race, and Islam*. Cambridge: Cambridge University Press.

Elleman, Bruce. 2001. *Modern Chinese Warfare, 1795–1989*. London: Routledge.

Elliott, Mark. 2001. *The Manchu Way: The Eight Banners and Ethnic Identity in Late Imperial China*. Palo Alto, CA: Stanford University Press.

Elton, Lord, ed. 1961. *General Gordon's Khartoum Journal*. London: William Kimber and Co.

Emery, Frank. 1986. *Marching Over Africa: Letters from Victorian Soldiers*. London: Hodder and Stoughton.

Enloe, Cynthia. 1980. *Ethnic Soldiers: State Security in Divided Societies*. New York: Penguin Books.

Ennaji, Mohammed. 1999. *Serving the Master: Slavery and Society in Nineteenth-Century Morocco*. New York: St. Martin's Press. Translated by Seth Graebner.

Enos, Ryan and Noam Gidron. 2018. "Exclusion and Cooperation in Diverse Societies: Experimental Evidence from Israel." *American Political Science Review* 112(4):742–57.

Enquay, S. 2005. *Tilmet*. Washington, D.C.: Artistic Publishing Company.

Epstein, Robert. 1994. *Napoleon's Last Victory and the Emergence of Modern War*. Lawrence: University of Kansas Press.

Erickson, Edward. 2001. *Ordered to Die: A History of the Ottoman Army in the First World War*. Westport, CT: Greenwood Press.

Erickson, Edward. 2007. *Ottoman Army Effectiveness in World War One*. Westport, CT: Greenwood Press.

Erickson, Edward. 2013. *Ottomans and Armenians: A Study in Counterinsurgency*. New York: Palgrave Macmillan.

Erickson, John. 1999*a*. *The Road to Berlin: Stalin's War with Germany*. Vol. II. New Haven, CT: Yale University Press.

Erickson, John. 1999*b*. *The Road to Stalingrad: Stalin's War with Germany*. Vol. I. New Haven, CT: Yale University Press.

Erlikhman, V. 2004. *Population Losses in the XX Century: Reference Book*. Moscow: Russian Panorama Press.

Esdaile, Charles. 2008. *Napoleon's Wars: An International History, 1803–1815*. New York: Penguin.

Fearon, James. 1995. "Rationalist Explanations for War." *International Organization* 49:379–414.

Fearon, James. 1999. "Why Ethnic Politics and 'Pork' Tend to Go Together." Unpublished Manuscript, Stanford University.

Fearon, James. 2018. "Cooperation, Conflict, and the Costs of Anarchy." *International Organization* 72:523–59.

Fearon, James and David Laitin. 1996. "Explaining Interethnic Cooperation." *American Political Science Review* 90:715–35.

Fearon, James and David Laitin. 2003. "Ethnicity, Insurgency, and Civil War." *American Political Science Review* 97:75–90.

Fearon, James and David Laitin. 2008. Integrating Qualitative and Quantitative Methods. In *The Oxford Handbook of Political Methodology*, ed. Janet Box-Steffensmeier, Henry Brady and David Collier. New York: Oxford University Press, pp. 756–776.

Featherstone, Donald. 2005. *Khartoum 1885: General Gordon's Last Stand*. Westport, CT: Praeger Security International.

Feaver, Peter. 2003. *Armed Servants: Agency, Oversight, and Civil-Military Relations*. Cambridge, MA: Harvard University Press.

Fennell, Jonathan. 2011. *Combat and Morale in the North African Campaign: The Eighth Army and the Path to El Alamein*. Cambridge: Cambridge University Press.

Ferejohn, John and Frances Rosenbluth. 2017. *Forged Through Fire: War, Peace, and the Democratic Bargain*. New York: W.W. Norton & Company.

Fessehatzion, Tekie. 2003. *Shattered Illusion, Broken Promise: Essays on the Eritrea-Ethiopia Conflict 1998–2000*. Trenton, NJ: Red Sea Press.

Figes, Orlando. 1990. "The Red Army and Mass Mobilization during the Russian Civil War." *Past & Present* 129:168–211.

Filippenkov, Michael. 2016. *Konev's Golgotha: Operation Typhoon Strikes the Soviet Western Front, October 1941*. New York: Helion and Company.

Fishman, Brian. 2016. *The Master Plan: ISIS, Al-Qaeda, and the Jihadi Strategy for Final Victory*. New Haven, CT: Yale University Press.

Fitzpatrick, John, ed. 1932. *The Writings of George Washington from the Original Manuscript Sources, 1745–1799*. Washington, D.C.: Government Printing Office.

Fitzpatrick, Sheila. 2000. *Everyday Stalinism: Ordinary Life in Extraordinary Times: Soviet Russia in the 1930s*. Oxford: Oxford University Press.

Fjelde, Hanne, Lisa Hultman and Desirée Nilsson. 2019. "Protection Through Presence: UN Peacekeeping and the Costs of Targeting Civilians." *International Organization* 73: 103–31.

Fletcher, Joseph. 1978. The Heyday of the Ch'ing Order in Mongolia, Sinkiang, and Tibet. In *The Cambridge History of China*, ed. John Fairbank. Vol. 10. Cambridge: Cambridge University Press, pp. 351–408.

Flores, Hilda Agnes Hübner. 1995. *Alemães Na Guerra Dos Farrapos*. Porto Alegre: EDIPUCRS.

Foner, Eric. 1999. *The Story of American Freedom*. New York: W. W. Norton.

Fontanellaz, Adrien and Tom Cooper. 2018. *Ethiopian-Eritrean Wars: Eritrean War of Independence, 1988–1991, and Badme War, 1998–2001*. Vol. 2. Warwick: Helion and Company.

Forrest, Alan. 1989. *Conscripts and Deserters: The Army and French Society During the Revolution and Empire*. New York: Oxford University Press.

Freedman, Lawrence. 2005. "A Theory of Battle or a Theory of War?" *Journal of Strategic Studies* 3:425–35.

Freedman, Lawrence. 2017. *The Future of War: A History*. New York: PublicAffairs.

Gaddis, John Lewis. 2018. *On Grand Strategy*. New York: Penguin Press.

Galántai, József. 1989. *Hungary in the First World War*. Budapest: Akadémiai Kiadó.

Galkina, M. N. 1868. *Ethograficheckie i istoricheskie materialy po Srednei Azii i Orenburgskomu Kraiu*. Sankt Peterburg: Izdanie Ia. A. Isakova.

Gapurov, Sh. A., A. M. Izraiilov and R. A. Tovsultanov. 2007. *Chechnia na zavershaiushchem etape Kavkazskoi voiny: stranitsy khroniki russko-gorskoi tragedii XIX veka*. Nal'chik: El'-Fa.

Gat, Azar. 2006. *War in Human Civilization*. Oxford: Oxford University Press.

Gavin, Francis. 2015. "What If? The Historian and the Counterfactual." *Security Studies* 24:425–30.

Gellner, Ernest. 1983. *Nations and Nationalism*. Ithaca, NY: Cornell University Press.

George, Alexander and Andrew Bennett. 2005. *Case Studies and Theory Development in the Social Sciences*. Cambridge, MA: MIT Press.

Gerring, John. 2012. *Social Science Methodology: A Unified Framework*. Cambridge: Cambridge University Press.

Gerring, John, Michael Hoffman and Dominic Zarecki. 2018. "The Diverse Effects of Diversity on Democracy." *British Journal of Political Science* 48:283–314.

Geukjian, O. 2012. *Ethnicity, Nationalism and Conflict in the South Caucasus*. Burlington, VT: Ashgate.

Geyer, Dietrich. 1987. *Russian Imperialism: The Interaction of Domestic and Foreign Policy, 1860–1914*. Berg: Bruce Little Leamington Spa.

Giddens, Anthony. 1985. *The Nation-State and Violence*. Vol. Two. Berkeley: University of California Press.

Gilpin, Robert. 1981. *War and Change in World Politics*. Cambridge: Cambridge University Press.

Giustozzi, Antonio. 2009. *Empires of Mud: Wars and Warlords in Afghanistan*. Oxford: Oxford University Press.

Glantz, David. 1999. "Forgotten battles of the German-Soviet War (1941–45), Part I." *Journal of Slavic Military Studies* 12:149–97.

Glantz, David. 2005a. *Colossus Reborn: The Red Army at War, 1941–1943*. Lawrence: University of Kansas Press.

Glantz, David. 2005b. *Slaughterhouse: The Handbook of the Eastern Front*. Bedford, PA: Aberjona Press.

Glantz, David and Jonathan House. 1999. *The Battle of Kursk*. Lawrence: University of Kansas Press.

Glantz, David and Jonathan House. 2014. *Endgame at Stalingrad*. Vol. 3 of *The Stalingrad Trilogy*. Lawrence: University of Kansas Press.

Glantz, David and Jonathan House. 2015. *When Titans Clashed: How the Red Army Stopped Hitler*. Revised and expanded ed. Lawrence: University of Kansas Press.

Glaser, Charles and Chaim Kaufmann. 1998. "What Is the Offense-Defense Balance and How Can We Measure It?" *International Security* 22:44–82.

Glavnoe upravlenie General'nogo shtaba. 1912. *Vooruzhennye sily Avstro-Vengrii*. Vol. Chast' 1. Organizatsiia, mobilizatsiia i sostav vooruzhennykh sil Sankt Peterburg: Voennaia tipografiia (v zdannii Glavnogo Shtaba).

Gleditsch, Kristian and Steve Pickering. 2014. "Wars Are Becoming Less Frequent: A Response to Harrison and Wolf." *Economic History Review* 67:214–30.

Gleichen, Edward. 1905. *The Anglo-Egyptian Sudan: A Compendium Prepared by Officers of the Sudan Government*. Vol. I. London: H. M. Stationary Office.

Godard, Léon. 1860. *Description et histoire du Maroc: comprenant la géographie et la statistique de ce pays d'après les renseignements les plus rècents et le tableau de règne des souverains qui l'ont gouverné depuis les temps les plus anciens jusque'á la paix de Tétouan en 1860*. Volume I. Paris: Ch. Tanera.

Goffman, Erving. 1961. *Asylums: Essays on the Social Situation of Mental Patients and Other Inmates*. New York: Doubleday.

Goldstein, Joshua. 2011. *Winning the War on War: The Decline of Armed Conflict Worldwide*. New York: Dutton Books.

Golovanov, A. A. 1992. *Krest'ianstvo Uzbekistana: Evoliutsiia Sotsial'nogo Polozheniia, 1917–1937 gg*. Tashkent': Iz. Fan Ak. Nauk. Respubliki Uzbekistan.

Gong, Gerrit. 1984. *The Standard of Civilization in International Society*. Oxford: Oxford University Press.

Gooch, John. 2014. *The Italian Army and the First World War*. Cambridge: Cambridge University Press.

Gordon, Grant. 2015. "Payment and Predation: The Politics of Wages in the Congolese Army." Unpublished manuscript.

Grauer, Ryan. 2016. *Commanding Military Power: Organizing for Victory and Defeat on the Battlefield*. Cambridge: Cambridge University Press.

Green, Dominic. 2007. *Three Empires on the Nile: The Victorian Jihad, 1869–1898*. New York: Free Press.

Greitens, Sheena. 2016. *Dictators and their Secret Police: Coercive Institutions and State Violence*. Cambridge: Cambridge University Press.

Griffiths, Arthur. 1897. Spanish Battles in Morocco, 1859–60: Castillejos, Tetuan, Guad el Ras. In *Battles of the Nineteenth Century*, ed. Archibald Forbes, G. A. Henty and Arthur Griffiths. Vol. II. London: Cassell and Company, pp. 105–15.

Grigor'ev, V. K. and L. S. Akhmetova. 2014. *Panfilovtsy: 60 dnei podviga, stavshikh legendoi*. Almaty: OO "Soiuz zhenshchin intellektual'nogo truda."

Grossman, Dave. 1996. *On Killing: The Psychological Cost of Learning to Kill in War and Society*. San Francisco: Back Bay Books.

Gumz, Jonathan. 2009. *The Resurrection and Collapse of Empire in Habsburg Serbia, 1914–1918*. Cambridge: Cambridge University Press.

Guo, Jianlin, Tang Aimin Su Quanyou and Qi Qingchang, eds. 2003. *Min chu Bei yang san da nei zhan ji shi*. Tianjin: Nan kai da xue chu ban she.

Gusterin, Pavel. 2014. *Istoriia Ibragim-beka. Basmachestvo odnogo kubashi s ero slov*. Saarbrukken: Lambert Academic Publishing.

Gutiérrez Maturana, José. 1876. *Bajo la tienda, 1859 y 1860: impresiones del momento: apuntes para el diario de operaciones de la 2ª División del 2° Cuerpo del Ejército de África por José Gutiérrez Maturana*. Madrid: Valladolid Imprenta, Librería, Estereo-galvanoplastia y Taller de Grabado de Gaviria y Zapatero.

Gutiérrez-Sanin, Francisco and Elisabeth Wood. 2017. "What Should We Mean by 'Pattern of Political Violence?' Repertoire, Targeting, Frequency, and Technique." *Perspectives on Politics* 15:20–41.

Habyarimana, James, Macartan Humphreys, Daniel Posner and Jeremy Weinstein. 2009. *Coethnicity: Diversity and the Dilemmas of Collective Action*. New York: Russell Sage Foundation.

Haggard, Andrew. 1895. *Under Crescent and Star*. Second edition. Edinburgh: William Blackwood and Sons.

Hainmueller, Jens and Dominik Hangartner. 2013. "Who Gets a Swiss Passport? A Natural Experiment in Immigration Discrimination." *American Political Science Review* 107: 159–87.

Hall, John and Siniša Malešević. 2013. Introduction: wars and nationalisms. In *Nationalism and War*, ed. John Hall and Siniša Malešević. Cambridge: Cambridge University Press, pp. 1–27.

Hamedi, Mohammad. 2010. "A Glance at Persian, European, and Russian Historical Sources on the Manghit Dynasty in the 19th Century." *Review of Middle East Studies* 44:33–47.

Hammond, Laura. 2004. *This Place Will Become Home: Refugee Repatriation to Ethiopia*. Ithaca, NY: Cornell University Press.

Hamner, Christopher. 2011. *Enduring Battle: American Soldiers in Three Wars, 1776–1945*. Lawrence: University Press of Kansas.

Hanmer, Michael and Kerem Ozan Kalkan. 2013. "Behind the Curve: Clarifying the Best Approach to Calculating Predicted Probabilities and Marginal Effects from Limited Dependent Variable Models." *American Journal of Political Science* 57:263–77.

Hanson, Victor Davis. 2002. *Carnage and Culture: Landmark Battles in the Rise to Western Power*. New York: Anchor.

Hardesty, Von and Ilya Grinberg. 2012. *Red Phoenix Rising: The Soviet Air Force in World War II*. Lawrence: University of Kansas Press.

Hardman, Frederick. 1860. *The Spanish Campaign in Morocco*. Edinburgh and London: William Blackwood and Sons.

Harrington, Peter and Frederic Sharf, eds. 1998. *Omdurman 1898: The Eye-Witnesses Speak*. London: Greenhill Books.

Harris, James, ed. 2013. *The Anatomy of Terror: Political Violence Under Stalin*. Oxford: Oxford University Press.

Hartmann, Christian. 2013. *Operation Barbarossa: Nazi Germany's War in the East, 1941–1945*. Oxford: Oxford University Press.

Hartzell, Caroline. 2014. Peacebuilding After Civil War. In *Routledge Handbook of Civil Wars*, ed. Edward Newman and Lark DeRouen Jr. New York: Routledge, pp. 376–86.

Hashim, Ahmed. 2018. *The Caliphate at War: Operational Realities and Innovations of the Islamic State*. Oxford: Oxford University Press.

Haslinger, Peter. 2014. Austria-Hungary. In *Empires at War, 1911–1923*, ed. Robert Gerwarth and Erez Manela. Oxford: Oxford University Press, pp. 73–90.

Hauser, William. 1980. The Will to Fight. In *Combat Effectiveness: Cohesion, Stress, and the Voluntary Military*, ed. Sam Sarkesian. New York: SAGE Publications, pp. 186–211.

Haythornthwaite, Philip. 2007. *The Waterloo Armies: Men, Organization and Tactics*. New York: Pen and Sword.

Headrick, Daniel. 2012. *Power over Peoples: Technology, Environments, and Western Imperialism, 1400 to the Present*. Princeton, NJ: Princeton University Press.

Healy, Maureen. 2004. *Vienna and the Fall of the Habsburg Empire: Total War and Everyday Life in World War I*. Cambridge: Cambridge University Press.

Hechter, Michael. 2000. *Containing Nationalism*. Oxford: Oxford University Press.

Hechter, Michael. 2013. *Alien Rule*. Cambridge: Cambridge University Press.

Hellbeck, Jochen. 2015. *Stalingrad: The City That Defeated the Third Reich*. New York: PublicAffairs.

Helmbold, Robert. 1990. Rates of Advance in Historical Land Combat Operations. Technical report U.S. Army Concepts Analysis Agency Research Paper No. CAA-RP-90-1.

Henderson, William. 1985. *Cohesion: The Human Element in Combat*. Washington, D.C.: National Defense University Press.

Henze, Paul. 2001. *Eritrea's War: Confrontation, International Response, Outcome and Prospects*. Addis Ababa: Shama Books.

Herrmann, David. 1989. "The Paralysis of Italian Strategy in the Italian-Turkish War, 1911–1912." *English Historical Review* 104:332–56.

Herwig, Holger. 2014. *The First World War: Germany and Austria-Hungary, 1914–1918*. 2nd ed. London: Bloomsbury Academic.

Ho, Daniel, Kosuke Imai, Gary King and Elizabeth Stuart. 2007. "Matching as Nonparametric Preprocessing for Reducing Model Dependence in Parametric Causal Inference." *Political Analysis* 15:199–236.

Hobsbawm, Eric. 1991. *Nations and Nationalism Since 1780: Programme, Myth, Reality*. Cambridge: Cambridge University Press.

Holt, P. M. 1958*a*. "The Source-Materials of the Sudanese Mahdia." *St. Antony's Papers* (4). London: Chatto & Windus.

Holt, P. M. 1958*b*. "The Sudanese Mahdia and the Outside World: 1881–9." *Bulletin of the School of Oriental and African Studies* 21:276–90.

Holt, P. M. 1970. *The Mahdist State in the Sudan, 1881–1898: A Study of Its Origins, Development, and Overthrow*. Second edition. Oxford: Clarendon Press.

Holt, P. M. and M. W. Daly. 2011. *A History of the Sudan from the Coming of Islam to the Present Day*. Sixth ed. London: Longman.

Hoover Green, Amelia. 2018. *The Commander's Dilemma: Violence and Restraint in Wartime*. Ithaca, NY: Cornell University Press.

Hopkins, B. D. 2008. "Race, Sex and Slavery: 'Forced Labour' in Central Asia and Afghanistan in the Early 19th Century." *Modern Asian Studies* 42:629–71.

Horowitz, Donald. 1985. *Ethnic Groups in Conflict*. Berkeley: University of California Press.

Horowitz, Michael, Erin Simpson and Allan Stam. 2011. "Domestic Institutions and Wartime Casualties." *International Studies Quarterly* 4:909–36.

House, Jonathan. 2001. *Combined Arms Warfare in the Twentieth Century*. Lawrence: University of Kansas Press.

House of Commons Debate. 1899. "Treatment of Wounded at Omdurman." *House of Commons Hansard* 66:1279–81.

Hovanissian, R. G. 1971. *The Republic of Armenia*. Vol. 1. Berkeley: University of California Press.

Huening, Lars-Christopher. 2013. "Making use of the past: the Rwandophone question and the 'Balkanisation of the Congo.'" *Review of African Political Economy* 40:13–31.

Hull, Isabel. 2005. *Absolute Destruction: Military Culture and the Practices of War in Imperial Germany*. Ithaca, NY: Cornell University Press.

Human Security Report Project. 2010. *Human Security Report 2009/2010: The Causes of Peace and the Shrinking Costs of War*. Vancouver: Simon Fraser University.

Humphreys, Macartan and Alan Jacobs. 2015. "Mixed Methods: A Bayesian Approach." *American Political Science Review* 109:653–73.

Huntington, Samuel. 1957. *The Soldier and the State*. Cambridge, MA: Harvard University Press.

Hutchinson, John. 2005. *Nations as Zones of Conflict*. London: SAGE Publications.

Hyde, Susan. 2015. "Experiments in International Relations: Lab, Survey, and Field." *Annual Review of Political Science* 18:403–24.

Iacus, Stefano, Gary King and Giuseppe Porro. 2012. "Causal Inference without Balance Checking: Coarsened Exact Matching." *Political Analysis* 20:1–24.

Iazov, D. T. 2011. *Panfilovtsy v boiakh za Rodinu*. Moskva: Krasnaia zvezda.

Institut rossiiskoi istorii Rossiiskoi Akademii Nauk. 2015. *Vklad uchenykh-istorikov v sokhranenie istoricheskoi pamiati o voine: Na materialakh Komissii po istorii Velikoi Otechestvennoi Voine AN SSSR, 1941–1945 gg*. Moskva: Tsentr gumanitarnykh initsiativ.

International Crisis Group. 2000. *Scramble for the Congo: Anatomy of an Ugly War*. Washington, D.C.: International Crisis Group.

Irace, Tullio. 1912. *With the Italians in Tripoli: The Authentic History of the Turco-Italian War*. London: John Murray.

Isgenderli, Anar. 2011. *Realities of Azerbaijan, 1917–1920*. Translated by Yusif Axundov ed. Moskva: Xlibris.

Jackson, H. C. 1926. *Osman Digna*. London: Methuen.

Jackson, Stephen. 2007. "Of 'Doubtful Nationality': Political Manipulation of Citizenship in the D. R. Congo." *Citizenship Studies* 11:481–500.

Jacquin-Berdal, Dominique and Martin Plaut, eds. 2004. *Unfinished Business: Ethiopia And Eritrea At War*. Trenton, NJ: Red Sea Press.

Jaggers, Keith and Ted Robert Gurr. 2004. *Polity IV: Regime Change and Political Authority, 1800–2004*. Ann Arbor, MI: Inter-University Consortium for Political and Social Research.

Jakiela, Pamela and Owen Ozier. 2019. "The Impact of Violence on Individual Risk Preferences: Evidence from a Natural Experiment." *Review of Economics and Statistics* 101:547–559.

Jalal, Ayesha. 1990. *The State of Martial Rule: The Origins of Pakistan's Politicl Economy of Defense*. Cambridge: Cambridge University Press.

Jalal, Ayesha. 1995. "Conjuring Pakistan: History as Official Imagining." *International Journal of Middle East Studies* 27:73–89.

Jensen, Geoffrey. 2007. The Spanish Army at War in the Nineteenth Century: Counterinsurgency at Home and Abroad. In *A Military History of Modern Spain*, ed. Wayne Bowen and Josè Alvarez. Westport, CT: Praeger Security International, pp. 15–36.

Jeřábek, Rudolf. 2002. The Eastern Front. In *The Last Years of Austria-Hungary: A Multi-National Experiment in Early Twentieth-Century Europe*, ed. Mark Cornwall. Exeter: University of Exeter Press, pp. 149–66.

Jervis, Robert. 1978. "Cooperation Under the Security Dilemma." *World Politics* 30:167–214.

Johnston, Iain. 1995. *Cultural Realism: Strategic Culture and Grand Strategy in Chinese History*. Princeton, NJ: Princeton University Press.

Joly, Alexandre. 1910. *Historia crítica de la campaña de 1859–1860*. Madrid: Imprenta y litografía de Bernardo Rodríguez.

Jones, Benjamin and Benjamin Olken. 2009. "Hit or Miss? The Effect of Assassinations on Institutions and War." *American Economic Journal: Macroeconomics* 1:55–87.

Judson, Pieter. 2016. *The Habsburg Empire: A New History*. Cambridge, MA: Belknap Press.

K.u.k. Hof-Kartographische Anstalt G. Freytag & Berndt. 1911. *Geographischer Atlas zur Vaterlandskunde an der österreichischen Mittelschulen*. Wien: K. u. k. Hof-Kartographische Anstalt G. Freytag & Berndt.

Kaldor, Mary. 1999. *New and Old Wars: Organised Violence in a Global Era*. Palo Alto, CA: Stanford University Press.

Kalyvas, Stathis. 2006. *The Logic of Violence in Civil War*. Cambridge: Cambridge University Press.

Kann, Robert A. 1950. *The Multinational Empire: Nationalism and National Reform in the Habsburg Monarchy, 1848–1918*. New York: Columbia University Press.

Kann, Robert A. 1974. *A History of the Habsburg Empire, 1526–1918*. Berkeley: University of California Press.

Karpat, Kemal. 1985. *Ottoman Population, 1830–1914: Demographic and Social Characteristics.* Madison: University of Wisconsin Press.

Karpat, Kemal. 1991. "Yakub Bey's Relations with the Ottoman Sultans: A Reinterpretation." *Cahiers du Monde russe et soviétique* 32:17–32.

Karpat, Kemal. 2002. *Studies on Ottoman Social and Political History.* New York: Brill.

Kay, Alex, Jeff Rutherford and David Stahel, eds. 2012. *Nazi Policy on the Eastern Front, 1941.* Rochester, NY: University of Rochester Press.

Keegan, John. 1976. *The Face of Battle.* New York: Viking.

Keegan, John. 1993. *A History of Warfare.* New York: Vintage.

Keegan, John. 1997. Towards a Theory of Combat Motivation. In *Time to Kill: The Soldier's Experience of War in the West, 1939–1945,* ed. Paul Addison and Angus Calder. London: Pimlico, pp. 3–11.

Kelly, Morgan. 2000. "Inequality and Crime." *Review of Economics and Statistics* 82:530–39.

Kennedy, Paul. 1984. "The First World War and the International Power System." *International Security* 9:7–40.

Kennedy, Paul. 1989. *The Rise and Fall of the Great Powers.* New York: Vintage.

Keown-Boyd, Henry. 1986. *A Good Dusting: A Centenary Review of the Sudan Campaigns 1883– 1889.* London: Leo Cooper.

Kerchnawe, Hugo. 1921. *Der Zusammenbruch der Österreichisch-Umgarischen Wehrmacht im Herbst 1918.* München: Lehmanns.

Khalfin, N. A. 1960. *Politika Rossii v Srednei Azii (1857–1868).* Moskva: Isd-vo vostochnoi literatury.

Khalfin, N. A. 1965. *Prisoedinenie Srednei Azii k Rossii (60-90-e gody XIX v.).* Moskva: Nauka.

Khalfin, N. A. 1974. *Rossiia i khantsva Srednei Azii (pervaia polovina XIX veka).* Moskva: Nauka.

Khlevniuk, Oleg. 2015. *Stalin: New Biography of a Dictator.* Translated by Nora Seligman Favorov. New Haven, CT: Yale University Press.

Kier, Elizabeth. 1999. "Homosexuals in the U.S. Military: Open Integration and Combat Effectiveness." *International Security* 23:5–39.

Kim, Hodong. 2004. *Holy War in China: The Muslim Rebellion and State in Chinese Central Asia, 1864–1877.* Palo Alto, CA: Stanford University Press.

King, Gary, Michael Tomz and Jason Wittenberg. 2000. "Making the Most of Statistical Analysis: Improving Interpretation and Presentation." *American Journal of Political Science* 44:341–55.

Kisangani, Emizet. 2003. "Conflict in the Democratic Republic of Congo: A Mosaic of Insurgent Group." *International Journal on World Peace* 20:51–80.

Kissi, Edward. 2006. *Revolution and Genocide in Ethiopia and Cambodia.* Lanham, MD: Lexington Books.

Kitchener, Herbert. 1898a. "Despatch from Major-General Sir Herbert H. Kitchener." *London Gazette* 30 September:5725–33.

Kitchener, Herbert. 1898b. "Despatch from Major-General Sir Herbert H. Kitchener." *London Gazette* 24 May:3231–35.

Knight, E. F. 1897. *Letters from the Sudan.* London: Macmillan and Co.

Knights, Michael. 2014. "ISIL's Political-Military Power in Iraq." *CTC Sentinel* 7:1–7.

Knyshevskii, P. N. 1992. *Skrytaia pravda voiny: 1941 god.* Moskva: Russkaia kniga.

Konev, I. S. 2014. *Zapiski komanduiushchego frontom.* Moskva: Izdatel'stvo Tsentrpoligraf.

König, Michael, Dominic Roehner, Mathias Thoenig and Fabrizio Zilibotti. 2007. "Networks in Conflict: Theory and Evidence from the Great War of Africa." *Econometrica* 85:1093–1132.

Kostenko, L. F. 1880. *Turkestanskii krai. Opyt voenno-statisticheskago obozreniia Turkestanskago voennago okruga.* Vol. 1–3. Sankt Peterburg: Tipografiia i khromolitografiia A. Transhchelia.

Kotkin, Stephen. 2017. *Stalin: Waiting for Hitler, 1929–1941.* New York: Penguin Books.

Kramer, Robert. 2010. *Holy City on the Nile: Omdurman During the Mahdiyya, 1885–1898.* Princeton, NJ: Markus Wiener Publishers.

Krebs, Ronald. 2004. "A School for the Nation? How Military Service Does Not Build Nations, and How It Might." *International Security* 28:85–124.

Krivosheev, G. F. 2009. *Velikaia Otechestvennaia bez grifa sekretnosti. Kniga poter'.* Moskva: Veche.

Kuneralp, S., ed. 2011. *Ottoman Diplomatic Documents on the Origins of World War One: The Turco-Italian War 1911–1912.* Vol. V. Istanbul: Isis Press.

Kuran, Timur. 1997. *Private Truths, Public Lies: The Social Consequences of Preference Falsification.* Cambridge, MA: Harvard University Press.

Kuznets, Simon. 1955. "Economic Growth and Income Inequality." *American Economic Review* 45:1–28.

Laitin, David. 1998. *Identity in Formation: The Russian-Speaking Population in the Near Abroad.* Ithaca, NY: Cornell University Press.

Lake, David. 1992. "Powerful Pacifists: Democratic States and War." *American Political Science Review* 86:24–37.

Lake, David. 2016. *The Statebuilder's Dilemma: On the Limits of Foreign Intervention.* Ithaca, NY: Cornell University Press.

Lake, Milli. 2017. "Building the Rule of War: Postconflict Institutions and the Micro-Dynamics of Conflict in Eastern DR Congo." *International Organization* 71:281–315.

Larson, Jennifer and Janet Lewis. 2017. "Ethnic Networks." *American Journal of Political Science* 61:350–64.

Last, Alexander. 2004. A Very Personal War, Eritrea-Ethiopia 1998–2000. In *Unfinished Business: Ethiopia and Eritrea at War,* ed. Dominique Jacquin-Berdal and Martin Plaut. Trenton, NJ: Red Sea Press, pp. 57–86.

Lato, Leenco. 2003. "The Ethiopian-Eritrea War." *Review of African Political Economy* 30:369–88.

Laudati, Ann. 2013. "Beyond minerals: broadening 'economies of violence' in eastern Democratic Republic of Congo." *Review of African Political Economy* 40:32–50.

Layish, Ahron. 1997. "The Legal Methodology of the Mahdi in the Sudan, 1881–1885." *Sudanic Africa: A Journal of Historical Sources* 8:39–41.

Lécuyer, M. C. and C. Serrano. 1976. *La Guerre D'Afrique et ses Répercussions en Espagne: Idéologies et colonialisme en Espagne, 1859–1904.* Paris: Presses Universitaires de France.

Ledonne, John. 1997. *The Russian Empire and the World, 1700–1917: The Geopolitics of Expansion and Containment.* Oxford: Oxford University Press.

Lehmann, Todd and Yuri Zhukov. 2019. "Until the Bitter End? The Diffusion of Surrender Across Battles." *International Organization* 73:133–69.

Lein, Richard. 2014a. Between Acceptance and Refusal: Soldiers' Attitudes Towards War (Austria-Hungary). In *1914–1918 online. International Encyclopedia of the First World War,* ed. Ute Daniel, Peter Gatrell, Oliver Janz, Heather Jones, Jennifer Keene, Alan Kramer and Bill Nasson. Berlin: Freie Universität Berlin.

Lein, Richard. 2014b. "The Military Conduct of the Austro-Hungarian Czechs of the First World War." *Historian* 76:518–49.

Leonhard, Jörn. 2018. *Pandora's Box: A History of the First World War*. Translated by Patrick Camiller ed. Cambridge, MA: Belknap Press.

Levi, Margaret. 1997. *Consent, Dissent, and Patriotism*. Cambridge: Cambridge University Press.

Levi, Scott. 2007. "The Ferghana Valley at the Crossroads of World History: The Rise of Khoqand, 1709–1822." *Journal of Global History* 2:213–32.

Levine, Donald. 2010. *Greater Ethiopia: The Evolution of a Multiethnic Society*. Chicago: University of Chicago Press.

Levy, Jack. 2015. "Counterfactuals, Causal Inference, and Historical Analysis." *Security Studies* 24:378–402.

Levy, Jack and William Thompson. 2011. *The Arc of War: Origins, Escalation, and Transformation*. Chicago: University of Chicago Press.

Lieberman, Evan. 2005. "Nested Analysis as a Mixed-Method Strategy for Comparative Research." *American Political Science Review* 99:435–52.

Liedtke, Gregory. 2016. *Enduring the Whirlwind: The German Army and the Russo-German War, 1941–1943*. West Midlands: Helion and Company.

Lieven, Dominic. 2015. *The End of Tsarist Russia: The March to World War I and Revolution*. New York: Viking.

Lister, Charles. 2015. *The Syrian Jihad: Al-Qaeda, the Islamic State and the Evolution of an Insurgency*. Oxford: Oxford University Press.

Lopukhovsky, Lev. 2013. *The Viaz'ma Catastrophe: The Red Army's Disastrous Stand Against Operation Typhoon*. Translated and edited by Stuart Britton ed. West Midlands: Helion and Company.

Lopukhovsky, Lev and Boris Kavalerchik. 2017. *The Price of Victory: The Red Army's Casualties in the Great Patriotic War*. South Yorkshire, UK: Pen and Sword.

Luttwak, Edward. 1968. *Coup D'Etat: A Practical Handbook*. London: Penguin.

Lyall, Jason. 2010. "Are Co-Ethnics More Effective Counterinsurgents? Evidence from the Second Chechen War." *American Political Science Review* 104:1–20.

Lyall, Jason. 2015. "Process Tracing, Causal Inference, and Civil War." In *Process Tracing in the Social Sciences: From Metaphor to Analytic Tool*, eds. Andrew Bennett and Jeffrey Checkel. Cambridge: Cambridge University Press, pp. 186–207.

Lyall, Jason. 2017. Forced to Fight: Coercion, Blocking Detachments, and Trade-offs in Military Effectiveness. In *The Sword's Other Edge: Trade-offs in the Pursuit of Military Effectiveness*, ed. Dan Reiter. Cambridge: Cambridge University Press, pp. 88–125.

Lyall, Jason, Graeme Blair and Kosuke Imai. 2013. "Explaining Support for Combatants in Wartime: A Survey Experiment in Afghanistan." *American Political Science Review* 107: 679–705.

Lynn, John. 1984. *The Bayonets of the Republic: Motivation and Tactics in the Army of Revolutionary France*. Urbana and Chicago: University of Illinois Press.

Lynn, John. 2003. *Battle: A History of Combat and Culture*. Boulder, CO: Westview Press.

MacCoun, Robert. 1993. *What Is Known about Unit Cohesion and Military Performance*. Santa Monica, CA: RAND, pp. 283–331.

MacCoun, Robert, Elizabeth Kier and Aaron Belkin. 2006. "Does Social Cohesion Determine Motivation in Combat? An Old Question with an Old Answer." *Armed Forces & Society* 32:646–54.

MacDonald, Paul. 2014. *Networks of Domination: The Social Foundations of Peripheral Conquest in International Politics*. Oxford: Oxford University Press.

Machiavelli, Niccolo. 1999. *The Prince*. New York: Penguin Books.

Mack, Andrew. 1975. "Why Big Nations Lose Small Wars: The Politics of Asymmetric Conflict." *World Politics* 27:175–200.

MacKenzie, David. 1969. "Expansion in Central Asia: St. Petersburg vs. the Turkestan Generals (1863–1866)." *Canadian Slavic Studies* 3:286–311.

MacKenzie, David. 1974. *The Lion of Tashkent: The Career of General M. G. Cherniaev*. Athens: University of Georgia Press.

Mahoney, James. 2010. "After KKV: The New Methodology of Qualitative Research." *World Politics* 62:120–47.

Malešević, Siniša. 2010. *The Sociology of War and Violence*. Cambridge: Cambridge University Press.

Malkasian, Carter. 2017. *Illusions of Victory: The Anbar Awakening and the Rise of the Islamic State*. Oxford: Oxford University Press.

Malte-Brun, Conrad. 1835. *Précis de la géographie universelle*. Brussels: Th. Lejeune.

Mampilly, Zachariah. 2011. *Rebel Rulers: Insurgent Governance and Civilian Life During War*. Ithaca, NY: Cornell University Press.

Manekin, Devorah. 2017. "The Limits of Socialization and the Underproduction of Military Violence: Evidence from the IDF." *Journal of Peace Research* 54:606–19.

Mann, Michael. 1993. *The Sources of Social Power*. Vol. II. Cambridge: Cambridge University Press.

Mann, Michael. 2018. "Have wars and violence declined?" *Theory and Society* 47:37–60.

Manz, Beatrice. 1987. "Central Asian Uprisings in the Nineteenth Century: Ferghana under the Russians." *Russian Review* 46:267–81.

Maringira, Godfrey. 2017. "Military corruption in war: stealing and connivance among Zimbabwean foot soldiers in the Democratic Republic of Congo (1998–2002)." *Review of African Political Economy* 44:611–23.

Marshall, Alex. 2006. *The Russian General Staff and Asia, 1800–1917*. New York: Routledge.

Marshall, S.L.A. 1947. *Men Against Fire: The Problem of Battle Command in Future War*. New York: William Morrow.

Martin-Màrquez, Susan. 2008. *Disorientations: Spanish Colonialism in Africa and the Performance of Identity*. New Haven, CT: Yale University Press.

Martin, Terry. 2001. *The Affirmative Action Empire: Nations and Nationalism in the Soviet Union, 1923–1939*. Ithaca, NY: Cornell University Press.

Marx, Anthony. 2003. *Faith in Nation: Exclusionary Origins of Nationalism*. Oxford: Oxford University Press.

Mawdsley, Evan. 2005. *The Russian Civil War*. New York: Pegasus Books.

May, Timothy. 2007. *The Mongol Art of War: Chinggis Khan and the Mongol Military System.* South Yorkshire, UK: Pen and Sword.

Mazower, Mark. 2009. *Hitler's Empire: How the Nazis Ruled Europe.* New York: Penguin Books.

Mccants, William. 2016. *The ISIS Apocalypse: The History, Strategy, and Doomsday Vision of the Islamic State.* New York: Picador.

McCaskie, T. C. 1995. *State and Society in Pre-Colonial Asante.* Cambridge: Cambridge University Press.

McClure, W. K. 1913. *Italy in North Africa: An Account of the Tripoli Enterprise.* London: Darf Publishers.

McCormick, Richard. 1859. *The war of 1859: being a succinct and accurate account of the contest between the Franco-Sardinian and Austrian armies, from the crossing of the Ticino to the treaty of Villafranca.* New York: Schonberg.

McCullagh, Francis. 1913. *Italy's War for a Desert: Being Some Experiences of a War-Correspondent with the Italians in Tripoli.* Chicago: F. G. Browne and Co.

McGurk, Brett. 2014. "Iraq at a Crossroads: Options for U.S. Policy." *Senate Foreign Relations Committee.*

McLauchlin, Theodore. 2014. "Desertion, Terrain, and Control of the Home Front in Civil Wars." *Journal of Conflict Resolution* 58:1419–1444.

McLauchlin, Theodore. 2015. "Desertion and Collective Action in Civil Wars." *International Studies Quarterly* 59:669–79.

McMeekin, Sean. 2013. *The Russian Origins of the First World War.* Cambridge: Belknap Press.

McMeekin, Sean. 2015. *The Ottoman Endgame: War, Revolution, and the Making of the Modern Middle East, 1908–1923.* New York: Penguin.

McNamara, Kevin. 2016. *Dreams of a Small Great Nation: The Mutinous Army that Threatened a Revolution, Destroyed an Empire, Founded a Republic, and Remade the Map of Europe.* New York: PublicAffairs.

McNeill, William. 1982. *The Pursuit of Power: Technology, Armed Force, and Society since A.D. 1000.* Chicago: University of Chicago Press.

McNerney, Michael, Ben Connable, S. Rebecca Zimmerman, Natasha Landar, Marek Posard, Jasen Castillo, Dan Madden, Ilana Blum, Aaron Frank, Benjamin Fernandes, In Hyo Seol, Christopher Paul and Andrew Parasiliti. 2018. *National Will to Fight: Why Some States Keep Fighting and Others Don't.* Santa Monica, CA: RAND.

McPherson, James. 1994. *What They Fought For, 1861–1865.* Baton Rouge: Louisana State University Press.

McPherson, James. 1997. *For Cause and Comrades: Why Men Fought in the Civil War.* New York: Oxford University Press.

McPherson, James. 2014. *Embattled Rebel: Jefferson Davis and the Confederate Civil War.* New York: Penguin.

Mearsheimer, John. 1989. "Assessing the Conventional Balance: The 3:1 Rule and Its Critics." *International Security* 13:54–89.

Melander, Erik, Therése Pettersson and Lotta Themnér. 2016. "Organized Violence, 1989–2015." *Journal of Peace Research* 53:727–42.

Meredith, John, ed. 1998. *Omdurman Diaries, 1898: Eyewitness Accounts of the Legendary Campaign.* South Yorks, UK: Leo Cooper.

Merridale, Catherine. 2005. *Ivan's War: Life and Death in the Red Army, 1939–1945*. London: Picador.

Merridale, Catherine. 2006. "Culture, Ideology, and Combat in the Red Army, 1939–45." *Journal of Contemporary History* 41:305–24.

Miguel, Edward and Mary Kay Gugerty. 2005. "Ethnic Diversity, Social Sanctions, and Public Goods in Kenya." *Journal of Public Economics* 89:2325–68.

Milanovic, Branko. 2005. *Worlds Apart: Measuring International and Global Inequality*. Princeton, NJ: Princeton University Press.

Milanovic, Branko. 2016. *Global Inequality: A New Approach for the Age of Globalization*. Cambridge, MA: Belknap Press.

Milanovic, Branko, Peter Lindert and Jeffrey Williamson. 2011. "Pre-industrial inequality." *Economic Journal* 121:255–72.

Miliutin, Dmitri Alexeevich. 2003. *Vospominaniia 1863–64*. Moskva: ROSSPEN.

Miller, Charles. 2013. Destructivity: A Political Economy of Military Effectiveness in Conventional Combat. PhD thesis. Duke University.

Millett, Allan and Williamson Murray. 1988. *Military Effectiveness*. Three Volumes. Boston: Allen and Unwin.

Ministero della Guerra. 1922. *Campagna di Libia: Parte generale—operazioni in Tripolitania dall'inizio della campagna alla occupazione di Punta Tagiura (Ottobre–Dicembre 1911)*. Vol. I. Roma: Stabilimento Poligrafico Per L'Amministrazione Della Guerra.

Ministero della Guerra. 1928. *Campagna di Libia: Operazioni in Tripolitania dal Dicembre 1911 (dopo l'occupazione di Punta Tagiura) alla fine dell'agosto 1912*. Vol. II. Roma: Stabilimento Poligrafico per l'Amministrazione della Guerra.

Mordacq, Jean Jule Henri. 1900. *La guerre au Maroc; enseignements tactiques des deux guerres franco-marocaine, 1844, et hispano-marocaine, 1859–1860*. Paris: H. Charles-Lavauzelle.

Morris, Ian. 2014. *War! What Is It Good For? Conflict and the Progress of Civilization from Primates to Robots*. New York: Farrar, Straus, and Giroux.

Morrison, Alexander. 2014a. "Introduction: Killing the Cotton Canard and getting rid of the Great Game: rewriting the Russian conquest of Central Asia, 1814–1895." *Central Asian Survey* 33:131–42.

Morrison, Alexander. 2014b. "'Nechto eroticheskoe,' 'courir aprés l'ombre'? Logistical imperatives and the fall of Tashkent, 1859–1865." *Central Asian Survey* 33:153–69.

Moskos, Charles. 1975. "The American Combat Soldier in Vietnam." *Journal of Social Issues* 31:25–37.

Mounteney-Jephson, A. J. 1890. *Emin Pasha and the Rebellion at the Equator: A Story of Nine Months' Experiences in the Last of the Soudan Provinces*. London: Sampson Low, Marston, Searle, and Rivington.

Mueller, John. 1989. *Retreat from Doomsday: The Obsolescence of Major War*. New York: Basic Books.

Müller, Rolf-Dieter. 2012. *The Unknown Eastern Front: The Wehrmacht and Hitler's Foreign Soldiers*. London: I. B. Tauris.

Murphy, Sean, Wan Kidane and Thomas Snider. 2013. *Litigating War: Mass Civil Injury and the Eritrea-Ethiopia Claims Commission*. New York: Oxford University Press.

Murray, Williamson and Kevin Woods. 2014. *The Iran-Iraq War: A Military and Strategic History*. Cambridge: Cambridge University Press.

Musa, Faisal. 2010. *The Institutions of the Mahdia State in the Sudan*. Khartoum: El-Nilien University Printing Press.

Mylonas, Harris. 2012. *The Politics of Nation-Building*. Cambridge: Cambridge University Press.

Naimark, Norman. 2010. *Stalin's Genocides*. Princeton, NJ: Princeton University Press.

Nalivkine, V. P. 1889. *Histoire du khanat de Khokand*. Paris: Ernest Leroux, Editeur.

Namier, Lewis. 1921. The Downfall of the Habsburg Monarchy. In *A History of the Paris Peace Conference*, ed. Harold Temperley. Volume Four. London: H. Frowde, Hodder & Stoughton, pp. 58–119.

Negash, Tekeste and Kjetil Tronvoll. 2000. *Brothers at War: Making Sense of the Eritrean-Ethiopian War*. Athens: Ohio University Press.

Neillands, Robin. 1996. *The Dervish Wars: Gordon and Kitchener in the Sudan, 1880–1898*. London: J. Murray.

Neufeld, Charles. 1899. *A Prisoner of the Khaleefa: Twelve Years in Captivity at Omdurman*. London: Chapman and Hall.

Newby, L. J. 2005. *The Empire and the Khanate: A Political History of Qing Relations with Khoqand c. 1760–1860*. Leiden: Brill.

Neyman, Jerzy. 1923. "On the Application of Probability Theory to Agricultural Experiments: Essays on Principles. Section 9." *Statistical Science* 5:465–72.

Ngolet, François. 2011. *Crisis in the Congo: The Rise and Fall of Laurent Kabila*. New York: Palgrave Macmillan.

Nicoll, Fergus. 2004. *The Sword of the Prophet: The Mahdi of the Sudan and the Death of General Gordon*. London: Sutton Publishing.

Nielsen, Richard. 2014. "Case Selection via Matching." *Sociological Methods and Research* 45:569–597.

Nolan, Cathal. 2017. *The Allure of Battle: A History of How Wars Have Been Won and Lost*. Oxford: Oxford University Press.

Nozick, Robert. 1974. *Anarchy, State, and Utopia*. New York: Basic Books.

Nushi, Muhammad Nushi. 1885. *General Report on the Seige [sic] and Fall of Khartoum*. Delhi: C.R.O.

Olcott, Martha Brill. 1981. "The Basmachi or Freemen's Revolt in Turkestan, 1918–1924." *Soviet Studies* 33:352–69.

Oloruntimehin, Benjamin. 1968. "Résistance Movements in the Tukulor Empire." *Cahiers d'études africaines* 8:123–43.

Oloruntimehin, Benjamin. 1972. *The Segu Tukulor Empire*. New York: Humanities Press.

O'Neil, Cathy. 2016. *Weapons of Math Destruction: How Big Data Increases Inequality and Threatens Democracy*. New York: Broadway Books.

Orlov, Andrei. 2012. *Shtrafbat: Prikazano unichtozhit'*. Moskva: Astrel'.

Österreichischen Bundesministerium für Heereswesen und Kriegsarchiv. 1930. *Österreich-Ungarns letzter Krieg 1914–1918*. Band 1: Vom Kriegsausbruch bis zum Ausgang der Schlacht bei Limanowa-Lapanów; 1. Das Kriegsjahr 1914 Wien: Verlag der Militärwissenschaftlichen Mitteilungen.

Ostler, Alan. 1912. *The Arabs in Tripoli*. London: John Murray.

Page, Scott. 2017. *The Diversity Bonus: How Great Teams Pay Off in the Knowledge Economy.* Princeton, NJ: Princeton University Press.

Paine, S. C. M. 2005. *The Sino-Japanese War of 1894–1895: Perceptions, Power, and Primacy.* Cambridge: Cambridge University Press.

Palat, M. K. 1988. "Tsarist Russian Imperialism." *Studies in History* 4:157–297.

Paluck, Elizabeth, Seth Green and Donald Green. 2018. "The Contact Hypothesis Re-Evaluated." *Behavioral Public Policy* 2:1–30.

Palut, M. 2005. The Conflict and Its Aftermath. In *Unfinished Business: Ethiopia and Eritrea at War,* ed. Dominique Jacquin-Berdal and Martin Plaut. Trenton, NJ: Red Sea Press, pp. 87–123.

Pantusov, N., ed. 1885. *Taarikh Shakhrokhi. Istoriia vladetelei Fergany.* Kazan': Tip. Imp. Univ.

Parker, Christopher. 2009. *Fighting for Democracy: Black Veterans and the Struggle Against White Supremacy in the Postwar South.* Princeton, NJ: Princeton University Press.

Parker, Geoffrey. 1996. *The Military Revolution: Military Innovation and the Rise of the West, 1500–1800.* Second ed. Cambridge: Cambridge University Press.

Pasher, Yaron. 2014. *Holocaust Versus Wehrmacht: How Hitler's "Final Solution" Undermined the German War Effort.* Lawrence: University of Kansas Press.

Patrushev, N. P., ed. 2000a. *Organy gosudarstvennoi bezopasnosti SSSR v Velikoi Otechestvennoi Voine. Sbornik dokumentov.* Tom vtoroi. Kniga 1. Nachalo. 22 iiunia–31 avgusta 1941 goda Izdatel'stvo "Rus'".

Patrushev, N. P., ed. 2000b. *Organy gosudarstvennoi bezopasnosti SSSR v Velikoi Otechestvennoi Voine. Sbornik dokumentov.* Tom vtoroi. Kniga 2. Nachalo. 1 sentiabria–31 dekabria 1941 goda Moskva: Izdatel'stvo "Rus'".

Paul, A. 1954. *A History of the Beja Tribes of the Sudan.* Cambridge: Cambridge University Press.

Pavlov, N. 1910. *Istoriia Turkestana: V sviazi s kratkim istoricheskim ocherkom sopredel'nykh stran.* Tashkent': Tipografiia pri kantseliarii Turkestanskago General-Gubernatora.

Pedroncini, Guy. 1983. *Les Mutineries de 1917.* Second edition. Paris: Presse Universitaires de France.

Peers, Chris. 2015. *Genghis Khan and the Mongol War Machine.* South Yorkshire, UK: Pen and Sword.

Peled, Alon. 1998. *A Question of Loyalty: Military Manpower in Multiethnic States.* Ithaca, NY: Cornell University Press.

Pennell, C. R. 2000. *Morocco since 1830.* New York: New York University Press.

Perlmutter, Amos. 1969. "The Praetorian State and the Praetorian Army: Toward a Taxonomy of Civil-Military Relations in Developing Polities." *Comparative Politics* 1:382–404.

Pettigrew, T. F. and L. R. Tropp. 2006. "A Meta-Analytic Test of Intergroup Contact Theory." *Journal of Personality and Social Psychology* 90:751–83.

Piketty, Thomas. 2013. *Capital in the Twenty-First Century.* Cambridge, MA: Belknap Press.

Pilster, Ulrich and Tobias Böhmelt. 2011. "Coup-Proofing and Military Effectiveness in Interstate Wars, 1967–99." *Conflict Management and Peace Science* 28:331–50.

Pilster, Ulrich and Tobias Böhmelt. 2012. "Do Democracies Engage in Less Coup-Proofing? On the Relationship Between Regime Type and Civil-Military Relations." *Foreign Policy Analysis* 8:1–17.

Pinker, Steven. 2011. *The Better Angels of Our Nature: Why Violence Has Declined*. New York: Viking.

Plaschka, Richard G., H. Haselsteiner and A. Suppan. 1974. *Innere Front: Militärassistenz, Widerstand und Umsturz in der Donaumonarchie 1918. Erster Band. Zwischen Streik und Meuterei*. München: R. Oldenbourg Verlag.

Platt, Stephen. 2012. *Autumn in the Heavenly Kingdom*. New York: Knopf.

Plaut, Martin and Patrick Silkes. 1999. *War in the Horn: The Conflict Between Eritrea and Ethiopia*. Discussion Paper No.82. London: Royal Institute of International Affairs.

Pogonii, Ia. F., ed. 2000. *Stalingradskaia epopeia: Materialy NKVD SSSR i voennoi tsenzury iz Tsentral'nogo arkhiva FSB RF*. Moskva: Zvonnitsa-MG.

Pollack, Kenneth. 2002. *Arabs at War: Military Effectiveness, 1948–1991*. Lincoln: University of Nebraska Press.

Porter, Patrick. 2009. *Military Orientalism: Eastern War Through Western Eyes*. New York: Columbia University Press.

Posen, Barry. 1993. "Nationalism, the Mass Army, and Military Power." *International Security* 18:80–124.

Posner, Daniel. 2004. "The Political Salience of Cultural Difference." *American Political Science Review* 98:529–46.

Posner, Daniel. 2005. *Institutions and Ethnic Politics in Africa*. Cambridge: Cambridge University Press.

President's Committee on Equality of Treatment and Opportunity in the Armed Services (22 May 1950). 1950. *Freedom to Serve: Equality of Treatment and Opportunity in the Armed Services*. Washington, D.C.: United States Government Printing Office.

Prunier, Gerard. 2009. *Africa's World War: Congo, the Rwandan Genocide, and the Making of a Continental Catastrophe*. Oxford: Oxford University Press.

Pugh, R.J.M. 2011. *Wingate Pasha: The Life of General Sir Francis Reginald Wingate, 1861–1953*. London: Pen and Sword.

Pyltsyn, Aleksandr. 2007. *Pravda o shtrafbatakh: Kak ofitserskii shtrafbat doshel do Berlina*. Moskva: Eksmo.

Quester, George. 1977. *Offense and Defense in the International System*. New York: John Wiley and Sons.

Quinlivan, J. T. 1999. "Coup-Proofing: Its Practice and Consequence in the Middle East." *International Security* 24:131–65.

Rachamimov, Alon. 2002. *POWs and the Great War: Captivity on the Eastern Front*. New York: Bloomsbury Academic.

Rachamimov, Alon. 2005. Arbiters of Allegiance: Austro-Hungarian Censors During World War I. In *Constructing Nationalities in East Central Europe*, ed. Pieter Judson and Marsha Rozenblit. New York: Berghahn Books, pp. 157–77.

Rahe, Paul. 2015. *The Grand Strategy of Sparta: The Persian Challenge*. New Haven, CT: Yale University Press.

Rahman, Tariq. 1996. *Language and Politics in Pakistan*. Oxford: Oxford University Press.

Raleigh, Clionadh, Andrew Linke Håvard Hegre and Joakim Karlsen. 2010. "Introducing ACLED-Armed Conflict Location and Event Data." *Journal of Peace Research* 47:651–60.

Rauchensteiner, Manfried. 2014. *The First World War and the End of the Habsburg Monarchy*. Vienna: Bohlau Verlag.

Raugh, Harold, Jr. 2008. *British Military Operations in Egypt and the Sudan*. Toronto: Scarecrow Press.

Razoux, Pierre. 2015. *The Iran-Iraq War*. Translated by Nicholas Elliott ed. Cambridge, MA: Belknap Press.

Reese, Roger. 2011. *Why Stalin's Soldiers Fought: The Red Army's Military Effectiveness in World War II*. Lawrence: University Press of Kansas.

Reiter, Dan. 2007. Nationalism and Military Effectiveness: Post-Meiji Japan. In *Creating Military Power: The Sources of Military Effectiveness*, ed. Risa Brooks and Elizabeth Stanley. Palo Alto, CA: Stanford University Press, pp. 27–54.

Reiter, Dan. 2017. Confronting Trade-offs in the Pursuit of Military Effectiveness. In *The Sword's Other Edge: Trade-offs in the Pursuit of Military Effectiveness*, ed. Dan Reiter. Cambridge: Cambridge University Press, pp. 1–30.

Reiter, Dan and Allan Stam. 1998a. "Democracy and Battlefield Effectiveness." *Journal of Conflict Resolution* 42:259–77.

Reiter, Dan and Allan Stam. 1998b. "Democracy, War Initiation, and Victory." *American Political Science Review* 92:377–89.

Reiter, Dan and Allan Stam. 2002. *Democracies at War*. Princeton, NJ: Princeton University Press.

Reiter, Dan and Allan Stam. 2003. "Identifying the Culprit: Democracy, Dictatorship, and Dispute Initiation." *American Political Science Review* 97:333–37.

Rémond, Georges. 1913. *Aux camps turco-arabes: notes de route et de guerre en Tripolitaine et en Cyréanaique*. Paris: Hachette.

Reynolds, Michael. 2011. *Shattering Empires: The Clash and Collapse of the Ottoman and Russian Empires*. Cambridge: Cambridge University Press.

Reyntjens, Filip. 2009. *The Great African War: Congo and Regional Geopolitics, 1996–2006*. Cambridge: Cambridge University Press.

Richards, Joanne. 2014. "Forced, coerced and voluntary recruitment into rebel and militia groups in the Democratic Republic of Congo." *Journal of Modern African Studies* 52: 301–26.

Rigg, Bryan. 2002. *Hitler's Jewish Soldiers: The Untold Story of Nazi Racial Laws and Men of Jewish Descent in the German Military*. Lawrence: University Press of Kansas.

Riker, William. 1962. *The Theory of Political Coalitions*. New Haven, CT: Yale University Press.

Roberts, Andrew. 2011. *The Storm of War: A New History of the Second World War*. New York: Harper.

Roberts, Les. 2001. *Mortality in Eastern Democratic Republic of Congo: Results from Eleven Mortality Surveys*. New York: International Rescue Committee.

Roberts, R. L. 1987. *Warriors, Merchants, and Slaves*. Palo Alto, CA: Stanford University Press.

Robinson, Amanda. 2017. "Ethnic Diversity, Segregation and Ethnocentric Trust in Africa." *British Journal of Political Science*, 1–23.

Robson, Brian. 1993. *Fuzzy-Wuzzy: The Campaigns in the Eastern Sudan, 1884–85*. Tunbridge Wells: Spellmount.

Roessler, Philip. 2011. "The Enemy Within: Personal Rule, Coups, and Civil War in Africa." *World Politics* 63:300–46.

Roessler, Philip. 2016. *Ethnic Politics and State Power in Africa: The Logic of the Coup-Civil War Trap*. Cambridge: Cambridge University Press.

Roessler, Philip and Harry Verhoeven. 2016. *Why Comrades Go to War: Liberation Politics and the Outbreak of Africa's Deadliest Conflict*. Oxford: Oxford University Press.

Rokossovsky, K. 1970. *A Soldier's Duty*. Moscow: Progress Publishers.

Roland, Alex. 2016. *War and Technology*. Oxford: Oxford University Press.

Rollman, Wilfred. 2004. "Military Officers and the Nizam al-Jadid in Morocco, 1844–1912." *Oriente Moderno* 23:205–25.

Romano, Sergio. 1977. *La Quarta Sponda: La Guerra Libia, 1911–1912*. Milano: Bompiani.

Rosen, Stephen. 1972. War Power and the Willingness to Suffer. In *Peace, War, and Numbers*, ed. Bruce Russett. Beverly Hills, CA: Sage, pp. 167–84.

Rosen, Stephen. 1995. "Military Effectiveness: Why Society Matters." *International Security* 19:5–31.

Rosen, Stephen. 1996. *Societies and Military Power: India and Its Armies*. Ithaca, NY: Cornell University Press.

Rosen, Stephen. 2005. *War and Human Nature*. Princeton, NJ: Princeton University Press.

Rosenbaum, Paul. 2002. *Observational Studies*. New York: Springer.

Rosenbaum, Paul. 2010. *Design of Observational Studies*. New York: Springer.

Ross, O. C. 1860. *Spain and the War with Morocco*. London: James Ridgway.

Rothenberg, Gunther Erich. 1976. *The Army of Francis Joseph*. West Lafayette, IN: Purdue University Press.

Rotte, Ralph and Christoph Schmidt. 2003. "On the Production of Victory: Empirical Determinants of Battlefield Success in Modern War." *Defense and Peace Economics* 14:175–92.

Royle, Charles. 1886. *The Egyptian Campaigns, 1882 to 1885, and the Events Which Led to Them*. London: Hurst and Blackett, Publishers.

Rubin, Donald. 2006. *Matched Sampling for Causal Effects*. Cambridge: Cambridge University Press.

Rupiya, Martin. 2002. A Political and Military Review of Zimbabwe's Involvement in the Second Congo War. In *The African Stakes in the Congo War*, ed. John Clark. New York: Palgrave Macmillan, pp. 93–108.

Russett, Bruce, J. David Singer and Melvin Small. 1968. "National Political Units in the Twentieth Century: A Standardized List." *American Political Science Review* 3:932–51.

Rutherford, Jeff. 2014. *Combat and Genocide on the Eastern Front: The German Infantry's War, 1941–1944*. Cambridge: Cambridge University Press.

Rutherford, Jeff and Adrian Wettstein. 2018. *The German Army on the Eastern Front: An Inner View of the Ostheer's Experiences of War*. Barnsley, S. Yorkshire: Pen & Sword.

Safranov, I. F. 1958. Oborona 316-i strelkovoi divizii v. raione g. Volokolamsk (oktiabr' 1941). In *Boevye deistviia strelkovoi divizii: Sbornik takticheskikh primerov iz Velikoi Otechestvennoi voiny*, ed. K. V. Sycheva. Moskva: Voenizdat, pp. 386–412.

Sahar, Bazza. 2010. *Forgotten Saints: History, Power, and Politics in the Making of Modern Morocco*. Cambridge, MA: Harvard University Press.

Salawi, Ahmad ibn Khalid al. 1917. *Versión Árabe de la Guerra de África (Años 1859–1860)*. Madrid: Biblioteca Hispano-Marroquí. Translated by Clemente Cerdeira.

Sambanis, Nicholas, Stergios Skaperdas and William Wohlforth. 2015. "Nation-Building through War." *American Political Science Review* 109:279–96.

Samsonov, A. M. 1989. *Stalingradskaia bitva*. 4-e izd. ed. Moskva: Nauka.

Samuelson, Paul. 1954. "Pure Theory of Public Expenditure." *Review of Economics and Statistics* 36:387–89.

Sanborn, Joshua. 2003. *Drafting the Russian Nation: Military Conscription, Total War, and Mass Politics, 1905–1925*. DeKalb: Northern Illinois University Press.

Sanchez de la Sierra, Raul. 2015. "On the Origins of States: Stationary Bandits and Taxation in Eastern Congo." Unpublished manuscript.

Sanderson, G. N. 1965. *England, Europe and the Upper Nile, 1882–1899*. Edinburgh: Edinburgh University Press.

Sanin, Francisco Gutierrez and Elisabeth Wood. 2014. "Ideology in civil war: Instrumental Adoption and beyond." *Journal of Peace Research* 51:213–26.

Sarkees, Meredith and Frank Wayman. 2010. *Resort to War, 1816–2007: A Data Guide to Inter-State, Extra-State, Intra-State, and Non-State Wars, 1816–2007*. Washington, D.C.: CQ Press.

Scanlon, T. M. 2018. *Why Does Inequality Matter?* Oxford: Oxford University Press.

Schaefer, Agnes, Radha Plumb, Srikanth Kadiyala, Jennifer Kavanagh, Charles Engel, Kayla Williams and Amii Kress. 2016. *Assessing the Implications of Allowing Transgender Personnel to Serve Openly*. Washington, D.C.: RAND.

Schake, Kori. 2018. "Introduction: A Strategist at Work." *Texas National Security Review*.

Scheidel, Walter. 2017. *The Great Leveler: Violence and the History of Inequality from the Stone Age to the Twenty-First Century*. Princeton, NJ: Princeton University Press.

Schelling, Thomas. 2008. *Arms and Influence*. New Haven, CT: Yale University Press.

Scherrer, Christian. 2002. *Genocide and crisis in Central Africa: Conflict roots, mass violence, and regional war*. Annapolis, MD: Greenwood Press.

Scheve, Kenneth and David Stasavage. 2012. "Democracy, War, and Wealth: Lessons from Two Centuries of Inheritance Taxation." *American Political Science Review* 106:81–102.

Schindler, John. 2015. *Fall of the Double Eagle: The Battle for Galicia and the Demise of Austria-Hungary*. Lincoln: University of Nebraska Press.

Schlagintweit, Eduard. 1863. *Der spanisch-marokkanische Krieg in den Jahren 1859 und 1860;*. Leipzig: F. A. Brockhaus.

Schneer, Aron. 2005. *Plen: Sovetskie voennoplennye v Germanii, 1941–1945*. Moskva: Mosty kul'tury.

Schuyler, Eugene. 1877. *Turkistan: Notes of a Journey in Russian Turkistan, Khokand, Bukhara, and Kuldja*. Volume I. New York: Scribner, Armstrong, and Co.

Scott, James. 1992. *Domination and the Arts of Resistance: Hidden Transcripts*. New Haven, CT: Yale University Press.

Scott, James. 1998. *Seeing Like a State: How Certain Schemes to Improve the Human Condition Have Failed*. New Haven, CT: Yale University Press.

Scott, Julius. 2018. *The Common Wind: Afro-American Currents in the Age of the Haitian Revolution*. New York: Verso Books.

Searcy, Kim. 2011. *The Formation of the Sudanese Mahdist State: Ceremony and Symbols of Authority: 1882–1898*. Leiden: Brill.

Serebrennikov, A. G., ed. 1914a. *Turkestanskii krai: Sbornik materialov dlia istorii ego zavoevaniia*. Vol. 17. Tashkent': Izdanie shtaba Turkestanskogo voennago okruga.

Serebrennikov, A. G., ed. 1914b. *Turkestanskii krai: Sbornik materialov dlia istorii ego zavoevaniia*. Vol. 18. Tashkent: Izdanie shtaba Turkestanskogo voennago okruga.

Serebrennikov, A. G., ed. 1914c. *Turkestanskii krai: Sbornik materialov dlia istorii ego zavoevaniia*. Vol. 19. Tashkent': Izdanie shtaba Turkestanskogo voennago okruga.

Serebrennikov, A. G., ed. 1914d. *Turkestanskii krai: Sbornik materialov dlia istorii ego zavoevaniia*. Vol. 20. Tashkent': Izdanie shtaba Turkestanskogo voennago okruga.

Sergeev, E. Iu. 2012. *Bol'shaia igra, 1856–1907: mify i realii rossiisko-britanskikh otnoshenii v Tsentral'noi Azii*. Moskva: Tovarishchestvo nauchnykh izdanii KMK.

Seton-Watson, Robert. 1926. *Sarajevo, a Study in the Origins of the Great War*. London.: Hutchinson and Co.

Shanafelt, Gary W. 1985. *The Secret Enemy: Austria-Hungary and the German Alliance, 1914–1918*. New York: Columbia University Press.

Shaposhnikov, B. M. 2006. *Bitva za Moskvu: Moskovskaia operatsiia zapadnogo fronta, 16 noiabria 1941 g–31 ianvaria 1942 g.* Moskva: AST Moskva.

Sharman, J. C. 2019. *Empires of the Weak: The Real Story of European Expansion and the Creation of the New World Order*. Princeton, NJ: Princeton University Press.

Sheehan, J. J. 2008. *Where Have All the Soldiers Gone? The Transformation of Modern Europe*. Boston: Houghton Mifflin Company.

Sheffield, Gary. 2001. *Forgotten Victory: The First World War: Myths and Realities*. London: Headline.

Shils, Edward and Morris Janowitz. 1948. "Cohesion and Disintegration in the Wehrmacht in World War II." *Public Opinion Quarterly* 12:280–315.

Shinn, D. H. and T. P. Ofcansky. 2013. *Historical Dictionary of Ethiopia*. Plymouth: Scarecrow Press.

Shirkey, Zachary. 2012. *Joining the Fray: Outside Military Intervention in Civil Wars*. Burlington, VT: Ashgate Publishing.

Showalter, Dennis. 2004. *Tannenberg: Clash of Empires, 1914*. Washington, D.C.: Brassey's.

Simmel, Georg. 1898. "The Persistence of Social Groups." *American Journal of Sociology* 3: 662–98.

Simon, Rachel. 1987. *Libya Between Ottomanism and Nationalism: The Ottoman Involvement in Libya During the War with Italy (1911–1919)*. Berlin: Klaus Schwarz Verlag.

Simou, Bahija. 1995. *Les Reformes Militaires au Maroc de 1844 à 1912*. Rabat: Publications de la Faculté des Lettres et des Sciences Humaines.

Singer, David. 1987. "Reconstructing the Correlates of War Dataset on Material Capabilities of States, 1816–1985." *International Interactions* 14:115–32.

Singer, David and David Small. 1972. *The Wages of War, 1816–1965: A Statistical Handbook*. New York: Wiley.

Singer, J. David and Melvin Small. 1966. "The Composition and Status Ordering of the International System, 1815–1940." *World Politics* 2:236–82.

Sked, Alan. 2001. *Decline and Fall of the Habsburg Empire, 1815–1918*. London: Longman.

Skilakie, Nikolaos, ed. 2013. *100 bitv, kotorye izmenili mir: Tashkent, 1846–1865*. Moskva: OOO "De Agostoni" Russia.

Skrine, Francis and Edward Ross. 1889. *The Heart of Asia: A History of Russian Turkestan and the Central Asian Khanates from the Earliest Times*. London: Methuen and Co.

Sky, Emma. 2015. *The Unraveling: High Hopes and Missed Opportunities in Iraq*. New York: PublicAffairs.

Slantchev, Branislav. 2004. "How Initiators End Their Wars: The Duration of Warfare and the Terms of Peace." *American Journal of Political Science* 48:813–29.

Slatin Pasha, Rudolf Carl. 1896. *Fire and Sword in the Sudan; A Personal Narrative of Fighting and Serving the Dervishes, 1879–1895*. London: E. Arnold. Translated by F. R. Wingate.

Slezkine, Yuri. 1994. "The USSR as a Communal Apartment, or How a Socialist State Promoted Ethnic Particularism." *Slavic Review* 53:414–52.

Small, Melvin and David Singer. 1982. *Resort to Arms: International and Civil War, 1816–1980*. Beverly Hills, CA: Sage.

Smele, Jonathan. 2015. *The "Russian" Civil Wars, 1916–1926: Ten Years That Shook the World*. London: Hurst and Company.

Smith, Adam. 2003. *An Inquiry Into the Nature and Causes of the Wealth of Nations*. New York: Bantam Classics.

Smith, Leonard. 2014. Mutiny. In *Cambridge History of the First World War: The State*, ed. Jay Winter. Vol. 2. Cambridge: Cambridge University Press, pp. 196–217.

Smith, Rogers. 1999. *Civic Ideals Conflicting Visions of Citizenship in U.S. History*. New Haven, CT: Yale University Press.

Smithers, A. J. 1992. *Cambrai: The First Great Tank Battle, 1917*. London: L. Cooper.

Snook, Mike. 2013. *Beyond the Reach of Empire: Wolseley's Failed Campaign to Save Gordon and Khartoum*. London: Frontline Books.

Snyder, Timothy. 2010. *Bloodlands: Europe Between Hitler and Stalin*. New York: Basic Books.

Sokolov, Boris. 2015. *Marshall K.K. Rokossovsky: The Red Army's Gentleman Commander*. West Midlands: Helion and Company.

Soviet General Staff. 2015. *The Battle of Moscow, 1941–1942: The Red Army's Defensive Operations and Counteroffensive along the Moscow Strategic Direction*. West Midlands: Helion and Company.

Spence, Jonathan. 1996. *God's Chinese Son: The Taiping Heavenly Kingdom of Hong Xiuquan*. New York: W. W. Norton and Company.

Spiers, Edward. 1998. Campaigning under Kitchener. In *Sudan: The Reconquest Reappraised*, ed. Edward Spiers. London: Frank Cass, pp. 55–81.

Spiers, Edward. 2004. *The Victorian Soldier in Africa*. Manchester: Manchester University Press.

Spiers, Edward. 2007. "Intelligence and Command in Britain's Small Colonial Wars of the 1890s." *Intelligence and National Security* 22:661–81.

Srhir, Khalid. 2004. "Britain and Military Reforms in Morocco During the Second Half of the Nineteenth Century." *Oriente Moderno* 23:85–109.

Stahel, David. 2012. *Kiev 1941: Hitler's Battle for Supremacy in the East*. Cambridge: Cambridge University Press.

Stahel, David. 2015. *The Battle for Moscow*. Cambridge: Cambridge University Press.

Stahel, David, ed. 2018. *Joining Hitler's Crusade: European Nations and the Invasion of the Soviet Union, 1941*. Cambridge: Cambridge University Press.

Stam, Allan. 1996. *Win, Lose, or Draw: Domestic Politics and the Crucible of War*. Ann Arbor: University of Michigan Press.

Stamford, Henry, Lewis Alford and William Sword. 1898. *The Egyptian Soudan: Its Loss and Its Recovery*. Volume I. London: Macmillan and Company.

Staniland, Paul. 2012. "States, Insurgents, and Wartime Political Orders." *Perspectives on Politics* 10:243–64.

Staniland, Paul. 2014. *Networks of Rebellion: Explaining Insurgent Cohesion and Collapse*. Ithaca, NY: Cornell University Press.

Stanton, Jessica. 2016. *Violence and Restraint in Civil War*. Cambridge: Cambridge University Press.

Stasavage, David. 2011. *States of Credit: Size, Power, and the Development of European Politics*. Princeton, NJ: Princeton University Press.

Statiev, Alex. 2012. "La Garde meurt mais ne se rend pas! Once Again on the 28 Panfilov Heroes." *Kritika: Explorations in Russian and Eurasian History* 13:769–98.

Stearns, Jason. 2011. *Dancing in the Glory of Monsters: The Collapse of the Congo and the Great War of Africa*. New York: PublicAffairs.

Stearns, Jason, Judith Verwijen and Maria Baaz. 2013. "The National Army and Armed Groups in the Eastern Congo: Untangling the gordian knot of insecurity." *RVI Usalama Project*.

Steevens, G. W. 1899. *With Kitchener to Khartum*. New York: Dodd, Mead and Company.

Stephensen, Charles. 2014. *A Box of Sand: The Italo-Ottoman War 1911–12*. East Sussex: Tattered Flag.

Stern, Jessica and J. M. Berger. 2015. *ISIS: The State of Terror*. New York: HarperCollins.

Stewart, Frances. 2008. Horizontal Inequalities and Conflict: An Introduction and Some Hypotheses. In *Horizontal Inequalities and Conflict: Understanding Group Violence in Multiethnic Societies*, ed. Frances Stewart. Houndsmill: Palgrave Macmillan, pp. 3–23.

Stewart, Nora Kinzer. 1991. *Mates and Muchachos: Unit Cohesion in the Falklands/Malvinas War*. Washington, D.C.: Brassey's.

Stockholm International Peace Research Institute (SIPRI). 2000. *SIPRI Yearbook 2000: Armaments, Disarmament, and International Security*. Oxford: Oxford University Press.

Stone, David. 2015. *The Russian Army in the Great War*. Lawrence: University of Kansas Press.

Stone, Norman. 1966. "Army and Society in the Habsburg Monarchy, 1900–1914." *Past & Present* 33:95–111.

Stone, Norman. 1975. *The Eastern Front: 1914–1917*. New York: Charles Scribner's Sons.

Stone, Norman. 2008. *The Eastern Front, 1914–1917*. 2nd revised edition. New York: Penguin.

Stouffer, Samuel, Edward Suchman, Leland DeVinney, Shirley Star and Robin Williams Jr. 1949. *The American Soldier: Adjustment during Army Life*. Princeton, NJ: Princeton University Press.

Strachan, Hew. 1988. *European Armies and the Conduct of War*. New York: Routledge.

Strachan, Hew. 2001. *The First World War*. Vol. I: To Arms. London: Oxford University Press.

Strachan, Hew. 2006. "Training, Morale, and Modern War." *Journal of Contemporary History* 41:211–27.

Strauss, Scott. 2015. *Making and Unmaking Nations: War, Leadership, and Genocide in Modern Africa*. Ithaca, NY: Cornell University Press.

Sullivan, Patricia. 2012. *Who Wins? Predicting Strategic Success and Failure in Armed Conflict*. Oxford: Oxford University Press.

Sun-tzu. 2009. *The Art of War*. New York: Penguin Books.

Sundberg, Ralph and Erik Melander. 2013. "Introducing the UCDP Georeferenced Event Dataset." *Journal of Peace Research* 50:523–32.

Tajfel, Henri. 1970. "Experiments in Intergroup Discrimination." *Scientific American* 223: 96–102.

Tajfel, Henri, ed. 2010. *Social Identity and Intergroup Relations*. Cambridge: Cambridge University Press.

Tajfel, Henri, Michael Billig, R. P. Bundy and Claude Flament. 1971. "Social Categorization and Integroup Behavior." *European Journal of Social Psychology* 1:149–78.

Talbot, Ian. 1998. *Pakistan: A Modern History*. London: Hurst and Company.

Talmadge, Caitlin. 2013. "The Puzzle of Personalist Performance: Iraqi Battlefield Effectiveness in the Iran-Iraq War." *Security Studies* 22:180–221.

Talmadge, Caitlin. 2015. *The Dictator's Army: Battlefield Effectiveness in Authoritarian Regimes*. Ithaca, NY: Cornell University Press.

Tareke, Gebru. 2009. *The Ethiopian Revolution*. New Haven, CT: Yale University Press.

Tashkandi, Mulla Muhammad Yunus Djan Shighavul Dadkhah. 2003. *Life of 'Alimqul: A Native Chronicle of Nineteenth Century Asia*. New York: RoutledgeCurzon. Edited and translated by Timur Beisembiev.

Taylor, A. J. P. 1948. *The Habsburg Monarchy, 1809–1918: A History of the Austrian Empire and Austria-Hungary*. London: H. Hamilton.

Taylor, Alan. 2014. *The Internal Enemy: Slavery and War in Virginia, 1772–1832*. New York: W. W. Norton & Company.

Tegegn, Y. 2014. *The Ethio-Eritrean War and the Tsorona*. In Amharic. Second Edition. Addis Ababa: Brana Publishing Enterprise.

Telitsyn, Vadim. 2010. *Mify o Shtrafbatakh*. Moskva: Eksmo.

Terent'ev, M. A. 1906. *Istoriia zavoevaniia Srednei Azii: s kartami i planami*. Volume I. St Petersburg: V. V. Komarov.

Theobald, A. B. 1951. *The Mahdiya: A History of the Anglo-Egyptian Sudan, 1881–1899*. London: Longsman, Green.

Thompson, William. 1999. "The Military Superiority Thesis and the Ascendancy of Western Eurasia in the World System." *Journal of World History* 10:143–78.

Tilly, Charles. 1975. Reflections on the History of European State-Making. In *The Formation of National States in Western Europe*, ed. Charles Tilly. Princeton, NJ: Princeton University Press, pp. 3–83.

Tilly, Charles. 1992. *Coercion, Capital, and European States: AD 990–1992*. New York: Wiley-Blackwell.

Tilly, Charles. 1999. *Durable Inequality*. Berkeley: University of California Press.

Tittoni, Renato. 1914. *The Italo-Turkish War (1911–12): Translated and Compiled from the Reports of the Italian General Staff*. Kansas City, MO: Franklin Hudson Publishing Company.

Tocqueville, Alexis de. 1856. *The Old Regime and the Revolution*. New York: Harper.

Tomz, Michael, Jason Wittenberg and Gary King. 2003. "Clarify: Software for Interpreting and Presenting Statistical Results." URL: http://gking.harvard.edu/clarify

Toptygin, A. 2002. *Neizvestnyi Beriia*. Moskva: Dom Neva/OLMA-press.

Tronvall, Kjetil. 2009. *War and the Politics of Identity in Ethiopia*. Rochester, NY: BOYE6.

Tshiband, Stean Nkumb. 2009. "Transnational Actors and the Conflict in the Great Lakes Region of Africa." Richardson Institute for Peace and Conflict Research.

Tunstall, Graydon A. 2010. *Blood on the Snow: The Carpathian Winter War of 1915*. Lawrence: University Press of Kansas.

Tunstall, Graydon A. 2016. *Written in Blood: The Battles for Fortress Przemyl in WWI*. Bloomington: Indiana University Press.

Turner, Thomas. 2013. *Congo*. Cambridge: Polity.

Turney-High, Harry. 1942. *The Practice of Primitive War: A Study in Comparative Sociology*. Missoula: Montana State University Press.

Tuunainen, Pasi. 2016. *Finnish Military Effectiveness in the Winter War, 1939–1940*. New York: Palgrave Macmillan.

UCDP/PRIO. 2015. *Armed Conflict Dataset Version 4-2015*. URL: https://www.prio.org/Data /Armed-Conflict/UCDP-PRIO/

United Nations. 2010. Democratic Republic of the Congo, 1993–2003: Report of the Mapping Exercise documenting the most serious violations of human rights and international humanitarian law committed within the territory of the Democratic Republic of the Congo between March 1993 and June 2003. United Nations.

Usenov, A., D. Snegin and D. Bulatov. 1985. *Panfilovtsy: Sbornik vospominanii veteranov 8-oi gvardeiskoi imeni I. V. Panfilova strelkovoi divizii*. Zhalyn: Alma-Ata.

Vagts, Alfred. 1959. *A History of Militarism: Civilian and Military*. Revised ed. London: Free Press.

Van Evera, Stephen. 1999. *Causes of War: Power and the Roots of Conflict*. Ithaca, NY: Cornell University Press.

Vandervort, Bruce. 1998. *Wars of Imperial Conquest in Africa, 1830–1914*. Bloomington: Indiana University Press.

Vandervort, Bruce. 2012. *To the Fourth Shore: Italy's War for Libya (1911–1912)*. Rome: Ufficio Storico SME - Roma.

Verner, W. W. C. 1886. *Sketches in the Soudan*. London: R. H. Porter.

Verweijen, Judith. 2013. "Military business and the business of the military in the Kivus." *Review of African Political Economy* 40:67–82.

Veselovskii, N. 1894. *Kirgizskii rasskaz" o russkikh" zavoevaniiakh v Turkestanskom" krae: Tekst", perevod" i prilozheniia*. Sankt Peterburg: P. O. Iablonskago.

Villalobos, Federico. 2004. *El Sueño Colonial: Las Guerras De España en Marruecos*. Barcelona: Ariel.

Vlassenroot, Koen. 2002. "Citizenship, identity formation and conflict in South Kivu: The case of the Banyamulenge." *Review of African Political Economy* 29:499–516.

Van Creveld, Martin. 1982. *Fighting Power: German and U.S. Army Performance, 1939–1945*. New York: Praeger.

Vzvarova, G. N. and H. M. Emel'ianova. 1989. "Dralis' do poslednego." *Voenno-istoricheskii zhurnal* (1):25–38.

Waldron, Arthur. 1995. *From War to Nationalism: China's Turning Point, 1924–1925*. Cambridge: Cambridge University Press.

Wallace, Geoffrey. 2012. "Welcome Guests, or Inescapable Victims? The Causes of Prisoner Abuse." *Journal of Conflict Resolution* 56:955–81.

Wang, Kevin and James Lee Ray. 1994. "Beginners and Winners: The Fate of Initiators of Interstate Wars Involving Great Powers Since 1495." *International Studies Quarterly* 38:139–54.

War By Spain on Morocco: Copies of Official Correspondence. 1860. Manchester: Taylor, Garnett, Evans and Co.

War Inquiry Commission. 2000. *The Report of the Hamoodur Rehman Commission into the 1971 War (As Declassified by the Government of Pakistan)*. Lahore: Vanguard.

Warner, Philip. 1973. *Dervish: The Rise and Fall of an African Empire*. London: Macdonald and Co.

Watson, Alexander. 2008. *Enduring the Great War: Combat, Morale, and Collapse in the German and British Armies, 1914–1918*. Cambridge: Cambridge University Press.

Watson, Alexander. 2014a. Morale. In *The Cambridge History of the First World War: The State*, ed. Jay Winter. Vol. 2. Cambridge: Cambridge University Press, pp. 174–95.

Watson, Alexander. 2014b. *Ring of Steel: Germany and Austria-Hungary at War, 1914–1918*. London: Allen Lane.

Watson, Bruce. 1997. *When Soldiers Quit: Studies in Military Disintegration*. Westport, CT: Praeger.

Wawro, Geoffrey. 2014. *A Mad Catastrophe: The Outbreak of World War I and the Collapse of the Habsburg Empire*. New York: Penguin.

Weber, Eugen. 1976. *Peasants into Frenchmen: The Modernization of Rural France, 1870–1914*. Palo Alto, CA: Stanford University Press.

Weber, Max. 1946. *From Max Weber: Essays in Sociology*. Oxford: Oxford University Press.

Weeks, Jessica. 2014. *Dictators in War and Peace*. Ithaca, NY: Cornell University Press.

Weiss, Michael and Hassan Hassan. 2015. *ISIS: Inside the Army of Terror*. New York: Regan Arts.

Weitsman, Patricia. 2014. *Waging War: Alliances, Coalitions, and Institutions of Interstate Violence*. Palo Alto, CA: Stanford University Press.

Weitz, Mark. 2005. *More Damning than Slaughter: Desertion in the Confederate Army*. Lincoln: University of Nebraska Press.

Weldetinsae, H. 2001. "Ex minister Haile Weldetinsae's seminar in Germany with introduction by ex Ambassador Adhanom Gebremariam." URL: https://www.youtube.com/watch?feature=player_embedded&v=Hos2BhVZ_RI

Weller, Nicholas and Jeb Barnes. 2014. *Finding Pathways: Mixed-Method Research for Studying Causal Mechanisms*. Cambridge: Cambridge University Press.

Wesbrook, Stephen. 1980. The Potential for Military Disintegration. In *Combat Effectiveness: Cohesion, Stress, and the Voluntary Military*. Beverly Hills, CA: Sage, pp. 244–78.

Wilcox, Vanda. 2015. The Italian soldiers' experience in Libya, 1911–1912. In *The Wars before the Great War: Conflict and International Politics before the Outbreak of the First World War*, ed. Dominik Geppert, William Mulligan and Andreas Rose. Oxford: Cambridge University Press, pp. 41–57.

Wilkinson, Steven. 2015. *Army and Nation: The Military and Indian Democracy Since Independence*. Cambridge, MA: Harvard University Press.

Williamson, Samuel and Ernest May. 2007. "An Identity of Opinion: Historians and July 1914." *Journal of Modern History* 79:335–87.

Wilson, Charles. 1886. *From Korti to Khartum: A journal of the desert march from Korti to Gubat and of the ascent of the Nile in General Gordon's steamers.* London: Blackwood.

Wimmer, Andreas. 2013. *Waves of War: Nationalism, State Formation, and Ethnic Exclusion in the Modern World.* Cambridge: Cambridge University Press.

Wimmer, Andreas. 2014. "War." *Annual Review of Sociology* 40:173–97.

Wimmer, Andreas. 2018. *Nation Building: Why Some Countries Come Together While Others Fall Apart.* Princeton, NJ: Princeton University Press.

Wimmer, Andreas, Lars-Erik Cederman and Brian Min. 2009. "Ethnic Politics and Armed Conflict: A Configurational Analysis of a New Global Data Set." *American Sociological Review* 74:316–37.

Wingate, F. R. 1891. *Mahdism and the Egyptian Sudan: Being an Account of the Rise and Progress of Madhism, and of Subsequent Events in the Sudan to the Present Time.* London: Macmillan and Co.

Wingate, F. R. 1892. *Ten Years' Captivity in the Madhi's Camp: From the Original Manuscripts of Father Joseph Ohrwalder.* 14th ed. London: Sampson Low, Marston and Company.

Woldemariam, Michael. 2015. "Partition Problems: Relative Power, Historical Memory, and the Origins of the Eritrean-Ethiopian War, Nationalism and Ethnic Politics." *Nationalism and Ethnic Politics* 21:166–190.

Woldemariam, Michael. 2018. *Insurgent Fragmentation in the Horn of Africa.* Cambridge: Cambridge University Press.

Woldemariam, Michael and Alden Young. 2018. "After the Split: Partition, Successor States, and the Dynamics of War in the Horn of Africa." *Journal of Strategic Studies* 41:684–720.

Wolseley, Field Marshal Viscount G. 1967. *In Relief of Gordon: Lord Wolseley's Campaign Journal of the Khartoum Relief Expedition, 1884–85.* London: Hutchinson and Co.

Wood, Elisabeth. 2008. "The Social Processes of Civil War: The Wartime Transformation of Social Networks." *Annual Review of Political Science* 11:539–61.

Wood, Elizabeth. 2003. *Insurgent Collective Action and Civil War in El Salvador.* Cambridge: Cambridge University Press.

Wright, H. C. Seppings. 1913. *Two Years Under the Crescent.* Boston: Small, Maynard and Co.

Wrong, Michela. 2006. *I Didn't Do It for You: How the World Betrayed a Small African Nation.* New York: Harper Perennial.

Wucherpfennig, Julian, Nils Weidmann, Luc Girardin, Lars-Erik Cederman and Andreas Wimmer. 2011. "Politically Relevant Ethnic Groups across Space and Time: Introducing the GeoEPR Dataset." *Conflict Management and Peace Science* 28:423–37.

Yapp, M. E. 1980. *Strategies of British India: Britain, Iran, and Afghanistan, 1798–1850.* Oxford: Clarendon Press.

Yorulmaz, Naci. 2014. *Arming the Sultan: German Arms Trade and Personal Diplomacy in the Ottoman Empire Before World War I.* New York: I. B. Tauris.

Young, Crawford. 2002. Contextualizing Congo Conflicts: Order and Disorder in Postcolonial Africa. In *The African Stakes in the Congo War*, ed. John Clark. New York: Palgrave Macmillan, pp. 33–52.

Yriarte, Charles. 1863. *Sous la Tente: Souvenirs du Maroc, Récits de Guerre et de Voyage*. Paris: Morizot, Libraire-Éditeur.

Zagorodnikova, T. N., ed. 2005. *"Bol'shaia Igra" v Tsentral'noi Azii. "Indiiskii Pokhod Russkoi Armii."* Moskva: IV RAN.

Zaitsev, V. N. 1882. *Istoriia 4-go Turkestanskogo lineinogo batal'ona, s kartoy, za period s 1771 po 1882 god, kak material k opisaniiu dvizheniia russkikh v Sredniuiu Aziiu*. Tashkent': Unknown.

Zamoyski, Adam. 2005. *Moscow 1812: Napoleon's Fatal March*. New York: Harper Perennial.

Zeitzoff, Thomas. 2014. "Anger, Exposure to Violence and Intragroup Conflict: A 'Lab in the Field' Experiment in Southern Israel." *Political Psychology* 35:309–55.

Zhilin, V. A., ed. 2001a. *Bitva pod Moskvoi: Khronika, Fakty, Liudi*. Vol. 1. Moskva: Olma-Press.

Zhilin, V. A., ed. 2001b. *Bitva pod Moskvoi: Khronika, Fakty, Liudi*. Vol. 2. Moskva: Olma-Press.

Zhukov, Georgii. 2013. *Marshal of Victory: The Autobiography of General Georgy Zhukov*. Vol. I. and II. South Yorkshire, UK: Pen and Sword.

Zolotarev, V. A., ed. 1996. *Glavnye politicheskie organy vooruzhyonnykh sil SSSR v Velikoi Otechestvennoi voine 1941–1945*. Vol. 17.6 of *Russkii Arkhiv: Velikaia Otechestvennaia*. Moskva: TERRA.

Zulfo, 'Ismat Hasan. 1980. *Karari: The Sudanese Account of the Battle of Omdurman*. London: Frederick Wane. Translated from the Arabic by Peter Clark.

Zürcher, Erik Jan. 1998. "The Ottoman Conscription System, 1844–1914." *International Review of Social History* 43:437–49.

Zviagintsev, Viacheslav. 2017a. *Tribunal dlia komdivov: 41-i*. Moskva: Ridero.

Zviagintsev, Viacheslav. 2017b. *Voina na vesakh Femidy: Voina 1941–1945 gg v. materialakh sledstvenno-sudebnykh del*. Moskva: Ridero.

Zwede, B. 1998. "The Military and Militarism in Africa: The Case of Ethiopia." In *The Military and Militarism in Africa*, ed. E. Hutchful and A. Bathily. Dakar: Conseil pour le développement de la recherche en sciences sociales en Afrique, pp. 257–89.

INDEX

Page numbers in *italics* refer to figures, maps, and tables.

A NOTE ON THE TYPE

THIS BOOK has been composed in Arno, an Old-style serif typeface in the classic Venetian tradition, designed by Robert Slimbach at Adobe.